San Antonio's Mission
San José

Books by Marion A. Habig

Biographies

Pioneering in China: Francis X. Engbring

The Franciscan Pere Marquette: Zénobe Membré

As the Morning Star: St. Francis

Everyman's Saint: St. Anthony

Man of Greatness: Junípero Serra
(with Francis Borgia Steck)

History

Heroes of the Cross: An American Martyrology

In Journeyings Often: Franciscans in the Orient

Heralds of the King: Chicago-St. Louis Province of Franciscans

Franciscan Book of Saints
(with Sr. M. Aquina Barth)

The Franciscans: St. Francis and His Three Orders
(with Alexandre Masseron)

The Franciscans at St. Augustine's and in Chicagoland

Franciscan Pictorial Book One
Franciscan Pictorial Book Two
(with Albert J. Nimeth)

A Short History of the Third Order
(with Mark Hegener)

San Antonio's Mission San José

Translations

Maggie: Life of Margaret Lekeux

Why Are You Fearful?

San Antonio's Mission San Jose

State and National Historic Site 1720-1968

By Fr. MARION A. HABIG, O.F.M.

The Naylor Company
Book Publishers of the Southwest
San Antonio, Texas

DAVID GLENN HUNT MEMORIAL LIBRARY GALVESTON COMMUNITY COLLEGE

TO THE BUILDERS OF SAN JOSÉ
IN COMMEMORATION OF THE
200TH ANNIVERSARY OF THE FOUNDATION-
BLESSING OF THE CHURCH OF
MISSION SAN JOSÉ Y SAN MIGUEL DE AGUAYO
THE QUEEN OF THE SAN ANTONIO MISSIONS
MARCH 19, 1768
AS WELL AS THE
250TH ANNIVERSARY OF THE FOUNDING OF
MISSION SAN ANTONIO DE VALERO
LATER CALLED THE ALAMO
MAY 1, 1718
THE VILLA AND PRESIDIO OF SAN ANTONIO
DE BÉXAR
MAY 5, 1718
FITTINGLY OBSERVED BY THE
CITY OF SAN ANTONIO'S
HEMISFAIR OF 1968

Preface

I̶T IS ALWAYS GRATIFYING TO READ A MANU-
script from the pen of Father Habig, but most especially is
this volume on old San José Mission welcome at this time
when San Antonio is celebrating the 250th anniversary of
its founding in 1718.

We Texans would like to say that we have the oldest
Cathedral in the United States here in San Antonio, but that
boast would be not entirely true since we can point with
pride to only the sanctuary of our historic San Fernando
Cathedral, begun as a parish church in 1738. The Indians
worshiped in the Alamo, San Antonio de Valero, and the
other citizens wanted a church of their own. They appealed
to the King of Spain for a donation and he sent them 12,000
pesos. A big campaign to build the new church was put on
and the people contributed 642 pesos. Later, when the
church had to be enlarged, the original edifice became the
sanctuary and a long nave and façade were added.

{ vii }

The Venerable Fray Antonio Margil O.F.M. was one of the early heroes of the pueblo of Saint Anthony and he founded old San José Mission here in 1720. Very early in its history this structure was called the "Queen of the Missions" and the "Glory of New Spain." With the cooperation of the Archdiocese it was declared "a National Historic Site" in 1941.

It is about this magnificent monument of the past that Father Habig writes in this book. It is here that one is privileged to see the famous "Rose Window" of old San José. It is to this Queen of the Missions that thousands of visitors come every year to admire its graceful façade, its beautiful lines and its imposing tower which rises so majestically toward the blue Texas sky.

As a sort of fringe benefit from his research on this mission, Father Habig came across additional historic information about our other old missions in San Antonio and these manuscripts, too, will be most welcome, since no other historian had previously discovered these interesting facts of the early days of Texas.

How did these missions happen to come to San Antonio? They are the result of political and religious forces operating here in the 17th and 18th centuries. The Spanish government believed that there was vast wealth in New Spain, a part of which is now the great state of Texas. The Spanish rulers also believed that the best way to make friends of the savage natives was not to murder them, but to give them the blessings of civilization. And so, Spain established presidios, or garrisons, of soldiers for security, and churches for religion, culture, and education. In Spanish America, where local civil and military authorities were sometimes cruel toward the natives, the padres were always the friends of the Indians.

And so it came about that Spain established some garrisons, in what is now East Texas, to prevent the French in Louisiana from penetrating into that area. And wherever the flag of Spain went, there was found a church for the people and a house for the priests. A Spanish mission, however, was not just a chapel and a friary; it included housing for the natives, a school in which to teach them the manual arts, the Spanish language, and religion. There was also the planting of crops and the raising of cattle and sheep. An acequia, or ditch, brought water from a nearby river. Whatever was required for the immense colonizing and civilizing work of Spain was found in the mission.

From this it will be seen that the work of the Franciscan padres was not secondary to that of the soldiers; the mission was not a mere appendage of the garrison; actually it was the padres who did the work. It was the Church which brought civilization to the Indians. The soldiers stood guard; they repelled the attacks of hostile forces. It was the missionaries, sons of Saint Francis, who changed the Indians from savages to Christians; it was the padres who taught the children of the wilderness to be children of God. Thus it happened not infrequently that the civil authority was not enthusiastic about organizing new garrisons and new missions; it was the clergy who insisted that this work be developed and enlarged; it was the padres who kept after the Viceroy insistently until he consented to furnish what was necessary to carry the cross and the flag still further into the wilderness. In all of this the flag was useful but it was the cross that really mattered; it was the cross in the hands of Franciscan padres that brought civilization to Texas.

And right here we might ask: What prompted these missionaries to leave their homes and their people to labor among the unlettered savages of the forest? Certainly they did not expect to find ease and comfort here in the wilderness. Surely they knew that the very natives whom they were trying to help could rise up against them and put them to death. They knew that they would not find, here on the endless prairies of Texas, anything that the world holds dear. At best they could expect pain and suffering; at worst, torture and death. But these missionaries were not men who sought the easy way to live and labor; they didn't think that martyrdom was a great misfortune. The thing that motivated them was love of God and neighbor. What happened to them personally didn't matter very much. Their love of God prompted them to serve their neighbor because fraternal charity is the visible test of our love for God. It was love that drove the missionaries into the wilderness.

We owe a debt of gratitude to Father Habig O.F.M. for the labor that he has so generously put into the writing of this volume. He has made a very valuable contribution to our knowledge of the past and the courageous soldiers of Christ who came here 250 years ago. These old missions are treasures of early Texas history. They are a tremendous asset to San Antonio. Although they belong to the Church, they are invested with a public interest. They are a precious heritage — spiritual, religious and historic — for the whole country. They are deathless monuments of the early days of charming San Antonio.

ROBERT E. LUCEY
Archbishop of San Antonio

Acknowledgments

TO ALL WHO WITH SUCH READY KINDNESS
and generosity have helped the author, he wishes to express
his sincere appreciation and heartfelt thanks — particularly
to the following:

His confreres Fr. Benedict Leutenegger of the Academy
of American Franciscan History, Washington, D.C., who
combed the Béxar Archives in Austin for all material they
contain about Mission San José; Fr. Fidel de J. Chauvet of
Mexico City; Fr. Raimundo M. Solano of Hebbronville,
Texas.

Fr. Eustace Struckhoff, pastor of San José Mission parish;
Fr. Gasper Meyer, his assistant; Brother Adrian Borer, and
the other Franciscans of the friaries in San Antonio.

Very Rev. Joseph Nuevo C.M.F., and his brethren of
San Fernando Cathedral; and Msgr. William H. Oberste of
Refugio, Texas.

Miss Carmen Perry, librarian-archivist of the Daughters

of the Republic of Texas Library at the Alamo; Dr. Chester Kielman and Mrs. Benson of the University of Texas Library, Latin American collection of documents and books; Brother Franklin Cullen C.S.C., chief librarian of St. Edward's University in Austin.

Mr. Pierson de Vries, superintendent of San José Texas State and National Historic Site; Mrs. Don F. Tobin, president of the San Antonio Conservation Society; Mr. Richard G. Santos, archivist of Bexar County; Mr. and Mrs. Ernst Schuchard of San Antonio; and Mrs. Joe O. Naylor and her staff of The Naylor Company.

Dr. L. Tuffly Ellis, Assistant Director of Texas State Historical Association, Austin, Texas; J. Dan Scurlock, Director, Park Interpretation, Texas Parks and Wildlife Department, Austin, Texas; Robert M. Utley, Chief Historian, and Roy E. Appleman, Acting Chief Historian, United States Department of the Interior, National Park Service, Washington, D.C.; the Most Rev. Robert E. Lucey, Archbishop of San Antonio, Texas.

The beautiful and historically correct poem about Mission San José by the late Janie F. Baskin of San Antonio, the several parts of which appear at the heads of some of the chapters in this book, was originally published November 4, 1926, in the San Antonio *Southern Messenger*.

List of Illustrations

Picture section between pages xiv and xv

Page 1   South side of San José Mission's church,
         showing sacristy window and tower.

Page 2   Painting of San José Mission by Seth Eastman, 1849.
         Painting of San José Mission by Theodore Gentilz, c. 1874.

Page 3   Photograph of San José Mission, before 1868.
         San José church and old friary, between 1928 and 1937.

Page 4   Doorway of the sacristy of San José, with original doors.

Page 5   The new doors of the main entrance of the church of San José.

Page 6   The church of Mission San José, after the restoration in 1937.
         The restored granary of Mission San José.

Page 7   View of San José's old friary and the church, from the east.
         The new Franciscan friary at San José, built in 1931.

Page 8   Façade and dome of San José's church, partially decorated as
         in the 1780's.

MAPS AND FACSIMILES

The Aguayo Map of 1729.   31
Memorial of the College of Zacatecas to the King, January 15, 1750.   59
Irrigation ditches and farms of San Antonio Mission and town of
    San Fernando (upper part).   71
Irrigation ditches and farms of Concepción Mission and town of
    San Fernando (lower part).   72
Irrigation ditches and farms of San José Mission.   73
Irrigation ditches and farms of Capistrano and Espada missions,
    and Espada aqueduct.   74
Letter of Fr. Ramírez from San José, July 6, 1776.   79
Letter of Fr. Pedrajo from San José, May 8, 1791.   93
Letter of Fr. Cárdenas from San José, September 13, 1794.   107
William Corner's plan of Mission San José, 1890.   154
William Corner's plan of San José's granary, 1890.   155
William Corner's map of San Antonio, 1890.   156
Boundaries of San José Parish, 1967.   170
St. Joseph Parish, southeast San Antonio.   171
Letter of Fr. Vallejo from San José, July 11, 1806.   205
Plan of San José State and National Historic Site.   228

View of south side of the church of Mission San José, showing the tower and the exterior of the sacristy with its famous "Rose Window." (H. L. Summerville photo; courtesy of San José Friary.)

The earliest picture of San José Mission, a painting made by Seth Eastman in 1849. (Courtesy of the Daughters of the Republic of Texas Library at the Alamo.)

Painting of San José Mission by Theodore Gentilz, showing the church after the collapse of the dome in 1874. (Courtesy of the Daughters of the Republic of Texas Library at the Alamo, where the original is on display.)

One of the first photographs of Mission San José, made about the same time as another by E. Raba, before the dome crashed. (From the Archives of San José Friary.)

Photo of San José, made between 1928 (after the tower fell and was rebuilt) and 1937 (before the restoration of the church was completed). (H. L. Summerville photo; courtesy of San José Friary.)

The doorway of the sacristy of Mission San José, with the original doors, looking out toward the arches of the old friary. (From the Archives of the new San José Friary.)

New doors of the main entrance of the church of Mission San José, carved by Peter Mansbendel; installed July, 1937. At left is Archbishop Arthur J. Drossaerts; Franciscan on right is Fr. Bonaventure Alerding, first superior of new San José Friary. (From the Archives of San José Friary.)

The restored church of Mission San José, a photo taken after the squat steeple of 1928 had been restored to its original shape in 1940. (Elicson photo, courtesy of San José Friary.)

The granary of Mission San José, after its restoration by the San Antonio Conservation Society had been completed in 1933. (H. L. Summerville photo; courtesy of San José Friary.)

View of San José church from the east, showing the arches of the old friary
and the tower after it was rebuilt, with a squat steeple, in 1928.
(H. L. Summerville photo; courtesy of San José Friary.)

The new Franciscan Friary of San José, built in 1931. In the left wing there is a chapel.
(From the Archives of San José Friary.)

Drawing by Ernst F. Schuchard, showing how the façade and dome of the church of Mission San José were decorated with color designs in the 1780's. (Courtesy of Mr. Schuchard.)

Contents

Preface by Archbishop Robert E. Lucey   vii

List of Illustrations   xiii

Introduction   xvii

   I   Spanish Texas   xxii

  II   The Founder of San José   6

 III   Founding of San José   24

 IV   Development of San José   34

  V   Heyday of San José   46

 VI   Queen of the Missions   60

VII   Decline of San José   80

VIII   Partial Secularization   94

 IX   Last Three Decades   108

  X   The Last of the Padres   118

 XI   Neglect and Reclaim of San José   134

XII   Return of the Franciscans   158

XIII   Restoration of San José   172

XIV   A Day at San José in 1778   190

XV   San José in Folklore and Art   206

XVI   A Tour of the Historic Site   224

Bibliography   241

Index   247

Introduction

SAN ANTONIO, TEXAS, IS CELEBRATING THE 250th anniversary of its founding in 1968; and the whole world joins the city in this celebration. The official World's Fair of 1968, known as HemisFair, opens April 6 and continues through October 6.

San Antonio had its beginning on May 1, 1718, when Fr. Antonio de Olivares founded Mission San Antonio de Valero, later called the Alamo, and on May 5, 1718, when Governor Martín de Alarcón established the Villa and Presidio of San Antonio de Béxar in present downtown San Antonio.

Less than two years later, a little farther south but within the present city limits, saintly Fr. Antonio Margil founded Mission San José y San Miguel de Aguayo on February 23, 1720.

After the lapse of eleven years, three more missions,

{ xvii }

originally established in eastern Texas in 1716, were moved to the San Antonio River and re-founded there in 1731: Mission Purísima Concepción, between the San Antonio and San José, and San Juan Capistrano and San Francisco de Espada a short distance to the south.

The City of San Antonio today enjoys the unique distinction of being the only one which has four old Spanish missions within its confines and a fifth just outside its southern boundary.

Mission San José, "the first mission in America . . . in point of beauty, plan, and strength," as Fr. Agustín Morfi described it in 1777, is also celebrating an anniversary in 1968. It was on March 19, 1768, that Fr. Solís and Governor Hugo Oconor laid the first stones of the mission's new church, the present restored edifice.

Today San José and the Alamo, as well as the restored missions of Nuestra Señora del Espíritu Santo de Zúñiga at Goliad and San Francisco de los Tejas near Weches in Houston County, are officially recognized as historic sites by the State of Texas.

Mission San José has also been designated as a National Historic Site, inasmuch as it is "a symbol of the faith, courage, and vigor of the Franciscan Fathers (the builders and missionaries of San José), and an example of the cultural and historical importance of the mission in the development of the United States." It is, in fact, the only one of the many colonial missions in our Spanish Borderlands upon which this national recognition and distinction has been conferred.

Although Mission San José holds such a unique rank and position in the State of Texas and in the United States of America, a complete and accurate history of the mission has not been written till now. It was long considered a rather hopeless task to write such a history, because most of the earlier records of the mission were destroyed in the Gutiérrez invasion of 1813.

In the recent past, however, scholars have uncovered not a little information about this mission, especially Dr. Carlos E. Castañeda, in his monumental work of seven volumes, *Our Catholic Heritage in Texas;* and there is considerable additional material concerning San José in contemporary manuscript and printed sources, which has not hitherto been exploited.

To observe in a fitting manner the two hundredth anniversary of the laying of the first stones of the present restored church of San José Mission, the historian of the Franciscans of the St. Louis-Chicago Province (who are now once more in charge of San José's church) began "to gather the fragments that were left over, lest they be lost," and to his surprise, "they filled more than twelve baskets." He found much more than he or anyone else had ever expected. The result was a more or less complete history, a fully documented and annotated manuscript, as yet unpublished, *Mission San José y San Miguel de Aguayo, 1720-1824.* It faithfully recounts in detail how Mission San José was founded, how it developed and reached its peak, and how it declined, during the 104 years of its existence as a Spanish mission.

But this is a work for students and scholars rather than for the general reading public. Convinced that the latter too would be interested in an authentic history of Mission San José, the writer has prepared the present work, omitting the copious footnotes and the full documentation contained in the former, condensing the background history of San José to a minimum, telling the story of San José's Spanish period in a simple narrative style, and adding an account of the subsequent vicissitudes of the mission, and its restoration, down to the present day.

To all who have helped the writer in this labor of love — more perhaps than they realized — by their encouragement, their suggestions, their assistance in gathering all available material, he wishes to express his heartfelt appreciation and thanks.

To all Americans, especially those of Texas and San Antonio and the visitors of HemisFair '68, we offer this illustrated but otherwise unembellished chronicle of a great and noble achievement and a precious heritage for all times.

M. A. H.

Spanish Texas

Only with extreme difficulty can we of this twentieth century age comprehend the ideal which inspired the missionary pioneer of our Southwest. We can understand why men should struggle to conquer a wilderness for the wealth it will yield. . . . But almost incomprehensible to us is the sixteenth-century ideal which brought to the Southwest its first pioneers of European civilization — the brown-mantled Franciscan and Jesuit missionaries.

— HERBERT E. BOLTON

1

TWO HUNDRED YEARS BEFORE THE FOUND-
ing of Mission San José y San Miguel de Aguayo, the Spanish
pioneers had discovered and claimed Texas. The year was
1519, the same in which Cortés landed in Mexico. It was
only six years after Ponce de León made his first voyage to
Florida, and less than twenty-seven years after Columbus
landed on Watling's Island in the Bahamas.

Alvárez de Piñeda, captain of a fleet of four ships, set
sail from Jamaica in the early summer of 1519, and explored
the entire gulf coast from Florida to Vera Cruz. He discovered the mouths of the Mississippi, the Rio Grande, and four
other rivers. They are shown on a map made during the voyage. On the way back, he tarried for forty days at the Rio
Grande in the fall of that year, and then returned the way
he had come. Twice, westward and eastward, he sailed along

the coast of Texas. Repeatedly during the voyage he went ashore to take formal possession of the newly discovered land and to trade with the Indians.

Two Hundred Years of Exploration

During the two centuries which followed, Spanish explorers and missionaries undertook more than forty expeditions into Texas or to its coast. But it was not until the latter part of the seventeenth century that the first missions were founded in Texas.

Between 1681 and 1684, three missions were founded at El Paso, two near Presidio, and one temporary mission as far inland as Ballinger, Texas. These belonged to the Spanish Province of Nuevo Mexico, which was established in 1598. So did the four missions which were founded in the Presidio area about 1715.

In the Spanish Province of Texas, which was not established until 1691, the first European settlement was not a Spanish but a French colony, namely La Salle's ill-fated Fort St. Louis on Garcitas Creek, 1684-1689. This bold intrusion into their territory made the Spaniards realize that they must occupy Texas if they wanted to keep it. And so the first two missions in eastern Texas, San Francisco de los Tejas (in the northeastern corner of Houston County) and Santísimo Nombre de María (in the southeastern part of Cherokee County) were founded in 1690. The following year, Don Domingo Terán de los Ríos, was appointed the first governor of the Province of Texas or Nuevas Filipinas; but he resigned the next year, and a year later the two missions in eastern Texas had to be abandoned.

Almost a quarter century passed before the Province of Texas was, at long last, permanently occupied. This was done by the expedition of Captain Domingo Ramón in

1716. Strangely enough, it was a Frenchman, Louis Juche-reau de St. Denis, who helped the Spaniards to do it.

This time six missions were founded in eastern Texas, four in 1716 and two in 1717. Near one of them, Mission Purísima Concepción, on the Angelina River, Captain Ramón established his Presidio of Nuestra Señora de los Dolores. The last of the chain of six missions, San Miguel de los Adaes, was beyond the Sabine River, near Robeline in present Louisiana; and not far away was the French post of Nachitoches.

The next step was the occupation of the San Antonio area, at the western end of the Province of Texas. On May 1, 1718, Governor Martín de Alarcón officially established Mission San Antonio de Valero, and on May 5 the Presidio of San Antonio de Béxar with the Villa de Béxar. San Antonio was from the beginning an important halfway station between the region around Nacogdoches in eastern Texas and the Presidio of San Juan Bautista which stood on the west side of the Rio Grande, not far from Eagle Pass.

The Spanish Province of Texas

The Spanish Province of Texas, it must be remembered, was not coextensive with the present State. The territory lying between San Antonio and San Juan Bautista belonged to the Province of Coahuila which had come into existence in 1674 through the efforts of the Franciscan pioneer, Fr. Juan Larios. The latter, in fact, had penetrated with Fernando del Bosque into this region as far as the Medina River, near San Antonio, already in 1675. The Presidio and El Paso areas were regarded as a part of the Province of Nuevo México. The Province of Nuevo León extended across the lower Rio Grande into Texas until 1747, when the new Province of Nuevo Santander was erected. At first this Province included all of southernmost Texas as far as the Guadalupe River; but in 1775 the boundary was moved west to the Nueces.

If San Antonio had not been founded in 1718, the occupation of the Province of Texas would not have been a permanent one in 1716. For, in 1719, the French drove the Spaniards out of eastern Texas, and they were not able to return until two years later. By their "invasion," the French really rendered a service to the Spaniards, for the result was the imposing expedition of Marqués de Aguayo which accomplished far more than any previous effort.

Not only did Aguayo re-establish the six missions in eastern Texas and the Presidio of Dolores, but near the Mission of San Miguel in Louisiana, he founded the Presidio de los Adaes, which remained the capital of the Province until 1772. Only in that year was San Antonio made the capital.

The first three of the missions in eastern Texas as well as Mission San Antonio were in the care of missionaries from the so-called Apostolic College of Santa Cruz de Querétaro. The other three eastern missions and Mission San José, on the San Antonio River, and Mission Nuestra Señora del Espíritu Santo, at Lavaca Bay, were in charge of missionaries from the College of Nuestra Señora de Guadalupe de Zacatecas.

These missionary colleges were units of the Franciscan Order similar to the so-called "provinces." But they had a twofold specialized purpose: the preaching of parish renewals or revivals in Christian towns and cities, which lasted a week or two; and missionary work among the Indians on the frontier. The superior of a college had the title of "Father Guardian," and he was assisted by an advisory council which was called a *discretorio*. The missionaries among the Indians in a certain area had as their immediate superior a Father *Presidente*.

Thus the *presidente* of the Querétaran missionaries who came to Texas in 1716 was Fr. Isidro Félix de Espinosa; and Fr. Antonio Margil held the same office for the Zacatecan missionaries.

The members of the colleges wore a grey habit, while those of most of the provinces in Mexico had a religious garment of a blueish color. There was only one province in Mexico, that of the Alcantarine or Discalced Friars, whose garb was of a light brown or coffee color.

It is not correct, therefore, to describe the missionaries in our Southwest as "brown-robed" Franciscans. Those of Texas and California (the latter belonged to the College of San Fernando, Mexico City) had a grey robe; and those of New Mexico had a blueish habit, since they were members of the Province of Santo Evangelio, Mexico City.

The Founder of San José

When did Your Reverence or I deserve that
our Savior should choose us to be his apostles
in these days? Happy are we, if we recognize
the favor. . . . Let us persevere unto death
like the Apostles. . . . Is there anything better?

— FR. ANTONIO MARGIL TO FR. ANDRADE

II

$\underline{\mathcal{LOC}\mathcal{LOC}\mathcal{LOC}\mathcal{LOC}\mathcal{LOC}\mathcal{LOC}\mathcal{LOC}\mathcal{O}}$

Mission San José was founded by one of
the greatest and saintliest missionaries of the New World —
the Venerable Fr. Antonio Margil de Jesús. As *presidente*
of the first group of missionaries from the College of Zacatecas who entered Texas, he was the founder, not only of San
José, but also of four other Texas missions: the Guadalupe,
Dolores, and San Miguel missions in east Texas and the
Espíritu Santo mission on Garcitas Creek near Lavaca
Bay, although he was not personally present at the establishment of the first and last of these. For this reason Fr.
Margil is sometimes called, and not altogether undeserved-
ly, the Apostle of Texas.

However, the six years which Fr. Margil spent in
Texas (1716-1722) were but the climax of a long missionary
career lasting forty-three years and extending from one

end of New Spain to the other. More perhaps than any of the great missionaries who preceded him, Fr. Margil deserves to be styled the Apostle of New Spain.

He was also one of the world's champion walkers. Except for one short trip in Coahuila, another from Tuxtla to Chiapa, and his last from Querétaro to Mexico City, he made all of his journeys on land and even some of his river crossings on foot — and not merely on foot, but barefoot. He called himself "God's donkey," and walked as fast or faster than a mule.

So extraordinary are the events of his life and so remarkable his achievements, that a writer of fiction could not narrate them because his story would be regarded as improbable or impossible. If they were not so indisputably established as facts, a historian would reject them as legendary. Fr. Margil's life-story is indeed a striking example of truth that is stranger than fiction.

Fr. Margil was born in Valencia, Spain, on August 18, 1657. He had two sisters, one of whom married while the other entered a Franciscan sisterhood. As a boy he was always a well-behaved lad, humble, obedient, prayerful, and at the same time endowed with a cheerful and friendly disposition. Cheerfulness and friendliness remained a characteristic mark of his even amid the most trying circumstances and the most austere self-imposed penances.

At the age of fifteen, he became a member of the Order of Friars Minor or Franciscans, April 22, 1673. He was a novice for one year in Valencia; and after taking his vows, he studied philosophy in Alicante for three years and theology in Valencia for five years. In philosophy he was good, in theology excellent. As a youthful friar he outstripped his elders in the perfect observance of the Franciscan rule of life. Several months after his twenty-fifth birthday, in 1682, he was ordained a priest.

Fr. Antonio Llinás was enlisting friars at this time for the first of the overseas missionary colleges which he was establishing at Querétaro, Mexico. Young Fr. Margil received permission to join him, paid his mother and sisters a last visit in Valencia, and made the journey to Cadiz on foot. On March 4, 1683, he set sail with Fr. Llinás and about twenty-two other Franciscans for Mexico. After a voyage of three months they reached Vera Cruz, just as the pirate Lorenzo de Gaff was leaving. They found the city in desolation, and Fr. Margil wept.

They tarried in Vera Cruz for a short time, helping to bury the dead and consoling the survivors. Then they set out for Puebla and Mexico City, going in pairs by different routes, walking all the way, and taking along only a crucifix, a breviary, and a staff. At the end of June they reached Mexico City. Fr. Margil was one of those present at the official opening of the missionary college in the friary of Santa Cruz at Querétaro on August 15, 1683. With twelve others, he preached his first parish mission in Mexico City during the month of October, and returned to Querétaro in November.

His Missionary Odyssey of Thirteen Years

In March of 1684 Fr. Margil took his leave from the College of Querétaro to enter upon a missionary journey which turned out to be an amazing odyssey lasting no less than thirteen years. During the greater part of this time, his constant companion was another great missionary, Fr. Melchor López. Together they traversed the southern Mexican states of Yucatán, Campeche, Tabasco, and Chiapas, and the Central American countries of Guatemala, El Salvador, Honduras, Nicaragua, and Costa Rica. Traveling on foot, they preached the word of God to the Christians in the towns and cities along the way, and made a series of prolonged excursions into the interior to carry the Gospel message to wild Indians who were still pagans.

During these years Fr. Margil founded no less than fifteen new missions among the Talamancas, Borucas, and Terrabas in Costa Rica, and ten among the Chols and Lacondons in Guatemala — a total of twenty-five. He and Fr. López baptized some ten thousand Indians during the ten years that they worked together (1684-1694).

Four times Fr. Margil was recalled to the College of Querétaro, but each time, except the last, the orders were revoked and he was permitted to continue his labors in Central America. Without special divine assistance, no human being could have survived the dangers, privations, and hardships which these two missionaries endured for long periods, far away from civilization.

With several companions Fr. Margil walked in March, 1684, from Querétaro to Vera Cruz, and sailed to Campeche, where they arrived on April 1. After a trip to Mérida, one hundred miles distant, Fr. Margil and Fr. López boarded a ship going toward Vera Cruz, but they disembarked on the coast of Tabasco and began to walk in a southerly direction, singing as they went.

By the time they reached the present Tuxtla Gutiérrez they were so weak, they could not stand and were on the point of death. Fr. Margil received the last sacraments. They were carried to Chiapa, and there gradually regained their strength. As soon as they were able to walk, they stole away and preached a mission in Ciudad Real (Chiapa de Españoles).

For about a year they remained in the province of Soconusco. At one time three to four thousand Indians, carrying tree branches, followed them. The crowd of natives seemed to be a moving forest. Followed by admiring and grateful Indians who called them San Antonio and San Melchor, they continued their journey to Santiago de Guatemala (the present Antigua) and arrived at the Franciscan friary in the city on September 21, 1685 — one and a half years after landing on the coast of Tabasco. In the cathedral they preached an eight-day mission in January, 1686. After a sojourn of about six months in the city and outlying districts, they resumed their apostolic wanderings and walked during the next three years through Guatemala, El Salvador, Honduras, Nicaragua, and Costa Rica as far as Cartago.

It was in the fall of 1689 that they set out for the Talamanca Indians who lived in the mountains of southern Costa Rica. For 118 years no missionary had been among these Indians. Fr. Margil and Fr. López baptized a large number of them and established twelve new missions with churches. They were reaping an abundant harvest when they were recalled, and other missionaries afterwards continued the good work.

When they returned to Cartago they were informed that they could extend their sojourn in Costa Rica; and so, in February, 1691, they went to the Indians called Ujambores on the frontier of Panama. But these Indians refused absolutely to listen to them, and the missionaries turned eastward to the Borucas. By March 19, 1691, they had Christianized one-third of these Indians. Next they directed their steps toward the Pacific Ocean and evangelized the fierce Terrabas, among whom they founded two missions with churches and remained for about five months. Once more they approached the Ujambores, and this time they enjoyed some measure of success and brought about peace between these Indians and the Terrabas.

They were on the point of moving on farther south, when they were recalled a second time and instructed to return to Querétaro. Their faces emaciated, their feet covered with sores, their habits torn and patched with the bark of the maxtate tree, they reached Guatemala on December 2, 1691.

They had accomplished much during the past two years, but they had also suffered much. Once the Indians had poisoned their food, but the poison did them no harm. Another time they were about to be burned at the stake, but the wood refused to burn. For three days and nights they were kept on their knees in a dense forest without food or drink; but seeing that they could not break their courage and determination, the Indians released them.

When they arrived in Guatemala, the Indians called Chols, in the province of Verapaz, lying to the east, were rioting; and the two missionaries were permitted to remain and to go among the Chols in the summer of 1692. After six months they were ordered back to Guatemala for the purpose of establishing a hospice (branch house) of the College of Querétaro there. But since this could not be done at the time, they returned to the Chols. Though at times they were tied to stakes and brutally lashed, they succeeded in establishing eight new missions with churches among the Chols in 1692-1693.

Asked to go among the hitherto unconquered Lacondon Indians in the mountains of northern Guatemala, they set out from Coban. But their guides did everything they could to prevent the missionaries from reaching their destination. It was only in the spring of 1694 that they reached the first village of the Lacondons, after they had almost starved to death. They were beaten and mistreated and held captives for five days without food. In the end they were able to leave without accomplishing anything, and for a short time they visited the Chols once more.

On May 14, 1694, they met four missionaries from Querétaro who were on their way to establish a hospice in

Guatemala. Together they went to the city, and the hospice was opened on June 10. Fr. Melchor was appointed superior and had to part company with Fr. Margil, whose co-worker he had been for ten years. With a new companion, Fr. Pedro de la Concepción, Fr. Margil was sent to the Chols at Belén to learn their language.

At this time it was decided to build a road from Guatemala to Tabasco through the country of the Lacondons. In fact, it was Fr. Margil's constant prodding of Jacinto de Barrios Leal, President of the Audiencia of Guatemala, that a triple expedition was organized for the purpose of blazing the new trail. Fr. Margil was chosen to be the confessor and associate of the president. He walked as fast as those who rode on horses. On April 20, 1695, they reached the Lacondon village where he and Fr. López had suffered so much the previous year.

A wooden fort and mission, named for Nuestra Señora de los Dolores, was built in the Lacondon village; and later another mission village, called San Ramón, was established some five miles distant. Together with other missionaries Fr. Margil remained here and devoted himself to the conversion of the Lacondons during the next two years. He knew their language and translated into it the greater part of Christian Doctrine.

In March, 1697, Fr. Margil received a letter, informing him that he had been chosen guardian of the College of Querétaro; and this time there was no cancellation. After a poignant leave-taking, he set out at once with crucifix, breviary, and vestments; and with amazing speed he walked all the way, through Chiapas, Oaxaca, and Puebla, to Querétaro. "I take short cuts," he explained, "and God helps me."

Five weeks after departing from the Lacondons, at sundown on April 22, he drew near to Querétaro. He had left as a young priest of 27. He came back an old and worn-out veteran, wearing an old patched habit. His feet were covered with thick calluses like those of an Indian. His complexion was deeply bronzed by the burning rays of the sun.

Taking up his new duties, he served as guardian of the college until November, 1700. After about a year, he undertook a preaching tour that took him through the province of Michoacan to Mexico City. At the college he lived an austere life, eating little and sleeping only three hours a day. At the same time he radiated cheerfulness and charity. He built an infirmary at the college and cared for travelers and the poor of the city.

Second Sojourn in Central America

After completing his term as guardian at Querétaro, he remained for a while as vicar and then set out once more for Central America. In ten days he walked the five hundred miles from Querétaro to Oaxaca; and leaving the latter city in mid April, 1701, he reached Guatemala by the end of May. He had come for a twofold purpose: to restore peace in the political struggle that was going on, and to raise the hospice in Guatemala to the rank of an independent missionary college. The political situation had quieted down when he arrived; and on the feast of St. Anthony, June 13, he officially established the College of Cristo Crucificado. Elected as its first guardian, he began to build a new church and friary on September 8, joining the laborers in the construction work.

But after Christmas, the following year (1702), he left the administration of the college in the hands of the vicar, and walked to Nicaragua. In the latter part of February, 1703, he was in the city of León; and during the first week of April he founded a hospice of his college in Granada.

Before returning to Guatemala, he made an excursion into the so-called land of the wizards north of Granada. The wizards were cannibal Indians who as yet had not been conquered by the Spaniards.

By the end of July, 1703, he was back at the college in Guatemala. His missionary journey had lasted seven months. On Christmas eve of that year he preached on the steps of the cathedral for three hours before midnight Mass. He had a stentorian voice, which reached the farthest corners of the plaza and was heard and understood a block away. In March, the following year (1704), he went once more to the wizards in the province of Suchitequez, and did not come back to the college until October. With the aid of Fr. Tomás Hidalgo, he then wrote a book about the wizards.

A new guardian was elected on August 13, 1705, and Fr. Margil was again free to undertake a missionary journey which took him back to Costa Rica. By the beginning of April, 1706, he was in Cartago; and in the middle of June he set out for the Talamanca Indians, among whom another member of the college and later a martyr, Fr. Pablo de Rebullida, was then working. But on July 25, he received a letter instructing him to return and to serve as the first guardian of the new College of Zacatecas.

He left at once; and during the first week of September, he reported in Guatemala that 8,000 Talamancas had been baptized. Now forty-nine years old, he was emaciated and bald, and his feet were deformed by calluses and deep cracks; his bearing was no longer erect, but he was still agile.

In October he reached Oaxaca, in November Mexico City, and by Christmas Querétaro. His second missionary odyssey from Querétaro to the south had lasted five years.

Guardian and Member of the Zacatecas College

The College of Zacatecas was really begun in 1703 when a hospice of the Querétaro College was opened there; but it was not till January, 1707, when Fr. Margil assumed his duties as guardian, that it was officially established as an independent college. Fr. Pedro de la Concepción, with whom Fr. Margil had worked in 1694 among the Indians of Verapaz, was the first to be appointed guardian of the new college; but he was named bishop of Puerto Rico and could not come. Fr. Margil held the office of guardian for two successive terms, 1707-1713.

As guardian of Zacatecas, Fr. Margil made a number of trips to preach parish missions. He did this in Guadalajara in 1707, in Durango, San Juan del Rio, and Santa María de los Lagos in 1708, and in San Luis Potosí in 1709. He also presided at the chapter of the Franciscan province of Zacatecas on February 23, 1709. But he was not able to absent himself more often and for longer periods, because, as he said, "the College of Zacatecas is like a nursing infant and it is my job to be the nurse."

However, after his first term as guardian came to an end in 1710, Fr. Margil, "the able and experienced missionary in apostolic excursions," received a very difficult assignment. Though he entered upon it with his old enthusiasm and dedication, this enterprise was not crowned with success. It was his first real failure, and he accepted it from the hands of God with as much humility as his triumphs.

A royal decree of July 31, 1709, had authorized the government of Guadalajara to undertake the conquest of the Cora and Huichole Indians of Nayarit. Fr. Margil was to be in charge of the spiritual conquest. When he was apprised of this by the beginning of 1711, he pleaded with the government to allow him to try peaceful missionary means first.

Nayarit was the name given to the mountainous region north and northwest of Guadalajara. Fr. Margil went to the city, and from nearby Zapópan he wrote to the Discalced Carmelite nun, Sister Leonor de San José, on March 28, 1711: "Let us all accompany Jesus. May He alone be the missionary and we . . . His beasts of burden!" Accompanied by Fr. Luís Delgado Cervantes and four Indian guides, of whom Pablo Felipe served as an interpreter, they set out for the Coras. But no matter how hard they tried and how persistent they were, the Coras remained adamant in their refusal to become Christians.

Sadly they left and reached Guadalajara on June 10. At the beginning of July, Fr. Margil was back at Zacatecas. Called back for consultation, we find him in Querétaro in May, 1712, and in Mexico City on August 18. But the expedition to Nayarit was postponed, and in September Fr. Margil was once more in Zacatecas. In the end, the expedition was not undertaken at all.

On November 11, 1713, Fr. Joseph Guerra was elected to succeed him and Fr. Margil now turned to the north and established the first Indian missions of the College of Zacatecas in the province of Coahuila. He was near sixty, thin and slightly bent, his feet encrusted and black like an Indian's. A fringe of white hair adorned his bald head like a halo. He walked slowly and grew tired on the way. Still he had some of his former vigor, which he showed by a certain firmness of step; and he was as enthusiastic for new projects and as cheerful as ever.

Querétaran missionaries had already been active in Coahuila for some time. Fr. Damian Massanet founded the Mission of Santiago at Candela in 1688. When he was guardian of Querétaro, Fr. Margil had sent Fr. Diego de Salazar and Fr. Francisco Hidalgo to Coahuila; and they founded the Mission of Nuestra Señora de los Dolores at

La Punta (so called because it was in the extreme north beyond the mountains of Lampazos) on November 12, 1698, and the Mission of San Juan Bautista on the Sabinas River in 1699. Fr. Antonio de Olivares re-established the latter about five miles west of the Rio Grande in January, 1700; and the following year the presidio of San Juan Bautista was established on the Mexican side of the Rio Grande, near the mission of the same name. Both the presidio and the mission played an important role in the history of Texas.

In January, 1714, accompanied by Fr. Matías Saenz, Fr. Margil walked the three hundred miles from Zacatecas to Saltillo, and then continued his march to the Sabinas River, on the banks of which he founded the first Mission of Nuestra Señora de Guadalupe on May 15. Buildings of wood, adobe, and straw were constructed, and Fr. Margil gathered a large number of Indians who consented to live at the mission. It was situated only five miles from the Mission of San Miguel Arcangel, which had been founded recently by the College of Querétaro.

Fr. Margil's mission lasted only three months. An attack of the Toboso Indians on San Miguel forced the missionaries of both missions to retreat to La Punta. At La Punta, on September 15, Fr. Margil wrote: "It is the will of God that there be a little suffering everywhere. We, that is my companion and I, will go to Christianize those settlements which we have not yet won over, until December. . . . Our intention is to persevere until we give them the Faith of Jesus Christ, or we give up our lives."

At the end of September he went to the town of Sabinas (now Sabinas Hidalgo), and returned in April, 1715, to La Punta. From the latter mission, he set out once more in July for the Sabinas River. He was not able to walk fast, and because the captain of the soldiers who went along asked it of him, Fr. Margil for the first time rode a horse.

But instead of being a relief, horseback riding was a torture for him, because he had been suffering from a double hernia for a long time. In spite of the pain he endured, he was in good spirits and cheered the rest.

In August or September, 1715, after two more missionaries from the College of Zacatecas had joined him, Fr. Margil founded the second Mission of Nuestra Señora de Guadalupe on the Salado River; but this mission, like the first, lasted only a short time. At the end of December, he opened a hospice of the College of Zacatecas at Boca de Leones, with an adobe house and chapel.

It was then decided that the two colleges of Querétaro and Zacatecas should both participate in the founding of missions in east Texas; and the Ramón expedition was organized. Fr. Margil was appointed *presidente* of the Zacatecan missionaries who were to take part in the venture. On February 26, 1716, he was still at Boca de Leones, getting together goats, oxen, and horses for the new missions. He followed in the tracks of Ramón's convoy when it finally proceeded to San Juan Bautista, but he could not keep up with it.

Alone and sick he trudged across the desert. He was afflicted with a fever which got so bad that he was barely able to stumble along to a stream, one day's journey distant from the camp. Someone found him there and he was carried to Mission San Juan Bautista. Fr. Espinosa gave him the last sacraments on April 25, and the expedition had to enter Texas without him. However, he recovered and arrived in east Texas before July 22. Early the following year he founded the two missions of Dolores and San Miguel, in easternmost Texas.

From his Mission of Nuestra Señora de los Dolores, when all were suffering great hardships, he wrote to Fr. Espinosa: "As gold in the furnace, so God tries his servants. If he is with us . . . in tribulation, it is no longer tribulation but glory." And to Fr. Francisco Andrade he wrote in March, 1717: "When did Your Reverence or I deserve that our Savior should choose us to be his apostles in these days? Happy are we if we recognize the favor. . . . Let us persevere unto death like the Apostles. . . . Is there anything better?"

In 1719, after the attack of the French on San Miguel Mission, he was forced to leave east Texas with the rest; but he returned in 1721 when the missions were re-established. It was during his sojourn at Mission San Antonio de Valero (1719-1721), that he founded Mission San José (1720) and sent Fr. Agustín Patrón to La Bahía (1721) to found the Mission of Nuestra Señora del Espíritu Santo (1722).

After Fr. Margil had arrived in east Texas for the first time, he was elected, at the end of 1716, for a third term as guardian of the College of Zacatecas; but the news of his election reached him only two years later, and so he was able to renounce the office for the one remaining year. At the beginning of 1722 he was informed that he was once more the college's choice for guardian. This time he had to accept the office. He bade farewell to the missions in east Texas and walked back to Zacatecas. It was June when he arrived at the college, eight and a half years after leaving it to begin missionary work in Coahuila.

In Zacatecas he preached a mission the same year; and in January, 1723, he accompanied Fr. Espinosa, now guardian of the Querétaro College, to Mexico City to secure greater help for the east Texas missions. Their efforts were not successful. But while he was in the capital, Fr. Margil preached for three hours on Good Friday afternoon, and during Easter week from six to nine in the morning and again in the afternoon, to a vast throng that filled the plaza in front of the cathedral.

He was back at Zacatecas in June, 1723. Some days after his return, he became very sick with a fever, the result of an hepatic tumor in the liver. For the third time in his life he received the last sacraments, but on August 7 he was convalescing again and wrote: "I desire to continue as I have up to now, the unworthy slave of all — of Jesus only, in all and each of my fellowmen."

After completing his term as guardian on February 17, 1725, he weakened visibly. He was now sixty-seven and felt the need of more sleep and rest, but later that year he undertook what was to be his last preaching tour and walked to Guadalajara, arriving on November 3. At two different places he had to escape on horseback at midnight; otherwise the Indians would have prevented his departure.

On May 1, 1726, he arrived at Valladolid and there preached his last mission. After the mission, he was confined to bed with a fever for seven days. On June 5 he went on to Querétaro. There his condition grew rapidly worse. At the suggestion of the commissary general, he was taken to the infirmary of the large friary of San Francisco el Grande in Mexico. During the first lap of the journey he rode a horse but during its latter part a carriage had to be hired. It was August 2, Portiuncula Day, when he arrived at San Francisco. He entered the church and spent a little time in prayer on his knees, and was then helped to his room in the infirmary.

He made a general confession of his whole life, but there was not a single serious violation of God's commandments that he had to confess. On August 5 he tenderly kissed an image of Nuestra Señora de los Remedios that was brought to him, and said: "Until tomorrow!" On the following day, August 6, 1726, at the age of 69 minus a few days, he expired peacefully between one and two in the afternoon. His last words were: "It is time now to go to God."

The many bells of the city tolled one after the other, and thousands came to pay their last respects to the great missionary and saintly friar, Fr. Antonio Margil. His body was laid out first in the infirmary chapel and then in the sacristy of the church. The solemn funeral was held on the 8th, and the burial took place in a vault in the church of San Francisco. In 1861, Fr. Margil's remains were transferred to the cathedral, first to the Chapel of La Soledad and then to that of La Purísima.

Immediately after his death, the investigation of his life was commenced with a view to beatification and canonization; but, due to the grave situation in Europe, there was an interruption for forty years. The cause was taken up once more, and on July 31, 1836 (the year of the independence of Texas), Pope Gregory XVI declared that Fr. Margil had practiced virtue in a heroic degree, thus bestowing on him the title of "Venerable." There the cause has rested, but there have been several attempts to reawaken interest in it.

Fr. Margil became great because he was so utterly humble. He called and signed himself "La misma nada" (Nothingness itself). And he really meant it. He found an example in Our Lady, who declared that God had "regarded the lowliness (the nothingness) of his handmaid." He loved to refer to her as "La Doña Nada" (Lady Nothingness). His was a total renunciation of self, so that he could be a tool in God's hands. He had a deep conviction that if he did not recognize his own nothingness, he would be worshipping his own ego and robbing God of some of the glory that is his. Everything that he was and had, he had received from God, and he surrendered himself and all his powers wholly to God. Thus he was able to love God with his whole being and to spend all of his energies in serving God's children, his fellowmen. "Jesus showed his love by his deeds," he wrote, "and we must prove our love of Jesus by our deeds, not mere words." And so, Fr. Antonio Margil, like St. Paul, the Apostle of the Gentiles, became as one "sorrowful, yet always rejoicing, as poor yet enriching many, as having nothing yet possessing all things."

Fr. Diego Miguel Bringas de Manzaneda (who preached the sermon at the solemn obsequies which were held when the remains of Fr. Francisco Garcés and his three companion martyrs were transferred to the College of Querétaro on July 19, 1794) wrote the following about Fr. Margil:

"What can we say of this new Apostle of the Indies, when so much has been written about him in America and even in Rome, where five folio volumes have already been printed in the prosecution of his cause of beatification. His wonderful life-story has been narrated by three chroniclers of the College, and in our own day a fourth, as yet unpublished, biography has been written. . . . For forty-four years he toiled indefatigably in America. . . . His whole life was an amazing kaleidoscope of leadership as superior, of preaching to sinners, of the founding of colleges and missions among pagans, of endless journeys of thousands of leagues made on foot, of constant growth in holiness and good example, and of the working of miracles. . . . All America was the witness and the scene of his virtues and miracles. To trace his journeys among the pagans, turn your eyes to east and west, to north and south, and you will find him in all these places, leading a very austere life, crossing mountains, struggling with the evil spirit until he has triumphantly planted his foundations. The widely scattered provinces of Nicaragua and Costa Rica, of Honduras and Chol and Panama, of Coahuila and Tejas — all of them heard his apostolic voice."

Founding of San José

According to what we have seen, this site on the San Antonio River and its vicinity, where we wish to establish the mission (San José), is destined to be the heart, as it were, from which we are to branch out in our work of founding missions.

— Fr. Antonio Margil

III

Fʀ. ANTONIO MARGIL AND MOST OF THE
other refugees from eastern Texas arrived at the San Antonio mission and presidio, with its little villa, early in
November, 1719; and they remained there for about a year
and a half, awaiting the arrival of the Marquis of Aguayo
and his army.

The Marquis had been commissioned to drive the French
from eastern Texas and to make the Spanish occupation of
the province a truly permanent one. Aguayo, a rich man
who owned a large part of the Province of Coahuila, had
been appointed Governor of both Coahuila and Texas; and
he was very much interested in the task assigned to him.
But it took time to raise an army and to gather the necessary supplies; and so he did not arrive in San Antonio until
April 4, 1721.

Fr. Margil at Mission San Antonio

During his sojourn at Mission San Antonio, Fr. Margil assisted Fr. Olivares. We find his signature in the baptismal register of Mission San Antonio, on February 4, 1720. On that day he administered the sacrament of baptism to the 32nd Indian neophyte to be baptized at the mission.

Near Mission San Antonio, Fr. Margil found three Indian tribes who were interested in settling down in a mission; but they did not want to join the Indians at the mission established the previous year, because they were not friendly with them. Fr. Margil conceived the idea of founding a second mission on the Río de San Antonio which would be in the care of the College of Zacatecas. It would also serve as a halfway station for this College, as the San Antonio Mission did for the College of Querétaro. In eastern Texas the two colleges had cooperated, each one having charge of three missions. The same cooperation could be expected on the Río de San Antonio, which was an ideal center from which both could expand their work, Querétaro toward the north and Zacatecas toward the south.

On the day after Christmas, 1719, Fr. Margil wrote a letter to the Marquis, with whom he was personally acquainted. He told Aguayo about his plan. For the present, some of the church furnishings which he had brought along from eastern Texas could be used; and he had a statue of St. Joseph which had been given to him for a mission which was to be named for the saint. All that was needed was the authorization of the Marquis, and a few oxen for plowing the fields and some corn seed for planting. He added that the new mission could be called San José y San Miguel de Aguayo in honor of the Marquis himself.

The Founding of Mission San José

The Marquis responded promptly. On January 22, 1720, he issued a decree, instructing Captain Juan Valdez of the Presidio of San Antonio de Béxar to proceed with the formal establishment of the new mission without further delay. He was to select a suitable site for the mission and to give the land to Fr. Margil, to be administered for the Indians by a missionary of the Father *Presidente's* choice. When Fr. Margil learned that his request had been granted, he sent two of his companions, Fr. Agustín Patrón and Fr. Miguel Núñez de Haro to select a place for the mission. They picked a spot, less than four miles south of Mission San Antonio on the east bank of the River, and there constructed a straw hut. It was "an elevated plain, spacious and very level."

Fr. Antonio de San Buenaventura y Olivares, the founder of San Antonio Mission, was opposed to the founding of a second mission so close to his. He was afraid there would be trouble between the Indians of the two missions who were anything but friendly with each other. However, Captain Valdez told him he had to go through with the orders he had received from the Marquis; and he assured Fr. Olivares that the law of the Indies which required missions to be three leagues apart would be observed.

On February 23, Valdez and three other officials, one of them Captain Lorenzo García who served as interpreter, Fr. Margil, Fr. Joseph Guerra, and a group of Indians went from the presidio to the place where Frs. Núñez and Patrón had built a straw hut. The Spanish officials rode horseback, and the missionaries and Indians walked. Fr. Margil always traveled on foot. Captain Valdez made sure that the distance was three leagues. This would be about seven and a half miles, but even the present site of the mission, which is a little farther south, is only about four and a half miles from the Alamo. However, they measured the distance, not in a straight line, but by going along the many windings of the San Antonio River; and their method of measuring distances was not very exact. Thus the Captain could say that the place selected was "more than three leagues" from the other mission.

In a colorful ceremony, Mission San José was then formally founded. Captain Valdez alighted from his horse. He told the Indians that the land was their property, but the missionaries would have full charge of everything at the mission, and would instruct and direct them. Joining hands with the three chiefs, he walked with them across the fields, and traced the course of an irrigation ditch which would be two miles long. The right to water from the San Antonio, and to the woods and timber was given to the Indians. The chiefs pulled up grass, cut branches from trees, and threw rocks and handfuls of ground across the fields as a sign of ownership. A spot, $333\frac{1}{3}$ feet square, was picked, around which the mission buildings were to be constructed. Finally Captain Valdez appointed one of the chiefs governor.

The Visit of Aguayo

About a year later, the Marquis of Aguayo and his army arrived. On April 26 he paid a visit to Mission San Antonio and distributed clothing and other articles to the 240 Indians who were congregated there. On another day he visited Mission San José and found that there were already 227 Indians living at the mission; and to each of these he gave similar gifts. He did the same to Chief Juan Rodríguez and his fifty followers, for whom Mission San Francisco Xavier was founded the following year at or near the site of the later Mission Concepción.

Accompanied by the refugees from the east, Aguayo then set out for eastern Texas, where he re-established the six missions and the presidio of Dolores near Mission Concepción; and near the easternmost mission, San Miguel de Linares de los Adaes, not far from present Robeline, Louisiana, he founded another presidio, which he made the capital of the Province of Texas. By January 23, 1722, he was back in San Antonio; and on March 16, he founded Mission San Francisco Xavier de Nájera. The same day he left for Lavaca Bay; and there, on April 6, he officially established another mission and presidio. A beginning had really been made for these new establishments the previous year by Fr. Agustín Patrón, who had been the companion of Fr. Núñez at Mission San José for one year, and by Captain Domingo Ramón, who had been in command of the presidio in eastern Texas.

The First Site

The Marquis was a sick man at this time; and returning to San Antonio, he left on May 5 for his capital in Coahuila. He did not again visit Texas; but he continued to take an interest in the Province. In 1729, when preparations were being made to bring a group of settlers from the Canary Islands to San Antonio, he made a map of the San Antonio area, showing Mission San José on the east side of the San Antonio River, below Mission San Antonio. He did not know that, by that time, Mission San José had been moved to the west bank.

That the original site of San José was on the east bank is clearly stated by Fr. Isidro Félix de Espinosa, who at this time was the Father President of the Querétaran missions in Texas; and he also tells us (in 1744) that the mission was moved to the west bank a little farther south, but he does not say at what time this was done.

Mission San José had been making excellent progress

The Aguayo Map of 1729. Rather than a map, this is a diagram drawn from memory by the Marques de Aguayo seven years after he had left the San Antonio area. At the left, on the east side of the San Antonio River, is Mission San Antonio de Valero; but the loop of the river is placed on the wrong side. At the right, on the east side, is Mission San Jose y San Miguel de Aguayo; but the juncture of San Pedro Creek is placed opposite this mission, whereas it should be farther north. Between the two missions, on the east side, Aguayo suggests that the new settlement of the Canary Islanders be located and that it be named Villa de San Antonio de Casafuerte (the name of the viceroy); but two years later, this settlement was established on the west side of the river and named Villa de San Fernando. Originally it was on the west side of the Presidio de San Antonio de Bexar, and shortly afterwards it was moved to the ground lying between the presidio and the river. (For the above redrawing of the map, the writer is indebted to the State Building Commission Archaeological Program, Report Number 1, *Historic Background of the Mission San Antonio de Valero* by Mardith K. Schuetz, November, 1966.)

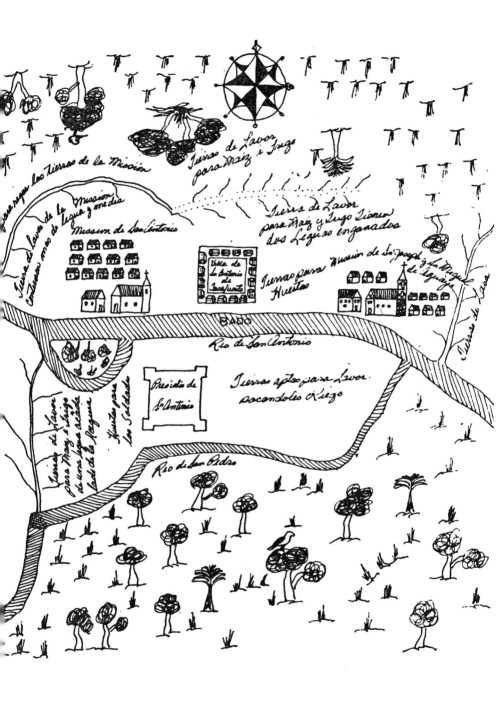

Para regar las Tierras de la Mission

Tierras de Lavor para Maiz é Trigo

Tierra del Lavor de la Mission Contienen mas de legua y media

Mission de San Antonio

Tierra de Lavor para Maiz y Trigo Tienen dos Leguas enganadas

Villa de la Batería de San Juanito

Tierras para Huertas

Mission de S.n Joseph y S.n Miguel de Aguayo

Tierras de Lavor

BADO

Rio de San Antonio

Presidio de S.n Antonio

Tierras de Lavor para Maiz é Trigo de una legua á lado de la laguna

Ajustar para los Soldados

Tierras aptas para Lavor dacandoles el riego

Rio de San Pedro

at its first site. Although Fr. Patrón had remained with Fr. Núñez for only one year, Captain Nicolás Flores y Valdez of the Presidio of San Antonio de Béxar had supplied two Spanish soldiers who had been very helpful. They not only served as a guard for the missionary and his Indian charges, but acted as *mayordomos* or overseers. They also taught the Indians various trades; and when some of the Indians ran away like truant school children, the soldiers went along with Fr. Núñez to go in quest of the runaways and to persuade them to return to the mission. In most instances the wayward Indians were glad to see their missionary and willingly went back with him.

By the spring of 1724, the irrigation ditch had been completed; and San José had a surplus crop of corn. In fact, Fr. Núñez was able to supply 100 *fanegas* (160 bushels) of corn, which was sent to the mission and presidio at La Bahía, which were in great need at that time.

The Second Site

In the spring of 1727, Brigadier General Pedro de Rivera arrived at San Antonio for an official inspection of the Province of Texas which lasted about a year. When he visited San José in 1727, the mission was no longer on the east side of the San Antonio River, but on its west bank. He mentions this fact in a letter of 1730, in which he points out that Aguayo's map of 1729 was mistaken. Aguayo had suggested that the Canary Islanders' settlement be located on the east bank, between the two missions, and named Villa de San Antonio de Casafuerte.

Sometime before 1727, therefore, Fr. Núñez had moved the mission to the other side of the river. This site, too, was not the present one, but closer to the river bank. Here Fr. Núñez constructed a church and other buildings of adobe. At least that is what Fr. Alto S. Hoermann, a Benedictine Father who resided at Mission San José, 1859 to 1864, states as a fact in his story about the mission, entitled *The Daughter of Tehuan*. He indicates that he got this information from some few people who had helped to erect the stone church at the present site and were still living in 1861. One of them, he writes, who died in 1860, had reached the age of 105 years. When Fr. Hoermann was at San José the spot was still marked by a pile of debris.

Fr. Hoermann's testimony is confirmed by a letter which the superiors of the College of Zacatecas wrote on January 15, 1750, to the Franciscan Commissary General of the Indies in Spain. It declares that Mission San José had been "placed in various locations," in order to achieve greater spiritual and temporal progress; and that evidently means that the mission had, not just two, but at least three different sites.

Development of San José

Where Danger lurked in countless hidden
    forms
And all relentless seized her luckless spoil,
They wrought unmoved. Brave pioneers of
    faith,
They called from wigwam and from forest
    haunt
The tawny dwellers of the wilderness,
Subdued the savage natures to their will,
And guided with their own the unskilled
    hands,
Till day by day the stately walls arose
In strength and beauty on the lonely plains;
And from the virgin soil, before untrod,
The golden grain sprang up in shining ranks.

— JANIE F. BASKIN

IV

THOUGH MISSION SAN JOSÉ HAD FARED WELL
at its first site on the eastern side of the San Antonio,
Fr. Núñez for some reason or other believed that
the west bank was a more advantageous place; and so he
moved the mission compound to the other side, a little
farther down the river.

Here new buildings of adobe, but still of a temporary
nature, were constructed. A new irrigation ditch also had
to be dug; but the irrigated fields at the original site were
no doubt cultivated, for a time at least, even after the
transfer was made.

At the second site, in the low lying terrain close to the
river bank, Mission San José prospered for more than a
decade. One cannot but admire the success that so quickly

crowned the patient and persevering efforts of Fr. Núñez in civilizing and Christianizing the mission Indians.

Only a short time before, these Indians had been pagan nomads with a very low culture and such a pronounced aversion to work of any kind that they preferred to go hungry rather than to do any work. They were the so-called Coahuiltecan Indians, a generic term used for some seventy different small tribes who roamed about in what is now southern Texas and the adjoining region of Mexico.

How the Indians Were Congregated

First of all, Fr. Núñez had to go in quest of them and attract them to the mission by giving them trinkets and food. That was the only language which they understood. Once they were at the mission, he slowly and gradually induced them to work for a living and instructed them in Christian doctrine. Only after they were well prepared, did he baptize them.

The products of the field were stored in a granary and distributed by the missionary. As long as the mission was under the supervision of the missionary and the Indians were under his guidance and tutelage, there was enough and more to satisfy the needs of all the residents.

The example of Fr. Núñez exerted a powerful influence on his charges. Seeing that the missionary sought no personal gain, but was solicitous only for their spiritual and temporal well-being, the neophytes must have realized before long that he was a true father and friend to them.

The early historian of Texas, Henderson Yoakum, praised the accomplishments of the missionaries; but he had erroneous ideas concerning the methods employed to gather the Indians in the missions and to keep them there. Yoakum writes: "Not content with the fruits of persuasion and kind treatment, they (the Franciscan fathers) made forays upon the surrounding tribes. The soldiers performed this duty. The prisoners taken, especially the young, were trained alike in the mysteries of the Christian faith and of agriculture. To effect their training, they were divided among the older and more deserving Indians of the mission who held them in servitude until they were of an age suitable to marry. At the proper time this rite was faithfully performed, and thus there grew up a race of domestic Indians around the mission."

There is no historical evidence that the missionaries or the mission guards used force or deception to bring the Indians into the mission and held them there as prisoners. In his *Crónica,* Fr. Espinosa, who had been a missionary in eastern Texas, wrote: "Rivera insinuates (March 23, 1728), the missionaries had intimated that the conversion of the savages must be effected by force of arms. He labors under a manifest misapprehension. It is one thing for the missionaries to have an armed guard in order to insure the respect of the savages, and another thing to impart the Faith by force of arms. This latter no one has even dreamed of. He adduces instances of troubles on the part of some friars who were maltreated by Indians. We may add that those Indians would never have been so bold and insolent, had they feared a castigation from some neighboring garrison. The very fact that the missionaries were seen to lack protection made the savages fearless and impudent."

San Fernando Villa and the Other Missions, 1731

Mission San José had been at its second site for some six years when it received several neighbors. Before 1731, there were only the Mission of San Antonio de Valero, on the east side of the San Antonio River, and on the other side the Presidio of San Antonio de Béxar, with a little villa or village of the same name. The Mission of San Francisco Xavier de Nájera had ceased to exist in 1726. Its Indians, who previously had insisted on having a separate mission, were at that time not only willing but desirous to join those at Mission San Antonio.

In 1731, a group of settlers from the Canary Islands came to the Villa de Béxar, and its name was changed to Villa de San Fernando; and although, later on, it was raised to the rank of a "ciudad," a city, the place was known more often, throughout the century that followed, by the name of the presidio — San Antonio de Béxar.

It was in 1731 also that three more missions were established in the San Antonio area. In 1729, after the inspection tour of Rivera, the presidio of Dolores in eastern Texas was suppressed; and the three Querétaran missions in its vicinity were transferred temporarily to the Colorado River in 1730, and the next year permanently to the San Antonio River. Mission Nuestra Señora de la Purísima Concepción, with the added appellation of "de Acuña," was located on the former site of the San Francisco Xavier Mission on the east side of the river, between San Antonio and San José. Mission San José de los Nazonis became San Juan Capistrano, likewise on the east bank of the San Antonio River, about three and a half miles south of San José. Mission San Francisco de los Neches, now called San Francisco de Espada, was re-established about two miles farther south on the west bank of the river.

The transfer of these three missions was quite a feat. While the Tejas Indians of these missions did not go along, all the moveable property and the stock were taken across numerous streams and rivers, more than three hundred miles, from present Cherokee and Nacogdoches counties to present Bexar County. At their new location, Coahuiltecan

Indians like those at the San Antonio and San José missions, were assembled; and a new beginning had to be made. The first mission buildings were flimsy temporary structures called *jacales*. Their walls consisted of stakes driven into the ground, interwoven with brush, and the interstices filled with mud which was soon hardened by the sun; and they had thatched roofs of straw.

Such also were the first structures of San José Mission at its first site; but at its second location adobe buildings had been constructed by 1731. The statement has often been made that "the church of San José Mission" was completed or dedicated on March 5, 1731, the day on which the three missions which were transferred from eastern Texas were established on the San Antonio River. If correct, this would have been the adobe church at the mission's second site; but the writer has looked in vain for any document that would serve as a basis for the assertion.

Anyhow, from the year 1731, the story of San José is intimately connected with that of the other four San Antonio missions, even though San José was the only Zacatecan mission until 1773 and the others were Querétaran missions. The latter too passed into the hands of the missionaries of the College of Zacatecas in 1773.

Apaches and Comanches

One of the difficulties with which San José and the other four missions had to contend, as long as they lasted, was the danger of attack by the Apaches, who came from the north, and by the Comanches who followed close upon their heels. Campaigns were conducted against them, treaties were made with them, missions were founded among them; but the Apache and Comanche menace was an ever present problem. For this reason the missions were built like fortresses; and the hostile Indians did not attempt to storm the mission compounds, but carried on a sort of guerilla warfare against the workers in the fields outside the walls and travelers, and made raids on the mission ranches stealing cattle and horses. That was the principal reason also, for Spanish guards at the mission during the earlier days and Indian soldiers during the later period. It was never safe to venture far beyond the mission walls without a guard of several soldiers.

Governor Franquis de Lugo, 1736-1737

San José and its neighbors, however, suffered less harm from the Apaches than from Governor Benites Franquis de Lugo, who came to Texas in 1736. He was a strange character who seemed to take delight in starting quarrels and exercising his authority in a dictatorial and arbitrary manner. At times he acted almost like a madman. Towards the missionaries especially he manifested a disrespectful and unjust attitude; and his evil example had a very bad influence on the Indians and the settlers.

The first thing he did was to reduce to one the Spanish guards, of whom there were two at San José and San Antonio and three at each of the other missions. At this time Fr. Núñez was assisted by Fr. Joseph Cosmé Borruel; and the latter, according to Franquis de Lugo, told the governor that San José Mission could get along without a guard and he could have both soldiers. The viceroy instructed Franquis that he should restore the usual three soldiers to each of the missions, but he disregarded the orders. It was only in September, 1737, that his successor sent the guards back to the missions.

In 1737 Fr. Borruel informed the governor that he had been transferred to the La Bahía mission, which was now on the Guadalupe River, and that another unnamed missionary was at San Juan Bautista with a train of supplies, waiting to take his place; but the captain of that presidio refused to furnish the usual escort of soldiers. This time, in his usual violent manner, Franquis sent a threatening letter to the captain in question, ordering him to supply the escort at once.

The previous year, the Tacame Indians who were at San José had left in a body and had gone to the Espada Mission. They were a fickle outfit; and the next year, they wanted to go to Mission San Antonio. When their request was refused, they departed and returned to the woods. The Querétaran missionaries tried to persuade them to come back — to San Antonio, if they wished; but their efforts were in vain. Then the two missionaries at San José (Fr. Núñez had an assistant at this time) endeavored to bring them back; and refusing to give up, continued to pursue this self-imposed task with an indomitable perseverance. After three years, they succeeded in leading seventy-seven Tacames, not to Mission San José, but to Mission San Antonio. Here is an example of the cooperation of the missionaries of the two colleges. While there was a friendly rivalry between the two colleges, it was not of the kind that some have thought it was.

Complaints of the Settlers

Franquis also tried to force the missionaries to permit the settlers to hire mission Indians for work on their farms. Knowing that this would have had many deplorable results, the missionaries refused. But after Franquis was removed from office, the settlers persisted in their attempts to get Indian laborers from the missions. A petition addressed to the viceroy in 1740 was not granted; but three years later, by making false accusations against the missionaries, they obtained the viceroy's consent. In 1745, after he had learned the true state of affairs from the missionaries, the viceroy reversed his decision.

One of the false charges made by the settlers against the missionaries was that they carried on competitive trade in products of the mission farms and shops. The viceroy believed the settlers and gave strict orders to the missionaries to abstain from such trade, which was forbidden to them. When he found out that the missions were rendering a service by supplying superfluous goods, the viceroy informed the captain of the presidio that he could get supplies either from the settlers or from the missionaries as he saw fit; and the settlers were not to do any trading with the Indians without the permission of the missionaries.

Another complaint of the settlers was that the mission cattle wandered into their fields and did considerable damage to their farms, which was a fact. However, Franquis de Lugo encouraged the settlers, not only to kill stray mission cattle, but also to go ostensibly on hunting trips and to steal cattle from the mission herds. The problem of stray cattle was solved to some extent, when the settlers hired a man to keep watch over their irrigated fields; and gradually they put up fences, as the viceroy told them to do. The mission farm of San José also had a fence around it.

Water rights to the San Antonio River was another moot question between the settlers and the missions. All of them drew water from the San Antonio for their irrigation ditches. The matter was finally settled amicably by an agreement made on August 14, 1745. Fr. Benito Fernández de Santa Ana, Father President of the Querétaran missions but acting also in the name of San José, proposed that a line be drawn from north to south on the west side of the San Antonio River, and that what lay west of the line belong to the settlers while the east side should be mission property. This proposal was accepted.

Franquis de Lugo also wanted the five missions reduced to two, and the settlers joined him in making this demand; but nothing came of it. It is interesting to note that, like the settlers, Franquis hailed from the Canary Islands.

The missions had begun to erect better buildings when Franquis appeared on the scene. But, because of the troubles that ensued, these activities came to an abrupt halt.

The Epidemic of 1739

To climax the evil days which had fallen on the missions, a calamitous smallpox and measles epidemic broke out in the entire San Antonio area in 1739. Many of the Indians died; many others fled from the missions. The missionaries also took sick; and the one at Espada, Fr. Ignacio Ysasmendi, the missionary who had been maligned by Franquis, died at his post.

Mission San José especially, perhaps because it was situated on low lying ground near the river bank, was hard hit. Its population, which had been near the three hundred mark, reached a low of forty-nine, less than that of any of the other missions. By the spring of 1740, Fr. Núñez and his assistant were convalescing; and even before the plague had run its course, one of them made long trips to bring back former mission Indians and to persuade new neophytes to join them. By the end of the year, there was a total of 249 Indians living at San José, more than in any of the other four missions, although San Antonio with 238 and Concepción with 210 were not far behind. The Capistrano Mission had 169 and Espada 120.

Testimony of Captain Urrutia, 1740

These figures are contained in a report made on December 17, 1740, by Captain Toribio de Urrutia of the Presidio of San Antonio de Béxar to the viceroy. The Captain had been living at Béxar ever since its establishment in 1718. He was well acquainted with Fr. Núñez, who had been serving San José since 1720. He had seen San José and the other missions develop, and was a witness of the disinterested and persevering labors of the missionaries. Unlike Governor Franquis, he was a friend and admirer of the missions and the padres.

From personal observation, he informed the viceroy, he knew the missionaries had carried out their difficult task with great care in both spiritual and temporal matters. They instructed the neophytes in Christian doctrine twice a day, in the early morning and in the late afternoon. With the Indians they went to the mission farms to work with them, and to show them by their personal example how to plant and to harvest the crops. They were solicitous to provide the Indians with all they needed. All had medicine chests; and when any of the Indians took sick, the missionaries administered to them the proper remedies. They did all they possibly could to make the Indians happy and contented.

To each missionary the government gave an annual allowance for their personal needs. Frequently, declares Captain Urrutia, the missionaries used a part of this sum to procure things for the comfort and welfare of their charges. At all times the sons of St. Francis showed great patience and kindness and love to their flock; and sometimes they traveled as much as 250 miles into unexplored territory in order to bring runaway Indians back to the missions.

An important statement of the Captain Urrutia concerning the mission buildings has often been overlooked. He says, and he was certainly in a position to know, that up to the time of his report, that is, the end of 1740, the buildings which had been erected in the missions, San José included, were still only of a temporary nature. The mission churches still had thatched roofs of straw; and in some of the missions these roofs had fallen down and were being rebuilt. The living quarters in some of the missions were as yet inadequate, because of the increased number of converts; but this defect was being remedied as quickly as the circumstances permitted it.

It was very probably in 1740, after the disastrous epidemic of 1739, that Fr. Núñez decided to move the mission for the second time, and this time to the higher ground it now occupies. The third site was about twenty-five feet higher and one-half mile distant from the second. For this we have the testimony of Fr. Hoermann who was at San José when some adobe ruins could still be seen at the second site of the mission.

Heyday of San José

The arts of peace bloomed in primeval wilds,
And nature's rude untutored were transformed
Through the all-quickening power of the Cross.
The spark divine that slumbered in their souls
Was kindled till it burned with steady flame;
And Indian hands toiled for the love of God,
While Indian hearts were turned to Him in
      prayer.
Here in this pile of ancient masonry
Was wrought the witness of their simple faith,
The sweet fruition of their hopes and fears.

— JANIE F. BASKIN

V

AFTER MISSION SAN JOSÉ HAD BEEN MOVED
to its present site at the beginning of the 1740's, it entered
upon its period of greatest development and achievement —
a period that lasted about four decades. For this period we
have a series of excellent reports by eyewitnesses and other
contemporary statements which describe in some detail not
only the mission buildings but also the condition and
activities of the neophytes who lived at the mission. All of
them are unanimous in praising the work of its missionaries
and declaring that San José was an outstanding mission, a
mission that was enjoying extraordinary success.

Fr. Espinosa's Statement, 1744

The first brief statement of this kind we find in the voluminous chronicle of the apostolic colleges which was printed in 1746, but completed at least two years earlier. Its author was Fr. Isidro Félix de Espinosa who had been a missionary in Texas three decades earlier, at the same time that Fr. Antonio Margil, the founder of San José, had been a Texas missionary.

Fr. Espinosa writes that San José was one of the most successful of the Zacatecan missions. Its Indians were fully instructed in Christian doctrine. It had an irrigation system, and a church with terraces. While it is possible that the church of which Fr. Espinosa speaks was the adobe structure at the mission's second site, it is more likely that it was the first church at the third, the present site. Having terraces, parts of it — if not the entire building — had a flat and probably earthen roof. Less than a quarter century later, it was torn down to make room for the present restored stone church.

Fr. Ciprián's Report, 1749

Besides the church, there were other buildings which were constructed of stone during the 1740's. This we learn from the report written in 1749 by Fr. Ignacio Antonio Ciprián, a missionary at the La Bahía Mission at least from 1747 to 1749, and he may have been the Father President of the Zacatecan missions in Texas.

Fr. Ciprián, who had been a missionary in Texas since 1731, could speak from personal observation. He declared that San José had made greater spiritual and temporal progress than any of the other missions of the College of Zacatecas in Coahuila, Nuevo León, and Nuevo Santander.

He described it as "a veritable fortress." The mission church, he says, was very beautiful and could accommodate two thousand persons. This was probably the terraced church mentioned by Fr. Espinosa; but, we believe, its capacity was two hundred, not two thousand. Even though two subsequent reports repeat the figure two thousand, it can hardly be explained except as an error that crept into Fr. Ciprián's report.

Adjoining the church there was a friary with a serrated cloister and a porter's office. This was, no doubt, the ground floor of the present stone *convento;* and it had a flat roof, the edge of which was notched or toothed like a saw.

The Indians were over two hundred in number. The letter of Fr. Guardian Francisco Vallejo and his council at the College of Zacatecas, dated January 15, 1750, states that the number of Indians at San José was two hundred and twenty. The houses of the Indians, continues Fr. Ciprián, were built of stone. The cotton and woolen clothes worn by the Indians were made of cloth that was woven at the mission.

The stock of the mission included two thousand head of cattle and one thousand sheep. The farm yielded a corn crop of twenty-four hundred bushels per year; and the corn was stored in a granary of stone — the first two sections of the present structure, then having a flat roof. Fr. Ciprián naively states that "if they planted more corn, they would have more," but he indicates they did not need more: "In every respect, all of them have everything they need."

The Indians were well instructed, and they were very good Christians. Not only did they fulfill their religious duties, but many of them frequented the sacraments during the year. On Saturdays they sang the Rosary outdoors, and they did so "very sweetly and with much devotion." The fourteen stations of the Way of the Cross had also been set up outdoors; and the Indians performed this religious exercise, walking from station to station, on the Fridays of Lent.

To good Fr. Núñez, who had established San José Mission three decades before, and had served it ever since, it must have been a great consolation to see his mission, at long last, in such a flourishing condition. Three years later, on December 2, 1752, he was called to his eternal reward. If he was thirty years old when he first came to Texas in 1718, he was sixty-four years old at the time of his death. The history of the Zacatecas College by Sotomayor records the fact that "his blessed body" was laid to rest at the Mission but later it was taken to Zacatecas and buried in the common cemetery of the College.

Report of Governor Barrios, 1758

About a decade after Fr. Ciprián made his report, Governor Jacinto Barrios y Jáuregui paid a visit to Mission San José on May 23, 1758. The missionary in charge of the mission was Fr. Ildefonso Joseph Marmolejo, who previously (1750-1753) had been the Father Guardian of the College of Zacatecas. Fr. Marmolejo welcomed the governor and took him on a tour of every part of the mission compound. He also showed him the mission records, which unfortunately have been lost. These revealed the fact that during the thirty-eight years of the mission's existence, 964 persons had been baptized, 145 couples had entered Christian marriages, and 466 had received Christian burial.

The governor was deeply impressed; and five days later he wrote a glowing report about San José. The arrangement of the mission buildings, as described by the governor, seems to have been quite different from what it was a decade later. However, when he says that the large square was divided into eight smaller squares of which four were formed by the Indian houses, each group having eighteen apartments, he is probably speaking of a mental division of the area. Since he mentions that the flat-roofed Indian houses were of stone and had parapets and loopholes, it appears that there was one row of eighteen houses along the east wall, another along the west wall, and two successive rows or thirty-six houses along the south wall. That makes a total of seventy-two houses. But Governor Barrios says the total was eighty-four; and hence there must have been twelve additional Indian apartments elsewhere.

Each Indian house consisted of one room and a kitchen, both well furnished. Each row of eighteen houses also had flowing water and a bathing pool. The flowing water came from the *acequia* just outside the north and east walls of the compound, or from an overflowing spring-fed well which is mentioned in 1768. The Indian population of the mission was 281, of whom 113 were men, all of them "capable of bearing arms." At night regular Indian guards made the rounds.

Four additional squares were occupied by the other buildings of the mission. The largest was the church, which was cruciform in shape, having one nave and a transept; and it could hold two thousand persons (sic). Inside the church there were beautiful images in relief; and at one corner stood a well-proportioned tower with a set of bells. It was the same church that Fr. Ciprián mentioned in 1749, except that the tower may have been added since then.

Adjoining the church, there was the *convento* and cloister, built of lime and stone, fairly large, and having two stories. On the second floor there was only one room; and on the ground floor were other rooms and the offices.

Opposite the church stood the soldiers' quarters, with another bathing pool. The fact that the governor calls them "cassas reales" (royal houses) indicates that the usual three Spanish guards were still stationed at San José at this time. They were still there in 1763. On May 11 of that year Captain Luís Antonio Menchaca of the Presidio of San Antonio de Béxar informed the viceroy that three Spanish guards were at each of the five San Antonio Missions. However, in 1768 the defence of the mission as well as the management of its farm and ranch were entirely in the hands of mission Indians; the Spanish soldiers were no longer stationed at San José.

The other buildings included the granary, in which there were 4,000 bushels of corn; the carpenter shop and other workshops; and a sugar mill, where cane syrup and brown sugar were made.

The cemetery, probably in front of the church, was 221½ feet square and had a rubble fence with three entrances. It served also as a military plaza, where the Indian soldiers had their arrow and rifle practice and their drills. The latter were different from those of Spanish soldiers, but they were carried out with remarkable precision.

On the mission ranch, the governor found 1,500 head of branded cattle, 3,376 sheep, 103 horses, 80 mares, and 30 yoke of oxen. In nine years, that is, since the treaty which the Spaniards had made with the Apaches in 1749, the latter had nevertheless killed and stolen no less than two thousand head of cattle from San José.

Every week seven beefs were slaughtered: four for those who lived inside the compound, one for the cowboys, one for the shepherds, and one from which jerked meat was made. There were also chickens; for, it is expressly stated that the sick received chicken and mutton. On Sundays the missionary gave each Indian one peck of corn and a slab of meat and also some tobacco. On Thursdays, he distributed beans, brown sugar bars, and to those who needed it more corn. On other days of the week, he supplied anything that was needed.

All the Indians of the mission were well dressed, "better than one would expect of their station." The missionary treated them with fatherly kindness, and they were happy and contented. So much so, that for some time, there had not been any fugitives. There was no need for a jail, or chains, or stocks. All the Indians then living at the mission were Christians. On Saturdays, they sang the Rosary in a most edifying manner. They had good voices, and also played musical instruments.

The mission Indians elected one of their number governor, and others for various civil and military offices. Their tribunals "administered justice without bloodshed"; for, the missionary used "his influence to see that the guilty were punished and all were drawn together in love." All of this, declared the governor, was accomplished with no aid from the government, and only by the use of the annual personal allowance of four hundred and fifty pesos which the government granted each missionary, and by the work of the Indians. And much more would have been achieved, if it had not been for the damaging raids of the thieving Apaches. The fact that Governor Barrios was no particular friend of the missionaries makes his report about Mission San José all the more impressive.

Visit of Bishop Martínez y Tejada, 1759

In 1762, Fr. Simon de Hierro, the Father Guardian of the College of Zacatecas, wrote a report about Mission San José, which seems to have been lost. However, Dr. Bolton wrote a summary of it in 1915; and this indicates that Fr. Hierro did not add anything new to the two previous reports (he repeats the statement that the church of San José could accommodate two thousand persons), except one important item. He states that Mission San José was highly praised by the bishop of Guadalajara, the Most Reverend Fray Francisco Martínez y Tejada.

The bishop visited San José in November, 1759, while making a tour of his vast diocese, which included the Province of Texas. At San José he no doubt administered confirmation to the Indian neophytes, as he did elsewhere along his route. Confirmation is the sacrament which confers special graces of the Holy Spirit on a baptized person, enabling him to profess and live his faith as a soldier of Christ.

The bishop had been the Father Guardian of the Franciscan friary in Seville in 1731, when he was named auxiliary bishop to the bishop of Cuba. In this capacity he resided at St. Augustine, Florida, for ten years, 1735-1745. Then he was appointed bishop of Yucatán; and in 1752 he was promoted to the see of Guadalajara. He died there, not long after his return from Texas, on December 20, 1760, at the age of about sixty-eight.

Visit and Report of Fr. Solís, 1768

Just ten years after Governor Barrios visited Mission San José, it was inspected and described by Fr. Gaspar José de Solís, official visitor or inspector of the seven missions which the College of Zacatecas had at that time in Texas. His account of Mission San José is even more detailed than that of Governor Barrios; and from it we learn that some changes had been made during the decade that had elapsed.

Fr. Solís' description of San José is a part of the diary he kept during his long journey which lasted almost a year, November 15, 1767, to October 13, 1768.

The actual visitation of the Texas missions was done in about a half year, from February to August, 1768. The first missions that Fr. Solís visited were the two at La Bahía. Then he went to San José, and remained there for three weeks, March 18 to April 7. Returning from eastern Texas, he spent another two weeks at San José, August 1 to 16, taking a well-deserved rest.

His account of San José is the entry he made in his diary on April 6; but on March 19 he records an important event in the history of the mission. The former church, which was supposed to have been large enough for two thousand, had been torn down; and the building of a new stone church on the same spot had been started. The foundations had been laid; and on the feast of St. Joseph, March 19, 1768, Fr. Solís blessed the foundation and the first stones. Then Governor Don Hugo Oconor laid one of the stones, and Fr. Solís laid another. There was no so-called "corner-stone" laying. When Fr. Morfi wrote his *History of Texas* about a decade later, he erroneously gave the date as May 19, 1768.

The mission compound consisted of one large square, 611 feet in length on each side. At each corner there was a gate; and on diagonal corners, two towers or bastions. An arched hall leading to the *convento* was being used temporarily as a church.

The Indian apartments were stone structures built along the walls, and formed a part of them. They were from fourteen to sixteen and one half feet in length and eleven feet in width. Each had a kitchen and a fireplace. In these homes, there were beds raised above the ground, and provided with fine large blankets made of wool and of cotton and sheets of gunny-sack, all of them manufactured in the mission shops. Bison hides served as mattresses.

The number of Indians living in the mission was three hundred and fifty, the largest recorded in the mission's history. Of these, one hundred and ten were warriors, forty-five of them armed with guns and the rest with bows and arrows, spears, and other weapons. Sentinels on horseback kept guard on the outside of the walls to prevent any surprise attack by hostile Indians.

The stone granary now had a vaulted roof. The workshops included a textile shop, tailor shop, carpenter shop, and a smithy. There were also lime and brick kilns. Also, a well "from which there comes as large a flow of water as from a small river; and the water from the well runs into a canal (irrigation ditch), which contains a great quantity of fish and irrigates many fertile fields." The mission was very fortunate in having such a spring-fed well within its walls.

Outside the walls was the mission farm and orchard, two and a half miles long, and all of it fenced in. It yielded abundant crops of corn, beans, lentils, melons, peaches and other fruits, potatoes, sugar cane, and all kinds of vegetables. The fruits of the peach trees, of which there were many, weighed as much as a pound each. San José was able to send supplies to the four presidios of San Antonio, La Bahía, Orcoquisac, and Los Adaes.

All the stock of the mission was kept at a ranch, called El Atascoso, twenty-five to thirty miles south of San José Mission. It included five thousand head of sheep and goats, fifteen hundred yoke of oxen (Fr. Solís must have meant fifteen hundred head of cattle, not three thousand oxen), ten droves of mares, and four of asses. This ranch probably was on the Atascosa River. "White overseers or administrators are not needed, for the Indians take complete charge of the ranch." They also did all the work in the shops and on the farm. "They are industrious and diligent, and are skilled in all kinds of labor. They act as mule-drivers, masons, cowboys, shepherds, etc., there being no need to employ anyone who does not belong to the mission. . . . The able-bodied men attend to the manual labor; the old men make arrows for the warriors; the grown-up girls weave cloth, card wool, and sew; the old women catch fish for the padres; and the younger boys and girls go to school and recite their prayers."

The Indians had attained a high degree of culture, despite the fact that, a short time before, they had been uncivilized nomads. All except the older ones spoke Spanish quite well, besides their Coahuiltecan language. Some played the guitar or violin or harp. All had good voices and could sing and dance like the Spaniards. Perhaps, says Fr. Solís, they performed the Spanish dances even more beautifully and gracefully than the Spaniards. They were decently dressed, and had two suits each, one for weekdays and one for Sundays and feastdays. They were "so polite and well-mannered and so refined, that one might imagine they had been civilized and living at the mission for a long time."

All of the mission Indians were baptized and well-instructed Christians; but the fathers (there were two at San José at this time) "are endeavoring to draw the pagans from the seacoast and from the frontiers, so that, emulating the example of the Indians at the mission, they may also be converted and educated."

On Saturdays, on the 19th of each month (St. Joseph's Day), and on the feasts of our Lord and the Blessed Virgin Mary, a choir of four voices sang the Rosary with musical accompaniment; and they did this "so beautifully, that it was a delight to hear them."

The records of the mission showed that since its inception in 1720, there had been, at San José, 1,054 baptisms, 287 Christian marriages, and 359 funerals of adults. The missionary in charge at the time of Fr. Solís' visit was the Father President of the Zacatecan missions in Texas, Fr. Pedro Ramírez de Arellano.

At the beginning of his account, Fr. Solís wrote: "This mission is so pretty and in such a flourishing condition, both materially and spiritually, that I cannot find words or figures with which to express its beauty." But he did find words after all to give us an engaging and graphic word-picture of Mission San José as it was in its heyday.

Last page of the copy, in the Biblioteca Nacional, Mexico City, of the memorial sent by the College of Zacatecas on January 15, 1750, to King Ferdinand VI. It was signed by Fr. Guardian Francisco Ballejo (Vallejo) and his councilors, among them Fr. Ildefonso Marmolejo, later missionary of San José, and Fr. Gaspar Joseph Solís.

deve à su Síndico de la obra material, la que aun està tan corta, que ni aun las Celdas correspondientes à los que estamos de familia tiene: y de el segundo, que es cerrarse el Noviciado para no recivir Pretendiente alguno, nos obliga à suplicar; el que atento el dicho crecido numero de Religiosos, carga de deudas, à estrechía de habitacion, nos vemos precisados à no recivir de una vez crecido numero de Religiosos; sino conforme se verifica estar vaco alguno de los lugares ytiles, recibimos uno, ò otro de los muchos Pretendientes que tenemos de lo que claramente se persuade la necesidad de tener abierto Noviciado. Razones porque no pide ahora este Colegio Misión à Vuestra Magestad las que si en su soberana comprehension no son de algun peso; y si su Real voluntad el embiarla determinarà lo que fuere servido, que à nuestra veneracion, y obediencia leal serà siempre el mayor acierto. — — — — —

Nuestro Señor guarde la Catholica Real persona de Vuestra Magestad los muchos años que la christiandad ha menester. Colegio Apostolico de propaganda fide de Nuestra Señora de Guadalupe de Zacatecas, y Enero quinze de mill setecientos cinquenta años. = Señor. = Fr. Fran.co Ballesse = Fr. Juan Gregorio de la Campa Cor.s = Fr. Ildephonso Joseph Marmolejo. = Fr. Gaspar Joseph Solís. = Fr. Joseph de S.n Miguel Dominguez. = Fr. Dimas Maria Chacón. — — — — —

Queen of the Missions

The sculptured façade, with its curving lines
Of grace and beauty, marks the master hand
Of some old artist whose rare skill has traced
Here in rude stone his fancy's quaint design.
The cunning of his art has glorified
The massive structure, touched its somber
　　strength
With vivid grace of carving, richly wrought,
And yet sublime in chaste sublimity.

— JANIE F. BASKIN

VI

THE MISSIONARY WHO LAUNCHED THE BUILD-
ing of the new church at Mission San José in 1768, Fr.
Pedro Ramírez de Arellano, hitherto has received little or
no recognition; and yet he was one of the outstanding
missionaries of Texas. He was a contemporary of the well
known Fr. Junípero Serra, who founded the first of the
California missions one year after the foundation of San
José's new church was blessed by Fr. Solís. As Fr. Serra
was the Father President of the California missions for
seventeen years (1767-1784), so was Fr. Ramírez the Father
President of the Zacatecan missions in Texas for about nine
years and of all the Texas missions for eight years more
(1764-1781). Fr. Serra died on August 28, 1784, and Fr.
Ramírez on September 30, 1781.

We first meet Fr. Ramírez in eastern Texas in 1751,

and then as the successor of Fr. Marmolejo at Mission San
José in 1759. In that year he supplied ten Indian soldiers
from San José for the campaign conducted by Colonel Ortíz
Parilla against the hostile northern tribes. Three years later,
he went to the Mission of Nuestra Señora del Espíritu Santo
at La Bahía. On June 5, 1762, he addressed an appeal to
Captain Manuel Ramírez de la Piscina for protection
against the marauding Apaches who were threatening the
very continuance of his mission and that of Rosario. Knowing the conditions prevailing at San José, he added that a
similar situation existed in the San Antonio area. At San
José the Apaches had, with impunity, reduced the mission
cattle from four thousand head to fifteen hundred, less than
one half. The captain fully agreed with Fr. Ramírez, but
was not in a position to render effective help. He added
his own testimony to the appeal of Fr. Ramírez and sent it
on to the viceroy.

Fr. Juan de Dios Camberos, 1764

The missionary who had taken Fr. Ramírez' place at
San José was Fr. Juan de Dios Camberos, the founder of
the second mission at La Bahía, Nuestra Señora del Rosario.
About the middle of October, 1764, Fr. Camberos granted
asylum at San José to Captain Rafael Martínez Pacheco,
who had been blamed wrongfully for the burning of the
presidio of Orcoquisac, near the mouth of the Trinity
River; and the captain remained at the mission for several
months. Later (1786-1790), the captain served as governor
of Texas.

Shortly after the arrival of Captain Martínez Pacheco,
Fr. Camberos died, November 7, 1764. We do not know
any details concerning his death, except that he was the
second missionary to die at his post in Mission San José.
He was no doubt buried in the sanctuary of the church;

and perhaps, as in the case of Fr. Núñez, his remains were taken to Zacatecas. This may have been done when the church was torn down to make room for the new stone church.

Fr. Ignacio María Lanuza, 1770-1771

It was probably after the death of Fr. Camberos that Fr. Ramírez returned to San José as Father President of the Zacatecan missions in Texas. He remained there until his death, except for about two years, which he spent in eastern Texas prior to the abandonment of the three remaining missions. During these years, 1770-1772, Fr. Ignacio María Lanuza, who had served as Fr. Solís' secretary when he visited the missions of Texas, took the place of Fr. Ramírez at San José.

On September 6, 1770, he informed Governor Ripperdá that he could furnish ten soldiers from San José for the defence of San Antonio and the pursuit of hostile Indians, only if the citizens of San Antonio likewise rendered military service. He joined Fr. Acisclos Valverde, the Father President of the Querétaran missions, in declaring that it would not be fair to expect the mission Indians to be more patriotic than the Spanish settlers.

The following year, Fr. Lanuza firmly refused — as did the other missionaries of the San Antonio area — to supply seven armed and mounted Indians from San José as well as forty-six horses for the presidio at La Bahía. Neither the Indians nor the horses could be spared at San José; it was simply a matter of self-preservation. Three times the governor tried to get what he wanted, but each time Fr. Lanuza replied it was impossible to carry out his demands. The missionary pointed out the reasons for this so convincingly that Ripperdá finally admitted that Fr. Lanuza was right. In 1780 Fr. Lanuza was back at the College in Zacatecas as a member of its *discretorio* or council.

Captain Martínez Pacheco, 1772

At the time that Fr. Ramírez returned to Mission San José (1772), Captain Martínez Pacheco, who was now in Mexico City, presented to the viceroy a special report on conditions in Texas. Except for the lack of horses, a result of the raids by the Apaches, said the captain, the missions in the San Antonio area were in a flourishing condition.

The Marqués de Rubí, who had inspected the presidios of Texas in 1767, had described the San Antonio missions as "opulent." Taking his cue from that remark, the captain asked why the missions were doing so well; and the question offered him an occasion for writing a well deserved eulogy of the work of the missionaries.

The reason why the missions, including San José, were "opulent," wrote the captain, was "the apostolic zeal of the missionaries, who have never failed to put up with fatigue and hardships at any time of the year, in order to promote the spiritual and temporal welfare of these missions. Religiously and unremittingly, they have devoted themselves to their work, going perseveringly in search of new converts as well as apostates, and visiting pagan tribes to bring new recruits into the mission pueblos."

Many a time, declared the captain, a lonely padre, accompanied by only two of his neophytes, would undertake such a trip and venture even into the camps of the Lipan Apaches to look for runaway Indians. He should have had an escort of soldiers, but the military commander would not grant the missionary's request when he was asked.

It is true, the captain admitted, that the mission churches and houses were of the best material and the best construction in the Province of Texas, the mission farms, ranches, and irrigation ditches were more successfully operated than any other in Texas, and the mission stock was more numerous; but all of this was due to the unselfish labors of the padres who directed these projects from the beginning.

At San José Mission the work on the new church had been going forward, slowly but steadily, ever since Fr. Ramírez had begun its construction in 1768; and although he was absent for two years while the church was being built, Fr. Ramírez deserves the title and distinction of being its builder. After his return to San José in 1772, he continued to superintend the rearing of this beautiful edifice until it was practically completed.

Visit of Fr. Morfi, 1777

At the end of 1777, when the church was nearing completion, Fr. Juan Agustín Morfi, the first historian of Texas, visited Mission San José; and he has left us an exact description of the mission and its new church — a description by a historian who was also an eyewitness. Fr. Morfi came to Texas as the chaplain and diarist of the inspection tour made by Teodoro de Croix, commandant general of the so-called Interior Provinces which included the entire frontier country of New Spain. During their journey, which lasted a half year, they covered some two thousand miles.

We can, therefore, accept Fr. Morfi's statement that San José was indeed the Queen of the Missions. In his *History of Texas, 1673-1779*, he wrote that San José "is, in truth, the first mission in America, not in point of time, but in point of beauty, plan, and strength, so that there is not a presidio along the entire frontier line that can compare with it."

The New Church of San José

Much of what Fr. Morfi records about San José pertains to the new church. "Next to the north side," he writes, "a new church was being built within the walls; and by now (1782), it has perhaps been completed. There was very little that remained to be done when I saw it at the close of 1777. It is a beautiful temple with three vaulted naves, twenty-seven and three-quarters feet wide and one-hundred and thirty-seven and three-quarters feet long with its transept."

By three naves he evidently meant three successive naves, although nowadays when we speak of three naves we mean three parallel naves; and the "transept" must have been the sanctuary or presbytery. There is no evidence that San José's church was ever cruciform in design. Actually, three distinct sections can be clearly distinguished in the single nave of the church, not counting the sanctuary.

The church, continues Fr. Morfi, "has a beautiful cupola, though it is overcrowded with unnecessary ornaments. This building, because of its size, good taste, and beauty, would grace a large city as a parish church. The whole structure is admirably proportioned and strongly built of stone and mortar, chiefly of a sandy limestone that is light and porous when freshly quarried, but in a few days hardens and becomes one with the mortar. For this reason, it is as useful for building as *tezontle* (a volcanic stone in Mexico, similar to the tufa used at San José). This stone is obtained from a quarry near the mission of Nuestra Señora de la Concepción."

It is well that Fr. Morfi thought the cupola was "overcrowded with unnecessary ornaments," for it made him record the fact that it was decorated. Ernst Schuchard has devoted years of study to the interior and exterior decoration of the original stone church of San José; and he has demonstrated that the flat surfaces of the façade and other parts of the exterior walls were plastered and then covered with geometrical color designs of yellow, red, blue, and black. Some of those who visited San José in the nineteenth century have mentioned these color designs in their writings; and even today a few faint traces can be detected by the close observer.

Fr. Morfi's description of the façade of the church is as follows: "The façade is very costly because of the statues and ornaments with which it is heavily decorated, detracting somewhat from its natural beauty. In the center, and immediately over the main entrance, a large balcony was constructed, which bestows much majesty on the building. The effect would have been enhanced, if the hexagonal window which admits light to the choir loft, and is the entrance to it, had been made to simulate a door. In a word, no one could have imagined that there were such good artists in so desolate a place."

Fr. Morfi was an art critic; but whether we agree with his tastes or not, we are glad to have his detailed description. However, he is mistaken when he speaks of a hexagonal window in the façade. It is oval in shape, and we have no reason for thinking that it was otherwise in 1777.

Of the sacristy, the large room on the south side of the church, which not a few writers have mistakenly called the baptistery, Fr. Morfi writes: "The sacristy of the new church is the place where divine services are held for the time being. It has a door that opens into the living quarters of the friars. It is a handsome and cheerful room, large and well decorated, with vaulted roof, good light, and everything in good taste."

The sacristy, therefore, was completed before the church proper; and, unlike the church it has never fallen into ruins. The large window which admits light into the sacristy is the world-famous so-called "Rose Window." The latter term is applied to the decoration on the outside of the window. Since Fr. Morfi makes no special mention of the latter, the exquisite stone carving of the exterior window frame appears to have been done after 1777. It is believed that the sculptor was Pedro Huizar, and that he did not complete this work of art until about 1790.

The Walled Mission Square

The rest of Fr. Morfi's account of Mission San José agrees for the most part with that of Fr. Solís; but he mentions some important changes and improvements that had been made during the past decade. Instead of two bastions on diagonal corners of the square, there were now four bastions, one at each corner. The wall, therefore, extended a little north of the granary, enough at least to allow room for a gate and a bastion at this point. In addition to the four gates at the four corners, there was now a fifth gate in the west wall.

"On the west side, facing the church, there is a fifth gate, with an iron grating; and this is the only one that is opened every day. It faces a wide plain on which the trees and brush have been cut down to prevent a surprise attack by hostile Indians."

The walled mission enclosure, says Fr. Morfi, was six hundred and eleven feet square on the outside; but on the inside it was six hundred feet square, because the Indian houses, which formed a part of the wall, extended eleven feet out from the wall. This implies that the Indian houses were along two walls or sides that formed a right angle; and since one of these was on the east side, the other was the south side wall.

"On the sides of the opening of each gate, loopholes have been bored through the walls of the adjoining rooms, where the most trusted Indians live, enabling them to fire safely upon the enemy, should the gates be stormed."

North of the fifth gate stood a well-stocked granary, having a vaulted roof and three naves, according to Fr. Morfi. Here, as in the case of the church, he evidently meant that there were three sections joined together to form a single nave.

On the north and west side of the square were various workshops: "There is also a loom, in which rich blankets, cotton cloth, sandcloth, and other heavy cotton and woolen cloth worn by the Indians are woven. There is a carpenter shop, a blacksmith shop, a tailor shop, and everything needed in a well regulated community. Lastly, everything is in such good order and so well planned, that even if the enemy would be able to lay siege to the mission, the besieged, having their granary well filled with food and plenty of good water in their wells, could afford to laugh at their opponents."

The Convento of San José

To the single room which was on the second floor of the *convento* in 1768, others had been added. "The *convento* or living quarters of the missionaries has two stories with spacious galleries. The one on the second floor opens out on the flat roofs of the Indian houses (along the east wall) and is very convenient. Sun dials were set up here on vertical columns. They were made of a species of limestone so soft when first brought from the quarry that it can be planed like wood; but, when exposed to the air, it hardens and can be polished like marble. The figures of the façade of the church, the balustrade of the stairway of the *convento*, and an image of St. Joseph standing on a pedestal — all were made more beautiful by the ease with which the stone can be cut. There are enough rooms for the missionaries (two in number) and for the convenience of a few guests, as well as the necessary offices for the friars, a large and well ordered kitchen, a comfortable refectory, and a pantry."

The fact that Fr. Morfi, after describing the friary, mentions an armory and a wardrobe, may indicate that these rooms were in or near the friary. "There is an armory where the guns, bows and arrows, and the lances are kept. With these the neophytes are armed in case of an attack; and with them they are equipped as auxiliary troops in a campaign. In the latter case the mission provides them not only with arms but also with ammunition and supplies. In a separate room are kept the decorations and dresses with which the Indians bedeck themselves for their dances, sometimes Spanish and at other times Mexican. These dances were introduced by the missionaries, so that the Indians might forget their native *mitotes* (pagan dances)."

The Irrigated Farm and the Ranch

Fr. Morfi, more accurately than Fr. Solís, says the mission farm outside the walls covered an area two and a half miles square; "and all of it is fenced, the fence being in good condition. For its benefit, water is taken from the San Antonio River and is distributed by means of a beautiful irrigation ditch to all parts of the field, where corn, beans, lentils, cotton, sugar cane, watermelons, melons, and sweet potatoes are raised. It has a patch for all kinds of vegetables; and there are some fruit trees."

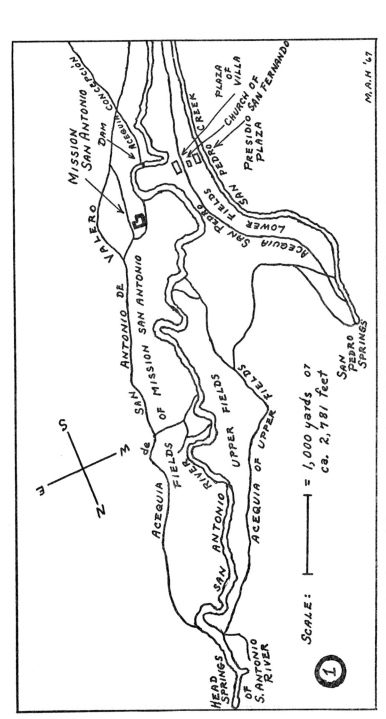

Part 1 of map of the *acequias* or irrigation ditches and the irrigated *labores* or farms in the San Antonio area, made by the Texas Civil Works Administration and the Texas Relief Commission, showing the *acequias* and *labores* of Mission San Antonio and the town of San Fernando. This map is continued in parts 2, 3, and 4, which follow.

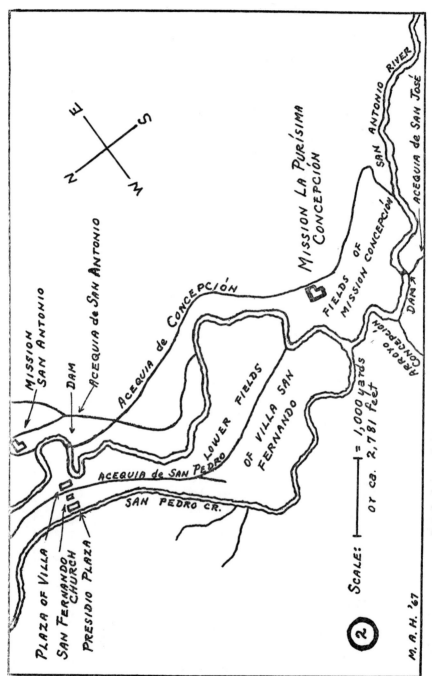

Part 2 of map of the San Antonio area, showing the *acequias* and *labores* of Mission Concepción and the town of San Fernando.

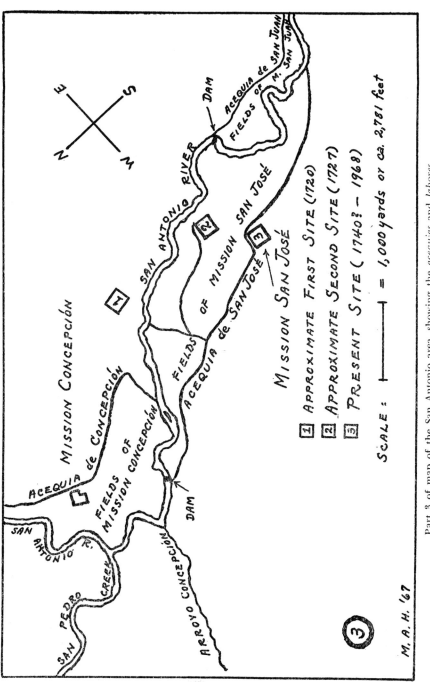

Part 3 of map of the San Antonio area, showing the *acequias* and *labores* of Mission San José and adjoining missions.

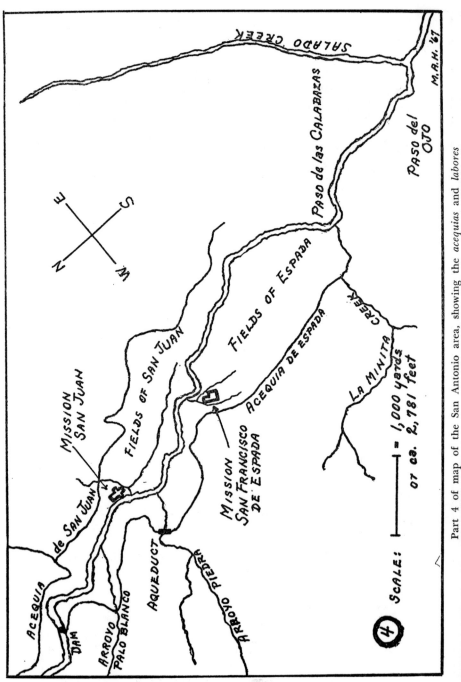

Part 4 of map of the San Antonio area, showing the *acequias* and *labores*

The Texas Civil Works Administration and the Texas Relief Commission made it one of their projects in the 1930's to trace the entire irrigation system of all five missions and of the town of San Fernando and the presidio of San Antonio de Béxar. The map which was drawn at the time shows that the irrigation canal of Mission San José began above a dam built across the river about a half mile below Arroyo Concepción. Thence its course ran south for about three and a half miles before it rejoined the river. At the mission square it passed from west to east outside the north wall and then south along the east wall. The irrigation ditch along the north wall, which supplied power for the flour mill, can still be seen.

Fr. Morfi also mentions the Rancho de las Cabras (Ranch of the Goats), which has been regarded as another name for San José Mission's ranch called El Atascoso; and he says that twenty-six persons were living at the ranch in 1777.

On a high plateau on the west bank of the San Antonio River in Wilson County, three miles from Floresville, there are some ruins which have been identified by some as those of buildings that belonged to the ranch of Mission San José. However, San José's ranch was probably situated on the Atascosa River in the vicinity of present Poteet.

Atascoso is mentioned as early as 1736 as being some thirty-five miles south of San Antonio Mission on the way to the Rio Grande; and when Fr. Solís visited El Atascoso ranch in 1768, he was traveling to Laredo. The day after he left the ranch, he crossed San Miguel Creek; the following day, he reached the Rio Frio; and the next day, he crossed the Nueces.

Possibly the Rancho de las Cabras and El Atascoso were two different ranches; and the site near Floresville may have been the place where Mission San Francisco de la

Espada had its ranch. The latter was likewise located at some distance from the mission in 1762, and had a good stone house where the Indian cowboys and shepherds could live comfortably.

The Mission Indians

Since 1768, says Fr. Morfi, the number of Indians living at the mission had been greatly reduced, but the missionaries were daily bringing in new Indians from the woods. Though he does not say how many there were in 1777, we can conclude from the general statistics of the San Antonio area that the population of San José at this time was about three hundred, including the Indians who were living at the ranch.

Of the Indians at the mission Fr. Morfi writes: "They are today well instructed and civilized, and know how to work very well at their mechanical trades and are proficient in some of the arts. They speak Spanish perfectly, with the exception of those who are daily brought in from the woods by the zeal of the missionaries. Many play the harp, the violin, and the guitar well, sing well, and dance the same dances as the Spaniards. They go about well dressed and are abundantly fed; and thus they arouse the envy of the less fortunate settlers of San Fernando, the indolence of many of whom obliges them to beg their food from these Indians, who enjoy so much plenty."

Fr. Pedro Ramírez de Arellano

Fr. Morfi concludes his account with a word of praise for the missionary who was both spiritual father and business director of the entire establishment: "The mission is in such opulence, thanks to the labors and exertions of Fray

Pedro Ramírez de Arellano of the College of Nuestra Señora de Guadalupe de Zacatecas, who is in charge of this mission and is the *presidente* of all the missions in the province, and whose dedication, zeal, and religious spirit deserve all praise."

Not long after Fr. Morfi's visit, Fr. Ramírez was empowered by an indult of Pope Clement XIV to administer the sacrament of confirmation throughout Texas. He exercised this unusual faculty, which is ordinarily reserved to a bishop, on May 10, 1778. It must have been a memorable fiesta day at Mission San José. Fr. Junípero Serra in California received the same faculty about the same time.

Shortly before the visit of Fr. Morfi, Fr. Ramírez had commenced a new register of baptisms, marriages, and burials at San José on September 1, 1777; and it was continued until the final secularization of the mission in 1824.

In the section containing the record of burials, entry number 862, we find a brief notice about the death and funeral of Fr. Ramírez. He died at 3:30 in the morning on September 30, 1781, "having received all the sacraments with a good disposition." On the same day, he was buried in the sacristy, which was then still serving as the church, because the sanctuary of the new stone church was not quite ready. The exact spot is indicated: "Outside the sanctuary, on the Gospel side, in the corner formed by the Communion railing and the wall, about one half *vara* (one and one third feet) from the wall." The notice pays the following simple but expressive tribute to the great missionary, the builder of San José's new church: "He was the universal father of all; and he distinguished himself especially by his charity towards the poor."

Fr. Ramírez had been a missionary in Texas for more than thirty years. He had held the office of *presidente* for about seventeen years, at first for the Zacatecan missions and then for all the Texas missions. For about eighteen years he resided at Mission San José. Probably he was about thirty years old when he first came to Texas in 1751; and so he must have been about sixty years old at the time of his death.

Letter, in the Béxar Archives, Austin, written to Governor Ripperdá of Texas by Fr. Pedro Ramírez at Mission San José on July 6, 1776, two days after the American Colonies' Declaration of Independence.

Sr. Baron de Ripperdá mi S.

Recibí el Oficio de V.S. con la
orden que luego recibí en mi
quarto, esta tarde, que los Pre-
sos vengan de sus destinos, y les
are saber el orden de V.S. y de mi
parte are los oficios posibles al
fin que el orden de V.S. sea bien
empleada.
Dios nuestro S.me Gde a
V.S. m[ucho]s a[ño]s Misión de S.S.S. Joseph, y
Julio 6 de 1776

Benito de Guerra Mro.
Capp.n y Pres.o

Fr. Pedro Ramirez

Decline of San José

It seems that these poor neophytes, in imitation of the Prophet Jeremia, might raise their voices, bewailing their fate as he does . . . and, taking the words from his mouth, say "Remember, O Lord, what has befallen us, look, and see our disgrace: our inherited lands have been turned over to strangers, our homes to foreigners (Lamentations 5, 1-2)."

— Fr. Jose Francisco Lopez

VII

WHILE THE NEW CHURCH WAS BEING BUILT
at San José, the decline of the mission had already begun,
at least to some extent. The number of Indians living in
the mission was less than before, although San José continued to have more than any of the other San Antonio
missions. The raids of the Apaches had considerably reduced
the number of mission cattle and especially the horses. In
1783, when there was another virulent epidemic, the number of Indians at San José dropped to 128; but it rose again
to 189 in 1786. Mission San José was still in a flourishing
condition. The other missions were less fortunate.

The principal reason for the decline of San José and
the other missions, the one which eventually brought about
the impoverishment of the once "opulent" missions, was a
decree issued by Teodoro de Croix after his visit to Texas

in 1777. This decree declared all unbranded cattle to be the property of the government; and anyone, including the missions, who slaughtered such cattle had to pay a fixed fee of four *reales* or half a peso per head. Thus the missions were deprived of their "wealth," their large herds of cattle, which were, for the most part, unbranded. As a result, the missions were unable to provide meat for a large number of Indians, and their population decreased.

Report of Fr. López, 1789

This and other causes of the decline of the missions are clearly set forth in a nine-thousand-word report on the missions of Texas, signed by Fr. President José Francisco López, at Mission San Antonio, on May 5, 1789. Fr. López had become the missionary in charge of Mission San Antonio in 1783; and when he was appointed *presidente* of the Texas missions about 1785, he remained at that mission. The missionary at San José at this time was Fr. José María de Salas, who had been the predecessor of Fr. López at the San Antonio Mission.

Fr. López first describes in detail the status of each of the seven missions which still existed in Texas at that time, and then points out the several causes for their decline. Besides the five missions in the San Antonio area, there was only one mission, Nuestra Señora del Espíritu Santo, at La Bahía, because the Rosario Mission had been temporarily abandoned. The seventh mission was the new settlement of Nacogdoches, where two Franciscan missionaries were stationed since 1775, not only to serve as pastors of the settlers, but "principally for the purpose of bringing about a reduction of the Orcoquisac, Vidai, Texas, and the other tribes of that region."

Description of San José in 1789

According to the report of Fr. López, Mission San José was still the Queen of the Missions although it had suffered a "notable decline." Fr. López' description of San José contains some interesting new details: the church had a pulpit which was entered from the *convento;* the latter had a flat roof; the church and *convento* were separated from the Indian houses on the north side by a street; mud was used as cement for the stone houses of the Indians; and the mission square now had six gates.

"This mission," writes Fr. López, "is situated on the west bank of the San Antonio River, south of those already described (San Antonio and Concepción), at a distance of about one league (two and one-half miles) from Mission Concepción and two (four and one-half miles) from that of San Antonio and the Royal Presidio. Situated on a broad plain, rather sparsely wooded, its grounds and buildings, surrounded by a rampart of stone-and-mud houses, offer an attractive sight.

"All the houses have hand-carved wooden doors, some with good locks. The rampart has four gates, each suitable for its purpose and directly facing one point of the compass. All have good strong locks. In addition to these main entrances there are two other smaller ones at places where they were deemed necessary on account of the growth of the pueblo, which from end to end may be said to be two hundred *varas* (555½ feet). These houses are built next to each other and have ample room, with a kitchen for each family. They are sufficiently protected against rain, wind, and other inclemencies of the weather.

"On the west corner (Fr. López got his directions mixed; he means the northeast corner), along the wall, separated from the habitations of the Indians by a street, stand the missionary's house, the church, and the sacristy." The houses along the north wall, therefore, which hitherto were believed to have been soldiers' quarters, were actually Indian houses; and between these and the *convento* and church there was a street.

The missionary's house, continues Fr. López, "contains, not only rooms for housing the missionaries, but also a kitchen, and the offices of the community. It is all of stone and lime and flat-roofed; the quarters for the missionary form a second story, and every part is in good taste.

"The church, with the sacristy, is contiguous to the other house so that, through the latter, one may enter a comparatively good pulpit in the presbytery" (that is, the sanctuary). One can still see the opening in the east wall which connected the sanctuary with the *convento*. Fr. López then makes a statement concerning San José that is similar to that of Fr. Morfi and justifies its title of Queen of the Missions:

"The church and the sacristy, because of their architecture, are the most beautiful structures to be seen anywhere this side of Saltillo (the capital of Coahuila). They may be valued without hesitation at thirty thousand pesos, and their furnishings at eight or ten thousand. The numerous ornaments, some of them of silver, include a frontal, a throne, and a baldaquin. It is evident that the lack of other ornaments is due to a notable decline, suffered by the mission as a result of influences which will be explained and discussed in the general report. The same happened to the other missions already referred to, and, in fact, to all of them, as will be seen when their funds will be discussed."

Statistics of the Indians living at San José follow in the report, indicating that these numbered 138, of whom 106 were Christians and 32 were still pagans. Fr. López then concludes his report about San José with the following remarks:

"With the exception of the thirty-two pagan Barrados, who came last year (1788) from the coast, the personnel is made up of the Pampopas (who were at the mission from the beginning) and Postitos; and their language is the usual one in this mission (Coahuiltecan), although most of them speak Spanish less incorrectly than in the other missions. Finally, this mission has always been the most populous, in spite of having been the most affected by the plague of buboes; and furthermore, it has been the richest, because the Indians are less indolent in the cultivation of the fields and the care of the herds."

San José Mission, therefore, was still faring quite well in May, 1789; and by December of the same year, the Indians living in the mission had again increased to 198. But it, too, could not escape the effect of the various factors which caused the decline of the missions; and in 1790 the number of mission Indians at San José decreased to 144, and the following year to 106.

The Work of the Missionaries

In his general report, which applies also to Mission San José, Fr. López presents details concerning the work of the missionaries, the languages spoken, the Indians' self-government and communal labor, and the mission records. These complete the picture of life at San José Mission as late as 1789, five years before its partial secularization.

Like the other missionaries, Fr. José María de Salas administered the temporal affairs of the mission in the style and fashion of a family. He was like "a common father who, being the spiritual head, also looks after the interests and wants of his children with as much careful exactness and punctuality as the best father could do. . . ."

The missionaries were not only "like fathers of a family,"

but also, "tutors or instructors of the Indians." They "determine everything that has to be done, even down to the very smallest details, such as adding to the fence rails what is needed, cleaning the fields by removing the stalks of the previous years, or the roots that sprout, digging, cleaning, or deepening the ditches and irrigation canals, etc."

The missionaries in the San Antonio area had reduced the many dialects of the Coahuiltecan Indians who were gathered in these missions to "one language, which is common or uniform in meaning;" and one of the Querétaran missionaries, Fr. Bartolomé García, had written a manual in this language for the use of his confreres. This manual was printed in 1760; and as Dr. Castañeda says, it is "aptly called the first textbook of Texas." The missionaries used this manual to instruct those Indians who knew little or no Spanish.

"As soon as these missionaries reach their respective assignments," writes Fr. López, "they make the most diligent attempt to learn, through use and daily intercourse, the language of their charges. This is the only means they have for communication, although usually the missionaries insist that the Indians understand and use Spanish, as is ordered by the laws of the kingdom. They comply with this order by speaking often with the adults, and by teaching the children usually or always to read, and, if it is deemed practical (which is not always the case) to write and figure." Some of the Indians, therefore, also learned to read and write Spanish.

"Spanish," says Fr. López, "is generally and commonly spoken among both Spaniards and Indians, although, in the case of the latter, with noticeable imperfection or, in the common expression, with stones in their mouth." Most of the Indians at San José, however, "speak Spanish less incorrectly than in the other missions."

By actual practice, the missionaries also instructed the

Indians "in civil and political life. The custom of electing annually two justices, who are called governor and *alcalde* (judge), has been introduced. This is done in the presence of the missionary, and thus there have been Indian governors in the (mission) towns. If the pueblos are lacking in men, married couples vote. The voting is done by secret ballot; and those who are elected by a plurality vote have their names submitted to the governor of the province, who confirms them by a written order. These men govern the towns in the province for a term of one year, under the direction and with the advice of the missionary."

It was only because the missionaries did their work so unselfishly and were prompted by higher and religious motives that the communal system was successful and produced such splendid results: "All the planting done in the missions, as well as the cultivation and distribution of the crops, is by communal labor. Those, however, who are considered most apt are assigned plots of land to cultivate with delicacies, such as vegetables, watermelons, cantaloups, and cucumbers. But here, just as in the case of the corn and beans that are gathered, the greatest care is taken to divide them equally among all, even though, to do this, it is necessary to act with thorough forethought and prudence."

The missionaries regarded themselves only as administrators, never as owners, of the mission properties. They were always able and ready to render an account of their stewardship; for, they kept exact records of all receipts and disbursements, "in which very punctilious note is made of each item."

Not only did the missionaries faithfully perform their duties without any remuneration, but they even used a part of the annual allowance which the government granted them for their personal needs, for the benefit of the missions: "Neither now nor ever have the missionaries demanded or received any compensation or fees, large or small, from either the Indians or the Spaniards. On the contrary, they added the prebend to the products from the missions, limiting themselves to a most meager allowance, and leaving the balance for the church expenses and the divine cult."

If such was the case, why were the missions no longer as successful as they had been formerly? To answer this question, Fr. López fully delineates the destructive forces which were at work, seven in number; and he makes one last eloquent plea in behalf of the missions. No lawyer in a court of justice could have pleaded his case better than did Fr. López. But he must have felt that his warnings would go unheeded; for, he predicted: "Unless it be by the grace of Heaven, that is, unless a remedy is found in the form of a particular or special intervention of Providence . . . all the missions will be depopulated, abandoned, and destroyed within a few years." Even now, he testified, "the Indians scarcely have enough to eat and wear, while previously they had enough to adorn their temples and lived in relative comfort. . . . We and our children see ourselves turned out to perish from hunger and even to desert the law and the faith in order to seek in the woods the sustenance of which we are deprived." Already, there has been "a great decrease in population; for, there are less than half as many individuals (in the missions) as there were in the past."

The Decree of Teodoro de Croix

The first and principal cause, as mentioned, was the decree of Teodoro de Croix. "Returning to his headquarters (in 1778), without being sufficiently informed, he declared that all wild or unbranded cattle within his jurisdiction belonged to the royal treasury. . . . He ordered no other formality to be observed in carrying out the new policy than the publication of his decree, which was to be obeyed to the letter. . . . Since the first decree, there have been issued many voluminous regulations with severe penalties for branding wild cattle, even those which can be logically proved the offspring of branded mothers and are found together with them in the pastures or private ranches. In accord with this principle, most of the cattle are unbranded and generally attract the smaller herds. An ultimate consequence is that all the cattle are now wild. They belong to the royal treasury."

A royal decree of September 21, 1787, confirmed that of De Croix. It gave the missions and the settlers a four-months period of grace for branding their cattle; but the missions could not have done the job in a much longer time, because they lacked the horses for making the necessary round-ups. The Comanches, writes Fr. López, "left the missions without a brood of horses, tame or untamed, with the result that nearly all the herds were left unbranded. . . . It is necessary for them to pay like any stranger the stipulated fee of four *reales* per head. And whereas in the past the income from the herds and the missionaries' allowance alone was enough to clothe the Indians and pay the expenses of divine cult, now without them (the herds), there is not enough for either. . . . And what is more important, there is an urgent need for the quota of cattle that, with the chief's permission, the missions are accustomed to take for their daily sustenance from the unmarked herds. This is done, even though it entails the selling of the grain, gathered with much labor, that is needed for the support of the missions. The Indians with their missionaries have been in need of it for some time, because there remain no other satisfactory means of satisfying their requirements."

Other Causes of Decline

Thus the decree of De Croix alone would have sufficed to bring about the eventual demise of the missions. However, the situation was aggravated by several contributing causes. Among these were the raids of the Apaches, the depredations of the soldiers, the hunting trips of the settlers, the recurring epidemics, the unrestrained flight of Indians from the missions, and the inability of the missionaries to gather new Indians in the missions.

"According to a moderate estimate," writes Fr. López, "the Apache Indians account for at least twenty head a day. . . . In the guise of friendship, these Indians carry on the most cruel, continuous, and wasting war against us, depriving us of human sustenance by the frightful destruction of our herds."

Instead of protecting the missions from the Apaches, the soldiers of the presidio "even add to the damages caused by them, killing and destroying our cattle in one endless slaughter." Every month, "the purveyors of the presidio do not fail to bring to the presidio more than 150 beefs." The twenty soldiers who were in charge of the horses and wandered with them from place to place "on occasions kill four beefs a day, and as a result most of the meat spoils or is thrown away." Of those troops who went out to reconnoiter or to bring in grass for fodder, "generally three or four, or as many as are able, lead a yearling apiece from their saddles. Usually they catch the offspring of the branded cows, and only seldom do they bring in that of unbranded ones. This they do every afternoon when they are able, and they hardly ever fail."

Among the Spanish settlers there were so-called hunters, "who kill more than a hundred head, and sometimes two hundred on each expedition, and these expeditions are undertaken weekly and sometimes more often."

And there were "those who have taken away whole herds during the last eight years, totaling more than 15,000 head, most of them cows." It is not clear whether Fr. López is speaking here of the Apaches or soldiers or settlers, or of all of them together.

Another cause for the decline of the missions was the Indians' susceptibility to the contagious diseases of smallpox and of buboes. "Many have died on account of the plague of buboes . . . and many others from smallpox." But there were also some Indians who pretended to be sick, because of their disinclination "to do the necessary work for raising corn. In some missions and in some years, like the present one (1789), there is a shortage sometimes because of this combination of causes."

Laziness was also the reason why some mission Indians left and rejoined their pagan countrymen; and now the missionaries no longer received an escort of soldiers to go with them in quest of the runaways. "As a result of the pressing need felt for the labor necessary to support the missions, they are experiencing great scarcity, while the renegades, like fierce brutes, scare and seduce the other civilized Indians who may be inclined to listen to the word of the Gospel."

The lack of an escort for the missionaries to bring in new Indians and the inability of the missions to support additional Indians because of the lack of cattle also rendered it prohibitive to increase the diminishing number of mission Indians by new converts. It was a kind of vicious circle.

Though the report of Fr. López was a correct diagnosis of the situation, the government took no steps to remedy it. It was no longer interested in the missions of Texas. French Louisiana had been ceded to Spain in 1763; and as far as the Apaches were concerned, they were regarded as an enemy that could neither be pacified nor civilized and Christianized.

Fr. José María de Salas

About a year after Fr. López sent in his report, Fr. José María de Salas died at Mission San José. The register of burials at San José states that Fr. Salas died on June 17, 1790, at one o'clock in the morning, and was buried the same day in the sanctuary of the church, on the Gospel side. The new church had been completed when Fr. Salas was appointed the missionary of San José in 1783. During his sojourn of seven years at the mission, "he was very exact in carrying out his obligations." Since March, it seems, he had been quite ill. At any rate, as the records show, he was a sick man for some time before his death; but he continued to fulfill his priestly duties to the end. All the missionaries in the San Antonio area were present at his funeral. The notice of Fr. Salas' death in the record of burials was signed by Father President López and Fr. José Manuel Pedrajo, who had been Fr. Salas' assistant for about a year and was his successor at San José. Fr. Salas was the fourth missionary who is known to have died at Mission San José.

Letter, in the Béxar Archives, Austin, written by Fr. José Manuel Pedrajo at Mission San José on May 8, 1791, to Governor Múñoz of Texas. The letter mentions the visit of three Lipan Apaches at San José. At the bottom is a note made by the governor.

Sõr Gov.or D.n Man.l Muñoz.

Muy Sñr mio, aqui se haya   y Indios Lipanes, lo
que participo a V.S. pues me parece se debo hacerlo p.r
ar novedades, que hay, y se pueden seguir, si estos bie-
sen de mala fée.

        D.s G.e a V.S. m.s a.s como desea su affmo. serv.or
        y Capp.n Q.S.M.B.

                Fr. Jose Manuel Pedrajo

S.to Jose
Mayo 8/
/91.
        S.r The vearm esta yaga um por
azer canse a s.n Jose y bearm que Indios son y que
es toque buscan deadonde vienen. pero esto sa-
ce concuidado y con disimulo.
        El P.e de la Espada medire que son
como 30 y como el P. Pedrajo, abla solo de tres
es menester saver adonde estan los demas y es
r.o. Con mucho cuidado   Muñoz

Partial Secularization

The Indians of the missions were expected soon to become self-supporting; and, indeed, in many cases they did acquire large wealth through stock-raising and agricultural pursuits. But not a penny of this belonged to the missionaries. . . . So long as the Indians were under the missionaries, their lands were secure from the land-grabber. . . . The missionaries always knew the danger, and they always resisted secularization until their work was finished.

— HERBERT E. BOLTON

VIII

~~~~~~

T HE SECULARIZATION OF A MISSION WAS NOT
something bad or undesirable in itself. If it was carried
out in the proper manner and at the right time, it was, in
fact, the fulfillment and the culmination of a mission. The
mission was then made a regular parish of Christian Indians,
and a "secular," that is, a diocesan priest was appointed its
pastor. The missionary moved on to new conquests.

In central Mexico, among the Indians of a higher culture, the mission ordinarily achieved its objective in about
ten years. In northern Mexico a much longer period was
required; and in Texas even more time was needed. The
Coahuiltecan nomads were on the lowest rung of civilization
when they became mission Indians. It is almost unbelievable
that the missionaries should succeed in making them civil-

ized Christians within a few short years; and yet that is what they achieved with some of them.

At Mission San José, the missionaries were particularly successful. However, at this and the other missions in the San Antonio area, new pagan Indians were constantly brought in to live with the Christian Indians; and the work of civilizing and instructing neophytes was continued as long as the mission existed. At no time were they ready to be converted into regular parishes. When finally they were completely secularized, they did not become regular parishes; but they were abandoned, and gradually fell into ruins.

A decree for the secularization of Mission San Antonio de Valero was issued in 1779 and again in 1781; but the governor of Texas delayed its execution, and it was not carried out. However, in 1793, after the mission had been in existence for seventy-five years, it was completely secularized. While some of the mission lands were distributed among the remaining Indians, and the church with its furnishings was turned over by Fr. President José Francisco López to the pastor of San Fernando parish, the secularization really amounted to a suppression of the mission because the mission chapel was no longer used as a chapel for the Christian Indians.

Decree of Secularization, 1794

The following year San José and the other three missions of the San Antonio area were likewise secularized; but it was a secularization of an entirely different kind. It consisted in the distribution of some of the irrigated fields and other mission property among the Christian Indians, and the appointment of a so-called justice to look after the temporal affairs of these Indians. Later, the justice was called the Spanish *alcalde* of the Indian pueblo. But the missionary remained at his post. As far as the Christian Indians who had become landowners were concerned, the missionary limited his activities to those of a pastor; but he continued to have complete charge of those Indians who were still under instruction. It was only a partial secularization. San José and its neighbors were still missions, although in a modified form; and the government as well as the missionaries regarded them as such until their complete and final secularization three decades later. Most of the historians who have written about San José, have made the mistake of saying that the mission came to an end in 1794. This did not happen until 1824.

The College of Zacatecas had no objections to the partial secularization of San José and its neighbors. On January 13, 1780, the *discretorio* of the College, consisting of the Father Guardian and his council, had in fact petitioned Commandant General Teodoro de Croix to relieve the missionaries in Texas from the temporal administration of the missions, so that they could devote themselves wholly to pastoral work. They suggested that a carefully chosen layman be appointed at each mission to supervise the temporal affairs of the Christian Indians, after the common property of the mission had been distributed among them. The missionary would take care of the church and friary and their furnishings; and he would be content with the annual allowance of four hundred fifty pesos for his personal needs. He would not ask the Indians for any contribution, except the services of a boy to run errands for him and a girl to grind corn and make tortillas for him. In other words, they requested the partial secularization of the Texas missions. Although no steps were taken in that direction in 1780, the petition of the College may have had some influence when San José and its three sister missions were secularized in 1794.

The Plan of Fr. Silva, 1792

After Fr. President José Francisco López had pointed out in his report of 1789 that the once opulent missions of Texas had been reduced to a state of penury by the decree of Teodoro de Croix, the College of Zacatecas elected one of its members who had been a missionary in eastern Texas, Fr. Manuel de Silva, "commissary and prefect of the missions," and commissioned him to go to Texas in order to see if anything could be done to improve the situation. They knew that there were still many Indians in Texas who had not been reached by the missions; and they were desirous to continue their missionary work among them.

Fr. Silva chose as his companion Fr. José María Francisco de la Garza, who had been the missionary in charge of San José as well as *presidente* for a short time in 1782-1783; and together they went to San Antonio. To renew the College's apostolic activities among the unconverted and uncivilized Indians in Texas, Fr. Silva proposed the following plan in 1792. A new mission should be established on the coast, not too far from the presidio at La Bahía; and eventually a new chain of missions, extending from the mouth of the Colorado to the Red River in the northeastern corner of the present State of Texas, should be founded.

Realizing that the biggest obstacle to the realization of this plan was the expense it would entail for the government, Fr. Silva suggested that Mission San Antonio de Valero be secularized, that the other four in the area be reduced to two, and that the two fathers who were at Nacogdoches be released. That would make six missionaries available for work elsewhere, without increasing the expenses of the government as far as the annual allowance for each missionary was concerned.

Fr. Silva and Fr. Garza, after overcoming many difficulties, succeeded in founding a new mission on the coast, Nuestra Señora del Refugio, in 1793; but it was the only one and the last one. Mission San Antonio was suppressed the same year. San José and the other three were partially secularized in 1794; and not long afterwards, one missionary residing at San José took care also of the Concepción Mission, and another living at the Espada Mission attended also that of Capistrano. The two fathers at Nacogdoches remained there, because they had been assigned to that settlement for the express purpose of continuing the missionary work, in as far as possible, among the Indians of eastern Texas.

When the decree for the partial secularization of San José and its three neighbors was promulgated, Fr. José Mariano Cárdenas, who had recently succeeded Fr. López as *presidente,* directed the missionaries to prepare the required inventories; and the secularization was carried out by Governor Manuel Múñoz in a formal manner during the summer of 1794.

Fr. Pedrajo's Flour Mill

The missionary at San José at this time was Fr. José Manuel Pedrajo. He had taken charge of the mission in 1789, and during the past five years he had been doing excellent work. A memorial written in 1801 and attributed to Brother José Alberola tells us that through love and understanding he succeeded in training the Indians to operate looms which produced cloth and blankets that were as good as those of Querétaro in Mexico. He also improved the products of the mission farm, which now included wheat; and he built a flour mill.

Wheat had not been raised at the missions during the earlier days, because the Indians did not care for it. As late as 1789, Fr. López wrote in his report: "Wheat is not sown, although it does well, because the Indians hold it in very low regard in comparison with corn, which is the daily bread of this land, and also because its cultivation would interfere with that of the latter, which is here considered absolutely necessary for human life."

In 1778, however, after he had visited Mission San José, Teodoro de Croix left special instructions that, not only corn, but also wheat, barley, and beans should be planted at this mission. The inventory of Mission San José which was prepared in 1794 mentions the fact that there were ninety sacks of wheat, containing about 432 bushels, in the granary of the mission.

At some time during his sojourn at San José, between 1789 and 1794, Fr. Pedrajo constructed a flour mill. But at the time of the secularization, the mill remained the property of the mission, that is, the missionary continued to have the care of it; for, in 1809 Governor Salcedo reported that San José Mission owned and operated a good wheat mill.

Fr. Pedrajo's mill is undoubtedly the same as the old mill which has been restored beside the old irrigation ditch outside the north wall of the mission square. There was a sugar mill at San José in 1758; but that was something quite different, and Governor Barrios' report apparently indicates that it was inside the mission walls.

The flour mill appears to have been in fairly good condition as late as 1859-1864, when Benedictine Father Alto S. Hoermann resided at San José. He described it as follows: "The mill was situated on the opposite side of the ditch.

The reservoir was built of rough hard rock, plastered with common mortar, and perfectly waterproof. It was supplied with water from the ditch. Next to the reservoir there was a vault built of solid tufa, which opened towards the field. The mill was erected directly over this vault, which contained the turbine. An opening near the bottom of the reservoir allowed the water to fall on the turbine from a height of about ten feet. After having furnished power for the turbine, the water flowed in a deep ditch to the fields. The mill stood on the ridge of the prairie."

The San José flour mill utilized not only the power derived from the flow of the water but the force given to the water by falling from a height on the turbine, thus causing it to revolve and to grind the wheat between two millstones. In other words, it operated on the same principle as that of the famous Pelton Wheel, which was thought to have been a new discovery.

In a paper which he prepared in 1955, Dr. Paul L. Czibesz of the Southwest Research Institute, writes: "The hydraulic machinery of the San José Mission mill is living proof that the impulse-turbine was invented a long time before Pelton had published his invention. . . . It is not an ordinary water-wheel. It is really a turbine-runner. Water-wheels work on gravity force or they use the velocity head of the water flow. The turbine wheel of the San José mill utilizes, obviously, the impulse energy. . . . Old-fashioned water-wheels utilized the weight of water on overshot wheels or they used the velocity of the flow by undershot assembly. Both methods could use only one-tenth of the available water power. Pelton's impulse wheel works on impact and impulse energy, and utilizes at least three-fourths of the hydraulic power available. It would appear that the San

José Mission mill is nothing less than the ancestor of Pelton's turbine."

Ernst F. Schuchard, the engineer who restored the old mill, wrote an unpublished monograph about it, in which he points out that it was a so-called Norse mill, a type which was in existence already in the days of Pliny; and the architect, Harvey P. Smith, in a published article, mentioned an old mill of the same type, near Mexico City, which was constructed in the eighteenth century. Scholars have hitherto thought that the San José mill was a grist mill for making corn meal; but it can now be definitely stated that it was a flour mill.

Formal Secularization

The partial secularization of Mission San José was carried out personally by Governor Múñoz on July 16, 1794. When the governor arrived at the mission, Fr. Pedrajo called together all of its Indians, a total of ninety-three persons. Of these seventy-eight were Christians and fifteen were still catechumens who had only recently come to the mission. The governor then announced to the Indians that the property of the mission, which they had held in common till now under the missionary's supervision, would be distributed among them. After the farm had been surveyed and subdivided, each family would receive a part of it and henceforth would have to provide for its own needs. However, there would still be a smaller common farm, to which everyone would have to contribute his labor for a specified time each year, to defray the expenses of the pueblo as a community.

A Spaniard by the name of José Herrera had come with the governor, and the latter introduced him to the Indians as his representative and the "justice" of the San José Indian pueblo. He would henceforth live among them as their advisor and protector in temporal matters. The padre would continue to serve them as their spiritual father. Only the church and friary and fifteen acres of land would remain in his care and under his direction.

After the farm had been surveyed by Pedro Huizar, the reputed sculptor of the famous so-called "Rose Window," Governor Múñoz paid another visit to Mission San José on July 23. Huizar had completed the task of subdividing the farm into forty-eight plats on the previous day. To each of the twenty-eight Christian heads of families or single persons he assigned one plat, measuring 555½ by 833 1/3 feet. To each of the six families of catechumens he gave two similar plats; but these were to remain under the supervision of the missionary as before, until the Indians were able to undertake the administration themselves. Eight plats, each measuring 555½ by 1,111 feet were set aside as the communal farm of the Indian pueblo; and it was Justice Herrera's task to see to it that this farm was managed properly.

There were thirty-four milk cows at the mission, just enough to give one to each head of a family and unmarried adult. The granary with the grain on hand, workshops, tools, supplies, and farm implements were then likewise turned over to the Indians as their common property, and hence they remained under the supervision of the justice. The houses which the Indians already occupied in the mission square became their private homes. While there were enough for all, the number of these Indian apartments had been greatly reduced. Only fifty-four remained and six of these were in ruins; but the other forty-eight were in fairly good condition, most of them having doors and windows.

Settling of Accounts

The mission accounts also had to be settled now, and Fr. Pedrajo had to balance the books as far back as 1761. He was still engaged in this task, when the new Father President, Fr. José Mariano de Cárdenas, took up his residence at Mission San José and assigned Fr. Pedrajo for a short time to the Rosario Mission and then to the new Refugio Mission as Fr. Silva's assistant.

About a year later, Fr. Silva sent Fr. Pedrajo to San Antonio for the purpose of procuring workers for the building of the Refugio Mission. To his great embarrassment, Fr. Pedrajo found the accounts of Mission San José to be still in the condition in which he had left them. For some reason or other Fr. Cárdenas had not been able to complete the settling of the accounts. Fr. Pedrajo immediately prepared a report of the loans which had been made by the mission and were still uncollected and another report of the debts of the mission. These he sent to Governor Múñoz with his apologies. In the meantime one of the debts had been paid. The creditor was the presidio of San Antonio from which the mission had borrowed certain goods, especially tobacco, grain, and clothes for the Indians, worth 458.23 pesos.

Fr. Pedrajo's statement, dated June 5, 1794, the one which he sent to the governor, showed that Mission San José was more than solvent. The mission owed a total sum of

2,230.20 pesos to two merchants in San Antonio and one at La Bahía; but there were thirty-eight other persons who owed the mission a total of 6,118.75 pesos. Thus, after the latter amount would be paid back to the mission, it would have a balance of 3888.55 pesos on hand. The debtors of the mission were mostly Spanish settlers, whom the mission had helped by making small loans to them. It took time, of course, to collect these debts; and while most of the accounts had been settled by September 1, 1795, some items were still outstanding in 1797.

After completing his task of hiring workers in San Antonio for the Refugio Mission, which did not prove to be very successful, Fr. Pedrajo returned to Refugio. But soon afterwards his health broke down, and he returned to Zacatecas by going directly from La Bahía to Laredo. His successor at Refugio was Fr. José Puelles, who had been at La Bahía with Fr. José de la Garza, the companion of Fr. Silva.

Before departing, Fr. Pedrajo sent a note of farewell to Governor Múñoz, thanking him for all past courtesies and offering him his good will as a humble and poor *fraile* (friar).

At Mission San José, after the partial secularization, a stranger would hardly have noticed that a change had been made. Fr. President Cárdenas carried out his duties at the church and instructed the catechumens as before. Justice Herrera saw to it that the Indian landowners cultivated their communal as well as individual farms. It was a rather thankless job, because no arrangement had been made for any salary to be paid to the "justices." Only three years later did the Commandant General Pedro de Nava give his consent to the proposal that two plats of farm land be given to each "justice," and then only as a reward for services faithfully rendered.

In September, 1794, Fr. Cárdenas, while residing at San José, began to take care also of Mission Concepción; and Fr. Pedro Noreña, who lived at the Espada Mission, began to attend also the Capistrano Mission. The government continued to grant to each of these two missionaries of the four missions the annual allowance for a while longer, that is, up to the beginning of 1816. From that time on, the missionaries in Texas no longer received any prebend from the government.

Last page of letter, in the Béxar Archives, Austin, written by Fr. Cárdenas at Mission San José, on September 13, 1794, to Governor Múñoz of Texas. The letter speaks of reducing the number of missionaries at the San Antonio missions from four to two, so that two could be sent to Sonora.

tes despues de verificada la Reunion
no se le podran embiar à su Seño-
ria, y en esta resolucion persiste
aun toda via dho P.e Guard.n como
Consta de la referida Carta de 23.
de Julio ultimo. La referida nese-
sidad, y prescicion de no poder Condesen-
der mi Prelado Con la Justa peticion
de dho Superior Gefe hasta g.e los dos
Ministros Sobrantes despues de la
Reunion de las Missiones, se regre-
sen al Coleg.o y Juntam.te la pia affec-
cion, cong.e V. S. mira a los Missioneros,
me haren esperar con la mayor Segu-
ridad, el favor g.e le he pedido de la Escolta
D.s q.e a V. S. m.s a.s Miss.n de S.r S.n Jose,
Sept.re 13. de 1794.
B. L. M. a V. S. Su aff.mo Serv.r y Capell.n

Fr. Jose M.a de Cardenas.

Sr. Gov.r D.n
Man.l Muñoz

Last Three Decades

The gray old walls stand out against the sky
In sharp relief, a lesson wrought in stone
That speaks sublimely to the souls of men.
For, who that gazes on the sculptured strength
Of arch and tower, rising from a past
Of toil and sacrifice, can fail to read
In every line the builder's patient thought?

— Janie F. Baskin

IX

FOR THREE DECADES AFTER ITS PARTIAL
secularization, the missionaries of the College of Zacatecas
continued to serve Mission San José and its three neighboring missions. During the greater part of this period there
were two padres who took care of the four missions; toward
the end, one missionary had the care of all four. They continued the work of former days as best they could; and at
San José a small number of new Indians were admitted
and instructed almost to the end. Never did the missionaries cease their efforts to improve the status of these missions. They even entertained the hope of restoring them in
some measure to their erstwhile flourishing condition.

Fr. Bernardino Vallejo, 1800-1816

Outstanding among those who were stationed at San
José during these years was Fr. Bernardino Vallejo, who
succeeded Fr. Cárdenas in 1800 both as missionary of San
José and Concepción and as *presidente* of the Texas missions. For more than fifteen years he persevered at his post,
serving both the Indians and the Spaniards who began to
settle at the missions; and he fulfilled his duties in such
an exemplary manner that all who were acquainted with
him held him in high esteem and regarded themselves
fortunate to have him in their midst. Twice, in 1810 and
in 1813, he was recalled to the College to serve on its governing board; but both times, at the request of the governor of
Texas, he was permitted to remain at Mission San José.
When finally he did go back to Zacatecas in April, 1816, he
was elected soon afterwards to the office of Father Guardian
(1816-1819); and subsequently he held the same office for a
second term (1831-1834).

Justices and Spanish Alcaldes

Justice José Herrera does not seem to have stayed at San
José very long. Two years later, Pedro Huizar, who had been
appointed to the same position at Mission Concepción when
it was secularized in 1794, appears to have succeeded Herrera
at San José. At any rate it was agreed in 1796, with the
consent of Justice Pedro Huizar, that Fr. Silva could have
the services of a blacksmith by the name of Vicente Bocanegra, provided that he pay the latter's debt to Mission
San José.

Letters and reports in the Béxar Archives reveal the names
of later "justices" of San José. Thus José Agustín Hernández
prepared a census of the San José pueblo in 1805, and San-

tiago Mandujano did the same in 1809. Mandujano was succeeded shortly afterwards by a son of Pedro Huizar, José Antonio Huisar (he spelled his name with an "s"). The latter was born at San José Mission in 1786, and hence he was still a young man of twenty-four in 1810. However, he was no longer called a "justice," but the Spanish *alcalde* of the Indian pueblo of San José; and he held this office for about ten years until December 13, 1819, when Tomás de León was appointed to succeed him. Tomás de León was still Spanish *alcalde* of San José in 1822.

As a reward for the services rendered by his father Pedro Huizar, José Antonio Huisar in 1806 asked Governor Cordero for a tract of land near Mission Concepción and the granary of San José. After the governor had first consulted Fr. Bernardino Vallejo, he granted the petition. Subsequently, José Antonio Huisar had his title to these properties confirmed by Governor Armiñán in 1815, and by the *Jefe Político* Saucedo in 1824.

On the last day of the year 1804, Fr. President Vallejo made out a report on the Texas missions in which he says that the number of Indians was practically the same as two years earlier, but the number of Spaniards living at San José and the other three missions had increased by thirty-seven. San José had a population of seventy-three persons, of whom fifty-seven were Indians and sixteen Spaniards.

Visit of Zebulon M. Pike, 1807

The soldier and explorer, Zebulon M. Pike, for whom Pike's Peak in the Rockies has been named, visited San Antonio on his way back to the United States from Mexico, June 7-14, 1807. Before reaching San Antonio, he stopped at Mission San José; and, as he tells us in his diary, he was welcomed in a friendly manner by the priest, whose name he does not mention but who was none other than Fr. Bernardino Vallejo. This priest, Pike wrote, was respected and loved by all who knew him, and he treated me with the kindest hospitality.

Governor Salcedo's Report, 1809

A survey compiled by Governor Salcedo in June, 1809, reported that the churches of San José and the other three missions were in fair condition and administered by two Franciscan missionaries. In the four missons there were only one hundred and twenty Indians, fifty-five of them at San José. But there were one hundred and eighty-six Spaniards who had settled on the mission lands, fifteen of them at San José.

The fifty-five Indians at San José and the sixty-five who were at the other missions all had houses within the mission walls. An adequate plot of ground had been allotted to each Indian family and unmarried adult, but no written titles to the real estate had been given to them. There remained a considerable amount of mission land which was not being used, even though some had been rented by Spaniards. Of the Indians and Spaniards who dwelt in or near the missions, Governor Salcedo did not have a very high opinion. He thought the missions were "a haven for idlers and gamblers" — a rather sweeping generalization. Not all the residents at San José deserved such unqualified condemnation.

Letters of Fr. Vallejo

Some interesting sidelights are contained in the letters written by Fr. Bernardino Vallejo during these years. An attempt was made to determine the boundary between Texas and Louisiana, and Fr. José María de Jesus Puelles, missionary and cartographer, was commissioned to study the question. For this purpose, Governor Cordero, in 1805, asked Fr. Vallejo for a copy of Fr. Espinosa's *Crónica;* but Fr. Vallejo had to get the volume from Zacatecas, and delivered it to Casa Calvo of Louisiana the following year. In 1806, he also informed the governor that there were no documents at San José that had any bearing on the boundary question. The following year, when Fr. Puelles' commission expired, he was staying temporarily at San José.

In January, 1809, Fr. Vallejo informed the governor that the Father Guardian of the College had asked him to solicit contributions for defraying the cost of the war against Napoleon; and in April, Justice Mandujano collected one peso from each of thirteen Indians and Spaniards at San José for this purpose.

A letter written by Fr. Vallejo to Governor Salcedo tells us that a change in weekly mail service between San Antonio and Coahuila was introduced in July, 1810. Henceforth, the mail carrier arrived on Wednesday and left on Saturday.

The following month Fr. Vallejo made use of the mail service to notify the College that the governor was interested in establishing a new mission among the Tahuacana Indians. In its reply, the College commended the zeal of the governor, and gave assurances that it would be ready to supply the necessary missionaries. However, the revolutions which followed and the cruel murder of Governor Salcedo in 1813 prevented the founding of the new mission.

For the same reason the plan which General Bernardo Bonavía proposed in 1809 did not materialize. He suggested that since only a few Indians remained at San José and the other three missions, four new towns should be established at these places. The *Junta de Guerra* (Council of War) adopted the plan with the modification that towns should be founded at San José and Espada, and haciendas at the other two missions. A section of land, four leagues square should be set aside for each, and a hundred families should be settled in the new town of San José and another hundred in that of Espada.

The Casas Rebellion followed in 1811, and that of Gutiérrez in 1813. The First Republic of Texas, established by the latter, lasted only a few months; and Spanish rule was re-established by General Arredondo in a ruthless manner. On October 5, 1811, Fr. Vallejo assured interim Governor Herrera that the Indian governors and the Spanish *alcaldes* of San José and the other three missions had remained loyal to the Spanish government throughout the Casas Rebellion. In his report on the status of the Texas missions at the end of 1814, Fr. Vallejo mentions the fact that, in the Gutiérrez campaign of 1813, many of the records of the four San Antonio missions which were kept at San José had been destroyed. However, the record book which Fr. Ramírez had started in 1777 survived.

Fr. Vallejo's Report, 1815

Fr. Vallejo was not able to submit his report on the Texas missions as of December 31, 1814, until February 11, 1815, because he had to wait for information from the Refugio mission. The total number of Indians in the four San Antonio missions was 107, and of these almost half, namely 49, were at San José. Almost twice as many Spaniards, a total of 202, had settled at the missions; and 60 of these were at San José. A total of 309 persons, therefore, was living at the four missions; and 109, or one third, were at San José. Every Sunday Fr. Vallejo and the Espada missionary gave instructions to all of them, Indians and Spaniards.

The churches of the four missions were still in a fair state of preservation; and Fr. Vallejo collected no fees for services rendered. The Indians were now practically destitute. They still raised some corn; but only some of the fields were irrigated, while others depended on rain.

San José and its neighbors, says Fr. Vallejo, were still exposed to attacks by hostile Indians from the north. This statement is corroborated by some of the entries he made in San José's register of burials. On March 10, 1813, for instance, he officiated at the funeral of a resident of the Capistrano mission who had been killed by savage Indians; and on February 15, 1815, he administered the last sacraments, except Viaticum, to a resident of the Espada Mission who was unable to receive Holy Communion because of the nature of the fatal wounds inflicted on him by the Comanches.

Successors of Fr. Vallejo

The 1815 report was the last one made by Fr. Vallejo. The next year he was succeeded by Fr. Manuel María Fellechea, who remained at San José only till the latter part of the following year.

The successor of Fr. Fellechea was Fr. Francisco Frexes, who likewise left San José after about a year and a half. That Fr. Frexes was also the Father President of the Texas Missions is expressly stated in a letter that he wrote to Governor Antonio Martínez, the last of the Spanish governors of Texas, on January 1, 1818. Fr. Frexes encountered unexpected difficulties at San José. Not only did he have to get along without the allowance, but the Indians now refused to render any services to him. They went farther and lodged serious charges against the missionary with the governor; and the latter made the mistake of accepting them at their face value. After Fr. Frexes had left, the governor apparently realized what the true situation had been and invited Fr. Frexes to return to Texas. Anyhow, from Boca de Leones, where the College of Zacatecas had a house called a hospice, Fr. Frexes, on April 22, 1820, wrote a letter to Martínez in which he thanked him for his good will and assured him that he would have liked to return to Texas, but for political reasons he had obtained permission to go back to the College.

That Fr. Frexes was not "an arrogant and quarrelsome character" and "of little or no use" as a missionary, as Martínez represented him to have been in a report he wrote in September, 1819, is shown by the esteem in which the missionary was held by his confreres at the College. For two terms he held the office of vicar of the College, and for three terms he served as one of its councillors. He distinguished himself also as an author and historian.

Shortly before Fr. Frexes left San José, on July 5, 1819, the San Antonio River overflowed its banks and caused considerable damage to the Indian and Spanish farmers at San José, Capistrano, and Espada. A fortnight after the flood, Fr. Miguel Muro arrived to take the place of Fr. Frexes; but the young priest was not disheartened. Until the latter part of 1820, he served San José and the other missions so well and managed to overcome all obstacles so successfully, that Governor Martínez became a close friend of his.

In Coahuila a collection was taken up for the flood sufferers in the San Antonio area. In March, 1820, the governor allotted one hundred and fifty pesos of the donations received to Fr. Muro; and the missionary distributed fifty pesos at each of the three missions of San José, Capistrano, and Espada, to both Indians and Spaniards. Fr. Muro was now the only missionary in the San Antonio area; and he had the care of all four missions. His two predecessors likewise seem to have attended not only San José and Concepción, but also Capistrano and Espada.

The Last of the Padres

*With my heart in my eyes and in my tears,
. . . I salute each and everyone who believes
in Jesus Christ. And let it be clear and well
known from this, that I beg, yes, I beg pardon
from each and everyone whom I have offended;
and likewise, prostrate in spirit on the ground,
I pardon with all my heart each and every
person who may have offended me, be it what
it may. I press all without exception to my
heart as my beloved children in the charity of
our Lord Jesus Christ.*

— Fr. Jose Antonio Diaz de Leon

X

THE LAST MISSIONARY OF THE COLLEGE OF Zacatecas who was stationed at Mission San José was also the last of the padres in Texas. His name was Fr. José Antonio Díaz de León. Like Fr. Miguel Muro, he was no doubt a native of Mexico; and it was in 1817, probably in the company of Fr. Muro, that he came to Texas as a missionary.

Since the revolutionary movement had gotten under way in Mexico, priests coming from Spain were no longer welcome; and, as a result, there was a lack of priests, both religious and secular. Fortunately the College of Zacatecas counted among its members quite a number of friars who were born in Mexico; but it too could not fill all the demands made upon it.

At the Refugio Mission

About the same time that Fr. Muro was assigned to the Mission of Nuestra Señora del Espíritu Santo at La Bahía, that is in the latter part of 1817, Fr. Díaz succeeded Fr. Gaitán at Mission Nuestra Señora del Refugio. This we learn from the baptismal register of the Refugio Mission. Extant also is a report which Fr. Díaz made in 1818 concerning the Refugio Mission. In it he says that the total number of persons residing in the mission pueblo, Indians and Spaniards, was 164. In 1804 it had been 224.

In September of 1818, a destructive storm, probably a hurricane from the gulf, struck the Refugio Mission. It killed many of the cattle, leveled the Indian dwellings, damaged the church's thatched roof; and the rain that poured into the interior ruined the furnishings. But Fr. Díaz succeeded in having the church repaired and the Indian houses rebuilt.

At Mission San José

On June 5, 1820, Fr. José Antonio Díaz de León, the missionary at the Refugio mission, informed Governor Martínez that he had been appointed interim *presidente* and missionary of San José and its neighbors. Not long afterwards he exchanged places with Fr. Muro; and Fr. Antonio de Jesús Anzar was assigned to the Espíritu Santo Mission at La Bahía. These three were the only missionaries in Texas at this time.

The Rosario Mission had practically ceased to exist; and the conditions in the six that remained presented a very discouraging outlook. Fr. Anzar returned to the College after some time; we do not know when. But Fr. Díaz and Fr. Muro never gave up. In fact they were as eager as any of their predecessors to rehabilitate the remaining missions and to make them the centers once more, of apostolic work among the Indians of Texas.

In 1821 Mexico finally gained its independence; and two years later the former Spanish Province of Texas became a part of the State of Coahuila. However, Texas was administered for the governor of Coahuila by a so-called *jefe político* (political chief). With the Mexican governor of Texas, José Trespalacios, and the political chiefs Antonio Saucedo and his successor Ramón Músquiz, Fr. Díaz was on the most friendly terms; and these government officials gave him their support, in as far as they could, when he tried with an amazing perseverance to save the last missions of Texas.

Early in 1822, the Reverend Refugio de la Garza, pastor of the parish of San Fernando, left San Antonio to go to the National Congress of Mexico as a delegate. Fr. Díaz was now the only priest in the San Antonio area; and alone, he took care, not only of San José and the other three missions, but also of the parish of San Fernando, until the military chaplain, the Reverend Francisco Maynes, came to San Antonio in November and assumed the duties of a substitute pastor. About the same time, a new missionary from the College, Fr. Ventura Bustamente, joined Fr. Díaz. The latter did not remain in Texas long; and the Reverend Refugio de la Garza returned to San Antonio only in 1824. Until he came back, Fr. Díaz continued to assist the Reverend Francisco Maynes in San Antonio; but as the records of San José show, he did not in any way neglect the missions during these years.

The Final Secularization

In September, 1813, the national legislature in Spain had issued a decree ordering the immediate secularization of all missions which had been in existence for ten years or more, and the distribution of their lands to private citizens, after a part of them had been given to the mission Indians. The decree was not carried out, because the very next year the acts of the Cortes were declared inoperative. However, when Iturbide became emperor of Mexico in 1822, he proclaimed the acts of the Cortes binding once more until new laws should be enacted.

The settlers in San Antonio were clamoring for the mission lands of San José and its neighbors at this time; and Delegate Garza seized upon Iturbide's order to demand that the decree of 1813 be carried out at once as far as the six remaining missions in Texas were concerned. The Provincial Deputation of Texas gave its approval on September 13, 1823; and two days later the secretary of state, Lucas Alamán, sent orders to Political Chief Saucedo to proceed with the complete secularization of San José and all the other missions of Texas.

The orders received by Saucedo recommended that each mission be converted into an autonomous village and that in each some of the land be reserved for the commons and for a jail and government buildings; but the lands of San José were to remain a unit administered by the town of San Fernando as a source of revenue for a public welfare fund.

When Fr. Díaz was apprised of the secularization decree, he did all he possibly could to save the remaining missions because he thought it was still possible to increase the number of Indian neophytes. He pointed out that Delegate Garza was mistaken when he stated that the missions had been abandoned, that the Indians were no longer living in them, and that the missions had been closed for a period of one year. He called attention to the fact that there could not be any true secularization for the simple reason that no diocesan priests were available to take over the missions. He insisted that he could not relinquish the missions until he received instructions from the Father Guardian of the College of Zacatecas to do so.

Political Chief Saucedo agreed with Fr. Díaz that the La Bahía and Refugio missions should not be closed, but he told the Father President that in the San Antonio area he had to carry out the orders received; and on October 31 he directed him to make an inventory of San José and the other three missions. After the superiors of the College gave their consent to the complete secularization of these missions on December 31, Fr. Díaz could no longer hold out.

Having drawn up the inventories, he signed them on February 29, 1824. On that day, San José, Concepción, Capistrano, and Espada were completely secularized and ceased to be missions. In the name of the bishop of Monterrey, Chaplain Maynes, the substitute pastor of San Fernando, took possession of the four churches and their furnishings. Fr. Díaz no longer had charge of them. Mission San José ceased to be a mission. It was now a part of the parish of San Fernando.

Last Years in Texas

Though it does not pertain directly to Mission San José, a brief account of the last years that Fr. Díaz de León spent in Texas will be of interest. It will complete the biographical sketch of the last missionary of San José, and serve as a counterpart to the life story of Fr. Antonio Margil, the founder of San José, which was presented at the beginning.

Fr. Díaz was still in San Antonio when the vicar forane or rural dean of Texas, the Rev. Juan Nepomuceno de la Peña, conducted a visitation of the parish of San Fernando during the first months of 1825. The pastor of San Fernando had failed to leave the records of the parish with Fr. Díaz when he left for the National Congress; and hence Fr. Díaz and Chaplain Maynes had to keep registers of their own. The Marriage Book showed no entries from February, 1822, to March 12, 1824. The dean ordered Fr. Díaz and Chaplain Maynes to transfer their records to the parish book and to sign their respective entries. The dean became angry with the two priests who had taken care of the parish of San Fernando during the pastor's absence; but they had done the best they could, going even beyond the call of duty. It was no fault of theirs that the Rev. Refugio de la Garza had gone off early in 1822 to the National Congress without making any arrangements for a substitute during his absence.

The two missionaries, Fr. Díaz and Fr. Muro, the only ones still in Texas at this time, presented their appointments and faculties to the dean, and he approved and reissued them on April 12, 1825. About five months later, it seems, Fr. Díaz joined Fr. Muro at La Bahía.

The missions of Nuestra Señora del Espíritu Santo, Nuestra Señora del Rosario, and Nuestra Señora del Refugio, had been included in the secularization decree of September, 1823. This decree was carried out for the four remaining San Antonio missions in 1824; but by his persevering efforts, Fr. Díaz succeeded in having its execution postponed in the La Bahía area for six and a half years.

Efforts to Save the Last Missions

Practically, the Rosario mission was already abandoned in 1806-1807, when its church furnishings were taken to the Refugio Mission and its Indians were assigned to the same mission. However, there were still a few Indians living at

Rosario; and its lands had not yet reverted to the government.

The Espíritu Santo Mission, too, was in a sad condition. It had been greatly damaged by the storm of 1818. It could not defend itself against the attacks of hostile Indians; and by the end of June, 1824, its moveable property had been transferred to the Presidio of La Bahía for safekeeping. But there were still some mission Indians left. Fr. Díaz gathered them; and taking along eleven carts of corn and seed corn, he led them to a place called Paraje del Oso (Place of the Bears), situated on the San Antonio River about ten miles below La Bahía. There they built four *jacales* of wood, and planned to cultivate a farm in common and to live according to a modified form of mission regularity. But the citizens of La Bahía objected, and Fr. Díaz had to give up the project.

He realized that he could no longer prevent the complete secularization of the Rosario and Espíritu Santo missions; but he continued to defend the Indians' right to the mission lands, despite the fact that the settlers of La Bahía were clamoring for them.

As far as the Refugio Mission was concerned, he felt that it should be maintained at all costs; and he continued his fight to save it from secularization. This he did despite the fact that Fr. Muro had to abandon the mission temporarily in 1824. After Fr. Muro gathered the Indians once more at Refugio in August, 1825, he was forced by the Comanches to abandon the mission a second time in May, 1826, and to transport its moveable property to La Bahía. But Fr. Díaz still did not give up.

After the abdication of Emperor Iturbide in 1823, the government of the Republic of Mexico joined Texas to Coahuila, making them one state. Texas was thus placed under the jurisdiction of Governor Rafael González of

Coahuila, while José Antonio Saucedo, with the title of Political Chief, administered Texas in the governor's name.

Fr. Díaz pleaded the cause of the La Bahía missions with these civil authorities and their successors (Governor Agustín Viesca and Political Chief Ramón Músquiz) so well that they agreed with him rather than with the persistent demands of the settlers that the missions be secularized and their lands be put on sale for them. The governor went so far as to forward Fr. Díaz' petition to the national government.

However, at the insistence of Goliad's deputy to the state legislature (La Bahía's name was changed to Goliad at this time), Governor Viesca, in March, 1829, ordered Political Chief Músquiz to carry out the secularization of the missions of Espíritu Santo and Refugio without further delay. Músquiz forwarded these orders to the *alcalde* of Goliad and to Father Presidente Díaz. Even then the missionary made one final, eloquent appeal in behalf of Refugio. Músquiz and Viesca again reconsidered the matter and decided that the missionary's plea should receive a hearing; and once more they sent his petition to the national government. The result was merely another delay.

The formal secularization of the last two missions of Texas finally took place on February 8, 1830, when Fr. Díaz, Fr. Muro, and the city officials of Goliad signed the inventories of the two missions.

The College of Zacatecas had agreed in October, 1829, not only to the secularization of these two missions, but also to the appointment of Fr. Díaz and Fr. Muro as parish priests of Nacogdoches and the Villa de San Felipe de Austin. Fr. Muro was willing to go to Austin's colony; but since the latter preferred to wait for an English-speaking priest, Fr. Muro continued to minister to the people of Goliad until his recall to the college in 1833. Later he served for a while as a missionary in California. He died at Zacatecas, June 20, 1848, about 58 years old.

At Nacogdoches

Fr. Díaz took up his duties at Nacogdoches as well as Liberty and San Augustine, shortly after the departure of the Rev. José Ignacio Galindo, who was pastor of Nacogdoches from the spring of 1828 to November 29, 1830. The new pastor had to use, as a church, the former home of Nathaniel Norris, because the church built in 1801 had been converted into a barracks during the Fredonian Rebellion at the end of 1826. Before 1801 the old church of the former Mission of Nuestra Señora de Guadalupe had served as a parish church. The people of Nacogdoches started to raise funds for a new church and a school in January, 1831; but it could not be started until after Texas gained its independence in 1836.

The Father Guardian of the College of Zacatecas had given Fr. Díaz a choice of going to east Texas or of returning to the College. The reason was the fact that some newcomers had entered east Texas who were filled with bitter and fanatical hatred of the Catholic Church and especially of its priests. From one of the Catholic empresarios in Texas, the Father Guardian had received a letter written in Latin, asking him not to allow the two remaining missionaries of the College to continue their work among the American settlers. He had knowledge, said the correspondent, that the attitude of several meetings of non-Catholic empresarios was such that a persecution of the missionaries was to be feared.

But, as Sotomayor tells us in his history of the College of Zacatecas, Fr. Díaz, who had spent years in the missions of Nuevo Santander, Mexico, more savage than those of

Texas, was not deterred by the danger of death. Besides, he did not think that white men of any nationality, ruffians though they might be, would be as dangerous as described.

At Nacogdoches and the surrounding area, Fr. Díaz, the veteran Indian missionary, "devoted himself to the task of guarding that flock in imitation of the Divine Shepherd" (Sotomayor). He soon won the esteem of the people of Nacogdoches, including such men as Prentiss Borden, Adolphus Sterne, and Colonel Elias Bean. Frequently he was a guest in the homes of John J. Linn and Martin de León. He counted among his friends and acquaintances, Austin, Kerr, DeWitt, Bastrop, Erasmo Seguín, De La Garza, outstanding empresarios and figures of early Texas history.

Fr. Díaz had only a limited knowledge of English, but his sincerity, humility, and friendliness were so genuine that his zealous labors for the spiritual welfare of the flock committed to his care were crowned with remarkable success. Soon the number of his parishioners increased considerably. Indifferent and poorly instructed so-called "Muldoon Catholics" began to take their religion seriously; and not a few non-Catholics asked to be instructed in Catholic doctrine and to be baptized.

Not long after his arrival at Nacogdoches, Fr. Díaz blessed the marriage of one of its outstanding citizens, Judge Charles S. Taylor; and the judge's good example was followed by many others.

In the home of Adolphus Sterne, on a May evening in 1833, Fr. Díaz poured the waters of baptism on the head of a man who had recently come to Texas. His name was Sam Houston, the hero of the battle of San Jacinto which won independence for Texas three years later. Mr. and Mrs. Sterne were his sponsors.

Missionary Trips

The Indians to whom Fr. Díaz had been a good shepherd were few in number, because he happened to come to Texas at a time when the missions were nearing their end; but now, among the colonists of east Texas, he had found a wide and fertile field for the priestly zeal with which he was animated. He was no longer a young man, but his energy seemed to have no bounds. Not satisfied with the care of souls in Nacogdoches only, he made frequent journeys from house to house through the pine forests in the surrounding area, and traveled as far as Liberty and San Augustine to bring the consolations of religion to those settlements as well. As a rule he went on foot; sometimes he rode his roan mare.

In January of 1834, he made one of these apostolic journeys, lasting about two weeks. On February 14, he celebrated a solemn Mass which had been requested by the governor. All the local officials attended the Mass; and twenty-five militiamen fired a salute at the Elevation.

Fr. Díaz was having too much success, as far as his enemies were concerned; and enemies there were. They informed him that it would be better for him if he left and went back to Mexico. Even in public they boldly threatened him. Some of his friends too warned him that it was not safe for him to take any risks. But he continued to make his trips to distant places unattended.

However, in October, 1834, the threats against his life had become so serious and persistent, that Fr. Díaz hesitated when Samuel C. Hirams asked him to come to the home of G. L. Thomas on the Trinity River for the celebration of Hirams' marriage. It was only toward the end of the month, after Hirams had repeated his request, that the good padre set out on what was to be his last journey.

He reached the Thomas home safely, and remained a few days to instruct the bride and groom and then blessed the marriage. Only three miles away, Peter J. Menard, whom the missionary trusted, had his home; and so he spent a few days there before beginning his return trip to Nacogdoches. He confided to Mr. Menard that he knew one or more persons had been hired to kill him on the way; but Mr. Menard said he did not think the priest would suffer any harm on the road. Nevertheless Fr. Díaz asked for ink and paper, wrote his last will and testament, and asked his host to give the message to his nephew Santos Antonio Áviles if anything should happen to him.

Farewell Message

There are several slightly differing versions of Fr. Díaz de León's farewell message, due to the fact perhaps that they are different translations from the Spanish. The following is the text given by J. M. Kirwin, in his *History of the Diocese of Galveston,* with some explanatory editing:

"This Sunday, November 4, 1834 (the date should be November 2, because the 4th in 1834 fell on a Tuesday), I returned to this house (of Mr. Menard), and as it seems to me to be the last day of my life — God knows why — I address my weak and languishing words to my beloved parishioners of Nacogdoches, bidding them, from the bottom of my heart, an earnest farewell. Adios! Adios! Let them inform His Excellency (the Governor of Coahuila-Texas?) of the state in which I am. I salute them, with my heart in my eyes and in my tears, especially Mr. Roberts, Lieutenant Colonel Elias Bean, Mr. Adolph (Sterne), my friends Allen, Reque (Rackey or Rickey), and Chones (Jones), and all and everyone who believes in Jesus Christ. And let it be clear and well known from this that I beg, as I do, pardon from each and all the persons whom I have offended, and likewise, prostrate in spirit on the ground, I pardon with all my heart all and every person who may have offended me, be what it may. I press all, without exception, to my heart as my beloved children in the charity of our Lord Jesus Christ. Also to the *alcalde* of the *ayuntamiento,* Don Juan Mora, farewell, I say, farewell. Amen. Amen. This letter, with like expressions of affection, I address to my dear friend, Dr. Manuel Santos, that he may send it to his correspondents, when he can, and to display my heart to all my parishioners, whom I beseech in the heart of our Savior Jesus Christ to persevere firmly in keeping the law of God and the sacred obligations they contracted in baptism. And I beg (him) to hand this to my nephew, Santos Antonio Áviles, that he may copy it, and live in the fear of the Author of his being. (Signed:) Fray Antonio Díaz de León."

Fr. Díaz asked Captain Hirams, for whose marriage he had come, to give him a companion on the return trip to Nacogdoches, and the captain hired a Kentuckian by the name of Philip Miller. It was also arranged that a servant of Mr. Menard, Manrico García, who was a native of Zacatecas, should go along; but at the last moment it was decided that this was not necessary. Mr. Menard also offered Fr. Díaz a pistol or gun to take along for his protection; but the padre said he would not have any use for either. Miller also declined the offer of a gun, saying it was too heavy to carry.

The Last Journey

About noon on Sunday, November 2, Fr. Díaz and Miller set out from the house of Mr. Menard. At the home of G. L. Thomas they ate supper. Continuing their journey, they stopped also at the house of H. B. Prentiss, because he wanted to send some letters to Nacogdoches. It was getting late, and they decided to spend the night there. Saying he was going to feed the horses, Miller went back to Menard that night and asked for a pistol, supposedly on the insistence of the padre — who had said he would not have any use for the weapon.

After breakfast on November 3, the travelers resumed their journey. By evening they had gone about twenty miles to Big Sandy Creek, but went a mile or so farther to a little branch of the creek and there pitched tent for the night. Miller had trouble trying to start a fire, but the padre took the flint and quickly had a fire going. About midnight Fr. Díaz awoke and saw Miller standing by the fire. They talked for a while about religion and the morrow, and went back to sleep.

Shortly before daybreak, said Miller, he was awakened by something, but not by a shot. Feeling chilly, so he testified, he went to the fire and found blood trickling from the mouth of Fr. Díaz and the pistol "near the body." Fr. Díaz had been murdered by a pistol shot into the region of his heart, which must have caused instant death. Miller went back to the house of G. L. Thomas, and together they returned, buried the body of the martyred missionary, and then went to Liberty to make a report to the *alcalde*.

The murderer or murderers of Fr. Díaz were not brought to justice. Miller, Hirams, García, and Menard made it appear that the padre had shot himself in a moment of despondency; and that explanation was apparently accepted by the court. But, as Dr. Castañeda writes, "a veteran missionary would never have preferred suicide to martyrdom. The inhabitants of Nacogdoches commonly believed that he was assassinated, and such was the tradition found in the area nineteen years later by Father Parisot when he visited Nacogdoches in 1853. The records which had escaped detection by investigators until now support the tradition of his martyrdom."

In his *History of Refugio Mission,* Msgr. William H. Oberste points out what is the best refutation of the slanderous blackening of the memory of the last missionary of San José Mission, the last of the padres of the College of Zacatecas in Texas, and the last of the Franciscan martyrs of Texas: "His known life of zeal and abnegation, the human pathos and sublime expressions embodied in his Last Will and Testament — all these belied the calculated rumor and unfounded claim that the saintly friar had committed suicide."

Some months before his death in 1936 (the year of the centennial of Texas independence), the Very Reverend Fr. Martin Strub, ex-provincial of the Chicago-St. Louis Franciscan Province, sent to the writer a letter he had received from a correspondent in Nacogdoches many years before. We quote from that letter: "The Franciscans should do something to commemorate his (Fr. Díaz de León's) memory. I firmly believe he was killed for the Faith, and is therefore a martyr. He foretold his death. If nothing else, a tablet should be placed in our little church here (in Nacogdoches) to perpetuate his blessed memory."

Neglect and Reclaim of San José

Deserted are the cloistered courts and cells;
Yet strange sweet memories haunt the grey
   old pile,
And breathe a message from the voiceless past,
Of men who wrought for higher than gold,
And dying, have bequeathed to future years
A heritage of noble thoughts and deeds.

— JANIE F. BASKIN

XI

AFTER SAN JOSÉ HAD PASSED INTO THE hands of the pastor of San Fernando, its church as well as those of Concepción, Capistrano, and Espada were completely neglected during the remaining years of the Mexican regime and the first years of the Republic of Texas. The pastor of San Fernando at this time was the Rev. Refugio de la Garza, who had returned from the National Congress in Mexico; and his assistant was the Rev. José Antonio Valdez.

Early Neglect of San José

Unfortunately the administrator of the diocese of Monterrey, Mexico, the Rev. José León Lobo (1821-1832), and the new bishop, the Franciscan Fray José de María Jesus Belauzarán y Ureña, had no other priests to send to Texas.

Two years after he came to Monterrey in 1832, the bishop had to flee in disguise from the state officials of Nuevo León. There was a Rev. Michael Muldoon in Texas at this time, but it is doubtful whether or not he was a genuine Catholic priest.

Other priests besides Fr. Díaz de León and Fr. Muro, who were in Texas during the Mexican period were: the Rev. Enrique Doyle, with the Irish settlers at Refugio in 1830; one Dominican and two Conventual Franciscans, also with Irish settlers in 1832; and the Rev. Maloney or Molloy, who became pastor of San Patricio in 1834.

None of these, except the latter, who was at Goliad when Fannin and his men were massacred by order of Santa Anna, and the two priests in San Antonio, seem to have been in Texas when it fought its war of independence (1835-1836).

Anglo-Americans in Texas

During the decade and a half that Texas belonged to the Republic of Mexico (1821-1836), the number of colonists increased more than ever before, and among them were not a few Catholics, who sorely felt the lack of priests. Moses Austin had received the permission of the last Spanish governor in 1820 to settle Texas with Americans; and his plan was carried out by his son, Stephen Austin, with the consent of the new government of independent Mexico. New towns were established, such as San Felipe de Austin, San Augustine, Brazoria, Columbia, Washington-on-the-Brazos, González, Velasco, San Patricio, Refugio, Victoria, Jackson, Galveston, Houston, Lavaca, Navidad, Copano; and the population of the older settlements of San Antonio, Nacogdoches, Goliad (the former La Bahía), was increased.

By 1835 there were about thirty thousand Anglo-Americans living in Texas. They were liberty-loving people, willing to be citizens of the Republic of Mexico, in which they expected to have some measure of self-government; but they were determined to die rather than to submit to a tyrant like General Antonio López de Santa Anna. Elected president of Mexico as a liberal in 1833, he threw off his mask the next year and began to rule as a dictator. In May, 1835, he crushed the revolt of the state of Zacatecas with savage cruelty.

The Texas War of Independence

The revolution in Texas followed. The first shot of its war for independence was fired on October 2, 1835, when the people of González refused to return a six-pound cannon to the Mexican troops and sent them back fleeing to San Antonio. Seven days later the insurgents drove the Mexican garrison from the fort at Goliad. On October 28 they won a battle with the Mexican army sent against them near Mission Purísima Concepción; and on December 10, they captured San Antonio. The Mexican soldiers retired to the Rio Grande; but the expedition of the Texans from San Antonio to Matamoros at the mouth of the Rio Grande was a mistake and ended in failure.

Meanwhile, at Washington-on-the-Brazos, the leaders of the settlers declared Texas independent of Mexico on March 27, 1836. Previously, on December 20, 1835, Captain Dimmitt's company of volunteers at Goliad had already signed a declaration of independence.

However, the Mexicans came back in greater numbers under Santa Anna himself; and after he and his army of 5,000 had re-entered Texas, the soldiers of the revolution suffered one defeat after another.

On February 27, 1836, Colonel Francis Johnson's Party

was surprised at San Patricio, eight or ten were killed and eighteen were taken prisoners.

On March 2, fourteen men of Dr. James Grant's party were killed at Agua Dulce, and six were taken prisoners.

On March 6, in the Battle of the Alamo, after a siege of thirteen days by Santa Anna's army, Colonel William Barret Travis and one hundred and eighty-three men died fighting rather than surrender.

On March 14-16, twenty-eight men under Colonel William Ward and Captain Amon B. King lost their lives in the fighting at Refugio.

On March 27, after the Battle of Coleto on the 19th, Colonel James Walker Fannin and more than three hundred and sixty other prisoners of war were inhumanly slaughtered by order of General Santa Anna.

These reverses and cruelties only made the Texans all the more determined never to give up; and in the decisive Battle of San Jacinto on April 21, General Sam Houston and his followers inflicted a complete defeat on the Mexican army, taking Santa Anna himself a prisoner and forcing the survivors to return to Mexico.

Bowie and Fannin at Espada

During these stirring events, Mission San José remained silent and deserted. But mention is made of the mission a few days before the battle near Mission Concepción (October 28, 1835), in a letter to Stephen F. Austin, the Father of Texas, written at twelve o'clock, Thursday night, October 22, at Espada Mission, by two heroes of the revolution, who had led an advance guard toward San Antonio to look for a place where the troops could be housed and if necessary defend themselves. They were James Bowie, who lost his life in the siege of the Alamo, and James W. Fannin who was killed at Goliad.

"At half past four o'clock P.M.," they wrote, "we took possession of this mission, without any resistance. A guard of five men escaped us by only a few minutes. We find the citizens well disposed and quite communicative. Owing to the late hour of our arrival, we have not examined the Missions above, but have had it done by our Pilot, who reports only five soldiers at St. José, known at San Juan. — We learn that no public stores are collected at either place. — The Bean crops are entirely destroyed. — There is corn in abundance, but the principal owners are in town, and couriers will be dispatched early for them, to make contracts with for the army. There is corn here, but owned by men who rent the Land, and will sell for cash only, and only in small quantities."

The next day, at five o'clock, they sent another letter to Austin, informing him that they had established headquarters at the Espada Mission, rather than at San José, because at the latter they would have been left "too much at the mercy of the enemy" and water was too far away. At San José they had found only one family, only a small crop of peas, and no corn. The corn crop had failed, because the dam which supplied water for irrigation had broken early in the season and the fields had been abandoned. They described the mission as being in a dilapidated state, although it still had fine quarters for the soldiers.

After the victory of San Jacinto, San José Mission was used at times as quarters for soldiers of the Republic of Texas. The mission was probably used for this purpose when Mexico made an attempt to win back Texas in 1842. On March 5th of that year General Rafael Vásquez took San Antonio and held it for two days; and on September 11, General Adrian Woll with sixteen hundred Mexican soldiers invaded San Antonio. The latter was a threat of a more serious nature; for, the defenders of the city had to surrender after four days. However, on September 15, in the Battle of Salado Creek, east of the city, the Texans once more defeated the Mexicans and compelled them to retire to the border.

Comanches at San José, 1840

The danger of attacks by hostile Indians was another menace with which the citizens of the Republic of Texas had to contend. Mary A. Maverick, who came to San Antonio as a bride in 1838, tells us in her memoirs of the boldness of the Comanches in San Antonio and at the former Mission San José. At the time, Lt. Colonel William S. Fisher and one hundred and sixty men of the First Infantry were quartered at San José. Chief Ismanica boldly rode into San Antonio on March 28, 1840, with two hundred and fifty to three hundred Comanches. When he was told that the soldiers were at the mission, he "took his braves to San José and with fearless daring bantered the soldiers for a fight. Colonel Fisher was lying on a sick bed and Captain (William D.) Redd, the next in rank, was in command. He said to the chief: 'We have made a twelve-day truce with your people in order to exchange prisoners. My country's honor is pledged, as well as my own, to keep the truce, and I will not break it. Remain here three days or return in three days, and the truce will be over. We burn to fight you.' Ismanica called him a liar, coward, and other opprobrious names, and hung around for some time, but at last the Indians left and did not return. Captain Redd remained calm and unmoved, but his men could with the greatest difficulty be restrained, and in fact some of them were ordered into the Mission church and the door guarded."

Fathers Odin and Calvo

In the same year (1840) Father John M. Odin with three other Vincentians, two priests and a brother, arrived in the Republic of Texas to come to the aid of its Catholic citizens, who had for so long a time been without the ministrations of a priest. Father John Timon had arrived at Galveston in 1838 as prefect apostolic of Texas; but since he could not remain in Texas he appointed Father Odin vice-prefect. Up to this time, nominally at least, Texas had still belonged to the diocese of Monterrey, Mexico.

Leaving Father Eudald Estany at Victoria, he accompanied the other two Vincentians to San Antonio. After he had removed from office the two aged priests, Frs. Garza and Valdez, who were still in San Antonio, he installed Father Michael Calvo on August 7 as pastor, with Brother Raymond Sala as a companion. In September, Father Odin visited the former missions. He found much to admire in the sturdy and artistically constructed churches of San José and Concepción, but described Capistrano and Espada as a mass of ruins. San José Mission, he thought, could easily be converted into a boys' school or college or seminary.

With Fr. Timon he then petitioned the Congress of the Republic of Texas at Austin to revalidate the Catholic Church's claim to San José and all other missions and buildings and adjoining lands which had been church property under the Spanish government. After the matter had been debated and a futile attempt had been made to make some exceptions, the Congress approved the following act on January 13, 1841:

"An Act Confirming the Use, Occupation, and Enjoyment of the Churches, Church lots, and Mission Churches to the Roman Catholic Congregations living in or near the vicinity of the same.

"Sec. 1. Be it enacted by the Senate and House of Representatives of the Republic of Texas, in Congress assembled, That the Churches of San Antonio, Goliad, and Victoria, the church lot of Nacogdoches, the churches at the Mission of Conception, San José, San Juan, Espada, and the Mission of Refugio, with outbuildings and lots, if any belonging to them, be, and they are hereby acknowledged and declared the property of the present chief pastor of the Roman Catholic Church in the Republic of Texas, and his successors in office in trust forever, for the use and benefit of the congregations residing near the same, for religious purposes and purposes of education, and none other; provided that nothing herein contained shall be so construed as to give title to any lands except the lots upon which the churches are situated, which shall not exceed fifteen acres."

Thus the church of Mission San José began to be used once more for religious purposes, at least occasionally. Father Odin, who was appointed vicar apostolic of Texas and consecrated a bishop in 1842, again visited San José, Concepción, and Capistrano in 1844, and organized catechism classes there in German, French, English, and Spanish. Father Estany joined Father Calvo and Brother Sala at San Antonio; and when their many duties there permitted it, one of the priests visited at times San José and the other former missions.

In 1844 Father Calvo reported that during the five years he had served as pastor of San Antonio and the nearby missions, he had heard more than five thousand confessions and he had given Holy Communion to over four thousand. In a report made by Father Timon in January, 1847, he expressly mentions San José, Capistrano, and Espada as "Mass stations" attended by the pastor of San Antonio. At this time there were ten priests in Texas; three years later there were twelve.

In the meantime, on December 29, 1845, the Republic of Texas had become one of the states of the United States of America. It was only then that women and children dared to return to San Antonio. The diocese of Galveston, comprising all of Texas, was erected in 1847, and Bishop Odin was appointed its first head.

William Bollaert, 1843

That Father Calvo occasionally offered up holy Mass at San José is confirmed by William Bollaert, an Englishman who arrived in Texas in 1842 and visited San José in 1843. In his observations he says that eight or ten Mexican families were living within the walls of the mission and that Mass was said for them occasionally. The church he found to be "still in good preservation," although it was "full of bats' nests." In the tower there was only one cracked bell. He admired the "exquisite work and labor" bestowed on the door and the window (the so-called "Rose Window") of the vestry or sacristy. "The images of the saints and other ornamental parts," he notes, "had been sadly mutilated by the soldiery during the wars."

George Kendall, 1841

This mutilation must have occurred only a year or two previously, because in 1841 they were still intact. In that year George Kendall, a noted journalist of the New Orleans *Picayune*, passed through San Antonio and visited the old missions. In his *Narrative of the Texan Santa Fe Expedition*, he reported that all the missions had walls of great thickness and were substantially built. Of San José in particular he writes: "The Mission of San José consists also of a large square, and numerous Mexican families still make it their residence. To the left of the gateway is the granary. The church stands apart from the other buildings in the square but not in the center. The west door (the front entrance) is surrounded with most elaborate stone carving of flowers, angels, and apostles. Though the Texan troops were long quartered here, the stone carvings have not been injured. The church has been repaired and divine service is performed in it" (by Father Calvo of San Antonio).

Ferdinand Roemer, 1846

The German scientist Ferdinand Roemer, who visited San José in 1846, mentions the fact that the walls of the San José Mission compound were still partially intact, and some Mexicans were living there in huts. Also, that traces of bright colors could still be seen on the statues.

John R. Bartlett, 1850

John Russell Bartlett, one of the United States commissioners who surveyed the boundary of the United States after the war with Mexico (1846), came to San Antonio in 1850. In his *Personal Narrative,* he writes that Mission San José was still in a fair state of preservation, although Seth Eastman had thought, in the previous year, that San José was "going to ruins."

Bartlett has the following to say about San José: "This was the largest and wealthiest Mission and its buildings were constructed with greater display of art and still remain in better preservation than the others. The principal doorway (of the church) is surrounded by elaborate carving, which includes numerous figures. The action of the weather has done much to destroy the figures, and the work of ruin has been assisted by the numerous military companies near here who, finding in the hands and features of the statues convenient marks for rifle and pistol shots, did not fail to improve the opportunity for showing their skill at arms. That portion of the front of the church not covered with carving was ornamented with a sort of stencilling in colors, chiefly red and blue. But few traces of this had withstood the rain. The interior presents but little of interest. The damp has destroyed the frescoes upon the wall, and the altar has been stripped of its decorations. It is now seldom used for religious purposes."

The former *convento* in the rear of the church, which was in a tolerable state of preservation, says Bartlett, was inhabited by an American who cultivated nearby fields. It may have been at this time that the old friary had the gable roof shown on an old picture of San José. In the neighborhood there were also Mexicans who were occasionally visited by Father Calvo, who was still serving as pastor of San Antonio and the old missions in 1850.

Frederick Olmsted, 1854

Four years later, Frederick Olmsted, the man who laid out New York City's Central Park, strange to say, found nothing of interest at Mission San José. In his *Journey through Texas,* he dismisses the old missions with the remark: "They are in different stages of decay, but all are real ruins, beyond any connection with the present — weird remains out of the silent past." His attitude reflected that of many Americans who were prejudiced against Spain and its culture and found nothing worth while in the achievements of the Spanish pioneers of our country.

Conventual Franciscans, 1852-1859

What Bishop Odin thought of the old mission of San José was quite different; and the hope that he had expressed in 1840 of making San José once more a religious center at long last enjoyed a temporary and partial fulfillment not long after Olmsted's visit. During the years 1852-1859 a group of five German Conventual Franciscans ministered to their Catholic countrymen in the San Antonio area, at New Braunfels, Fredericksburg, Castroville, D'Hanis, and other places; and the Polish Conventual Fr. Leopold Moczygemba, who came already in 1851, founded the parish of Panna Maria in 1854, his successor being Fr. Anthony Rossadowski, a confrere from London, who remained in Texas until after 1860.

Even before the German Conventual Franciscans left in 1859, Bishop Odin turned for help to Abbot Boniface Wimmer of St. Vincent's Abbey at Latrobe, Pennsylvania. When his first request remained fruitless, Bishop Odin went in person to St. Vincent's Abbey and persuaded the abbot to send some fathers to Texas.

Father Hoermann and the Benedictines, 1859-1868

Bishop Odin was at St. Vincent's in June, 1858. After he had submitted to Abbot Wimmer his plan for the establishment of a large Benedictine monastery at the old Mission San José, the abbot's interest was aroused at once and he yielded to the bishop's plea without further delay. In fact, as his letters show, the abbot became the soul of the enterprise. Not only a monastery but also a seminary was planned. Fr. Alto S. Hoermann was appointed prior of San José and received instructions to begin repairs and construction as soon as possible.

On July 1, 1859, Father Hoermann and four other Benedictines, two priests and two brothers, left for Texas. They were Fathers Emil or Aemilian Wendel and Peter Baunach, and Brothers Michael Boehns and Norbert Rossberger. Subsequently these were joined by others; and during the decade that the Benedictines remained in Texas, they also served as pastors of German parishes in San Antonio and the vicinity. While he resided at San José, Father Hoermann took care of the German-speaking members of St. Mary's parish in San Antonio.

Father Hoermann took a deep interest in the mission and its past history; and he made a valiant effort to restore the old *convento* and to add to it. The Gothic arches which still remain were no doubt built at this time. This construction work was done at the cost of great effort and many hardships. Father Hoermann's health was undermined, and he contracted lung trouble. He had to return to St. Vincent's, and spent the last years of his life in pastoral and literary work. From 1864 to 1867 he served as parish priest at Augusta, Kentucky; and on June 29, 1867, he died of tuberculosis at Covington, Kentucky.

At San José, Father Hoermann was succeeded first by Father Armand Kramer, and then by Father Aemilian Wendel. Bishop Odin was made archbishop of New Orleans in 1861. His successor as bishop of Galveston, Bishop DuBuis, was likewise very much interested in the Benedictine venture at San José. The chapter held at St. Vincent's Abbey in 1862 resolved to send a petition to the Holy See for the establishment of an independent priory, but the Civil War interfered. Several of the Benedictines died in Texas, and the survivors were recalled in 1868. The building and lands at San José were returned to Bishop DuBuis.

After the Benedictines left San José, another great lover of the old missions, the diocesan priest Rev. Francis Bouchu was doing restoration work single-handed at Mission San Francisco de Espada. For almost forty years, 1868 to 1907, he resided at Espada, serving the Catholics who lived in the neighborhood and at Carmen.

In the same year in which the Benedictines reluctantly left San José, a part of the north wall of the church collapsed during a storm, the night of December 10, 1868. For wellnigh a century the church had stood intact for the most part. People apparently had been digging for imagined buried treasures along the foundations on the north side, thus weakening the wall and causing it to fall in the storm. The spacious sacristy then served as a church, as it did in the 1770's while the church was being completed.

After the departure of the Benedictines, San José was more or less abandoned again for several years until the arrival of the Holy Cross Fathers from Notre Dame, Indiana, in 1872.

Sidney Lanier, 1872

In Sidney Lanier's historical sketch, written in 1872, we find the following reference to Mission San José: "Further down the river a couple of miles, one comes to the Mission *San José de Aguayo*. This is more elaborate and on a larger scale than the buildings of the first Mission (San Antonio), and is still very beautiful. Religious services are regularly conducted here; and one can do worse things than to steal out here from town on some wonderfully calm Sunday morning, and hear a mass, and dream back the century and a half of strange, lonesome, devout, hymn-haunted and Indian-haunted years that have trailed past these walls. Five or six miles (sic) further down the river are the ruins of the Mission San Juan in much dilapidation."

For a decade and a half, until 1888, the Holy Cross

Fathers attended Mission San José. Two years after they took charge, the church's dome, "the day star of Manitou" as the Indians called it, which had not fallen with the north wall of the church in 1868, and the greater part of the roof crashed to the floor of the church. This happened while midnight Mass was being celebrated in the sacristy chapel on December 25, 1874. The fact that the dome had remained suspended on one side in mid air for a half dozen years shows how well it had been built.

A Visitor in 1876

A visitor of San José in 1876 described the mission in the following words: "The ruins are very extensive. More than half of the walls have fallen. A few Mexicans live near and care for the chapel, which was a model of rude neatness. The nice, clever, and evidently pious Mexican matron, who brought the key for our entrance, had hung the altar with gaudy patchwork quilts of her own manufacture. The most exquisite tapestry could not have told the story of her devout love more plainly. . . . Every part of the ruined chapel was arranged with neatness and decency. The floor of the sacristy and that of the baptistry, which we could not enter, had been paved with tiles of home manufacture. The clay was procured in the vicinity, and they were equal to any of European manufacture. This clay will one day be made the foundation of a valuable industry (sic)" (R. Sturmberg, *History of San Antonio*, p. 126).

William Corner, 1890

In the "Guide and History" of San Antonio, which William Corner wrote and published in 1890, we find a detailed description of Mission San José as he found it at that time. "The gateway is gone to-day," he writes. "The granary, with its strong and curious flying buttresses and arched stone roof, is still there and in it families make a home. The road still enters the Mission Square just at the right of the granary, where the old entrance was.

"Here you are in full view of the façade of the Mission Buildings with the square spreading out to the right or south of the long main building of the Mission. The Mexican families still exist in huts erected upon the ruins of the ramparts of the Mission Square, and in a few years these now hardly to be defined foundations will have been 'improved' from the place.

"At the southwestern corner of the Mission buildings is a belfry tower, about sixty feet high. It has four lookout windows and a pyramidical stone roof. Tucked in the angle made by this tower and the south wall of the large Chapel, is a peculiar round tower to accommodate the winding stair-way of solid hewn wooden steps to the second story of the belfry tower. From the second story are very curious stairs or ladders made of solid tree trunks notched and dressed with an axe, leading to the upper lookout of the tower. Here are to be had some fine views of the country. All over the tower chamber's walls are thousands of names of visitors.

"Only a small portion of the large stone roof of the main Chapel remains and much of the north wall has gone, leaving a great ugly gap on this side and the remnant of the roof (over the choir loft) very unsafe in appearance. These portions of the Chapel with its dome fell in with a great crash on a stormy night of December, 1868 (and 1874).

"To the south of the main Chapel is a smaller one, the window and carving of which were referred to above. This is roofed by three domes, the tops of the enclosing walls being serrated, all quite in Moorish style. The entrance to this Chapel is from the east from the ante-chamber or wing of the cloisters. The arch and side-stones of the entry door are beautifully sculptured, and here, there still remain, much chipped, once finely carved, cedar double doors, and although so badly damaged they suggest to one's mind what the beauty of the front doors or gates at the façade of the main Chapel might have been. In this little Chapel services are still occasionally held. Its altar is decked with gaudy patchwork of a distinctly Mexican design, and many a little trumpery, by way of offering is placed there by the simple and believing women folk of the place. . . .

"There are two ancient Spanish pictures, one hanging each side of the altar, much the worse for age, scenes from the life of St. Joseph. One is very plainly the 'Flight into Egypt.' The other, more difficult to make out, is most likely a picture of the Circumcision. The fan-like fluted canopies of the window and recesses have a pretty architectural effect.

"The cloisters and cells, which were of two stories, are quite extensive with a double series of arches stretching eastwardly from the main building. The outside arches are plain, wide semicircular arches, and pointed Gothic arches inside and on the second floors. These monastic additions to the Mission had formerly fallen very much into decay, but in 1859 some Benedictine fathers arrived here from St. Vincent's Abbey in the Pittsburgh Diocese, Pennsylvania, with the intention of rebuilding these rooms and cloisters for scholastic purposes. The intention was only partially carried into effect.

"The industrious fathers rebuilt many of the upper Gothic arches, as far as can be learned, manufacturing their own red bricks for that purpose and the making of the big oven at the east end. What finally interfered with this purpose of the Benedictines it is difficult to discover, but it is more than likely that wars and rumors of wars and an unsettled epoch had much to do with the abandonment of their project, adding one more unfinished chapter to the heroic history of the Catholic Church in Texas."

Corner's reference to the sacristy window, which precedes the above account of Mission San José, together with a description of the façade, is as follows: "The south window of the Baptistery (the sacristy-chapel) is considered by good judges the finest gem of architectural ornamentation existing in America to-day. Its curves and proportions are a perpetual delight to the eye, and often as the writer has seen and examined it, it is of that kind of art which does not satiate, but ever reveals some fresh beauty in line or curve. . . . If stones ever do cry out, it is when they are alive with this touch of genius."

Of the façade, he writes: "San José Mission is the most beautiful of all, and its carving is surely 'a joy forever.' The hand that chiseled the wonderful façade at the main entrance of the Church, the doorway, window, and pillar capitals of the smaller Chapel, that now goes by the name of the Baptistery, was one of marvelous cunning.

"The façade is rich to repletion with the most exquisite carving. Figures of Virgins and Saints with drapery that looks like drapery, cherubs' heads, sacred hearts, ornate pedestals and recesses with their conch-like canopies, and cornices wonderful. The doorway pillar and arch, is daring in its unique ornamentation — showing in its combination of form the impression of Moorish outlines.

"Otherwise the whole façade is rich Rennaissance — figures and hearts alone with anything realistic about them. All other ornamentation is conventional, but with nothing stiff, every curve showing a free hand. The window above the archway is a simple wreath of such acanthus-like curves and conchoids of surpassing workmanship."

Corner deplored the ruthless defacing of the façade by desecrators who had no kinship with Art and took pieces of the stone for the sake of possessing a piece of the material. From his account we learn too that the front doors had been taken away by 1890. He also points out that, after the Holy Cross Fathers had ceased attending San José in 1888, "services were still held occasionally" in the sacristy-chapel.

The Redemptorists, 1923-1931

But it was not until April 22, 1923, that the Redemptorist Fathers of San Antonio were officially placed in charge of the old missions of San José, Concepción, Capistrano and Espada. They conducted divine services in the sacristy of San José until the return of the Franciscans in 1931, after an absence of one hundred and eight years. Also after 1931, the Redemptorists continued to visit Capistrano and Espada until 1956, when these two missions were placed in the care of diocesan priests.

Mission Concepción had become an adjunct of St. John's Diocesan Seminary at the time it was built in 1920. When the second building of the seminary was added in 1935, it was named Margil Hall in memory of the founder of Mission San José.

In 1928, while the Redemptorist Fathers had the care of San José, the tower of the church likewise collapsed. There was some suspicion of sabotage at the time, but this could not be verified. Anyhow, the tower was immediately reconstructed, stone for stone; and the work was done so well with the original materials that there is little evidence of a restoration. There was an aged resident at San José who knew the old tower so well that he was able to replace the stones in their proper place.

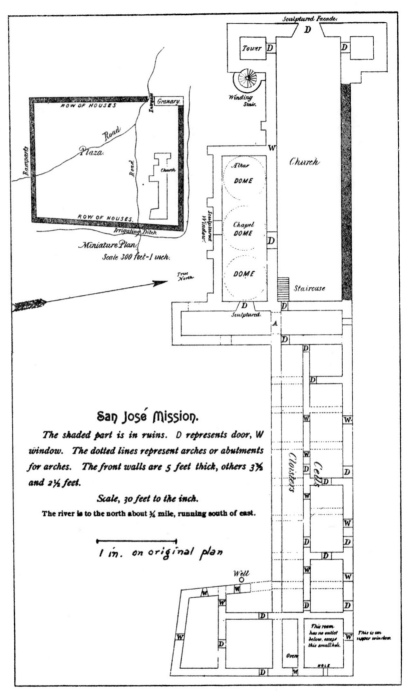

Sculptured Facade.

D

Tower   D   D

Winding
Stair.

Granary.

ROW OF HOUSES   W   Church

Road

Plaza.   Road

Church

ROW OF HOUSES.

Irrigating Ditch.

Miniature Plan.
Scale 300 feet—1 inch.

Ramparts

Altar
DOME

Chapel
DOME

DOME

True
North

D

Sculptured.

A

D

Staircase

San José Mission.

The shaded part is in ruins. D represents door, W
window. The dotted lines represent arches or abutments
for arches. The front walls are 5 feet thick, others 3½
and 2½ feet.

Scale, 30 feet to the inch.

The river is to the north about ¾ mile, running south of east.

1 in. on original plan

Cloisters   Cells

D

W

W

D

W

W

D

Well

W

W

W

W

D

W

D

W

D

D

W

This room
has no outlet
below, except
this small hole.

This is an
upper window.

Oven   W

HOLE

D   W

William Corner's plan of San José Mission, 1890.

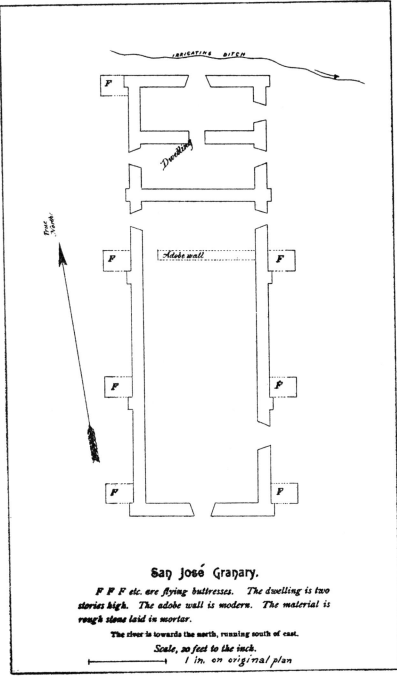

San José Granary.

*F F F etc. are flying buttresses. The dwelling is two
stories high. The adobe wall is modern. The material is
rough stone laid in mortar.*

The river is towards the north, running south of east.

Scale, 20 feet to the inch.
1 in. on original plan

William Corner's plan of the San José Granary, 1890.

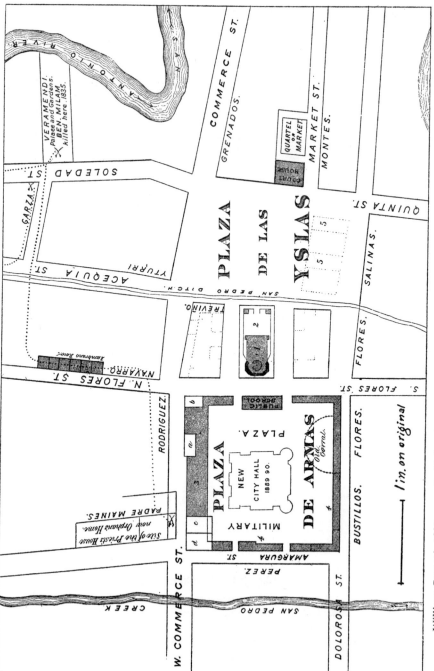

William Corner's 1890 map of old San Antonio. His references to the numbers on the map are on the next page.

References

Illustrating the Villa Capital de San Fernando, Spanish Garrison, Etc.

1. The old Church of San Fernando.

2. Churchyard Burying Ground, now covered by the Cathedral of 1868-72.

3. The Presidio Garrison Barracks, long since removed.

4. The old Plaza de Armas Dwellings and Ramparts. All 3 and 4 were claimed by the city as city property and in most cases the city substantiated its claims, and, acquiring it, cleared the old buildings away. The lot marked *b* was the last private property to disappear–1889. In the '40s and '50s a man named Goodman gave much trouble before he was finally ousted by law by the city. Plats of most of these properties, and the names of claimants, may be found in Book 1, City Engineer's Records. The City Hall of 1850-90, with City Jail, occupied N. W. corner, *c d*.

5. Properties of N. Lewis, Callaghan, Groesbeeck, et al., on Main Plaza, claimed and cleared by the city similarly to those on Military Plaza (See note 4).

6. The isolated Spanish family names on the plan are those of some of the original property holders.

7. The faintly dotted lines to and from the Veramendi and Garza Houses are the approximate routes to Zambrano Row and to the Priest House taken by the besieging companies under Milam and F. W. Johnston in 1835. The capitulation of Cos to Burleson followed in 1835.

This plan is about 75 varas to the inch, Rampart Dwellings from 6 to 12 varas wide, Garrison Barracks, 20 varas wide.

Return of the Franciscans

The broad-arched cloisters, strangely silent
    now,
Are peopled with the thoughts of long ago.
Dim figures of the past, in robe and cowl,
Move through the shadowed courts with noise-
    less tread;
And peaceful benediction hovers still
About the quiet cells where once they toiled.

— JANIE F. BASKIN

XII

THE LAST FRANCISCAN MISSIONARY OF THE Apostolic College of Zacatecas, Fr. José Antonio Díaz de León, bade a sad farewell to Mission San José when it was completely secularized in 1824 by decree of the Republic of Mexico. More than a hundred years elapsed before other Franciscans of an American Province returned to San José in 1931.

Five years before the centennial of the independence of Texas, Archbishop Arthur J. Drossaerts of San Antonio invited the Very Rev. Fr. Vincent Schrempp, minister provincial of the Franciscan Province of the Most Sacred Heart of Jesus, known also as the Chicago-St. Louis Province of Franciscans, to establish a friary at old Mission San José.

Building of a New Friary

The invitation was accepted and the same year the Franciscan architect, Brother Christopher Hugenschmidt, built a stone friary on a three-acre tract of land at the northeast corner of the mission square. In a small room on the third floor of St. Francis Home for the Aged, which served as office, living room, and bed room, Brother Christopher began his work. Daily he toiled over his plans; and after the construction of the friary got under way, he was constantly on the scene superintending the work being done by some thirty native workmen.

Being a Franciscan who had taken the vow of poverty, the Brother Architect was not inspired in his tasks by the modern percentage methods. For him it was a labor of love. It was his aim to put up a building that would blend perfectly with the ruins of San José and in some measure reflect the mission's past glory. Every stone was cut by hand and the building went up in leisurely fashion, much as the mission church itself was constructed in the 1770's, though of course modern improved methods were also used. Among the native workmen it is not unlikely that there were descendants of the Indians who once dwelt in the mission.

When the cornerstone was laid on Sunday, October 25, 1931, more than seven thousand persons attended the ceremonies. The Rev. Mariano S. Garriga, who did so much to bring about the restoration of the old mission church, gave the principal address. He welcomed back to the old mission the sons of St. Francis, the successors and brethren of the illustrious pioneers who founded San José and made it the Queen of the Missions. He asked the modern friars to shoulder the same burdens, to make the same sacrifices, and to continue the same work.

"San José," said Father Garriga, "contributed much to

the civilizing processes of the North American continent; but the prime purpose and motivating influence of the Spanish Franciscans who founded and maintained the mission was purely a religious and a missionary endeavor. Although San José, together with the other four San Antonio missions at one time were possibly worth in present-day commercial terms upwards of a hundred million dollars, yet the Franciscan Fathers never at any time owned a foot of the land they cultivated; they never owned for their own benefit a single cow of the thousands that later on became the foundation herds of the American cattle industry; they never asked or received a penny in emoluments other than their daily food."

"In these times," continued Father Garriga, "it is hard for the casual reader to understand the reason for persons making the sacrifice they made — some half hundred of them were martyred and killed by the savages they sought to civilize (in Texas alone there were nine Franciscan Martyrs, and in the territory now a part of the continental United States at least seventy-two); others of them worked their lives out that the work might go on, and never a one of them profited a penny from this. They only wanted to baptize into Christianity the pagan Indians, and in this they were successful. In this missionary work they received their recompense."

Cornerstone of the Friary

In the cornerstone of the new friary were placed a current issue of the San Antonio *Express* and of the *Southern Messenger,* mementos of the bicentennial celebration held the previous March (commemorating the dedication of San José's church at the mission's second site, which some writers claimed took place on March 5, 1731), and a parchment with the following inscription in Latin:

"In the year of our Lord 1931, the 25th day of October, on the feast of Our Lord Jesus Christ the King, at 4:00 P.M., Pope Pius XI being bishop of Rome, the Most Reverend Arthur J. Drossaerts being archbishop of the archdiocese of San Antonio, Fr. Bonaventure Marani being superior general of the Franciscans of the entire world, Fr. Vincent Schrempp being provincial of the Province of the Sacred Heart, Herbert Hoover being president of the United States, Ross S. Sterling being governor of the State of Texas, C. M. Chambers being mayor of the City of San Antonio, William A. Wurzbach being county judge of Bexar County, His Excellency the Most Reverend Arthur J. Drossaerts laid this cornerstone of the Franciscan Friary of San José (St. Joseph), Spouse of the most illustrious Virgin Mary, for the greater glory and honor of God and in memory of that great leader, the Venerable Anthony Margil and of those other illustrious Spanish Franciscan missionaries, who more than two centuries ago founded the adjoining old mission.

"It will be to the everlasting glory, both of the Most Reverend Archbishop A. J. Drossaerts, that he invited the Franciscans to return to the old field of labor of their confreres, and of the Very Reverend Provincial Vincent Schrempp that he gave heed to this invitation and sent his men back to San José Mission.

"May this house and all who dwell in it, their friends and benefactors, as also their enemies — if such there be — be richly blessed by God, the Almighty and All-good.

"(Signed) Fr. Vincent Schrempp O.F.M., Provincial; Fr. Bonaventure Alerding O.F.M., Superior; Fr. F. Emery O.F.M.; Bro. Christopher Hugenschmidt O.F.M."

The Friary and Chapel

San José Friary, with a chapel of its own and accommodations for eight friars, was completed the same year; and Fr. Bonaventure Alerding, the first superior, and his confreres moved into the new building. On one day during the following month of November there was a record number of four hundred visitors at old Mission San José. This was attributed, not only to San Antonio's growing tourist business, but also to the return of the Franciscans.

Although the church of San José was in ruins when the Franciscans came back, the archdiocese of San Antonio committed itself to its restoration at this time; but this was not achieved until six years later, at the cost of $100,000, even though the work was done with relief labor. In the meantime the sacristy of the old mission and the chapel of the new friary were used for divine services.

About a year after the new friary was completed, it was the scene of a memorable event, when the San Antonio Knights of Columbus, Fourth Degree Assembly, observed Columbus Day at Mission San José, October 12, 1932.

Six permanent flagstaffs had been erected in front of the new friary; and at the base of each had been placed a bronze tablet with the name of the donor. It will be of interest to record the inscriptions on these tablets. If one stands in front of and with back turned to the friary, the three on the right, starting in the middle, are for the flags of the United States, the Republic of Texas, and Spain.

(1) The United States:

OUR FLAG
RADIANT WITH COLOR AND
THE GATHERED GLORY
OF OUR PAST
PORTER LORING, DONOR

(2)   The Republic of Texas:

THE MAVERICK FAMILY
MAURY MAVERICK
DONOR

(3)   Spain:

S. A. PUBLIC SERVICE CO.
W. B. TITTLE, PRES.
DONOR

The three on the left, starting in the middle, are for the flags of the Confederacy, Mexico and France.

(4)   The Confederacy:

IN MEMORY OF THE
CONFEDERATE DEAD
ARCHDIOCESAN COUNCIL
OF CATHOLIC WOMEN
OF SAN ANTONIO
DONATED BY
MARY McCORMICK

(5)   Mexico:

DEDICATED TO THE MEMORY OF
JOSÉ ALEJANDRO GUERRA
ROYAL SURVEYOR TO THE KING OF SPAIN
IN THE PROVINCE OF NUEVO SANTANDER
1763
OUR FOREFATHER

(6) France:

HON. C. M. CHAMBERS, MAYOR
PAUL STEFFLER, COMM.
PHIL WRIGHT, COMM.
JACOB RUBIOLA, COMM.
FRANK H. BUSHICK, COMM.

In the chronological order the six flags of Texas are those of Spain, France, Mexico, the Republic of Texas, the Confederacy, and the United States. If there had been an Indian flag, a seventh could have been added and put in the first place.

On Columbus Day in 1932, after a solemn pontifical field Mass, celebrated by the Franciscan Archbishop Albert J. Daeger of Santa Fe, New Mexico, officers and soldiers from Fort Sam Houston carried out the impressive ceremony of the six flag raisings. During the pauses, Dr. Carlos E. Castañeda delivered an eloquent address summarizing the history of the six epochs of Texas.

Speaking of the period which followed the founding of missions San Antonio and San José, Dr. Castañeda said: "The history of the next sixty years is replete with the heroic sacrifices of the brown-robed ("grey-robed" it should be) Franciscans, who labored long and faithfully to bring the roving children of the plains to a realization of our Christian faith and to teach them the habits and customs of civilized life.

"Every mission — and there were many founded during their period — became a vocational school, where the Indians were gathered and taught, not only the fundamental truths of religion, but the rudiments of civilized life.

"The missionaries themselves set them an example. With plow or hoe in hand, they showed the Indians how to till the soil, how to plant the seed, how to raise the crop. In the long winter days, the neophytes learned manual trades, repairing the rude furniture of the mission and their own quarters. Under the direction of the kindly padres, they learned to carve stone and wood, to weave, to make sandals, to sew, to mend things, and to play various instruments. Each mission had its armory, its carpenter shop, its blacksmith shop, its loom, and its amusement room where the Indians played and danced on feast days.

"It was in this manner that the great task of civilizing the Indians was carried on. In addition to their cultivated fields, well-kept orchards where excellent fruits were raised, and their tanneries and workshops, the Indians of the missions had their cattle, their stock, and their sheep.

"But this growth was not all a garden of roses. Many were the hardships, the trials, and the tribulations which the unselfish and suffering soldiers of Christ had to endure in the daily routine of their simple lives.

"During these sixty years, they were often forced to carry on their work without the full cooperation of the officials, and frequently against their open opposition. The Indians were fickle by nature. Unaccustomed to regular work and habits of industry, they soon tired, became discouraged, and ran away. Sickness was a constant source of trouble for the missionaries. The Indian medicine men, who saw their power destroyed by the new order of things, naturally hinted that the epidemics were due to the waters of baptism.

"Against this and many other influences, that were constantly undoing their work, the missionaries labored patiently, with love in their hearts, with faith and hope in their souls for ultimate success. Be it said to the honor of the sons of Saint Francis that, through it all, they never faltered. They worked with exemplary Christian resignation to bring to the fold, through patience, kindness, and love, the thousands of Indians that roamed the vast plains. Before their task was half accomplished, some of them made the supreme sacrifice and gladly gave their lives. The Texas historian cannot pass in silence the heroic virtues of the saintly Margil, founder of San José Mission, nor the martyred Fray Alonso Giraldo Terreros and Fray Santiesteban, murdered by the infuriated Comanches at San Sabá. . . .

"The long Spanish period, during which the real work of civilization was carried on by the Church and the missionaries, lasted from the beginning of the eighteenth century to almost the end of the first quarter of the nineteenth."

Dr. Castañeda concluded his address with the following words: "It is significant that the pioneers in the real beginnings of civilization in the state (of Texas) were the humble and pious Franciscan missionaries who, almost three centuries ago, when there were no material incentives to stimulate interest in the country, braved the hardships of the wilderness, risked their lives, and gave the best they had in them to save the souls of the natives and to implant the seeds of Christian civilization in Texas, the land of God's special predilection. May the Stars and Stripes wave over the state forever, a guarantee of justice and liberty!"

Spanish-speaking Americans now constitute a large part of the population of the southern section of the city of San Antonio. It is among these people that the modern Franciscans were called to engage in apostolic and social activities, together with other religious and diocesan priests; and a much wider field was opened to them than the one in which their confreres of the eighteenth century toiled,

Christianizing and civilizing the Indians of many different tribes in the five old missions of San Antonio.

In 1932 Archbishop Drossaerts separated from St. Leo's parish a section of southeastern San Antonio and constituted it the new parish of Mission San José, entrusting it to the Franciscans. In the beginning the membership of this parish was small, and progress was slow even after 1937. But by 1968, it counted some five hundred families, of whom about one-half are Latin-Americans. A parochial school was opened in September, 1948. Although this school had to be closed in 1965, a Saturday and Sunday school of Christian Doctrine is still being conducted; and it is hoped that it will be possible to reopen the parochial school at some future date.

It would lead us too far afield to present even a short account of the work of present-day Franciscans in San Antonio. A brief summary will suffice. Another new parish, which likewise had St. Joseph as its patron and comprised the greater part of southwestern San Antonio, was established in 1935 and committed to the care of the Franciscans. For ten years it was attended from San José Friary; and then a second friary, that of St. Joseph, was erected.

Von Ormy, outside the city limits, was added to St. Joseph parish in 1949. A decade later two new parishes were carved out of St. Joseph parish, Our Lady of the Angels and St. Leonard.

At the request of Archbishop Robert E. Lucey, the Franciscans in 1967 also assumed the care of old missions San Francisco de Espada and San Juan Capistrano, together with Southton and Villa Coronado.

Today, twenty-one Franciscan friars, residing in five friaries, all of them in southern San Antonio, have the care of five parish churches and six chapels. Two of the parish churches are old missions, San José and San Francisco de la Espada. One of the chapels is likewise an old mission, San Juan Capistrano.

To a great extent, they are engaged in the same work that was done by the eighteenth-century missionaries of the Apostolic Colleges of Querétaro and Zacatecas in their five missions of San Antonio. For, they are devoting themselves to the spiritual, and in as far as they can, also the temporal welfare of predominantly poor people, most of whom are descendants of the Spaniards and the Indians of a bygone day.

NOTE

A fuller account of the work of the Franciscans of the Chicago-St. Louis Province in southern San Antonio is presented in the writer's "Modern Missions in Old San Antonio," *Lesser Brothers,* (Chicago) , I, pp. 4-16, 24-30, 37.

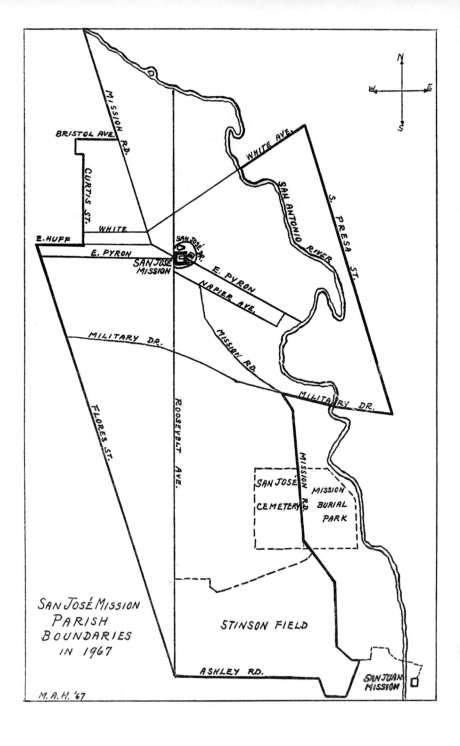

N
W   E
S

MISSION RD.

BRISTOL AVE.

CURTIS ST.

WHITE AVE.

SAN ANTONIO RIVER

S. PRESA ST.

E. HUFF

WHITE

E. PYRON

SAN JOSE MISSION

SAN JOSE RD.

E. PYRON

NAPIER AVE.

MILITARY DR.

MISSION RD.

MILITARY DR.

FLORES ST.

ROOSEVELT AVE.

MISSION RD.

SAN JOSE CEMETERY

MISSION BURIAL PARK

SAN JOSÉ MISSION
PARISH
BOUNDARIES
IN 1967

STINSON FIELD

ASHLEY RD.

SAN JUAN MISSION

M. A. H. '67

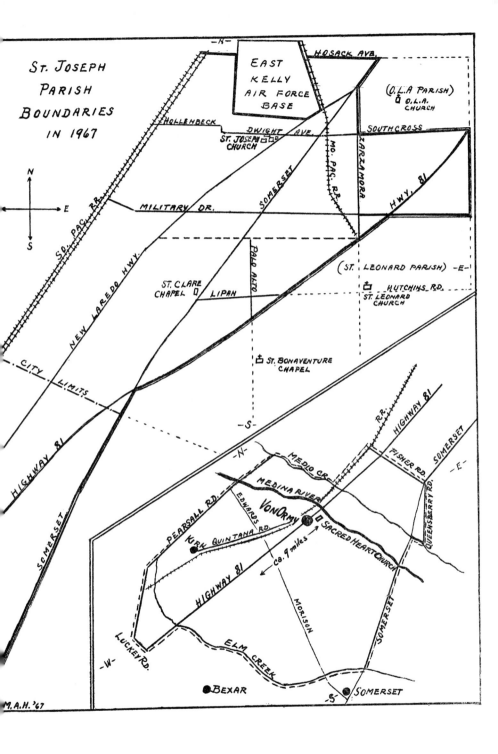

ST. JOSEPH PARISH BOUNDARIES IN 1967

Restoration of San José

The belfry rears aloft its towered height
To shield from harm the deep-toned messenger
That once rang out across the vibrant air
And startled sleeping echoes on the plain,
While in the chapel with its lowly shrine
Abides the mystic hush of other days.

— JANIE F. BASKIN

XIII

F OR MORE THAN A HALF CENTURY MISSION
San José lay in ruins. The Indian houses, the workshops, and the walls of the square disappeared completely except for some foundations. The dome and greater part of the roof and north wall of the church crashed to the ground in 1868 and 1874; and some time later the roof of the granary caved in. The *convento* too became roofless. The only structure that remained intact was the sacristy of the church, which continued to be used as a chapel.

To many it seemed that San José was an irreparable ruin and that nothing could be done to prevent it from eventually disappearing completely and becoming a mere memory.

A postcard picture sold to visitors about 1890 showed the roofless shell of the church minus the north wall, the interior filled with rubble from the stately dome, brush growing among the fallen rocks and cactus thriving on top of the tower. On the back of the picture was printed the sad comment: "The Mission, between the elements and the festive vandal, will soon be no more." To tourists small pieces of the wall and roof were sold for a few cents as souvenirs.

But in that same year William Corner published his book, *San Antonio de Bexar,* and awakened some interest in the city's old missions. There were not lacking those who were hopeful that San José should not fall into oblivion; and eventually they took steps, not only to save what was left of the mission, but to restore it in some measure to its pristine glory.

"The saving of San José," writes Charles Ramsdell, "the slow painstaking task of bringing it back to life, has been achieved through the tireless efforts of a good many people, working together and separately, but all devoted to the same ideal" *(San Antonio,* p. 136).

Among these interested persons were ecclesiastical and government leaders and organizations as well as private individuals and societies, all of whom contributed to the marvel of causing San José to rise phoenix-like from its ruins.

First Steps toward Restoration

The first who took definite steps toward the restoration of Mission San José, as far as the writer could ascertain, were the Texas Historic Landmarks Association and the De Zavala Chapter of the Daughters of the Republic of Texas. A donation for the purpose of saving what was left of the mission was given to the Archdiocese of San Antonio, and this was used to defray the expenses of some rebuilding. The De Zavala Chapter "propped up the beautiful front doorway to keep the arch from falling, repaired the roof of the sacristy, and tried to retain all stones and woodwork in place" (James M. Day in *Six Missions of Texas*, p. 160).

William Wheeler Hume

One of those who played a leading role in making the people of San Antonio conscious of the treasures they possessed in their long neglected old missions was Msgr. William Wheeler Hume. He was born on the Isle of Wight in 1873, one year before the diocese of San Antonio was erected — with the Most Rev. Anthony Pellicer as its first bishop, the Most Rev. John Claude Neraz as the second bishop in 1881, and the Most Rev. John Anthony Forest as the third bishop in 1894.

It was at the invitation of the Most Rev. John William Shaw, who was made coadjutor to Bishop Forest in 1910 and his successor from 1911 to 1918, that Father Hume came to San Antonio. He was later honored with the title of monsignor, and died in New Orleans in 1924.

The many tasks that Father Hume performed in the diocese of San Antonio did not prevent him from taking a lively interest in the old missions and their restoration. His first step was to reopen them as houses of worship; and he personally assumed the pastorate of the Espada Mission.

About 1918 he undertook the work of rehabilitating San José Mission, with the generous assistance of Mrs. H. P. Drought. At that time the ruins completely hid from view the carved doorway leading to the sacristy. He had the debris removed from the interior of the church, and the north wall partly rebuilt. The sacristy was repaired and furnished; and from that time it continued to serve as a chapel until the church itself was restored.

On the right side of the doorway leading from the

sacristy into the church, a tablet has been affixed to the wall. It has the following Latin inscription: "Pro Henrico Patritio Drought, in cujus memoriam hoc sacellum vetus An. Ch. MCMXVIII instauratum ac cultui Divino denuo dicatum, ora." Translated, it reads: "Pray for Henry Patrick Drought, in whose memory this old chapel was renovated and once more dedicated to divine worship in the year of Christ 1918."

Msgr. Hume also had the cracks of the façade of the church mended, and thus perhaps saved it from collapsing. The structure of the spiral staircase beside the tower had fallen in 1903, but the steps still lay scattered about; and he had these replaced. He also had the lower arches of the *convento* filled in.

Drossaerts, Garriga, Morkovsky

The successor of Bishop Shaw, the Most Rev. Arthur Jerome Drossaerts, who became San Antonio's first archbishop in 1926, brought back the Franciscans in 1931 and at this time decided upon the complete restoration of the church of Mission San José. As supervisor of the project he chose the Rev. Mariano S. Garriga.

A native of Port Isabel, Texas, and a former missionary in the Big Bend country, Father Garriga was likewise an ardent admirer of San José and what it represented. He planned to have the restoration of the church completed for the Texas Centennial year of 1936. Only the materials had to be purchased, since the government supplied the labor of the unemployed during the Great Depression. But by May of 1935 the San José Mission Fund reached rock bottom, and the workers had to be dismissed.

Seventeen months of idleness slipped by. Father Garriga was made a domestic prelate in 1935; and the following year he was called to Corpus Christi as coadjutor bishop. He succeeded to that see in 1949, and died in 1965.

Not until October 26, 1936, could the restoration of San José's church be resumed under the direction of the Rev. Alois J. Morkovsky. To raise funds for the project and to promote the cause of the beatification of Fr. Antonio Margil, the founder of San José, the Margil Society had been organized in 1933. Each member contributed a minimum of one dollar annually. Archbishop Drossaerts headed the membership list with a donation of twenty dollars. People were not able to contribute much in those years; but the little offerings of many were a big help.

In the spring of 1937 the restoration of the church had advanced far enough to make it available for divine worship; and it was rededicated on Sunday, April 18. At ten in the morning, Archbishop Drossaerts celebrated a pontifical Mass; and Bishop Garriga, Coadjutor of Corpus Christi, preached the festive sermon. All the bishops of the ecclesiastical province of San Antonio as well as other bishops attended the Mass and dedication ceremonies.

The Restored Church of San José

The mutilated statues on the façade had not as yet been repaired; nor had the large, richly carved wooden doors, which had been taken away between 1880 and 1890, been replaced. And the altar in the sanctuary was only a temporary one. But otherwise the church of San José now looked very much as it did when the mission came to an end.

At the time of its rededication the church was described as follows. The dome conforms as faithfully as possible to old photographs dating from the 1860's. A massive chandelier of wrought iron, having a simple Spanish design and decorated with scroll-work not unlike that of the old cross on top of the tower, is suspended by a stout chain from the lofty dome more than sixty feet above the floor. Its giant proportions are hardly noticed because they harmonize so well with those of the dome.

On the six pilasters of the wall are mounted six wrought-iron brackets with five candles each. They fittingly recall the candlesticks of the same material in the crypt of the Archbasilica of San Francesco in Assisi, containing the tomb of St. Francis, the founder of the religious order to which the missionaries of San José belonged.

Under the arch of the choir loft, the meager but precious traces of the original stencil design of fresco has been reproduced in delicate colors of ocher, red, and blue.

Throughout the nave of the church, there is a new flagstone floor, which had to be placed about four inches above the old level.

The pews of oak are a necessary compromise with our modern times, but their simple details of ornament make them harmonize with the age and architecture of San José.

The two steps to the higher level of the sanctuary are duplicates of the old ones which had almost disappeared.

The turned balusters of the Communion railing follow the outlines of those which remained of the choir loft balustrade.

The door in the wall to the right of the altar opened from the missionary's quarters in the *convento* at the rear of the church on a pulpit which has not been replaced.

The lamp, which is now in the sanctuary, at one time hung in the old cathedral of Galveston. It is not too rich an ornament for San José.

The Façade and Portal

The two steps of flagstone at the main entrance and a quadrangular area on the outside have been sunk to the original ground level and thus was uncovered the graceful molding at the base of the façade, which had been hidden for at least fifty years.

Above the main entrance a wrought iron railing now replaces the original balcony which once completed the beauty of the façade. For want of more exact information, the ornamental details of this railing were made to follow the designs of the grating of the so-called "Rose Window" outside the sacristy, since the stone sculpture of this window displays the same art as that of the façade.

Not long after the rededication of San José, during the first week of July, 1937, the two main doors, another door leading into the baptistry inside the church near the entrance, and the gates of the Communion railing, all of them carved from black walnut by Peter Mansbendel of Austin, a noted sculptor, were put in place.

Though the original doors disappeared, the artist was able to make faithful copies of them from old photographs which were in the possession of Father Morkovsky. Each of the main doors, which are made of Kentucky black walnut, measures nine by fifteen feet, is two and a half inches thick, and weighs several hundred pounds. They are too heavy for hinges, and hence they are mounted on pivots. The designs on the doors are old Spanish baroque scrolls, with leaves of traditional Moorish origin. The Moslem Moors refrained from copying any living thing in their sculpture.

For Peter Mansbendel the carving of these huge doors was a work of love. He said of it: "Ever since I saw the most beautiful of all the missions, San José, for the first time I had hopes that some day I might be identified with the project of its restoration. Carving the doors of the Spanish Governor's Palace and my pleasant connections with Harvey P. Smith, architect, seemed a sort of introduction to the portals of San José.

"Though bent over my work-table, I spent part of my time in thoughts in front of San José, keeping well in mind the scale and beautiful character of the building, trying not only to reproduce as faithfully as possible the Spanish baroque style, but also to give it the power and beauty, not only of the building, but also of the faith which it stands for. This was not just another commission, but a rare privilege to be able to express my gratitude and esteem to those who made it possible, and to my beloved Texas."

The project of restoring the church of San José was completed by Archbishop Robert E. Lucey in 1947-1952, when the mutilated statues on the façade were repaired and replaced by E. Lenarduzzi, artist and sculptor of Houston (in 1948), and two arches of the *convento* were reconstructed. A suitable altar of hand-carved stone, as well as a hand-carved walnut tabernacle, a crucifix, and candlesticks were placed in the sanctuary. At this time too it was found that the entire structure needed reinforcing, and every part of it was strengthened. The famous "Rose Window" was also rejointed and made waterproof.

The San Antonio Conservation Society

For the restoration of the granary and the adjoining area of San José Mission a great debt of gratitude will always be due to the San Antonio Conservation Society, which was founded in 1924. A group of public-spirited women organized this society, making "one of its chief objectives the preservation of the Spanish missions and mission lands around San Antonio, with special concentration and interest in San José and its deteriorated granary."

The granary's walls were crumbling; the vaulted roof had caved in; only three flying buttresses remained; and all the doors but one had long since been split up into kindling wood. What remained of the granary belonged at this time to Señor Ignacio Salcedo. A member of the new society, Mrs. Essie Castanola, had taught most of the children living in the neighborhood of San José. She was acquainted with Mr. Salcedo, and she purchased the remaining door from him for the sum of $50.00.

The Society then collected funds in various ways and bought parcels of land, a few feet at a time, around the granary. Mrs. Perry J. Lewis, president, persuaded her husband to serve as the Society's lawyer without fee and to purchase the first piece of ground as a birthday present for her at the cost of $500.00. Mrs. Elizabeth Graham procured the ownership of another strip of fifty feet. Several other pieces were picked up from their Mexican owners; and what nobody seemed to own was fenced in.

For the granary itself and the ground on which it stood Mr. Salcedo at first wanted $10,000; but when he got himself into trouble, he was ready to accept half that amount, provided that he would receive $2,500 immediately. With the assistance of their husbands' signatures, the ladies of the Society borrowed the necessary sum from a local bank and bought the granary ruin in 1930. Eventually they repaid the bank with donations they received and with the proceeds of various fund-raising projects. In 1932 they paid the last amount of their debt on the granary.

Now that they had the ruins of the granary, the task of restoring the structure remained. With the aid of professional advice, they gathered materials and tools; and in 1933 unemployed workmen, furnished by the government, reconstructed the granary. A substantial donation from the 1936 Texas Centennial Committee helped pay for the materials. Inside the restored building is a plaque with the following inscription:

"The Granary of the Mission San José de Aguayo. Reconstruction completed 1933 by the San Antonio Conservation Society. Mrs. Lane Taylor, Pres. Mrs. Rena M. Green, Chairman of Missions. Miss Anna Ellis, Historian. Harvey P. Smith, A.I.A., Architect. J. W. Beretta, Engineer. A. J. Modlem, Sup't of Cons't. Labor furnished by Central Relief Committee."

The stone below the only window in the building, on the west side, "honors the memory of Mrs. Perry J. Lewis, President of the San Antonio Conservation Society." The entrance doors "honor the memory of Mrs. Essie Crawford Castanola, Secretary and Treasurer of the San Antonio Conservation Society, 1926-1932."

The Society also restored the north wall of the mission compound and some of the rooms forming a part of it; and with the thought of creating a park-like setting for the mission, it purchased the land on the other side of the wall. When workmen cleaned out the old irrigation ditch in 1933, they discovered the lower part of the old mill. It was reconstructed in 1936 with the help of gifts of money from the National Society of the Colonial Dames of America in the State of Texas, and the gift of the machinery from the Pioneer Flour Mills of San Antonio, the engineer being Ernst Schuchard. The gates in the north wall were likewise presented by the Colonial Dames of Texas.

The land acquired by the San Antonio Conservation Society included an abandoned gravel pit beyond the irrigation ditch and old mill. This was converted into a small outdoor theater already in the early 1930's. After more land had been donated to make it possible for the stage to be enlarged, the theater was entirely rebuilt in 1958 through the cooperation of various organizations and many individuals. The pit was filled in and terraced, and a new stage was built.

After the Society had made a gift of the theater to the State of Texas, the governor proclaimed it the Official Texas State Historical Theater in the same year (1958). It had its opening season during the summer of that year, when *A Cloud of Witnesses: The Drama of the Alamo*, written by the Texas playwright Ramsey Yelvington, was produced by the Baylor Theater under the direction of Paul Baker. During subsequent seasons other historical pageants have been presented in San José's open-air theater. In 1962 it was the *San José Story*. In 1965, both *Lightning from the East* and *Los Indios de San José* were staged.

The San Antonio Conservation Society has continued to give financial aid for the upkeep of the mission through the years. In a letter, dated October 13, 1965, Mrs. Don F. Tobin, President, states that the Society includes in its budget for this year "the same contribution we have been making to the Granary Fund of San José Mission." The Archdiocese likewise makes an annual contribution for the maintenance of the mission square.

The County of Bexar

The county in which Mission San José is situated has likewise had a large share in the restoration of the mission square, inasmuch as it rebuilt the mission walls and Indian quarters on the west, south, and east sides of the square with relief labor. Several hundred men, engaged in excavating at San José and the other missions, uncovered the foundations of the walls and Indian houses at San José, discovered the location of its wells, and traced its entire irrigation system. They found "hundreds of bones of all kinds, utensils of that early day and later periods, such as copper, shovels, knives, spoons, gems, old Spanish spurs, locks, bronze candlesticks, candle snuffers and wick trimmers, brass uniform buttons of the Texas Republic period 1836-1845, fragments of pottery, wrought iron, etc." (C. M. Brooks, *Texas Missions,* pp. 94-115).

On the wall at the western gate of San José, there is a plaque with the following inscription: "Founded 1720 — Restored 1932. Restoration of Mission Plaza Walls, San José y San Miguel de Aguayo, by County of Bexar. Frost Woodhull, County Judge. Albert G. Trawalter, Com'r Pct. 1, part term. James W. Donnell, Com'r Pct. 2. Robert F. Uhr, Commissioner Pct. 3. Thomas H. Abbott Jr., Com'r Pct. 4. Edgar G. Garvey, County Auditor. Harvey P. Smith, A.I.A., Architect."

The Friendly Suit of 1936-1937

To determine exactly which parts of the mission grounds were owned by the three interested parties, namely the Catholic Archdiocese of San Antonio, the Conservation Society of San Antonio, and the County of Bexar, Archbishop Drossaerts filed a "friendly suit" in December, 1936, at which time the restoration work on the mission church was nearing completion. A settlement was reached on November 8 of the following year, when Judge S. G. Tayloe, in the 45th District Court, decided the extent of the several titles of ownership.

A Texas State Historic Site

In 1941, the San Antonio Conservation Society deeded the restored granary and other property it had acquired at the mission to the County of Bexar. The County, in turn, surrendered the title to this and the other parts of the mission square of which it was the owner to the State of Texas.

At this time, too, the Catholic Archdiocese of San Antonio, while retaining the ownership of the church and *convento* and an undivided half interest in the main plaza, entered a cooperative agreement with the State of Texas, thus making it possible for the entire mission compound to become a State Historic Site. In the same year, the old mission was also declared to be a National Historic Site.

San José is the only such Historic Site in our country, at which an active parish church is in operation. It was agreed that the church and *convento* be maintained by the Archdiocese, and that the mission square be administered by the Texas State Parks Board, which has been a part of the Texas Parks and Wildlife Department since 1963.

The map of the Texas Highway Department still designates San José as a State Park, but the Park Services of Texas have classified the old mission as an Historic Site; and hence it is now properly called a State Historic Site.

Because of the unique manner in which the restoring agencies had given the land and buildings of Mission San José to the State of Texas and placed them in the care of its Park Services, an Advisory Board was created to give them a voice in matters pertaining to the old mission and its conservation. Thus the Texas Parks and Wildlife Department now administers the Historic Site in cooperation with the Archdiocese of San Antonio, the National Park Service, the San Antonio Conservation Society, and the County of Bexar.

A National Historic Site

Besides the twenty-five National Historic Sites in the United States which are the property of the Federal Government, there are ten others which are not federally owned; and Mission San José is one of these. Of all the old missions in our Spanish Borderlands, San José is the only one which has been included among our National Historic Sites.

It will be of interest to list the other nine National Historic Sites, not federally owned. They are:

Chicago Portage, Ill.   Jamestown, Va.
Chimney Rock, Neb.   McLoughlin House, Oregon
Dorchester Heights, Mass.   St. Paul's Church, Bill of
Gloria Dei, Pa.   Rights Shrine,
Golden Spike, Utah   Mt. Vernon, N. Y.
                                 Touro Synagogue, R. I.

We should add, however, that there is in San Antonio also a Registered National Historic Landmark, namely the Espada Aqueduct, a part of that mission's irrigation canal, built in 1740-1745. The certificate and plaque designating it as such was presented on April 25, 1965. The restored Presidio of La Bahía and its chapel of Nuestra Señora de Loreto were likewise declared to be a National Historic Landmark in 1967.

The formal dedication and designation of Mission San José as a National Historic Site took place on May 8, 1941. At the dedication ceremonies, the Honorable Alvin J. Wirtz, Under-Secretary of State, gave an address in which he said among other things: "The importance of San José is shown by its date. It was begun in the wilderness fourteen years before the birth of George Washington, and twenty-five years before that of Thomas Jefferson. . . . It was a center of culture and religion, decades before our country became a Federal Union under the Constitution."

Address of Archbishop Lucey

Archbishop Robert E. Lucey of San Antonio, on this memorable occasion, gave the following address:

"When a Spanish king sought to colonize Mexico early in the sixteenth century, he sent his soldiers with the flag of Spain and Franciscan Padres with the Cross of Christ. These courageous individuals, armed only with the shield of faith and the sword of God's grace, gave battle to the powers of darkness until at last the ferocious tribes of Mexico knelt in humble submission beneath the banner of the Cross. . . .

"They (the Franciscan missionaries) walked bravely into the wilderness to lead the savages to the Church of Christ. They left Mexico City far behind them; and at last they planted the Cross of Christ here, in this dear and sunny land. At the risk of their lives they brought Christian faith and virtue to the Indians.

"The ignorant natives had to be instructed in handicraft, cattle-raising, and agriculture. Water had to be brought from the distant streams for crops and animals. Houses had to be provided, and first of all the House of God. And so Mission San Fernando, San Antonio de Padua, Concepción, San Francisco de Espada, and San Juan de Capistrano were built under the sky of Texas.

"But the most magnificent, the most artistic, the most beautiful of all was San José, the 'Queen of the Missions'. . . .

"Here the rugged children of the forest came to kneel

in silent prayer. The gentle sons of St. Francis had taken the primitive Indian and had formed and fashioned him into a devout follower of the Crucified Christ. . . .

"And so under the watchful eyes of the Saints in silent stone, this temple of worship was a center of spiritual life from birth to death — one hundred and sixty-four years ago.

"In that far-distant day we see the missions in their glory. But all too soon we find them deserted and abandoned. The Spanish Crown withdrew its support from these far-flung outposts in the New World. Gradually the Padres themselves were forced to retire from this field. The Franciscan Fathers held on in this center as they could. Early in the nineteenth century they were compelled to go. Gray days came to this gem of architecture, this House of God, lovely San José. For years it stood lonely, weatherbeaten, and forgotten.

"But it was not the will of God that Mission San José with all its beauty and charm should be forever forgotten or allowed to sink into the silent dust of oblivion. Too much had been invested in San José that it should continue to crumble and decay — too much of human labor and sweat, too much of faith and courage, too much of genius and grandeur, that it should remain a broken and tragic ruin. . . .

"You all know how this treasure of religion, history, and art was brought back to life. . . . But much remains to be done. Those jewels of architecture, the lovely arches of the cloister, still stand in all their silent beauty and charm. But their hold on life is precarious. We shall see to it that they are protected from the ravages of time and the elements, that they may stand strong and beautiful through the years, eloquent of the faith that builded them and the artistry that made them immortal.

"This evening, as the sun is sinking in the west, 'Il

Poverello, the Poor Man of Assisi,' no longer dressed in rags and tatters, but a glorious Saint of Heaven, stands beside the Great White Throne beyond the stars. He looks with joy upon this scene, because in this solemn hour a temple built by his sons is now bequested to the centuries.

"The United States of America, the incomparable State of Texas, and the ancient Church join hands today in a spirit of friendship and cooperation, to the end that lovely, historic San José may be fully restored and preserved for all time.

"Seven hundred and fifty years have passed since St. Francis walked through the plains and valleys of his native land; one hundred and sixty-four years have gone since his sons reared near the City of St. Anthony this temple of worship to the glory of God and the honor of San José! I am sure that good St. Francis gives us his blessing today as this hallowed ground, sacred in Texas history, holy in religious associations, is dedicated to the ages."

A Day at San José in 1778

Now silent, gray, it towers above the plain
And mutely tells its story of a past
Filled with brave deeds and loyal sacrifice,
With daily toil and patience infinite.
Around it stretch the glowing harvest fields,
Where, mid the glory of their ripened sheaves,
It rises up in stately majesty.

— Janie F. Baskin

XIV

As THE FIRST RAYS OF THE RISING SUN LIGHT
up the eastern horizon on Saturday, May 9, 1778, Miguel,
the Indian sacristan of Mission San José, climbs the narrow
winding stairway beside the tower of the church. Reaching
the level of the choir loft, he seizes the two ropes hanging
down from the belfry and rings both bells for several minutes merrily and harmoniously.

Some 275 Indians who have their homes in the stone
apartments along the walls of the mission square, both old
and young, except the little ones under nine years of age,
get up from their comfortable beds and begin a new day.
The raised wooden beds have buffalo hides for mattresses
and sheets of gunnysack or cotton.

Morning Mass, Angelus, and Instruction

Fifteen minutes later, the Indians have gathered at the chapel on the south side of the church, some inside and others in the arcade beside the *convento*. Although the new church is nearing completion, it is not yet ready; and the large sacristy serves in the meantime as a temporary church. Two Indian *fiscales* make a careful check of those who are present. If anyone has absented himself without a reasonable excuse, he will receive a mild form of punishment in the evening from one of the Indian officials. In many respects these neophytes, who but lately roamed about as uncivilized nomads, are like little children who are still growing up; and they must needs be treated sometimes like youngsters who do not behave themselves.

After all the Indians have assembled, Miguel, the sacristan, rings the morning Angelus Bell: three short rings of one of the bells, each followed by a pause, then the ringing of both bells for a minute or two. The Angelus recited by the Indians is still said in many places at the present day:

> The Angel of the Lord declared unto Mary;
> And she conceived of the Holy Spirit.
> > Hail Mary. . . .

> Behold the handmaid of the Lord;
> Be it done to me according to your word.
> > Hail Mary. . . .

> And the Word was made flesh;
> And dwelt among us.
> > Hail Mary. . . .

Pray for us, O holy Mother of God;
That we may be made worthy of the
    promises of Christ.

Let us pray: Pour forth, we beseech you,
O Lord, your grace into our hearts, that
we, to whom the Incarnation of Christ, your
Son, was made known by the message of an
angel, may, by his Passion and Cross, be
brought to the glory of his Resurrection.
Through the same Christ our Lord. Amen.

The grey-robed missionary has been up for a half hour or more before the Indians were roused from their slumber. He has been preparing for the celebration of holy Mass by private prayer and the recitation of the divine office or breviary. He is Padre Fray Pedro Ramírez de Arellano, who has served San José with fatherly kindness during the greater part of the past decade.

Since today is a Saturday, he puts on, over his grey habit, a white alb and a white chasuble; for, he will offer up the votive Mass in honor of the Immaculate Conception of the Virgin Mary. Under this title, Nuestra Señora de la Purísima Concepción, our Lady is honored as the principal and universal Patroness throughout the Spanish empire. The supreme pontiff formally gave his approval to this choice in 1760.

The Doctrina Cristiana

During the Mass, the Indian men, women, and children, led by the pueblo's *gobernador,* recite from memory the

Spanish *Doctrina Cristiana,* the principal doctrines and prayers which the missionary has taught them:

Por la señal de la Santa Cruz, de nuestros enemigos libranos, Señor Dios nuestro: En el nombre del Padre, y del Hijo, y del Espiritu Santo. Amen. (Through the sign of the holy Cross, from our enemies deliver us, O Lord, our God: In the name of the Father, and of the Son, and of the Holy Spirit. Amen.)

Gloria al Padre, y al Hijo, y al Espiritu Santo. Como era en el principio, ahora y siempre y por los siglos de los siglos. Amen. (Glory be to the Father, and to the Son, and to the Holy Spirit. As it was in the beginning, is now, and ever shall be world without end. Amen.)

Padre nuestro que estas en los cielos, sanctificado sea el tu nombre. . . . (Our Father, who art in heaven, hallowed be thy name. . . .)

Dios te salve María, llena eres de gracia. . . . (Hail Mary, full of grace. . . .)

Creo en Dios Padre, Todopoderoso, Criador del cielo y de la tierra. . . . (I believe in God the Father Almighty, Creator of heaven and earth. . . .)

Yo pecador, me confiese a Dios Todopoderoso, y a la bienaventurada siempre Virgen María. . . . (I, a sinner, confess to Almighty God, to the Blessed, ever-Virgin Mary. . . .)

Los mandamientos de la ley de Dios son diez: los tres primeros pertenecen al honor de Dios, y los otros siete al provecho del prójimo. El primero: amarás a Dios sobre todas las cosas. . . . (The commandments of the law of God are ten in number: the first three pertain to the honor of God, and the others to the good of one's neighbor. The first: Thou shalt love God above all things. . . .)

Los mandamientos de la Santa Madre Iglesia son cinco. El primero: oir misa entera los domingos y fiestas de guar-

dar. . . . (The commandments of Holy Mother Church are five in number. The first is: to hear the entire Mass on Sundays and Holy Days of obligation. . . .)

Los sacramentos de la Santa Madre Iglesia son siete. El primero: Bautismo. . . . (The sacraments of Holy Mother Church are seven in number. The first is: Baptism. . . .)

The Alabado

After the Mass, during which some of the Indians have received Holy Communion, all join in singing the seven stanzas of the *Alabado,* as it was introduced by Fr. Margil in all the missions which he founded:

Alabado y ensalzado
Sea el divino Sacramento
En quien Dios oculto asiste
De las almas el sustento

Lift your heart in joy and exalt Him
In the Blessed Sacrament all Holy,
Where the Lord, His glory veiling,
Comforts souls true and lowly.

Y la limpia Concepción
De la Reina de los cielos
Que, quedando virgen pura,
Es Madre del verbo eterno.

Laud the glorious Conception
Of the Queen in God's Kingdom supernal,
Who remaining Virgin stainless,
Bore for men the Word eternal.

Y el glorioso San José
Electo por Dios inmenso
Para padre estimativo
De su Hijo, el divino Verbo

Honor Joseph, spouse of Mary,
The chosen of God in heaven,
To his paternal arms so tender
The Incarnate Son was given.

Y esto por todos los siglos
Y de los siglos. Amen.
Amen. Jesús y María;
Jesús, María, y José.

And so for endless ages
Shall it be for evermore.
Amen. Jesus and Mary.
Jesus, Mary, and Joseph.

Oh! Dulcísimo Jesús!
Yo te doy mi corazon,
Para que estampes en el
Tu santísima pasión.

O dearest Jesus,
To you I give my heart.
Imprint on it, dear Lord,
Your most holy Passion.

Madre, llena de dolor,
Haced que cuando expiremos
Nuestras almas entreguemos
Por tus manos al Señor.

Mother, full of sorrow,
Grant that when we come to die
Our souls we shall surrender
To God through your most holy hands.

Quién a Dios quiera seguir	Whoever seeks to follow God
Y a su gloria quiera entrar	And strives to enter in His glory
Una cosa ha de asentar	One thing he has to do
Y de corazón decir:	And from his heart to say:
"Morir, antes que pecar;	"Die, rather than sin!
Antes que pecar, morir!"	Rather than sin, die!"

Meanwhile Father Pedro has taken off his vestments, and he now gives an instruction in Spanish to the assembled Indians outside the chapel. All of them understand and speak the Spanish language, except a few pagans from the coast who have recently come to San José. The latter receive special instructions from the missionary in the Coahuiltecan language. Father Pedro is a veteran missionary and knows this common Indian language well; and he has the help of the *Manual* written by Fr. Bartolomé García.

Today the subject of his instruction is the sacrament of confirmation, the sacrament by which the Holy Spirit will come in a special manner to the neophytes and confirm them in the Faith. Father Pedro, who is also the *presidente* of all the missions in Texas, was notified a short time before that the Holy Father in Rome had conferred on him the power to administer this sacrament; and on the morrow, Sunday, May 10, he will exercise his new faculty for the first time.

Many years ago, in 1759, Bishop Martínez y Tejada of Guadalajara had visited Mission San José and confirmed the Christian Indians; but most of the Indians now at the mission have not received the sacrament as yet. Tomorrow Father Pedro will anoint the forehead of those who are ready, with holy chrism, the blessed oil made of olives and balsam, and say to them: "I sign you with the sign of the cross and confirm you with the chrism of salvation, in the name of the Father, and of the Son, and of the Holy Spirit."

Breakfast and Work

The Indians listen attentively and then go back to their apartments for their breakfast of *atole,* a kind of gruel, made of corn or other grain which was roasted before it was ground. It is cooked in iron kettles, and served in earthen or bark bowls. The natives have no desire at all for wheat, but they love Indian corn or maize, especially when served as *atole.* There is a plentiful supply of corn in the granary, more than will be needed until the next harvest.

Three quarters of an hour are set aside for breakfast; and then the Indians take up the work assigned to them by the *gobernador* and his assistants, the *alcalde* and *regidores.* A few of the men and older boys go to the smithy and the carpenter shop inside the walls. A large number go out through the fifth gate, the one on the west side of the square, to work in the cultivated fields which extend for several miles along San José's *acequia.* They are accompanied by armed and mounted sentinels who will remain on the lookout in the surrounding area for any marauding bands of Apaches or Comanches.

Another group, also armed and mounted, sets out for the mission's Rancho El Atascoso, situated between the Medina and the Atascosa rivers, some twenty-five miles distant from the mission, where there are about five thousand sheep and fifteen hundred head of cattle. They will relieve some of the shepherds and cowboys at the ranch, and send them back to the mission with a supply of beef and mutton. Formerly there were four thousand head of cattle on the ranch, but the raids of the Apaches have reduced the herd to less than half that number.

All the men who can be spared in the shops and on the farm and ranch, continue the work on the new church.

Though the greater part of the imposing edifice has been constructed, it will take at least four more years to complete it. Among the workers is Pedro Huizar, who has come up from Mexico to contribute his skill as a builder and sculptor.

The grown-up girls go to the textile and tailor shops to card wool, to weave cotton and woolen cloth, and to cut and sew the cloth into garments for men, women, and children. The housewives take care of the children, prepare meals, make pottery, and weave baskets. The old men make arrows for the hunters and warriors. The old women go down to the river bank to catch fish. And the little boys and girls, five years and older, come running to the arcade at the *convento* and greet Padrecito Pedro with shouts of joy and beaming faces.

Teacher, Doctor, Superintendent

The little ones closest to the padre take hold of the white cord with three knots hanging from his right side, and others finger the seven-decade rosary attached to his cord on the left side. Father Pedro then tells them to be quiet, spends some time teaching the children how to read and write the Spanish language, and explaining to them in simple words the catechism and prayers. Some Indian women, who themselves received their education at the mission, continue the school work; for, the missionary has many other matters that claim his attention.

First, he takes his little medicine chest and visits several sick Indians in their apartments. The home remedies which he administers to them have surprising effect; but more than the medicines, it is the Padre's blessing and consoling words that cheer up the patients and make them feel better.

Then Padre Pedro goes to the textile shop with its several looms, where Indian women are weaving cloth of various kinds, woolen, cotton, and gunnysack. Also the tailor shop, where the cloth is made into clothing for young and old. After that, the carpenter shop and the smithy. The Indian supervisors in each of these shops are well able to direct the work, but the interest and encouragement of the padre is an incentive for all to do their job better.

Padre Pedro also takes a brief look at the irrigated fields outside the walls, where some of the corn will be ripe in another month. During the earlier years of the mission, the missionary in charge, or his companion, taught the Indians how to till the soil not only by word but also by example. That is no longer necessary now. Indian overseers take care of everything.

Work on the Church

On the way back to the *convento,* Padre Pedro pauses in the church to inspect the work being done by a crew of Indians in the sanctuary. In a few years the new church will be completed. Here too he speaks a word of approval. He has hardly done so, when two Indians, who apparently were merely looking on, yoke a pair of oxen and hitch the team to a two-wheeled cart; and walking beside the cart, they set out for the quarry at Mission Concepción. The light and soft tufa stone is quarried only as needed, because it hardens rapidly after it is exposed to the air and sun.

Fr. Alto S. Hoermann, who lived at San José in the 1860's, described the road that linked the two missions as follows: "The road to the next mission across the river ran inside the irrigation ditch along the ridge of the prairie. It was not a wagon road, but rather a good path filled up in swampy places. . . . To the left, young trees and shrubs rose above

the ridge of the prairie and the ditch. To the right, the
field was open and only bounded by strips of forest along
the river. . . . At the end of the field, where the path entered
the woods, it became so narrow that riding in single file
was necessary; then, widening again at the river, and crossing
it, the path led through a shady grove of pecan trees to La
Concepción."

Father Presidente's Letters

Padre Pedro does not stay long in the church. He sees
a rider on horseback enter the open western gate. He is the
mail carrier and he delivers several letters to the missionary.
As the *presidente* of all the missions in Texas, Fr. Ramírez
must take care of not a little correspondence with Governor
Domingo Cabello who resides in the governor's palace near
the Presidio of San Antonio de Béxar, and with the padres
in the other missions.

Besides the letters he has just received there are several
others which he has not yet answered. He goes to his office
on the first floor of the *convento* and sits down at a table
to write a few replies. One he addresses to Fr. José María
Salas. He too is building a new church at Mission San Antonio de Valero on the site of the former one which has
collapsed; but the new church will never be completed.
Another letter goes to Fr. José Francisco López at Mission
Concepción. He is fortunate in having a beautiful stone
church which was completed already in 1755. Other letters
that Fr. Pedro must answer are from Fr. José Mariano de
Cárdenas at San Juan Capistrano, and Fr. Pedro Noreña
at San Francisco de la Espada. The latter's church had to be
torn down, because it threatened to fall; and another building of considerable size is being used as a chapel.

There are still other letters he will have to write, though

he cannot do it now. At the Rosario Mission near La Bahía, Fr. José Escovar, who was so highly praised by Solís in 1768, is still carrying on his excellent work; he has been doing this for the past twenty-five years, ever since 1754. Father Pedro must get a younger man to take his place, so that the deserving old missionary can return to Zacatecas and spend his last years at the College.

Two more missionaries are at the struggling settlement of Bucareli, namely, Fr. José Francisco Mariano de la Garza and Fr. Juan García Botello. Though he was loathe to do so, since they were badly needed in the other missions, Father Pedro sent them to Bucareli at the request of Governor Ripperdá to care for the settlers and to work among the Indians in that region.

These and the padre of Espíritu Santo Mission at La Bahía are the missionaries who look to Fr. Presidente Pedro as their superior and leader. All of them present their problems to him, and it is his task to encourage them in their labors.

Dinner, Siesta, Work

While Father Pedro is busy with his correspondence, the sacristan Miguel once more ascends the stairs beside the church tower to ring the Angelus Bell. The position of the sun in the sky tells him it is midday; and the sun dial on the second floor of the *convento* confirms his estimate of the time of day.

When the workers in the shops, on the farm, and at the church hear the sound of the bell, they pause to pray the Angelus and then come together for their noonday meal. This consists of *pozole,* a tasty soup to which is added meat and beans or peas, lentils, garbanzos.

After dinner most of the Indians, except the sentinels

who are on guard, retire to their apartments for a siesta. About two o'clock they resume their work and continue it till about five, when Miguel rings the Angelus Bell for the third time. Thus they work about seven hours a day. On Sundays and Holy Days and many other fiesta days they do no manual work; they spend these days in religious exercises and amusements such as games, dances, plays, song, and music.

Rosary, Supper, Recreation

On other work days the Indians gather in front of the church after the work ends, to recite the *Doctrina Cristiana* again, to listen to another instruction given by the missionary, and to sing the *Alabado* once more. But today is Saturday, the day on which they sing the Rosary, in four voices and with musical accompaniment. This they do with edifying devotion and harmony, really putting their heart into it. At the end they sing the *Salve Regina* in Spanish:

Dios te salve, Reina y Madre de misericordia, vida y dulzura, esperanza nuestra, Dios te salve. A ti llamamos. . . . (Hail holy Queen, Mother of mercy, our life, our sweetness, and our hope, hail. To you do we cry. . . .)

And then follows the tender and touching Evening Hymn:

> Hail Mary, blessed of God and full of grace,
> The Lord is with thee, purest of our race!
>
> Blessed art thou, Dove of purest, spotless white,
> Only woman never touched by sin's chill blight.
>
> With one voice earth and heaven thee acclaim
> As Queen, God's Mother, Virgin free from stain!

So shall it be; forever sound our strain!
With one voice earth and heaven thee acclaim.

About six o'clock they have a supper of *atole,* the same as breakfast. They are very fond of *atole.* The rest of the evening until sundown they spend in recreation — in games and dances and singing and music. Those who make up the choir, practice the Sunday high Mass for tomorrow, with the musical accompaniment of violin and guitar.

On other work days the missionary conducts another class for the school children after supper; but this evening he hears the confessions of the men and boys who will be confirmed tomorrow. He has already done that for the women and girls in the afternoon. The Indians also take a bath in their pool before retiring; and the housewives get the Sunday clothes ready for the family.

Soon after the setting sun casts a golden glow over the mission and the countryside, young and old begin to retire for the night. They get up at sunrise and they go to bed at sunset — all, except the guards who are on duty. Father Pedro also stays up a little longer, praying his breviary and preparing his Sunday sermon.

While this placid and happy life goes on at Mission San José, the English colonies on the Atlantic Coast are fighting their war of independence against Great Britain; and the tide has begun to turn in their favor. France has already recognized their independence. In another five years the war will be over. Spain too is on the side of the colonies, and in 1779 joins the war against Great Britain. At the close of the war in 1783, the colony of Florida, which had been lost to Great Britain twenty years earlier, is returned to Spain. France has already ceded Louisiana to Spain (in 1762); and it remains a part of the Spanish empire until

1801, when it is given back to France. Two years later France sells Louisiana to the United States.

NOTE

For the translation of the first three stanzas of Fr. Margil's *Alabado* and also of the Evening Hymn, the writer is indebted to Fr. Owen da Silva, who published them in *Mission Music of California* (Los Angeles, 1941).

Letter written by Fr. Bernardino Vallejo at Mission San José on July 11, 1806, informing Governor Cordero that there was nothing in the archives of the mission concerning the boundary between Texas and Louisiana. Original in the Bexar Archives, Austin.

97

En vista de el oficio de V.S. rho.
el dia de hoy, pasé luego a registrar
los Papeles, y Docum.ros q.e se hallan en ese
Archivo de mi cargo, y en ninguno de
ellos he encontrado noticia alg.a q.e
de luzes sobre la linea divisoria
de esa Prov.a con la de la Luciana;
eso no obstante seguiré Registrando
Papeles Sueltos, y Viejos y siempre q.e
en ellos halle alg.a noticia util la pa-
sare a V.S. sin perdida de t͠po.

Dios g.e a V.S. m.s a.s Miss.n de
S.r S.n Jose 11. de Julio de 1806.

Fr. Bernardino Vallejo

S.r Gov.r D.n
Ant.o Cordero.

San José in Folklore and Art

The Spaniard kept his childhood — his
ideals and imagination and love of mystery
and adventure, his chivalry and warm humanity. He wasn't ashamed to show that he had
feelings. It is no wonder that the discovery
and the taming of the New World by such
spirits has given us four centuries of uninterrupted and infinitely varied Romance.

— CHARLES F. LUMMIS

XV

IT IS NOT SURPRISING TO FIND THAT THE MIS-
sionaries of Mission San José and the beautiful stone church
of the mission with its artistic sacristy window have played
a role in folklore, literature, and the arts. Legends are not
history, but they reflect the life and spirit of a people who
pass them on from father to son. They are, as a rule, stories
which have a historical setting or background. Sometimes
the tales themselves have a historical basis; sometimes they
are pure fiction. Actual historical events may be presented
in a rather muddled and inaccurate manner; and what happened at different times may be merged into one narrative,
so that the dates given cannot be taken seriously.

In this history of San José, we have adhered strictly to
the records contained in bona fide documents. But it would
not be complete if we did not make mention of the legends

about San José. We offer an abridged version of them for what they are — not as history but as legends.

The Bells of San José

At the time of the founding of Mission San José in 1720, a youth whose name was Angel de León enlisted as a private in the army of Spain. He was engaged to a beautiful maiden called Teresa. Desirous of giving her more than a private's meager salary, he sought and received an assignment to New Spain where he could more easily attain an officer's commission. He bade his fiancée a sad farewell at Xeres, Spain, and she promised to await his return.

Arriving in New Spain, he was sent to the presidio of San Antonio de Béxar. In several battles with the Comanches, he displayed such courage and leadership that he was soon promoted to the rank of lieutenant. Only six months of his enlistment remained, when it was learned that the Comanches were gathering en masse to attack San Antonio. General Bustillos decided to carry the war into the country of the Comanches before they could strike. He assembled troops from all the presidios of Texas. Just before setting out on the expedition, General Bustillos gave Lieutenant Angel de León a document signed by the viceroy of New Spain, the Marqués de Casa Fuerte. It promoted him to the rank and salary of a captain of the royal cavalry. Angel was very happy; for, now he could marry Teresa.

It was late in the evening when the Spaniards reached the encampment of the Comanches about thirty miles northwest of San Antonio. The next morning the mounted soldiers were arranged in a wedge-shaped formation, with Captain Angel de León at their head. They approached the Comanches at a trot, while the Comanches stood ground and prepared to fight. A short distance from the enemy,

Angel gave a signal and they rode right into the midst of the astounded Comanches at a furious gallop.

The savages were overwhelmed and scattered, but Angel rode with such speed and force that he was carried forward, and his companions lost sight of him as he disappeared behind a cloud of dust. They found him afterwards, shot through with two arrows. He was still alive, and they carried him to Mission San José. But all attempts to save his life proved futile. He was buried with honors in the campo santo in front of the church of San José.

Since 1720 there were direct though infrequent sailings for Spain from Matagorda Bay. Teresa knew this and was waiting to hear from her beloved Angel. One day a letter arrived, but it was from the padre who was stationed at Mission San José. He related as gently as he could what had happened and enclosed a short farewell message written by Angel shortly before he died.

For several days Teresa was so afflicted with grief that she hovered between life and death. Then she heard that bells were soon to be cast nearby for Mission San José. Teresa asked to be taken there; and the crowd, which always gathered for such an occasion, made room for her so she could go right up to the fire-clay caldron containing the molten metal, ready to be poured into the moulds. From her neck she took the gold crucifix and from her finger the gold ring which she had received from Angel, and threw them into the blinding caldron, saying: "Take these with you, dear mission bells; and when you ring the Angelus above Angel's grave for the first time, he will hear and know that I have been faithful."

Teresa was carried away in a faint and taken back home. From day to day she grew weaker. She no longer had any will to live, and yet she hung on as if waiting for something. Many months later, her parents were standing at her bedside one night when suddenly they saw her thin face wreathed in a sweet smile. And they heard Teresa say distinctly: "The Angelus! The bells of San José are ringing the Angelus. Angel is hearing them and understands." Then she died and the smile of happiness remained on her countenance. Later it was learned that at that very hour the bells in the lofty tower of San José Mission in faraway Texas for the first time rang out the Angelus.

A similar legend is associated with Mission San Gabriel in California, but it was told in Texas at an earlier date. The bells of San Gabriel did not come from Spain, but one or more bells of San José were cast in Spain, it is claimed, before 1631.

Another version of this legend of the bells of San José places Angel and Teresa among the aristocracy of Spain. Don Luís Angel de León did not go to New Spain to win promotion and a captain's salary, but to serve his king and country and to gain the laurels of a brave soldier. He lost his life in a running fight with raiding Apaches near Mission San José when an arrow pierced his heart; and he was buried in the mission cemetery. Teresa cast her jewelry into the molten metal for the bells of San José; and some time later, hearing the Angelus rung by these bells at San José, she fell lifeless to the ground. In still another version Angel is called Carlos.

When a new mission was founded, even on the most distant frontier, one or more bells were always taken along. No mission was complete without a bell. The missions also had their sun-dials, but for most of the Indians the ringing of the Angelus Bell, morning, noon, and evening, sufficed to indicate the time of day, while it invited them to pause for a few moments of prayer.

The Legend of the Rose Window

Juan Huizar (Huisar, Huicar) — so the story goes — was born in Málaga, Spain, about 1696. A lineal descendant of the architect who designed the Alhambra, he manifested an unusual talent for sculpture at an early age. His parents provided for him the best instructors in Spain and then sent him to Italy to complete his studies.

Returning to Málaga, he fell hopelessly in love with a rich señorita, Inés Yánez de Loja. But the latter's parents objected to the match because Juan possessed no wealth except his skill as a sculptor. He was a true artist and cared not for riches; but he decided to acquire them by using his talents, and then he would ask for the hand of Inés. He proposed to go back to Italy, but Inés objected because there were too many attractive girls in that country. So Juan Huizar swallowed his pride and went to America as a gold-seeker.

Stories were still circulated about a Gran Quivira in Texas, as yet undiscovered, where the Indians had immense treasures of silver and gold. In the year 1720 Juan arrived at San Antonio de Béxar and planned to undertake a small expedition toward the north, where the Indians told him Quivira was situated. Just then a train of supplies for the presidio and the missions, brought by a ship from Spain to Matagorda Bay, reached San Antonio. It also delivered to Juan a message from the king of Spain. The king wanted to keep men like Juan Huizar at home, and he offered Juan an ample annuity as long as he would devote himself to his art in Spain.

Juan's problems were solved, and he went joyfully to La Bahía, to the mission of Nuestra Señora del Espíritu Santo near the bay. In four months another ship, bound for Spain, was due to touch at this port. When the ship arrived, Juan was there, ready to go on board. The officer of the ship who came ashore in a boat was none other than Juan's old friend, Alonso Gardenas; and Juan told him about his good fortune and his plans. Alonso congratulated his friend with a certain restraint, and then informed him that his former fiancée had married another. It was a crushing blow for poor Juan, and Alonso left him standing there on the sands of the coast for a long time.

Juan did not sail for Spain. He went back to the mission at La Bahía and unburdened his heart to the fatherly missionary. The padre tried to console him by revealing to him that he had the same experience in his youth; and he told him that the best cure for sorrow was work. "Go to Mission San José," he said. "Your talents are needed there for the new church they are building. At San José you can dedicate your life and work to God. That will make it possible for you to forget your pains."

The next morning Juan Huizar took the road back to San Antonio. At Mission San José his services were joyfully accepted, and he was shown every kindness. For eleven years Juan worked diligently with his mallet and chisel, sculpturing the façade and the sacristy window of the Queen of the Missions. But he led a solitary life and never spoke much. He grew prematurely old, and at the end he sent a short message to the padre at the La Bahía mission: "Work has not eased my pain." Shortly afterwards he was found dead in his cabin.

There are several other versions of this legend. One, more correctly, gives Huizar the name of Pedro. We are told that he was sent by King Philip V for the express purpose of executing the carvings at San José Mission. His fiancée was Rosita González. She set out to join Pedro, and was on the same ship that brought over the Canary-Islanders who in 1731 founded the town of San Fernando beside the presidio of San Antonio de Béxar. On the voyage sickness broke out among the passengers, and Rosita nursed the sick until she herself was stricken and died. The Canary-Islanders brought the sad news to Pedro, and he was disconsolate; but Fr. Antonio Margil persuaded him to complete his work at San José. Shortly after he had completed the "Rose Window," he died.

Another version has it that Pedro Huizar's betrothed bore the name of Rosa. Pedro came to New Spain to seek fame and fortune, and reached Mission San José in the late 1780's when the new stone church was practically completed. He offered to decorate the sacristy window's exterior with his carvings, which would symbolize for him all the grace and beauty of his loved one. It would be Rosa's window — the "Rose Window." It would be the most beautiful window in all the world; and after he had almost completed it, he would send for Rosa and marry her at San José.

Five years later, Pedro invited Rosa to join him, and she took the next ship that sailed for New Spain. Pedro was awaiting her arrival as he put the finishing touches to his masterpiece. The padre came to him and gently placing his hand on Pedro's shoulder told him the tragic news. Rosa had died at sea. According to one version the ship sank, and she was drowned. Pedro was grief-stricken for a long time; but he took a new interest in life when he undertook to ornament the simple façade of the church with many beautiful carvings and statues. The task occupied him for the rest of his life.

The Ghostly Procession and Voices

Still another variation of the Rose Window legend, together with the legend of the procession and voices at the window, was related in 1931 by James B. Cunningham of

San Antonio. When he was a boy, he said, he paused one evening to chat with an aged Mexican who had spent his entire life in the shadow of San José Mission.

When Huizar was a young gallant in Spain, the old man told him, the sculptor joined a band of adventurers who were going to the New World. The reason why he went was not the lure of gold or fame but the hope of regaining his health. He was already acclaimed as the King's sculptor; and he had a sweetheart in Spain, to whom he made the promise that he would soon return. At Mission San José he won back his vigor and strength, while rendering some valuable assistance in the construction of the new stone church.

He was getting ready to return to Spain when the news reached him that his loved one had died. Having no desire now to go back to Spain, he made up his mind to erect a memorial to his deceased fiancée by spending the rest of his life in beautifying the church of San José.

Thirty years later, after completing his task, he was standing outside the sacristy window on a moonlit night. Suddenly, he seemed to hear, as from a distance, the voice of his beloved, singing a lover's song. As he called to her, he was overcome by a strange faintness and fell to the ground; but he saw a troop of slowly moving figures approaching the window. They passed the window, and the last of the ghostly band, a lady in the royal robes of the court of Spain, paused and knelt down beside him as he lay prone on the ground. He heard her addressing him with words of endearment and speaking of a love that was stronger than death; and she placed in his right hand the very ring he had given to his fiancée. Then she moved on with the others in the group.

Loud he called and reeled and staggered, falling there
upon the ground,
As those loving accents (a song of a lonely lover, floating
o'er a distant hill) reached him, dealing deep a
mortal wound.
Then from margin of the river, suddenly appeared
in sight,
Troops of moving, ghostly figures, spirit things of
shining light. . . .
When the light of day was breaking by that window
near the stair,
Good Antonio, Gentle Padre, found a figure lying there.
T'was the body of the artist, who through thirty years
alone,
Carved and wrought in wondrous beauty matchless
poems on the stone. . . .

These lines are from a poem written by Mr. Cunningham to recount the legend. He says the old man concluded his story by saying: "It may not be true, Señor. But my grandfather told it to me when I was a boy like you, and his grandfather told it to him. Buenas noches, Señor. Buenas noches!"

Pedro Huizar

It is hardly necessary to call attention to the historical inaccuracies in some of these versions of the "Rose Window" legends. The stone church of San José was not built in the 1720's; and Fr. Margil was not at San José in 1731. But there was a man named Pedro Huizar in the San Antonio area during the latter part of the eighteenth century. He was born at Aguascalientes, Mexico in 1740. In 1778, when the present restored church of San José was being completed, he was thirty-eight years old and married to a woman called María de la Trinidad Henriques. About that time, a daughter, María Josefa, was born to them at Mission Concepción; and she married José María de Herrera, who was chosen to be the first "justice" of San José at the time of its partial secularization in 1794. A few years later, the latter was residing at the Espada Mission; and he had a son who was baptized at San José by Fr. José Mariano Cárdenas on July 22, 1797.

According to his own testimony, José Antonio Huizar, a son of Pedro, was born at San José in 1786. The records of San José mention two other sons of Pedro. Josef Lucas was baptized at San José by Fr. Josef Agustín Falcón Mariano on October 19, 1785; and the entry in San José's register of baptisms (no. 924) calls Pedro Huizar a "carpintero of the mission." Another son, Josef Gerónimo, was baptized at San José by Fr. Josef María Salas on October 7, 1789 (no. 982).

San José's register of marriages tells us that after his first wife had died, Pedro Huizar, on February 5, 1798, married María Gertrudis Martínez, who was the widow of Juan Antonio Flores. Fr. Juan Joseph Aguilar officiated at this wedding. In 1959 there were at least eighteen heads of families in San Antonio who bore the name of Huizar, all of them apparently descendants of Pedro.

The fact that Pedro Huizar was living near Mission San José in 1778, and, in 1785-1786 at least, at this mission, seems to confirm the oral tradition that he was the sculptor of the "Rose Window" and the façade of San José church. He was known also as a surveyor, and hence was a man of some accomplishments.

When Mission San Antonio de Valero was suppressed in 1793, it was Pedro Huizar who made a survey of the mission lands and was present with Governor Múñoz at their distribution among twenty-three adult Indians, nine couples and five individuals; and in payment for his services, Huizar received a parcel of land just like the Indians, that is, a tract suitable for the planting of about one and a half bushels of seed. Huizar was one of those who signed the document recording the distribution of land.

Huizar also surveyed the lands of the other four San Antonio missions when they were partially secularized; and he assisted Governor Múñoz in distributing definite plats to the Indians in July, 1794. This was done at the Espada Mission on July 12, at San Juan Capistrano on July 14, at San José on July 16-23, and at Concepción on July 31-August 1.

At Concepción Huizar was appointed the *justicia*, who was to supervise the temporal affairs of the Indians; and he received one plat "to cultivate or rent for his benefit and his family's in lieu of a salary for his services." By 1796, he seems to have been the "justice" of Mission San José, perhaps of both Concepción and San José.

Some years earlier, in 1790, Huizar had been sent to La Bahía by Governor Múñoz to make a report on the practicability and cost of irrigating the lands at the presidio. In his report of March 4, 1791, Huizar declared the cost would be prohibitive and an aqueduct was not feasible. His report was accepted by the *Junta Superior de Hacienda* in Mexico.

And on December 10, 1790, Huizar was commissioned by Governor Múñoz to draw plans for the reconstruction of the presidio of San Antonio de Béxar and the improvement of its defences. He submitted drawings and estimates of the cost; but the project was never carried out.

If Pedro Huizar was the sculptor of San José, he was not only a man skilled in practical affairs but also an artist of the first rank. Harvey P. Smith wrote the following about the so-called Rose Window: "This one piece of work alone is worth coming a long way to see, and is considered by connoisseurs to be the finest single piece of Spanish-colonial ornamentation existing in America. . . . The carving is bold and daring, but exquisite in line and curve, with a freedom and freshness in its composition that denotes the hand of an inspired genius."

Charles Ramsdell calls attention to one feature which the casual visitor can easily overlook: "At a short distance, the doorway (of the façade) gives the viewer a sense of perfect symmetry, though there is but slight formal symmetry of pattern. Instead, there is the most delicate and subtle balance of forms." The same is true of the Rose Window.

The Legend of San José's Tunnel

For years it was thought that Mission San José had an underground passage way, leading from somewhere within the walls to some distant point outside, possibly along the bank of the San Antonio River. The purpose of this tunnel was supposed to have been to provide a means of escape in case the mission was besieged and the hostile Indians could no longer be held off. Actually San José was so well fortified and so abundantly provided with food and water that the mission could "laugh at its enemies," and the Apaches and Comanches never tried to attack the compound.

Anyhow, the legend of the tunnel persisted. "In searching for an entrance to this tunnel," writes Charles M. Brooks, "in the nave of the church, three complete skeletons were unearthed, a man, woman, and a baby, apparently Indians, from the shape of the skulls. Just inside the sacristy, a hollow spot was found under the tile floor. . . . But when opened, something like a hundred skulls were uncovered." When workmen cleaned out the irrigation ditch on the north side of the mission, it was again thought at first that they had found the tunnel; but what they found was the lower part of the old mill.

There have also been legends of buried treasure at San José and the other San Antonio missions; but it is hardly worth while mentioning the fact. When several hundred men of the CWA were engaged in excavating at the missions under the direction of Harvey P. Smith, he was besieged with requests to be allowed to dig in various spots.

Legend about San José's Dome

The majestic dome or cupola of the church of San José was completed before the end of 1777. It was indeed a remarkable achievement. How was it done? A legend has it that, as the walls were constructed, the interior of the building was filled with ground and capped by a mound of dirt which had the shape of the dome. This served as a mould and support of the masonry of the dome until the cement had hardened. Then the little mountain of earth inside the church was gradually removed by the shovels of the Indians and carted away.

Charles Mattoon Brooks Jr. rightly observes that this "seems a fabulous sort of tale. More than likely, wooden sub-forms were built for the construction, much as they are today in poured concrete buildings." In the thirties, the writer saw workers reconstruct the dome of a chapel in Mexico which had fallen down. They made use of a tall tree trunk with arms attached to it near the top, something like a telegraph pole. This pole enabled them to rebuild the dome and to put the keystone in its place; and it held the stones in place until the cement hardened.

A Novel and a Romance

The novel about San José (292 pages), written by the Benedictine Fr. Alto S. Hoermann and entitled *The Daughter of Tehuan*, has already been mentioned. Charles Ramsdell dismisses it as being "without merit." However, it contains not a few valuable historical observations; and, the writer is of the opinion that it captures the atmosphere and spirit of the days when San José was an Indian mission. It has an authentic historical setting, except inasmuch as it speaks of a "prefecture," which was supposed to have been the residence of a royal representative who was stationed at the mission. There never was such an official at San José, unless the "justices" or Spanish *alcaldes* who were appointed for San José after its partial secularization in 1794 be called "prefects."

Jane Maury Maverick wrote a five-page *Romance* about Mission San José, a piece of pure fiction about Fr. José Francisco López, who was the *presidente* of the Texas missions, c.1785-1794, and resided at Mission San Antonio but never at Mission San José. The story relates that Don José Francisco López, a young soldier, became a Franciscan friar when Juanita, whom he had hoped to marry, took the veil in a convent. Huicar came to San José when its new church was being built, and contributed to the ornamentation of the church by his skill as a sculptor. Padre Margil and Padre Núñes directed the construction of the church, including its spiral staircase beside the tower. The new church was to be consecrated on Easter morning, when the Comanches attacked the mission. Don José Francisco López, who was now Padre José, quickly ascended the staircase to ring the bell in warning; but a Comanche who had entered the mission compound pursued him and felled him with his tomahawk.

Paintings of San José

The earliest known picture of Mission San José is a painting made by Seth Eastman, an artist and member of a party comprising forty-seven soldiers, eight wagons, nine teamsters, and one wagon master who stopped at San José in August, 1849. He got the facts wrong in his historical sketch of the mission, but he made a good painting of San José's church as it was before the dome collapsed. Eastman's painting of San José measures 15⅝ by 21⅛ inches.

Another old painting made toward the end of the 1860's by an unknown amateur artist is in the possession of Mr. Frank Walsh of San Antonio. "It is lacking in perspective, but not devoid of an academic sense of proportion and color values," and it is the only picture of San José that shows a little dome over the structure at the rear of the church with Gothic windows, which was constructed by the Benedictines.

After the collapse of the church's dome in 1874, the San Antonio artist Theodore Gentilz made his paintings of San José, a large one that is now at St. Mary's University in San Antonio and a smaller one that is in the Library of the Daughters of the Republic of Texas at the Alamo. Gentilz was born in France, 1820, and died in San Antonio, 1906. He came to Texas with Henri Castro in 1844, moved to San Antonio in 1846, went back to France in 1849, but returned after he had married. For many years he was a teacher of art at St. Mary's College, which is now a university. He also made paintings of the Alamo, of San Francisco de Espada, of San Juan Capistrano, and of Concepción, all of which are in the DRT Library at the Alamo.

Another early painting of San José is that of Thomas Allen, who was born in St. Louis, 1849, and died, 1924. He spent a part of the winter of 1878-1879 in Texas, and at that time made a painting of the main doorway and façade of the church of San José. It shows the doors hanging loosely on their hinges and a shepherd wearing a cap and serape, sitting in front of the church, patiently tending his flock.

The oldest picture of San José after Eastman's painting of 1849 is an engraving made by Loudenback Hoffman and used as the frontispiece in H. Yoakum's *History of Texas*, first volume, published in New York, 1856. In this picture, a part of the *convento* has a gable roof, but no Gothic arches (which were built by the Benedictines in the 1860's), and a house with a thatched roof is standing in front of the church. A larger framed copy of this engraving, and another old engraving can be seen in the granary of San José, hanging on the east wall.

A painting, portraying the building of San José's present restored church in a composite picture, showing the sacristy with its "Rose Window" in a section separate from the church proper, was used some years ago on the covers of *Catholic Digest*.

A more recent and very beautiful oil painting of San José's church is the one done by Granville Bruce of Irving, Texas. This and five other paintings of the other four San Antonio missions and the presidio chapel at Goliad were donated by Mr. and Mrs. John B. Godfrey of Austin to the Texas State Library, where they are on display. They have been reproduced in four colors in *Six Missions of Texas*, published in Waco, 1965.

Replicas of San José

Two more or less faithful replicas of the mission church of San José have been built in Texas. One is the St. Anthony Shrine on Lorenz Road in Alamo Heights, San Antonio, which at least resembles the church of San José.

The idea of building this shrine was conceived by the Rev. Father M. Baque and then furthered by the Missionary Sons of St. Anthony and their friends who erected it at the cost of $118,000. The cornerstone was laid on June 12, 1932; and the church was dedicated on Sunday, December 1, 1957, by Archbishop Robert E. Lucey.

In 1924 a group of Spanish Franciscan Friars of the Third Order Regular came to Waco, Texas. They have built a beautiful replica of San José at Waco and called it the Church of St. Francis of Assisi. Its dimensions on the outside are one hundred and twenty-five by sixty-one feet; and it was constructed of bricks and concrete, the roof being of tile. Inside the church are three interesting paintings on canvas, depicting the arrival of the early Franciscan missionaries in Texas, the death of the Franciscan martyrs, and the building of the missions.

At the Alamo Plaza entrances to Joske's department store in San Antonio, there are a half dozen replicas of San José's famous "Rose Window."

A Tour of the Historic Site

Each stone is eloquent of weary years
When brave hearts of the ages long gone by
Labored upon the prairie's broad expanse
And reared amid its early solitude
This monument of human faith and love.
Each carven arch and pillar tells again
The story of their daily toil and hope.

— JANIE F. BASKIN

XVI

MISSION SAN JOSÉ HAS BEEN RESTORED, TO A great extent, to the condition in which it was in 1768, except for the church which was begun in that year and completed in 1782. When the mission was founded in 1720 — to summarize briefly what has been related in several chapters of this book — it occupied a site, a mile or less to the north, on the east bank of the San Antonio River. Before 1727, the mission was moved to the low lying ground on the west bank about a half mile from the present site. It was moved to the elevated spot it now occupies about 1740. By the end of 1740, San José as well as the other San Antonio missions did not, as yet, have any permanent buildings. The first stone structures of San José and the other four neighboring missions were built in the 1740's. San José continued to be an Indian mission, not only till 1794 when it was partially secularized, but till its final secularization in 1824.

San José State and National Historic Site is situated about four and one-half miles south of the Alamo. Roosevelt Avenue, a part of Highway 281, runs almost parallel with the western walls of the mission. The entrance to the grounds is at the southwestern corner; and there are ample parking facilities outside the south wall.

San José Mission is open to visitors from 9:00 a.m. to 8:00 p.m., April 1 to September 30, and from 9:00 a.m. to 6:00 p.m., October 1 to March 31. During the year 1967 the number of visitors has risen fifteen per cent over that of 1966; and by the end of the year it is expected, at the present writing, that the total will be slightly more than 125,000.

At the entrance gate the visitor receives a plan of the mission compound, with numbered trail keys and explanatory notes; and this plan together with interpretive signs which have been set up along the suggested route enable the visitor to make a self-conducted tour.

What follows are the writer's comments concerning the points of interest indicated on the plan that is given to the visitor:

(1) *Entrance.* The present entrance, called the South Gate, is a new one, and was completed in 1954 with the cooperation of the National Park Service, the Texas Parks and Wildlife Department, the State Highway Department, the County of Bexar, and the City of San Antonio. In 1950, a tablet with the American Eagle and bearing the following inscription was set up at the entrance to San José Mission:

NATIONAL HISTORIC SITE
SAN JOSÉ MISSION
SAN JOSÉ Y SAN MIGUEL DE AGUAYO
FOUNDED IN 1720
WAS DESCRIBED BY FATHER MORFI
IN 1778 AS
"THE QUEEN OF THE MISSIONS
OF NEW SPAIN IN POINT OF BEAUTY,
PLAN AND STRENGTH"
AND IS A SYMBOL OF THE FAITH,
COURAGE AND VIGOR OF THE
FRANCISCAN FATHERS —
AN EXAMPLE OF THE CULTURAL
AND HISTORICAL IMPORTANCE OF
THE MISSION IN THE DEVELOPMENT
OF THE UNITED STATES.
BUILDING OF THE PRESENT CHURCH
WAS BEGUN IN 1768.

(Seal)

UNITED STATES
DEPARTMENT OF THE INTERIOR
NATIONAL PARK SERVICE

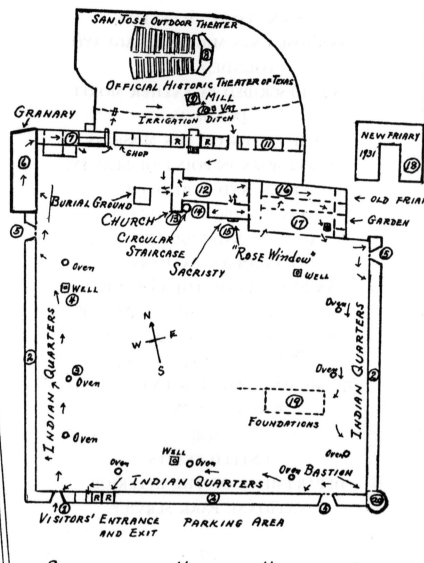

PLAN OF MISSION SAN JOSÉ

SAN JOSE OUTDOOR THEATER

OFFICIAL HISTORIC THEATER OF TEXAS

MILL
VAT

GRANARY

IRRIGATION DITCH

SHOP

NEW FRIARY
1931

OLD FRIARY

GARDEN

BURIAL GROUND

CHURCH

CIRCULAR
STAIRCASE

SACRISTY

"ROSE WINDOW"

WELL

Oven

WELL

Oven

Oven

Oven

INDIAN QUARTERS

INDIAN QUARTERS

N
W E
S

Oven

FOUNDATIONS

WELL

Oven

Oven

Oven BASTION

Oven

INDIAN QUARTERS

VISITORS' ENTRANCE
AND EXIT

PARKING AREA

ROOSEVELT AVENUE — U.S. HIGHWAY 281

STATE AND NATIONAL HISTORIC SITE

M. A. H. '67

(2) *Indian Quarters.* In 1758 there were 84 Indian apartments, built of stone, for a total of 281 persons. Ten years later there were 350 Indians, and their apartments, one for each family, were built mainly along the east and south walls. They extended 11 feet from the wall, and varied in length from 14 to 16½ feet. The result was that the square measured 611 feet on the outside and 600 feet on the inside, on each of the four sides. These measurements are given in the report of Fr. Solís (1768) and that of Fr. Morfi (1777). Fr. Solís also tells us that each Indian apartment had a small kitchen, which was a separate, narrow room extending eleven feet from the wall. All of them had raised beds, with bison hides for mattresses, and with sheets of gunny-sack or cotton and blankets of wool, which were manufactured at the mission. Each Indian had two sets of clothing, one for weekdays and one for Sundays and fiestas.

(3) *Ovens.* There are nine outdoor ovens in the restored mission, placed at intervals along the Indian apartments, so that each one could serve a group of families. Besides the ovens, each Indian apartment had a fireplace in its kitchen (Fr. Solís). The restored ovens, except the one in the northeastern corner, could not now be used for baking purposes, because they are built of tufa. The one in the northeastern part of the square, according to William Corner (p. 19), was built by the Benedictine Fathers when they were at San José Mission in 1859-1868. He writes: "The industrious fathers rebuilt many of the upper Gothic arches, as far as can be learned, manufacturing their own red bricks for that purpose and the making of the big oven at the east end."

(4) *Water Wells.* Four dry wells are within the mis-

sion square. These were reconstructed over the original sites. One of them, as Fr. Solís tells us, was spring-fed; and in 1768 the volume of water that gushed forth from this well was like a small river that flowed off to the irrigated fields outside the square.

(5) *West Gate.* In 1768 the square had four gates, one at each corner. By 1777, writes Fr. Morfi, a fifth gate had been added, opposite the church, on the west side. The latter was the most frequently used, and the only one kept open during the day. Each gate could be defended by firing through the loopholes in the wall beside it and in the parapet above it. The whole mission was built like a fortress, because there was always the danger of an attack by hostile Apaches or Comanches. By 1789, according to Fr. López, a sixth gate had been put into the wall, probably on the east side.

(6) *Granary.* The granary was one of the first buildings erected at the present site. By 1749, two sections of the stone structure, with a flat roof, had been built. In 1768, it had a vaulted roof; and before 1777, a third section had been added. The flying buttresses were constructed no doubt to reinforce the walls when or after the building received a vaulted roof. The granary was never used as a church, as some have thought. The first church at the mission's present site stood where the present one was built, 1768-1782. Already in 1758 no less than four thousand bushels of corn were stored in the granary. According to Fr. Morfi's description of the mission (1777), it seems that the several workshops of the mission were located near the granary on the west and north side. These have not been restored. They included a textile shop in which gunny, cotton, and woolen cloth was woven, a tailor shop, a carpenter shop, and

a smithy. There were also lime and brick kilns. These workshops, together with the fenced and irrigated mission farm and orchard, which were outside the walls and about two and one-half miles square, and the stock ranch which was some thirty miles farther south in 1768, made the mission an independent and self-sufficient community. Everything that its residents needed was raised or manufactured by the mission.

(7) *Prefecture.* Because Fr. Hoermann, who lived at San José from 1859 to 1864, postulated — in his novel about San José, *The Daughter of Tehuan* — a prefecture, which was supposed to have been the residence of a royal representative in whom the civil and military authority at the mission was vested and who made reports to the king, many have been misled into thinking that the "prefecture" existed at San José in the middle of the eighteenth century. However, until Mission San José was partially secularized in 1794, it was the resident missionary who alone administered both the spiritual and the temporal affairs of the mission, kept all the accounts, and made all the reports. It was only in 1794 that a so-called "justice," later called the Spanish *alcalde* of the mission pueblo of Indians, was appointed by the government to look after the temporal interests of the Christian Indians who had been made landowners. From 1794 to 1824, the missionary restricted his activities principally to the sacred ministry, although also during these years he continued to have full charge of a few new Indian converts who were under instruction, in the same way as before 1794. The "prefecture," therefore, can be considered authentic only if it is regarded as the residence of the "justice" or Spanish *alcalde* during the last three decades of the mission's existence, or as the quarters of the

two or three Spanish soldiers stationed at San José until about 1765.

(8) *Official Historic Theater of Texas.* Passing through a gate in the north wall, at *La Mission Tienda,* a souvenir store, the visitor crosses a little bridge built over a remnant of the mission's irrigation ditch and sees before him a 1,000-seat open-air amphitheater. This theater was designated the Official Historic Theater of Texas in 1958; and it is operated by the Texas Historic Theater Foundation, a non-profit tax-exempt corporation. During the summer months, plays which are of a cultural or historical character are staged in this theater.

(9) *Old Mill and Acequia.* Along the *acequia* or irrigation ditch is the reconstructed flour mill of San José, which was built by Fr. José Pedrajo between 1790 and 1794. The upper room and the machinery have been restored, but the lower part of the structure is original. The *acequia* which conducted water from the San Antonio River to the mission farm outside the walls was tapped at this point to power the mill, and the water then flowed off to irrigate the fields. The *acequia* itself continued to flow along the northern and eastern walls outside the square and rejoined the river a short distance above the dam where the Espada *acequia* commenced.

(10) *Unrestored Leather Vat.* This rock pit may have been a vat in which hides of animals were cured. They would have been tanned, of course, after they had been removed from the vat.

(11) *Unrestored Rooms.* Formerly it was thought that these had been soldiers' quarters. Although Governor Bar-

rios in 1758 still speaks of soldiers' quarters at Mission San José, which were opposite the church, no such quarters are mentioned in 1768 by Fr. Solís; and it is evident from his account that there were no Spanish soldiers at San José in that year. It was only from 1720 to about 1765 that two, or at most three, Spanish soldiers were stationed at San José; and these soldiers assisted the missionary also as instructors and overseers of the Indians. In 1768 San José had one hundred and ten Indian "warriors, of whom forty-five were armed with guns and sixty-five with bows and arrows, spears, and other weapons." But this was done only in case of need. Only a few of them were on guard at all times. In 1789 Fr. López expressly states that there were Indian houses along the north wall, and that these were separated from the church and *convento* by a street.

(12) *Church.* The earlier church which stood on the site of the present one was built during the 1740's, when the first two sections of the stone granary, the lower floor of the stone *convento,* and the first Indian houses of stone were likewise constructed. This church, whether of stone or adobe we do not know, seems to have been a large structure with a flat roof and with terraces extending from the sides of the building and having flat earthen roofs. Governor Barrios in 1758 described it as cruciform in shape and having a tower with a set of bells. The transepts at this time may have been terraces. The reports of 1749, 1758, and 1762, all say that this church was large enough to accommodate two thousand persons; but this statement seems to have been a repetitive error. There was no need for such a huge building at Mission San José. The figure two thousand seems to have been used instead of two hundred. Anyhow, this church was torn down before 1768 to make room for the present (restored) stone church. The foundation of the latter was blessed on March 19, 1768; and it was not completed until 1782. At that time it was the most beautiful

church along the entire frontier of New Spain, "the rim of Christendom."

With Charles M. Brooks, "we walk a little to the west in order to turn about and better contemplate the famed façade from an adequate distance. Here the tour-de-force of all American Mission Architecture greets our eyes . . . the soaring beauty of the tower is lost, the color of the plaster wall (which once covered the flat surfaces) fades, the rest of the building is forgotten, as all the light and shadow in the enclosure seems concentrated at this rippling curtain of stone."

The figures on the façade are statues of the following saints: in the center of the upper part St. Joseph, on his right St. Dominic, on his left St. Francis; in the center of the lower part, above the entrance, Our Lady of Guadalupe, on her right St. Joachim, and on her left St. Anne.

You are invited to enter the church, which is still used as a house of worship by the present parish of San José. The Blessed Sacrament is reserved in the tabernacle on the altar, which now faces the people. Just inside the entrance there is a message from the Archbishop of San Antonio which reads as follows:

"Ladies and Gentlemen: We welcome you to the sacred soil of this National Historic Site and to the quiet grandeur of old San José Mission. The church which you have just entered is nearly two hundred years old. The first stones were laid on March 19, 1768, by Governor Hugo Oconor and Father Gaspar Solís. The whole structure is admirably proportioned and strongly built of solid limestone called tufa. The walls in places are over five feet in thickness.

"This church is a living symbol in stone and mortar of the faith and dedication of the early Franciscan Fathers in their efforts to bring the religion and culture of Christian civilization to the Indians of New Spain. The Fathers had to use whatever tools were at their disposal — kindness, patience, and good example. They also very wisely made use of the natural interests and talents of the Indians, such as fondness for music, dance, story-telling, color, and design, to gain the confidence of these children of the forest, so that they could be instructed in the Christian faith. The success of the Franciscan founders is evident today, not only in the physical accomplishments of the Indians, such as assisting in the carvings on the façade of the church, but also by the fact that the Christian faith is deeply rooted in the descendants of the Indians. . . ."

The little room on the left is the baptistery. It has an old baptismal font. On the right-hand wall of the church a tablet will be placed to commemorate the memory of San José's first missionary, Fr. Miguel Núñez de Haro, who served the mission for thirty-two years and developed it into the most successful mission of Texas. He died in 1752 and was buried at the mission; but later his remains were taken to Zacatecas, Mexico.

Walking up the aisle of the church to the sanctuary, you will find on the left side of the altar, as you face it, the grave of Fr. José María Salas, who died on June 17, 1790, after serving this mission for seven years. Previously he had been the missionary at San Antonio Mission (the Alamo) for about five years.

Turn to the right and enter the large sacristy. This was the first part of the church to be completed, and then it was used as a chapel until the church proper was ready in 1782. The sacristy never fell into ruins as did the church; and it was again used as a chapel while the church was being restored. Just outside the railing in the sacristy, on the left side, is the grave of Fr. Pedro Ramírez, the builder of the present restored church and *presidente* of all the Texas missions. He died on September 30, 1781, and was buried in the sacristy, because the church was not quite ready at the time.

Take a look at the old carved doors leading out of the sacristy and at the old statues in a cabinet on the left; and then return through the church to the main portal. The massive wooden doors there are nine and one-half feet high. They were carved to resemble the original ones, which were stolen by someone between 1880 and 1890.

Exact measurements of all the buildings at the four old missions of San José, Concepción, Capistrano, and Espada were made by the United States Government through the WPA Official Project No. 265-6907 in 1934. The drawings with measurements, comprising seventeen sheets, are now part of the Historic American Buildings Survey, more than twenty-six thousand sheets of drawings, which are in the custody of the Prints and Photographs Division of the Library of Congress in Washington. According to these measurements, the façade of San José is forty-one feet and three inches wide; and the hight of the tower to the apex of its pyramidical roof or steeple (in 1934) was sixty-eight and one-half feet. Since the tower had a squat roof in 1934 (the one which it received when the tower was rebuilt in 1928), and since this roof was restored in 1940 to its original shape which is a few feet higher, we can say that the tower is approximately seventy feet high, without the cross on top of it.

In front of the church there are a few graves. One tombstone still clearly marks the grave of Juan Huizar, whose father very probably was Josef Bruno Huizar (baptized at San José by Fr. Bernardino Vallejo on October 17, 1810), whose grandfather was José Antonio Huizar (Spanish *alcalde* of San José, 1810-1819), and whose great-grandfather was Pedro Huizar (the reputed sculptor of the so-called "Rose Window"). The inscription on the tombstone is: "Juan

Huizar. Fallecio el dia 30 Marzo 1893 a la edad de 59 anos" (Juan Huizar. He died on March 30, 1893 at the age of fifty-nine years).

In 1758 Governor Barrios mentioned the fact that there was a large cemetery, 221½ feet square in the space between the church and the soldiers' quarters which were opposite the church. The cemetery no doubt remained where it was; and hence the space in front of the church must have been the cemetery throughout the latter half of the eighteenth century.

(13) *Tower and Restored Designs.* In the tower there is only one bell, size thirty, made in Hillsboro, Ohio, November 27, 1919. However, in the granary there is a small bell, suspended from a wooden yoke; and it may date from the mission days. At the base of the tower, on the south side, can be seen the color designs which once covered the flat surfaces of the façade and tower, and, it seems, also the other outer walls of the church. For the restoration of these designs the same methods were employed as those used for their original application.

(14) *Winding Stairway.* The steps of this stairway, beside the tower, were hand hewn from live-oak logs when the church was built. The entrance to it, which is locked, is from the outside only. It leads to the choir loft of the church; and from there the belfry can be reached by means of a ladder.

(15) *Rose Window.* This is the most famous window of colonial times; but it seems to have been extolled at the expense of the façade of the church, which is undoubtedly a greater work of art. It is not really a rose window, but the exterior decoration of the rectangular window in the

south wall of the sacristy. The name of "Rose Window" may have been given to it because of the legend — and it is no more than a legend — that Pedro Huizar dedicated it to his lost love Rosa. Although the sacristy had been completed and was used temporarily as a church in 1777, Fr. Morfi makes no mention of the "Rose Window." Probably it was not completed until about 1790.

(16) *Old Convento or Friary.* These roofless arches and cloisters housed the offices of the mission and the living quarters of the missionary and his assistant (when he had one) and their guests. The Roman arches are original, while the Gothic arches probably date from the 1860's when the Benedictine Fathers lived at the mission and tried to establish a priory and seminary here. The lower part of the *convento* had been built by 1749 (Fr. Ciprián); by 1758, there was one room on the second floor (Governor Barrios); and before 1777 other rooms were added on the second floor (Fr. Morfi).

(17) *Rose Garden.* The roses in the garden outside the *convento* "were contributed by the San Antonio Rose Society. The age of introduction ranges from before the time of Christ (Rosa Damascena Bifera) to 1878 (Mabel Morrison)."

(18) *New Friary.* The building beyond the locked gate is the residence of the Franciscans who now have the care of the church of Mission San José. It was built in 1931, and a part of it stands on the northeast corner of the original mission square. In the morning on Sundays and feast days and in the evening of the First Fridays, holy Mass is celebrated in the mission church; and then the east gate

is left open for worshippers. On other days the chapel in the west wing of the friary is used by the public.

(19) *Old Foundations.* The building which rested on these foundations probably was one of the workshops. Because of the four isolated stone foundations at the farther end, it is thought to have been the carpenter shop which was described in 1794 as having three open arches.

(20) *Corner Bastions.* From this lookout, sentinels could see the exterior of two walls of the compound. In 1768, according to Fr. Solís, there were two such bastions on diagonal corners; and in 1777, according to Fr. Morfi, there were four, one at each corner. Along the walls there are, and during the mission days there were, Indian apartments. The entrance gate of the San José Mission National and State Historic Site is also the gate by which visitors leave the grounds.

Anyone who has the opportunity to visit Mission San José, should not miss it. A visit to San José will be a rewarding experience for young and old — one which will never be forgotten.

NOTE

The Texas State Parks Board was merged in 1963 with the former Texas Game and Fish Commission to form the Texas Parks and Wildlife Department. The Texas Park Services, a division of the new Department, now administers most of the state parks, but not all. The Alamo, for instance, is administered by the Daughters of the Republic of Texas. (Letter to the writer from J. Dan Scurlock, Director, Park Interpretation, July 17, 1967; and E. B. Camiade, *Development of the Texas State Park System*, a detailed history from the beginning in 1923 to 1963.)

Barbara Jaska, Parks Interpretation Assistant, in an article entitled "Why State Parks?" (*Texas Parks and Wildlife*, June, 1967, pp. 7-11), has pointed out that all "state parks constitute resources for the wholesome enjoyment of outdoor recreation, recreation here meaning mental and physical, passive and active, expressive as well as receptive activities. . . . To emphasize certain of these purposes, the State of Texas has classified its parks into four types: recreation types, scenic parks, historic parks, and historic sites. . . . Historic parks and historic sites preserve historic structures and memorialize historic events with few, if any, recreational facilities" (p. 10). Mission San José belongs to the last mentioned of the four types.

Bibliography

A complete bibliography of manuscript and printed sources and other printed works on Mission San José is contained in the writer's as yet unpublished manuscript, *Mission San José y San Miguel de Aguayo, 1720-1824*. Here we will list only some of the more important printed sources, some other works of unequal value, and a few manuscripts.

Alcocer, Fr. José Antonio. *Bosquejo de la Historia del Colegio de Nuestra Señora de Guadalupe y sus Misiones, Año de 1788*. Introducción, bibliografia, acotaciones e ilustraciones del R. P. Fr. Rafael Cervantes. Mexico, 1958.

Batz, Richard. *The Acquisition and Restoration of the San José Mission Granary by the San Antonio Conservation Society, 1924-1933*. Ms. of 39 pp. in the Archives of the San Antonio Conservation Society, San Antonio.

Bolton, H. E. *Texas in the Middle Eighteenth Century*. Berkeley, 1915. A new printing of this work has been made recently.

Brooks, Jr., C. M. *Texas Missions: Their Romance and Architecture*. Dallas, 1936.

Castañeda, C. E. *Our Catholic Heritage in Texas*. 7 vols. Austin, 1936-1958.

Corner, W. *San Antonio de Bexar: A Guide and History*. San Antonio, 1890.

Cuellar Ximenez, B. *Gallant Outcasts*. San Antonio, 1890.

Cunningham, J. B. *A Legend of the Mission San José*. Copy in the Daughters of the Republic of Texas Library at the Alamo.

Czibesz, P. L. *Unknown Facts About Technical History in San Antonio*. Ms. San Antonio, 1955.

Engelhardt, Z. "Missionary Labors of the Franciscans among the Early Days (Texas)" in *Franciscan Herald* (Chicago), vols. II to V (1914-1917).

————.*Mission San Carlos Borromeo*, edited by Felix Pudlowski. Santa Barbara, Calif., 1934.

————.*The Missions and Missionaries of California*. 4 vols. and Index. San Francisco, Calif., 1908-1916.

Enciclopedia universal ilustrada Europeo-Americana. 70 vols. Barcelona, 1918-1930.

Espinosa, Fr. Isidro Félix de. *Crónica de los Colegios de Propaganda Fide de la Nueva España*. Mexico, 1746. New edition, with Notes and Introduction by Lino G. Canedo, Washington, 1964. The Introduction and Notes of Fr. Canedo are a valuable contribution to the history of Texas.

Friedrichs, I. H. *History of Goliad*. Victoria, Texas, 1961.

Gannon, M. V. *The Cross in the Sand: The Early Catholic Church in Florida, 1513-1870*. Gainesville, Fla., 1965.

Gilbert, M. J., ed. *Archdiocese of San Antonio, 1874-1949*. San Antonio, 1949.

Grimes, R. *Goliad 130 Years After (Refugio and Guadalupe Victoria), March 1836-1966*. Victoria, Texas, 1966.

Habig, M. A. *Heroes of the Cross: An American Martyrology*, 3rd edn. Paterson, N. J., 1947.

————. *The Franciscan Pere Marquette: A Critical Biography of Father Zénobe Membré O.F.M. (Franciscan Studies, XIII)*. New York, 1934.

————, and F. B. Steck. *Man of Greatness: Father Junípero Serra*. Chicago, 1963.

Hallenbeck, C. and J. H. Williams. *Legends of the Spanish Southwest*. Glendale, Calif., 1938.

Harris, E. W. *San José Mission, Queen of the Missions*, 13th edn. San Antonio, 1942.

Heusinger, E. W. *Early Explorations and Mission Establishments in Texas*. San Antonio, 1936.

Hodge, F. W., ed. *Handbook of American Indians North of Mexico* (Bulletin 30, Smithsonian Institution, Bureau of American Ethnology). 2 vols. Washington, 1907-1910. Vol. I, 2nd edn., New York, 1959.

Hoermann, A. S. *The Daughter of Tehuan, or Texas of the Past Century*, translated by A. Braun. San Antonio, 1932.

Ilg, J. *San José, Queen of the Missions*, 5th edn. San Antonio, 1940.

Kirwin, J. M. *Diamond Jubilee, 1847-1922, of the Diocese of Galveston and St. Mary's Cathedral*. Galveston, 1922.

López, Fr. José Francisco. *The Texas Missions in 1785* (sic — the year should be 1789), translated by J. Autry Dabbs *(Preliminary Studies of the Texas Catholic Historical Society, III, 6)*. Austin, 1940.

Madlem, W. *San José Mission: Its Legends, Lore, and History. Story of the Queen of the Missions*. San Antonio, 1934.

Maverick, J. M. *Mission San José: A Romance*. 5 pages. Copy in the DRT Library at the Alamo.

Maverick, Mary A. *Memoirs of Mary A. Maverick,* arranged by Mary A. Maverick and her son Geo. Madison Maverick, edited by Rena Maverick Green. San Antonio, 1921. These *Memoirs* are also included in Rena Maverick Green, ed., *Samuel Maverick, Texan* (San Antonio, 1952).

Morfi, Fr. Juan Agustín. *History of Texas, 1673-1779,* translated with biographical introduction and annotations by C. E. Castañeda *(Quivira Society Publications,* VI). 2 vols. Albuquerque, N. Mex., 1935.

McCaleb, W. F. *The Spanish Missions of Texas.* San Antonio, 1954 and 1961.

McCloskey, M. B. *The Formative Years of the Missionary College of Santa Cruz of Querétaro, 1683-1733.* Washington, 1955.

Oberste, W. H. *History of the Refugio Mission.* Refugio, Texas, 1942.

———. *Remember Goliad.* 2nd edn. Austin, 1949.

O'Connor, K. S. *The Presidio La Bahia del Espiritu Santo de Zúñiga, 1721 to 1846.* Austin, 1966.

O'Rourke, T. P. *The Franciscan Missions in Texas, 1690-1793.* Washington, 1927.

Parisot, P. F., and C. J. Smith. *History of the Catholic Church in the Diocese of San Antonio, Texas, 1685-1897.* San Antonio, 1897.

Peña, Juan Antonio de la. *Peña's Diary of the Aguayo Expedition,* translated by Peter P. Forrestal *(Texas Catholic Historical Society Preliminary Studies,* II, 7). Austin, 1935.

Porrua Turanzas, José, and José y Enrique Porrua Venero, eds. *Documentos para la Historia eclesiastica y civil de la provincia de Texas o Nuevas Philipinas, 1720-1779 (Colección Chimalistac de libros y documentos acerca de Nueva España,* XII). Madrid, 1961.

Robles, Vito Alessio. *Coahuila y Texas en la Epoca Colonial.* Mexico, 1938.

Roemer, F. von. *Roemer's Texas,* translated by O. Mueller. San Antonio, 1935, and Waco, 1967.

Rotchford, W. P. et al. Map of the acequias and farm lands of the Presidio of San Antonio de Béxar, the town of San Fernando, and the five San Antonio missions. Project of the Texas CWA. Original at Mission San José.

Schuchard, E. F. *Fresco Paintings of the Missions.* Ms. San Antonio, 1935.

———.*The Old Mill at Mission San José.* Ms.

Shea, J. G. *The Catholic Church in Colonial Days, 1521-1763 (A History of the Catholic Church within the Limits of the United States, I).* New York, 1886.

Silva, O. da. *Mission Music of California: A Collection of Old California Mission Hymns and Masses, Transcribed and Edited.* Los Angeles, 1941.

Simpson, L. B., ed. *The San Sabá Papers: A Documentary Account of the Founding and Destruction of San Sabá Mission,* translated by Paul D. Nathan. San Francisco, 1959.

Smith, H. P. *Romantic San Antonio.* 16 pages. San Antonio, 1918. A copy in the DRT Library at the Alamo.

———. "Old Mill of San José Mission" in *Plaza Parade,* Sept., 1935, pp. 121-123.

Solís, Fr. Gaspar José de. *The Solís Diary of 1767,* translated by Peter P. Forrestal *(Preliminary Studies of the Texas Catholic Historical Society, I, 6).* Austin, 1931. Another translation by Margaret Kenney Kress, in *Southwestern Historical Quarterly,* XXXV, 30-76.

Sotomayor, José Francisco. *Historia del Apostólico Colegio de Nuestra Señora de Guadalupe de Zacatecas desde su fundación hasta nuestros dias* (a single volume). Zacatecas, 1874. Second edition in 2 vols., Zacatecas, 1889.

Streit, R. *Der Letzte Franziskaner von Texas.* Dülmen i. W., Germany, 1907.

Sturmberg, R. *History of San Antonio and of the Early Days in Texas.* San Antonio, 1920.

Tiscareño, Fr. Angel de los Dolores. *El Colegio de Guadalupe desde su origen hasta nuestros dias.* 4 vols. Vol. I and II, Mexico, 1902 and 1905; Vol. III and IV, Zacatecas, 1907 and 1909. The title is misleading; the work is mostly about Zacatecas and has little about the Colegio.

Wantland, C. *History and Guide: The Five San Antonio Missions.* San Antonio, 1962.

Waugh, J. N. "The Return of the Franciscans to San Antonio" in *America* (New York), Oct. 24, 1931, pp. 62-63; reprinted in *Southern Messenger* (San Antonio), Nov. 12, 1931.

Weddle, R. S. *The San Sabá Mission, Spanish Pivot in Texas.* Austin, 1964.

Winfrey, J., et al. *Six Missions of Texas.* Waco, Texas, 1965.

Winsor, J. ed. *Narrative and Critical History of America.* 8 vols. Boston, 1889.

Winkler, E. W., ed. *Manuscript Letters and Documents of Early Texians, 1821-1845, in Facsimile, Folio Collection of Original Documents.* Austin, 1937.

Yoakum, H. *History of Texas from Its First Settlement in 1785 to Its Annexation to the United States in 1846.* 2 vols. New York, 1856. Reprinted, Austin, 1935.

Zavala, A. de. *History and Legends of the Alamo and the Other Missions.* San Antonio, 1917.

Index

Alabado, The, mission hymn, 195-196, 202, 204

Alamán, Lucas, Secretary of State of Mexico, 122

Alamo, Siege of the, 139

Allen, Thomas, artist, 221-222

Alvárez de Piñeda, Alonso, explorer, 1-2

Angelina River, 3

Angelus Bell, The, 192-193, 201-202

Apostolic Colleges, Franciscan, 4-5

Arredondo, General José Joaquín, 114

Atascosa River, 56, 75

Atascoso, El, ranch of Mission San José, 56, 197

Austin, Stephen F., 126, 138

Avilés, Santos Antonio, 130-131

Ballinger, Texas, 2

Baque, Rev. M., 223

Barrios Leal, Jacinto de, of Guatemala, 13

Bartlett, John R., 144-145

Baskin, Janie F., 34, 46, 60, 108, 134, 158, 172, 224

Bean, Colonel Elias, 128, 130

Benedictine Fathers at San José, 146-147, 151, 222, 238

Béxar, Villa de, 3, 38; County of, 183-185, 226; Presidio de San Antonio de, 3, 27, 38, 44, 52, 56, 75, 200, 217

Bishops of San Antonio, 175

Boca de Leones, Hospice of, 19, 116

Bocanegra, Vicente, blacksmith, 110

Bollaert, William, 143

Bolton, Herbert E., 1, 53, 94

Bonavía, General Bernardo, 113

Borden, Prentiss, 128

Bosque, Fernando del, explorer, 3

Bouchu, Rev. Francis, 147

Bowie, James, at Espada, 138-139

Brooks, Charles Mattoon, 184, 218, 234

Bucareli, settlement on the Trinity, 201

Calvo C. M., Rev. Michael, 141-145

Casa Calvo, Marqués de, governor of Louisiana, 113

Casas Rebellion, 114

Castañeda, Carlos E., 86, 132-133, 165-167

Castanola, Essie Crawford, 181-182

Chambers, C. M., Mayor, 165
Cherokee County, Texas, 2, 38
Clement XIV, Pope, 77
Colonial Dames of America, 182
Colorado River, 38, 98
Columbus, Christopher, 1
Concepción, Arroyo de, 75
Corner, William, 149-157, 174
Cortés, Hernan, 1
Croix, Teodoro de, commandant
  general, 65, 81, 88-90, 97, 100
Cunningham, James B., 213-215
Cuba, 54
Czibesz, Paul L., 101

Daughters of the Republic of
  Texas, 174-175; Library of, at
  the Alamo, 221
Doctrina Cristiana, The, 193-195
Doyle, Rev. Enrique, 136
Drossaerts, Archbishop Arthur J.,
  159, 162, 168, 176-177, 184
Drought, Henry Patrick, 176
Drought, Mrs. H. P., 175
DuBuis, Bishop Claude, 147
Durango, Mexico, 16

Eagle Pass, Texas, 3
Eastman, Seth, artist, 221
El Paso, Texas, 2, 3
Estany C.M., Rev. Eudald, 141-142
Evening Hymn, sung at the mis-
  sions, 202-203

Fannin, James Walker, at Espada,
  136, 138-139
Fisher, Lt. Col. William S., at San
  José, 140
Flood of the San Antonio River, 116
Flores y Valdez, Captain Nicolás, 32
Floresville, Texas, 75
Florida, 203
Fort of Natchitoches, La., French, 3
Fort St. Louis, French, 2
Fort Sam Houston, 165
Franciscans (see also Missionaries
  and Reports):
    Alberola, Brother José, 99
    Alerding, Fr. Bonaventure,

162-163
Andrade, Fr. Francisco, 20
Belauzarán y Ureña, Bishop
  José de María Jesús, 135-136
Bringas de Manzaneda, Fr. Di-
  ego, 23
Ciprián, Fr. Ignacio Antonio,
  48, 51
Concepción, Fr. Pedro de la,
  13, 16
Daeger, Archbishop Albert J.,
  165
Delgado Cervantes, Fr. Luís, 17
Espinosa, Fr. Isidro Félix de,
  19-20, 29, 37, 48
Escovar, Fr. José, 201
Fernández de Santa Ana, Fr.
  Benito, 42
Gaitán, Fr. José Manuel, 120
Garcés, Fr. Francisco, 23
García, Fr. Bartolomé, 86, 196
García Botello, Fr. Juan, 201
Guerra, Fr. Joseph, 17, 27
Hidalgo, Fr. Francisco, 17
Hidalgo, Fr. Tomás, 15
Hierro, Fr. Simón de, 53-54
Hugenschmidt, Brother Chris-
  topher, 160, 162
Larios, Fr. Juan, 3
López, Fr. José Francisco, 82-
  92, 96, 98-100, 200
López, Fr. Melchor, 9-13
Llinás, Fr. Antonio, 9
Martínez y Tejada Díez de Ve-
  lasco, Bishop Francisco de
  San Buenaventura, 54, 196
Massanet, Fr. Damián, 17
Morfi, Fr. Juan Agustín, 65-77,
  227-230, 238-239
Olivares, Fr. Antonio de San
  Buenaventura y, 18, 26
Puelles, Fr. José María de
  Jesús, 105, 112-113
Rebullida, Fr. Pablo, 15
Sáenz, Fr. Matías, 18
Santiesteban, Fr. José, 167
Schrempp, Fr. Vincent, 159-162
Serra, Fr. Junípero, 61, 77
Silva, Fr. Manuel de, 98-99,

104, 110
Solís, Fr. Gaspar José, 54-60, 68, 70, 229-230, 238-239
Strub, Fr. Martin, 133
Terreros, Fr. Alonso Giraldo, 167
Vallejo, Fr. Francisco, 49, 59
Valverde, Fr. Asisclos, 63
Ysasmendi (Isasi Isasmendi), Fr. Ignacio, 43
Franciscans of the Chicago-St. Louis Province, 153, 158, 167-169, 176
Franciscans, Conventual, in the San Antonio area, 146
Franciscans of the Third Order Regular, in Waco, 223
Fredonian Revolution, 127
French, The, in Louisiana, 2, 4
Friendly Suit of 1936-1937, 184
Frio River (Rio Frio), 75

Galindo, Rev. José Ignacio, 127
Galveston, Cathedral of, 178; Diocese of, 143, 147
García, Lorenzo, 27
García, Manrico, 131
Garcitas Creek (River), 2, 7
Garriga, Bishop Mariano S., 160-161, 176-177
Garza, Rev. Refugio de, 121-122, 124, 135, 141
Gentilz, Theodore, artist, 221
Godfrey, John B., 222
Goliad (see also La Bahía), Church of, 142
Governors of Texas:
Aguayo, Marqués de, Joseph de Azlor Virto de Vera (1719-1722), 4, 25-31
Alarcón, Martín de (1716-1719), 3
Armiñan, Benito (1814-1815), 111
Barrios y Jáuregui, Jacinto (1750-1759), 50-53, 100, 232-233, 237-238
Cabello, Domingo (1777-1786), 200
Cordero, Manuel Antonio

(1805-1808), 111, 113
Franquis de Lugo, Carlos Benites (1736-1737), 40-43
González, Rafael (1823-1827), of Coahuila-Texas, 125
Herrera, Simón de (1811), 114
Martínez, Antonio (1817-1822), 115-116
Martínez Pacheco, Rafael (1786-1790), 62
Múñoz, Manuel (1790-1797), 99, 103-105, 216-217
Oconor, Hugo (1767-1770), 55, 234
Ripperdá, Juan María Vicencio Barón de (1770-1777), 63, 201
Salcedo, Manuel María de, 1808-1811, 1811-1813), 100, 112
Terán de los Ríos, Domingo (1691-1692), 2
Trespalacios, José Félix (1822-1823), 121
Viesca, Agustín, of Coahuila-Texas (1827-1832), 126
Graham, Elizabeth, 181
Granville, Bruce, artist, 222
Great Depression, The, 176
Gregory XVI, Pope, 22
Guadalajara, Mexico, 16-17, 54
Guadalupe River, 4, 41
Guatemala, Colegio de Cristo Crucificado de, 14
Guerra, Henry A., 165
Guerra, José Alejandro, 165
Gutiérrez Revolution, 114

Hernández, Justice José Agustín, 110
Herrera, Justice José María, 103, 110, 216
Hirams, Samuel C., 129-130
Historic American Buildings Survey, 236
Hoermann O.S.B., Rev. Alto S., 33, 45, 100, 146-147, 199, 220, 231
Hoffmann, Loudenback, artist, 222
Holy Cross Fathers, at San José, 148-149, 153
Houston County, Texas, 2, 38
Houston, Sam, 128, 138

Huisar, José Antonio, Spanish
 alcalde, 111, 216, 236
Huizar, Josef Bruno, 236; Juan, 236-
 237; Pedro, 68, 103, 110, 111, 198,
 212, 215-217, 220, 236, 238
Hume, Msgr. William Wheeler, 175-
 176
Indians:
  Apaches (Lipan Apaches), 39, 40,
   62, 64, 81, 90-92
  Barrados, 85
  Borrucas (C.A.), 10-11
  Chols (C.A.), 10-13
  Coahuiltecans, 17-18, 26, 28, 36,
   38, 86, 95
  Comanches, 39-40, 89, 125, 140,
   167
  Coras (Nayarit), 16-17
  Huicholes (Nayarit), 16
  Lacondons (C.A.), 10, 12-13
  Orcoquisacs, 82
  Pampopas, 85
  Postitos, 85
  Tacames, 41
  Tahuacanas, 113
  Talamancas (C.A.), 10-11, 15
  Tejas (Texas), 2, 38, 82
  Terrabas (C.A.), 10-11
  Tobosos (Coahuila), 18
  Ujambores (C.A.), 11
  Vidais, 82
  Wizards (C.A.), 15
Ismanica, Comanche chief, 140
Iturbide, Agustín de, emperor of
 Mexico, 122, 125

Jamaica, 1
Joske's Department Store,
 San Antonio, 223
Juchereau de St. Denis, Louis, 3

Kendall, George, 143-144
Kirwin, Rev. J. M., 130
Knights of Columbus, 163

La Bahía (Goliad), Texas, 105,
 124-126, 137
Language, Coahuiltecan, 86
Lanier, Sidney, 148
La Punta, Mexico, 17-18

Laredo, Texas, 75, 105
La Salle, Robert Cavelier Sieur de, 2
Lavaca Bay, 4, 7, 29
Legends about San José:
  Bells, The, 208-210
  Buried Treasure, 219
  Dome, The, 219
  Ghostly Procession, The, and
   Voices, 213-215
  Rose Window, The, 211-213
  Tunnel, The, 218-219
Lenarduzzi, E., sculptor, 180
León, Martín de, 128
León, Tomás de, Spanish *alcalde*, 111
Leonor de San José, Sister,
 Carmelite nun, 17
Lewis, Mrs. Perry J., 181
Liberty, Texas, 129, 132
Linn, John J., 128
Lobo, Rev. José León, 135
López de Santa Anna, General
 Antonio (see Santa Anna)
Lorenzo de Gaff, pirate, 9
Loring, Peter, 163
Louisiana, 91, 203-204
Lucey, Archbishop Robert E., 168,
 180, 187-189, 223, 234-235
Lummis, Charles, 206

Maloney (Molloy), Rev., 136
Mandujano, Justice Santiago, 111, 113
Mansbendel, Peter, sculptor, 179-180
Manual of missionaries, Coahuilte-
 can, 86, 196
Margil Hall, St. John Seminary, 153
Margil Society, 177
Martínez Pacheco, Captain Rafael,
 62, 64-65
Martyrs, Franciscan, in Texas and
 the U.S., 161
Maverick, Mary A., 140; Jane Maury,
 220; Maury, 164
Maynes, Rev. Francisco, 121-124
McCormick, Mary, 164
Medina River, 3
Menard, Peter J., 130-132
Menchaca, Captain Luís Antonio, 52
Mexico City, Mexico, 9, 17
Mexico, Republic of, 159

Miller, Philip, 131-132
Missions in Texas:
Nuestra Señora de Guadalupe de
  Nacogdoches (1716-1773),
  7, 127
Nuestra Señora del Pilar de
  Bucareli (1776-1779), 98
Nuestra Señora del Pilar de
  Nacogdoches (1779-1820), 82
Nuestra Señora de la Purísima
  Concepción (1716-1824), 3, 28-
  29, 38, 43, 66, 99, 106, 110-111,
  117, 120, 123, 125-126, 137-138,
  141-142, 153, 199-200, 217, 221,
  236
Nuestra Señora del Espíritu Santo de Zúñiga (1722-1830), 4,
  40, 48, 62, 82, 124-125, 201
Nuestra Señora de los Dolores de
  los Ais (1717-1773), 7, 19
Nuestra Señora del Refugio
  (1793-1830), 99, 104-105, 114,
  120, 124-126, 142
Nuestra Señora del Rosario
  (1754-1807), 62, 82, 104, 120,
  124-125, 201
San Antonio de Valero (1718-
  1793), 3-4, 20, 26-27, 41, 43, 82,
  96, 98-99, 200, 221, 236
San Francisco de la Espada
  (1731-1824), 41, 43, 75-76, 99,
  106, 114-117, 123, 138-139, 141-
  142, 148, 153, 168-169, 200, 217,
  221, 236
San Francisco de los Neches
  (1721-1729), 38
San Francisco de los Tejas
  (1690-1693), 2, 16
San Francisco Xavier de Nájera
  (1722-1726), 28, 38
San José y San Miguel de
  Aguayo (1720-1824) (see also
  Legends about, Missionaries of,
  Reports about San José):
Accounts, Settling of, 104, 106
Attacks by Apaches, 39-40; by
  Comanches, 39-40, 140
Bastions, 55, 68, 239
Bell, 237

Brick kilns, 56
Cemetery, 52, 237
Church, at second site, 35, 48;
  first at present site, 48-49, 51,
  55; second at present site, 66-
  68, 83-84; collapse of dome,
  149; collapse of north wall,
  148; in 1890, 150; restora-
  tion, 163, 173-189; today,
  233-236
Communal life, 87
Congregating Indians, Manner
  of, 36-37
Day, A, in 1778, 190-204
Decoration, Exterior, 67, 144-
  145, 237
Development, 34-45
Ditches, Irrigation, 71-74, 182,
  232
Doors of church entrance, 153,
  177-179
Epidemic, of 1739, 43; of 1783,
  81
Façade of church, 67, 152, 176,
  179, 234
Farm, 70-76
Foundation, Blessing of, 55
Founder, 6-23
Founding, 27-28
Franquis de Lugo, Governor,
  40
Friary (Convento), Old, 49, 69-
  70, 83-84, 145, 151, 176, 185,
  238; New, 160-163, 238-239
Gates, 68-69, 230
Granary, 49, 52, 56, 69, 150,
  181, 230-231
Heyday, 46-59
Houses of Indians, 68-69, 183,
  229
Indians, 76, 160
Justices (Spanish *alcaldes*), 97,
  110-111
Last three decades, 108-117
Leather vat, 232
Mail service, 113
Mill, Flour, 99-101, 182, 219,
  232
Mill, Sugar, 52

Neglect, 135-136, 173
Neighbors, 37-39
Odin, Father, 141-142
Old foundations, 239
Opposition of Fr. Olivares, 27
Ovens, 151, 229
Paintings, 221-222
Plan of Fr. Silva (1792), 98-99
"Prefecture," 220, 231
Queen of the missions, 60-79
Ranch, 56, 70, 75-76, 197
Records, 57, 87
Replicas, 222-223
Rose garden, 238
Rose Window, 68, 152, 217-218, 222-223, 236-238
Sacristy, 67-68, 84; sacristy-chapel, 150-151, 175
Settlers, Complaints of, 41-43; Cattle hunting by, 90-91
Secularization, Partial, 94-107; Final, 121-123, 159, 217
Services, Divine, 142
Sicknesses of Indians, 91
Site, 235-236; First, 29; Second, 32-33, 35; Third, 45-47
Soldiers of the presidio, 90-91
Soldiers' quarters, 52, 83, 139, 231
Spanish spoken, 86
Square, Walled, 55, 68-69, 83; in 1890, 150
Stairway, Winding, 150, 176, 237
Statistics, 81, 84-85
Stock, 49, 52, 56, 75, 161
Tower of church, 150, 153, 236
Unrestored rooms, 232-233
Visit of Aguayo, 28; of Bishop Martínez y Tejada, 53-54; of Fr. Solís, 54-58; of Fr. Morfi, 65-77; in 1876, 149
Visitors, in 1931, 163; in 1967, 226
Walls, 183
Wells, 56, 229-230
Wheat grown, 100
San José de los Nazonis, 38 (1716-1729)

San Juan Capistrano (1731-1824), 43, 99, 115-117, 123, 139, 141-142, 153, 168-169, 200, 217, 221, 236
San Miguel de Linares de los Adaes (1717-1773), 3, 4, 7, 29
Santísimo Nombre de María (1691-1692), 2
Missionaries of San José:
Aguilar, Fr. Juan Joseph (1798), 216
Anzar, Fr. Antonio de Jesús (1820), 120
Borruel, Fr. Joseph Cosmé (1736-1737), 40
Bustamente, Fr. Ventura (1822), 121
Camberos, Fr. Juan de Dios (1762-1764), 62
Cárdenas, Fr. José Mariano (1792-1799), 99, 104-107, 200-216
Díaz de León, Fr. José Antonio (1820-1824), 119-133, 159; quoted, 118; at Refugio Mission, 120; at San José, 120-123; last years in Texas, 123-133; efforts to save last missions, 124-127; at Nacogdoches, 127-133; farewell message, 130-131; last journey, 131-132
Falcón Mariano, Fr. Josef Agustín (1784-1785), 216
Fellechea, Fr. Manuel María (1816-1817), 115
Frexes, Fr. Francisco (1817-1819), 115-116
Garza, Fr. José María (Mariano) Francisco de la (1782-1783), 98-99, 105, 201
Lanuza, Fr. Ignacio María (1770-1772), 63-64
Margil, Fr. Antonio (1720) founder of five missions in Texas, 6-28, 123, 167, 177, 215, 220; early life, 8; as a walker, 8; arrival in Mexico, 9; first sojourn in C. A., 9-14; second sojourn in C. A., 14-15; at the

College of Zacatecas, 16-17, 21-22; in Nayarit, 16-17; in Coahuila, 17-19; in eastern Texas, 19-20; missions founded by, 7; founder of San José, 25-28; at San Antonio, 26; letter to Aguayo, 26; last years, 21-22; greatness of, 22-23; letter to Fr. Andrade, 6; quoted, 6, 24

Marmolejo, Fr. Ildefonso Joseph (1753-1758), 50, 59, 61

Muro, Fr. Miguel (1819-1820), 116, 119-120, 124-127

Noreña, Fr. Pedro (1786), 106, 200

Núñez de Haro, Fr. Miguel (1720-1752), 27, 29, 32, 35-36, 41, 43-45, 220, 235

Patrón y Guzmán, Fr. Agustín (1720-1721), 20, 27, 29, 32

Pedrajo, Fr. José Manuel (1789-1794), 92-93, 99-100, 102, 104-105, 232

Ramírez de Arellano, Fr. Pedro (1759-1762, 1764-1781), 57, 61, 65, 76-79, 114, 193-203, 235-236

Salas, Fr. José María (de) (1783-1790), 82, 85, 92, 200, 235

Vallejo, Fr. Bernardino (1800-1816), 110-114, 205, 236

Missionary Sons of St. Anthony, 223

Mississippi River, 1

Monterrey, Diocese of, 141

Mora, Juan, 131

Morkovsky, Rev. Alois J., 177

Muldoon, Rev. Michael, 128, 136

Músquiz, Ramon, jefe político, 121, 126

Nacogdoches, Texas, 3, 126-130, 133; church of, 142

Napoleon Bonaparte, 113

Natchitoches, La., 3

National Historic Site, San José Mission, 186, 226-239

National Park Service, 185, 226-227

Nava, Pedro de, commandant general, 105

Nayarit, Mexico, 16-17

Norris, Nathaniel, 127

Nueces River, 4, 75

Nuestra Señora de los Dolores de los Lacondones Mission, in C.A., 13

Nuestra Señora de los Dolores Mission, in Coahuila, 17-18

Nuestra Señora de Guadalupe Mission, in Coahuila, 18-19

Nuevo León, Province of, 3, 48

Nuevo Mexico, Province of, 2

Nuevo Santander, Province of, 3, 48, 127, 164

Oberste, Msgr. William H., 133

Odin C.M., Bishop John M., 141-143, 146-147

Olmsted, Frederick, 145

Ortiz Parilla, Coloniel Diego, 62

Paraje del Oso, near Goliad, 125

Parish of Our Lady of the Angels, San Antonio, 168, 171; of St. Joseph, 168, 171; of San José Mission, 168, 170; of St. Leonard of Port Maurice, 168-171; of Von Ormy, Texas (Sacred Heart), 168, 171

Parisot, Rev. P. F., 132-133

Peña, Rev. Juan Nepomuceno de la, 123-124

Pike, Zebulon M., 111-112

Pioneer Flour Mills, San Antonio, 182

Poteet, Texas, 75

Prentiss, H. B., 132

Presidios:
Nuestra Señora de los Dolores de los Tejas, 3, 4, 29
Nuestra Señora de Loreto de la Bahía del Espíritu Santo, 56, 63, 98, 125, 186, 217
Nuestra Señora de la Luz de Orcoquisac, 56, 62
Nuestra Señora del Pilar de los Adaes, 4, 56
San Antonio de Béxar, 3, 27, 38, 44, 52, 56, 75, 200, 217
San Juan Bautista del Rio Grande, 3, 18, 19

Presidio, Texas, 2, 3

Puebla de los Angeles, Mexico, 9

Quarry at Mission Concepción, 66
Querétaro, Mexico, 9-15, 20-21, 23, 99
Querétaro, Colegio de la Santa Cruz de, 4-5, 9, 12-13, 17-18, 20, 23, 26, 39, 169

Ramírez de la Piscina, Captain Manuel, 62
Ramón, Captain Domingo, 2-3, 19, 29
Ramsdell, Charles, 174, 218-220
Rancho de las Cabras, 75
Red River, 98
Redd, Captain William D., 140
Redemptorist Fathers, 153
Religious garb of Franciscans, Color of, 5
Reports about San José:
    Barrios y Jáuregui, Governor Jacinto (1758), 50-53, 232-233, 237-238
    Ciprián, Fr. Ignacio Antonio (1749), 48-50, 238
    Hierro, Fr. Simón de (1762), 53-54
    Martínez Pacheco, Captain Rafael (1772), 64-65
    Morfi, Fr. Juan Agustín (1777), 65-77, 227-230, 238-239
    López, Fr. José Francisco (1789), 82-91, 230
    Salcedo, Governor Manuel María de (1809), 112
    Solís, Fr. Gaspar José (1768), 54-58, 60, 68, 70, 229-230, 238-239
    Urrutia, Captain Toribio de (1740), 44-45
    Vallejo, Fr. Bernardino (1804), 111; (1815), 114-115
Rio Grande, 1, 3, 18
Rivera, Brigadier General Pedro de, 32
Road to Mission Concepción, 199-200
Robeline, La., 3, 29
Rodríguez, Chief Juan, 28
Roemer, Ferdinand, 144
Rosary, The, 202
Rubí, Marqués de, 64

Sabinas River, Mexico, 18
Sabinas Hidalgo, Mexico, 18
Sabine River, 3
St. Anthony Shrine, San Antonio, 222-223
St. Augustine, Fla., 54
St. Francis Church, Waco, 223
St. Francis Home for the Aged, San Antonio, 160
St. John Seminary, 153
St. Mary's University, 221
St. Vincent's Abbey, Latrobe, Pa., 146-147
Sala C.M., Brother Raymond, 141
Salado Creek, Battle of, 140
Salado River, Mexico, 19
Salcedo, Ignacio, 181
Saltillo, Mexico, 18
San Antonio, Archdiocese of, 174-175, 183, 185
San Antonio, City of, 226; in 1890, 156-157
San Antonio Conservation Society, 180-183, 185
San Antonio *Express*, 161
San Antonio River, 4, 24, 26, 28, 32, 35, 37-39, 42, 116
San Augustine, Texas, 129
San Felipe de Austin, Villa de, 126
San Fernando, Villa de, 37-38, 75, 96, 121, 123; church of, 142-143
San Fernando, Colegio de, Mexico City, 5
San Jacinto, Victory of, 139
San Juan Bautista Mission, Coahuila, 18-19
San Luís Potosi, Mexico, 16
San Miguel Creek, 75
San Miguel Arcangel Mission, Coahuila, 18
San Ramón de los Lacondones Mission, in C.A., 13
Santa Anna, General Antonio López de, 136-137
Santa María de los Lagos, Mexico, 16
Santos, Dr. Manuel, 131
Salve Regina, The, 202
Saucedo, José Antonio, *jefe politico*, 111, 122-123, 126

Schuchard, Ernst F., 67, 102, 182
Secularization, Meaning of, 95
Smith, Harvey P., 102, 180, 217-219
Sotomayor, Rev. José Francisco, 50, 127
Southern Messenger, 161
Sterne, Adolphus, 128, 130

Taylor, Charles S., 128
Taylor, Mrs. Lane, 182
Texas:
  Anglo-Americans in, 136-137
  Centennial in 1936, 176, 182
  Centennial Commission, 182
  Civil Works Adminstration, 75
  Discovery of, 1
  Exploration of, 2-3
  Historic Landmarks Association, 174
  Historic Theater Foundation, 232
  Relief Commission, 75
  Republic of, Act of Congress, 141-142
  Spanish Province of, 3-4
  State Library, 222
  State Highway Department, 226
  State Historic Theater, Official, 182-183, 232
  State and National Historic Site, San José Mission:
    Entrance to, 226-227
    Location of, 226, 239
    Naming of, 184-185
    Plan of, 228
    Self-conducted tour, 226

Tablet at entrance, 227
Visiting Hours, 226
State Parks and Wildlife Department, 185, 226, 239
War of Independence, 137-138
Tezontle (tufa), 66
Thomas, G. L., 129-132
Timon C. M., Rev. John, 141-142
Tittle, W. B., 164
Tobin, Mrs. Don F., 183

Urrutia, Captain Toribio de, 44-45
U.S. Library of Congress, 236
U.S. War of Independence, 203

Vásquez, General Rafael, 139
Valdez, Captain Juan, 27-28
Valdez, Rev. José Antonio, 135, 141
Valladolid (Morelia), Mexico, 21
Victoria, Texas, Church of, 142

Waco, Texas, 223
Walsh, Frank, 221
Watling's Island, 1
Wimmer, Abbot Boniface, 146
Wirtz, Alvin J., 186-187
Woll, General Adrian, 139-140

Yoakum, Henderson, 36-37, 222

Zacatecas, Mexico, Colegio de Nuestra Señora de Guadalupe de, 4-5, 7, 15-21, 26, 39, 48-50, 59, 97, 110, 119, 123, 126, 137, 159, 169

What role did the Jews have in the formation of our modern economic system? What forces peculiar to their religious ethic and to their patterns of life fitted the Jews for their role? This pioneer work examines these two fundamental questions. In developing his theses, Sombart discusses such matters as the part played by Jews in the trade in precious stones, Jewish participation in the development of stock exchanges, and the role of the Jews in the colonization of Latin America. In Chapter 10 he takes up in detail the "pariah" position of the Jews and their resulting need to keep their funds as liquid as possible.

In the opinion of Professor Hoselitz, the questions posed by Sombart and the standard of comparison he set for later work will make *The Jews and Modern Capitalism* required reading for a long time to come.

WERNER SOMBART

THE

AND MODERN

JEWS

CAPITALISM

Translated by M. EPSTEIN

With an Introduction to the American Edition by

BERT F. HOSELITZ

COLLIER BOOKS
NEW YORK, N.Y.

Contents

Translator's Introductory Note 7
Introduction to the American Edition 9

Part I
The Contribution of the Jews to Modern Economic Life

1. Introductory 27
2. The Shifting of the Centre of Economic Life
   since the Sixteenth Century 34
3. The Quickening of International Trade 44
4. The Foundation of Modern Colonies 49
5. The Foundation of the Modern State 67
6. The Predominance of Commerce in Economic Life 77
7. The Growth of a Capitalistic Point of View in
   Economic Life 124

Part II
The Aptitude of the Jews for Modern Capitalism

8. The Problem 159
9. What is a Capitalist Undertaker? 162
10. The Objective Circumstances in the Jewish
    Aptitude for Modern Capitalism 169
11. The Significance of the Jewish Religion in
    Economic Life 187
12. Jewish Characteristics 238

Part III
The Origin of the Jewish Genius

13. The Race Problem 263
14. The Vicissitudes of the Jewish People 299

Notes and References 327
Bibliographical Note 385
Index 401

Contents

Translator's Introductory Note
Introduction to the American Edition

Part I
The Contribution of the Jews to Modern Economic Life

1. Introductory
2. The Shifting of the Centre of Economic Life since the Sixteenth Century
3. Children of Importance/Fame
4. The Foundation of Modern Colonies
5. The Foundation of the Modern State
6. The Predominance of Commerce in Economic Life
7. The Growth of a Capitalist State of View of Economic Life

Part II
The Attitude of the Jews to Modern Capitalism

8. The Problem
9. Who is a Capitalist Undertaker?
10. The Objective Circumstances in the Jewish Attitude to Modern Capitalism
11. The Significance of the Jewish Religion in Economic Life
12. Jewish Characteristics

Part III
The Origin of the Jewish Genius

13. The Race Problem
14. The Vicissitudes of the Jewish People

Notes and References
Bibliographical Note
Index

Translator's Introductory Note

WERNER SOMBART is undoubtedly one of the most striking personalities in the Germany of to-day. Born in 1863, he has devoted himself to research in economics, and has contributed much that is valuable to economic thought. Though his work has not always been accepted without challenge, it has received universal recognition for its brilliance, and his reputation has drawn hosts of students to his lectures, both at Breslau, where he held the Chair of Economics at the University (1890-1906), and now in Berlin at the Handelshochschule, where he occupies a similar position.

But Sombart is an artist as well as a scholar; he combines reason with imagination in an eminent degree, and he has the gift, seldom enough associated with German professors, of writing in a lucid, flowing, almost eloquent style. That is one characteristic of all his books, which are worth noting. The rise and development of modern capitalism has been the theme that has attracted him most, and his masterly treatment of it may be found in his *Der moderne Kapitalismus* (2 vols., Leipzig, 1902). In 1896 he published *Sozialismus und soziale Bewegung,* which quickly went through numerous editions and may be described as one of the most widely read books in German-speaking countries.[1] *Die deutsche Volkswirtschaft im 19ten Jahrhundert* appeared in 1903, and *Das Proletariat* in 1906.

For some years past Sombart has been considering the revision of his *magnum opus* on modern capitalism, and in the course of his studies came across the problem, quite accidentally, as he himself tells us, of the relation between the Jews and modern capitalism. The topic fascinated him, and he set about inquiring what that relationship precisely

---

[1] An English version was prepared by the present writer and issued by Messrs. J. M. Dent & Co. in 1909, under the title *Socialism and the Social Movement.*

was. The results of his labours were published in the book[2] of which this is an English edition.

The English version is slightly shorter than the German original. The portions that have been left out (with the author's concurrence) are not very long and relate to general technical questions, such as the modern race theory or the early history of credit instruments. Furthermore, everything found within square brackets has been added by the translator.

My best thanks are due to my wife, who has been constantly helpful with suggestions and criticisms, and to my friend Leon Simon for the verse rendering on pp. 201-202.

M. E.

LONDON, *April 21, 1913.*

[2] *Die Juden und das Wirtschaftsleben.* Leipzig: Duncker und Humblot. 1911.

Introduction to the American Edition

By BERT F. HOSELITZ

ALTHOUGH WERNER SOMBART'S *Die Juden und das Wirt-schaftsleben* appeared in an English translation shortly after its publication in German, both the original and the translation have become very scarce. The decision to reprint the work must, therefore, be warmly welcomed. For although Sombart's achievements have sometimes been exaggerated no one can deny that his work has attained a lasting position in the field of social and economic history. Few writers on the economic development of the western world have roamed over such vast areas and can boast of such a voluminous output. But in spite, or rather because, of Sombart's great productivity, his work is marred by frequent blemishes. His imagination was fertile, but not always too critical. His reading was wide, but he was often indifferent to the qualities of his sources. He had the capacity to integrate ideas drawn from a wide variety of social relations, and to present them persuasively, but his logic was sometimes superficial and his reasoning based on intuition rather than on strict evidence.

For these reasons Sombart's life work did not turn out what he had planned it to be: the definitive explanation of the origin and dynamics of capitalism. On the contrary, its chief value consists in its suggestiveness, in the stimulus it provides for the fuller exploration of the areas which he sketches in broad but often indistinct outlines, and in the impetus it gives to other scholars to adduce by diligent historical and sociological analysis the evidence which may serve to evaluate the plausibility of Sombart's often highly imaginative hypotheses.

Hardly any work of Werner Sombart shows his strength and weakness more clearly than *The Jews and Modern Capitalism*. But in addition the very decision to write such a book in the Germany of his day, plagued as it was by a strong and unceasing undercurrent of antisemitism, was an act of courage. For no matter what his conclusions, and no matter how dispassionate and "objective" his presentation, the book was likely to please no one. This is precisely what happened. On its publication the book was denounced by Jews and liberals as giving comfort to antisemites. Similarly it was attacked by the Jew-baiters for failing to confirm the viciousness, parasitism, and moral depravity which they attributed to the Jews. To see his writing so attacked was no novelty to Sombart. His earlier studies on *Socialism and the Social Movement* (1896 and later editions) and the first edition of *Der moderne Kapitalismus* (1902), had been criticized by conservatives as propaganda tracts for socialism and conversely by socialists as apologia for the existing order.

The burning of books—in a literal or figurative sense—cannot destroy the validity of the truths contained in them, although it may make authentic editions scarce—a plague to scholarship. But the critical evaluation of the propositions in a work and the proof that the author's facts or reasoning are at fault may seriously impair his reputation. Thus more important than the politically or emotionally inspired attacks have been the scientific criticisms leveled against this study on the role of the Jews in the rise of modern capitalism. Sombart's work was designed to attract a good deal of scholarly scrutiny. For one reason, already indicated, the book explicitly and frankly dealt with a delicate topic, whose very raising created multiple repercussions in the politics of his day—and ours. Secondly, although no one seriously questioned Sombart's competence as an economic and social historian, the fact was that he had no training in theology, or knowledge of Jewish culture and religious philosophy before he undertook the research on *The Jews and Modern Capitalism.* Thirdly, Sombart did not know Hebrew and had to use secondary sources or translations whose reliability and bias he was unable to check; thus some primary material supporting his case, and other original sources that tend to invalidate it, remained inaccessible to him. Finally, the methodological difficulties involved in making such vast sociohistorical generalizations, in relating religious thought and ethics to economic practice, are very great. In the "leap" from limited fact to large-scale theory it is easy to employ faulty reasoning, guesswork, and inconclusive evidence. Hence the suspicions of scholars are easily aroused.

In the face of these difficulties Sombart's courage in publishing this book must evoke our admiration. He not only exposed himself to political attack in an area where feeling ran high, but he risked his scholarly reputation. Since the first appearance of the German edition of the book in 1911 criticism of his scholarship has not been lacking. Many of his important conclusions have been disproved. But the freshness of the work has remained, and its suggestiveness has continued to challenge students of social and religious history. The lasting value of Sombart's work thus does not consist in his results, but in the fact that it is a point of departure. Many scholars have labored to fill the gaps left by him, to follow up some remarks he made sometimes almost as if in passing, and to supply data which are designed to resolve the differences between Sombart and his critics. Although I do not propose to list this literature in detail, it is perhaps not improper to say that a fair number of books on Jewish history as well as numerous articles and essays in the *Revue des études juives* and in the *Jewish Social Studies* directly or indirectly follow up suggestions made originally by Sombart.

But Sombart's *The Jews and Modern Capitalism* has not only inspired students to follow up the hints made by him, it has also evoked profound and often vehement criticisms. Since sections of the work have come through the critical fire with varying degree of success it may be in order to survey briefly the literature dealing with the book.

The work can be divided in two parts. The first, historical-empirical, seeks to define the role played by the Jews in the formation of the modern economic system. The second examines the peculiar socio-psychological and moral forces in the Jewish religious ethic and in Jewish patterns of life which fitted the Jews to promote this new set of economic relations.

The second problem is more fundamental, for unless it can be established that elements in the culture of medieval

Jews were instrumental in making them into "founders of
modern capitalism" (p. vii of the German original) the vast
work of collecting facts on Jewish participation in the trading, colonial and financial enterprises of the early modern
age is almost useless.

Sombart acknowledges that his interest in Jewish law and
Jewish religion was evoked by Max Weber's hypothesis on
the relation between the Puritan ethic and the growth of
capitalism. Sombart makes the astounding discovery that
"those parts of the Puritan dogma which appear to be of
real importance for the formation of the spirit of capitalism,
are borrowed from the realm of ideas of the Jewish religion"
(p. v of the German original). His fundamental thesis, therefore, is that the impersonal, rational, "materialistic commercialism" characteristic of the capitalist spirit can be traced
back to Jewish religion and philosophy, as one of its indispensable sources.

The full acceptance of Sombart's reasoning ultimately depends upon our agreement on the determining role assigned
by him to the "spirit of capitalism" and capitalist rationality
in the development of modern industrialism. But such an
assessment would have to question not only *The Jews and
Modern Capitalism*, but also the logic of Sombart's entire
work and to some extent that of Max Weber and others as
well. For the sake of argument (although noting that Marxian criticism takes another view), let us grant that the role
assigned by Sombart to capitalist rationality, accountability,
and related character traits, is correct.

In his efforts to find elements favorable to the formation
of the capitalist spirit Sombart examines various aspects of
Jewish law and religion and brings to bear, wherever appro-
priate, rules of behavior and tenets of conduct drawn from a
multitude of sources. But already here his defective knowledge of Hebrew and of adequate sources makes him miss
some important pieces of evidence. The medieval Jews (just
as the gentiles) had an abundance of "moralities" and books
of conduct. Although the precepts enunciated in these works
do not have "binding" character (such as, for example, passages in the Pentateuch) they provide invaluable insights

into the actual standards of conduct and, particularly, economic behavior of medieval Jews. Sombart ignores these writings completely, and, in general, rejects all sources, except the canonical books of the Bible, the Talmud, and three medieval codes, by Maimonides (1135-1204), Asher ben Yehiel (ca. 1250-1327), and Joseph Caro (1488-1575). He arrives at the conclusion that the Jewish religion is essentially rationalistic and almost entirely devoid of elements of mysticism. But Sombart's view is untenable; not only does he underestimate the profoundly mystical character of the Cabbala, he misinterprets the deep penetration of mysticism in eastern Chassidism. Moreover Sombart attributes to the literate Jew who has learned to read and interpret the Talmud a rationalism which is entirely foreign to him. This notion is a product of Sombart's "rationalistic capitalist" bias rather than of any sound inference from the Jewish sources. For even to the literate Jew the binding power of the law does not consist in his rational acceptance of its rules, but in his piety and almost child-like belief in the truth of his religion and the wisdom of his God. Julius Guttmann in particular does not tire of pointing out that mystical traits are not foreign to later Judaism, and he refers above all to the writings of Philo, Solomon ibn Gabirol, Judah Halevi, and more recently, Martin Buber.[1] Even that great rationalist, Spinoza, is not quite free from lapses into mysticism.

Even less tenable than Sombart's view of the paucity of mystical elements in later Jewish theology and philosophy, is his theory of the contractual "quasi-commercial" relationship to the deity. Guttmann, Güdemann, Hoffmann, and Feuchtwanger deny, in particular, Sombart's analysis of the

---

[1] Julius Guttmann, "Die Juden und das Wirtschaftsleben," *Archiv für Sozialwissenschaft und Sozialpolitik,* XXXVI (1913), 175 ff; other critics of the points raised in this and the following paragraphs are M. Güdemann, "Die Juden und das Wirtschaftsleben," *Monatsschrift für Geschichte und Wissenschaft des Judentums,* LV (1911), 257-275; Moses Hoffmann, *Judentum und Kapitalismus,* Berlin, 1912; Ludwig Feuchtwanger, "Die Juden und das Wirtschaftsleben," *Jahrbuch für Gesetzgebung, Verwaltung und Volkswirtschaft,* XXXV (1911), 1436 ff.

accounting of sins. On the one hand they point to the fact that Sombart uses only that part of the evidence which supports his thesis, and omits other elements of Jewish doctrine, notably the ritual of the Day of Atonement, which tends to contradict his theory; on the other hand, they adduce evidence from Catholic and Protestant writers alike who express a similar balancing of sins against virtues to that found by Sombart in the Jewish religion.

Similarly, Sombart's argument on the commercial acumen of the Jewish rabbis is based on a misunderstanding of the role of the rabbi in Jewish culture. The rabbi, as is well known, was (and is) not a priest, but a teacher. In this capacity he had to familiarize himself with all aspects of law and the rules of daily commercial and personal intercourse of the members of his community. But the wisdom of a "good" rabbi extended far beyond his knowledge of the rules of trade and commercial equity. The characteristic most appreciated in a rabbi was not his knowledge of and acumen in matters of money, credit, and commerce, but his wisdom and understanding of *all* phases of life; this included technological questions (agriculture and crafts) as well as human relations (family problems, education, rules of communal propriety), etc.

I have drawn attention only to a few important aspects of Jewish religion which were ignored or missed by Sombart. But more important than his interpretation of certain rabbinical rules or certain elements of the "spirit" of Jewish philosophy is Sombart's disregard of the impact of cultural tradition on the one hand and the effects of acculturation on the other. Jewish law in its primitive form, especially as laid down in the earlier parts of the Pentateuch (chiefly Exodus, Numbers, and parts of Leviticus) was the law of a people living on a primitive level of economic development. It was the law of a group of tribes engaged chiefly in cattle and sheep herding and, to some extent, agriculture. Most passages referred to by Sombart originated at a time when the Jews had ceased to have a common homeland and were scattered over the face of the ancient world. The old rules and regulations applicable primarily to a community of small peasants had to be applied to the economic relations of a people that was found chiefly in urban centers, that had lost its country of origin and that was in constant intercourse with peoples whose religion, language, and entire set of customs were foreign to the Jews. Thus the later parts of Talmudic law, as well as medieval Jewish codices and commentaries on the law, attempt to achieve a double aim. On the one hand they endeavor to maintain the purity and simplicity of ancient Hebrew legal and religious rules and practices in as complete a fashion as possible. On the other hand they seek the avenues by which Jews can make the adjustments necessary to their changed economic situation and their role as a pariah people with the least infringement of the duties imposed upon them by the divine word in the Bible. It was inevitable in this process for many legal precepts arising outside of traditional Jewish legal philosophy to be adopted and incorporated so that to a later generation some of them might appear as autochthonous. Thus it is correct to regard the Jews as carriers of parts of ancient culture into more modern times; but the same can be said of the Arabs, various monastic orders, and the citizens of Venice, Genoa and other Mediterranean towns who transmitted ancient economic precepts, some of which show resemblance to capitalist maxims, to the modern period and who constantly modified and adapted them to the needs of changing economic life.

The history of usury is an example of this process. The persistence in Jewish law of the prohibition of taking usury from one's brother is based on the fundamentally binding force attributed to the prescription of Deuteronomy. The prohibition was gradually relaxed among Jews, as well as among gentiles. The relaxation of the prohibition to take usury—in the face of opposing legal and religious sanctions—was not based primarily on factors in Jewish law or commercial relations which loosened the strictness of the prohibitions, but on the objective fact of the gradual development of economic relations which made the taking of interest an indispensable factor in the further growth of commerce and production. To these factors must be added for the Jews in particular, the fact that they experienced keenly the impact of a foreign culture in which they felt themselves alienated and to whose hostility they were almost constantly exposed.

This impact of external circumstances as well as the tight interlacing of traditional Jewish cultural elements with borrowed foreign ones brought about a conflict in Jewish economic practice and the economic views of Jewish philosophers. Maimonides went so far as to interpret the permissive regulation of Deuteronomy to take interests from strangers (gentiles) as an imperative prescription. This view was repudiated by others, some of whom contended that the lending activities of Jews to gentiles should be tolerated only to a strictly limited extent.[2] Jewish medieval casuistry was profuse on this as well as other economic questions, but the wide divergence of opinions (and practices) is only an expression of the internal conflict in which medieval Jewish communities lived. It is beyond doubt that this situation, which was clearly the outcome of the prolonged pariah existence of the Jews, exercised a profound influence on the personality structure of medieval Jews. Hence the rationalism and "chaffering" spirit of medieval Jews was the expression of their personalities in an environment which strictly limited and rigorously circumscribed their activity. The interrelations between Jewish religion, Jewish personality structure, and Jewish "racial" characteristics is a point to which I shall come back later.

Sombart's explanation of the development of Jewish "rationalism" and "impersonal commercialism" thus confounds cause and effect. Not the legal philosophy or the religious rationalism of Judaism were responsible factors for the development of capitalism, but the growth of opportunities for gain from commercial and financial transactions, the need to

---

[2] Cf. Benjamin N. Nelson, *The Idea of Usury: From Tribal Brotherhood to Universal Otherhood*, Princeton, 1949, pp. xvi-xvii. My discussion in this and the preceding paragraphs owes much to this excellent study.

adapt to a foreign hostile world—after the warm personal bonds of the brotherhood of the Jewish tribes had been broken—modified Jewish law and religious practice in such a way as to make them a fertile field for the development of the capitalist spirit. Not the Jews as they were made capitalism, but capitalism made the Jews what they are.

We have found that the fundamental socio-historical hypothesis of Sombart can by no means be regarded as proven, or even as plausible. Yet even his factual account of the part played by Jews in the growth of capitalism is subject to severe criticism. The main objection against Sombart's historical reconstructions is that they are made often not on the basis of carefully checked factual sources, but that they are "mental pictures" (p. 63) of Sombart's imagination. In other words, instead of describing what did happen, he explains what he supposes might or must have happened. In what follows I propose to give a few examples of this method and the errors to which it leads.

Sombart's major thesis is that the shift of the commercial center of the Western world from the Mediterranean basin to Antwerp, and later to Holland, was in no mean degree a consequence of the expulsion of the Jews from Spain, and the later limitation of Jewish and Marrano* settlement in Antwerp. He contends that the economic importance of the Jews for the countries to which they migrated was their active participation in (and their virtual monopoly of) the trade with the Levant, their leadership in Dutch colonial enterprises, and their role as money lenders and financial administrators to princes. The latter role particularly was instrumental in aiding the rise of the modern centralized state, a condition regarded by Sombart as an indispensable basis on which a capitalistic economy can be built (Chapters 1-5). Sombart is probably on firmest ground with respect to the role of the Jews in the development of centralized states. His findings on this point have been supplemented by later researches, notably the studies of Max Grunwald on the

---

* Appears as "Maranno" throughout text.—PUBLISHER'S NOTE.

Austrian Jews, of Felix Priebatsch on the Jews in western Germany, of Paul Sundheimer on the Bavarian Jews and of Selma Stern on the Jews in Prussia.[3] But even then it should be noted that these studies as well as most of Sombart's examples deal primarily with the late seventeenth and early eighteenth century, a period following the decline of the great financial and commercial houses of the Fugger, the Welser, the Höchstetter, and others. The services of these non-Jewish financiers to the most powerful and most absolute monarchs of their day are well known. Sombart and his epigones discuss the period after the Thirty-Years' War, a time when the financial resources of most German states were at rock-bottom, and when the princes were inclined therefore to make concessions to and gain support from any group in a position to ease their financial stringency. By this time the issue of territorial centralization versus local municipal autonomy had long been settled. So, while the claim can be made that Jewish financiers in the late seventeenth and early eighteenth centuries contributed to the *stability* of several centralized territorial— i.e., modern absolutist—states, the fact of centralization and the elimination of prosperous and economically powerful free cities which might challenge the princes was accomplished in the sixteenth and early seventeenth centuries, when the German princes depended not on Jews but on the Christian merchants of Augsburg, Frankfurt, Nuremberg, etc.

Sombart's claims regarding the importance of Jewish migration to Antwerp and Holland, the participation of the Jews in colonial enterprises, and the importance of the Jewish monopoly in the Levantine trade are also quite exaggerated. Felix Rachfahl, who did research in this field, argues that the Levantine trade of Holland in the seventeenth century

[3] Max Grunwald, [*History of the Jews in*] *Vienna*, Philadelphia, 1936, esp. pp. 75 ff.; Felix Priebatsch, "Die Judenpolitik des fürstlichen Absolutismus im 17. und 18. Jahrhundert," in *Forschungen und Versuche zur Geschichte des Mittelalters und der Neuzeit; Festschrift Dietrich Schäfer zum 70 Geburtstag, Jena, 1915, pp. 564-651; Paul Sundheimer, "Die jüdische Hochfinanz und der bayrische Staat im 18 Jahrhundert," *Finanzarchiv*, XLI (1924), 1-44 and 259-308; Selma Stern, *Der preussische Staat und die Juden*, Berlin, 1925.

did not exceed three per cent of the total Dutch trade.[4] Actually, if Sombart had consulted the book by Wätjen, which was available to him, he would have found that the Jewish monopoly in the Dutch trade to the Mediterranean was non-existent and that Rachfahl was correct in asserting that the claim that the Jews of Holland were the chief promoters of Dutch trade was "bragging on the part of [the Jewish historians] Graetz and Koenen."[5] This is a clear instance where Sombart was more concerned with painting a "mental picture" than with the actual facts.

Other instances of this predilection for fiction rather than fact occur in Sombart's analysis of Jewish participation and leadership in Dutch colonial enterprise. In one instance he claims on the basis of their portraits that several directors of the East India Company were Jews (Chapter 4). Since a Dutch law, in effect until 1657, barred Jews from becoming company directors, and several portraits to which Sombart apparently refers date from an earlier time, the evidence is less than conclusive. With a similar high-handed disregard for the elementary laws of evidence Sombart "proves" the role of Jewish leadership in Dutch colonial enterprise by arguing that Jan Pieterszoon Coen, Governor General of the East India Company between 1617 and 1629, was a Jew because Coen and Cohn are the same name (Chapter 4). It does not occur to Sombart to check Coen's family history. If he had done this, he would have found that Coen was a name adopted by Jan Pieterszoon, and that therefore Rachfahl's explanation relating the name Coen to the German Conrad, or Wätjen's assertion that Coen derives from the honorific surname "kühn" (valiant), are infinitely more likely

[4] Felix Rachfahl, "Das Judentum und die Genesis des modernen Kapitalismus," *Preussische Jahrbücher,* CXLVIII (1912), pp. 33 and 51.
[5] Hermann Wätjen, *Die Niederländer im Mittelmeergebiet zur Zeit ihrer höchsten Machtstellung,* Berlin, 1909; Rachfahl, *op. cit.,* p. 52. See also Herbert I. Bloom, *The Economic Activities of the Jews of Amsterdam in the Seventeenth and Eighteenth Centuries,* Williamsport, Penna., 1937, esp. pp. 219-21.

explanations than Sombart's guess.[6] For a historian who is challenging an accepted theory these "impressionistic" procedures were gravely inadequate. In fact, as the researches of Wätjen and others show, the part played by Jews in Dutch colonial enterprise was no more spectacular than their participation in the Levantine trade or in the development of Holland to the leading trading nation of the world. Certainly the Jews took part in these trading enterprises, and the relative share of Jewish capital in Dutch trade and colonial enterprises, notably from the late seventeenth century on, was far from small. This point has never been denied but it is a far cry from this statement to the sweeping new theory that the Jews *originated* the development of capitalism in Holland.

Finally we come to the central proposition of Sombart's historical analysis, that capitalist procedures, capitalist modes of enterprise, life, and thinking were carried northwards by the Jews from Spain, Portugal, and Italy to Antwerp and Holland, and ultimately to England. The weakness of this theory was already pointed out by early reviewers of Sombart's book, notably by Rachfahl, Oppenheimer, Feuchtwanger, and Guttmann.[7] More recent work, notably that of Pirenne, Strieder, and Tawney, has completely exploded the theory. These men either built on the hypothesis first enunciated by Max Weber in his *Protestant Ethic and the Spirit of Capitalism,* or proceeding independently arrived at an explanation of the origin and development of capitalism in northwestern Europe without appeal to the role assigned to the Jews by Sombart.[8]

[6] Rachfahl, *op. cit.,* p. 56; Hermann Wätjen, "Das Judentum und die Aufänge der modernen Kolonisation," *Vierteljahrschrift für Sozial-und Wirtschaftsgeschichte,* XI (1913), p. 354.

[7] Rachfahl, *op. cit.,* passim, esp. pp. 29 ff.; Franz Oppenheimer, "Die Juden und das Wirtschaftsleben," *Die Neue Rundschau,* XXII (1911), 889 ff.; Feuchtwanger, *op. cit.,* 1436 ff.; Guttmann, *op. cit.,* p. 155.

[8] Henri Pirenne, *Economic and Social History of Medieval Europe,* New York, n.d. [1937], and other works; R. H. Tawney, *Religion and the Rise of Capitalism,* London, 1926; Jakob Strieder, *Studien zur Geschichte kapitalistischer Organisationsformen,* Leipzig, 1925.

Interspersed with Sombart's "impressionistic" accounts are occasional masterful expositions of Jewish participation in important areas of modern western economic development. Some of the more successful are the discussion of the part played by Jews in the trade of luxury goods and precious stones (Chapter 3); the analysis of Jewish participation in the colonization of Latin America (Chapter 4); the development of markets for negotiable instruments and Jewish participation in the development of stock exchanges (Chapter 6); the discussion of the pariah position of the Jews and the resulting need for keeping their funds as liquid as possible (Chapter 10).

Moreover, in the course of his analysis Sombart raises a host of other fascinating problems, some of which are of absorbing interest. I should like to draw attention particularly to his analysis of the impact of Jewish religious teaching on sexual asceticism and its connection with Jewish preoccupation with money matters. Without any knowledge of the works of Sigmund Freud, Sombart here expressed views which call for further investigation and clarification by men trained in psychoanalytic or psychodiagnostic techniques of character study. It is significant that Guttmann—also without benefit of psychoanalytic insights—in spite of his severe criticism of many of Sombart's facts and interpretations—arrives at the statement that "the only element in the Jewish religion favorable to a capitalist style of economic action is the formation of a formal personality structure, which through rationalization of the style of life enables its possessor to engage in capitalist activity."[9] This admission is of great interest, for it shows that Sombart's theory of the socio-psychological impact of the Jewish religious ethic has definite merit if used with caution. Unfortunately Sombart overstates his case and Guttmann inadvertently follows him by conceding the possibility of a peculiarly Jewish character, *unchanged over the ages;* in other words, he admits one of the central points of Sombart's entire theoretical structure, the existence of peculiar "racially" determined mental predisposi-

[9] Guttmann, *op. cit.,* p. 198.

tions of the Jews. This racial theory is essentially a "romantic" theory, that is, it is founded on imaginary speculation rather than empirical evidence; it does not explain Jewish life and Jewish destiny at *a given time* on the basis of the predominant character orientation of the Jews participating in the process of change under study. Sombart could speak of Jewish "essence" (jüdisches Wesen), because he considered the racial hypothesis as valid. But once it is recognized that the peculiarities of any particular group of Jews at any particular time can be interpreted in terms of the prevailing character orientation of the members of the group, any racial interpretation becomes manifestly defective. For character orientation is, as I have pointed out already, to a large extent a function of the cultural environment. The most constant element in medieval Jewish culture was, admittedly, religion. But religion—even in a people as closely bound to "the book" as the Jews—is only one, albeit an important factor in cultural life. If personality structure is, at least in part, a function of culture then the variables exerting an influence on the formation of a Jewish "national character" appear again hopelessly confounded. For in spite of segregation, in spite of the ghetto, and the yellow patch on their coats, the very fact that the Jews for centuries continued to exist as a pariah people made them accept and integrate into their culture elements that were not indigenous with them. And the Jewish character, if it could be discovered, would turn out to combine, as time went on, elements stemming from Hellenistic, Roman, Arab, Germanic, Turkish, and even Slavonic sources, inseparably fused with the survivals from the Israelite or Canaanite culture some of whose intellectual aspects are distilled in the Old Testament and the other sacred books of the Jews. The history of a group or a people cannot be retraced. Once the bonds of the tribal brotherhood of the Jews were broken by the Babylonian exile, once the soil on which the Temple of Jerusalem had stood was ploughed over by Titus' legionnaires, the long diaspora began which reshaped the Jews fundamentally, since they became full-fledged members of what Benjamin Nelson has recently called the Universal Otherhood. And the Jews who wandered from country to country, from continent to continent, were always different Jews. The Jews who flew from Spain and Portugal in the fifteenth and sixteenth centuries were as different from the Jewish refugees from Hitler Germany as these latter were from the Russian Jews who became the first pioneers in modern Palestine. Hence all the talk by Sombart, as well as by others, of a Jewish "race" distinguished by peculiar mental or physical characteristics is sheer nonsense, and what is worse, a dangerous nonsense as the sad experience with antisemitic movements has so clearly shown.

What misled Sombart and others was the external similarity of Jewish destiny for so many centuries. They lived almost permanently as a pariah people. But although this kind of existence presents external similarities, the actual conditions under which the Jews lived among the Romans, in feudal Europe, and finally in modern capitalist countries differ greatly. The very migrations of the Jews were an important factor in the changes which their national character was undergoing. Hardly a generation of Jews escaped the harrowing experience of participating in some process of violent social change. In such circumstances personality structures undergo rapid and irretrievable changes. One can point to clear instances of this from the experience of other peoples as well as from recent Jewish history. The wretched and half-starved Irish peasant became within a generation a pioneer in America and Australia; the son of a cottager of "Merrie England" developed into a wage-slave or an ironmaster; and the children of timid, cowed orthodox Jews whose most valued aspiration was eminence in peaceful scholarship, braved the assault of the united Arab armies. Surely it cannot be denied that such profound changes in personality structure from one generation to the next were conditioned by the imperative need of adjustment to a new environment. Similarly, by their migration from feudal Spain to "capitalist" Antwerp and Holland, Jewish personality patterns changed. In a generation or two the Jews developed the faculties which enabled them to carry on a successful existence in the new environment. And so we come to the same result by way of the "psychological" history of the Jews, which we reached by way of their intellectual history: not the Jews as they were made capitalism, but capitalism made the Jews what they are!

Thus we come to the conclusion that much of Sombart's *The Jews and Modern Capitalism* must be rejected or severely modified. His historical facts are often faulty or imaginary; his analysis based on them is often methodologically assailable; his social theory is defective, and his interpretation of Jewish religion, law, and philosophy deduced in considerable part from biased and incomplete sources; last but not least his views of national character and the "racial" characteristics of Jews are derived from untenable theories or purely romantic speculation.

Why then print a new edition of the book? Two simple answers come to mind. Firstly, because in spite of its defects the work poses often in sharp and unusually keen and penetrating manner all the crucial questions of the role played by the Jews not merely in the development of capitalism but of human civilization in general. And secondly because *The Jews and Modern Capitalism* is a classic which inaugurated a new era in the study of Jewish social relations. As such it shares the role of almost all—major and minor—classics. The fate of *The Jews and Modern Capitalism* is the same as that of many influential works in social science. Works of this kind open up new avenues of research, and in this process many theories contained in the path-breaking work are amended or rejected. But later generations of scholars will only appreciate the significance of a new approach in social science fully if they do not content themselves with the latest results in a field but if they descend to the original sources. For this reason, perhaps more than for any other, *The Jews and Modern Capitalism* will be required reading for a long time to come.

PART I

THE CONTRIBUTION OF THE JEWS TO MODERN ECONOMIC LIFE

Chapter 1

Introductory

Two POSSIBLE METHODS may be used to discover to what extent any group of people participated in a particular form of economic organization. One is the statistical; the other may be termed the genetic.

By means of the first we endeavour to ascertain the actual number of persons taking part in some economic activity—say, those who establish trade with a particular country, or who found any given industry—and then we calculate what percentage is represented by the members of the group in which we happen to be interested. There is no doubt that the statistical method has many advantages. A pretty clear conception of the relative importance for any branch of commerce of, let us say, foreigners or Jews, is at once evolved if we are able to show by actual figures that 50 or 75 per cent. of all the persons engaged in that branch belong to either the first or the second category named. More especially is this apparent when statistical information is forthcoming, not only as to the number of persons but also concerning other or more striking economic factors—*e.g.*, the amount of paid-up capital, the quantity of the commodities produced, the size of the turnover, and so forth. It will be useful, therefore, to adopt the statistical method in questions such as the one we have set ourselves. But at the same time it will soon become evident that by its aid alone the complete solution cannot be found. In the first place, even the best statistics do not tell us everything; nay, often the most important aspect of what we are trying to discover is omitted. Statistics are silent as to the dynamic effects which strong individualities produce in economic, as indeed in all human life—effects which have consequences reaching far beyond the limits of their immediate surroundings. Their actual importance for the general tendency of any particular develop-

27

ment is greater far than any set of figures can reveal. Therefore the statistical method must be supplemented by some other.

But more than this. The statistical method, owing to lack of information, cannot always be utilized. It is indeed a lucky accident that we possess figures recording the number of those engaged in any industry or trade, and showing their comparative relation to the rest of the population. But a statistical study of this kind, on a large scale, is really only a possibility for modern and future times. Even then the path of the investigator is beset by difficulties. Still, a careful examination of various sources, including the assessments made by Jewish communities on their members, may lead to fruitful results. I hope that this book will give an impetus to such studies, of which, at the present time, there is only one that is really useful—the enquiry of Sigmund Mayr, of Vienna.

When all is said, therefore, the other method (the genetic), to which I have already alluded, must be used to supplement the results of statistics. What is this method? We wish to discover to what extent a group of people (the Jews) influence or have influenced the form and development of modern economic life—to discover, that is, their qualitative or, as I have already called it, their dynamic importance. We can do this best of all by enquiring whether certain characteristics that mark our modern economic life were given their first form by Jews, *i.e.*, either that some particular form of organization was first introduced by the Jews, or that some well-known business principles, now accepted on all hands as fundamental, are specific expressions of the Jewish spirit. This of necessity demands that the history of the factors in economic development should be traced to their earliest beginnings. In other words, we must study the childhood of the modern capitalistic system, or, at any rate, the age in which it received its modern form. But not the childhood only: its whole history must be considered. For throughout, down to these very days, new elements are constantly entering the fabric of capitalism and changes appear in its characteristics. Wherever such are noted our aim must be to discover to whose influence they are due. Often enough this will not be easy; sometimes it will even be impossible; and scientific imagination must come to the aid of the scholar.

Another point should not be overlooked. In many cases the people who are responsible for a fundamental idea or innovation in economic life are not always the inventors (using that word in its narrowest meaning). It has often been asserted that the Jews have no inventive powers; that not only technical but also economic discoveries were made by non-Jews alone, and that the Jews have always been able cleverly to utilize the ideas of others. I dissent from this general view in its entirety. We meet with Jewish inventors in the sphere of technical science, and certainly in that of economics, as I hope to show in this work. But even if the assertion which we have mentioned were true, it would prove nothing against the view that Jews have given certain aspects of economic life the specific features they bear. In the economic world it is not so much the inventors that matter as those who are able to apply the inventions: not those who conceive ideas (*e.g.*, the hire-purchase system) as those who can utilize them in everyday life.

Before proceeding to the problem before us—the share of the Jews in the work of building up our modern capitalistic system—we must mention one other point of importance. In a specialized study of this kind Jewish influence may appear larger than it actually was. That is in the nature of our study, where the whole problem is looked at from only one point of view. If we were enquiring into the influence of mechanical inventions on modern economic life the same would apply: in a monograph that influence would tend to appear larger than it really was. I mention this point, obvious though it is, lest it be said that I have exaggerated the part played by the Jews. There were undoubtedly a thousand and one other causes that helped to make the economic system of our time what it is. Without the discovery of America and its silver treasures, without the mechanical inventions of technical science, without the ethnical peculiarities of modern European nations and their vicissitudes, capitalism would have been as impossible as without the Jews.

In the long story of capitalism, Jewish influence forms but one chapter. Its relative importance to the others I shall show in the new edition of my *Modern Capitalism*, which I hope to have ready before long.

This *caveat* will, I trust, help the general reader to a proper appreciation of the influence of Jews on modern economic life. But it must be taken in conjunction with another. If on the one hand we are to make some allowance, should our studies apparently tend to give Jews a preponderating weight in economic affairs, on the other hand, their contribution is very often even larger than we are led to believe. For our researches can deal only with one portion of the problem, seeing that all the material is not available. Who to-day knows anything definite about the individuals, or groups, who founded this or that industry, established this or that branch of commerce, first adopted this or that business principle? And even where we are able to name these pioneers with certainty, there comes the further question, were they Jews or not?

Jews—that is to say, members of the people who profess the Jewish faith. And I need hardly add that although in this definition I purposely leave out any reference to race characteristics, it yet includes those Jews who have withdrawn from their religious community, and even descendants of such, seeing that historically they remain Jews. This must be borne in mind, for when we are determining the influence of the Jew on modern economic life, again and again men appear on the scene as Christians, who in reality are Jews. They or their fathers were baptized, that is all. The assumption that many Jews in all ages changed their faith is not far fetched. We hear of cases from the earliest Middle Ages; in Italy, in the 7th and 8th centuries; at the same period in Spain and in the Merovingian kingdoms; and from that time to this we find them among all Christian nations. In the last third of the 19th century, indeed, wholesale baptisms constantly occurred. But we have reliable figures for the last two or three decades only, and I am therefore inclined to doubt the statement of Jacob Fromer that towards the end of the twenties in last century something like half the Jews of Berlin had gone over to Christianity.[1] Equally improbable is the view of Dr. Werner, Rabbi in Munich, who, in a paper which he recently read, stated that altogether 120,000 Jews have been baptized in Berlin. The most reliable figures we have are all against such a likelihood. According to these, it was in the nineties that apostasy on a large scale first showed itself, and even then the highest annual percentage never exceeded 1.28 (in 1905), while the average percentage per annum (since 1895) was 1. Nevertheless, the number of Jews in Berlin who from 1873 to 1906 went over to Christianity was not small; their total was 1869 precisely.[2]

The tendency to apostasy is stronger among Austrian Jews, especially among those of Vienna. At the present time, between five and six hundred Jews in that city renounce their faith every year, and from 1868 to 1903 there have been no less than 9085. The process grows apace; in the years 1868 to 1879 there was on an average one baptism annually for every 1200 Jews; in the period 1880 to 1889 it was one for 420-430 Jews; while between 1890 and 1903 it had reached one for every 260-270.[3]

But the renegade Jews are not the only group whose influence on the economic development of our time it is difficult to estimate. There are others to which the same applies. I am not thinking of the Jewesses who married into Christian families, and who, though they thus ceased to be Jewish, at any rate in name, must nevertheless have retained their Jewish characteristics. The people I have in mind are the crypto-Jews, who played so important a part in history, and whom we encounter in every century. In some periods they formed a very large section of Jewry. But their non-Jewish pose was so admirably sustained that among their contemporaries they passed as Christians or Mohammedans. We are told, for example, of the Jews of the South of France in the 15th and 16th centuries, who came originally from Spain and Portugal (and the description applies to the Marannos everywhere): "They practised all the outward forms of

Catholicism; their births, marriages and deaths were entered on the registers of the church, and they received the sacraments of baptism, marriage and extreme unction. Some even took orders and became priests."[4] No wonder then that they do not appear as Jews in the reports of commercial enterprises, industrial undertakings and so forth. Some historians even to-day speak in admiring phrase of the beneficial influence of Spanish or Portuguese "immigrants." So skilfully did the crypto-Jews hide their racial origin that specialists in the field of Jewish history are still in doubt as to whether a certain family was Jewish or not.[5] In those cases where they adopted Christian names, the uncertainty is even greater. There must have been a large number of Jews among the Protestant refugees in the 17th century. General reasons would warrant this assumption, but when we take into consideration the numerous Jewish names found among the Huguenots the probability is strong indeed.[6]

Finally, our enquiries will not be able to take any account of all those Jews who, prior to 1848, took an active part in the economic life of their time, but who were unknown to the authorities. The laws forbade Jews to exercise their callings. They were therefore compelled to do so, either under cover of some fictitious Christian person or under the protection of a "privileged" Jew, or they were forced to resort to some other trick in order to circumvent the law. Reliable authorities are of opinion that the number of Jews who in many a town lived secretly in this way must have been exceedingly large. In the forties of last century, for example, it is said that no less than 12,000 Jews, at a moderate estimate, were to be found in Vienna. The wholesale textile trade was at that time already in their hands, and entire districts in the centre of the city were full of Jewish shops. But the official list of traders of 1845 contained in an appendix the names of only sixty-three Jews, who were described as "tolerated Jewish traders," and these were allowed to deal only in a limited number of articles.[7]

But enough. My point was to show that, for many and various reasons, the number of Jews of whom we hear is less than those who actually existed. The reader should therefore bear in mind that the contribution of the Jews to the fabric of modern economic life will, of necessity, appear smaller than it was in reality.

What that contribution was we shall now proceed to show.

Chapter 2

The Shifting of the Centre of Economic Life since the Sixteenth Century

ONE OF THE MOST IMPORTANT FACTS in the growth of modern economic life is the removal of the centre of economic activity from the nations of Southern Europe—the Italians, Spaniards and Portuguese, with whom must also be reckoned some South German lands—to those of the North-West—the Dutch, the French, the English and the North Germans. The epoch-making event in the process was Holland's sudden rise to prosperity, and this was the impetus for the development of the economic possibilities of France and England. All through the 17th century the philosophic speculators and the practical politicians among the nations of North-Western Europe had but one aim: to imitate Holland in commerce, in industry, in shipping and in colonization.

The most ludicrous explanations of this well-known fact have been suggested by historians. It has been said, for example, that the cause which led to the economic decline of Spain and Portugal and of the Italian and South German city states was the discovery of America and of the new route to the East Indies; that the same cause lessened the volume of the commerce of the Levant, and therefore undermined the position of the Italian commercial cities which depended upon it. But this explanation is not in any way satisfactory. In the first place, Levantine commerce maintained its pre-eminence throughout the whole of the 17th and 18th centuries, and during this period the prosperity of the maritime cities in the South of France, as well as that of Hamburg, was very closely bound up with it. In the second place, a number of Italian towns, Venice among them, which in the 17th century lost all their importance, participated to a large extent in the trade of the Levant in the 16th century, and that despite the neglect of the trade route. It is a little difficult to understand why the nations which had played a leading part until the 15th century—the Italians, the Spaniards, the Portuguese—should have suffered in the least because of the new commercial relations with America and the East Indies, or why they should have been placed at any disadvantage by their geographical position as compared with that of the French, the English or the Dutch. As though the way from Genoa to America or the West Indies were not the same as from Amsterdam or London or Hamburg! As though the Spanish and Portuguese ports were not the nearest to the new lands—lands which had been discovered by Italians and Portuguese, and had been taken possession of by the Portuguese and the Spaniards!

Equally unconvincing is another reason which is often given. It is asserted that the countries of North-Western Europe were strong consolidated states, while Germany and Italy were disunited, and accordingly the former were able to take up a stronger position than the latter. Here, too, we ask in wonder whether the powerful Queen of the Adriatic was a weaker state in the 16th century than the Seven Provinces in the 17th? And did not the empire of Philip II excel all the kingdoms of his time in power and renown? Why was it, moreover, that, although Germany was in a state of political disruption, certain of its cities, like Hamburg or Frankfort-on-the-Main, reached a high degree of development in the 17th and 18th centuries, such as few French or English cities could rival?

This is not the place to go into the question in all its many-sidedness. A number of causes contributed to bring about the results we have mentioned. But from the point of view of our problem one possibility should not be passed over which, in my opinion, deserves most serious consideration, and which, so far as I know, has not yet been thought of. Cannot we bring into connexion the shifting of the economic centre from Southern to Northern Europe with the wanderings of the Jews? The mere suggestion at once throws a flood of light on the events of those days, hitherto shrouded in semi-darkness. It is indeed surprising that the parallelism has not before been observed between Jewish wanderings and settlement on the one hand, and the economic vicissitudes of the different peoples and states on the other. Israel passes over Europe like the sun: at its coming new life bursts forth; at its going all falls into decay. A short résumé of the changing fortunes of the Jewish people since the 15th century will lend support to this contention.

The first event to be recalled, an event of world-wide import, is the expulsion of the Jews from Spain (1492) and from Portugal (1495 and 1497). It should never be forgotten that on the day before Columbus set sail from Palos to discover America (August 3, 1492) 300,000 Jews are said to have emigrated from Spain to Navarre, France, Portugal and the East; nor that, in the years during which Vasco da Gama searched for and found the sea-passage to the East Indies, the Jews were driven from other parts of the Pyrenean Peninsula.[1]

It was by a remarkable stroke of fate that these two occurrences, equally portentous in their significance—the opening-up of new continents and the mightiest upheavals in the distribution of the Jewish people—should have coincided. But the expulsion of the Jews from the Pyrenean Peninsula did not altogether put an end to their history there. Numerous Jews remained behind as pseudo-Christians (Marannos), and it was only as the Inquisition, from the days of Philip II onwards, became more and more relentless that these Jews were forced to leave the land of their birth.[2] During the centuries that followed, and especially towards the end of the 16th, the Spanish and Portuguese Jews settled in other countries. It was during this period that the doom of the economic prosperity of the Pyrenean Peninsula was sealed.

With the 15th century came the expulsion of the Jews from the German commercial cities—from Cologne (1424-5), from Augsburg (1439-40), from Strassburg (1438), from Erfurt (1458), from Nuremberg (1498-9), from Ulm (1499), and from Ratisbon (1519).

The same fate overtook them in the 16th century in a

number of Italian cities. They were driven from Sicily (1492), from Naples (1540-1), from Genoa and from Venice (1550). Here also economic decline and Jewish emigration coincided in point of time.

On the other hand, the rise to economic importance, in some cases quite unexpectedly, of the countries and towns whither the refugees fled, must be dated from the first appearance of the Spanish Jews. A good example is that of Leghorn,[3] one of the few Italian cities which enjoyed economic prosperity in the 16th century. Now Leghorn was the goal of most of the exiles who made for Italy. In Germany it was Hamburg and Frankfort[4] that admitted the Jewish settlers. And remarkable to relate, a keen-eyed traveller in the 18th century wandering all over Germany found everywhere that the old commercial cities of the Empire, Ulm, Nuremberg, Augsburg, Mayence and Cologne, had fallen into decay, and that the only two that were able to maintain their former splendour, and indeed to add to it from day to day, were Frankfort and Hamburg.[5]

In France in the 17th and 18th centuries the rising towns were Marseilles, Bordeaux, Rouen—again the havens of refuge of the Jewish exiles.[6]

As for Holland, it is well-known that at the end of the 16th century a sudden upward development (in the capitalistic sense) took place there. The first Portuguese Marannos settled in Amsterdam in 1593, and very soon their numbers increased. The first synagogue in Amsterdam was opened in 1598, and by about the middle of the 17th century there were Jewish communities in many Dutch cities. In Amsterdam, at the beginning of the 18th century, the estimated number of Jews was 2400.[7] But even by the middle of the 17th century their intellectual influence was already marked; the writers on international law and the political philosophers speak of the ancient Hebrew commonwealth as an ideal which the Dutch constitution might well seek to emulate.[8] The Jews themselves called Amsterdam at that time their grand New Jerusalem.[9]

Many of the Dutch settlers had come from the Spanish

Netherlands, especially from Antwerp, whither they had fled on their expulsion from Spain. It is true that the proclamations of 1532 and 1539 forbade the pseudo-Christians to remain in Antwerp, but they proved ineffective. The prohibition was renewed in 1550, but this time it referred only to those who had not been domiciled for six years. But this too remained a dead letter: "the crypto-Jews are increasing from day to day." They took an active part in the struggle for freedom in which the Netherlands were engaged, and its result forced them to wander to the more northerly provinces.[10] Now it is a remarkable thing that the brief space during which Antwerp became the commercial centre and the money-market of the world should have been just that between the coming and the going of the Marannos.[11]

It was the same in England. The economic development of the country, in other words, the growth of capitalism,[12] ran parallel with the influx of Jews, mostly of Spanish and Portuguese origin.[13]

It was believed that there were no Jews in England from the time of their expulsion under Edward I (1290) until their more or less officially recognized return under Cromwell (1654-56). The best authorities on Anglo-Jewish history are now agreed that this is a mistake. There were always Jews in England; but not till the 16th century did they begin to be numerous. Already in the reign of Elizabeth many were met with, and the Queen herself had a fondness for Hebrew studies and for intercourse with Jews. Her own physician was a Jew, Rodrigo Lopez, on whom Shakespeare modelled his Shylock. Later on, as is generally known, the Jews, as a result of the efforts of Manasseh ben Israel, obtained the right of unrestricted domicile. Their numbers were increased by further streams of immigrants including, after the 18th century, Jews from Germany, until, according to the author of the *Anglia Judaica*, there were 6000 Jews in London alone in the year 1738.[14]

When all is said, however, the fact that the migration of the Jews and the economic vicissitudes of peoples were coincident events does not necessarily prove that the arrival of Jews in any land was the only cause of its rise or their departure the only cause of its decline. To assert as much would be to argue on the fallacy "post hoc, ergo propter hoc." Nor are the arguments of later historians on this subject conclusive, and therefore I will not mention any in support of my thesis.[15] But the opinions of contemporaries always, as I think, deserve attention. So I will acquaint the reader with some of them, for very often a word suffices to throw a flood of light on their age.

When the Senate of Venice, in 1550, decided to expel the Marannos and to forbid commercial intercourse with them, the Christian merchants of the city declared that it would mean their ruin and that they might as well leave Venice with the exiles, seeing that they made their living by trading with the Jews. The Jews controlled the Spanish wool trade, the trade in Spanish silk and crimsons, sugar, pepper, Indian spices and pearls. A great part of the entire export trade was carried on by Jews, who supplied the Venetians with goods to be sold on commission; and they were also bill-brokers.[16]

In England the Jews found a protector in Cromwell, who was actuated solely by considerations of an economic nature. He believed that he would need the wealthy Jewish merchants to extend the financial and commercial prosperity of the country. Nor was he blind to the usefulness of having moneyed support for the government.[17]

Like Cromwell, Colbert, the great French statesman of the 17th century, was also sympathetically inclined towards the Jews, and in my opinion it is of no small significance that these two organizers, both of whom consolidated modern European states, should have been so keenly alive to the fitness of the Jew in aiding the economic (*i.e.*, capitalistic) progress of a country. In one of his Ordinances to the Intendant of Languedoc, Colbert points out what great benefits the city of Marseilles derived from the commercial capabilities of the Jews.[18] The inhabitants of the great French trading centres in which the Jews played an important rôle were in no need of being taught the lesson; they knew it from their own experience and, accordingly, they brought all their influence to bear on keeping their Jewish fellow-citizens within their walls. Again and again we hear laudatory accounts of the Jews, more especially from the inhabitants of Bordeaux. In 1675 an army of mercenaries ravaged Bordeaux, and many of the rich Jews prepared to depart. The Town Council was terrified, and the report presented by its members is worth quoting. "The Portuguese who occupy whole streets and do considerable business have asked for their passports. They and those aliens who do a very large trade are resolved to leave; indeed, the wealthiest among them, Gaspar Gonzales and Alvares, have already departed. We are very much afraid that commerce will cease altogether."[19] A few years later the Sous-Intendant of Languedoc summed up the situation in the words "without them (the Jews) the trade of Bordeaux and of the whole province would be inevitably ruined."[20]

We have already seen how the fugitives from the Iberian Peninsula in the 16th century streamed into Antwerp, the commercial metropolis of the Spanish Netherlands. About the middle of the century, the Emperor in a decree dated July 17, 1549 withdrew the privileges which had been accorded them. Thereupon the mayor and sheriffs, as well as the Consul of the city, sent a petition to the Bishop of Arras in which they showed the obstacles in the way of carrying out the Imperial mandate. The Portuguese, they pointed out, were large undertakers; they had brought great wealth with them from the lands of their birth, and they maintained an extensive trade. "We must bear in mind," they continued, "that Antwerp has grown great gradually, and that a long space of time was needed before it could obtain possession of its commerce. Now the ruin of the city would necessarily bring with it the ruin of the land, and all this must be carefully considered before the Jews are expelled." Indeed, the mayor, Nicholas Van den Meeren, went even further in the matter. When Queen Mary of Hungary, the Regent of the Netherlands, was staying in Ruppelmonde, he paid her a visit in order to defend the cause of the New Christians, and excused the conduct of the rulers of Antwerp in not publishing the Imperial decree by informing her that it was contrary to all the best interests of the city.[21] His efforts, however, were unsuccessful, and the Jews, as we have already seen, left Antwerp for Amsterdam.

Antwerp lost no small part of its former glory by reason of the departure of the Jews, and in the 17th century especially it was realized how much they contributed to bring about material prosperity. In 1653 a committee was appointed to consider the question whether the Jews should be allowed into Antwerp, and it expressed itself on the matter in the following terms: "And as for the inconveniences which are to be feared and apprehended in the public interest—that they (the Jews) will attract to themselves all trade, that they will be guilty of a thousand frauds and tricks, and that by their usury they will devour the wealth of good Catholics—it seems to us on the contrary that by the trade which they will expand far beyond its present limits the benefit derived will be for the good of the whole land, and gold and silver will be available in greater quantities for the needs of the state."[22]

The Dutch in the 17th century required no such recommendations; they were fully alive to the gain which the Jews brought. When Manasseh ben Israel left Amsterdam on his famous mission to England, the Dutch Government became anxious; they feared lest it should be a question of transplanting the Dutch Jews to England, and they therefore instructed Neuport, their ambassador in London, to sound Manasseh as to his intentions. He reported (December 1655) that all was well, and that there was no cause for apprehension. "Manasseh ben Israel hath been to see me, and did assure me that he doth not desire anything for the Jews in Holland but only for those as sit in the Inquisition in Spain and Portugal."[23]

It is the same tale in Hamburg. In the 17th century the importance of the Jews had grown to such an extent that they were regarded as indispensable to the growth of Hamburg's prosperity. On one occasion the Senate asked that

permission should be given for synagogues to be built, otherwise, they feared, the Jews would leave Hamburg, and the
city might then be in danger of sinking to a mere village.[24]
On another occasion, in 1697, when it was suggested that
the Jews should be expelled, the merchants earnestly en-
treated the Senate for help, in order to prevent the serious
endangering of Hamburg's commerce.[25] Again, in 1733, in
a special report, now in the Archives of the Senate, we may
read: "In bill-broking, in trade with jewellery and braid and
in the manufacture of certain cloths the Jews have almost
a complete mastery, and have surpassed our own people.
In the past there was no need to take cognizance of them,
but now they are increasing in numbers. There is no section
of the great merchant class, the manufacturers and those who
supply commodities for daily needs, but the Jews form an
important element therein. They have become a necessary
evil."[26] To the callings enumerated in which the Jews took
a prominent part, we must add that of marine insurance
brokers.[27]

So much for the judgment of contemporaries. But as a
complete proof even that will not serve. We must form our
own judgment from the facts, and therefore our first aim
must be to seek these out. That means that we must find from
the original sources what contributions the Jews made to the
building-up of our modern economic life from the end of
the 15th century onward—the period, that is, when Jewish
history and general European economic progress both tended
in the same direction. We shall then also be able to state
definitely to what extent the Jews influenced the shifting of
the centre of economic life.

My own view is, as I may say in anticipation, that the
importance of the Jews was twofold. On the one hand, they
influenced the outward form of modern capitalism; on the
other, they gave expression to its inward spirit. Under the
first heading, the Jews contributed no small share in giving
to economic relations the international aspect they bear
to-day; in helping the modern state, that framework of capitalism, to become what it is; and lastly, in giving the capital-

istic organization its peculiar features, by inventing a good many details of the commercial machinery which moves the business life of to-day, and co-operating in the perfecting of others. Under the second heading, the importance of the Jews is so enormous because they, above all others, endowed economic life with its modern spirit; they seized upon the essential idea of capitalism and carried it to its fullest development.

We shall consider these points in turn, in order to obtain a proper notion of the problem. Our intention is to do no more than ask a question or two, and here and there to suggest an answer. We want merely to set the reader thinking. It will be for later research to gather sufficient material by which to judge whether, and to what extent, the views as to cause and effect here propounded have any foundation in actual fact.

Chapter 3

The Quickening of International Trade

THE TRANSFORMATION OF European commerce which has taken place since the shifting of the centre of economic activity owed a tremendous debt to the Jews. If we consider nothing but the quantity of commodities that passed through their hands, their position is unique. Exact statistics are, as I have already remarked, almost non-existent; special research may, however, bring some figures to light that will be useful. At present there is, to my knowledge, only some slight material on this head, but its value cannot be over-estimated.

It would appear that even before their formal admission into England—that is, in the first half of the 17th century—the extent of the trade in the hands of Jews totalled one-twelfth of that of the whole kingdom.[1] Unfortunately we are not told on what authority this calculation rests, but that it cannot be far from the truth is apparent from a statement in a petition of the merchants of London. The question was whether Jews should pay the duty on imports levied on foreigners. The petitioners point out that if the Jews were exempted, the Crown would sustain a loss of ten thousand pounds annually.[2]

We are remarkably well informed as to the proportion of trading done by Jews at the Leipzig fairs,[3] and as these were for a long period the centre of German commerce, we have here a standard by which to measure its intensive and extensive development. But not alone for Germany. One or two of the neighbouring countries, especially Bohemia and Poland, can also be included in the survey. From the end of the 17th century onwards we find that the Jews take an increasing share in the fairs, and all the authorities who have gone into the figures are agreed that it was the Jews who gave to the Leipzig fairs their great importance.[4]

It is only since the Easter fair of 1756 that we are able
to compare the Jewish with the Christian traders, as far as
numbers are concerned, for it is only from that date that
the Archives possess statistics of the latter. The average
number of Jews attending the Leipzig fair was as follows:—

1675-1680	416	1767-1769	995
1681-1690	489	1770-1779	1652
1691-1700	834	1780-1789	1073
1701-1710	854	1790-1799	1473
1711-1720	769	1800-1809	3370
1721-1730	899	1810-1819	4896
1731-1740	874	1820-1829	3747
1741-1748	708	1830-1839	6444

Note especially the speedy increase towards the end of the
17th and 18th centuries and also at the beginning of the
19th.

If we glance at the period 1766 to 1839, we see that the
fairs were visited annually by an average of 3185 Jews and
13,005 Christians—that is to say, the Jews form 24.49 per
cent., or nearly one-quarter of the total number of Christian
merchants. Indeed, in some years, as for example between
1810 and 1820, the Jewish visitors form 33⅓ per cent. of the
total of their colleagues (4896 Jews and 14,366 Christians).
This is significant enough, and there is no need to lay stress
on the fact that in all probability the figures given in the
table are underestimated.

The share taken by Jews in the commerce of a country
may sometimes be ascertained by indirect means. We know,
for example, that the trade of Hamburg with Spain and
Portugal, and also with Holland, in the 17th century was
almost entirely in the hands of the Jews.[5] Now some 20 per
cent. of the ships' cargoes leaving Hamburg were destined
for the Iberian Peninsula, and some 30 per cent. for Holland.[6]

Take another instance. The Levant trade was the most
important branch of French commerce in the 18th century.

A contemporary authority informs us that it was entirely controlled by Jews—"buyers, sellers, middlemen, bill-brokers, agents and so forth were all Jews."[7]

In the 16th and 17th centuries, and even far into the 18th, the trade of the Levant as well as that with, and *via,* Spain and Portugal, was the broadest stream in the world's commerce. This mere generalization goes far to prove how pre-eminent, from the purely quantitative point of view, the Jews were in forwarding the development of international intercourse. Already in Spain the Jews had managed to obtain control of the greater portion of the Levant trade, and everywhere in the Levantine ports Jewish offices and warehouses were to be found. Many Spanish Jews at the time of the expulsion from Spain settled in the East; the others journeyed northwards. So it came about that almost imperceptibly the Levantine trade became associated with the more northerly peoples. In Holland, more especially, is the effect of this seen: Holland became a commercial country of world-wide influence. Altogether, the commercial net, so to say, became bigger and stronger in proportion as the Jews established their offices, on the one hand further afield, on the other in closer proximity to each other.[8] More particularly was this the case when the Western Hemisphere—largely through Jewish influence—was drawn into the commerce of the world. We shall have more to say on this aspect of the question in connexion with the part the Jews played in colonial foundations.

Another means by which we may gain a clear conception of what the Jews did for the extension of modern commerce is to discover the kind of commodities in which they for the most part traded. The quality of the commerce matters more than its quantity. It was by the character of their trade that they partially revolutionized the older forms, and thus helped to make commerce what it is to-day.

Here we are met by a striking fact. The Jews for a long time practically monopolized the trade in articles of luxury, and to the fashionable world of the aristocratic 17th and 18th centuries this trade was of supreme moment. What sort of commodities, then, did the Jews specialize in? Jewellery, precious stones, pearls and silks.[9] Gold and silver jewellery, because they had always been prominent in the market for precious metals. Pearls and stones, because they were among the first to settle in those lands (especially Brazil) where these are to be found; and silks, because of their ancient connexions with the trading centres of the Orient.

Moreover, Jews were to be found almost entirely, or at least predominantly, in such branches of trade as were concerned with exportation on a large scale. Nay, I believe it may with justice be asserted that the Jews were the first to place on the world's markets the staple articles of modern commerce. Side by side with the products of the soil, such as wheat, wool, flax, and, later on, distilled spirits, they dealt throughout the 18th century specially in textiles,[10] the output of a rapidly growing capitalistic industry, and in those colonial products which for the first time became articles of international trade, viz., sugar and tobacco. I have little doubt that when the history of commerce in modern times comes to be written Jewish traders will constantly be met with in connexion with enterprises on a large scale. The references which quite by accident have come under my notice are already sufficient to prove the truth of this assertion.[11]

Perhaps the most far-reaching, because the most revolutionary, influence of the Jews on the development of economic life was due to their trade in new commodities, in the preparation of which new methods supplanted the old. We may mention cotton,[12] cotton goods of foreign make, indigo and so forth.[13] Dealing in these articles was looked upon at the time as "spoiling sport," and therefore Jews were taunted by one German writer with carrying on "unpatriotic trade"[14] or "Jew-commerce, which gave little employment to German labour, and depended for the most part on home consumption only."[15]

Another great characteristic of "Jew-commerce," one which all later commerce took for its model, was its variety and many-sidedness. When in 1740 the merchants of Montpelier complained of the competition of the Jewish traders, the Intendant replied that if they, the Christians, had such well-assorted stocks as the Jews, customers would come to them as willingly as they went to their Jewish competitors.[16] We hear the same of the Jews at the Leipzig fairs: "The Jewish traders had a beneficial influence on the trade of the fairs, in that their purchases were so varied. Thus it was the Jews who tended to make trade many-sided and forced industry (especially the home industries) to develop in more than one direction. Indeed, at many fairs the Jews became the arbiters of the market by reason of their extensive purchases."[17]

But the greatest characteristic of "Jew-commerce" during the earlier capitalistic age was, to my mind, the supremacy which Jewish traders obtained, either directly or by way of Spain and Portugal, in the lands from which it was possible to draw large supplies of ready money. I am thinking of the newly discovered gold and silver countries in Central and South America. Again and again we find it recorded that Jews brought ready money into the country.[18] The theoretical speculator and the practical politician knew well enough that here was the source of all capitalistic development. We too, now that the mists of Adam Smith's doctrines have lifted, have realized the same thing. The establishment of modern economic life meant, for the most part, and of necessity, the obtaining of the precious metals, and in this work no one was so successfully engaged as the Jewish traders. This leads us at once to the subject of the next chapter, which deals with the share of the Jews in colonial expansion.

Chapter 4

The Foundation of Modern Colonies

WE ARE ONLY NOW beginning to realize that colonial expansion was no small force in the development of modern capitalism. It is the purpose of this chapter to show that in the work of that expansion the Jews played, if not the most decisive, at any rate a most prominent part.

That the Jews should have been keen colonial settlers was only natural, seeing that the New World, though it was but the Old in a new garb, seemed to hold out a greater promise of happiness to them than cross-grained old Europe, more especially when their last Dorado (Spain) proved an inhospitable refuge. And this applies equally to all colonial enterprises, whether in the East or the West or the South of the globe. There were probably many Jews resident in the East Indies even in mediæval times,[1] and when the nations of Europe, after 1498, stretched out their hands to seize the lands of an ancient civilization, the Jews were welcomed as bulwarks of European supremacy, though they came as pioneers of trade. In all likelihood—exact proofs have not yet been established—the ships of the Portuguese and of the Dutch must have brought shoals of Jewish settlers to their respective Indian possessions. At any rate, Jews participated extensively in all the Dutch settlements, including those in the East. We are told that Jews were large shareholders in the Dutch East India Company.[2] We know that the Governor of the Company who, "if he did not actually establish the power of Holland in Java, certainly contributed most to strengthen it,"[3] was called Cohn (Coen). Furthermore, a glance at the portraits of the Governors of the Dutch colonies would make it appear that this Coen is not the only Jew among them.[4] Jews were also Directors of the Company;[5] in short, no colonial enterprise was complete without them.[6]

49

It is as yet unknown to what extent the Jews shared in the growth of economic life in India after the English became masters there. We have, however, fairly full information as to the participation of the Jews in the founding of the English colonies in South Africa and Australia. There is no doubt that in these regions (more particularly in Cape Colony), well-nigh all economic development was due to the Jews. In the twenties and thirties of the 19th century Benjamin Norden and Simon Marks came to South Africa, and "the industrial awakening of almost the whole interior of Cape Colony" was their work. Julius Mosenthal and his brothers Adolph and James established the trade in wool, skins, and mohair. Aaron and Daniel de Pass monopolized the whaling industry; Joel Myers commenced ostrich farming. Lilienfeld, of Hopetown, bought the first diamonds.[7] Similar leading positions were occupied by the Jews in the other South African colonies, particularly in the Transvaal, where it is said that to-day twenty-five of the fifty thousand Jews of South Africa are settled.[8] It is the same story in Australia, where the first wholesale trader was Montefiore. It would seem to be no exaggeration therefore that "a large proportion of the English colonial shipping trade was for a considerable time in the hands of the Jews."[9]

But the real sphere of Jewish influence in colonial settlements, especially in the early capitalistic period, was in the Western Hemisphere. America in all its borders is a land of Jews. That is the result to which a study of the sources must inevitably lead, and it is pregnant with meaning. From the first day of its discovery America has had a strong influence on the economic life of Europe and on the whole of its civilization; and therefore the part which the Jews have played in building up the American world is of supreme import as an element in modern development. That is why I shall dwell on this theme a little more fully, even at the risk of wearying the reader.[10]

The very discovery of America is most intimately bound up with the Jews in an extraordinary fashion. It is as though the New World came into the horizon by their aid and for them alone, as though Columbus and the rest were but managing directors for Israel. It is in this light that Jews, proud of their past, now regard the story of that discovery, as set forth in the latest researches.[11] These would seem to show that it was the scientific knowledge of Jewish scholars which so perfected the art of navigation that voyages across the ocean became at all possible. Abraham Zacuto, Professor of Mathematics and Astronomy at the University of Salamanca, completed his astronomical tables and diagrams, the *Almanach perpetuum,* in 1473. On the basis of these tables two other Jews, Jose Vecuho, who was Court astronomer and physician to John II of Portugal, and one Moses the Mathematician (in collaboration with two Christian scholars), discovered the nautical astrolabe, an instrument by which it became possible to measure from the altitude of the sun the distance of a ship from the Equator. Jose further translated the Almanack of his master into Latin and Spanish.

The scientific facts which prepared the way for the voyage of Columbus were thus supplied by Jews. The money which was equally necessary came from the same quarter, at any rate as regards his first two voyages. For the first voyage, Columbus obtained a loan from Louis de Santangel, who was of the King's Council; and it was to Santangel, the patron of the expedition, and to Gabriel Saniheg, a Maranno, the Treasurer of Aragon, that the first two letters of Columbus were addressed. The second voyage was also undertaken with the aid of Jewish money, this time certainly not voluntarily contributed. On their expulsion from Spain in 1492, the Jews were compelled to leave much treasure behind; this was seized by Ferdinand for the State Exchequer, and with a portion of it Columbus was financed.

But more than that. A number of Jews were among the companions of Columbus, and the first European to set foot on American soil was a Jew—Louis de Torres. So the latest researches would have us believe.[12]

But what caps all—Columbus himself is claimed to have been a Jew. I give this piece of information for what it is worth, without guaranteeing its accuracy. At a meeting of the Geographical Society of Madrid, Don Celso Garcia de la Riega, a scholar famous for his researches on Columbus, read a paper in which he stated that Christobal Colon (not Columbus) was a Spaniard who on his mother's side was of Jewish descent. He showed by reference to documents in the town of Pontevedra, in the province of Galicia, that the family of Colon lived there between 1428 and 1528, and that the Christian names found among them were the same as those prevalent among the relatives of the Spanish admiral. These Colons and the Fonterosa family intermarried. The latter were undoubtedly Jews, or they had only recently been converted, and Christobal's mother was called Suzanna Fonterosa. When disorders broke out in the province of Galicia the parents of the discoverer of America migrated from Spain to Italy. These facts were substantiated by Don Celso from additional sources, and he is strengthened in his belief by distinct echoes of Hebrew literature found in the writings of Columbus, and also because the oldest portraits show him to have had a Jewish face.

Scarcely were the doors of the New World opened to Europeans than crowds of Jews came swarming in. We have already seen that the discovery of America took place in the year in which the Jews of Spain became homeless, that the last years of the 15th century and the early years of the 16th were a period in which millions of Jews were forced to become wanderers, when European Jewry was like an ant-heap into which a stick had been thrust. Little wonder, therefore, that a great part of this heap betook itself to the New World, where the future seemed so bright. The first traders in America were Jews. The first industrial establishments in America were those of Jews. Already in the year 1492 Portuguese Jews settled in St. Thomas, where they were the first plantation owners on a large scale; they set up many sugar factories and gave employment to nearly three thousand Negroes.[13] And as for Jewish emigration to South America, almost as soon as it was discovered, the stream was so great that Queen Joan in 1511 thought it necessary to take measures to stem it.[14] But her efforts must have been without avail, for the number of Jews increased, and finally, on May 21, 1577, the law forbidding Jews to emigrate to the Spanish colonies was formally repealed.

In order to do full justice to the unceasing activity of the Jews in South America as founders of colonial commerce and industry, it will be advisable to glance at the fortunes of one or two colonies.

The history of the Jews in the American colonies, and therefore the history of the colonies themselves, falls into two periods, separated by the expulsion of the Jews from Brazil in 1654.

We have already mentioned the establishment of the sugar industry in St. Thomas by Jews in 1492. By the year 1550 this industry had reached the height of its development on the island. There were sixty plantations with sugar mills and refineries, producing annually, as may be seen from the tenth part paid to the King, 150,000 arrobes of sugar.[15]

From St. Thomas, or possibly from Madeira,[16] where they had for a long time been engaged in the sugar trade, the Jews transplanted the industry to Brazil, the largest of the American colonies. Brazil thus entered on its first period of prosperity, for the growth of the sugar industry brought with it the growth of the national wealth. In those early years the colony was populated almost entirely by Jews and criminals, two shiploads of them being brought thither annually from Portugal.[17] The Jews quickly became the dominant class, "a not inconsiderable number of the wealthiest Brazilian traders were New Christians."[18] The first Governor-General was of Jewish origin, and he it was who brought order into the government of the colony. It is not too much to say that Portugal's new possessions really began to thrive only after Thomé de Souza, a man of exceptional ability, was sent out in 1549 to take matters in hand.[19] Nevertheless the colony did not reach the zenith of its prosperity until after the influx of rich Jews from Holland, consequent on the Dutch entering into possession in 1642. In that very year, a number of American Jews combined to establish a colony in Brazil, and no less than six hundred influential Dutch Jews joined them.[20] Up to about the middle of the 17th century all the large sugar plantations belonged to Jews,[21] and contemporary travellers report as to their many-sided activities and their wealth. Thus Nieuhoff, who travelled in Brazil from 1640 to 1649, says of them:[22] "Among the free inhabitants of Brazil that were not in the (Dutch West India) Company's service the Jews were the most considerable in number, who had transplanted themselves thither from Holland. They had a vast traffic beyond the rest; they purchased sugar-mills and built stately houses in the Receif. They were all traders, which would have been of great consequence to the Dutch Brazil had they kept themselves within the due bounds of traffic." Similarly we read in F. Pyrard's *Travels*:[23] "The profits they make after being nine or ten years in those lands are marvellous, for they all come back rich."

The predominance of Jewish influence in plantation development outlasted the episode of Dutch rule in Brazil, and continued, despite the expulsion of 1654,[24] down to the first half of the 11th century.[25] On one occasion, "when a number of the most influential merchants of Rio de Janeiro fell into the hands of the Holy Office (of the Inquisition), the work on so many plantations came to a standstill that the production and commerce of the Province (of Bahio) required a long stretch of time to recover from the blow." Later, a decree of the 2nd March 1768 ordered all the registers containing lists of New Christians to be destroyed, and by a law of 25th March 1773 New Christians were placed on a footing of perfect civic equality with the orthodox. It is evident, then, that very many crypto-Jews must have maintained their prominent position in Brazil even after the Portuguese had regained possession of it in 1654, and that it was they who brought to the country its flourishing sugar industry as well as its trade in precious stones.

Despite this, the year 1654 marks an epoch in the annals of American-Jewish history. For it was in that year that a goodly number of the Brazilian Jews settled in other parts of America and thereby moved the economic centre of gravity.

The change was specially profitable to one or two important islands of the West Indian Archipelago and also to the neighbouring coastlands, which rose in prosperity from the time of the Jewish influx in the 17th century. Barbados, which was inhabited almost solely by Jews, is a case in point.[26] It came under English rule in 1627; in 1641 the sugar cane was introduced, and seven years later the exportation of sugar began. But the sugar industry could not maintain itself. The sugar produced was so poor in quality that its price was scarcely sufficient to pay for the cost of transport to England. Not till the exiled "Dutchmen" from Brazil introduced the process of refining and taught the natives the art of drying and crystallizing the sugar did an improvement manifest itself. As a result, the sugar exports of Barbados increased by leaps and bounds, and in 1661 Charles II was able to confer baronetcies on thirteen planters, who drew an annual income of £10,000 from the island. By about the year 1676 the industry there had grown to such an extent that no fewer than 400 vessels each carrying 180 tons of raw sugar left annually.

In 1664 Thomas Modyford introduced sugar manufacturing from Barbados into Jamaica,[27] which in consequence soon became wealthy. Now, while in 1656, the year in which the English finally wrested the island from Spain, there were only three small refineries in Jamaica, in 1670 there were already 75 mills at work, many of them having an output of 2000 cwts. By 1700 sugar was the principal export of Jamaica and the source of its riches. The petition of the English merchants of the colony in 1671, asking for the exclusion of the Jews, makes it pretty plain that the latter must have contributed largely to this development. The Government however, encouraged the settlement of still more Jews, the Governor in rejecting the petition remarking[28] that "he was of opinion that his Majesty could not have more profitable subjects than the Jews and the Hollanders; they had great stocks and correspondence." So the Jews were not expelled from Jamaica, but "became the first traders and merchants of the English colony."[29] In the 18th century they paid all the taxes and almost entirely controlled industry and commerce.

Of the other English colonies, the Jews showed a special preference for Surinam.[30] Jews had been settled there since 1644 and had received a number of privileges—"whereas we have found that the Hebrew nation . . . have . . . proved themselves useful and beneficial to the colony." Their privileged position continued under the Dutch, to whom Surinam passed in 1667. Towards the end of the 17th century their proportion to the rest of the inhabitants was as one to three, and in 1730 they owned 115 of the 344 sugar plantations.

The story of the Jews in the English and Dutch colonies finds a counterpart in the more important French settlements, such as Martinique, Guadeloupe, and San Domingo.[31] Here also sugar was the source of wealth, and, as in the other cases, the Jews controlled the industry and were the principal sugar merchants.

The first large plantation and refinery in Martinique was established in 1655 by Benjamin Dacosta, who had fled thither from Brazil with 900 co-religionists and 1100 slaves.

In San Domingo the sugar industry was introduced as early as 1587, but it was not until the "Dutch" refugees from Brazil settled there that it attained any degree of success.

In all this we must never lose sight of the fact that in those critical centuries in which the colonial system was taking root in America (and with it modern capitalism), the production of sugar was the backbone of the entire colonial economy, leaving out of account, of course, the mining of silver, gold and gems in Brazil. Indeed, it is somewhat difficult exactly to picture to ourselves the enormous significance in those centuries of sugar-making and sugar-selling. The Council of Trade in Paris (1701) was guilty of no exaggerated language when it placed on record its belief that "French shipping owes its splendour to the commerce of the sugar-producing islands, and it is only by means of this that the navy can be maintained and strengthened." Now, it must be remembered that the Jews had almost monopolized the sugar trade; the French branch in particular being controlled by the wealthy family of the Gradis of Bordeaux.[32]

The position which the Jews had obtained for themselves in Central and South America was thus a powerful one. But it became even more so when towards the end of the 17th century the English colonies in North America entered into commercial relations with the West Indies. To this close union, which again Jewish merchants helped to bring about, the North American Continent (as we shall see) owes its existence. We have thus arrived at the point where it is essential to consider the Jewish factor in the growth of the United States from their first origins. Once more Jewish elements combined, this time to give the United States their ultimate economic form. As this view is absolutely opposed to that generally accepted (at least in Europe), the question must receive full consideration.

At first sight it would seem as if the economic system of North America was the very one that developed independently of the Jews. Often enough, when I have asserted that modern capitalism is nothing more or less than an expression of the Jewish spirit, I have been told that the history of the United States proves the contrary. The Yankees themselves boast of the fact that they throve without the Jews. It was an American writer—Mark Twain, if I mistake not—who once considered at some length why the Jews played no great part in the States, giving as his reason that the Americans were as "smart" as the Jews, if not smarter. (The Scotch, by the way, think the same of themselves.) Now, it is true that we come across no very large number of Jewish names to-day among the big captains of industry, the well-known speculators, or the Trust magnates in the country. Nevertheless, I uphold my assertion that the United States (perhaps more than any other land) are filled to the brim with the Jewish spirit. This is recognized in many quarters, above all in those best capable of forming a judgment on the subject. Thus, a few years ago, at the magnificent celebration of the 250th anniversary of the first settlement of the Jews in the United States, President Roosevelt sent a congratulatory letter to the Organizing Committee. In this he said that that was the first time during his tenure of office that he had written a letter of the kind, but that the importance of the occasion warranted him in making an exception. The persecution to which the Jews were then subjected made it an urgent duty for him to lay stress on the splendid civic qualities which men of the Jewish faith and race had developed ever since they came into the country. In mentioning the services rendered by Jews to the United States he used an expression which goes to the root of the matter—"The Jews participated in the up-building of this country."[33] On the same occasion ex-President Cleveland remarked: "I believe that it can be safely claimed that few, if any, of those contributing nationalities have directly and indirectly been more influential in giving shape and direction to the Americanism of to-day."[34]

Wherein does this Jewish influence manifest itself? In the first place, the number of Jews who took part in American business life was never so small as would appear at the first glance. It is a mistake to imagine that because there are no Jews among the half-dozen well-known multi-millionaires, male and female, who on account of the noise they make in the world are on all men's lips, therefore American capitalism necessarily lacks a Jewish element. To begin with, even among the big Trusts there are some directed by Jewish hands and brains. Thus, the Smelters' Trust, which in 1904 represented a combination with a nominal capital of 201,000,000 dollars, was the creation of Jews—the Guggenheims. Thus, too, in the Tobacco Trust (500,000,000 dollars), in the Asphalt Trust, in the Telegraph Trust, to mention but a few, Jews occupy commanding positions.[35] Again, very many of the large banking-houses belong to Jews, who in consequence exercise no small control over American economic life. Take the Harriman system, which had for its goal the fusion of all the American railways. It was backed to a large extent by Kuhn, Loeb & Co., the well-known banking firm of New York. Especially influential are the Jews in the West. California is for the most part their creation. At the foundation of the State Jews obtained distinction as Judges, Congressmen, Governors, Mayors, and so on, and last but not least, as business men. The brothers Seligman—William, Henry, Jesse and James—of San Francisco; Louis Sloss and Lewis Gerstle of Sacramento (where they established the Alaska Commercial Company), Hellman and Newmark of Los Angeles, are some of the more prominent business houses in this part of the world. During the gold-mining period Jews were the intermediaries between California and the Eastern States and Europe. The important transactions of those days were undertaken by such men as Benjamin Davidson, the agent of the Rothschilds; Albert Priest, of Rhode Island; Albert Dyer, of Baltimore; the three brothers Lazard, who established the international banking-house of Lazard Frères of Paris, London and San Francisco; the Seligmans, the Glaziers and the Wormsers. Moritz Friedlaender was one of the chief "Wheat kings." Adolph Sutro exploited the Comstock Lodes. Even to-day the majority of the banking businesses, no less than the general industries, are in the hands of Jews. Thus, we may mention the London, Paris and American Bank (Sigmund Greenbaum and Richard Altschul); the Anglo-Californian Bank (Philip N. Lilienthal and Ignatz Steinhart); the Nevada Bank; the Union Trust Company; the Farmers' and Merchants' Bank of Los Angeles; John Rosenfeld's control of the coalfields; the Alaska Commercial Company, which succeeded the Hudson Bay Company; the North American Commercial Company, and many more.[36]

It can scarcely be doubted that the immigration of numerous Jews into all the States during the last few decades must have had a stupendous effect on American economic life everywhere. Consider that there are more than a million Jews in New York to-day, and that the greater number of the immigrants have not yet embarked on a capitalistic career. If the conditions in America continue to develop along the same lines as in the last generation, if the immigration statistics and the proportion of births among all the nationalities remain the same, our imagination may picture the United States of fifty or a hundred years hence as a land inhabited only by Slavs, Negroes and Jews, wherein the Jews will naturally occupy the position of economic leadership.

But these are dreams of the future which have no place in this connexion, where our main concern is with the past and the present. That Jews have taken a prominent share in American life in the present and in the past may be conceded; perhaps a more prominent share than would at first sight appear. Nevertheless, the enormous weight which, in common with many others who have the right of forming an opinion on the subject, I attach to their influence, cannot be adequately explained merely from the point of view of their numbers. It is rather the particular kind of influence that I lay stress on, and this can be accounted for by a variety of complex causes.

That is why I am not anxious to overemphasize the fact, momentous enough in itself, that the Jews in America practically control a number of important branches of commerce; indeed, it is not too much to say that they monopolize them, or at least did so for a considerable length of time. Take the wheat trade, especially in the West; take tobacco; take cotton. We see at once that they who rule supreme in three such mighty industries must perforce take a leading part in the economic activities of the nation as a whole. For all that I do not labour this fact, for to my mind the significance of the Jews for the economic development of the United States lies rooted in causes far deeper than these.

As the golden thread in the tapestry, so are the Jews interwoven as a distinct thread throughout the fabric of America's economic history; through the intricacy of their fantastic design it received from the very beginning a pattern all its own.

Since the first quickening of the capitalistic spirit on the coastlands of the ocean and in the forests and prairies of the New World, Jews have not been absent; 1655 is usually given as the date of their first appearance.[37] In that year a vessel with Jewish emigrants from Brazil, which had become a

Portuguese possession, anchored in the Hudson River, and the passengers craved permission to land in the colony which the Dutch West India Company had founded there. But they were no humble petitioners asking for a favour. They came as members of a race which had participated to a large extent in the new foundation, and the governors of the colony were forced to recognize their claims. When the ship arrived, New Amsterdam was under the rule of Stuyvesant, who was no friend to the Jews and who, had he followed his own inclination, would have closed the door in the face of the newcomers. But a letter dated March 26, 1665, reached him from the Court of the Company in Amsterdam, containing the order to let the Jews settle and trade in the colonies under the control of the Company, "also because of the large amount of capital which they have invested in shares of this Company."[38] It was not long before they found their way to Long Island, Albany, Rhode Island and Philadelphia.

Then their manifold activities began, and it was due to them that the colonies were able to maintain their existence. The entity of the United States to-day is only possible, as we know, because the English colonies of North America, thanks to a chain of propitious circumstances, acquired a degree of power and strength such as ultimately led to their complete independence. In the building up of this position of supremacy the Jews were among the first and the keenest workers.

I am not thinking of the obvious fact that the colonies were only able to achieve their independence by the help of a few wealthy Jewish firms who laid the economic foundations for the existence of the New Republic. The United States would never have won complete independence had not the Jews supplied the needs of their armies and furnished them with the indispensable sinews of war. But what the Jews accomplished in this direction did not arise out of specifically American conditions. It was a general phenomenon, met with throughout the history of the modern capitalistic States, and we shall do justice to instances of it when dealing with wider issues.

No. What I have in mind is the special service which the Jews rendered the North American colonies, one peculiar to the American Continent—a service which indeed gave America birth. I refer to the simple fact that during the 17th and 18th centuries the trade of the Jews was the source from which the economic system of the colonies drew its life-blood. As is well known, England forced her colonies to purchase all the manufactured articles they needed in the Mother-country. Hence the balance of trade of the colonies was always an adverse one, and by constantly having to send money out of the country they would have been drained dry. But there was a stream which carried the precious metals into the country, a stream diverted in this direction by the trade of the Jews with South and Central America. The Jews in the English colonies maintained active business relations with the West Indian Islands and with Brazil, resulting in a favourable balance of trade for the land of their sojourn. The gold mined in South America was thus brought to North America and helped to keep the economic system in a healthy condition.[39]

In the face of this fact, is there not some justification for the opinion that the United States owe their very existence to the Jews? And if this be so, how much more can it be asserted that Jewish influence made the United States just what they are—that is, American? For what we call Americanism is nothing else, if we may say so, than the Jewish spirit distilled.

But how comes it that American culture is so steeped in Jewishness? The answer is simple—through the early and universal admixture of Jewish elements among the first settlers. We may picture the process of colonizing somewhat after this fashion. A band of determined men and women—let us say twenty families—went forth into the wilds to begin their life anew. Nineteen were equipped with plough and scythe, ready to clear the forests and till the soil in order to earn their livelihood as husbandmen. The twentieth family opened a store to provide their companions with such necessaries of life as could not be obtained from the soil, often no doubt hawking them at the very doors. Soon this twentieth family made it its business to arrange for the distribution of the products which the other nineteen won from the soil. It was they, too, who were most likely in possession of ready cash, and in case of need could therefore be useful to the others by lending them money. Very often the store had a kind of agricultural loan-bank as its adjunct, perhaps also an office for the buying and selling of land. So through the activity of the twentieth family the farmer in North America was from the first kept in touch with the money and credit system of the Old World. Hence the whole process of production and exchange was from its inception along modern lines. Town methods made their way at once into even the most distant villages. Accordingly, it may be said that American economic life was from its very start impregnated with capitalism. And who was responsible for this? The twentieth family in each village. Need we add that this twentieth family was always a Jewish one, which joined a party of settlers or soon sought them out in their homesteads?

Such in outline is the mental picture I have conceived of the economic development of the United States. Subsequent writers dealing with this subject will be able to fill in more ample details; I myself have only come across a few. But these are so similar in character that they can hardly be taken as isolated instances. The conclusion is forced upon us that they are typical. Nor do I alone hold this view. Governor Pardel of California, for example, remarked in 1905: "He (the Jew) has been the leading financier of thousands of prosperous communities. He has been enterprising and aggressive."[40]

Let me quote some of the illustrations I have met with. In 1785 Abraham Mordecai settled in Alabama. "He established a trading-post two miles west of Line Creek, carrying on an extensive trade with the Indians, and exchanging his goods for pinkroot, hickory, nut oil and peltries of all kinds."[41] Similarly in Albany: "As early as 1661, when Albany was but a small trading post, a Jewish trader named Asser Levi (or Leevi) became the owner of real estate there."[42] Chicago has the same story. The first brick house was built by a Jew, Benedict Schubert, who became the first merchant tailor in Chicago, while another Jew, Philip Newburg, was the first to introduce the tobacco business.[43] In Kentucky we hear of a Jewish settler as early as 1816. When in that year the Bank of the United States opened a branch in Lexington, a Mr. Solomon, who had arrived in 1808, was made cashier.[44] In Maryland,[45] Michigan,[46] Ohio[47] and Pennsylvania[48] it is on record that Jewish traders were among the earliest settlers, though nothing is known of their activity.

On the other hand, a great deal is known of Jews in Texas, where they were among the pioneers of capitalism. Thus, for example, Jacob de Cordova "was by far the most extensive land locator in the State until 1856." The Cordova's Land Agency soon became famous not only in Texas but in New York, Philadelphia and Baltimore, where the owners of large tracts of Texas land resided. Again, Morris Koppore in 1863 became President of the National Bank of Texas. Henry Castro was an immigration agent; "between the years 1843-6 Castro introduced into Texas over 5000 immigrants . . . transporting them in 27 ships, chiefly from the Rhenish provinces. . . . He fed his colonists for a year, furnished them with cows, farming implements, seeds, medicine, and in short with everything they needed."[49]

Sometimes branches of one and the same family distributed themselves in different States, and were thereby enabled to carry on business most successfully. Perhaps the best instance is the history of the Seligman family. There were eight brothers (the sons of David Seligman, of Bayersdorf, in Bavaria) who started a concern which now has branches in all the most important centres in the States. Their story began with the arrival in America in the year 1837 of Joseph Seligman. Two other brothers followed in 1839; a third came two years later. The four began business as clothiers in Lancaster, moving shortly after to Selma, Ala. From here they opened three branches in three other towns. By 1848 two more brothers had arrived from Germany and the six moved North. In 1850, Jesse Seligman opened a shop in San Francisco—in the first brick house in that city. Seven years later a banking business was added to the clothing shop, and in 1862 the house of Seligman Brothers was established in New York, San Francisco, London, Paris and Frankfort.[50]

In the Southern States likewise the Jew played the part of the trader in the midst of agricultural settlers.[51] Here also (as in Southern and Central America) we find him quite early as the owner of vast plantations. In South Carolina indeed, "Jew's Land" is synonymous with "Large Plantations."[52] It was in the South that Moses Lindo became famous as one of the first undertakers in the production of indigo.

These examples must suffice. We believe they tend to illustrate our general statement, which is supported also by the fact that there was a constant stream of Jewish emigration to the United States from their earliest foundation. It is true that there are no actual figures to show the proportion of the Jewish population to the total body of settlers. But the numerous indications of a general nature that we do find make it pretty certain that there must always have been a large number of Jews in America.

It must not be forgotten that in the earliest years the population was thinly scattered and very sparse. New Amsterdam had less than 1000 inhabitants.[53] That being so, a shipful of Jews who came from Brazil to settle there made a great difference, and in assessing Jewish influence on the whole district we shall have to rate it highly.[54] Or take another instance. When the first settlement in Georgia was established, forty Jews were among the settlers. The number may seem insignificant, but when we consider the meagre population of the colony, Jewish influence must be accounted strong. So, too, in Savannah, where in 1733 there were already twelve Jewish families in what was then a tiny commercial centre.[55]

That America early became the goal of German and Polish Jewish emigrants is well known. Thus we are told: "Among the poorer Jewish families of Posen there was seldom one which in the second quarter of the 19th century did not have at least one son (and in most cases the ablest and not least enterprising) who sailed away across the ocean to flee from the narrowness and the oppression of his native land."[56] We are not surprised, therefore, at the comparatively large number of Jewish soldiers (7243)[57] who took part in the Civil War, and we should be inclined to say that the estimate which puts the Jewish population of the United States about the middle of the 19th century at 300,000 (of whom 30,000 lived in New York)[58] was if anything too moderate.

Chapter 5

The Foundation of the Modern State

THE DEVELOPMENT of the modern colonial system and the establishment of the modern State are two phenomena dependent on one another. The one is inconceivable without the other, and the genesis of modern capitalism is bound up with both. Hence, in order to discover the importance of any historic factor in the growth of capitalism it will be necessary to find out what, and how great a part that factor played in both the colonial system and the foundation of the modern State. In the last chapter we considered the Jews in relation to the colonial system; in the present we shall do the same for the modern State.

A cursory glance would make it appear that in no direction could the Jews, the "Stateless" people, have had less influence than in the establishment of modern States. Not one of the statesmen of whom we think in this connexion was a Jew—neither Charles the Fifth, nor Louis the Eleventh, neither Richelieu, Mazarin, Colbert, Cromwell, Frederick William of Prussia nor Frederick the Great.[1] However, when speaking of these modern statesmen and rulers, we can hardly do so without perforce thinking of the Jews: it would be like Faust without Mephistopheles. Arm in arm the Jew and the ruler stride through the age which historians call modern. To me this union is symbolic of the rise of capitalism, and consequently of the modern State. In most countries the ruler assumed the role of protector of the persecuted Jews against the Estates of the Realm and the Gilds—both pre-capitalistic forces. And why? Their interests and their sympathies coincided. The Jew embodied modern capitalism, and the ruler allied himself with this force in order to establish, or maintain, his own position. When, therefore, I speak of the part played by the Jews in the foundation of modern States, it is not so much their direct influence as organizers

67

that I have in mind, as rather their indirect co-operation in the process. I am thinking of the fact that the Jews furnished the rising States with the material means necessary to maintain themselves and to develop; that the Jews supported the army in each country in two ways, and the armies were the bulwarks on which the new States rested. In two ways: on the one hand, the Jews supplied the army in time of war with weapons, and munition and food; on the other hand, they provided money not only for military purposes but also for the general needs of courts and governments. The Jews throughout the 16th, 17th and 18th centuries were most influential as army-purveyors and as the moneyed men to whom the princes looked for financial backing. This position of the Jews was of the greatest consequence for the development of the modern State. It is not necessary to expatiate on this statement; all that we shall do is to adduce instances in proof of it. Here, too, we cannot attempt to mention every possible example. We can only point the way; it will be for subsequent research to follow.

The Jews as Purveyors

Although there are numerous cases on record of Jews acting in the capacity of army-contractors in Spain previous to 1492, I shall not refer to this period, because it lies outside the scope of our present considerations. We shall confine ourselves to the centuries that followed and begin with England.

In the 17th and 18th centuries the Jews had already achieved renown as army-purveyors. Under the Commonwealth the most famous army-contractor was Antonio Fernandez Carvajal, "the great Jew," who came to London some time between 1630 and 1635, and was very soon accounted among the most prominent traders in the land. In 1649 he was one of the five London merchants entrusted by the Council of State with the army contract for corn.[2] It is said that he annually imported into England silver to the value of £100,000. In the period that ensued, especially in the wars of William III, Sir Solomon Medina ("the Jew Medina") was "the great contractor," and for his services he was knighted, being the first professing Jew to receive that honour.[3]

It was the same in the wars of the Spanish Succession; here, too, Jews were the principal army-contractors.[4] In 1716 the Jews of Strassburg recall the services they rendered the armies of Louis XIV by furnishing information and supplying provisions.[5] Indeed, Louis XIV's army-contractor-in-chief was a Jew, Jacob Worms by name;[6] and in the 18th century Jews gradually took a more and more prominent part in this work. In 1727 the Jews of Metz brought into the city in the space of six weeks 2000 horses for food and more than 5000 for remounts.[7] Field-Marshal Maurice of Saxony, the victor of Fontenoy, expressed the opinion that his armies were never better served with supplies than when the Jews were the contractors.[8] One of the best known of the Jewish army-contractors in the time of the last two Louis was Cerf Beer, in whose patent of naturalization it is recorded that ". . . in the wars which raged in Alsace in 1770 and 1771 he found the opportunity of proving his zeal in our service and in that of the State."[9]

Similarly, the house of the Gradis, of Bordeaux, was an establishment of international repute in the 18th century. Abraham Gradis set up large storehouses in Quebec to supply the needs of the French troops there.[10] Under the Revolutionary Government, under the Directory, in the Napoleonic Wars it was always Jews who acted as purveyors.[11] In this connexion a public notice displayed in the streets of Paris in 1795 is significant. There was a famine in the city and the Jews were called upon to show their gratitude for the rights bestowed upon them by the Revolution by bringing in corn. "They alone," says the author of the notice, "can successfully accomplish this enterprise, thanks to their business relations, of which their fellow citizens ought to have full benefit."[12] A parallel story comes from Dresden. In 1720 the Court Jew, Jonas Meyer, saved the town from starvation by supplying it with large quantities of corn. (The Chronicler mentions 40,000 bushels.)[13]

All over Germany the Jews from an early date were found in the ranks of army-contractors. Let us enumerate a few of them. There was Isaac Meyer in the 16th century, who, when Cardinal Albrecht admitted him a resident of Halberstadt in 1537, was enjoined by him, in view of the dangerous times, "to supply our monastery with good weapons and armour." There was Joselman von Rosheim, who in 1548 received an imperial letter of protection because he had supplied both money and provisions for the army. In 1546 there is a record of Bohemian Jews who provided greatcoats and blankets for the army.[14] In the next century (1633) another Bohemian Jew, Lazarus by name, received an official declaration that he "obtained either in person, or at his own expense, valuable information for the Imperial troops, and that he made it his business to see that the army had a good supply of ammunition and clothing."[15] The Great Elector also had recourse to Jews for his military needs. Leimann Gompertz and Solomon Elias were his contractors for cannon, powder and so forth.[16] There were numerous others: Samuel Julius, remount contractor under the Elector Frederick Augustus of Saxony; the Model family, court-purveyors and army-contractors in the Duchy of Ansbach in the 17th and 18th centuries are well known.[17] In short, as one writer of the time pithily expresses it, "all the contractors are Jews and all the Jews are contractors."[18]

Austria does not differ in this respect from Germany, France and England. The wealthy Jews, who in the reign of the Emperor Leopold received permission to re-settle in Vienna (1670)—the Oppenheimers, Wertheimers, Mayer Herschel and the rest—were all army-contractors.[19] And we find the same thing in all the countries under the Austrian Crown.[20] Lastly, we must mention the Jewish army-contractors who provisioned the American troops in the Revolutionary and Civil Wars.[21]

The Jews as Financiers

This has been a theme on which many historians have written, and we are tolerably well informed concerning this aspect of Jewish history in all ages. It will not be necessary for me, therefore, to enter into this question in great detail; the enumeration of a few well-known facts will suffice.

Already in the Middle Ages we find that everywhere taxes, salt-mines and royal domains were farmed out to Jews; that Jews were royal treasurers and money-lenders, most frequently, of course, in the Pyrenean Peninsula, where the Almoxarife and the Rendeiros were chosen preferably from among the ranks of the rich Jews. But as this period does not specially concern us here, I will not mention any names but refer the reader to the general literature on the subject.[22]

It was, however, in modern times, when the State as we know it to-day first originated, that the activity of the Jews as financial advisers of princes was fraught with mighty influence. Take Holland, where although officially deterred from being servants of the Crown, they very quickly occupied positions of authority. We recall Moses Machado, the favourite of William III; Delmonte, a family of ambassadors (Lords of Schoonenberg); the wealthy Suasso, who in 1688 lent William two million gulden, and others.[23]

The effects of the Jewish *haute finance* in Holland made themselves felt beyond the borders of the Netherlands, because that country in the 17th and 18th centuries was the reservoir from which all the needy princes of Europe drew their money. Men like the Pintos, Delmontes, Bueno de Mesquita, Francis Mels and many others may in truth be regarded as the leading financiers of Northern Europe during that period.[24]

Next, English finance was at this time also very extensively controlled by Jews.[25] The monetary needs of the Long Parliament gave the first impetus to the settlement of rich Jews in England. Long before their admission by Cromwell, wealthy crypto-Jews, especially from Spain and Portugal, migrated thither *via* Amsterdam: the year 1643 brought an exceptionally large contingent. Their rallying-point was the house of the Portuguese Ambassador in London, Antonio de Souza, himself a Maranno. Prominent among them was

Antonio Fernandez Carvajal, who has already been mentioned, and who was as great a financier as he was an army-contractor. It was he who supplied the Commonwealth with funds. The little colony was further increased under the later Stuarts, notably under Charles the Second. In the retinue of his Portuguese bride, Catherine of Braganza, were quite a number of moneyed Jews, among them the brothers Da Sylva, Portuguese bankers of Amsterdam, who were entrusted with the transmission and administration of the Queen's dowry.[26] Contemporaneously with them came the Mendes and the Da Costas from Spain and Portugal, who united their families under the name of Mendes da Costa.

About the same period the Ashkenazi (German) Jews began to arrive in the country. On the whole, these could hardly compare for wealth with their Sephardi (Spanish) brethren, yet they also had their capitalistic magnates, such as Benjamin Levy for example.

Under William III their numbers were still further increased, and the links between the court and the rich Jews were strengthened. Sir Solomon Medina, who has also been already mentioned, followed the King from Holland as his banker, and with him came the Suasso, another of the plutocratic families. Under Queen Anne one of the most prominent financiers in England was Menasseh Lopez, and by the time the South Sea Bubble burst, the Jews as a body were the greatest financial power in the country. They had kept clear of the wild speculations which had preceded the disaster and so retained their fortunes unimpaired. Accordingly, when the Government issued a loan on the Land Tax, the Jews were in a position to take up one quarter of it. During this critical period the chief family was that of the Gideons, whose representative, Sampson Gideon (1699-1762), was the "trusted adviser of the Government," the friend of Walpole, the "pillar of the State credit." In 1745, the year of panics, Sampson raised a loan of £1,700,000 for the assistance of the Government. On his death his influence passed to the firm of Francis and Joseph Salvador, who retained it till the beginning of the 19th century, when the Rothschilds succeeded to the financial leadership.

It is the same story in France, and the powerful position held by Samuel Bernard in the latter part of the reign of Louis XIV and in the whole of that of Louis XV may serve as one example among many. We find Louis XIV walking in his garden with this wealthy Jew, "whose sole merit," in the opinion of one cynical writer,[27] "was that he supported the State as the rope does the hanged man." He financed the Wars of the Spanish Succession; he aided the French candidate for the throne of Poland; he advised the Regent in all money matters. It was probably no exaggeration when the Marquis de Dangeau spoke of him in one of his letters[28] as "the greatest banker in Europe at the present time." In France also the Jews participated to a large extent in the re-consolidation of the French East India Company after the bursting of the South Sea Bubble.[29] It was not, however, until the 19th century that they won a really leading position in financial circles in France, and the important names here are the Rothschilds, the Helphens, the Foulds, the Cerfbeers, the Duponts, the Godchaux, the Dalemberts, the Pereires and others. It is possible that in the 17th and 18th centuries also a great many more Jews than those already mentioned were active as financiers in France, but that owing to the rigorous exclusion of Jews they became crypto-Jews, and so we have no full information about them.

It is easier to trace Jewish influence in finance in Germany and Austria through that clever invention—the status of "Court Jew." Though the law in these countries forbade Jews to settle in their boundaries, yet the princes and rulers kept a number of "privileged" Jews at their courts. According to Graetz,[30] the status of "Court Jew" was introduced by the Emperors of Germany during the Thirty Years' War. Be that as it may, it is an undoubted fact that pretty well every State in Germany throughout the 17th and 18th centuries had its Court Jew or Jews, upon whose support the finances of the land depended.

A few examples by way of illustration. In the 17th century[31] we find at the Imperial Court Joseph Pinkherle, of Goerz, Moses and Jacob Marburger, of Gradisca, Ventura Parente of Trieste, Jacob Bassewi Batscheba Schmieles in Prague, the last of whom the Emperor Ferdinand raised to the ranks of the nobility under the title von Treuenburg on account of his faithful services. In the reign of the Emperor Leopold I we meet with the respected family of the Oppenheimers, of whom the Staatskanzler Ludewig wrote in the following terms.[32] After saying that the Jews were the arbiters of the most important events, he continues: "In the year 1690 the Jew Oppenheimer was well known among merchants and bankers not only in Europe but throughout the world." No less famous in the same reign was Wolf Schlesinger, purveyor to the court, who in company with Lewel Sinzheim raised more than one large loan for the State. Maria Theresa utilized the services of Schlesinger and others, notably the Wertheimers, Arnsteins and Eskeles. Indeed, for more than a century the court bankers in Vienna were Jews.[33] We can gauge their economic influence from the fact that when an anti-Jewish riot broke out in Frankfort-on-the-Main, the local authorities thought it wise in the interest of credit to call upon the Imperial Office to interfere and protect the Frankfort Jews, who had very close trade relations with their brethren in Vienna.[34]

It was not otherwise at the smaller German courts. "The continually increasing needs of the various courts, each vying with the other in luxury, rendered it imperative, seeing that communication was by no means easy, to have skilful agents in the commercial centres." Accordingly the Dukes of Mecklenburg had such agents in Hamburg; Bishop John Philip of Würzburg was in 1700 served by Moses Elkan in Frankfort. This activity opened new channels for the Jews; the enterprising dealer who provided jewels for her ladyship, liveries for the court chamberlain and dainties for the head cook was also quite willing to negotiate a loan.[35] Frankfort and Hamburg, with their large Jewish population, had many such financial agents, who acted for ruling princes living at a distance. Besides those already mentioned we may recall the Portuguese Jew, Daniel Abensur, who died in Hamburg in 1711. He was Minister-resident of the King of Poland in that city, and the Polish Crown was indebted to him for many a loan.[36] Some of these agents often moved to the court which borrowed from them, and became "Court Jews." Frederick Augustus, who became Elector of Saxony in 1694, had a number of them: Leffmann Berentz, of Hanover, J. Meyer, of Hamburg, Berend Lehmann, of Halberstadt (who advanced money for the election of the King of Poland) and others.[37] Again, in Hanover the Behrends were Chief Court Purveyors and Agents to the Treasury;[38] the Models, the Fraenkels and the Nathans acted in a similar capacity to the Duchy of Ansbach. In the Palatinate we come across Lemte Moyses and Michel May, who in 1719 paid the debt of 2½ million gulden which the Elector owed the Emperor,[39] and lastly, in the Marggravate of Bayreuth, there were the Baiersdorfs.[40]

Better known perhaps are the Court Jews of the Brandenburg-Prussian rulers—Lippold, under Joachim II; Gomperz and Joost Liebmann, under Frederick III; Veit, under Frederick William I; and Ephraim, Moses, Isaac and Daniel Itzig, under Frederick II. Most famous of all the German Court Jews, the man who may be taken as their archetype, was Suess-Oppenheimer, who was at the court of Charles Alexander of Würtemberg.[41]

Finally, we must not leave unmentioned that during the 18th century, more especially in the Revolutionary Wars, the Jews played no small role as financiers in the United States of America. Haym Salomon[42] ranks side by side with the Minis and the Cohens in Georgia,[43] but the most prominent of them all was Robert Morris, the financier *par excellence* of the American Revolution.[44]

And now comes an extraordinary thing. Whilst for centuries (especially during the 17th and the 18th—the two so momentous in the growth of the modern State) the Jews had personal financial dealings with the rulers, in the century that followed (but even during the two already mentioned) the system of public credit gradually took a new form. This forced the big capitalist from his dominating position more and more into the background, and allowed an ever-increasing number of miscellaneous creditors to take his place. Through the evolution of the modern method of floating loans the public credit was, so to speak, "democratized," and, in consequence, the Court Jew became superfluous. But the Jews themselves were not the least who aided the growth of this new system of borrowing, and thus they contributed to the removal of their own monopoly as financiers. In so doing they participated to a greater degree than ever before in the work of building up the great States of the present.

The transformation in the public credit system was but a part of a much vaster change which crept over economic life as a whole, a metamorphosis in which also the Jews took a very great share. Let us consider this change in its entirety.

Chapter 6

The Predominance of Commerce in Economic Life

IT IS A MATTER of common knowledge that the Stock Exchange in modern times is becoming more and more the heart of all economic activities. With the fuller development of capitalism this was only to be expected, and there were three clear stages in the process. The first was the evolution of credit from being a personal matter into one of an impersonal relationship. It took shape and form in securities. Stage two: these securities were made mobile—that is, bought and sold in a market. The last stage was the formation of undertakings for the purpose of creating such securities.

In all the stages the Jew was ever present with his creative genius. We may even go further and say that it was due specifically to the Jewish spirit that these characteristics of modern economic life came into being.

The Origin of Securities[1]

Securities represent the standardization of personal indebtedness.[2] We may speak of "standardization" in this sense when a relationship which was originally personal becomes impersonal; where before human beings directly acted and reacted on each other, now a system obtains. An instance or two will make our meaning clear. Where before work was done by man, it is now done by a machine. That is the standardization of work. In olden times a battle was won by the superior personal initiative of the general in command; nowadays victory falls to the leader who can most skilfully utilize the body of experience gathered in the course of years and can best apply the complicated methods of tactics and strategy; who has at his disposal the best guns and who has the most effective organization for provisioning his men. We may speak in this instance of the "standardization" of war. A business becomes standardized when the head of the firm who came into personal contact with his employees on the one hand and with his customers on the other, is succeeded by a board of directors, under whom is an army of officials, all working on an organized plan, and consequently business is more or less of an automatic process.

Now, at a particular stage in the growth of capitalism credit became standardized. That is to say, that whereas before indebtedness arose as the result of an agreement between two people who knew each other, it was now rearranged on a systematic basis, and the people concerned might be entire strangers. The new relationship is expressed by negotiable instruments, whether bill of exchange or security or banknote or mortgage deed, and a careful analysis of each of them will prove this conclusively.

Of the three persons mentioned in a bill of exchange, the specified party in whose favour the document is made out (the payee) or, if no name is mentioned, the bearer of the document may be quite unknown to the other two; he may have had no direct business relation with the party making out the bill (the drawer), yet this document establishes a claim of the former on the latter—general and impersonal.[3]

The security gives the owner the right to participate in the capital and the profit of a concern with which he has no direct personal contact. He may never even have seen the building in which the undertaking in question is housed, and when he parts with his security to another person he transfers his right of participation.

Similarly with a banknote. The holder has a claim on the bank of issue despite the fact that he personally may never have deposited a penny with it.

So, in short, with all credit instruments: an impersonal relationship is established between either an individual or a corporation on the one hand (the receiver of moneys), and an unknown body of people (we speak of "the public") on the other—the lender of moneys.

What share did the Jews take in the creation of this credit machinery? It would be difficult, perhaps impossible, to show what that share was by reference to documentary evidence, even if we had a very full account of the position of the Jews in the early economic history of most lands. But unfortunately that aspect of economic development which would have been invaluable for the solution of the problem in hand has been sadly neglected. I refer to the history of money and of banking in the Pyrenean Peninsula during the last centuries of the Middle Ages. But even if such a history were at our disposal, the question would still be difficult to answer. We must remember that the origins of economic organization can no more be discovered by referring to documentary evidence than the origins of legal institutions. No form of organization or tendency in economic life can be traced to a particular day or even a particular year. It is all a matter of growth, and the most that the economic historian can do is to show that in any given period this or that characteristic is found in business life, this or that organization dominates all economic activities. Even for this the ludicrously inadequate sources at our disposal are hardly sufficient. The historian will have to turn to the general history of the particular group in which he happens to be interested.

To take an instance. The history of bills of exchange can scarcely be written merely by referring to the few mediæval bills which chance has left to us. Such documents are certainly useful to supplement or correct general theories. But we must formulate the general theories first. Let us take a case in point. The bill which for a long time was held to be the oldest extant was drawn by a Jew, Simon Rubens, in the year 1207. This is hardly sufficient evidence on which to base the assertion that the Jews were the inventors of this form of credit instrument.[4] Earlier bills have come to light recently, drawn by non-Jews, but they do not render testimony strong enough for the statement that the Jews were *not* the inventors of bills. Do we know how many thousands of bills circulated in Florence or Bruges, and how can we be sure which section of the population issued them? We do know, however, that the Jews were occupied throughout the

Middle Ages in money-dealing, that they were settled in various parts of Europe and that they carried on a continuous intercourse with each other. From these facts we may draw the tolerably certain conclusion that "the Jews, the intermediaries in international trade, utilized on a large scale the machinery of foreign exchanges, then traditionally current in the Mediterranean lands, and extended it."[5]

That this method of reasoning requires great caution is self-evident. Yet it may lead to useful conclusions for all that. There are cases, as we shall see, where the share of the Jews in the extension of some economic policy or machinery may be proved by a fund of documentary evidence. In other instances, and they are numerous, we must content ourselves if it can be shown that, at any particular time and in any given place, there must have been some special reason for the utilization by Jews of a form of economic organization then current.

Bearing this in mind, let us enquire into the genesis of one or two types of credit instruments.

The Bill of Exchange

Not merely the early history of the bill of exchange but rather that of the modern endorsable bill is what we are concerned with most of all. It is generally accepted that the endorsing of bills of exchange had been fully developed prior to the 17th century, and the first complete legal recognition of such endorsement was found in Holland (Proclamation in Amsterdam of January 24, 1651).[6] Now, as we shall see presently, all developments in the money and credit systems of Holland in the 17th century were due more or less to Jewish influence. Some authorities trace the origin of endorsable bills of exchange to Venice, where they were made illegal by a law of December 14, 1593.[7] It is fairly certain that the use of circulating endorsable bills in Venice must have been first commenced by Jews, seeing that we know that nearly all bill-broking in the Adriatic city in the 16th century was in their hands. In the petition of the Christian merchants of Venice of the year 1550 (to which reference has already been made) the passage relating to the bill business of Jews reads as follows[8]:—

> We carry on the same commerce with them also in matters of exchange, because they continually remit to us their money . . . sending cash, in order that we may change it for them for Lyons, Flanders and other parts of the world on our Exchange, or indeed that we may buy for them silken cloths and other merchandise according to their convenience, gaining our usual commission.
>
> That which we say of the inhabitants of Florence holds good also of the other merchants of the same Spanish and Portuguese nation, who dwell in Flanders, Lyons, Rome, Naples, Sicily and other countries, who lay themselves out to do business with us, not only in exchanges but in sending hither merchandise of Flanders, selling corn from Sicily and buying other merchandise to transport to other countries.

A further development in the endorsing of bills appears to have taken place at the fairs of Genoa in the 16th century. Who, we may ask, were the "Genoese," met with everywhere throughout that century, but especially at the famous fairs of Besançon, dominating the money market, and who all of a sudden showed a remarkable genius for business and gave an impetus to the growth of new methods, hitherto unknown, for cancelling international indebtedness? It is true that the ancient wealthy families of Genoa were the principal creditors of the Spanish Crown as well as of other needy princes. But to imagine that the descendants of the Grimaldis, the Spinolas, the Lercaras exhibited that extraordinary commercial ability which gave a special character to the activity of the Genoese in the 16th century; to think that the old nobility gadded about the fairs at Besançon or elsewhere, or even sent their agents with never-failing regularity— this appears to me an assumption hardly warranted without some very good reason. Can the explanation be that the Jews brought new blood into the decrepit economic body of Genoa? We know[9] that fugitives from Spain landed at Genoa, that some of the settlers became Christians, that the rest were admitted into Novi, a small town near Genoa, and that the Jews of Novi did business with the capital; we know, too, that the newcomers were "for the most part intelligent Jewish craftsmen, capitalists, physicians," and that in the short space of time between their arrival and 1550 they had become so unpopular in Genoa that they had aroused the hatred of the citizens; we know, finally, that there were constant communications between the Genoese bankers and the Jewish, or rather Maranno, banking houses of the Spanish cities, *e.g.*, with the Espinosas, the leading bankers in Seville.[10]

Securities (Stocks and Shares)

If we should wish to speak of securities in those cases where the capital of a business concern is split up into many parts, and where the liability of the capitalists is limited, we have ample justification for so doing in the case of the Genoa Maones, in the 14th century,[11] the Casa di San Giorgio (1407) and the important trading companies of the 17th century. But if stress is laid on the standardization of the credit-relationship, it will not be before the 18th century that we shall find instances of joint-stock enterprise and of securities. For the early contributions to a joint-stock never lost their personal character. The Italian Montes were impregnated through and through with the personality of their founders. In the case of the Maones, the personal factor was no less important than the financial; while at the Bank of St. George in Genoa, the families concerned jealously guarded the principle that each one should obtain its proper share in the directing of the work of the bank. The trading companies too had a strong personal element. In the English East India Company, for instance, it was not until 1650 that shares could be transferred to strangers, but they had to become members of the Company.

In all early instances the security was for unequal and varying sums. The personal relationship thus showed itself plainly enough. In some companies shares could not be transferred at all except by consent of all the other members. In fact, the security was just a certificate of membership, and throughout the 18th century such securities as were made out in the name of a specified person predominated.[12] Even where there was freedom of transfer from one person to another (as in the case of the Dutch East India Company) the process was beset with innumerable obstacles and difficulties.[13]

The modern form of security can therefore not be found before the 18th century. If now it be asked what share did the Jews have in the extension of this form of credit in modern times, the reply is obvious enough. During the last hundred and fifty or two hundred years, Jews have been largely instrumental in bringing about the standardization of what was before a purely personal relationship between the holder of stock and the company in which he participated. I am bound to admit, however, that I cannot adduce direct proofs in support of my thesis. But indirectly the evidence is fairly conclusive. Jews were great speculators, and speculation must of necessity tend to substitute for the security wherein the holder is specified one which has no such limitation. A little reflection will show therefore that Jews must have had no small influence on the standardization of securities. In some cases it may even be demonstrated that speculation was responsible for the change from securities of differing amounts to those of equal value. The Dutch East India Company is a case in point. Originally its shares were of all values; later only 3000 florin shares were issued.[14]

Banknotes

Many opinions prevail as to the precise occasion when banknotes first came into use. For my own part I lay stress on the standardization here also. The first time any banker issued a note without reference to some specific deposit a new type of credit instrument, the modern banknote, came into being. There were banknotes in existence long before that.[15] But they bore the depositor's name and referred to his money.[16] I believe that in all probability the personal banknote became a general (impersonal) one in Venice about the beginning of the 15th century. There are on record instances dating from that time of banks making written promises to pay over and above the sums deposited with them. An edict of the Venetian Senate as early as 1421 made it an offence to deal in such documents.[17] The first permission to establish a bank was granted to two Jews in 1400, and their success was so great that the *nobili* made haste to follow their example.[18] The question arises, may these two Jews be regarded as the fathers of the modern (impersonal) banknote?

But perhaps no particular firm introduced the new paper money. It may have come into existence in order to satisfy the needs of some locality. Nevertheless, if we take as the place of its origin the town where the earliest banks reached a high degree of perfection, we shall surely be on the safe side. From this point of view Venice is admirably qualified. Now Venice was a city of Jews, and that is wherein its interest for us lies in this connexion. According to a list dating from the year 1152, there were no fewer than 1300 Jews in Venice.[19] In the 16th century their number was estimated at 6000; and Jewish manufacturers employed 4000 Christian workmen.[20] These figures, to be sure, have no scientific value, but they do show that the Jews must have been pretty numerous in Venice. From other sources we are acquainted with some of their activities. Thus, we find Jews among the leading bankers—one of the most influential families were the Lipmans; and in 1550, as we have already noted, the Christian merchants of Venice stated that they might as well emigrate if trade with the Marannos were forbidden them.

It is possible that the Marannos may have founded the business of banking even while they were yet in Spain. We have, however, no satisfactory information, though many writers have dealt with the subject.[21] There is a strong probability that at the time when measures were taken against them (16th century) the Jews were the leading bankers in the Pyrenean Peninsula. If this be so, is not the presumption justifiable that before then, too, the Jews engaged in banking?

Furthermore, Jews were prominent and active figures wherever in the 17th century banks were established. They participated in the foundation of the three great banks of that period—the Bank of Amsterdam, the Bank of England and the Bank of Hamburg. But as none of these owed its origin to purely commercial causes, I shall not emphasize their importance in connexion with the Jews. The facts, nevertheless, are interesting, and I would therefore state that the experience which the Jews gathered when the Bank of Amsterdam was founded served them in good stead when in 1619 the Hamburg Bank came into being. No less than forty Jewish families took shares in the new concern. As for the Bank of England, the latest authorities[22] on its history are agreed that the suggestion for the Bank came from Jewish immigrants from Holland.

Public Debt Bonds

The earliest bonds issued for public loans were addressed to some individual lender, and it was long before they changed their character and became "general" instruments. In Austria, to take one example, it was not until the Debt of 1761 was contracted that the bonds had coupons attached which gave the bearer the right to receive interest.[24] Previous to that, the bond was of the nature of a private agreement; the Crown or the Treasury was the debtor of some specific lender.[25]

To what extent the Jews were responsible for the "standardization" of public credit it is difficult to estimate. So much is certain, that William III's advisers were Jews; that public borrowing in the German States was commenced on the model of Holland, most probably through the influence of Dutch Jews who, as we have already seen, were the chief financiers in German and Austrian lands. Speaking generally, Dutch Jews were most intimately concerned in European finance in the 18th century.[26]

As for private loan-bonds or mortgage-deeds, we know

very little of their history, and it is almost impossible to compute the direct influence of the Jews here. But indirectly the Jews were, in all likelihood, the originators of this species of credit instrument, more especially of mortgage deeds. We have it on record that Dutch bankers, from about the middle of the 18th century onward, advanced money to colonial planters on the security of their plantations. Mortgage-deeds of this kind were bought and sold on the Stock Exchange, just like Public Debt bonds. The bankers who dealt in them were called "correspondentie" or "Directeurs van de negotiatie," and the instruments themselves "obligatie." Documents to the value of no less than 100,000,000 gulden were in circulation before the crash of the 1770's.[27]

I must confess that nowhere have I found any mention of Jewish bankers participating in these speculations. Yet even the most superficial acquaintance with the Dutch money-market in the 18th century can scarcely leave room for doubt that Jews must have been largely interested in this business. It is a well-known fact (as I hope to show) that in those days anything in Holland connected with money-lending, but especially with stocks and shares and speculation, was characteristically Jewish. We are strengthened in this conclusion through knowing that most of the business in mortgage-banking was carried on with the colony of Surinam. Of the 100,000,000 gulden of mortgage-deeds already mentioned, 60,000,000 worth was from Surinam. Now Surinam, as we noted above, was the Jewish colony *par excellence*. The possibility that the credit relationship at that time between Surinam and the Motherland was maintained by other than Jewish houses is well-nigh excluded.

So much for the "sources" regarding the Jewish share in the development of modern credit instruments. The sum-total is not much; it is for subsequent research to fill in the details and to add to them. Yet I believe the evidence sufficient for the general conclusion that in the standardization of modern credit the Jews took no inconsiderable share. This impression will only be deepened if we think for a moment of the means by which the standardization was brought about or, at any rate, facilitated. I mean the legal form of the credit instruments, which in all probability was of Jewish origin.

There is no complete agreement among authorities on the history of legal documents as to the origin of credit instruments.[28] But in my opinion the suggestion that they owe their modern form to Jewish influence has much to be said for it. Let it be remembered that such documents first came into use among merchants, in whose ranks the Jewish element was not insignificant. The form that became current received recognition in judicial decisions, and eventually was admitted into the body of statute law, first of all presumably in Holland.

The only question is, Can we possibly deduce modern credit instruments from Rabbinic law? I believe we can.

In the first place, the Bible and the Talmud are both acquainted with credit instruments. The Biblical passage is in the Book of Tobit, iv. 20; v. 1, 2, 3; ix. 1, 5.

The best known passage in the Talmud is as follows (*Baba Bathra*, 172):—

"In the court of R. Huna a document was once produced to this effect: 'I, A.B., son of C.D., have borrowed a sum of money from you.' R. Huna decided that 'from you' might mean 'from the Exilarch or even from the King himself.' "

Second, in later Jewish law, as well as in Jewish commercial practice, the credit instrument is quite common. As regards practice, special proof is hardly necessary; and as for theory, let me mention some Rabbis who dealt with the problem.[29]

First in importance was Rabbenu Asher (1250-1327), who speaks of negotiable instruments in his Responsa (lxviii. 6, 8). "If A sends money to B and C, and notes in his bill 'payable to bearer by B and C,' payment must be made accordingly." So also R. Joseph Caro in his *Choshen Mishpat:* "If in any bill no name is mentioned but the direction is to 'pay bearer,' then whoever presents the bill receives payment" (lxi. 10; cf. also 1.; lxi. 4, 10; lxxi. 23). R. Shabbatai Cohen in his *Shach.* (l. 7; lxxi. 54) is of the same opinion.

Thirdly, it is very likely that the Jews, in the course of business, independently of Rabbinic laws, developed a form of credit instrument which was quite impersonal and general in its wording. I refer to the *Mamre* (*Mamram, Mamran*).[30] It is claimed that this document first appeared among the Polish Jews in the 16th century, or even earlier. Its form was fixed, but a space was left for the name of the surety, sometimes, too, for the amount in question. There is no doubt that such documents were in circulation during three centuries and were very popular, circulating even between Christians and Jews. Their value as evidence consists in that they already had all the characteristics of modern instruments: (1) the holder put the document in circulation by endorsement; (2) there is no mention of the personal relationship of the debtor and the creditor; (3) the debtor may not demand proof of endorsement or transfer; (4) if the debtor pays his debt without the presentation of the *Mamre* having been made to him, it is considered that he has not really discharged his obligation; and lastly (5) the cancellation of the document is almost the same as it is to-day—if it is lost or stolen the holder of the document informs the debtor; public notice is given by a declaration posted up for four weeks in the synagogue, wherein the bearer of the instrument is requested to come forward; at the end of four weeks, if nothing happens, the creditor demands payment of the debtor.

In the fourth place, it would appear that Jewish influences were potent in the development of many weighty points of legal practice. Let me mention some.

(1) During the 16th century there circulated in different parts of Europe credit instruments with blanks for filling in names. What was their origin? Is there not a possibility that they emanated from Jewish commercial circles, having been modelled on the pattern of the *Mamre?* They are met with in the Netherlands,[31] in France[32] and in Italy.[33] In the Netherlands they appeared towards the beginning of the 16th century at the Antwerp fairs, just when the Jews began to take a prominent part in them. An Ordinance of the year

1536 states explicitly that "at the Antwerp fairs payment for commodities was made by promissory notes, which might be passed on to third persons without special permission." It would seem from the wording that the practice of accepting notes in payment for goods was a new one. What sort of documents were these notes? Can they have been Christian *Mamrem?* Even more Jewish were the documents in vogue in Italy a century later. I mean the first known "open" note, issued by the Jewish bill-brokers, Giudetti, in Milan. The note was for 500 scudi, payable through John Baptist Germanus at the next market day in Novi to the personal order of Marcus Studendolus in Venice for value received. Studendolus sent the bill to de Zagnoni Brothers in Bologna "with his signature, leaving a sufficient blank space at the end for filling in the amount, and the name of the person in whose favour the de Zagnonis preferred payment to be made." The recorder of this instance remarks[34] that "Italian financial intercourse could hardly have thought of a facility of this kind, had there not been a model somewhere to imitate. Such a model is found in France, where from the 17th century onward bearer bonds were in general circulation." The question at once suggests itself, how did this document arise in France. Will the example of Holland account for it? Even in Italy it may be a case of Maranno influence—Studendolo(?) in Venice, Giudetti in Milan!

(2) Of very great significance in the development of modern credit instruments is the Antwerp Custom of 1582, wherein it is for the first time admitted that the holder of a note has the right of suing in a court of law.[35] This conception spread rapidly from Antwerp to Holland—as rapidly, indeed, as the Jewish refugees from Belgium settled down among the Dutch.[36]

(3) In Germany the first State to adopt credit instruments was Saxony. In the year 1747 an adventurer of the name of Bischopfield suggested to the Minister of Finance the plan of a Public Loan, and it seems that Bischopfield was in communication with Dutch Jews at the time.[37] Further, an ordinance of 20th September 1757 forbade Dutch Jews to

speculate in Saxon Government Stock. All of which points
to Jewish influence—on the one side of the Dutch Jews,
and on the other of Polish Jews, owing to the connexion of
the royal houses of Saxony and Poland. So great was this
influence that one authority comes to the definite conclusion
that the *Mamre* became the model for credit instruments.[38]

(4) Among the instruments wherein the name of the
holder was inserted we must include marine insurance policies. It is recorded that the Jewish merchants of Alexandria
were the first to use the formulæ *"o qual si voglia altera
persona," "et quævis alia persona"* and *"sive quamlibet aliam
personam"* ("or to any other person desired").[39]

Now why did the Jewish merchants of Alexandria adopt
this legal form? The answer to this question is of the gravest
import, more especially as I believe that the causes for which
we are seeking were inherent in the conditions of Jewish
life.

(5) That leads me to my fifth consideration. It was to
the interest of the Jews to a very large degree—in some
respects even it was to the interest of the Jews alone—to
have a proper legal form for credit instruments. For what
was it that impelled the Jewish merchants of Alexandria to
make out their policies to bearer? Anxiety as to the fate of
their goods. Jewish ships ran the risk of capture by Christian
pirates and the fleets of His Catholic Majesty, who accounted
the wares of Jews and Turks as legitimate booty. Hence the
Jewish merchants of Alexandria inserted in their policies
some fictitious Christian name, Paul or Scipio, or what you
will, and when the goods arrived, received them in virtue
of the "bearer" formula in their policies.

How often must the same cause have actuated Jews
throughout the Middle Ages! How often must they have
endeavoured to adopt some device which concealed the fact
that they were the recipients either of money or of commodities sent from a distance. What more natural than that
they should welcome the legal form which gave "the bearer"
the right of claiming what the document he had entitled him
to. This formula made it possible for fortunes to vanish if

the Jews in any locality passed through a storm of persecution. It enabled Jews to deposit their money wherever they wanted, and if at any time it became endangered, to remove it through the agency of some fictitious person or to transfer their rights in such a way as not to leave a trace of their former possessions.[40] It may seem inexplicable that while throughout the Middle Ages the Jews were deprived of their "all" at very short intervals, they managed to become rich again very quickly. But regarded in the light of our suggestion, this problem is easily explained. The fact was that the Jews were never mulcted of their "all"; a good portion of their wealth was transferred to a fictitious owner whenever the kings squeezed too tight.

Later, when the Jews commenced to speculate in securities and commodities (as we shall see in due course) it was only to be expected that they would extend the use of this form of bond, more particularly in the case of securities.[41] It is obvious that if a big loan is subscribed by a large number of comparatively small contributors bearer bonds offer facilities of various kinds.[42]

The remark of a Rabbi here and there demonstrates this conclusively. One passage in the commentaries of R. Shabbatai Cohen is distinctly typical. "The purchaser of a bond," he says, "may claim damages against the debtor if he pays the debt without obtaining a receipt, the reason being that as there is no publicity in the transaction this practice is detrimental to dealings in such instruments. It is true that Rabbenu Asher and his school expressed no view concerning *Shetarot* (instruments) of all kinds, which the Rabbis introduced in order to extend commerce. That is because dealings in such instruments were not very common, owing to the difficulty of transfer. But the authorities were thinking only of personal bonds. In the case of bearer bonds, the circulation of which at the present time (*i.e.*, the 17th century) is greater far than that of commodities, all ordinances laid down by the Rabbis for the extension of commerce are to be observed."

(6) Here again we touch a vital question. I believe that if

we were to examine the whole Jewish law concerning bearer
bonds and similar instruments we should find—and this is
my sixth point—that such documents spring naturally from
the innermost spirit of Jewish law, just as they are alien to
the spirit of German and Roman law.

It is a well-known fact that the specifically Roman conception of indebtedness was a strictly personal one.[43] The
obligatio was a bond between certain persons. Hence the
creditor could not transfer his claim to another, except under
exceedingly difficult conditions. True, in later Roman law
the theory of delegation and transmission was interpreted
somewhat liberally, yet the root of the matter, the personal
relationship, remained unchanged.

In German law a contract was in the same way personal;
nay, to a certain extent it was even more so than in Roman
law. The German principle on the point was clear enough.
The debtor was not obliged to render payment to any one
but the original creditor to whom he had pledged his word.
There could in no wise be transference of claim—as was
the case in English law until 1873. It was only when Roman
law obtained a strong hold on Germany that the transfer of
claims first came into vogue. The form it took was that of
"bearer bonds"—the embodiment of an impersonal credit
relationship.

It is admitted that the legal notion underlying all "bearer"
instruments—that the document represents a valid claim for
each successive holder—was not fully developed either in the
ancient world or in the Middle Ages.[44] But the admission
holds good only if Jewish law be left out of account. Jewish
law was certainly acquainted with the impersonal credit
relationship.[45] Its underlying principle is that obligations may
be towards unnamed parties, that you may carry on business
with Messrs. Everybody. Let us examine this principle a
little more closely.

Jewish law has no term for obligation: it knows only debt
("Chov") and demand ("Tvia"). Each of these was regarded
as distinct from the other. That a demand and a promise
were necessarily bound up with some tangible object is

proved by the symbolic act of acquisition. Consequently there could be no legal obstacles to the transfer of demands or to the making of agreements through agents. There was no necessity therefore for the person against whom there was a claim to be defined, the person in question became known by the acquisition of certain commodities. In reality claims were against things and not against persons. It was only to maintain a personal relationship that the possessor of the things was made responsible. Hence the conception that just as an obligation may refer to some specified individual, so also it may refer to mankind as a whole. Therefore a transference of obligations is effected merely by the transference of documents.

So much would appear from the view held by Auerbach. Jewish law is more abstract in this respect than either Roman or German law. Jewish law can conceive of an impersonal, "standardized" legal relationship. It is not too much to assume that a credit instrument such as the modern bearer bond should have grown out of such a legal system as the Jewish. Accordingly, all the external reasons which I have adduced in favour of my hypothesis are supported by what may be termed an "inner" reason.

And what is this hypothesis? That instruments such as modern bearer bonds owe their origin chiefly to Jewish influences.

Buying and Selling Securities

The Evolution of a Legal Code Regulating Exchange

In modern securities we see the plainest expression of the commercial aspect of our economic life. Securities are intended to be circulated, and they have not served their true purpose if they have not been bought and sold. Of course it may be urged that many a security rests peacefully in a safe, yielding an income to its owner, for whom it is a means to an end rather than a commodity for trading in. The objection has a good deal in it. A security that does not circulate is in reality not a security at all; a promissory note might replace it equally well. The characteristic mark of a security is the ease with which it may be bought and sold.

Now if to pass easily from hand to hand is the real *raison d'être* of the security, everything which facilitates that movement matters, and therefore a suitable legal code most of all. But when is it suitable? When it renders possible speedy changes in the relationship between two people, or between a person and a commodity.

In a society where every commodity continues as a rule in the possession of one and the same person, the law will strive all it can to fix every relationship between persons and things. On the other hand, if a body of people depends for its existence on the continued acquisition of commodities, its legal system will safeguard intercourse and exchange.

In modern times our highly organized system of intercommunication, and especially dealings in securities and credit instruments of all kinds, has facilitated the removal of old and the rise of new legal relationships. But this is contrary to the spirit of Roman and German law, both of which placed obstacles in the way of commodities changing hands. Indeed, under these systems any one who has been deprived of a possession not strictly in accordance with law may demand its return from the present owner, without the need of any compensation, even though his *bona-fides* be established. In modern law, on the other hand, the return of the possession can be made only if the claimant pays the present owner the price he gave for it—to say nothing of the possibility that the original owner has no claim whatever against the present holder.

If this be so, whence did the principle, so alien to the older systems, enter into modern law? The answer is that in all probability it was from the Jewish legal code, in which laws favouring exchange were an integral part from of old.

Already in the Talmud we see how the present owner of any object is protected against the previous owners. "If any one," we read in the "Mishna" (*Baba Kama*, 114*b* and 115*a*), "after it has become known that a burglary took place at

his house finds his books and utensils in the possession of
another, this other must declare on oath how much he paid
for the goods, and on his receiving the amount returns them
to the original owner. But if no burglary has taken place,
there is no need for this procedure, for it is then assumed
that the owner sold the goods to a second person and that
the present owner bought them." In every case, therefore,
the present owner obtains compensation, and in certain
given circumstances he retains the objects without any further ado. The "Gamara," it is true, wavers somewhat in the
discussion of the passage, but in general it comes to the
same conclusion. The present owner must receive "market
protection," and the previous owner must pay him the price
he gave.

The attitude of the Talmud, then, is a friendly one towards
exchange, and the Jews adopted it throughout the Middle
Ages. But more than that—and this is the important point—
they succeeded quite early in getting the principle recognized
by Christian law-courts in cases where Jews were concerned.
For centuries there was a special enactment regulating the
acquisition of moveables by Jews; it received official recognition for the first time in the "Privileges" issued by King
Henry IV to the Jews of Speyers in 1090. "If a commodity
that has been stolen," we read therein, "is found in the possession of a Jew who declares that he bought it, let him swear
according to his law how much he paid for it, and if the
original owner pays him the price, the Jew may restore the
commodity to him." Not only in Germany, but in other
lands too[46] (in France already about the middle of the 12th
century), is this special ordinance for Jews to be met with.[47]

The Stock Exchange

But when all is said, the principal thing was to establish
a suitable market for credit instruments. The Stock Exchange
answered the purpose. And just as the commodities there to
be bought and sold were impersonal embodiments of claims,
so, too, was the dealing divested of its personal character.
Indeed, this is a feature of the Stock Exchange which dif-

ferentiates it from other markets. It is no longer the trust-worthiness that a merchant enjoys in the estimation of his fellow-merchants, based upon personal experience, that underlies business activities, but the general, abstract valuation of credit, the *ditta di Borsa*. Prices are no longer formed by the higgling of two or more traders talking over their transactions, but rather by a mechanical process, representing the average of a thousand and one units.[48]

As for the history of the Stock Exchange (in the broadest connotation of the term), it may be divided into two periods—(1) from its beginning in the 16th to the end of the 18th century, an epoch of growth and development, and (2) from the 19th century to the present day, when the Stock Exchange dominates all economic activities.

It is now generally agreed that the origin of Stock Exchange dealing most likely began with the associating of bill-brokers.[49] The centres where the famous exchanges first arose in the 16th and 17th centuries were previously well known for a brisk trade in bills.

The important thing for us is that just when the Stock Exchanges came into being the Jews almost entirely monopolized bill-broking. In many towns, indeed, this business was regarded as a Jewish specialty. That such was the case in Venice we have already seen.[50] It was also true of Amsterdam, though we must add that the first mention of Jews in that capacity was not until the end of the 17th century.[51] Despite this, however, I believe we shall be safe in assuming that previous to that date also they were influential bill-brokers.

In Frankfort-on-the-Main we hear the same story. Already in the 16th century a contemporary[52] says of the Jews who came to the fairs that their presence was "hardly ornamental but certainly very useful, especially in the bill-discounting business." Again, in 1685, the Christian merchants of Frankfort complained that the Jews had captured the whole of the business of bill-broking.[53] Lastly, Glückel von Hameln states in her *Memoirs* that friends of her family dealt in bills, "as was customary among Jews."[54]

As for Hamburg, Jews certainly introduced the business of bill-broking there. A hundred years after the event (1733) a document in the Archives of the Senate expressed the opinion that "Jews were almost masters of the situation in bill-broking and had quite beaten our people at it."[55] And even as late as the end of the 18th century the Jews were almost the only purchasers of bills in Hamburg. Among other German towns, it is recorded that in Fürth bill-broking (in the 18th century) was almost entirely in Jewish hands.[56]

The position in Vienna was no different. The Austrian capital, as is well known, became a notable centre as a stock market at the end of the 18th century, and the State Chancellor Ludewig remarks concerning the activities of the Jews under Leopold I, "chiefly in Vienna by the influence and credit of the Jews business of the greatest importance is often transacted. Especially exchanges and negotiations of the first import in the market."

So in Bordeaux, where we are told[57] "the chief business activity is buying bills and introducing gold and silver into the realm." Even from so far north as Stockholm the same story reaches us.[58] There also the Jews dominated the bill-broking market in the early 19th century (1815).

As the principal bill-brokers of the period, the Jews must have had much to do with the establishment of the Stock Market. But more than that. They gave the Stock Exchange and its dealings their peculiar features in that they became the "originators of speculation in futures," and, indeed, of speculation generally.

When speculation in stocks first arose is as yet difficult to determine. Some have held[59] that the Italian cities furnish examples of this kind of dealing as early as the 15th century.[60] But to my mind this has not yet been conclusively proved.[61]

Not in Italy in the 15th, but in Amsterdam in the 17th century will the beginnings of modern speculation have to be more correctly placed. It is almost certain that the Dutch East India Company's shares called stock-jobbing into existence. The large number of shares of equal value that were suddenly put into circulation at that time, the strong speculative temper of the age, the great interest taken in the Company ever since its foundation, the changing rates of profit that its activities produced—all these must surely have given an impetus to stock and share dealing on the Amsterdam Exchange,[62] then already a highly developed institution. In the space of only eight years dealing in stock became so general and so reckless that it was regarded as an evil by the authorities, who tried to abolish it. A proclamation by the Government of the 26th February, 1610, forbade merchants to sell more shares than they actually possessed. Similar prohibitions were issued in 1621, 1623, 1677, 1700 and so on, all equally without effect.

Who were the speculators? The answer is, all those irrespective of religion who had sufficient money to enable them to participate. Nevertheless the assumption will not be too bold that the Jews were more prominent than others in this activity. Their contribution to the growth of Stock Exchange business was their specialization in stockbroking and the device of dealing in futures. We are not without evidence on both points. Towards the end of the 18th century it was a generally accepted fact that Jews had "discovered" the stock and share business.[63] This belief does not necessarily prove anything; yet that it was without any foundation is hardly likely, especially as there are witnesses to give it support. Nicolas Muys van Holy, who has already been mentioned, says that Jews were the principal stockholders— already in the second half of the 17th century. Later they are found as large investors in both the Dutch India Companies. De Pinto[64] is the authority as regards the Dutch East India Company, and for the West India Company there is the letter of the Directors to Stuyvesant,[65] the Governor of New Amsterdam, requesting him to allow the Jews to settle in the Company's colony, "also because of the large amount of capital which they have invested in shares of the Company." Referring to both companies, Manasseh ben Israel[66] reported to Cromwell "that the Jews were enjoying a good part of the Dutch East and West India Company."

Most significant of all, however, the book which for the first time exhaustively treated of Stock Exchange business in all its branches was written by a Portuguese Jew in Amsterdam, towards the end of the 17th century. I refer to Don Joseph de la Vega's *Confusion de confusiones*, etc., which appeared in 1688,[67] and which a Stock Exchange specialist has described as "being still the best description, both in form and substance, of stock and share dealing even to-day." The book bears witness to the fact that a Jew was the first "theorist" in the sphere of speculations in futures. De la Vega was himself engaged in commerce and his treatise clearly reflects the atmosphere in which he lived.

De la Vega's book in conjunction with the other evidence quoted cannot but lead to the conclusion that if the Jews were not actually the "fathers" of Stock Exchange business they were certainly primarily concerned in its genesis.

Should this view nevertheless be sceptically received by some, I have a trump card in the way of direct proof in support of it.

We possess a report, probably of the French Ambassador in The Hague, written for his Government in the year 1698, wherein he distinctly states that the Jews held the Stock Exchange business in their hands, and shaped its development as they willed. The most salient passages[68] here follow in full:—

In this State (Holland) the Jews have a good deal of power and according to the prognostications of these pretended political speculators, themselves often unreliable, the prices of these stocks vary so considerably that they cause transactions to take place several times a day, transactions which merit the term wager or bet rather than business; the more so, as the Jews who dominate this kind of activity are up to all manner of tricks which take in people, even if they be ever so skilled. . . . Their Jewish brokers and agents, the cleverest of their kind in all the world. . . . Bonds and shares, of all of which they hold large amounts.

The author, acquainted as he is with all the secrets of Stock Exchange activity, describes at length how the Jews succeeded in obtaining the influential position they held on the Amsterdam Stock Exchange. I shall refer to this in due course.

Much light is thrown on the conditions of the Stock Exchange in the Dutch capital when compared with those in other centres. Let us take London first, which from the 18th century onward succeeded Amsterdam as the chief financial centre in Europe. The predominance of Jews in the Stock Exchange in London is perhaps more apparent even than in the case of Amsterdam. The growing activity in the London Stock market towards the end of the 17th century may be traced to the exertions of Amsterdam Jews, who at that time began to settle in England. If this be so, it is proof positive that the Jews were in large measure responsible for the expansion of Stock Exchange dealing in Amsterdam. Else how could they have been so influential in the London Exchange, highly developed as it then already was?

One or two particulars in the story of the accession to power of the Jews in the London Exchange may be noted.

In 1657 Solomon Dormido applied for admission as a member of the Exchange, from which Jews were officially excluded. The law which ordered this exclusion seems to have been conveniently forgotten. Anyhow, towards the end of the 17th century the Exchange (which since 1698 had become known as 'Change Alley) was full of Jews. So numerous did they become that a special corner of the building was designated the "Jews' Walk." "The Alley throngs with Jews," wrote a contemporary.[69]

Whence these throngs?[70] The answer is obvious. They came in the train of William III from Amsterdam, and brought with them the machinery of Stock Exchange dealings in vogue there. The events, as related by John Francis, are regarded as a true presentation by many authorities, even on the Jewish side.

The Stock Exchange was like Minerva: it appeared on

the scene ready armed. The principal participants in the
first English loan were Jews: they assisted William III with
their advice, and one of them, the wealthy Medina, was
Marlborough's banker, giving the General an annual grant
of £6,000 and receiving in return the advantage of being
first in the field with news of the wars. The victories of the
English troops were as profitable to Medina as they were
honourable for England. All the tricks bound up with rising
and falling prices, lying reports from the seat of war, the
pretended arrival of couriers, the formation of financial
cliques and cabals behind the scenes, the whole system of
Mammon's wheels—they knew them all, the early fathers
of the Stock Exchange, and utilized them to the full to their
own advantage.

By the side of Sir Solomon Medina ("the Jew Medina,"
as he was called), who may be regarded as having originated
speculation in the public funds in England, we may place a
number of other wealthy Jews of the reign of Anne, all of
whom speculated on the Stock Exchange. Manasseh Lopez
was one. He amassed a fortune in the panic which followed
the false news that the Queen was dead, buying up all Government Stock which had fallen in price in consequence.
A similar story is told of Sampson Gideon, known among
the Gentiles as "the great Jew broker."[71] A notion of the
financial strength of the Jews in the London of those days
may be obtained when it is recalled that at the beginning
of the 18th century the number of Jewish families with an
annual income between £1000 and £2000 was put by
Picciotto at 100; those with an annual income of £300 at
1000; whilst some individual Jews, such as Mendes da Costa,
Moses Hart, Aaron Frank, Baron d'Aguilar, Moses Lopez
Pereira, Moses or Anthony da Costa (who towards the end
of the 17th century was a Director of the Bank of England)
and others were among the wealthiest merchants in London.

It is evident then that the wealth of the Jews brought
about Stock Exchange speculation on a large scale. But more
striking still, the business of stock-jobbing as a specialized
profession was introduced into the London Exchange by

Jews, probably in the first half of the 18th century. As far as I am aware this fact has hitherto passed unnoticed. But there is abundant proof in support of it.

Postlethwayt, who is pretty reliable in matters of this kind, asserts[72] that "Stock-jobbing . . . was at first only the simple occasional transferring of interest and shares from one to another as persons alienated their estates; but by the industry of the stockbrokers, who got the business into their hands, it became a trade; and one, perhaps, which has been managed with the greatest intrigue, artifice, and trick that ever anything which appeared with a face of honesty could be handled with; for, while the brokers held the box, they made the whole exchange the gamesters, and raised and lowered the prices of stocks as they pleased and always had both buyers and sellers, who stood ready, innocently to commit their money to the mercy of their mercenary tongues."

That Jews formed a considerable proportion of brokers is well-known. As early as 1697, out of one hundred sworn brokers on the London Exchange, no fewer than twenty were Jews and aliens. Doubtless their number increased in the centuries that followed. "The Hebrews flocked to 'Change Alley from every quarter under heaven," wrote Francis. Indeed, a reliable observer of the 1730's (that is to say, a generation after their first appearance on the London Exchange) remarks[73] that there were too many Jewish brokers for them all to do business, consequently this "has occasioned almost one half of the Jew brokers to run into stock-jobbing." The same authority puts the number of Jews then in London at 6000.

This process, by which stock-jobbing was in a sense the outcome of stockbroking, was not limited to London. The same tendencies showed themselves in Frankfort. Towards the end of the 17th century the Jews there were in possession of the entire broking business,[74] and gradually no doubt worked their way into stock-jobbing. In Hamburg[75] the Portuguese Jews had four brokers in 1617, whilst a little later there were twenty.

Taking these facts into consideration, taking into consideration also that public opinion regarded the Jews as responsible for the growth of arbitrage business on the London Exchange,[76] and that Jews participated to a great degree in the big speculations in Government Stock towards the end of the 18th century, we shall be forced to agree with the view that has been expressed by a first-rate authority,[77] that if to-day London is the chief financial centre of the world, it owes this position in large measure to the Jews.

In the period of early capitalism, the Stock Exchanges of other towns lagged far behind those of Amsterdam and London. Even in Paris it was not until towards the end of the 18th century that business became at all brisk. The beginnings of stock speculation (or *Agiotage,* as it is called in France) can be traced to the early 18th century; Ranke[78] discovered the term *Agioteur* in a letter of Elisabeth Charlotte, dated 18th January, 1711. The writer is of the opinion that the term had some connexion with the *billets de monnaye* (bills) but that it was unknown before. It would seem, therefore, that the Law period left no lasting impression. For even in the 1730's the economic pre-eminence of England and Holland, both more capitalistically advanced than their neighbour, was felt in France. One writer of the time[79] makes this clear. "The circulation of stock is one of the sources of great wealth to our neighbours; they have a bank, dividends are paid, and stock and shares are sold." Apparently then such was not the case in France. Even in 1785, an edict (7th August) proclaimed that "the King is informed that for some time past a new kind of commodity has been introduced into the capital"—viz., stocks and shares.

The condition of comparative unimportance which Stock Exchange activities occupied in France during the 18th century is a direct indication that the Jews had little influence on the economic life of France (and especially of Paris) in that period. The cities in which they resided, such as Lyons or Bordeaux, were hardly favourable to the development of stockbroking. In Lyons, however, there was for a short space, in the 16th century, a fairly brisk trade in what would

to-day be called securities, but no satisfactory reasons have
as yet been offered to explain it.[80] Anyhow, it had no after-
effects.

But to return to Paris. What stockbroking it had it probably owed to the Jews. The centre of this business was in
the Rue Quincampoix, which later became notorious through
the swindles connected with the name of Law. Now in this
particular street there lived, in the words of a reliable authority,[81] "many Jews." Be that as it may, the man with
whom the first stock speculations in France were connected,
one who was a greater master of the art of manipulation
than even Law, was Samuel Bernard, the well-known financier of Louis XIV. No wonder then that the *billets de monnaye,* when they became merely bits of valueless paper,
were nicknamed *Bernardines.*[82] And as for John Law, his
knowledge of the mechanism of the Stock Exchange had
been acquired in Amsterdam.[83] Whether he was himself a
Jew (it has been held[84] that Law = Levy) I have been unable to discover. It is, however, quite possible. Was not his
father a "goldsmith" (and banker)? He was, it is true, a
Christian, but that is not necessarily a proof of his non-
Jewishness. The Jewish appearance of the man in portraits
(for example, in the German edition (1720) of his *Money
and Trade Considered*) rather supports the thesis that he
was a Jew. On the other hand, the peculiar mixture of the
lordling and the adventurer which characterized his nature
is against the assumption.

In Germany the Exchanges of Frankfort and Hamburg,
the two Jewish towns *par excellence,* alone reached a position of any importance. Illustrations of the Jewish influence
have already been dealt with.

As for Berlin, it may be said that the Stock Exchange
there was a Jewish institution from its very inception. At
the beginning of the last century, even before 1812, when
they were emancipated, the Jews predominated numerically
on the Exchange. Of the four Presidents, two were Jews;
and the whole Stock Exchange Committee was made up as
follows:—4 Presidents, 10 Wardens of the two Gilds, 1 of

the Elbe Seamen's Gild, and 8 "of the merchants of the Jewish nation, elected thereto." Out of a total of 23, therefore, 10 were Jews. That is to say, professing Jews: it is impossible to determine whether, and how many, baptized Jews and crypto-Jews were in the committee.

As it is, their number shows plainly enough that stockbroking had its large quota of Jews. Of six sworn billbrokers three were Jews. Further, of the two sworn brokers in cotton and silk, one was a Jew, and his substitute was also a Jew. That is to say, of a total of three, two were Jews.[85]

Stockbroking so far as Germany in the 18th century was concerned was carried on only in Hamburg and Frankfort. Already at the beginning of that century trading in securities was forbidden. A proclamation of the Hamburg Council, dated 19th July, 1720, expresses itself as follows:—"The Council has heard to its abhorrence and great disgust, that certain private citizens, under the pretext of founding an assurance company, have on their own authority commenced business as dealers in shares. The Council fears that harmful consequences may ensue therefrom as well to the public at large, as also to the said private citizens."[86] It seems that the powers that be were only voicing the general feeling in the matter; "the dangerous and wickedly ruinous trade in stocks and shares" a writer of the time[87] indignantly called it.

Were Jews here also the originators? So much at least is certain, that the impetus to stock-dealing came from the circles of the assurers, as is apparent from the above-mentioned proclamation of 1720. Now, as a matter of fact, it is known that Jews actively stimulated the growth of marine insurance in Hamburg.[88] Any further evidence as to Stock Exchange influences is only indirect. The same applies to Frankfort. The first certain trace dates from 1817, and refers to Augsburg. There is on record the decision of a court of law in a bill case of the 14th February in the year mentioned. A motion to enforce payment of the difference in the price of a credit-instrument which rose owing to the rise of the market-rate was dismissed, on the ground that it was of the nature of a game of hazard. The sum in question was 17,630 florins, and the original contract was for delivery of 90,000 florins' worth of lottery tickets in the Bavarian State Lottery. The plaintiff's name was Heymann, the defendant's H. E. Ullmann! This is the first attested case of speculation in bonds in Germany.[89]

But with the year 1817 we reach a period which differed from the preceding one, and which I consider as opening a new epoch in the history of Stock Exchange transactions. Why new? What were its special features that it should be described by that dreadful word "modern"?

Judgments on the Stock Exchange by contemporaries then and now show how widely different a position it occupies to-day from what it did even a hundred years ago.

Until well on in the 18th century, even in capitalistic circles, speculation in the public funds was looked at askance. The standard commercial handbooks and dictionaries in English, French, Italian and German, which have come down to us from the 18th century, either make no mention at all of dealings in stocks (especially in the economically "backward" countries), or if, like Postlethwayt, they do treat of the subject, they cannot sufficiently express their contempt for it. The view concerning the Stock Exchange which is to-day held by the petty trader, the small shopkeeper or the farmer was in the 18th century that of the rich merchant. When in 1733 Sir John Barnard's Bill (to prevent the "infamous practice of stock-jobbing") was being discussed in the House of Commons, all the speakers were unanimous in their condemnation of the business. Half a generation later the same harsh terms are to be found in the pages of Postlethwayt, who refers to "those mountebanks we very properly call stockbrokers." Stock-jobbing he regards as a "public grievance," which has become "scandalous to the nation."[90] No wonder that the legislation of the period completely forbade the business.

But the dislike of the Stock Exchange went deeper still. It was bound up with an aversion for what the Exchange rested on—securities in general. Naturally the interests of the State coincided with those who defended the trade in securities, so that Ruler and Jobber were ranged as a lonely couple on one side, while everybody else was on the other—save only those who indulged in the purchase of securities. In truth, the National Debt was looked upon as something of which States had need to be ashamed, and the best men of their generation were agreed that its growth was an evil which should be combated by all possible means. Thinkers and practical men were united on this point. In commercial circles the question was seriously discussed how the public debt could be paid off, and it was even suggested that the State should disavow its responsibilities in connexion with the debt, and so wipe it out. And this in England in the second half of the 18th century![91] Nor were the theorists of the time differently minded. The system of public borrowing is called by David Hume "a practice . . . ruinous beyond all controversy;"[92] Adam Smith writes of "the ruinous practice of funding," "the ruinous expedient of perpetual funding . . . has gradually enfeebled every State which has adopted it" . . . "the progress of the enormous debts, which at present oppress and will in the long run probably ruin all the great nations of Europe."[93] In these opinions, as always, Adam Smith is the mirror of the economic conditions of his age, a period of early capitalistic development, and nothing distinguishes it from our own so well as the fact that in the complete system of Adam Smith there is no niche available for the study of securities, or of the Stock Exchange and its business.

About the same time, however, a book appeared which dealt only with credit and its blessings, with the Stock Exchange and its significance; a book which may be justly termed the "Song of Songs" of Public Debts and share-dealing; a book which looked to the Future, as the *Wealth of Nations* looked to the Past. I refer to the *Traité du crédit et de la circulation*, published in 1771 from the pen of Joseph de Pinto. Now Pinto was a Portuguese Jew, hence my special reference to him in this connexion. In his pages may be found the very arguments which have been put forward in the 19th century in defence of public credit, of dealings in securities and of speculation in the public funds. If Adam Smith in his system be said to stand at the end of the period in which the Stock Exchange was in its infancy, Pinto may be regarded as standing at the beginning of the modern era with its theory of credit, in which stock and share speculation have become the centre of economic activity, and the Stock Exchange the heart of the body economic.

Silently, but none the less surely, public opinion veered round in favour of dealings in securities and of the recognition of the Stock Exchange as a necessity. Public opinion grew as these grew, and step by step, hostile legislation was removed, so that when the Napoleonic wars were over and peace reigned once more, the Stock Exchange began to take on enormous dimensions.

We see, then, that there is some justification for speaking of a new period in the history of the Stock Exchange. What were the actual changes? And to what extent were the Jews concerned in bringing about the new state of affairs?

There was not much modification in the mechanism of the Stock Exchange; that was complete as early as 1688, when de la Vega published his book. Naturally, subsidiary kinds of business activities cropped up here and there, and of these, too, Jews were generally the originators. Thus I have discovered[94] that the business of insurance was established (in Germany) by W. Z. Wertheimer in Frankfort, and that of the peculiar form of ship chartering known as *"Heuergeschäft"* Jews were the founders.

But the rise of subsidiary businesses was not the salient point in the development of Stock Exchange activities. It was rather the extensive and intensive growth of the volume of business.

The enormous increase in the number of securities which have appeared in the market since the beginning of the 19th century, and the rapidity with which they came before the public, are facts too well known to need repetition. But with this increase came also an extension of speculation. Until about the middle of the 18th century, speculation in London and Amsterdam may be compared to little ripples on the face of the water. It was not till 1763, as a reliable informant tells us, that the first private loan was floated in Amsterdam. Previously what speculation there was was limited to public bonds, "but during the last war a vast ocean of annuities flooded the market."[95] Even so, there were only forty-four different kinds of securities on the Amsterdam Exchange about the middle of the century. Of these, twenty-five were bonds of internal, and six of German loans. When the century closed, the first category of bonds numbered eighty, and the second thirty.[96] Then came a sudden upward movement, especially after the defeat of Napoleon. From the first establishment of the Amsterdam Exchange until the year 1770, a total debt of 250,000,000 Gulden had been dealt in; whereas in fourteen years (1808-22) one London firm alone issued a greater sum—22,000,000 pounds. All this is common knowledge; and the identity of that one London firm, which in a decade floated so vast a sum on the market, does not need further indication.

With the mention of this firm, and of its four branches, we have touched on the connexion between the extensive growth of Stock Exchange activities and the Jewish influence upon it. For the expansion of the share market between 1800 and 1850 was also the expansion of the house of Rothschild and its appendages. The name Rothschild refers to more than the firm: it stands for the whole of Jewish influence on the Stock Exchange. By the aid of that influence the Rothschilds were enabled to attain to their powerful position—it may even be said to their unique position—in the market for Government securities. It was no exaggeration to assert that in many a land the minister of finance who could not come to an agreement with this firm might as well close the doors of his exchequer. "There is only one power in Europe," was a dictum well-known about the middle of the 19th century, "and that is Rothschild: a dozen other banks are his underlings, his soldiers are all honest merchants and workmen, and speculation is his sword" (A. Weil). Heine's wit, in passages that are surely too well-known to need quoting, has demonstrated the importance of the family better far than any table of figures.

I have not the least intention of writing here a history of the Rothschilds, even in outline. The reader will find ample material[97] at his disposal should he wish to acquaint himself with the fortunes of this remarkable family. All I shall do will be to point out one or two characteristics which the modern Stock Exchange owes to them, in order to make clear that not only quantitatively, but also qualitatively, the Stock Exchange bears the impress of the Rothschilds (and therefore of the Jew).

The first feature to be observed is that, since the appearance of the Rothschilds, the stock market has become international. This was only to be expected, considering the enormous extension of Stock Exchange activities, which necessitated the flow of vast sums from all parts of the inhabited world to the borrowing centres. To-day the internationalization of the stock market is an accepted fact; at the commencement of the 19th century it was regarded with nothing short of amazement. When in 1808, during the Peninsular War, Nathan Rothschild undertook in London to attend to the pay of the English army in Spain, his action was regarded as a stupendous achievement, and indeed, laid the foundation of all his influence. Until 1798 only the Frankfort firm had been in existence; in that year one of the sons of Mayer Amschel established a branch in London, another son settled in Paris in 1812, a third in Vienna in 1816, and a fourth in Naples in 1820. The conditions were thus given whereby a foreign loan might be treated as though it were an internal loan, and gradually the public became accustomed to investing their capital in foreign securities, seeing that the interest could be paid at home in coins of the realm. Writers of the early 19th century describe it as a marvellous thing that "every holder of Government stock . . . can receive his dividends in various places at his convenience without any difficulty. The Rothschilds in Frankfort pay interest for many

Governments; the Paris house pays the dividends on the Austrian Métalliques, the Neapolitan Rentes, the Anglo-Neapolitan Loan either in London, Naples or Paris."[98]

The circle of possible investors was thus enlarged. But the Rothschilds were also alive to the importance of obtaining every available penny that could be borrowed, and for this purpose they skilfully utilized the machinery of the Stock Exchange for floating loans.

As far as can be judged from contemporary records,[99] the issue by the Rothschilds of the Austrian bonds in 1820-1 was an epoch-making event, both in public borrowing and in Stock Exchange business. For the first time all the ropes were pulled to create a demand for the shares, and speculations in Government stocks may be stated to have begun on this occasion, at least on the Continent.

"To create a demand" was henceforth the watchword of the Stock Exchange. "To create a demand" was the object in view when, by means of systematic buying and selling, changes were brought about in price; and the Rothschilds devoted themselves to the business from the first.[100] In a sense, they carried on what the French called *agiotage*, and this was something quite new for a great banking firm to do. In reality the Rothschilds only adopted the methods of the Amsterdam Jews for artificially influencing the market, but they applied them to a new purpose—the placing of fresh securities before the public.

The changed relation of the banker to the Stock Exchange on the one hand, and to the public on the other, will become more apparent when we have glanced at the new activities which loomed on the horizon at this period—the age of the Rothschilds—and began to play an independent rôle. I mean the business of bringing out loans.

The Creation of Securities

The business of bringing out loans is an attempt to obtain profit by means of the creation of securities. It is important because it represents a capitalistic force of exceedingly great power. Henceforth, stocks and shares come into being not because of the needs of those who require money and depend on credit, but quite independently, as a form of capitalistic enterprise. Hitherto the possible investor was waited for until he came; now he is sought out. The loan-floater becomes, as it were, aggressive; he gives the impetus to the borrowing movement. But this is hardly ever notice-able. We see how it works, however, when small States require loans; we may imagine a kind of "commercial travel-ler in loans." "Now we have wealthy firms with large ma-chinery, whose time and staff are devoted to hunting about the world for Powers for whom to bring out loans."[101]

Naturally, the loan-floater's relation to the Stock Exchange and the public changes. He must be aggressive and pushful, now that his main work is to get people to take up shares.

There is as yet no satisfactory history of the business of bringing out loans. We do not know, therefore, when it first began; its origins, however, no doubt reach back into the 18th century, and probably there were three well marked stages in its growth.

In the first of these, either a bank or a wealthy individual (who, in the pre-Stock Exchange period himself made the loan) was entrusted with the placing of the debt in return for a commission. Such was the method adopted in Austria throughout the whole of the 18th century: "Loans of fairly large sums, especially those contracted abroad, were usually obtained through the intervention of a bank or a group of financiers. The firm in question arranged, by means of public subscription, for the supply of the amount needed; handed over the sum to the borrower or his agent; undertook the payment of interest and portions of the principal to the individual lenders—out of their own funds if need be; all, of course, for a consideration."[102]

But about the middle of the 18th century there were already "dealers in loans." In 1769 there were Italian and Dutch firms who would willingly undertake the floating of loans.[103] Adam Smith's description of this business makes the matter plainer still. "In England . . . the merchants are generally the people who advance money to Government. But by advancing it they do not mean to diminish, but, on the contrary, to increase their mercantile capitals; and unless they expected to sell with some profit their share in the subscription for a new loan, they never would subscribe." In France, on the other hand, those concerned in the finances were people of private means, who advanced their own money.[104]

Where did the specialists in this business come from? Not from among the bankers, who in the 18th century floated loans, but in all probability from among the dealers in stock and shares. Towards the end of the 18th century the charmed circle of London bankers who had the monopoly of bringing out Government loans was broken through by competition from the ranks of the stockholders. Here, too, it was a Jewish firm that took the initiative, and brought the emission of loans into connexion with the Stock Exchange. I refer to the "Rothschilds of the 18th century," the men who predominated in 'Change Alley in those days—Abraham and Benjamin Goldsmid. In 1792 they came forward as the first members of the Stock Exchange[105] to compete with the bankers of London in the bringing out of the new loan, and from that date until the death of the second brother, Abraham, which occurred in 1810, this firm controlled the money market. Perhaps we may account them as the first "loan specialists," whom the Rothschilds succeeded. But even if there is some doubt about the Goldsmids' claim, there can be no possible doubt about the Rothschilds', who were thus certainly the first in the field.

But it is obvious that only a few wealthy firms could subsist by the business of issuing public loans. After all, the demand was comparatively limited. But as soon as opportunities offered themselves for the creation of securities for private needs, a very wide field of activity was ready for ploughing. All that was necessary was to create a big demand artificially, and this tendency gave birth to company-promoting and mortgage business.

Company-promoting is carried on by firms "whose business it professedly is to make money by manufacturing stocks and shares wholesale and forcing them upon the public"

(Crump). The strength of the motive power that thus began to actuate economic activities need scarcely be described. It was not to the interest of undertakers, some of no small importance, to create fresh capital by the issue of new stock or by extending the old, without any reference at all to the question as to whether there was a demand for the stock or not.

Who first started this form of business? It will not be difficult to show that even if the Jews did not actually establish it, they certainly helped forward its development.

The first ray of light on this matter, as far as we can make out, is once again the activity of the Rothschilds. The railway boom of the 1830's made it possible to carry on company-promoting on a large scale. The Rothschilds, as well as other Jewish houses (the d'Eichthals, the Foulds, etc.), were the first in the field, and brought this branch of business to a flourishing condition.

The extent of the participation may be gathered in some degree from the length of the lines built, or the amount of capital subscribed. But the actual share of the individual firms cannot be estimated. Nevertheless, we know that the Rothschilds "built" the Northern Railway in France, the Northern Railway in Austria, the Austro-Italian Railway, and many more.

Further, judging from the views of contemporaries, it would appear that the Rothschilds were really the first "Railway Kings." In 1843 the *Augsburger Allgemeine Zeitung* wrote as follows: "When in the last few years speculation became rife in industrial undertakings, and railways grew to be a necessity for the Continent, the Rothschilds took the plunge and placed themselves at the head of the new movement." The house of Rothschild set the fashion in railway building as it had done before in public loans. "Scarcely a company that was started in Germany but looked to the goodwill of Rothschild. Those in which he had no say were not very successful, and little could be made out of them."[106] Statements such as these, in which friend and foe agree, are significant enough.

Ever since those days the activity of floating companies has become a specialty of Jewish undertakers. In the first place, the very biggest men, such as Baron Hirsch or Dr. Strousberg, were Jews. But the rank and file, too, have many Jews among them. A glance at the figures on the next page concerning the promotion of companies in Germany in the two years 1871-3 suffices to show that an astoundingly large number of Jews participated in the work.[107] But these figures do not tell the whole story. In the first place, they form only a selection of the whole, and refer (of set purpose) to the "shaky" companies, from which the Jews will probably have kept away; and secondly, in many cases, the Jews were behind the scenes as controlling influences, and those in the foreground were merely puppets. Even so the figures will serve a useful purpose.

The tendency is perhaps best seen where private banking is still important, as it is in England. Here, as I am told on the best authority, of the 63 banks in the *Bankers' Almanack* for 1904, 33 were Jewish firms, or at least with a strong Jewish interest, and of these 33, 13 were first-class concerns.

It is more difficult to determine the proportion of Jews in this calling in countries (*e.g.*, Germany) where the private banker has been displaced by the joint-stock bank. But everything points to Jewish influence in the tendency of the joint-stock banks to act as company promoters.

None of the decades of company-flotation, neither the fifties nor the seventies, nor still less the nineties, would have been conceivable without the co-operation of the speculative bank. The stupendous undertakings in railway construction owe their very existence to the banks, which advanced capital to limited companies of their own creation. Private firms, it is true, did no little in the same direction, but their means did not allow of rivalry with the great banks. In France, between 1842 and 1847, no less than 144 million francs were spent in railway building; in the following four years 130 millions, while from 1852 to 1854 the sum had reached 250 millions; in 1855 alone it was 500 millions, and in 1856 520 millions.[108] It was the same in Germany. "The entire work

Nature of Establishment	Total Number of Founders	Number of Jews
Twenty-five firms of first-rate importance that floated companies	25	16
Two of the biggest mining syndicates	13	5
Continental Railway Company (capital 1½ million sterling)	6	4
Twelve land-purchase companies in Berlin	80	27
Building Society, "Unter den Linden"	8	4
Nine building banks	104	37
Nine Berlin breweries	54	27
Twenty North German machine building companies	148	47
Ten North German gasworks	49	18
Twenty paper factories	89	22
Twelve North German chemical works	67	22
Twelve North German textile factories	65	27

of building our net of railways in this period (1848-70) . . . was carried through . . . with the assistance of banks."[109]

The reason for this is not far to seek. On the one hand, the increase of available capital, which was due to the rise of new joint-stock banks, paved the way for proportionately larger undertakings. On the other hand, since the joint-stock company in trying to obtain greater profits strove harder than a private firm to add to its activities, all possible opportunities that presented themselves were utilized to the full.[110]

How did this special banking activity originate?[111] I believe it may be traced to 1852, when the *crédits mobiliers*[112] were first established.

The history of the *crédit mobilier* is well known.[113] What interests us specially is that it owes its inception to two Portuguese Jews, Isaac and Emil Pereire, and that other Jews participated in it. The list of subscribers showed that the two Pereires together held 11,446 shares, and Fould-Oppenheim 11,445, that among the other large shareholders were Mallet Frères, Benjamin Fould, Torlonia (of Rome), Solomon Heine (of Hamburg), Oppenheim (of Cologne)—in other words, the chief representatives of European Jewry. The Rothschilds were not found in the list, for the *crédit mobilier* was directed against them.

The French *crédit mobilier* produced in the years that followed a number of offshoots, legitimate and illegitimate, all of Jewish blood. In Austria there was the "Kaiserlich-Koenigliche privilegierte oesterreichische Kreditanstalt," established in 1855 by S. M. Rothschild. In Germany the first institution modelled on the new principle was the Bank für Handel und Industrie (Darmstädter Bank), founded in 1853, on the initiative of the Oppenheims of Cologne.[114] One of the first directors of this bank was Hess, who had been a high official in the *crédit mobilier*. The Berliner Discontogesellschaft was the second institution of the same kind. Its origin was Christian, but its transformation into what it is to-day is the work of David Hausemann. It was the same with the third German instance—the Berliner Handelsgesellschaft, which was called into being by the Cologne firms already mentioned in connexion with the Darmstädter Bank, and by the best known Berlin bankers, such as Mendelssohn & Co., S. Bleichröder, Robert Warschauer & Co., Schickler Brothers, and others Finally, in the case of the Deutsche Bank (1870) the Jewish element again predominated.

The Commercialization of Industry

With the speculative banks capitalistic development reached its zenith, at any rate, for the time being. They pushed the

process of the commercialization of economic life as far
forward as it could go. Themselves children of the Stock
Exchange, the speculative banks brought Stock Exchange
activities (*i.e.,* speculation) to their fullest bloom.[115] Trade
in securities was extended to undreamt-of proportions. So
much so, that the opinion has been expressed that, in Germany at any rate, the speculative joint-stock banks will replace the Stock Exchange.[116] There may be a grain of truth
in this, provided the terms be properly understood. That the
Stock Exchange may cease to be an open market and be
dominated by *la haute finance* is possible; but as an economic
organization it is bound to gain, if anything, by modern
developments, seeing that its sphere is continuously being
widened.

That is what I mean by the commercialization of industry. The Stock Exchange activities of the joint-stock banks
are becoming more and more the controlling force in every
department of economic life. Indeed, all undertakings in the
field of industry are now determined by the power of finance.
Whether a new industrial concern shall be established or an
old one enlarged, whether a "universal provider" shall receive
an increase of capital in order to extend his business—all
this is now decided in the private offices of banks or bankers.
In the same way the distribution of commodities is becoming more and more a financial problem. It is not too much
to say that our chief industries are as much financial as
industrial concerns. The Stock Exchange determines the price
of most international manufactured articles and raw materials, and he who hopes to survive the competitive strain
must be able to command the Stock Exchange. In a word,
it may be safely asserted that all economic activities nowadays are tending to become commercial dealings.

The electrical industry is the best example. From its first
foundations it represented a new type. Hitherto the great
capitalistic industries regarded their work as finished when
they had obtained and carried out their orders. A particular
factory would appoint an agent in every big town, who in
most cases represented other factories as well, and whose

search for customers could not be marked by any very striking initiative. In the electrical industry all this was changed. Its organizers were the first to see that one of the primary duties of an industry was to create a market for itself. What did they do? They endeavoured to capture the customer. On the one hand, they attempted to control buyers. For example, by purchasing shares either in tram companies about to be turned into electric tramways, or in entirely new undertakings, they could obtain a dominating influence over the body which gave orders for the commodities they were manufacturing. In case of need, the directors of electrical undertakings would themselves call into being limited companies for such activities as would create a demand for their goods. The most successful electrical works have to-day become in an increasing degree similar to banks for floating companies.

Nor is this all. Another policy they adopted was to establish branches in all parts in order to seize upon as much of the market as they could. Whereas formerly reliance was placed on general agents, now the work of extending the connexion is delegated by each firm to a special representative of its own. What is the result? The customer is seen at closer quarters; his needs are better understood and, therefore, better supplied; his wishes more easily met, and so forth.

It is well known that such was the system adopted by the Allgemeine Elektrizitäts-Gesellschaft and that Felix Deutsch was foremost in its extension. The older companies have but slowly followed suit. Siemens and Halske long thought themselves "too grand to run after customers," until Berliner, one of their directors, accepted the new plan to such good effect, that his company soon regained the lost ground from its rival.

This instance is typical, and we may say generally that the commercialization of industry was the gap in the hedge through which the Jews could penetrate into the field of the production and transportation of commodities, as they had done earlier in commerce and finance.

By this we are not asserting that the history of the Jews

as industrialists commences here. Far from it. As soon as modern capitalism differentiated between the technical and commercial aspects of all economic processes, so soon was the Jew found engaged in both. It is true that commerce attracted him more, but already in the early capitalistic period Jews were among the first undertakers in one industry or another.

Here they established the tobacco industry (Mecklenberg, Austria); there, whisky distilling (Poland, Bohemia); in some countries they were leather manufacturers (France, Austria), in others silk manufacturers (Prussia, Italy and Austria); they made stockings in Hamburg; looking-glasses in Fürth; starch in France; cotton in Moravia. And almost everywhere they were pioneers in the tailoring trade. I could show by reference to the materials I have collected that in the 18th and early 19th centuries there were many other instances of Jews as capitalistic industrialists.[117] But I hold that an account of this aspect of Jewish economic history is useless, seeing that it contains nothing specifically Jewish. Jews were driven into an industry by mere chance, and in all probability it would have thriven without them equally well. Let us take an instance or two. In Poland and Austria the position of the Jews as the stewards of the nobility brought it about that they became whisky distillers. In other countries their enterprise in the tobacco industry was a direct result of their status as Court Jews, in connexion with which they very often held the tobacco monopoly. In the majority of instances their commercial activities led to their stocking manufactured articles, and eventually to their making of them, as in the case of textiles. But the process is a common one, and non-Jews passed through it equally with Jews. There was, however, an exception in the case of old clo' dealing. That was an essentially Jewish business, and led first to the sale of new clothes, and eventually to tailoring.

But when all is said, Jewish influence on industrial undertakings was not very great until their commercialization came about; that is, until in almost every modern industry the work of directing and organizing has become common to all, and a man may pass from one industry to another without thereby diminishing his skill. The technical side is now in all cases a subdivision by itself. It is no uncommon thing therefore to find that a man who started in the leather industry ends up as an ironmaster, after having been in turn (shall we say?) a manufacturer of alcoholic liquors and of sulphuric acid. The capitalistic undertaker of old bore a technical impress, the modern undertaker is quite colourless. Can you imagine Alfred Krupp manufacturing anything but guns, Borsig anything but machines, Werner von Siemens anything but electrical apparatus? Can you picture H. H. Myer at the head of any other concern but the Nord-deutscher Lloyd? On the other hand, if Rathenau, Deutsch, Berliner, Arnold, Friedländer, Ballin changed positions to-morrow they would be no less successful than in their present capacities. And what is the reason? They are all men of commerce, and the particular sphere of their activity matters not in the least.

It has been put thus: the Christian makes his way up, starting as technician; the Jew as commercial traveller or clerk.

The extent of Jewish participation in industrial undertakings to-day would be very useful to know, but there is little material to go upon. We shall have to be content with an approximate estimate, based on the numbers of Jews who are directors of industrial concerns. The method is unsatisfactory—naturally so. How is it possible to say with certainty who is a Jew and who is not? How many people are aware, for example, that Hagen of Cologne, who holds more directorships than any other man in Germany, was originally called Levy? But apart from this, mere numbers are no criterion of the extent of influence. Moreover, in some companies business ability alone does not determine the membership of the Board of Directors; in others there is an unwritten law to exclude Jews from positions of trust. In any case, therefore, the figures that have been obtained relate only to a small portion of the Jewish influence.

MANAGING DIRECTORS

Industry	Total	Number of Jews	Percentage of Jews
Leather and rubber	19	6	31.5
Metal	52	13	25.0
Electrical	95	22	23.1
Brewing	71	11	15.7
Textiles	59	8	13.5
Chemicals	46	6	13.0
Mining	183	23	12.8
Machinery	90	11	12.2
Potash	36	4	11.1
Cement, timber, glass, china	57	4	7.0
Total	808	108	13.3

BOARD OF DIRECTORS

Industry	Total	Number of Jews	Percentage of Jews
Brewing	165	52	31.5
Metal	130	40	30.7
Cement, timber, glass, china	137	41	29.9
Potash	156	46	29.4
Leather and rubber	42	12	28.6
Electrical	339	91	26.8
Mining	640	153	23.9
Chemicals	127	29	22.8
Machinery	215	48	21.4
Textiles	141	19	13.5
Total	2092	511	24.4

For all that I quote them; they have been compiled for me from the last edition of the *Handbook of German Joint-Stock Companies*. In the case of the electrical industries, only those with a capital of 6 million mark have been noted; in the chemical industries those with 5 millions; machinery and textiles with 4 millions, and the remainder with 3 millions.

What do these figures suggest? Is the Jewish influence in the industries named great or small? I think it is very large, at any rate quantitatively. Bear in mind that the social group which occupies almost a seventh part of all directorships, and nearly a quarter of all the boards of directors, forms exactly only a hundredth part of the entire population of the German Empire.

Chapter 7

The Growth of a Capitalistic Point of View in Economic Life

IT IS EVIDENT from the survey in the previous chapters that Jewish influence extended far beyond the commercial institutions which it called into being. In other words, the Stock Exchange is not merely a piece of machinery in economic life, it is the embodiment of a certain spirit. Indeed, all the newest forms of industrial organization are the products of this spirit, and it is to this that I wish specially to call the reader's attention.

The outer structure of the economic life of our day has been built up largely by Jewish hands. But the principles underlying economic life—that which may be termed the modern economic spirit, or the economic point of view—may also be traced to a Jewish origin.

Proofs for the statement will have to be sought in directions other than those hitherto followed. Documentary evidence is obviously of little avail here. But what will certainly be a valuable guide is the feeling that prevailed in those circles which first became alive to the fact that the Jewish attitude of mind was something alien. Non-Jewish merchants or their spokesmen expressed opinions which, though one-sided and often harsh, are nevertheless of immense help, because they naïvely set forth the dislike of the Jewish spirit, reflecting it, as it were, as in a mirror (though often enough, to be sure, it was a convex mirror). The people who voiced the opinions to which we are about to refer looked on the Jews as their worst enemies, and therefore we must try to read between the lines, and deduce the truth from statements which were meant to convey something very different. The task is made the more easy because of the uniformity in the opinions formulated—a uniformity due by no means to thoughtless imitation, but rather to similarity of conditions. Their very similarity adds to their forcefulness as proofs.

In the first place, it must be noted that wherever Jews appeared as business competitors, complaints were heard that Christian traders suffered in consequence: their livelihood, we are told, was endangered, the Jews deprived them of their profits, their chances of existence were lessened because their customers went to Jews, and so forth.

A few extracts from documents of the 17th and 18th centuries, the period which concerns us most, will illustrate what has been mentioned. Let us turn first to Germany. In 1672 the Estates of Brandenburg complain that the Jews "take the bread out of the mouths of the other inhabitants."[1] Almost the same phrase is found in the petition of the merchants of Danzig, of March 19th, 1717.[2] In 1712 and 1717 the good citizens of the old town of Magdeburg object to the admission of Jews into their midst, "because the welfare of the city, and the success of traders, depends upon the fact that . . . no Jewish dealing is permitted here."[3]

In 1740 Ettenheim made a communication to its Bishop, wherein it was stated that "as is well-known, the Jews' low ways make only for loss and undoing." The same idea is voiced in the proverb, "All in that city doth decay, where Jews are plentiful as hay."[4] In the preamble to the Prussian Edict of 1750, mention is made that "the big merchants of our town complain . . . that the Jews who deal in the same commodities as they do, lessen their business considerably." It was the same in the South of Germany. In Nuremberg, for example, the Christian traders had to sit by and see their customers make purchases of Jews. In 1469 the Jews were expelled from Nuremberg; a very large number of them settled in the neighbouring town of Fürth, and their customers from the first-named city, seeking the best advantage for themselves as buyers, journeyed to Fürth to do their shopping.* No wonder that the City Fathers of Nuremberg showered ordinances on the town throughout the 17th and 18th centuries, forbidding dealings with Jews from Fürth.[5]

---

* The first German railway was built between Nuremberg and Fürth (1835). Whether the Jewish influence mentioned in the text had anything to do with it is difficult to say. But it is a curious fact.—Trans.

That Jews all through the 18th century were refused admission to the merchant-gilds, no less than to the craft-gilds, is too well-known to need further emphasis.[6]

Was it different in England? By no means. Says Josiah Child, "The Jews are a subtil people . . . depriving the English merchant of that profit he would otherwise gain"; they carry on their business "to the prejudice of the English merchants."[7] When in 1753 the Jews' Naturalization Bill became law, the ill-will of the populace against the hated race was so great that the Act had to be repealed the very next year. One great fear was that if the Jews became English citizens they would "oust the natives from their employment."[8]

From Marseilles to Nantes the same tones were heard in France. The merchants of the latter city in 1752 bewailed their fate in the following terms: "The prohibited trade carried on by these strangers . . . has caused considerable loss to the merchants of this town, so much so, that if they are not favoured by the good-will of these gentry, they are in the predicament of being able neither to provide for their families nor to pay their taxes."[9] Seven years earlier, in 1745, the Christian traders of Toulouse regretfully declared that "everybody runs to the Jewish traders."[10] "We beseech you to bar the onward march of this nation, which otherwise will assuredly destroy the entire trade of Languedoc"—such was the request of the Montpelier Chamber of Commerce.[11] Their colleagues in Paris compared the Jews to wasps who make their way into the hive only to kill the bees, rip open their bodies and extract the honey stored in their entrails.[12]

In Sweden,[13] in Poland,[14] the same cry resounded.[15] In 1619 the civic authorities of Posen complained, in an address to King Sigismund, that "difficulties and stumbling-blocks are put in the way of merchants and craftsmen by the competition of Jews."

But all this does not suffice. We want to know more than that the Jews endangered the livelihood of the others. We want to find out the reason for this. Why were they able to become such keen competitors of the Christian traders? Only when this question has been answered will we understand the peculiar nature of Jewish business methods, "les secrets du négoce," as Savary calls them.

Let us refer to contemporary opinion, to the men who were sufficiently in touch with everyday life to know the reason. Here again the answer is pretty well unanimous. And what is it? The Jews were more successful because of their dishonest dealing. "Jews . . . have one law and custom whenever it pays them; it is called lying and cheating," you may read in the pages of Philander von Sittewald.[16] Equally complimentary is the *Comic Lexicon of Cheating,* compiled by George Paul Hönn,[17] where under "Jews," the only interpolation in the whole book is made as follows: "Jews are cheats, collectively and individually. . . ." The article "Jews," in the *General Treasury for Merchants,* is of the same calibre,[18] while an anonymous writer on manners and morals declares that the Jews of Berlin "make their living by robbing and cheating, which, in their opinion, are no crimes."[19]

Similar views were current in France. "The Jews," says Savary, "have the reputation of being good at business, but they are supposed not to be able to carry it on with strict honesty and trustworthiness."[20]

Now what do these accusations amount to? Even if the term "cheating" be given a very wide connotation, the commercial practices of many Jews hardly came within its scope. When it was asserted that Jews were cheats, that was only an epithet to describe the fact that Jews in their commercial dealings did not always pay regard to the existing laws or customs of trade. Jewish merchants offended in neglecting certain traditions of their Christian compeers, in (now and again) breaking the law, but above all, in paying no heed to commercial etiquette. Look closely into the specific accusations hurled against Jewish traders, examine their innermost nature, and you shall find that the conflict between Jewish and Christian merchants was a struggle between two outlooks, between two radically differing—nay, opposite—views on economic life.

To understand this conflict in its entirety, it will be necessary to obtain some idea of the spirit that dominated economic activities, activities in which from the 16th century onwards the Jews were obtaining a surer footing from day to day. So much did they seem to be out of harmony with that spirit that everywhere they were looked upon as a disturbing element.

During the whole of the period which I have described as the "early capitalistic age," and in which the Jews began to make their influence felt, the same fundamental notions generally prevailed in regard to economic life as characterized the Middle Ages—feudal relationships, manual labour, three estates of the realm, and so forth.

The centre of this whole was the individual man. Whether as producer or as consumer, his interests determined the attitude of the community as of its units, determined the law regulating economic activities and the practices of commercial life. Every such law was personal in its intent; and all who contributed to the life of the nation had a personal outlook. Not that each person could do as he liked. On the contrary, a code of restrictions hedged about his activities in every direction. But the point is that the restrictions were born of the individualistic spirit. Commodities were produced and bought and sold in order that consumers might have their wants sufficiently satisfied. On the other hand, producers and traders were to receive fair wages and fair profits. What was fair, and what sufficient for your need, tradition and custom determined.

And so, producer and trader should receive as much as was demanded by the standard of comfort in their station in life. That was the mediæval view; it was also the view current in the early capitalistic age, even where business was carried on along more or less modern lines. We find its expression in the industrial codes of the day, and its justification in the commercial literature.[21]

Hence, to make profit was looked upon by most people throughout the period as improper, as "unchristian"; the old economic teaching of Thomas Aquinas was observed,[22] at least officially. The religious or ethical rule was still supreme;[23] there was as yet no sign of the liberation of economic life from its religious and ethical bonds. Every action, no matter in what sphere, was done with a view to the Highest Tribunal—the will of God. Need it be pointed out that the attitude of Mammon was as opposed to this as pole is to pole?

Producer and trader should receive sufficient for their need. One outstanding result of this principle was strictly to circumscribe each man's activity in his locality. Competition was therefore quite out of the question. In his own sphere a man might work as he willed—when, how, where—in accordance with tradition and custom. But to cast a look at his neighbour's sphere—that he was forbidden to do. Just as the peasant received his holding—so much field, with pasture and woodland, as would keep him and his family, just as he never even dreamt of adding to his possessions, so, too, the craftsman and the merchant were to rest content with their portions and never covet their neighbour's. The peasant had his land, the town-dweller his customers: in either case they were the source whence sprang his livelihood; in either case they were of a size sufficient for the purpose. Hence, the trader had to be assured of his custom, and many were the ordinances which guarded him against competition. Besides, it was commercial etiquette. You did not run after customers. You waited until they came, "and then" (in the words of De Foe's sermon), "with God's blessing and his own care, he may expect his share of trade with his neighbours."[24] The merchant who attended fairs did not do otherwise; "day and night he waits at his stall."[25]

To take away your neighbour's customers was contemptible, unchristian, and immoral.[26] A rule for "Merchants who trade in commodities" was: "Turn no man's customers away from him, either by word of mouth or by letter, and do not to another what you would not have another do to you."[27] It was, however, more than a rule; it became an ordinance, and is met with over and over again. In Mayence its wording was as follows:[28] "No one shall prevent another from buying, or by offering a higher price make a commodity dearer, on pain of losing his purchase; no one shall interfere in another's business undertaking, or carry on his own on so large a scale as to ruin other traders." In Saxony it was much the same.[29] "No shopkeeper shall call away the customers from another's shop, nor shall he by signs or motions keep them from buying."

But to attract customers even without interfering with your neighbour's business was regarded as unworthy. As late as the early 18th century in London itself it was not considered proper for a shopkeeper to dress his window tastefully, and so lure purchasers. De Foe, no less than his later editors, did not mince words in expressing his contempt for such a course, of which, as he mentions apparently with some satisfaction, only a few bakers and toymen were guilty.[30]

To the things that were not permitted belonged also advertising your business and praising your wares. The gentle art of advertising first appeared in Holland sometime about the middle of the 17th century, in England towards its end, in France much later. The *Ghentsche Post-Tijdingen,* founded in 1667, contained the first business advertisement in its issue of October 3rd of that year.[31] At this time none of the London news-sheets published advertisements; even after the Great Fire not one business thought of advertising its new address. It was not until 1682, when John Houghton established *The Collection for the Improvement of Husbandry and Trade,* that the merchant community of London became accustomed to utilizing the Press as a medium for advertising.[32] This had been preceded by the practice, in a small way, of distributing bills in the streets to passers-by.

Two generations later Postlethwayt[33] gave currency to the then existing views. "Advertising in the newspapers, in regard to matters of trade and business, is now grown a pretty universal practice all over the kingdoms of England, Scotland and Ireland; . . . and however mean and disgraceful it was looked upon a few years since, by people of reputation in trade, to apply to the public by advertisements in the papers; at present (1751) it seems to be esteemed quite otherwise; persons of great credit in trade experiencing it to be the best, the easiest and the cheapest method of conveying whatever they have to offer to the knowledge of the whole kingdom."

They were not quite so far advanced in France at that time. In his Dictionary (1726) Savary[34] says nothing of the economic aspect of the term *réclame*. Not until six years later—in 1732, when his supplement was published—does he add: "A poster exhibited in public thoroughfares to make something generally known." And what does he instance? The sale of ships; the time of sailing; the announcement by the big trading companies of the arrival of goods from distant parts, but only in cases where they are to be publicly sold; the establishment of new factories; change of address. The business advertisement in its most elementary form is lacking. It is lacking also in the newspapers of the period until the second half of the 18th century. Surprising as it may seem, the first issue of the famous advertisement sheet, *Les Petites Affiches*, which appeared on May 13, 1751, contained no real business advertisement.[35] In other words, the simple announcement "I sell such-and-such wares at such-and-such a place" did not become general in England until the 18th century, and in France not till much later. In Germany only one or two towns were to the fore in this respect. Berlin and Hamburg may be instanced, but even there the innovations are isolated, the only exception being books, which were originally much advertised.

To praise your goods or to point out wherein your business was superior to others was equally nefarious. But the last word in commercial impropriety was to announce that your prices were lower than those of the man opposite. "To undersell" was most ungentlemanly: "No blessing will come from harming your neighbour by underselling and cutting prices."[36]

Bad as underselling itself was in the eyes of the people of those days, it was beneath contempt to advertise it. "Since the death of our author," say the editors of the fifth edition (1745) of De Foe's *Complete English Tradesman*,[37] "this underselling practice is grown to such a shameful height that particular persons publickly advertise that they undersell the rest of the trade." It may be asked, Why were the editors so concerned about the matter? The reason is manifest in a subsequent passage. "We have had grocers advertising their underselling one another at a rate a fair trader cannot sell for and live." It is the old cry: fixed profits, a fixed livelihood, a fixed production and fixed prices.

We possess a French instance which shows even more strikingly how heinous this offence was thought to be, even in Paris. An Ordinance of 1761[38] proclaimed to all and sundry in the French capital that to advertise that you are selling your goods at a price below the customary one must be regarded as the last resource of a merchant in difficulties, and that such action deserved severe condemnation. The Ordinance proceeded to forbid the traders of Paris and its suburbs "to run after one another trying to find customers, and above all, to distribute hand-bills calling attention to their wares."

Like the producers, the consumers also received attention. In a certain sense the consumer received even more, for the naïve conception that all production was in the interests of consumption had not yet disappeared. Hence the stress laid on *good* wares, on the principle that commodities should really be what they pretended; and innumerable were the ordinances that were everywhere promulgated to this intent, more especially in the 17th and 18th centuries.

It was long before the purely capitalistic notion gained acceptance that the value in exchange of any commodity was what influenced the undertaker most. We may see how slow its progress was from the conflicting opinions on the subject in England in the 18th century. Sir Josiah Child appears to have been in the minority on this, as on most other questions, when he formulated the demand that every manufacturer should be allowed to judge for himself as to the kind of commodity, and the quality, that he brought into the market. It is curious enough nowadays to read Child's plea for the right of the manufacturer to make shoddy goods. "If we intend to have the trade of the world," he cries,[39] "we must imitate the Dutch, who make the worst as well as the best of all manufactures, that we may be in a capacity of serving all markets and all humours."

In a world of economic ideas such as these, the theory of "just price" was an organic element. Price was not something in the formation of which the individual had a say. Price was determined for him; it was a subject to religious and ethical principles as everything else in economic life. It was to be such as would make for the common good, as well of the consumer as of the producer. Different ages had their own standard for determining it; in Luther's day, for example, the cost of production was the deciding factor. But as commercial intercourse widened, the doctrine of the just price was found to be more and more impossible, and the view that price must be determined by the factors in the market[40] found general acceptance. But be that as it may, the point to accentuate is that price was based on ethical and not (as was held to be the case later) on natural principles. Then people said that the individual *must* not determine price at his own will; whereas later the view was that he *could* not so determine it.

What manner of world was that in which opinions such as these predominated? If we had to describe it in a word, we should say that it was "slow." Stability was its bulwark and tradition its guide. The individual never lost himself in the noise and whirl of business activity. He still had complete control of himself; he was not yet devoid of that native dignity, which does not make itself cheap for the sake of profit. Trade and commerce were everywhere carried on with a dash of personal pride. And all this to a greater extent in the country than in the large towns, where advancing capitalism made itself soonest felt. "The proud and haughty demeanour of the country merchant" is noted by a keen observer of his time.[41] We can almost see the type, in his knee-breeches and long coat, his head bewigged and his manner somewhat stiff. Business with him was an even process; he got through it without much thought or worry, serving his circle of customers in the traditional way, knowing nothing of excitement, and never complaining that the way was too short.

To-day one of the best signs of a flourishing trade is a universal hurry and scurry, but towards the end of the 18th century that was regarded as a sure token of idleness. The man of business was deliberately slow of stride. "In Paris people are in one continuous haste—because there is nothing to do there; here (in Lyons, the centre of the silk industry, and a town of some commercial importance) our walk is slow because every one is busy." Such is the verdict of the observer,[42] already mentioned, in the year of grace 1788.

In this picture the Nonconformist, the Quaker, the Methodist, is a fitting figure, even though we are accustomed to think of him as one of the first to be associated with capitalistic ideas. As his inner life, so was his outward bearing to be. "Walk with a sober pace, not tinkling with your feet," was a canon of the Puritan rule of life.[43] "The believer hath, or at least ought to have, and, if he be like himself, will have, a well-ordered walk, and will be in his carriage stately and princely."[44]

This was the world the Jews stormed. At every step they offended against economic principles and the economic order. That seems clear enough from the unanimous complaints of the Christian traders everywhere.

But were the Jews the only sinners in this respect? Was it fair to single out "Jewish dealing" and to stigmatize it as inclined to be dishonest, as contrary to law and practice, as characterized by lying and deception? There can be little doubt that the practices of Christian manufacturers and traders were not always blameless in the matter of being opposed to custom and regulation. Human nature being what it is, this was only to be expected. But apart from that, the age with which we are concerned could not boast of a very high standard of commercial morality. Else why the necessity for the plethora of ordinances and prohibitions which touched economic activities at every point? Contemporary evidence certainly leaves no doubt on the subject.

We have already mentioned the *Cheating Lexicon* which

was published at the beginning of the 18th century. It must have been widely read, for in the space of a few years several editions were issued. Turn to its pages, and you will ask in amazement whether there was any honesty left in the world. True, this impression is created by the concentration within a small space of very many instances and illustrations of cheating and swindling. But even making allowance for this fact, the impression cannot be eradicated that there must have been a good deal of questionable conduct in those days. And if any doubt still lurks on this point other witnesses soon obliterate it. "You can find but few wares nowadays (1742) that have not been adulterated," is the plaint of one German writer.[45] Numerous are the prohibitions of the evil; imperial edicts (such as that of 1497), police regulations (such as that of Augsburg, of 1548) and rules originating in merchant circles (such as that of Lübeck, of 1607) all deal with the practice. But falsification was by no means limited to the production of commodities; it was not unknown in commerce too. Fraudulent bankruptcies must have occurred very frequently in the 17th and 18th centuries, and must have formed a problem difficult of solution. Again and again there were complaints about their uninterrupted reappearance.[46] Indeed, the loose commercial morality of English merchants in the 17th century was proverbial.[47] Cheating and falsifying were said to be "the besetting sin of English tradesmen." "Our merchants," says a 17th-century writer,[48] "by their infinite over-asking for commodities proclaim to the world that they would cheat all if it were in their power."

Such being the case, what reason was there for marking out the Jews? And can we really speak of something specially characteristic in the conduct of Jews over against the established principles of the time? I believe we can. I believe that the specifically Jewish characteristic consisted in that it was not an individual here and there who offended against the prevailing economic order, but the whole body of Jews. Jewish commercial conduct reflected the accepted point of view among Jewish traders. Hence Jews were never conscious of doing wrong, of being guilty of commercial immorality; their policy was in accordance with a system, which for them was the proper one. They were in the right; it was the other outlook that was wrong and stupid. We are not here speaking of capital delinquencies generally acknowledged to be wrong, and generally condemned. For a distinction must be drawn between the fundamental regulations of any legal institution (e.g., property), and those which vary with the progress of society. Stealing will be looked upon as a capital offence as long as property exists; but there will be much difference of opinion from age to age on the question of taking interest. The first falls under the former category; the second under the latter.

No doubt, in their peculiar commercial activity, Jews were guilty of both sorts of misdemeanours. In early times Jews committed wrongs which were universally regarded as such. They were constantly accused, for example, of receiving and dealing in stolen property.[49] But Jews, as a body, themselves condemned practices of this kind; and for that matter, there were honest and dishonest Jews as there were honest and dishonest Christians. If any Jews were addicted to systematic cheating, they in so far set themselves up against the majority of Jews and Christians, both of whom were agreed that such conduct was not in accord with the accepted standards of right. We are not without records that illustrate this very forcibly. The history of the Jews in Hamburg is an instance. In the 17th century, the Portuguese Jews undertook to a certain extent to be responsible to the authorities for the proper commercial conduct of the newly arrived German Jews. As soon as the *Tedescos* came into the city, they had to promise their Portuguese brethren not to buy stolen property, nor otherwise to carry on shady business. On one occasion the Elders of the German Jews were summoned before the *Mahamad** and warned because several

---

* The governing body of the Portuguese Jewish congregation. The term is still used among the Spanish and Portuguese Jews in London.—Trans.

of them had broken their pledge; on another occasion because they had bought stolen goods from soldiers.[50]

The point I am emphasizing must be remembered in considering the accusations hurled against the Jews in the early capitalistic age, accusations which, on the whole, were not unfounded. Universally accepted offences, such as stealing or receiving stolen property, must not be included under this heading. Jews equally with Christians abhorred such crimes. The practices, however, common to all Jews, which overstepped law and custom, but which Jews did not feel as being wrong, the practices which may be looked upon as being the result of a specifically Jewish outlook, these must come within our ken. And what do we find on examining them?

We find that the Jew rises before us unmistakably as more of a business-man than his neighbour; he follows business for its own sake; he recognizes, in the true capitalistic spirit, the supremacy of gain over all other aims.

I know of no better illustration than the *Memoirs of Glückel von Hameln,* a mine of information, by the way, about Jewish life and thought in the early capitalistic age. Glückel, the wife of a merchant in Hamburg, lived between 1645 and 1724, the period when the Jewish communities of Hamburg and Altona shot up to a position of prosperity, and in almost every respect we may regard this remarkable woman as a type of the Jew of that day. Her narrative grips the reader because of its natural simplicity and freshness. As I read these *Memoirs,* in which a complete personality is revealed to us in a life rich in experience, I was again and again reminded of the famous Frau Rat (Goethe's mother).

If I cite just this splendid book in order to show the predominating interest of money among Jews in those days, it is because I believe that this characteristic must have been general, seeing that even in so gifted a woman as Glückel it also stands out. In very truth, money is the be-all and end-all with her, as with all the other people of whom she has anything to say. Accounts of business enterprise occupy but a small space in the book, but on no less than

609 occasions (in 313 pages) does the authoress speak of money, riches, gain and so forth. The characters and their doings are mentioned only in some connexion or other with money. Above all, we are told of good matches—good from the financial point of view. To marry her children is in fact the chief object of Glückel's business activities. "He also saw my son, and they were almost on the point of coming to terms, but they could not close because of a thousand marks." Incidents of this kind abound in the book. Of her second marriage she says, "in the afternoon my husband wedded me with a valuable gold ring an ounce in weight." I cannot help regarding the peculiar conception of marriage-making, which used to be current among Jews, as symptomatic of the way they looked upon money, and especially the tendency among them of appraising even the most precious things in life from a purely business point of view. Children, for example, have their value. That was a matter of course among Jews in those days. "They are all my darling children, and may they all be forgiven, as well those on whom I had to spend a lot of money as those on whom I spent nothing," writes Glückel. It was as marriageable persons that they had a price, which varied with the state of the market. Scholars, or the children of scholars, were much in demand. In one case we are told that a father speculated in his children. The fortunes of Solomon Maimon, as related by Graetz, are well known and frequently cited in this connexion. "At eleven years of age he had so complete a mastery of the Talmud that he . . . became much sought after as a possible husband. His needy father, in a speculating spirit, provided him with two brides at once, without his being able to see . . . either of them." Similar incidents are abundant enough to warrant the conclusion that they must have been typical.

But the objection may be urged that among Christians also money was no less valued, only the fact was not admitted; people were hypocritical. There is perhaps a certain element of truth in this objection. In that case I should say what was specifically Jewish was the naïveté with which money was made the pivot of life; it was a matter of course; no attempt was made to hide it.

What light does contemporary opinion in the 17th and 18th centuries shed upon the characteristic to which we have called attention? There appears to be universal agreement on the subject, which lends support to our theory. The Jew in those days of undeveloped capitalism was regarded as the representative of an economic outlook, wherein to obtain profit was the ultimate goal of all commercial activity. Not his "usury" differentiated him from the Christian, not that he sought gain, not that he amassed wealth; only that he did all this openly, not thinking it wrong, and that he scrupulously and mercilessly looked after his business interests. But more awful things are related of Christian "usurers" who "are worse than Jews." "The Jews wears his soul on his sleeve and is not ashamed, but these carry on their devil's trade with hypocritical Christian countenances."[51]

One or two more contemporary opinions must be quoted. "These people have no other God but the unrighteous Mammon, and no other aim than to get possession of Christian property . . . they . . . look at everything for their profit."[52] Such is the verdict of the Rev. John Megalopolis, who wrote on March 18th, 1655. Another judgment is harsher still.[53] "No trust should be put in the promises made there (in Brazil) by the Jews, a race faithless and pusillanimous, enemies to all the world and especially to all Christians, caring not whose house burns so long as they may warm themselves at the coals, who would rather see a hundred thousand Christians perish than suffer the loss of a hundred crowns." The statement of Savary,[54] who was amicably disposed towards the Jews, is also to the point. "A usurious merchant or one too keen, who tries to get a mean advantages and flays those who have dealings with him, is termed 'a real Jew.' People say 'he has fallen into the hands of Jews' when those with whom a man does business are hard, immovable and stingy." It is true that a very Christian merchant first coined the phrase "Business is business," but

Jews undoubtedly were the first to mould their policy in accordance with it.

In this connexion we ought to mention also that the proverbs of all nations have always depicted the Jew as the gain-seeker, who had a special love of money. "Even to the Jew our Lady Mary is holy" (Hungarian)—in reference to the Kremnitzer gold ducats. "Yellow is the colour that suits the Jew best" (Russian). "Yellow is the dearest colour for the Jew" (German).

This profit-seeking, which the Jew held to be legitimate, will account for his business principles and practices, of which complaints were so frequently made. In the first place, he paid no attention to the strict delimitation of one calling or of one handicraft from another, so universally insisted on by law and custom. Again and again we hear the cry that Jews did not content themselves with one kind of activity; they did whatever they could, and so disturbed the order of things which the gild system wished to see maintained. Their aim was to seize upon all commerce and all production; they had an overpowering desire to expand in every direction. "The Jews strive to destroy the English merchants by drawing all trade towards themselves," is a further complaint of the Rev. John Megalopolis in 1655.[55] "The Jews are a subtil people prying into all kinds of trade," said Sir Josiah Child.[56] And Glückel von Hameln thus describes her father's business: "He dealt in precious stones, and in other things—for every Jew is a Jack-of-all-trades."

Innumerable were the occasions when the German gilds complained of this Jewish ubiquitousness in trade, which paid no heed to the demarcation of all economic activities into strictly separate categories. In 1685, the city authorities of Frankfort-on-the-Main were loud in their cry that Jews had a share in all kinds of business—e.g., in linen and silk retailing, in cloth and book selling.[57] In the other Frankfort (on the Oder)[58] Jews were blamed for selling foreign braid to the detriment of the gold-lace makers, and so forth.

Perhaps the reason for this tendency to universal trading may be found in that a large number of miscellaneous articles, all forfeited pledges, brought together by mere chance, collected in the shops of Jews, and their sale would naturally enough interfere with the special business of all manner of dealers. The very existence of these second-hand shops—the prototype of the stores in modern times—was a menace to the prevailing order of commerce and industry. A vivid picture of such a collection of second-hand goods is given in an old Ratisbon song, dating from the 15th century,[59] and the details could not but have become more well-marked as time went on.

> No handicraft however mean,
> But the Jew would damage it i' the extreme.
> For if any one had need of raiment
> To the Jew he'd hie with payment;
> Whether 'twas silver or linen or tin,
> Or aught his house was lacking in,
> The Jew was ready to serve his need,
> With pledges he held—right many indeed.
> For stolen goods and robbers' plunder
> They and the Jew were seldom asunder.
>
> *   *   *   *   *   *   *
>
> Mantle, hose or damsel's veil,
> The Jew he had them all for sale.
> To the craftsman, then, there came but few,
> For all the world dealt with the Jew.

Here an interesting question presents itself. Is there any connexion between the breach of gild regulations and the stress laid on pure business ends on the part of the Jews, and their hostile attitude to mercantilism? Was it their aim to establish the principle that trade should be untrammelled, regardless of the commercial theory which guided the mercantilist States? It looks like it. "Jewish trade," was the term applied to the commerce of Frankfort in the 18th century, because it was mostly import trade, "which gives useful employment to but few German hands and flourishes only by reason of home consumption."[60] And when in the early 19th century Germany was flooded with the cheap products of England, which were sold for the most part at auctions, Jews were held to be the mainstay of this import trade. The Jew almost monopolized the auctions. "Since dealing in manufactured articles is to a great extent in the hands of Jews, the commerce of England is for the most part with them." The Jew had "his shop full of foreign hats, shoes, stockings, leather gloves, lead and copper ware, lacquer work, utensils, ready-made clothing of all sorts—all brought over by English ships."[61] It was the same story in France.[62] Nor was this all. The Jews were guilty of another deadly sin in the mercantilist calendar: they imported raw materials.[63]

We see, then, that the Jews, in following their business interests, gave as little heed to the barriers between States as to those between industries. Still less did they have regard to the prevailing code of etiquette in any industry. We have already seen how custom-chasing was looked upon in the early capitalistic age. Here the Jews were continual offenders. Everywhere they sought out sellers or buyers, instead of waiting for them in their shops, as commercial custom prescribed. Of this we have abundant proof.

A complaint was lodged by the furriers of Königsberg[64] in 1703 against "the Jews Hirsch and Moses, who with their agents are always first in the field in buying raw material and selling the ready-made furs, whereby they (the supplicants) suffer much loss." In 1685 the jewellers and goldsmiths of Frankfort had a similar experience.[65] They were forced to buy all the old gold and silver they needed from Jews, who, by means of their numerous "spies," snapped it away from under the very noses of the Christians. A few years previously the whole of the trading body of that town had protested against Jews "spying out the business of Christian merchants." Earlier still, in 1647, the tailors of Frankfort petitioned[66] that the Jews should be forbidden to engage in the sale of new clothing. "A source of bitter weeping it is, that the Jews may freely wander up and down the streets, laden with all manner of goods and cloth, like so many camels and asses, running to meet every newcomer to Frankfort, be he of high or low degree, and offering to sell him what he wants; and so deprive us of our daily bread."[67] Still earlier even than this, in 1635, was the petition of the silk merchants, who bemoaned the fact that the Jews "wait about in the city outside the bounds of the Jewish quarter, in inns and wherever opportunity offers; they run through many a street, both openly and in secret, to meet the soldiers and their officers, when these come to town. They have arranged with certain master-tailors to give them facilities for exhibiting their wares at their shops when troops march past."[68]

In 1672 a complaint is heard from Brandenburg.[69] "Jews go about as chapmen among the villages and in the towns and force their wares on people." A similar story comes from Frankfort-on-the-Oder,[70] wherein the details are fuller. Jews run after customers—the travellers to their hotels, the nobility to their castles and the students to their lodgings. And in Nikolsburg, in Austria, we are told[71] that "the Jews have drawn to themselves all the trade, all the money, all the goods. They wait outside the city, try to strike up an acquaintance with travellers while they are yet on the road, and endeavour to take away their custom from Christian citizens."

How the Jews were ever on the look-out for new customers is described by a well-informed writer of the early 19th century.[72] It was a practice with them, he says, "to pay frequent visits to all and sundry places of public resort where, by reading the many news-sheets, they sought to obtain knowledge of possibilities for doing business, and especially of noting what strangers were expected to arrive; and by listening to every conversation, to find out whose houses were in danger in order to make bargains or contracts with them."

The streets in which the Jewish old clo' men lived were the scenes of similar activities, the end in view always being the same. In fact, the dealers sometimes seized the passer-by by the arm and tried to force him to make purchases. This method of carrying on business is not unknown in our modern cities; it was known in the Paris of the 18th century, where it was associated with the *fripiers*, the old clo' dealers, who, as we are informed,[73] were for the most part Jews. One description of such a scene is too good not to be quoted.[74] "The touts of these disorderly shops call to you uncivilly enough; and when one of them has invited you, all the other shopkeepers on your road repeat the deafening invitation. The wife, the daughter, the servant, the dogs, all howl in your ears. . . . Sometimes these fellows seize an honest man by the arm, or by his shoulder, and force him to enter in spite of himself; they make a pastime of this unseemly game. . . ."

We hear the same tale from a traveller who journeyed in Western Germany about that time. "To walk in the streets of those places where there are many Jews has become a nuisance. You are badgered by them every minute and at every turn. You are constantly being asked, Can I sell you anything? Won't you buy this, that or the other?"[75]

Or they turn into wandering traders in order to sweep in custom. "The Jew thinks nothing of turning the seats in the porches into a shop counter, often extending them by means of planks; he places a form or table against the wall of any house he can get at, or even makes the front passage into a shop; or, he hires a cart which becomes his moving shop, and often enough he has the bad manners to pull up in front of a shop which sells the same wares as he."[76]

"Get hold of the customers"—that was the end and aim. Is it not the guiding principle of the big industries of to-day? Is not the splendid organization of a concern like the Allgemeine Elektrizitäts-Gesellschaft, for example, directed to the same object?

The policy was first systemized when advertising was resorted to. The "deafening invitation" which, as we have just noted, came from the small *fripier*, is now made by the million-voiced advertisements of our business life. If the Jews are to be considered the originators of the system of "getting hold of the customers," their claim to be the fathers of modern advertising is equally well established. I am, however, unable to adduce conclusive evidence for this. What is needed is a careful study of the files of the earliest newspapers, in order to discover the names of the people who advertised. As a matter of fact, the whole subject of advertising has as yet been dealt with but scantily. The only branch which has received adequate attention is the history of business announcements. Nevertheless, I am able to give one or two instances which show the connexion of Jews with the practice of advertising.

The very earliest advertisement with which I am acquainted is to be found in No. 63 of the *Vossische Zeitung,* of May 28, 1711, which is to this effect: "This is to inform all and sundry that a Dutch (Jewish?) merchant has arrived at Mr. Boltzen's in the Jews' Street, with all kinds of tea of the finest quality, to be sold cheap. Any one who may care to buy should come early, as the visitor will not stay for more than eight days."

The first known advertisement in the text of the paper dates from 1753, and hails from Holland. The advertiser was an eye-specialist of the name of Laazer.[77] A very old advertisement in the United States—whether the oldest I cannot say—appeared on August 17, 1761, in the *New York Mercury,* as follows[78]:—"To be sold by Hayman Levy, in Bayard Street, Camp Equipages of all sorts, best soldiers' English shoes . . . and everything that goes to make up the pomp and circumstance of glorious war."

Finally, the Jews are the founders of the modern Press, *i.e.,* the machinery for advertising, more especially of the cheap newspapers.[79] Polydore Millaud, who established the *Petit Journal,* was the father of the "half-penny Press."

But to obtain likely addresses, to intercept travellers on their way, to sing the praises of your wares—that was only one side of the game of catching customers. It was supplemented by another, which consisted in so decking-out the goods for sale as to attract people. In this art the Jews were great adepts. Nay more, there is sufficient evidence that they were the first to stand up for the general principle, that it is the right (and the duty) of every trader to carry on his business in such a way as will obtain for him as much of the available custom as possible, or by creating new demands, will increase the circle of buyers.

Now in a community where quality was regulated, the only effective means of achieving this end was price-cutting. We shall therefore not be surprised to find the Jews availing themselves of this weapon, and we shall see that it was just this that made them so disliked among Christian traders, whose economic outlook was all for maintaining prices. The Jew undersells; the Jew spoils prices; the Jew tries to attract customers by low prices—that was the burden of the complaints heard in the 17th and 18th centuries wherever Jews did business.

Our pages would be overloaded did we attempt to cite all the proofs on this point. A few, therefore, will have to suffice.

First for England where, in 1753, the storm burst forth against the Jews on the passing of the Naturalization Bill. One of the principal fears was that if they became recognized citizens, they would oust the natives from their means of livelihood by underselling them.[80]

Next for France. "The stuffs . . . which the Jews bring to the fairs . . . are worth more at the price at which they sell them than those in the traders' shops," is the reply[81] of the Intendant of Languedoc to the plaints of the merchants of Montpelier (May 31, 1740). The merchants of Nantes[82] were of opinion that the public, which dealt with Jews under the impression that they were making a good bargain, were generally duped. At the same time, they admit that prices at Jewish shops are lower than elsewhere. The same admission is made by the Paris traders: the Jews sell even more cheaply than the factories.[83] Concerning a Fürth Jew, of the name of Abraham Oulman,[84] the bronze-dealers of Paris reported that "he sells the same bronzes below the price for which they are sold in this country." In Lyons the master silk-weavers passed a resolution (October 22, 1760) in which they ascribed the bad times to the influence of the Jews, who had cut prices, and thereby made themselves masters of the silk industry in all the provinces.[85]

The Swedish Parliament in 1815 debated the question whether the Jews should be allowed entire liberty of trade, and one of the chief reasons which prevailed against the motion was that Jews lowered prices.[86]

From Poland the same strains reach us. Jews tell Christian traders that if they (the latter) sold their goods as cheaply as the Jews, they too would attract customers.[87]

It is no different in Germany. From Brandenburg (1672),[88] from Frankfort (17th century),[89] from Madgeburg (1710)[90] the old story is repeated. A Wallachian traveller in Germany[91] about the same time reports the ubiquity of this accusation. The General Prussian Edict of 1750 takes cognizance of it. "The merchants of our towns . . . complain . . . that the Jewish traders who sell the same goods do them great harm, because they sell at a lower price." Right up to the 19th century it is still met with. In the Supplication of the Augsburg wholesale merchants against the admission of the Jews[92] (1803) we may read that "the Jews understand how to derive advantages from the general depression of trade. They obtain goods from people who need money badly at shameful prices, and then spoil the market by selling them at a cheaper rate."

In many branches of industry Christian manufacturers and merchants even to-day regard the cutting of prices by Jews as a serious endangering of their trade. That this is an open secret and often enough discussed, is well known. I hope to touch upon the matter again in due course.

One more instance from the history of Finance, as showing that the Jews had the reputation of making lower terms. When the Austrian Government early in the 18th century determined on raising another loan, as usual, in Holland, an order was issued (December 9, 1701) to Baron Pechmann, who was negotiating the matter, to make private enquiries whether, in view of the fact that the Hungarian Copper Mines were being pledged to guarantee the loan, a greater sum might not be raised. More especially was he to communicate with the Portuguese Jews in Holland, since the other subjects of the United Provinces asked for an additional guarantee beside the general one.[98] In a report of the Court Chancery of Vienna (May 12, 1762) the view is expressed that "it is advisable to come to terms with the Jews in reference to contracts for the army . . . seeing that they are prepared to quote lower prices than others."

Here, then, was a problem for all the wiseacres to put their heads together and try to solve. They did, asking each other again and again, at their work and in their shops, on Sunday afternoons in their walks outside the city rampart, and in the evenings at the social pint of beer: How is it possible? How on earth is it done? How can the Jew carry through his "dirty trick" of underselling? What was the reason for it?

The answer differed in accordance with the capacity and the prejudice of each enquirer. And so the numberless explanations on record cannot be accepted without testing their value; unlike the assertion that Jews lowered prices, which, in view of its unanimity, there is no reason to doubt. In any case, for the present only those opinions will be of interest to us which give indication of a special way of carrying on business, or of a special commercial morality.

The commonest explanation is that of dishonesty, and the conclusion was arrived at in some such way as this. Seeing that the Jews have the same expenses, seeing that the cost of production is also the same, if the price is below the current one, everything is not quite above-board. The Jews must have obtained possession of their wares by dishonest means. They were doubtless stolen goods. The bad reputation of the Jews generally must have given probability to this explanation, and the low prices must have lent support to the accusation levelled against them that they were receivers.

I have no intention of citing instances where this line of argument is taken, for in reality it is the least interesting of any. In many cases, no doubt, it was correct. But if that were the only reason forthcoming to account for low prices among Jewish traders, there would be no need to mention the matter at all, for then it would not have the significance which it actually possesses.

As a matter of fact, even the extremists among gild members could not but cast about for other causes to account for the underselling of Jewish traders, and they found them close at hand, not in actual breach of the law, but in practices that were not all they should be. And what were these? That the Jews dealt in prohibited articles (contraband of war, etc.); in lapsed pledges; in goods that had been confiscated (*e.g.,* by customs officials); in goods that had been bought for a mere song from the owners, who were deep in debt and whose necessity, therefore, was great,[94] or from those who needed money badly;[95] in old goods, bought for next to nothing at auctions; in bankrupt stock;[96] in goods the quality of which was not up to the standard of the ordinances of the industrial code;[97] or, finally, that the Jew cut prices with the intention of going into bankruptcy himself.[98]

To what extent instances such as these—"the miserable methods of the Jews" as they were termed by the traders of Metz[99]—were general or only sporadic, it is difficult to say. Nor does it much matter for our purpose. As to their probability, it is hardly likely that they were all pure inventions. The important thing to note, however, is that shady practices such as those enumerated were laid to the Jews' door. And even if only a minute proportion were in accordance with actual fact, that would be enough to make them symptomatic, and they would be very useful as supporting the result obtained in other ways. I shall return to this question later. Here we will continue the catalogue of reasons which were urged in explanation of the Jews' lower prices.

Side by side with those already mentioned was the accusation that the commodities sold by the Jews were of an inferior quality. So frequently is this statement met with that its correctness can hardly be doubted. An official report from Magdeburg, a petition from Brandenburg, a complaint from Frankfort[100]—all harp on this same string. And the *Traders' Lexicon,* to which I have already more than once referred as a reliable authority, states that Jews sold inferior goods "which they know how to polish up, to colour anew, to show off at their best, to provide with a fresh cover, smell and taste that even the greatest connoisseur is often taken in."

This is repeated almost verbally in the Report of the merchants of Nantes, with which we are by this time so well acquainted. The goods of the Jews are really dear, despite their cheapness. For they sell things that are out of fashion or that cannot be used any longer. Silk stockings they re-dye, pass them through a calender, and then sell them as new. But they cannot be worn more than once. The silk weavers of Lyons tell the same tale:[101] the Jews have ruined the silk industry because, in order to be able to sell at low prices, they order goods of second-rate quality only. So, too, the Governor of Bohemia in 1705:[102] "The Jews have got hold of all manual occupations and all commerce, but as for the most part they make only poor stuff, there is no chance for a profitable export trade to spring up." The opinion of Wegelin in the Swedish Parliament (1815), likewise referred to already, is only in accord with the preceding. "It is true," he said, "that the Jews alone engaged in calico-printing, but they have completely spoiled this branch of industry because of their low quality goods—the so called "Jews' calico."

This complaint, which started in the early capitalistic period, has not yet ceased. The cry of the Christian manufacturers that the Jews cut prices has been followed by the corollary that, in order to maintain low prices at all costs, Jews lowered the quality of goods.

Summing up all the facts adduced, we shall perceive that the Jews originated the principle of substitution.

What was called inferior quality in the wares of the Jews was not in reality so. It was not as if the articles were of the same sort as those of other traders, except that they were worse in quality. It was rather that they were new articles, intended for similar use as the old, but made of a cheaper material, or by new processes which lessened the cost of production. In other words, the principle of substitution was brought into play, and Jews may thus be regarded as the pioneers in its application. The most frequent cases occurred in textile fabrics; but other instances are also on record—for example, substitutes for coffee. In one sense, too, dyeing must be mentioned in this connexion. Jewish influence aided its growth. Originally, the inventors of artificial alizarine used expensive chemicals to mix with their red colouring matter; the Jews introduced cheaper materials, and thus gave an impetus to the dyeing industry.

There is yet one other, though less frequent, accusation levelled against the Jews. It was that the Jews could sell more cheaply than Christians because they gave less weight or short measure.[103] They were taunted with this in Avignon, where woollen articles were mentioned, and in the case of German Jews an actual illustration is given. "The Jew is on the look-out for the least advantage. If he measured 10 ells there were only 9⅞. The Christian (customer) is aware of this, but he says to himself, 'Jews' measure is short, ten ells are never quite ten, but then the Jew sells cheap.' "[104]

In all this the point for us to discover is whether, and if so to what extent, the different courses, which were alleged to have been taken by the Jewish traders in order to reduce prices, may be traced to some general business principle characteristic of the Jews. To my mind, the whole case can be summed up by saying that the Jew to a certain extent held that in business the means justified the end. His consideration for the other traders and his respect for legal enactments and social demands were not very great, while on the other hand, the idea of value in exchange in relation to goods, and the idea that all business activity had reference to wealth and to that only—these became keen. What I have elsewhere described as the inherent tendency in capitalism to obtain profit, regardless of all else, is here seen in its early origin.

But we have not yet done with the inventory of methods adopted by Jews to lower prices. We now turn to those which were of equal fundamental importance with the others already mentioned, but which differed from them materially. While the first brought about only apparent reductions, or actual reductions at other people's expense, these produced lower prices really and absolutely. What were they? Innovations which decreased the total cost of production in some way or other. Either the producer or the dealer was content with less

for himself, or the actual expenses of production were reduced in that wages were lowered or the manufacturing and
distributing processes made more efficient.

That all these means of cheapening commodities were
adopted by Jews, and by them first, is amply evidenced by
records in our possession.

First, the Jew could sell more cheaply because he was
satisfied with less than the Christian trader. Unprejudiced
observers remarked this fact on many occasions, and even
the competitors of the Jews admitted its truth. Let us once
again quote the Magdeburg official report. The Jews sell
cheaply, "whereby the merchants must suffer loss. For they
need more than the Jew, and, therefore, must carry on their
business in accordance with their requirements."[105] In another
document it is also stated that "the Jew is satisfied with a
smaller profit than the Christian."[106] And what did the Polish
Jews tell the Christian Poles?[107] That if they (the Poles) did
not live so extravagantly, they would be able to sell their
goods at the same prices as the Jews. A keen-eyed traveller
in Germany towards the end of the 18th century came to the
same conclusion. "The reason for the complaint (that Jews
sell cheaply) is apparent: it lies in the extravagant pride of
the haughty shopkeeper, who in his dealings requires so much
for mere show, that he cannot possibly charge low prices. The
Jew, therefore, deserves the gratitude of the public, to whom
he brings gain by his frugal habits, and forces the shopkeeper
with his large expenditure either to be more economical, or
to go to the wall."[108] The Report of the Vienna Court Chancery (May 12, 1762) was of the same opinion. The Jews can
deliver at a lower rate than the Christians "because they are
more thrifty and live more cheaply." The tale was repeated in
a Hungarian document of January 9, 1756, wherein the proposed reduction by Joseph II of Jewish spirit-licences was
discussed. It was there pointed out[109] that Jews were able to
pay more for their licences because of their cheap and poor
living.

No less explicit on the point is Sir Josiah Child for the
England of his age. "They are a penurious people, living

miserably," he says,[110] "and therefore can, and do afford to trade for less profit than the English." By the middle of the 18th century this belief was still current, for the cry went up that the Jews by reason of their extreme frugality were able to undersell the natives.[111] The identical view prevailed in France. "It is my firm belief," said the Intendant of Languedoc,[112] in reply to the chronic complaints of the traders of Montpellier, "that Jewish commerce . . . does less harm to the merchants of Montpellier than their own lack of attention to the requirements of the public, and their rigid determination to make as large profits as they can."

But this is not all. There were people who asserted—and they must have been gifted with no little insight—that the Jews had discovered yet another trick, by means of which they succeeded in obtaining as great, or even greater, profits than their Christian neighbours despite their comparatively low prices—they increased their turnover. As late as the early part of the 19th century this was regarded as a specifically "Jewish practice"[113]—"small profits with a frequent turnover of your capital pay incomparably better than big profits and a slow turnover." This is no isolated opinion; it occurs very frequently indeed.[114]

Small profits, quick returns—obviously this was a breaking away from the preconceived idea of an economic organization of society, where one of the cardinal doctrines was to produce for subsistence only. And the Jews were the fathers of this new business-principle. Profit was considered as something fixed by tradition; hence-forward it was determined by each individual trader. That was the great novelty, and again it emanated from Jews. It was a Jewish practice to settle the rate of profit as each trader thought fit; it was a Jewish practice to decide whether to sell at a profit at all, or for a time to do business without making profits in order to earn more afterwards.[115]

Lastly, we have still to mention the taunt levelled against Jews, that they sought to reduce the cost of production, either by employing the cheapest labour, or by utilizing more economical methods.

With regard to the first, numerous plaints abound. The woollen manufacturers of Avignon,[116] the merchants of Montpellier,[117] the civic authorities of Frankfort-on-the-Oder[118] and the Tailors' Craft of the other Frankfort are a few cases in point. But none of these disaffected people could realize that the Jews were the earliest undertakers in industries with capitalistic organizations, and, consequently, utilized new forms of production, just as they had utilized them in commerce.

And here we must not pass over another characteristic of Jewish business methods, one, however, which is not mentioned in the literature of the early capitalistic period, probably because it was developed at a later date. I refer to the conscious endeavour of attracting new customers by some device or other—whether it was the placing of goods for sale in a new juxtaposition, or a new system of payment, or a new combination of departments, or the organization of some new service. It would be a most fascinating study to compile a list of all the inventions (exclusive, of course, of technical inventions) which trade and commerce owe to the Jews. Let me refer to a few, about which we are tolerably certain that they are of Jewish origin. I say nothing as to whether Jews were merely the first to apply them, or whether they were actually created by Jews.

First in order I would mention the trade in old and damaged goods, the trade in remnants and rubbish—the Jews were able "here and there to maintain themselves and make a profit out of the commonest articles, which before had no value whatever, such as rags, rabbit-skins and gall-nuts."[119] In short, we may term the Jews the originators of the waste-product business. Thus, in the 18th century in Berlin, Jews were the first feather-cleaners, the first vermin-killers and the inventors of the so-called "white beer."[120]

To what extent the general store owes its existence to the Jew it is impossible to say. Anyhow, the Jews, in that they held pledges, were the first in whose shops might be found a conglomeration of wares. And is it not one of the distinguishing marks of a modern store to have for sale articles of various kinds, intended for various uses? The result is that the owner of the store is but little concerned with what he sells, so long as he does sell. His aim is to do business, and this policy is in accordance with the Jewish spirit. But apart from that, it is well-known that to-day stores in the United States[121] and in Germany[122] are for the most part in the hands of Jews.

An innovation of no little importance in the organization of retail trading at the time of its introduction was the system of payment by instalments when goods to a large amount or very costly goods were sold. In Germany, at any rate, it is possible to say with tolerable certainty, that in this, too, Jews were pioneers. "There is a class of shopkeeper among Jews," we may read in an early 19th-century writer, "indispensable to the ordinary man, and of exceeding great benefit to trade. They are the people who sell clothes or material for clothes to the ordinary customer, and receive payment for it in small instalments."[123]

Of Jewish origin also are a number of innovations in the catering business. Thus, the first coffee-house in England (perhaps the first in the world) was opened in Oxford in 1650, or 1651, by a Jew of the name of Jacobs.[124] It was not until 1652 that London obtained its first coffee-house. And to come to a later period, everybody knows that a new era dawned in catering when Kempinsky* introduced the standardization of consumption and of prices as the guiding principles of the business.

In all these instances it is not so much the innovations themselves that interest us, as the tendency to which they bear witness—that a new business ideal had come into existence: the adoption of new tricks. Hence my treatment of this subject in the present chapter, which deals with the Jewish spirit, Jewish commercial morality and the specifically Jewish economic outlook.

Reviewing the ground we have traversed, we see clearly the strong contrast between the Jewish and the non-Jewish outlooks in the early capitalistic period. Tradition, the subsistence

---

* Kempinsky is the Lyons of Berlin.—Trans.

ideal, the overpowering influence of status—these were the fundamentals of the latter. And the former—wherein lay its novelty? How may it be characterized? I believe one all-comprehensive word will serve our purpose, and that word is "modern." The Jewish outlook was the "modern" outlook; the Jew was actuated in his economic activities in the same way as the modern man. Look through the catalogue of "sins" laid at the door of the Jews in the 17th and 18th centuries, and you will find nothing in it that the trader of to-day does not regard as right and proper, nothing that is not taken as a matter of course in every business. Throughout the centuries the Jews championed the cause of individual liberty in economic activities against the dominating views of the time. The individual was not to be hampered by regulations of any sort, neither as to the extent of his production nor as to the strict division between one calling and another: he was to be allowed to carve out a position for himself at will, and be able to defend it against all comers. He should have the right to push forward at the expense of others, if he were so able; and the weapons in the struggle were to be cleverness, astuteness, artfulness; in economic competition there should be no other consideration but that of overstepping the law; finally, all economic activities should be regulated by the individual alone in the way he thinks best to obtain the most efficient results. In other words, the idea of free-trade and of free competition was here to the fore; the idea of economic rationalism; in short, the modern economic outlook, in the shaping of which Jews have had a great, if not a decisive influence. And why? It was they who introduced the new ideas into a world organized on a totally different basis.

Here a pertinent question suggests itself. How are we to explain that even before the era of modern capitalism, Jews showed a capacity for adopting its principles? The question must be expanded into a much larger one. What was it that enabled the Jew to exercise so decisive an influence in the process that made modern economic life what it is, an influence such as we have observed in the foregoing enquiry?

PART II

THE APTITUDE OF THE JEWS
FOR MODERN CAPITALISM

Chapter 8

The Problem

BEFORE US LIES a great problem. We are to explain why the Jews played just the part they did in the economic life of the last two or three centuries. That this *is* a problem will be admitted with but few exceptions by all. There are a few faddists who deny that the Jews occupied any special position in modern economic life, asserting as they do that there are no Jews. These will object. Then, too, there is that other small category of people who hold that the Jews were economically of such slight import that they were without any influence whatever on modern economic life. But we shall pay little heed to either class in our considerations, which are for all those who think with me that the Jews had a decisive influence on the structure of modern economic life.

I have spoken of the aptitude of the Jews for modern capitalism. If our researches are to be fruitful of results we shall have to make two things absolutely clear: (1) their aptitude—for what? and (2) their aptitude—how developed?

Their aptitude for what? For everything which in the first part of the book we have seen them striving to achieve— founding and promoting international trade, modern finance, the Stock Exchange and the commercialization generally of all economic activities; supporting unrestricted intercourse and free competition, and infusing the modern spirit into all economic life. Now in my superscription of this part of our subject all these activities are summed up in the word "capitalism." In a special chapter (the ninth) we shall show that all the single facts that have been mentioned hang together, and that they are kept together by means of capitalistic organization. The essentials of the latter, at least in their outline, will therefore also have to be dealt with, in order to demonstrate the special functions of the individual in the capitalistic system. This method will give the death-blow to such vague conceptions, usually met with in connexion with the Jewish problem, as "economic capacity," "aptitude for commerce and haggling" or other equally dilettante phrases, which have already done too much mischief.

As for the second point, how, by what means, is it possible to achieve any result? If any one rescues a drowning man, it may be that it was because he happened to be standing at the water's edge, just where a boat was tied, or on a bridge, where a life-belt was ready to hand. In a word, his accidental presence in a particular spot made it possible for him to do the deed, by rowing out in the boat to the man in danger, or by throwing the life-belt to him. Or he may have done it because he was the only one among the crowd on the shore who had the courage to jump into the water, swim out to the sinking man and bring him safely to land. In the first case we might term the circumstances "objective," in the second "subjective." The same distinction can be applied to the Jews in considering their aptitude for capitalism: it may be due to objective or to subjective circumstances.

My immediate business will be to deal with the first set of causes, and for many reasons. To begin with, every explanation that is put forward must be closely scrutinized, in order to make sure that no unproved hypothesis is its basis, and that what has to be proved is not a dogma. Dangerous in most cases, it is particularly so in the problem before us, in which racial and religious prejudices may work havoc, as, indeed, they have done in the writings of the great majority of my precursors on this question. I shall do my utmost to avoid their error in this respect, and shall be at great pains to see to it that my considerations are above criticism. My aim is to discover the play of cause and effect as it really was, without any preconceived idea influencing my reasoning, and I shall adduce my proofs in such a way, that they may be easily followed by all—by the assimilationist Jew no less than by the Nationalist; by him who pins his faith to the influence of race as by the warmest supporter of the doctrine of environment; by the anti-Semite as by his opponent. Hence my starting-point will always have to be from facts admitted on all

hands. That will preclude any appeal to "special race characteristics" or arguments of that ilk.

Any one who does not admit that the Jews have special
gifts may demand that the part played by this people in modern economic life should be explained without any reference
to national peculiarities, but rather from the external circumstances in which Jews were placed by the accident of history.
I shall endeavour to satisfy this demand in the tenth chapter.

Finally, if it becomes apparent that the contribution of the
Jews to modern economic life cannot be entirely explained by
the conditions of their historic situation, then will be the time
for looking to subjective causes, and for considering the Jews'
special characteristics. This shall be the purpose of the twelfth
chapter.

Chapter 9

What is a Capitalist Undertaker?

CAPITALISM[1] IS THE name given to that economic organization wherein regularly two distinct social groups co-operate—the owners of the means of production, who at the same time do the work of managing and directing, and the great body of workers who possess nothing but their labour. The co-operation is such, that the representatives of capital are the subjective agents, that is, they decide as to the "how" and the "how much" in the process of production, and they undertake all risks.

Now what are the mainsprings of the whole system? The first, and perhaps the chiefest, is the pursuit of gain or profit. This being the case, there is a tendency for undertakings to grow bigger and bigger. Arising from that, all economic activities are strictly logical. Whereas in the pre-capitalistic period *quieta non movere* was the watchword and Tradition the guiding star, now it is constant movement. I characterize the whole as "economic rationalism," and this I would term the second mainspring of the capitalistic system.

Economic rationalism expresses itself in three ways. (1) There is a *plan*, in accordance with which all things are ordered aright. And the plan covers activities in the distant future. (2) *Efficiency* is the test applied in the choice of all the means of production. (3) Seeing that the "cash nexus" regulates all economic activity, and that everywhere and always a surplus is sought for, exact *calculations* become necessary in every undertaking.

Everybody knows that a modern business is not merely, say, the production of rails or cotton or electric motors, or the transport of stones or of people. Everybody knows that these are but parts in the organization of the whole. And the characteristics of the undertaker are not that he arranges for the carrying out of the processes named. They are to be found elsewhere, and for the present we may put it roughly that they are a constant buying and selling of the means of production, of labour or of commodities. To vary the phrase somewhat, the undertaker makes contracts concerning exchanges, wherein money is the measure of value.

When do we speak of having accomplished a successful piece of business? Surely when the contract-making has ended well. But what is meant precisely by "well"? It certainly has no reference to the quality or to the quantity of the goods or services given or received; it refers solely and only to the return of the sum of money expended, and to a surplus over and above it (profit). It is the aim of the undertaker so to manipulate the factors over which he has control as to bring about this surplus.

Our next step must be to consider what functions the capitalistic undertaker (the subjective economic factor) has in the sphere of capitalism, seeing that our purpose is to show the capacity of the Jews in this direction. We shall try to discover what special skill is necessary in order to be successful in the competitive struggle. In a word, we shall seek for the type.

To my mind, the best picture of the modern capitalistic undertaker is that which paints him as the combination of two radically different natures in one person. Like Faust, he may say that two souls dwell within his breast; unlike Faust's, however, the two souls do not wish to be separated, but rather, on the contrary, desire to work harmoniously together. What are these two natures? The one is the undertaker (not in the more limited sense of capitalistic undertaker, but quite generally), and the other is the trader.

By the undertaker I mean a man who has an object in view to which he devotes his life, an object which requires the co-operation of others for its achievement, seeing that its realization is in the world of men. The undertaker must thus be differentiated from the artist or the prophet. Like them he has a mission; unlike them he feels that he must bring it to realization. He is a man, therefore, who peers into the distant future, whose every action is planned and done only in so far as it will help the great whole. As an instance of an undertaker in this (non-capitalistic) sense we may mention an African or a North Pole explorer. The undertaker becomes a capitalistic undertaker when he combines his original activities with those of the trader.

And what is a trader? A man whose whole being is set upon doing profitable business; who appraises all activities and all conditions with a view to their money value, who turns everything into its gold equivalent. The world to such a man is one great market-place, with its supply and demand, its conjunctures—good and bad—and its profits and losses. The constant question on his lips is, "What does it cost? What can I make out of it?" His last question would in all probability be, "What is the price of the universe?" The circle of his thoughts is circumscribed by one piece of business, to the successful issue of which he devotes all his energies.

In the combination I have endeavoured to sketch, the undertaker is the constant factor, the trader the variant one.

Constant the undertaker must be, for, having set his heart upon some far-distant goal, he is of necessity bound to follow some plan in order to reach it. Change in his policy is contrary to his nature. Constancy is the basis of his character. But the trader is changeable, for his conduct wavers with the conditions of the market. He must be able to vary his policy and his aim from one moment to another if the prevailing conjuncture so demands it. "Busy-ness" marks him out above all else.

This theory of the two souls in one body is intended to clarify our conception of the capitalistic undertaker. But we must analyse the conception still further, this time into its actual component parts.

In the undertaker I perceive the following four types:—

(1) The Inventor—not merely in the technical sense, but in that of the organizer introducing new forms which bring greater economies into production, or transport, or marketing.

(2) The Discoverer—of new means of selling his commodities, either intensively or extensively. If he finds a new sphere for his activities—let us say he sells bathing-drawers to Eskimos, or gramophones to Negroes—we have a case of

extensive discovery; if he creates new demands in markets where he already has a footing, we may speak of intensive discovery.

(3) The Conqueror. An undertaker of the right kind is always a conqueror, with the determination and will-power to overcome all the difficulties that beset his path. He must also be able to risk much, to stake his all (that is to say, his fortune, his good name, even his life), if need be, to achieve great results for his undertaking. It may be the adoption of new methods in manufacture, the extension of his business though his credit is unstable, and so on.

(4) The Organizer. Above all else the undertaker must be an organizer; *i.e.*, he must be able so to dispose of large numbers of individuals as to bring about the most successful result; must be able to fit the round man into the round hole and the square man into the square; must be able to give a man just the job for which he is best equipped, so as to obtain the maximum of efficiency. To do this satisfactorily demands many gifts and much skill. For example, the organizer must be able to tell at a glance what a man can do best, and which man among many will best suit his purpose. He must be able to let others do his work—*i.e.*, to place in positions of trust such persons as will be able to relieve him of responsibility. Finally, he must be able to see to it that the human factors in the work of production are sufficient for the purpose, both quantitatively and qualitatively, and that their relationship to each other is harmonious. In short, the management of his business must be the most efficient possible.

Now business organization means a good deal more than the skilful choice of men and methods; it means taking into consideration also geographical, ethnological and accidental circumstances of all sorts. Let me illustrate my point. The Westinghouse Electric Company is one of the best organized concerns in the United States. When the Company decided to capture the English market it set up a branch in this country, the organization of which was modelled exactly on that of the parent concern. After a few years, what was the result? The financial break-up of the English branch, chiefly because sufficient allowance had not been made for the difference in English conditions.

This leads us to the activities of the trader. A trader has no definite calling; he has only certain well-defined functions in the body economic. But they are of a very varied kind. For example: to provision ships and supply them with men and ammunition, to conquer wild lands in distant parts, to drive the natives from hearth and home and seize their goods and chattels, to load the ships with these latter and bring them home in order to sell them at public auctions to the highest bidder—all this is a form of trading.

Or, it may be a different form—as when a dealer obtains a pair of old trousers from a needy man of fashion, to whose house he comes in vain five times in succession, and then palms those same trousers off on a stupid yokel.

Or, again, it may take the form of arbitrage dealing on the Stock Exchange.

Clearly there are differences in these instances, as there were between trading in modern and in mediæval times. In the pre-capitalistic period, to trade meant to trade on a big scale, as the "royal merchants" did in the Italian and German cities, and the trader had to be an undertaker (in the general, and not merely in the capitalistic sense). "Each (of the citizens of Genoa) has a tower in his house; if civil war breaks out, the battlements of these towers are the scenes of conflict. They are masters of the sea; they build them ships, called galleys, and roam for plunder in the most distant parts, bringing the spoil back to Genoa. With Pisa they live in continual enmity." "Royal merchants" these, if you like; but not traders in my sense.

I regard those as traders who set out with the intention of doing good business; who combine within themselves two activities—calculation and negotiation. In a word, the trader must be (1) a speculating calculator, and (2) a business man, a negotiator.

As a speculating calculator, he must buy in the cheapest market and sell in the dearest. Which means that he must obtain his labour and his raw material at as low a rate as possible, and not waste anything in the process of manufacture. And when the commodity is ready for sale, he must part with it to the man whose credit is sound, and so forth. For all this he must calculate, and he must speculate. By speculation in this sense I mean the drawing of several conclusions from particular instances—let us call it the power of economic diagnosis, the complete survey of the market, the evaluation of all its symptoms, the recognition of future possibilities and the choice of that course which will have the greatest utility in the long run.

To this end the dealer must have a hundred eyes, a hundred ears and a hundred feelers in all directions. Here he may have to search out a needy nobleman, or a State bent on war, in order to offer them a loan at the psychological moment; there, to put his hand on a labour group that is willing to work a few pence below the prevailing rate of wages; here he may have to form a right estimate of the chances that a new article is likely to have with the public; there, to appraise the true effect of a political crisis on the Stock Exchange. In every case the trader expresses the result in terms of money. That is where the calculation comes in. "A wonderfully shrewd calculator" is a term common in the United States for an adept in this direction.

But a discerning eye for a profitable piece of business is not sufficient: the trader must also possess the capacity for doing business. In this, his negotiating powers will come into play, and he will be doing something very much more akin to the work of an arbitrator between two litigants. He will talk to his opponent, urge reasons and counter-reasons in order to induce him to embark on a certain course. To negotiate is to fence with intellectual weapons.

Trading, then, means to negotiate concerning the buying and selling of some commodity, be it a share, a loan, or a concern. Trading must be the term applied to the activity of the hawker at the back-door, trying to sell the cook a "fur" collar, or to that of the Jewish old clo' man, who talks for an hour to the bucolic driver to persuade him to purchase a pair of trousers. But it must be equally applied to the activities of a Nathan Rothschild, who negotiated with the representative of the Prussian Government for a loan of a million. The difference is not one of kind, but of extent, for the essence of all trading is negotiation, which need not necessarily be by word of mouth. The shopkeeper who recommends his goods to the public, be his method what you will, is in reality negotiating. What is all advertisement but "dumb show" negotiation? The end in view is always the same—to convince the possible buyer of the superiority of a particular set of goods. The ideal of the seller is realized when everybody purchases the article he has recommended.

To create interest, to win confidence, to stir up a desire to buy—such is the end and aim of the successful trader. How he achieves it is of little moment. Sufficient that he uses not outward force but inner forces, his customers coming to him of their own free will. He wins by suggestion, and one of the most effective is to arouse in the heart of the buyer the feeling that to buy at once will be most advantageous. "We shall have snow, boys, said the Finns, for they had Aander (a kind of snow-shoe) to sell," we read in the Magnus Barford Saga (1006 A.D.). This is the prototype of all traders and the suggestion of the Finns the prototype of all advertising—the weapon with which the trader fights. No longer does he dwell in fortified towers, as did his precursor in Genoa in the days of Benjamin of Tudela, nor does he wreck the houses of the natives with his guns if they refuse to "trade" with him, as did the early East India settlers in the 17th century.

Chapter 10

The Objective Circumstances in the Jewish Aptitude for Modern Capitalism

Now THAT we know what a capitalist undertaker is our next question must be, What were the outward circumstances that made it possible for the Jews to do so much in shaping the capitalistic system? To formulate an answer we shall have to review the position of the Jews of Western Europe and America from the end of the 15th century until the present time—the period, that is, in which capitalism took form.

How can that position be best characterized?

The Governor of Jamaica in a letter he wrote (December 17, 1671) to the Secretary of State was happy in his phraseology.[1] "He was of opinion," he said, "that His Majesty could not have more profitable subjects than the Jews: *they had great stocks and correspondence.*" These two reasons, indeed, will account in large measure for the headway made by Jews. But we must also bear in mind their peculiar status among the peoples with whom they dwelt. They were looked upon as strangers and were treated not as full, but as "semi-citizens."

I would therefore assign four causes for the success of the Jews: (1) their dispersion over a wide area, (2) their treatment as strangers, (3) their semi-citizenship, and (4) their wealth.

Jewish Dispersion over a Wide Area

The fact of primary significance is that the Jews were scattered all over the world. Scattered they had been from the time of the first Exile; they were scattered anew after their expulsion from Spain and Portugal, and again when great masses of them left Poland. We have already accompanied them on their wanderings during the last two or three centuries, and have noted how they settled in Germany and

France, in Italy and in England, in the Near East and in the Far West, in Holland, in Austria, in South Africa and in Eastern Asia.

One result of these wanderings was that off-shoots of one and the same family took root in different centres of economic life and established great world-famed firms with numerous branches in all parts. Let us instance a few cases.[2]

The Lopez family had its seat in Bordeaux, and branches in Spain, England, Antwerp and Toulouse. The Mendès family, well-known bankers, also hailed from Bordeaux, and were to be found in Portugal, France and Flanders. The Gradis, relatives of the Mendès, were also settled in all directions. So, too, the Carceres in Hamburg, in England, in Austria, in the West Indies, in Barbados and in Surinam. Other famous families with world-wide branches were the Costas (Acostas, D'Acostas), the Coneglianos, the Alhadibs, the Sassoons, the Pereires, the Rothschilds. We might continue the list *ad infinitum*; suffice it to say that Jewish business concerns that had a footing in at least two places on the face of the globe may be counted in hundreds and in thousands.

What all this means is obvious enough. What Christian business houses obtained only after much effort, and even then only to a much less degree, the Jews had at the very beginning—scattered centres from which to carry on international commerce and to utilize international credit; "great correspondence" in short, the first necessity for all international organization.

Let us recall what I observed about the participation of the Jews in Spanish and Portuguese trade, in the trade of the Levant, and in the economic growth of America. It was of great consequence that the great majority of Jews settling in different parts hailed from Spain; they were thus agents in directing colonial trade, and to an even greater extent the flow of silver, into the new channels represented by Holland, England, France and Germany.

Was it not significant that the Jews directed their footsteps just to these countries, all on the eve of a great economic revival, and were thus the means of allowing them to benefit

by Jewish international connexions? It is well known that
Jews turned away the flow of trade from the lands that
expelled them to those that gave them a hospitable reception.

Was it not significant that they were predominant in Leghorn, which in the 18th century was spoken of as "one of the
great depôts in Europe for the trade of the Mediterranean,"[3]
significant that they forged a commercial chain binding North
and South America together, which assured the North American Colonies of their economic existence, significant above all,
that by their control of the Stock Exchanges in the great
European centres they were the means of internationalizing
public credit?

It was their distribution over a wide area which enabled
them to do all this.

An admirable picture of the importance of the Jews from
this point of view was drawn by a clever observer who made
a study of that people two hundred years ago. The picture has
lost none of its freshness; it may be found in the *Spectator* of
September 27, 1712[4]:—

> They are so disseminated through all the trading Parts of
> the World, that they are become the Instruments by which
> the most distant Nations converse with one another and by
> which mankind are knit together in a general correspond-
> ence. They are like the pegs and nails in a great building,
> which though they are but little valued in themselves, are
> absolutely necessary to keep the whole frame together.

How the Jews utilized for their own advantage the special
knowledge that their scattered position gave them, how they
regulated their activities on the Stock Exchange, is related in
all detail in a Report of the French Ambassador in The
Hague, written in the year 1698.[5] Our informant is of opinion
that the dominance of the Jews on the Amsterdam Stock
Exchange was due in a large degree to their being so well-
informed. This piece of evidence is of such great value that I
shall translate the whole of the passage:—

They carry on a correspondence on both these subjects (news and commerce) with those they call their brotherhoods (congregues). Of these, Venice is considered to be the most important (although neither the richest nor the most populous) because it is the link, by way of the brotherhood of Salonica, between the East and the West as well as the South. Salonica is the governing centre for their nation in these two parts of the world and is responsible for them to Venice, which together with Amsterdam, rules the northern countries (including the merely tolerated community of London, and the secret brotherhoods of France). The result of this association is that on the two topics of news and commerce they receive, one might almost say, the best information of all that goes on in the world, and on this they build up their system every week in their assemblies, wisely choosing for this purpose the day after Saturday, *i.e.*, the Sunday, when the Christians of all denominations are engaged in their religious exercises. These systems, which contain the minutest details of news received during the week, are, after having been carefully sifted by their rabbis and the heads of their congregations, handed over on the Sunday afternoon to their Jewish stockbrokers and agents. These are men of great cleverness, who after having arranged a preconcerted plan among themselves, go out separately to spread news which should prove the most useful for their own ends; ready to start manipulations on the morrow, the Monday morning, according to each individual's disposition: either selling, buying, or exchanging shares. As they always hold a large reserve of these commodities, they can always judge of the most propitious moment, taking advantage of the rise or fall of the securities, or even sometimes of both, in order to carry out their plans.

Equally beneficial was their dispersion for winning the confidence of the great. Indeed, the progress of the Jews to *la haute finance* was almost invariably as follows. In the first instance their linguistic ability enabled them to be of service to crowned heads as interpreters, then they were sent as intermediaries or special negotiators to foreign courts. Soon they were put in charge of their employer's fortunes, at the same time being honoured through his graciousness in allowing them to become his creditors. From this point it was no long step to the control of the State finances, and in later years of the Stock Exchanges.

It is no far-fetched assumption that already in ancient times their knowledge of languages and their acquaintance with foreign civilizations must have made them welcome visitors at the courts of kings and won for them royal confidence. Think of Joseph in Egypt; of the Alabarch Alexander (of whom Josephus tells), the intimate of King Agrippa and of the mother of the Emperor Claudius; think of the Jewish Treasurer of Queen Candace of Ethiopia, of whom we may read in the Acts of the Apostles (viii. 27).

As for the Court Jews in the Middle Ages, we have definite information that they won their spurs in the capacity of interpreters or negotiators. We know it of the Jew Isaac, whom Charlemagne sent to the court of the Caliph Haroun al Rashid; of Kalonymus, the Jewish friend and favourite of the Emperor Otto II; of the famous Chasdai Ibn Shaprut (915-70), who achieved honour and renown as the diplomatic representative of the Caliph Abdul-Rahman III in his negotiations with the Christian courts of Northern Spain.[6] Similarly when the Christian princes of the Iberian Peninsula required skilful negotiators they sought out Jews. Alphonso VI is a good example. Intent on playing off the petty Mohammedan rulers against each other, he chose Jewish agents, with their linguistic abilities and their insight into foreign ways, to send to the courts of Toledo, Seville and Granada. In the period which followed, Jewish emissaries are met with at all the Spanish courts, including those Jews, learned in ethnography, whom James II commissioned to travel into Asia in order to supply his spies with information and who tried to discover the mythical country of Prester John;[7] including also the many interpreters and confidential agents associated with the discovery of the New World.[8]

Considering the importance of the Spanish period in Jewish history not only from the general, but also from the special economic point of view, these cases are worthy of note in that they clearly show the reason for the rise of Jews to influential positions. But they are not limited to the Spanish period; they abound in subsequent epochs also. Thus, Jewish diplomatists were employed by the States-General in their intercourse with the Powers; and names like Delmonte, Mesquita[9] and others are well-known. Equally famous is the Seigneur Hebræo, as Richelieu called the wealthy Ildefonso Lopez, whom the French statesman sent on a secret mission to Holland, and on his return bestowed upon him the title of "Conseiller d'Etat ordinaire."[10]

Finally, the dispersion of the Jews is noteworthy in another way. Their dispersion internationally was, as we have seen, fruitful enough of results; but their being scattered in every part of some particular country had consequences no less potent. To take one instance—the Jews were army-purveyors (and their activities as such date from the days of antiquity, for do we not read that when Belisarius besieged Naples, the Jewish inhabitants offered to supply the town with provisions?).[11] One reason was surely that they were able to accumulate large quantities of commodities much more easily than the Christians, thanks to their connexions in the different centres. "The Jewish undertaker," says one 18th-century writer, "is free from these difficulties. All he need do is to stir up his brethren in the right place, and at a moment's notice he has all the assistance he requires at his disposal."[12] In truth, the Jew at that time never carried on business "as an isolated individual, but always as a member of the most extended trading company in the world."[13] In the words of a petition of the merchants of Paris in the second half of the 18th century,[14] "they are atoms of molten money which flow and are scattered, but which at the least incline reunite into one principal stream."

The Jews as Aliens

During the last century or two Jews were almost everywhere strangers in the sense of being new-comers. They were never old-established in the places where their most successful activities were manifest; nor did they arrive in such centres from the vicinity, but rather from distant lands, differing in manners and customs, and often in climate too, from the countries of their settlements. To Holland, France and England they came from Spain and Portugal and then from Germany; they journeyed to Hamburg and Frankfort from other German cities; later on they dispersed all over Germany from Russian Poland.

The Jews, then, were everywhere colonists, and as such learned the lesson of speedy adaptation to their new surroundings. In this they were ahead of the European nations, who did not become masters of this art until the settlements in America were founded.

New-comers must have an observant eye in order to find a niche for themselves amid the new conditions; they must be very careful of their behaviour, so that they may earn their livelihood without let or hindrance. While the natives are still in their warm beds the new-comers stand without in the sharp morning air of dawn, and their energy is all the keener in consequence. They must concentrate their thoughts to obtain a foothold, and all their economic activities will be dictated by this desire. They must of necessity determine how best to regulate their undertakings, and what is the shortest cut to their goal—what branches of manufacture or commerce are likely to prove most profitable, with what persons business connexions should be established, and on what principles business itself should be conducted. What is all this but the substitution of economic rationalism for time-honoured Tradition? That the Jews did this we have already observed; why they were forced to do it becomes apparent when we recall that everywhere they were strangers in the land, new-comers, immigrants.

But the Jews were strangers among the nations throughout many centuries in yet another sense, which might be termed psychological and social. They were strangers because of the inward contrast between them and their hosts, because of their almost caste-like separation from the peoples in whose midst they dwelt. They, the Jews, looked upon themselves as a peculiar people: and as a peculiar people the nations regarded them. Hence, there was developed in the Jews that conduct and that mental attitude which is bound to show itself in dealings with "strangers," especially in an age in which the conception of world-citizenship was as yet non-existent. For in all periods of history innocent of humani-tarian considerations the mere fact that a "stranger" was being dealt with was sufficient to ease the conscience and loosen the bonds of moral duty. In intercourse with strangers people were never quite so particular. Now the Jews were always brought into contact with strangers, with "others," especially in their economic activities, seeing that everywhere they were a small minority. And whereas the "others" dealt with a stranger, say, once in ten times or even in a hundred, it was just the reverse with the Jews, whose intercourse with strangers was nine out of the ten or ninety-nine out of the hundred times. What was the consequence? The Jew had recourse to the "ethics for strangers" (if I may use this term without being misunderstood) far more frequently than the non-Jew; for the one it was the rule, whilst for the other it was only the exception. Jewish business methods thus came to be based on it.

Closely interwoven with their status as strangers was the special legal position which they occupied everywhere. But this has an importance of its own, and we shall therefore assign an independent section to it.

Jews as Semi-Citizens

At first glance the legal position of the Jews would appear to have had an immense influence on their economic ac-tivities in that it limited the callings to which they might devote themselves, and generally closed the avenues to a live-lihood. But I believe that the effect of these restrictions has been over-estimated. I would even go so far as to say that they were of no moment whatever for the economic growth of Jewry. At least, I am not aware that any of the traces left by Jews on the development of the modern economic system were due to the restraining regulations. That these could not have left a very deep impress is obvious, seeing that during the period which is of most interest to us the laws affecting Jews differed greatly according to locality. For all that we note a remarkable similarity in Jewish influence throughout the whole range of the capitalistic social order.

How varied the laws in restraint of Jews were is not always sufficiently realized. To begin with, there were broad differences between those of one country and of another. Thus, while the Jews in Holland and England were in a position of almost complete equality with their Christian neighbours so far as their economic life was concerned, they laboured under great disabilities in other lands. But even in these last their treatment was not uniform, for in certain towns and districts they enjoyed entire economic freedom, as, for example, in the papal possessions in France.[15] Moreover, even the disabilities varied in number and in kind in each country, and sometimes in different parts of the same country. In most instances they appeared to be quite arbitrary; nowhere was there any underlying principle visible. In one place Jews might not be hawkers, and in another they were not allowed to be shopkeepers. Here they received permission to be craftsmen; there this right was denied them. Here they might deal in wool, there they might not. Here they might sell leather, there it was forbidden them. Here the sale of alcoholic liquors was farmed out to them, there such an idea seemed preposterous. Here they were encouraged to start factories, there they were strictly enjoined to desist from all participation in capitalistic undertakings. Such examples might be continued indefinitely.

Perhaps the best is furnished by Prussia's treatment of her Jews in the 18th century. Here in one and the same country the restrictive legislation for one locality was totally opposed to that of another. The revised General Privileges of 1750 (Article 2) forbade Jews the exercise of handicrafts in many places; yet a royal order of May 21, 1790, permitted the Jews in Breslau "to exercise all manner of mechanical arts," and went on to say that "it would be a source of much pleasure to Us if Christian craftsmen of their own

free will took Jewish boys as apprentices and eventually
received them into their gilds." A similar enactment was
made in the General Reglement for the Jews of South-East
Prussia, dated April 17, 1797 (Article 10).

Again, while the Jews of Berlin were forbidden (by Articles 13 and 15 of the General Privileges of 1750) to sell
meat, beer and brandy to non-Jews, all the native-born Jews
of Silesia had complete freedom of trade in this respect (in
accordance with an Order of February 13, 1769).

The list of commodities in which they were allowed or
forbidden to trade seems to have been drawn up with an
arbitrariness that passes comprehension. Thus, the General
Privileges of 1750 allowed the Jews to deal in foreign or
home leather prepared though undyed, but not in raw or
dyed leather; in raw calf and sheep skins, but not in raw
cow or horse hides; in all manner of manufactured woollen
and cotton wares, but not in raw wool or woollen threads.

The picture becomes still more bewildering when we take
into consideration the varying legal status of the different
classes of Jews. The Jewish community of Breslau, for instance, was (until the Order of May 21, 1790, changed
things) composed of four groups: (1) those with "general
privileges," (2) those with "privileges," (3) those who were
only tolerated, and (4) temporary residents.

The first class included those Jews who were on an equal
footing with Christians so far as trade and commerce were
concerned, and whose rights in this respect were hereditary.
In the second were comprised such Jews as had "special
(limited) privileges" given them, wherein they were allowed
to trade in certain kinds of goods specifically mentioned.
But their rights did not pass to their children, though the
children received preference when privileges of this kind
were being granted. The third class was composed of Jews
who had the right of living in Breslau, but whose economic
activities were even more limited than those in the second
class. As for the fourth, it contained the Jews who received
permission to dwell in the town for a temporary period only.

But even of such rights as they had they were never sure.

In 1769, for example, the Silesian Jews who lived in country districts were allowed to receive in farm the sale of beer, brandy and meat; in 1780 the permission was withdrawn; in 1787 it was renewed.

Yet in all this it must not be forgotten that regulations in restraint of industry and commerce during the last two or three centuries were for the most part a dead letter; as a matter of fact, capitalistic interests found ways and means of getting round them. The simplest method was to overstep the law, a course to which as time went on the bureaucratic State shut its eyes. But there were lawful means too of circumventing inconvenient paragraphs: concessions, privileges, patents, and the whole collection of documents granting exceptional treatment which princes were always willing to issue if only an additional source of income accrued therefrom. The Jews were not slow in obtaining such privileges. The proviso mentioned in the Prussian Edicts of 1737 and 1750—that all restraints referring to Jews might be removed by a special royal order—was tacitly held to apply in all cases. Some way out must have been possible, else how could the Jews have engaged in those trades (*e.g.*, leather, tobacco) which the law forbade them?

At one point, however, industrial regulations made themselves felt as very real checks to the progress of the Jew, and that was wherever economic activities were organized on a corporate basis. The gilds were closed to them; they were kept back by the crucifix which hung in each gild-hall, and round which members assembled. Accordingly, if they wished to engage in any industry or trade monopolized by a gild, they were forced to do so as "outsiders," interlopers and free traders.

But a still greater obstacle in their path were the laws regulating their position in public life. In all countries there was a remarkable uniformity in these; everywhere the Jew was shut out from public offices, central or local, from the Bar, from Parliament, from the Army, from the Universities. This applied to the States of Western Europe—France, Holland, England—and also to America. But there is no need to consider with any degree of fullness the legal status of the Jews in the pre-emancipation era, seeing that it is fairly generally known. Only this we would mention here—that their condition of semi-citizenship continued in most countries right into the 19th century. The United States was the first land in which they obtained civil equality; the principle was there promulgated in 1783. In France the famous Emancipation Law dates from 27th September 1791; in Holland the Batavian National Assembly made the Jews full citizens in 1796. But in England it was not until 1859 that they were granted complete emancipation, while in the German States it took ten years longer. On 3rd July 1869 the North German Confederation finally set the seal on their civil equality; Austria had already done so in 1867, and Italy followed suit in 1870.

Equally well-known is it that in many cases the emancipation laws have become dead letters. Open any Liberal paper in Germany (to take a good instance) and day by day you will find complaints that Jews are never given commissions in the Army, that they are excluded from appointments to the Bench, and so on.

This set-back which the Jews received in public life was of great use to industry and commerce in that the Jew concentrated all his ability and energy on them. The most gifted minds from other social groups devoted themselves to the service of the State; among the Jews, in so far as they did not spend themselves in the *Beth Hamidrash* [the Communal House of Study], such spirits were forced into business. Now the more economic life aimed at profit-making and the more the moneyed interests acquired influence, the more were the Jews driven to win for themselves by means of commerce and industry what was denied them by the law—respect and power in the State. It becomes apparent why gold (as we have seen) was appraised so highly among Jews.

But if exclusion from public life was of benefit to the economic position of the Jews in one direction, giving them a pull over their Christian neighbours, it was equally beneficial in another. It freed the Jews from political partisanship. Their attitude towards the State, and the particular Government of the day, was wholly unprejudiced. Thanks to this, their capacity to become the standard-bearers of the international capitalistic system was superior to that of other people. For they supplied the different States with money, and national conflicts were among the chief sources from which Jews derived their profit. Moreover, the political colourlessness of their position made it possible for them to serve successive dynasties or governments in countries which, like France, were subjected to many political changes. The history of the Rothschilds illustrates the point. Thus the Jews, through their inferior civil position, were enabled to facilitate the growth of the indifference of capitalism to all interests but those of gain. Again, therefore, they promoted and strengthened the capitalistic spirit.

The Wealth of the Jews

Among the objective conditions which made possible the economic mission of the Jews during the last three or four centuries must be reckoned that at all times and in all places where their rôle in economic life was no mean one, they disposed of large sums of money. But this assertion says nothing about the wealth of the whole body of Jews, so that it is idle to urge the objection that at all periods there were poor Jews, and very many of them. Any one who has ever set foot in a Jewish congregation on the Eastern borders of Germany, or is acquainted with the Jewish quarter of New York, knows that well enough. But what I maintain—a more limited proposition—is that much wealth and great fortunes were to be found, and still are to be found, among Jews ever since the 17th century. Put in a slightly different way, there were always many wealthy Jews, and certainly the Jews on an average were richer than the Christians round them. It is beside the mark to say that the richest man in Germany or the three richest in America are not Jews.

A good many of the exiles from the Pyrenean Peninsula must have been very wealthy indeed. We are informed that their flight brought with it an "exodo de capitaes," a flow of capital from the country. However, in many instances they sold their property, receiving foreign bills in exchange.[16] The richest among the fugitives probably made for Holland. At any rate it is recorded that the first settlers in that country—Manuel Lopez Homen, Maria Nunez, Miguel Lopez and others—had great possessions.[17] Whether other wealthy Spaniards followed in the 17th century, or whether those already resident added to their fortunes, it is not easy to discover. But certain it is that the Jews of Holland in the 17th and 18th centuries were famed for their riches. True, there are no statistics to illustrate this, but an abundance of other weighty evidence exists. Travellers could not sufficiently admire the splendour and the luxury of the houses of these refugees who dwelt in what were really palaces. And if you turn to a collection of engravings of that period, do you not very soon discover that the most magnificent mansions in, say, Amsterdam or The Hague were built by Jews or inhabited by them—those of Baron Delmonte, of the noble Lord de Pinto, of the Lord d'Acoste and others? (At the close of the 17th century de Pinto's fortune was estimated at 8,000,-000 florins.) Of the princely luxury at a Jewish wedding in Amsterdam, where one of her daughters married, Glückel von Hameln draws a vivid picture in her *Memoirs*.[18]

It was the same in other lands. For 17th and 18th century France we have the generalization of Savary, who knew most things. "We say," these are his very words, "we say that a tradesman is 'as rich as a Jew' when he has the reputation of having amassed a large fortune."[19]

As for England, actual figures are extant concerning the wealth of the rich Sephardim soon after their arrival. A crowd of rich Jews followed in the train of Catharine of Braganza, Charles II's bride, so that while in 1661 there were only 35 Jewish families in London, two years later no less than 57 new-comers were added to the list. In 1663, as appears from the books of Alderman Blackwell, the following was the half-yearly turnover of the wealthy Jewish merchants:[20] Jacob Aboab, £13,085; Samuel de Vega, £18,309; Duarte de Sylva, £41,441; Francisco da Sylva, £14,646;

Fernando Mendes da Costa, £30,490; Isaac Dazevedo, £13,605; George and Domingo Francia, £35,759; and Gomez Rodrigues, £13,124.

The centres of Jewish life in Germany in the 17th and 18th centuries were, as we have already observed, Hamburg and Frankfort-on-the-Main. For both cities it is possible to compute the wealth of the resident Jews by the aid of figures.

In Hamburg, too, it was Spanish and Portuguese Jews who were the first settlers. In 1649, 40 of their families participated in the foundation of the Hamburg Bank, which shows that they must have been fairly comfortably off. Very soon complaints were made of the increasing wealth and influence of the Jews. In 1649 they were blamed for their ostentatious funerals and for riding in carriages to take the air; in 1650 for building houses like palaces. In the same year sumptuary laws forbade them too great a show of magnificence.[21] Up to the end of the 17th century the Sephardic Jews appear to have possessed all the wealth; about that time, however, their Ashkenazi brethren also came quickly to the fore. Glückel von Hameln states that many German-Jewish families which in her youth were in comparative poverty later rose to a state of affluence. And Glückel's observations are borne out by figures dating from the first quarter of the 18th century.[22] In 1729 the Jewish community in Altona was composed of 279 subscribing members, of whom 145 were wealthy, possessing between them 5,434,300 mark [£271,715], that is, an average of more than 37,000 mark [£1850] per head. The Hamburg community had 160 subscribing members, 16 of whom together were worth 501,-500 mark [£25,075]. These figures appear to be below the actual state of things, if we compare them with the particulars concerning each individual. In 1725 the following wealthy Jews were resident in Hamburg, Altona and Wandsbeck: Joel Solomon, 210,000 mark; his son-in-law, 50,000; Elias Oppenheimer, 300,000; Moses Goldschmidt, 60,000; Alex Papenheim, 60,000; Elias Salomon, 200,000; Philip Elias, 50,000; Samuel Schiesser, 60,000; Berend Heyman, 75,000; Samson Nathan, 100,000; Moses Hamm, 75,000;

Sam Abraham's widow, 60,000; Alexander Isaac, 60,000; Meyer Berend, 400,000; Salomon Berens, 1,600,000; Isaac Hertz, 150,000; Mangelus Heymann, 200,000; Nathan Bendix, 100,000; Philip Mangelus, 100,000; Jacob Philip, 50,-000; Abraham Oppenheimer's widow, 60,000; Zacharias Daniel's widow and widowed daughter, 150,000; Simon del Banco, 150,000; Marx Casten, 200,000; Abraham Lazarus, 150,000; Carsten Marx, 60,000; Berend Salomon, 600,000 rthlr.; Meyer Berens, 400,000; Abraham von Halle, 150,000; Abraham Nathan, 150,000.

In view of this list it can scarcely be doubted that there were many rich Jews in Hamburg.

Frankfort presents the same picture; if anything the colours are even brighter. The wealth of the Jews begins to accumulate at the end of the 16th century, and from then onwards it increases steadily. In 1593 there were 4 Jews and 54 Christians (making 7.4 per cent.) in Frankfort who paid taxes on a fortune of over 15,000 florins; in 1607 their number had reached 16 (compared with 90 Christians, i.e., 17.7 per cent.).[23] In 1618 the poorest Jew paid taxes on 100 florins, the poorest Christian on 50. Again, 300 Jewish families paid as garrison and fortification taxes no less than 100,900 florins in the years 1634 to 1650.[24]

The number of taxpayers in the Frankfort Jewish community rose to 753 by the end of the 18th century, and together they possessed at least 6,000,000 florins. More than half of this was in the hands of the twelve wealthiest families:[25] Speyer, 604,000 florins; Reiss-Ellissen, 299,916; Haas, Kann, Stern, 256,500; Schuster, Getz, Amschel, 253,075; Goldschmidt, 235,000; May, 211,000; Oppenheimer, 171,-500; Wertheimer, 138,600; Flörsheim, 166,666; Rindskopf, 115,600; Rothschild, 109,375; Sichel, 107,000.

And in Berlin the Jews in the early 18th century were not by any means poor beggars. Of the 120 Jewish families resident in the Prussian capital in 1737 only 10 owned less than 1000 thalers, the rest all had 2000 to 20,000 thaler, and over.[26]

That the Jews were among the richest people in the land

is thus attested, and this state of affairs has continued through the last two or three hundred years right down to our own day, except that to-day it is perhaps more general and more widespread. And its consequence? It can scarcely be over-estimated for those countries which offered a refuge to the wanderers. The nations that profited by the Jews' sojourn with them were well equipped to help forward the development of capitalism. Hence it should be specially noticed that the wanderings of the Jews had the effect of shifting the centre where the precious metals had accumulated. Obviously it could not but influence the trend of economic life that Spain and Portugal were emptied of their gold and England and Holland enriched.

Nor is it difficult to prove that Jewish money called into existence all the large undertakings of the 17th century and financed them. Just as the expedition of Columbus would have been impossible had the rich Jews left Spain a generation earlier, so the great India Companies might never have been founded and the great banks which were established in the 17th century might not so quickly have attained their stability had it not been that the wealth of the Spanish exiles came to the aid of England, Holland and Hamburg; in other words, had the Jews been expelled from Spain a century later than was actually the case.

This in fact was why Jewish wealth was so influential. It enabled capitalistic undertakings to be started, or at least facilitated the process. To establish banks, warehouses, stock and share broking—all this was easier for the Jew than for the others because his pockets were better lined. That, too, was why he became banker to crowned heads. And finally, because he had money he was able to lend it. This activity paved the way for capitalism to a greater degree than anything else did. For modern capitalism is the child of money-lending.

Money-lending contains the root idea of capitalism; from money-lending it received many of its distinguishing features. In money-lending all conception of quality vanishes and only the quantitative aspect matters. In money-lending the contract becomes the principal element of business; the agreement about the *quid pro quo*, the promise for the future, the notion of delivery are its component parts. In money-lending there is no thought of producing only for one's needs. In money-lending there is nothing corporeal (*i.e.*, technical), the whole is a purely intellectual act. In money-lending economic activity as such has no meaning; it is no longer a question of exercising body or mind; it is all a question of success. Success, therefore, is the only thing that has a meaning. In money-lending the possibility is for the first time illustrated that you can earn without sweating; that you may get others to work for you without recourse to force.

In fine, the characteristics of money-lending are the characteristics of all modern capitalistic economic organizations.

But historically, too, modern capitalism owes its being to money-lending. This was the case wherever it was necessary to lay out money for initial expenses, or where a business was started as a limited company. For essentially a limited company is in principle nothing but a matter of money-lending with the prospect of immediate profit.

The money-lending activities of the Jews were thus an objective factor in enabling the Jews to create, to expand and to assist the capitalistic spirit. But our last remarks have already touched upon a further problem, going beyond objective considerations. Is there not already a specific psychological element in the work of the money-lender? But more than this. It may be asked, Can the objective circumstances alone entirely explain the economic rôle of the Jews? Are there not perhaps special Jewish characteristics which must be taken into account in our chain of reasoning? Before proceeding to this chapter, however, we must turn to an influence of extreme importance in this connexion—to the Jewish religion.

Chapter 11

The Significance of the Jewish Religion in Economic Life

Introductory Note

THREE REASONS HAVE ACTUATED ME in devoting a special chapter to the consideration of the religion of the Jewish people and the demonstration of its enormous influence on Jewish economic activities. First, the Jewish religion can be fully appreciated in all its bearings from the economic standpoint only when it is studied in detail and by itself; secondly, it calls for a special method of treatment; and thirdly, it occupies a position midway between the objective and the subjective factors of Jewish development. For, in so far as any religion is the expression of some particular spiritual outlook, it has a "subjective" aspect; in so far as the individual is born into it, it has an objective aspect.

The Importance of Religion for the Jewish People

That the religion of a people, or of a group within a people, can have far-reaching influences on its economic life will not be disputed. Only recently Max Weber demonstrated the connexion between Puritanism and Capitalism. In fact, Max Weber's researches are responsible for this book. For any one who followed them could not but ask himself whether all that Weber ascribes to Puritanism might not with equal justice be referred to Judaism, and probably in a greater degree; nay, it might well be suggested that that which is called Puritanism is in reality Judaism. This relationship will be discussed in due course.

Now, if Puritanism has had an economic influence, how much more so has Judaism, seeing that among no other civilized people has religion so impregnated all national life. For the Jews religion was not an affair of Sundays and Holy Days; it touched everyday life even in its minutest action, it regulated *all* human activities. At every step the Jew asked himself, Will this tend to the glory of God or will it profane His name? Jewish law defines not merely the relation between man and God, formulates not merely a metaphysical conception; it lays down rules of conduct for all possible relationships, whether between man and man or between man and nature. Jewish law, in fact, is as much part of the religious system as are Jewish ethics. The Law is from God, and moral law and divine ordinances are inseparable in Judaism.[1] Hence in reality there are no special ethics of Judaism. Jewish ethics are the underlying principles of the Jewish religion.[2]

No other people has been so careful as the Jews in providing for the teaching of religion to even the humblest. As Josephus so well put it: Ask the first Jew you meet concerning his "laws" and he will be able to tell you them better than his own name. The reason for this may be found in the systematic religious instruction given to every Jewish child, as well as in the fact that divine service partly consists of the reading and explanation of passages from Holy Writ. In the course of the year the Torah is read through from beginning to end. Moreover, it is one of the primary duties of the Jew to study the Torah. "Thou shalt speak of them when thou sittest in thine house and when thou walkest by the way and when thou liest down and when thou risest up" (Deut. vi. 5).[3]

No other people, too, has walked in God's ways so conscientiously as the Jews; none has striven to carry out its religious behests so thoroughly. It has indeed been asserted that the Jews are the least religious of peoples. I shall not stay to weigh the justice of this remark. But certain it is that they are the most "God-fearing" people that ever were on the face of the earth. They lived always in trembling awe, in awe of God's wrath. "My flesh trembleth for fear of Thee, and I am afraid of Thy judgments," said the Psalmist (Ps. cxix. 120), and the words may be taken as applicable to the Jews in every age. "Happy is the man that feareth alway" (Prov. xxviii. 14). "The pious never put away their fear"

(*Tanchuma Chukkath*, 24).[4] One can understand it when one thinks of the Jewish God—fearful, awful, curse-uttering Jehovah. Never in all the world's literature, either before or since, has humanity been threatened with so much evil as Jehovah promises (in the famous 28th chapter of Deuteronomy) to those who will not keep His commandments.

But this mighty influence (the fear of God) did not stand alone. Others combined with it, and together they had the tendency of almost forcing the Jews to obey the behests of their religion most scrupulously. The first of these influences was their national fate. When the Jewish State was destroyed the Pharisees and Scribes—*i.e.*, those who cherished the traditions of Ezra and strove to make obedience to the Law the end and aim of life—the Pharisees and Scribes came to the head of affairs and naturally directed the course of events into channels which they favoured. Without a State, without their sanctuary, the Jews, under the leadership of the Pharisees, flocked around the Law (that "portable Fatherland," as Heine calls it), and became a religious brotherhood, guided by a band of pious Scribes, pretty much as the disciples of Loyola might gather around them the scattered remnants of a modern State. The Pharisees now led the way. Their most distinguished Rabbis looked upon themselves as the successors of the ancient Synhedrium, and were indeed so regarded, becoming the supreme authority in spiritual and temporal affairs for all the Jews in the world.[5] The power of the Rabbis originated in this fashion, and the vicissitudes of the Jews in the Middle Ages only helped to strengthen it. So oppressive did it eventually become that the Jews themselves at times complained of the burden. For the more the Jews were shut off, or shut themselves off, from the people among whom they dwelt, the more the authority of the Rabbis increased, and the more easily could the Jews be forced to be faithful to the Law. But the fulfilment of the Law, which was urged upon them by the Rabbis, must have been a necessity for the Jews for inner reasons: it satisfied their heart's desire, it appeared the most precious gift that life had to offer. And why? Because amid all the persecution and suffering which was meted out to the Jews on all sides, that alone enabled them to retain their dignity, without which life would have been valueless. For a very long period religious teaching was enshrined in the Talmud, and hence Jews through many centuries lived in it, for it and through it. The Talmud was the most precious possession of the Jew; it was the breath of his nostrils, it was his very soul. The Talmud became a family history for generation after generation, with which each was familiar. "The thinker lived in its thought, the poet in its pure idealism. The outer world, the world of nature and of man, the powerful ones of the earth and the events of the times, were for the Jew during a thousand years accidents, phantoms; his only reality was the Talmud."[6] The Talmud has been well compared (and the comparison to my mind applies equally to all religious literature) to an outer shell with which the Jews of the Diaspora covered themselves; it protected them against all influences from without and kept alive their strength within.[7]

We see, then, what forces were at work to make the Jews right down to modern times a more God-fearing people than any other, to make them religious to their inmost core, or, if the word "religious" be objected to, to keep alive among high and low a general and strict observation of the precepts of their religion. And for our purpose, we must regard this characteristic as applicable to all sorts and conditions of Jews, the Marannos of the 16th, 17th and 18th centuries included. We must look upon these too as orthodox Jews. Says the foremost authority on that period of Jewish history,[8] "The great majority of the Marannos were Jews to a much larger extent than is commonly supposed. They submitted to force of circumstance and were Christians only outwardly. As a matter of fact they lived the Jewish life and observed the tenets of the Jewish religion. . . . This admirable constancy will be appreciated to the full only when the wealth of material in the Archives of Alcalia de Henares, Simancas and other places has been sorted and utilized."

But among professing Jews the wealthiest were often

enough excellent Talmudic scholars. Was not a knowledge of the Talmud a highway to honour, riches and favour among Jews? The most learned Talmudists were also the cleverest financiers, medical men, jewellers, merchants. We are told, for example, of some of the Spanish Ministers of Finance, bankers and court physicians that they devoted to the study of the Holy Writ not only the Sabbath day but also two nights of each week. In modern times old Amschel Rothschild, who died in 1855, did the same. He lived strictly according to Jewish law and ate no morsel at a stranger's table, even though it were the Emperor's. One who knew the Baron well says of him that "he was looked upon as the most pious Jew in all Frankfort. Never have I seen a man so afflict himself—beating his breast, and crying to Heaven— as Baron Rothschild did in the synagogue on the Day of Atonement. The continual praying weakens him so that he falls into a faint. Odorous plants from his garden are held to his nose to revive him."[9]* His nephew William Charles, who died in 1901 and who was the last of the Frankfort Rothschilds, observed all the religious prescriptions in their minutest detail. The pious Jew is forbidden to touch any object which under certain circumstances has become unclean by having been already touched by some one else. And so a servant always walked in front of this Rothschild and wiped the door-handles. Moreover, he never touched paper money that had been in use before; the notes had to be fresh from the press.

If this was how a Rothschild lived, it is not surprising to come across Jewish commercial travellers who do not touch meat six months in the year because they are not absolutely certain that the method of slaughtering has been in accordance with Jewish law.

However, if you want to study orthodox Judaism you must go to Eastern Europe, where it is still without disintegrating elements—you must go there personally or read the

* Sombart in the German text quotes this as an occurrence on the Sabbath. It is obvious that the description refers to the Day of Atonement.—Trans.

books about it. In Western Europe the orthodox Jews are a small minority. But when we speak of the influence of the Jewish religion it is the religion that held sway until a generation ago that we mean, the religion that led the Jews to so many victories.

The Sources of the Jewish Religion

Mohammed called the Jews "the people of the Book." He was right. There is no other people that lived so thoroughly according to a book. Their religion in all its stages was generally incorporated in a book, and these books may be looked upon as the sources of the Jewish religion. The following is a list of such books, each originating at a particular time and supplementing some other.

1. The Bible, *i.e.*, the Old Testament, until the destruction of the Second Temple. It was read in Hebrew in Palestine and in Greek (Septuagint) in the Diaspora.
2. The Talmud (more especially the Babylonian Talmud), from the 2nd to the 6th century of the Common Era, the principal depository of Jewish religious teaching.
3. The Code of Maimonides, compiled in the 12th century.
4. The Code (called the *Turim*) of Jacob ben Asher (1248-1340).
5. The Code of Joseph Caro—the *Shulchan Aruch* (16th century).

These "sources" from which the Jewish religion drew its life appear in a different light according as they are regarded by scientific research or with the eyes of the believing Jew. In the first case they are seen as they really are; in the second, they are idealized.

What are they in reality? The Bible, *i.e.*, the Old Testament, is the foundation upon which the entire structure of Judaism was built up. It was written by many hands at different periods, thus forming, as it were, a piece of literary mosaic.[10] The most important portion of the whole is the Torah, *i.e.*, the Pentateuch. It received its present shape by the commingling of two complete works some time in the period after Ezra. The one was the old and the new (the Deuteronomic) Law Book (650 B.C.) and the other, Ezra's Law Book (440 B.C.).* And its special character the Torah owes to Ezra and Nehemiah, who introduced a strict legal system. With Ezra and the school of *Soferim* (scribes) that he founded, Judaism in the form which it has to-day originated; from that period to the present it has remained unchanged.

Beside the Torah we must mention the so-called Wisdom Literature—the Psalms, Job, Ecclesiastes, Ecclesiasticus and the Proverbs. This section of Jewish literature is wholly post-exilic; only in that period could it have arisen, assuming as it did the existence of the Law, and the prevailing belief that for obeying the Law God gave Life, for transgressing it Death. The Wisdom Literature, unlike the Prophetic Books, was concerned with practical life. Some of the books contain the crystallized wisdom of many generations and are of a comparatively early date. The Book of Proverbs, for example, the most useful for our purpose, dates from the year 180 B.C.[11]

Two streams flow from the Bible. The one, chiefly by way of the Septuagint, ran partly into Hellenistic philosophy and partly into Pauline Christianity. That does not concern us further.

The other, chiefly by way of the Hebrew Bible current in Palestine, ran into Jewish "Law," and the course of this we shall have to follow.

The specifically Jewish development of the Holy Writ already began as early as Ezra's day; it was due to the first schools of *Soferim* (scribes), and the later schools of Hillel and Shammai only extended and continued the work. The actual "development" consisted of explanations and amplifi-

I.e. Deut. v. 45.-xxvi. 69 (about 650 B.C.) and Exod. xii. 25-31, xxxv. to Lev. xv.; Numb. i.-x.; xv.-xix; xxvii.-xxxvi. (about 445 B.C.).

cations of the Holy Writ, arrived at as the result of disputa-
tion, the method in vogue in the Hellenistic World. The
development was really a tightening of the legal formalism,
with the view of protecting Judaism against the inroads of
Hellenistic Philosophy. Here, as always, the Jewish religion
was the expression of a reaction against disintegrating forces.
The Deuteronomic Law was the reaction against Baal worship; the Priestly Code against Babylonian influences; the
later Codes of Maimonides and Rabbenu Asher and Caro
against Spanish culture; and the teaching of the *Tannaim*
[Tannai—teacher] in the century preceding and that com-
mencing the Common Era against the enervating doctrines
of Hellenism.[12]

The old oral tradition of the "Wise" was codified about
the year 200 A.D. by R. Judah Hanassi (the Prince), usually
called Rabbi. His work is the *Mishna*. Following on the
Mishna are further explanations and additions which were
collected and given a fixed form in the 6th century (500-550
A.D.) by the *Saboraim* [Saborai—those who give opinions].
Those portions which had reference to the Mishna alone were
termed the *Gemara*, the authors of which were the *Amoraim*
[Amorai—speaker]. Mishna and Gemara together form the
Talmud, of which there are two versions, the Palestinian and
the Babylonian. The latter is the more important.[13]

The Talmud, as edited by the Saboraim, has become the
chief depository of Jewish religious teaching, and its universal authority resulted from the Mohammedan conquests.
To begin with, it became the legal and constitutional foundation for Jewish communal life in Babylon, at the head of
which stood the "Prince of the Captivity" and the Presidents
of the two Talmudic colleges, the *Gaonim* [Gaon—Excel-
lency]. As Islam spread further and further afield the Jewish
communities in the lands that it conquered came into closer
relation with the Gaonate in Babylon; they asked advice on
religious, ethical and common law questions and loyally
accepted the decisions, all of which were based on the Talmud. Indeed, Babylonian Jewry came to be regarded as the
new centre of Jewish life.

As soon as the Gemara was written down, and so received permanent form, the development of Judaism ceased. Nevertheless we must mention the three codes which in the post-Talmudic period embodied all the substance of the religion, first, because they presented it in a somewhat different garb, and secondly, because in their regulation of the religious life they could not but pay some heed to changed conditions. All the three codes are recognized by Jews as authoritative side by side with the Talmud, and the last, the *Shulchan Aruch,* is looked upon to-day by the orthodox Jew as containing the official version of religious duties. What is of interest to us in the case of all the codes is that they petrified Jewish religious life still more. Of Maimonides even Graetz asserts as much. "A great deal of what in the Talmud is still mutable, he changed into unmodifiable law. . . . By his codification he robbed Judaism of the power of developing. . . . Without considering the age in which the Talmudic regulations arose, he makes them binding for all ages and circumstances." R. Jacob ben Asher went beyond Maimonides, and Joseph Caro beyond Jacob ben Asher, reaching the utmost limit. His work tends to ultra-particularism and is full of hair-splitting casuistry. The religious life of the Jews "was rounded off and unified by the *Shulchan Aruch,* but at the cost of inwardness and unfettered thought. Caro gave Judaism the fixed form which it has retained down to the present day."[14]

This, then, is the main stream of Jewish religious life; these the sources from which Judaism drew its ideas and ideals. There were, of course, tributary streams, as, for instance, that of the Apocalyptic literature of the pre-Christian era, which stood for a heavenly, a universal, an individualistic Judaism;[15] or that of the Kabbala, which busied itself with symbols and arithmetical figures. But these had small share in the general development of Jewish life, and may be neglected so far as their effect on historic Judaism is concerned. Nor were they ever recognized by "official" Judaism as sources of the Jewish religion.

So much for the realistic conception of these sources. But

what of that current in orthodox Jewish circles? In many respects the belief of the pious Jew touching the origin of the Jewish system is of much more consequence than its real origin. We must therefore try and acquaint ourselves with that belief.

The traditional view, which every orthodox Jew still holds, is that the Jewish system has a twofold birth: partly through Revelation and partly in the inspiration of the "Wise." Revelation refers to the written and the oral tradition. The former is contained in the holy books of the Bible—the Canon as it was fixed by the members of the Great Synagogue. It has three parts[16]:—the Torah or Pentateuch, the Prophetical Books and the "Writings" (the remaining books). The Torah was given to Moses on Sinai and he "gradually instructed the people in it during their forty years' wandering in the wilderness. . . . It was not until the end of his life that he finished the written Torah, the five books of Moses, and delivered them unto Israel, and we are in duty bound to consider every letter, every word of the written Torah as the Revelation of God."[17] The remaining books were also the outcome of divine revelation, or, at any rate, were inspired by God. The attitude towards the Prophetical literature and the Hagiographa, however, is somewhat freer than that towards the Torah.

The Oral Tradition, or the Oral Torah, is the explanation of the written one. This, too, was revealed to Moses on Sinai, but for urgent reasons was not allowed to be written down at once. That took place at a much later date—only after the destruction of the second Temple—and was embodied in *Mishna* and *Gemara,* which thus contain the only correct explanation of the Torah, seeing that they were divinely revealed. In the Talmud are included also rabbinic ordinances and the *Haggada, i.e.,* the interpretation of those portions of Holy Writ other than the legal enactments. The interpretation of the latter was called the *Halacha,* and *Halacha* and *Haggada* supplemented each other. Beside these were placed the collection of decisions, *i.e.,* the three codes already referred to.

What was the significance of all this literature for the religious life of the Jews? What was it that the Jew believed, what were the commands he obeyed?

In the first place it must be premised that so far as I am aware there is no system of dogmas in Judaism.[18] Wherever compilation of such a system has been attempted it was invariably the work of non-Jews.[19] The nature of the Jewish religion and more especially the construction of the Talmud, which is characterized by its lack of order, is inconsistent with the formulation of any dogmatic system. Nevertheless certain principles may be discovered in Judaism, and its spirit will be found expressed in Jewish practices. Indeed, it will not be difficult to enumerate these principles, since they have remained the same from the very beginning. What has been termed the "spirit of Ezekiel" has been paramount in Judaism from Ezra's day to ours. It was only developed more and more, only taken to its logical conclusions. And so to discover what this "spirit" is we need only refer to the sources of the religion—the Bible, the Talmud and the later Rabbinic literature.

It is a harder task to determine to what extent this or that doctrine still finds acceptance. Does, for example, the Talmudic adage, "Kill even the best of the Gentiles," still hold good? Do the other terrible aphorisms ferreted out in Jewish religious literature by Pfefferkorn, Eisenmenger, Röhling, Dr. Justus and the rest of that fraternity, still find credence, or are they, as the Rabbis of to-day indignantly protest, entirely obsolete? It is obvious, of course, that the single doctrines were differently expressed in different ages, and if the whole literature, but more especially the Talmud, is referred to on particular points, opposite views, the "pros" and the "cons," will be found. In other words, it is possible to "prove" absolutely anything from the Talmud, and hence the thrust and counter-thrust between the anti-Semites and their Jewish and non-Jewish opponents from time immemorial; hence the fact that what the one proved to be black by reference to the Talmud the others proved to be white on the same authority. There is nothing surprising in this when it is remembered that to a great extent the Talmud is nothing else than a collection of controversies of the different Rabbinical scholars.

To discover the religious ordinances which regulated actual life we must make a distinction which, to my mind, is very real—the distinction between the man who by personal study strives to find out the law for himself, and the one who accepts it on the authority of another. In the case of the first, the thing that matters is that some opinion or other is found expressed. It is of no consequence that its very opposite may also be there. For the pious Jew who obtains edification by the study of his literature the one view was enough. It may have been the spur to a particular course of action; or it may have provided him with an additional reason for persisting in a course upon which he had already entered. The sanction of the book was sufficient in either event, most of all if it was the Bible or, better still, the Torah. Since all was of divine origin, one passage was as binding as another. This held good whether applied to the Bible, to the Talmud or to the later Rabbinic writings.

The matter assumes a different aspect if the individual does not, or cannot, study the sources himself but relies on the direction of his spiritual adviser or on books recommended by him. Such a one is confronted with only one opinion, arrived at by the proper interpretation of contradictory texts. Obviously these views must have varied from time to time, in accordance with the Rabbinic traditions in each epoch. Hence, to find the laws that in any period were binding we much search for its Rabbinic traditions—no great task since the publication of the Rabbinic law-books. From the 11th to the 14th century we have the *Yad Hachazaka* ["Strong Hand"] of Maimonides, from the 14th to the 16th the *Tur* of R. Jacob ben Asher, and after the 16th the *Shulchan Aruch* of Caro. Each of these gives the accepted teachings of the age, each is the decisive authority. For the last three hundred years the *Shulchan Aruch* has thus laid down the law wherever there were differences of opinion. As the text-book I have already quoted says, "First and foremost the *Shulchan Aruch* of R.

Joseph Caro, together with the notes of R. Moses Isserlein and the other glosses, is recognized by all Israel as the Code on which we model our ritual observances." The Law is also summed up in the 613 precepts which Maimonides derived from the Torah and when even to-day are still in force. "According to the tradition of our Teachers (of blessed memory) God gave Israel by the hand of Moses 613 precepts, 248 positive and 365 negative. All these are binding to all eternity; only those which have reference to the Jewish State and agricultural life in Palestine and to the Temple service in Jerusalem are excepted, as they cannot be carried out by the Jews of the Diaspora. We can obey 369 precepts, 126 positive and 243 negative; and in addition the seven Rabbinic commands."[20]

The lives of Orthodox Jews were governed by these manuals during the last century and still are so to-day, in so far as the guidance of the Rabbinic law was followed and opinions based on a personal study of the sources were not formed. From the manuals we have mentioned, therefore, we must gather the ordinances which were decisive for each individual instance in religious life. Hence Reformed Judaism is of no concern to us, and books trimmed to suit modern ideas, such as the great majority of the latest expositions of the "Ethics of Judaism," are absolutely useless for our purpose—which is to show the connexion between capitalism and genuine Jewish teaching, and its significance in modern economic life.

The Fundamental Ideas of the Jewish Religion

Let me avow it right away: I think that the Jewish religion has the same leading ideas as Capitalism. I see the same spirit in the one as in the other.

In trying to understand the Jewish religion—which, by the way, must not be confused with the religion of Israel (the two are in a sense opposites)—we must never forget that a *Sofer* was its author, a rigidly minded scribe, whose work was completed by a band of scribes after him. Not a prophet, mark you; not a seer, nor a visionary nor a mighty king; a *Sofer* it was. Nor must we forget *how* it came into being: not as an irresistible force, not as the expression of the deepest needs of contrite souls, not as the embodiment of the feelings of divinely inspired votaries. No; it came into being on a deliberate plan, by clever deductions, and diplomatic policy which was based on the cry "Its religion must be preserved for the people." The same calm consideration, the same attention to the ultimate goal were responsible in the centuries that followed for the addition of line to line and precept to precept. That which did not fit in with the scheme of the *Soferim* from before the days of Ezra and that which grew up afterwards, fell away.

The traces of the peculiar circumstances which gave it birth are still visible in the Jewish religion. In all its reasoning it appeals to us as a creation of the intellect, a thing of thought and purpose projected into the world of organisms, mechanically and artfully wrought, destined to destroy and to conquer Nature's realm and to reign itself in her stead. Just so does Capitalism appear on the scene; like the Jewish religion, an alien element in the midst of the natural, created world; like it, too, something schemed and planned in the midst of teeming life. This sheaf of salient features is bound together in one word: Rationalism. Rationalism is the characteristic trait of Judaism as of Capitalism; Rationalism or Intellectualism—both deadly foes alike to irresponsible mysticism and to that creative power which draws its artistic inspiration from the passion world of the senses.

The Jewish religion knows no mysteries, and is perhaps the only religion on the face of the globe that does not know them. It knows not the ecstatic condition wherein the worshipper feels himself at one with the Godhead, the condition which all other religions extol as the highest and holiest. Think of the Soma libation among the Hindoos, think of entranced Indra himself, of the Homa sacrifice of the Persians, of Dionysus, the Oracle of Greece and of the Sibylline books, to which even the staid Romans went for advice, only because they were written by women who in a state of frenzy prophesied the future.

Down to the latest days of the Roman Empire the characteristic of religious life which remained the same in all aspects of heathenism continued to manifest itself—the characteristic which spread far and wide and infected large masses of people, of working yourself up by sheer force to a pitch of bodily or mental excitement, often becoming bacchanalian madness, and then regarding this as the deity's doing and as part of his service. It was a generally accepted belief that certain sudden impulses or bursts of passion or resolutions were roused in the soul of a man by some god or other; and conduct of which a man was ashamed or which he regretted, was usually ascribed to the influence of a god.[21] "It was the god who drove me to it"—so, in Plautus's comedy, the young man who had seduced a maiden excused himself to his father.

The same thing must have been experienced by Mohammed in his morbid condition when his fits of ecstasy were upon him, and there is a good deal of mysticism in Islam. At least Mohammedanism has its howling dervishes.

And in Christianity, too, so far as it was not Judaism, room was found for emotional feeling—witness the doctrine of the Trinity, the sweet cult of Mariolatry, the use of incense, the communion. But Judaism looks with proud disdain on these fantastic, mystical elements, condemning them all. When the faithful of other religions hold converse with God in blissful convulsions, in the Jewish synagogue, called a *Shool* [*i.e.,* School] not without significance, the Torah is publicly read. So Ezra ordained, and so it is done most punctiliously. "Ever since the destruction of the State, study became the soul of Judaism, and religious observances without knowledge of the ordinances which enjoined them was considered as being of little worth. The central feature of public service on Sabbaths and Holy Days was the lesson read from the Law and the Prophets, the translation of the passages by the *Targumists* [Interpreters] and the homiletic explanation of them by the *Haggadists* [Preachers]."

> Radix stultitiæ, cui frigida sabbata cordi
> Sed cor frigidus relligione sua
> Septima quæque dies turpi damnato veterno
> Tanquam lassati mollis imago dei.

> [The Sabbath—monstrous folly!—fills the need
> Of hearts still icier than their icy creed,
> Each seventh day in shameful sloth they nod,
> And ape the languor of their weary God.]

Such was the Roman view.[22]

Judaism then looked askance at mysteries. With no different eye did it regard the holy enthusiasm for the divine in the world of feeling. Astarte, Daphne, Isis and Osiris, Aphrodite, Fricka and the Holy Virgin—it would have none of them. It banished all pictorial art from its cult. "And the Lord spake unto you out of the midst of the fire: ye heard the sound of words but ye saw no form" |Deut. iv. 12). "Cursed be the man that maketh a graven or molten image, an abomination unto the Lord, the work of the hands of the craftsman. . . ." (Deut. xxvii. 15). The command, "Thou shalt not make unto thee any graven image" finds acceptance to-day, and the pious Jew has no statues made, nor does he set them up in his house.[23]

The kinship between Judaism and Capitalism is further illustrated by the legally regulated relationship—I had almost said the businesslike connexion, except that the term has a disagreeable connotation—between God and Israel. The whole religious system is in reality nothing but a contract between Jehovah and His chosen people, a contract with all its consequences and all its duties. God promises something and gives something, and the righteous must give Him something in return. Indeed, there was no community of interest between God and man which could not be expressed in these terms— that man performs some duty enjoined by the Torah and receives from God a *quid pro quo*. Accordingly, no man should approach God in prayer without bringing with him something of his own or of his ancestors' by way of return for what he is about to ask.[24]

The contract usually sets forth that man is rewarded for duties performed and punished for duties neglected; the rewards and punishments being received partly in this and partly in the next world. Two consequences must of necessity follow: first, a constant weighing up of the loss and gain which any action needs must bring, and secondly, a complicated system of bookkeeping, as it were, for each individual person.

The whole of this conception is excellently well illustrated by the words of Rabbi [164-200 A.D.]: "Which is the right course for a man to choose? That which he feels to be honourable to himself and which also brings him honour from mankind. Be heedful of a light precept as of a grave one, for you do not know what reward a precept brings. Reckon the loss incurred by the fulfilment of a precept against the reward secured by its observance, and the gain gotten by a transgression against the loss it involves. Reflect on three things and you will not come within the power of sin. Know what is above thee—a seeing eye, and a hearing ear, and all your deeds written in a book."[25] So that whether one is accounted "righteous" or "wicked" depends on the balance of commands performed against commands neglected. Obviously this necessitates the keeping of accounts, and each man therefore has his own, in which his words and his deeds, even the words spoken in jest, are all carefully registered. According to one authority (*Ruth Rabba*, 33a) the prophet Elijah keeps these accounts; according to another (*Esther Rabba*, 86a) the duty is assigned to angels.

Every man has thus an account in heaven: Israel a particularly large one (*Sifra*, 44b). And one of the ways of preparing for death is to have your "account" ready (*Kohelet Rabba*, 77c). Sometimes "extracts" from the accounts are forthcoming (by request). When the angels brought an accusation against Ishmael, God asked, "What is his position at present? Is he a righteous man or a wicked?" (*i.e.*, do the commands performed outweigh those neglected?). And the angels replied, "He is a righteous man." When Mar Ukba died, he asked for a statement of his account (of the money he had given to charity). It totalled 7000 zuzim. As he was afraid that this would not suffice for his salvation he gave away half of his fortune in order to be on the safe side (*Kethuboth*, 25; *Baba Bathra*, 7). The final decision as to the righteousness or wickedness of any man is made after his death. The account is then closed, and the grand total drawn up. The result is inserted in a document (*Shetar*) which is handed to each individual after it has been read out.[26]

It is not difficult to perceive that the keeping of these accounts was no easy matter. In Biblical times, so long as rewards and punishments were meted out in the life on earth, the task was no great one. But in the period that followed, when rewards and punishments were granted partly in this life and partly in life everlasting, the question grew to be troublesome, and in the Rabbinic theology an intricate and artistic system of bookkeeping was evolved. This distinguished between the capital sum or the principal, and the fruits or the interest, the former being reserved for the future world, the latter for this. And in order that the reward which is laid up in heaven for the righteous may not be diminished, God does not lessen the stock when He grants him ordinary earthly benefits. Only when he receives extraordinary, *i.e.*, miraculous, benefits on earth does the righteous man suffer a diminution of his heavenly reward. Moreover, the righteous is punished for his sins at once on earth, as the wicked is rewarded for his good deeds, so that the one may have only rewards in heaven and the other only chastisements.[27]

Another conception is bound up with this of divine bookkeeping and is closely akin to a second fundamental trait of capitalism—the conception of profit. Sin or goodness is regarded as something apart from the sinner. Every sin, according to Rabbinic theology, is considered singly and by itself. "Punishment is according to the object and not the subject of the sin."[28] The quantity of the broken commandments alone counts. No consideration whatever is had for the personality of the sinner or his ethical state, just as a sum of money is separated from persons, just as it is capable of being added to another abstract sum of money. The ceaseless striving of the righteous after well-being in this and the next world must needs therefore take the form of a constant endeavour to increase his rewards. Now, as he is never able to tell whether at a particular state of his conscience he is worthy of God's goodness or whether in his "account" the rewards or the punishments are more numerous, it must be his aim to add reward after reward to his account by constantly doing good deeds to the end of his days. The limited conception of all personal values thus finds no admission into the world of his religious ideas and its place is taken by the endlessness of a pure quantitative ideal.

Parallel with this tendency there runs through Jewish moral theology another which regards the getting of money as a means to an end. The conception is frequently found in books of religious edification, the authors of which realizing but seldom that in their warnings against the acquisition of too much wealth they are glorifying this very practice. Usually the treatment of the subject is under the heading "covetousness," forbidden by the tenth commandment. "A true Israelite," remarks one of the most popular of modern "helps to faith,"[29] "avoids covetousness. He looks upon all his possessions only as a means of doing what is pleasing in the sight of God. For is not the entire purpose of his life to use all his possessions, all enjoyment as the means to this end? Indeed it is a duty . . . to obtain possessions and to increase one's enjoyments, not as an end in themselves but as a means to do God's will on earth."

But if it is urged that this is no conclusive proof of the connexion between the religious idea and the principle of getting gain, a glance at the peculiar ordering of divine service will soon be convincing. At one stage in the service there is a veritable public auction. The honorary offices connected with the reading of the law are given to the highest bidder. Before the scrolls are taken from the Ark, the beadle walks round the central platform (the Almemor) and cries out: "Who will buy *Hazoa vehachnosa?* (*i.e.*, the act of taking the scrolls from the Ark and of replacing them). Who will buy *Hagboha?* (the act of raising the scroll in the sight of the people). Who will buy *Gelilah?*" (the act of rolling up the scroll when the reading is finished). These honours are knocked down to the highest bidder, and the money given to the synagogue poor-box. It need hardly be said that to-day this practice has long been eliminated from synagogue worship. In days of long ago it was quite general.[30]

Again, the words of some of the Talmudic doctors, who at times dispute over the most difficult economic questions with all the skill of experienced merchants, cannot but have a curious connotation, and must needs lead to the conclusion that they preached the getting of gain. It would be fascinating to collect those passages of the Talmud wherein the modern practice of making profit is recommended by this or that Rabbi, in many cases themselves great traders. I will quote an instance or two. "R. Isaac also taught that a man should always have his money in circulation." It was R. Isaac, too, who gave this piece of good advice. A man should divide his fortune into three parts, investing one in landed property, one in moveable goods, and holding the third as ready cash (*Baba Mezia, 42a*). "Rav once said to his son, Come let me instruct thee in worldly matters. Sell your goods even while the dust is yet upon your feet." (What is this but a recommendation to have a quick turnover?) "First open your purse and then unloose the sack of wheat. . . . Have you got dates in the box? Hasten at once to the brewer" (*Pesachim, 113a*).

What is the meaning of this parallelism between the Jewish religion and capitalism? Is it a mere chance? A stupid joke perpetrated by Fate? Is the one the effect of the other, or are both traceable to the same causes? Questions such as these naturally suggest themselves to us, and I hope to answer them as we proceed. Here it will suffice to have called attention to them. Our next step will be the comparatively simpler one of showing how individual customs, conceptions, opinions and regulations of the Jewish religion influenced the economic conduct of Jews, of showing whether they facilitated the extension of capitalism by the Jews, and, if so, to what degree. We shall limit ourselves in this to primary psychological motives, avoiding all speculative difficulties. Our first problem will be to discover the goal set up by the Jewish religion and its influence on economic life, and the next section is devoted to it.

The Idea of Rewards and Punishments

The idea of contract, which is part and parcel of the underlying principles of Judaism, must perforce have the corollary that whoever carries out the contract receives reward, whoever breaks it receives punishment. In other words, the legal and ethical assumption that the good prosper and the evil suffer punishment was in all ages a concept of the Jewish religion. All that changed was the interpretation of prosperity and punishment.

The oldest form of Judaism knows nothing of another world. So, weal and woe can come only in this world. If God desires to punish or to reward, He must do so during man's lifetime. The righteous therefore is prosperous here, and the wicked here suffer punishment. Obey my precepts, says the Lord, "so that thou mayest live long and prosper in the land which the Lord thy God hath given unto thee." Hence the bitter cry of Job, "Wherefore do the wicked live, become old, yea, wax mighty in power? . . . But my way He hath fenced up, that I cannot pass . . . He hath broken me down on every side . . . He hath also kindled His wrath against me" [Job xxi. 7; xix. 8, 10, 11]. "Why hath all this evil come upon me, seeing that I walked in His path continually?"

A little after Ezra's time the idea of another world (*Olam Habo*) finds currency in Judaism, the idea, too, of the immortality of the soul and of the resurrection of the body. These beliefs were of foreign origin, coming probably from Persia. But like all other alien elements in Judaism they, too, were given an ethical meaning, in accordance with the genius of the religion. The doctrine grew up that only the righteous and the pious would rise up after death. The belief in eternity was thus made by the *Soferim* to fit in with the old teaching of rewards and punishments, in order to heighten the feeling of moral responsibility, *i.e.*, of the fear of the judgment of God.[31]

The idea of prosperity on earth is now extended. It is no longer the only reward of a good life, for a reward in the world to come is added to it. Still, God's blessing in this world is no small part of the total reward. Moreover, the very fact that a man is prosperous here was proof positive that his life was pleasing to God, and that therefore he might expect reward in the next world also. Then, too, the idea of a blind fate is no longer troublesome. What appeared as such is now regarded as God's punishment on earth to the righteous for his transgressions, so that his heavenly recompense may suffer no diminution.

The "doctrine of possession" (if the term may be allowed in connexion with the Jewish religion) received some such shape as this, more especially through the Wisdom Literature. The great aim of life is to obey God's commandments. Earthly happiness apart from God has no existence. Hence it is folly to seek to obtain earthly possessions for their own sake. But to obtain them in order to use them for divine ends, so that they become at one and the same time the outward symbols and guarantees of God's pleasure, as signs of His blessing—such a course is wise. Now earthly possessions in this view of them include a well-appointed house and material well-being—in a word, wealth.

Look through Jewish literature, more especially through the Holy Writ and the Talmud, and you will find, it is true, a few passages wherein poverty is lauded as something higher and nobler than riches. But on the other hand you will come across hundreds of passages in which riches are called the blessing of the Lord, and only their misuse or their dangers warned against. Here and there, too, we may read that riches alone do not necessarily bring happiness, other things are essential in addition (such as health, for example), that there are "goods" (in the broadest use of the word) more valuable or as valuable as riches. But in all this nothing is said *against* riches; and never is it stated that they are an abomination to the Lord.

I once gave expression to this view in a public lecture, and it was severely criticized on all sides. Just this point more than any other was controverted—the statement that riches are in the Jewish religion accounted as a valuable good. Many of my critics, among them several distinguished Jewish rabbis, went to the trouble of compiling lists of passages from the

Bible and Talmud which confuted my opinion. I admit that there are many places in the Bible and the Talmud which regard wealth as a danger to the righteous, and in which poverty is extolled. There are some half-dozen of them in the Bible; the Talmud has rather more. But the important thing is that each of these passages may be capped by ten others, which breathe a totally different spirit. In such cases numbers surely count.

I put the question to myself in this way. Let us imagine old Amschel Rothschild on a Friday evening, after having "earned" a million on the Stock Exchange, turning to his Bible for edification. What will he find there touching his earnings and their effect on the refinement of his soul, an effect which the pious old Jew most certainly desired on the eve of the Sabbath? Will the million burn his conscience? Or will he not be able to say, and rightly say, "God's blessing rested upon me this week. I thank Thee, Lord, for having graciously granted the light of Thy countenance to Thy servant. In order to find favour in Thy sight I shall give much to charity, and keep Thy commandments even more strictly than hitherto"? Such would be his words if he knew his Bible, and he did know it.

For his eye would rest complacently on many a passage in the Holy Writ. In his beloved Torah he would be able to read again and again of the blessing of God. "And He will love thee and bless thee and multiply thee, He will also bless the fruit of thy body and the fruit of thy ground, thy corn and thy wine and thine oil . . . thou shalt be blessed above all peoples" (Deut. vii. 13-15). And how moved he would be when he reached the words, "For the Lord, thy God, will bless thee, as He promised thee: and thou shalt lend unto many nations, but thou shalt not borrow" (Deut. xv. 6). Then suppose he turns to the Psalms, what would he find there?

O fear the Lord, ye His saints: for there is no want to them that fear Him (Psa. xxxiv. 10).

Blessed is the man that feareth the Lord. . . . Wealth and riches are in his house (Psa. xc. 1-3).

Our garners are full, affording all manner of store, our sheep bring forth thousands and ten thousands in our fields (Psa. cxliv. 13).

He would rejoice with Job when on concluding the story of his trials he found that his latter end was more blessed than his beginning, and that "he had 14,000 sheep, 6000 camels, 1000 yoke of oxen and 1000 she-asses" and the rest. (Happily our friend Amschel knew nothing of modern Biblical criticism, and was not aware therefore that this particular portion of Job is a later interpolation in the story.)

The prophets also promised Israel earthly rewards if it kept to God's way and walked therein. If Amschel turned to the 60th chapter of Isaiah he would find the prophecy that one day the Gentiles should bring their gold and silver to Israel.

But perhaps Amschel's favourite book would be Proverbs,[32] "which expresses in a most pregnant form the ideas of life current in Israel" (as a rabbi wrote to me who quoted this book in proof of my error, Prov. xxii. 1, 2; xxiii. 4; xxviii. 20, 21; xxx. 8). Here he would be warned that riches alone do not bring happiness (xxii. 1, 2), that God must not be denied amid great wealth (xxx. 8), that "he that maketh haste to be rich shall not be unpunished" (xxviii. 20). (Perhaps he will say to himself that he does not "hasten" to be rich.) The only verse that may disquieten him is when he reads "Weary not thyself to be rich; cease from thine own wisdom" (xxiii. 4). But only for a moment, for his mind will be eased when he observes the connexion with the preceding passage. Possibly these six little words may not after all trouble him much when he remembers the numerous passages in this very book which commend riches. So numerous indeed that it may be said they give the tone to the whole of Proverbs.[33] A few only shall be quoted:—

Length of days are in her right hand; in her left are riches and honour (iii. 16).
Riches and honour are with me; yea, durable riches and righteousness" (viii. 18).

The rich man's wealth is his strong city (x. 15).

Their riches are a crown unto the wise (xiv. 24).

The reward of humility and the fear of the Lord is riches and honour and life (xxii. 4).

The Wisdom Literature included Ecclesiastes and the Wisdom of Solomon. The first[34] certainly does not breathe a uniform spirit; the many accretions of later times make it full of contradictions. Yet even here the pious Jew found never a passage which taught him to despise wealth. On the contrary, wealth is highly valued.

Every man also to whom God hath given riches and wealth, and hath given him power to eat thereof . . . this is the gift of God (v. 19).

A feast is made for laughter and wine maketh glad the life: and money answereth all things (x. 19).

The Wisdom of Solomon likewise praises riches. No less does the Book of Jesus, the son of Sirach, that fund of wise saws, which old Amschel must have conned with delight. If any Rabbi had told him that Ben Sirach's books regard the wealthy man almost as a sinner and wealth as the source of evil, instancing chapters x.-xiii. in proof, Amschel would have replied, "My dear Rabbi, you are mistaken. Those passages are a warning against the dangers of wealth. But a rich man who avoids the dangers is thereby the more righteous. 'Blessed is the rich that is found without blemish . . . his goods shall be established and the congregation shall declare his alms' (xxxi. 8, 11). And why, my dear Rabbi" (so Amschel might continue), "do you not mention the passages which speak of the man who has amassed millions, passages like the following?

Better is he that laboureth and aboundeth in all things, than he that boasteth himself and wanteth bread (x. 27).

The poor man is honoured for his skill, and the rich man is honoured for his riches (x. 30).

Prosperity and adversity, life and death, poverty and riches come of the Lord' (xi. 14).

Gold and silver make the foot stand sure (xl. 25).

Riches and strength lift up the heart (xl. 26).

Better it is to die than to beg (xl. 28).

"Should I be ashamed of my millions, my dear Rabbi" (Amschel would conclude the imaginary conversation), "should I not rather look upon them as God's blessing? Recall what the wise Jesus ben Sirach said of great King Solomon (xlvii. 18): 'By the name of the Lord God, which is called the Lord God of Israel, thou didst gather gold as tin, and didst multiply silver as lead.' I also will go, Rabbi, and in the name of the Lord God will gather gold as tin and silver as lead."

In the Talmud the passages that express the same point of view are frequent enough. Riches are a blessing if only their owner walk in God's ways, and poverty is a curse. Hardly ever are riches despised. Let us quote a few Talmudic sayings on the subject.

Seven characteristics are there which are "comely to the righteous and comely to the world." One of them is riches (*Aboth*, vi. 8).

In prayer a man should turn to Him who owns wealth and possessions. . . . In reality both come not from business, but according to merit" (*Kidushin*, lxxxiia).

R. Eleazer said, "The righteous love their money more than their bodies" (*Sota*, xiia).

Rabba honoured the wealthy, so did R. Akiba (*Erubin*, lxxxvia).

In time of scarcity a man learns to value wealth best (*Aboth de Rabbi Nathan*).

Doctrines concerning wealth such as these could not but encourage a worldly view of life. This the Jewish view was, despite the belief in another world. There were indeed attempts at ascetic movements in Judaism (*e.g.*, in the 9th century the Karaites combined to live the life of monks;* in the 11th century Bachja ibn Pakuda preached asceticism in Spain), but none of them ever took root. Judaism even in times of great affliction was always optimistic. In this the Jews differ from the Christians, whose religion has tried to rob them all it could of earthly joys. As often as riches are lauded in the Old Testament they are damned in the New, wherein poverty is praised. The whole outlook of the Essenes, turning its back upon the world and the flesh, was incorporated in the Gospels. One can easily recall passage after passage to this effect. (Cf. Matt. vi. 24; x. 9, 10; xix. 23, 24.) "It is easier for a camel to go through a needle's eye than for a rich man to enter into the Kingdom of God." This is the keynote of Christianity on the point, and the difference between it and Judaism is clear enough. There is no single parallel to the saying of Jesus in the whole of the Old Testament, and probably also none in the entire body of Rabbinic literature.

There is no need to expatiate on the different attitude of the good Jew and the good Christian towards economic activities. The Christian is forced by all manner of mental gymnastics to interpret away the Essene conception of riches from his Scriptures. And what anxious moments must the rich Christian live through as he thinks of heaven locked against him! Compare with him the position of the rich Jew, who, as we have seen, "in the name of the Lord God" gathers gold as tin and silver as lead.

It is well known that the religion of the Christians stood in the way of their economic activities. It is equally well known that the Jews were never faced with this hindrance. The more pious a Jew was and the more acquainted with his religious literature, the more he was spurred by the teachings of that literature to extend his economic activities. A beautiful illustration of the way religion and business were fused in the mind of pious Jews may be found in the delightful *Memoirs*

* Sombart is mistaken in this. The characteristic of the Karaites was that they accepted and lived by the *letter* of the Torah.— Trans.

of Glückel von Hameln, to which we have already referred. "Praise be to God, who gives and takes, the faithful God, who always made good our losses," she says. And again, "My husband sent me a long, comforting letter, urging me to calm my soul, for God, whose name be blessed, would restore to us what we had lost. And so it was."

The Rationalization of Life

Since Judaism rests upon a contract between God and His people, *i.e.*, upon a two-sided legal agreement, each party must have definite responsibilities. What were those of the Jews?

Again and again was the answer to this question given by God through His servant Moses. Again and again the Israelite was informed that two great duties were his. He was to be holy and to obey God's law. (Cf. Exod. xix. 6; Deut. iv. 56.) God did not require sacrifices of him; He demanded obedience (Jer. vii. 22, 23).

Now it is generally known that in the course of events the Jews came to regard righteousness as a minute fulfilment of the Law. The inward holiness that may have existed in early days soon vanished before formalism and legalism. Holiness and observation of the Law became interchangeable terms. It is generally known, too, that this legalism was a device of the Rabbis to protect the Jews against the influences first, of Hellenism, then of Christianity, and finally, when the Second Temple was destroyed, to maintain by its means the national consciousness. The struggle with Hellenism resulted in Pharisaism; the struggle with Pauline Christianity which aimed at replacing the Law by faith, transformed the religion of the Pharisees into that of the Talmud, and the old policy of the Scribes "to encompass the whole of life with regulation" made greater progress than ever. In their political isolation the Jewish communities submitted entirely to the new hierarchy. They desired to see the end attained and so accepted the means. The school and the Law outlasted the Temple and the State, and Pharisaic Rabbinism had unlimited sway.

Righteousness henceforth meant living in strict accordance with the Law. Piety, under the influence of the legally minded Scribes, was given a legal connotation. Religion became the common law. In the Mishna all this finds admirable expression. The commands of the Pentateuch and the commands deduced from these are all divine ordinances which must be obeyed without questioning. More and more stress is laid on externals, and between important and insignificant commands there is less and less differentiation.[35]

So it remained for two thousand years; so it is to-day. Strict orthodoxy still holds fast to this formalism and the principles of Judaism know no change. The Torah is as binding to-day in its every word as when it was given to Moses on Sinai.[36] Its laws and ordinances must be observed by the faithful, whether they be light or grave, whether they appear to have rhyme or reason or no. And they must be strictly observed, and only because God gave them. This implicit obedience makes the righteous, makes the saint. "Saintly or holy in the Torah sense is he who is able to fulfil the revealed will of God without any struggle and with the same joy as carrying out his own will. This holiness, this complete fusion of the will of man with the divine will, is a lofty goal attainable in its entirety by a few only. Hence the law of holiness refers in the first instance to the striving towards this goal. The striving all can do; it demands a constant self-watchfulness and self-education, an endless struggle against what is low and vulgar, what is sensual and bestial. And obedience to the behests of the Torah is the surest ladder on which to climb to higher and higher degrees of holiness."[37]

These words show clearly enough how holiness and legalism are connected; they show that the highest aim of Israel still is to be a kingdom of priests and a holy nation; and that the path to that end is a strict obedience to God's commandments. Once this becomes apparent, we can imagine the importance the Jewish religion has for the whole of life. In the long run, external legalism does not remain external; it exercises a constant influence on the inner life, which obtains its peculiar character from the observance of the law.

The psychological process which led to the shaping of Judaism appears to me to be this. At first God's behests were those that mattered, regardless of their contents. But slowly the contents must needs make themselves manifest to the observer, and a clearly defined ideal of Life evolved itself from the word of God. To follow this ideal, to be righteous, to be holy was the heart's desire of each believer.

Before continuing, let us strive to obtain some notion of what the pious Jew meant, and means, by holiness in the material sense.

Let us recall what was said in the last section about the "worldliness" of the Jewish religion. In accordance with this it can scarcely be holy to deny the natural instincts or to crush them, as other religions teach—e.g., Buddhism or Primitive Christianity. Other-worldly asceticism was always antagonistic to Judaism. "The soul which has been given thee—preserve it, never kill it"—that is the Talmudic maxim on which to build up the conduct of life and which found currency at all times.[38]

The negation of life cannot therefore be holiness. Nor can the exercise of man's passions and appetites be holiness. For if it were, it could not be put as an ideal before the righteous; it would then be accessible to everybody. There remains therefore only one other possibility—to live your life of set purpose in accordance with some ideal plan based on supernatural rules, and either utilizing the desires within you or crushing them. In fine, holiness is the rationalization of life. You decide to replace the natural existence with its desires and inclinations by the moral life. To be holy is to become refined, and to realize this is to overcome all your natural tendencies by means of moral obedience.[39]

A rugged Dualism—the terrible Dualism which is part and parcel of our constitution—characterizes the Jewish conception of ethical worth. Nature is not unholy, neither is she holy. She is not yet holy. She may become holy through us. All the seeds of sin are in her; the serpent still lurks in the grass as he did long ago in the Garden of Eden. "God certainly created the evil inclination, but he also created the

Torah, the moral law, an an antidote to it."[40] The whole of human life is one great warfare against the inimical forces of Nature: that is the guiding principle of Jewish moral theology, and it is in accordance with it that the system of rules and regulations was instituted by which life might be rationalized, de-naturalized, refined and hallowed without the necessity of renouncing or stifling it. In this we see the marked difference between the Christian (Essene) and the Jewish (Pharisaic) ideas of morality. The former leads quite logically away from the world into the silent hermitage and the monastery (if not to death); the latter binds its faithful adherent with a thousand chains to the individual and social life. Christianity makes its devotee into a monk, Judaism into a rationalist; the first ends in asceticism outside the world; the second in asceticism within it (taking asceticism to mean the subjugation of what is natural in man).

We shall gain a clearer insight of what Jewish Ethics (and therefore also the Jewish religion) stands for if we examine its regulations one by one.

The effect of Law is twofold. Its very existence has an influence; so have its contents.

That there is a law at all, that it is a duty to obey it, impels one to think about one's actions and to accomplish them in harmony with the dictates of reason. In front of every desire a warning finger-post is set; every natural impulse is nullified by the thousand and one milestones and danger-signals in the shape of directions to the pious. Now, since obedience to a multifariousness of rules (the well-known commands compiled by Maimonides numbered 365—of which 243 are still current—and his prohibitions 248) is well-nigh impossible wtihout a pretty good knowledge of what they are, the system includes the command to study the Holy Writ, and especially the Torah. This very study itself is made a means of rendering life holy. "If the evil inclination seizes hold of you, march him off to the House of Study," counsels the Talmud.

The view that all the enactments were for the purpose of ennobling the life of the faithful was accepted at all times, and is still held to-day by many orthodox Jews.

God wished to refine Israel, therefore He increased the number of the commandments (*Makkoth*, 23*b*).

The commandments were given by God to ennoble mankind (*Vajikra Rabba*, 13).[41]

It would have been better for a man never to have been born, but once he is in the world let him continually examine his actions (*Erubin*, 13*b*).

Every night a man should critically examine his deeds of the day (*Magen Abraham* on *Orach Chajim*, 239, § 7).[42]

"Observe" and "remember" were ordained in a single utterance."[43]

Deum respice et cura[44] is still the motto of the Jew. If he meets a king or sees a dwarf or a Negro, passes a ruined building or takes his medicine or his bath, notes the coming storm or hears its roaring thunder, rises in the morning and puts on his clothes or eats his food, enters his house or leaves it, greets a friend or meets a foe—for every emergency there is an ordinance which must be obeyed.

Now what of the contents of the ordinances? All of them aim at the subjugation of the merely animal instincts in man, at the bridling of his desires and inclinations and at the replacing of impulses by thoughtful action; in short, at the "ethical tempering of man."

You must think nothing, speak nothing, do nothing without first considering what the law about it is, and then apply it to the great purpose of sanctification. You must therefore do nothing merely for its own sake, spontaneously, or from natural instinct.

You must not enjoy Nature for the sheer pleasure of it. You may do so only if you think thereby of the wisdom and the goodness of God. In the spring when the trees put on their blossom the pious Jew says, "Blessed art Thou, O Lord our God, . . . who hast made Thy world lacking in nought, but hast provided therein goodly creatures and trees wherewith to give delight to the children of men." At the sight of the rainbow he brings to mind the Covenant with God. On high mountains, in vast deserts, beside mighty rivers—in a

word, wherever his heart is deeply moved by Nature's won-
ders—he expresses his feelings in the benediction, "Blessed
art Thou, O Lord our God, . . . who hast made the Creation."

You must not enjoy art for its own sake. Works of plastic
art should be avoided, for they may easily lead to a breach of
the second commandment. But even the poet's art is not
looked upon with favour, except it refer to God. All reading
is good, provided it has some practical end in view. "It is best
to read the books of the Torah or such as refer to them. If
we desire to read for recreation, let us choose books that are
able to teach us something useful. Among the books written
for amusement and to while away the time there are some
that may awake sinful wishes within us. The reading of these
books is forbidden."[45]

You must not indulge in harmless pleasures. "The seat of
the scornful [Psa. i. I],—the theatres and circuses of the
heathen are meant." Song, dance and wine, save when they
are connected with religious ceremonial, are taboo. "Rabbi
Dosa ben Hyrkanus used to say, Morning sleep and midday
wine and childish talk and attending the houses where the
ignorant foregather put a man out of the world."[46] "He that
loveth pleasure shall be a poor man; he that loveth wine and
oil shall not be rich" (Prov. xxi. 17).

If this be so, those qualities which may lead a man to
"unseemly" conduct are useless or even harmful. Such are
enthusiasm (for while a man is in this state he may do something useless),[47] kindness of heart (you must exercise kindness only because the idea of benevolence actuates you; you
must never let pity carry you away, so that the nobility and
dignity of the ideal law may always be before you);[48] a
sensual temperament ("the source of passion—and of sin—
is in sensuality"),[49] ingenuousness, in short anything that
marks the natural (and therefore unholy) man.

The cardinal virtues of the pious are, on the other hand,
self-control and circumspection, a love of order and of work,
moderation and abstemiousness, chastity and sobriety.

Self-control and circumspection especially and in regard to
your words is a constant theme of the moralists. "In the multi-

tude of words there wanteth not transgression: but he that refraineth his lips doth wisely" (Prov. x. 19).[50]

No less insistent was the later tradition. "Raba held that whoso carries on an unnecessary conversation transgresses a command" (*Joma*, 19b). "Our sanctification," says a modern book for popular edification, "depends to a large extent on the control of our tongues, on the power of holding our peace. The gift of speech . . . was given to man for holy purposes. Hence all unnecessary talk is forbidden by our wise men."[51]

But self-control and circumspection generally are urged on the pious Jew.

Who is the strongest of the strong? He who controls his passions (*Aboth de R. Nathan*, xxiii. 1).

The thoughts of the diligent tend only to plenteousness: but every one that is hasty hasteth only to want (Prov. xxi. 5).

He that hasteth with his feet sinneth (Prov. xix. 2).

And as for industry and thrift, innumerable are the exhortations to that end.

The Jew must wake the day, not the day the Jew—so taught the Rabbis, as a homily on Psalm lvii. 9.[52]

It is just the strongest instincts of man that must be curbed, directed into right channels, deprived of their natural force and made to serve useful ends. In short, they must be rationalized.

Take the instinct which desires to satisfy hunger. It is forbidden to appease the appetite merely because it happens to be there; it should be appeased only for the body's sake. And when the good man sits down to eat, let him do so according to the precepts of his Maker. Hence the large number of rules concerning food; hence the command to be serious at meals—to begin and to close with prayer; hence the advice to be moderate and the appeal to banish the pleasure of feeding. "It is only through God's goodness that you are enabled to use His creatures as food, and therefore if your entire eating and drinking is not to be beastly, it must be hallowed; it must be looked upon as the getting of strength for His service."[53] "The Jew should make the satisfaction of his appetite for food a sacrament; should regard his table as an altar and the food thereon as sacrifice, which he enjoys only in order to obtain more strength for the fulfilment of his duties."[54] (Jewish cooking, by the way, is excellent.)

Finally—and this of course matters most—just like hunger, Love also must be rationalized, that is to say, its natural expression must be held in check. Nowhere more than in the erotic sphere does the hard dualism show itself so well. The world, and certainly the civilized nations, owes this conception of the sexual to the Jews (through the agency of Christianity, which was infected with the idea). All earlier religions saw something divine in the expression of sex, and regarded sexual intercourse as of the nature of a heavenly revelation. All of them were acquainted with Phallus-worship in a grosser or finer form. None of them condemned what is sensuous, or looked upon women as a source of sin. But the Jews from Ezra's day to this held, and hold, the opposite view.

To sanctify himself, to make himself worthy of his converse with God, Moses "drew not nigh unto his wife." And Job mentions as being in his favour that he made a covenant with his eyes not to look upon a maid. The whole Wisdom Literature abounds in warnings against women,* and the same spirit dominates the Talmud. "Better to die than to be guilty of unchastity" (*Sanhedrin, 75a*). Indeed, the three capital crimes for which even death does not atone are murder, idol-worship and adultery. "Hast thou business with women? See to it that thou art not with them alone" (*Kiddushin, 82a*). This dread runs through all the codes. The *Eben Ha-ezer* condemns to death by stoning any one who has had guilty intercourse with a woman related to him within the prohibited degrees. The very clothes or the little finger of a woman of such close consanguinity must not be looked at "to get pleasure from it." It is forbidden a man to allow

---

* Sombart instances Prov. v. 3-4. But does not the passage clearly refer to *bad* women?—Trans.

himself to be waited on by a woman, or to embrace his aunt or his grown-up sister.

Teachers of to-day are no less explicit. "Guard yourself against any contact with impurity," says one of the most popular of them. "Look at nothing, hear nothing, read nothing, think of nothing which may in any wise occupy your thoughts unchastely or make you familiar with what is not clean. Do not walk in the street behind a woman; if you cannot help yourself, look not at her with desire.* Do not let your eye rest longingly on a woman's hair, nor your ears on her voice; do not take pleasure in her form; yea, a woman's very clothes should not be looked at if you know who has worn them. In all things go out of the way of Opportunity. . . . The two sexes should not jest together. Even in make-believe little pressures of the hand, winking of the eyes, embracing and kissing are sinful."[55]

Warnings such as these were not neglected, as may be seen from the autobiographies of pious Jews, some of which may now be read in modern languages.[56]

But the point of it all must not be overlooked. Other religions also show signs of being terrified at women. Ever since the notion became prevalent that woman brought sin into the world there have always been morbid souls who spent their lives exciting themselves with all manner of lascivious imaginings but avoiding woman as though she were the devil incarnate. In other religions the man fled to the hermit's cave in the wilderness or to a monastery. In either case, his religion forced "chastity" upon him, with all the horrid resultants well known to students of monastic life. Not so Judaism. Judaism does not forbid sexual intercourse; it rationalizes it. Not that it does not regard sexual intercourse as sinful. Sinful it must always be, but its sinfulness may to some extent be removed by sanctification. Hence Judaism advocates early marriages and regulates the relationship between husband and wife as something "ever in the great Taskmaster's eye."

"A man should not be without a wife, nor a woman without

* Cf. Robert Louis Stevenson: "To remember the faces of women without desire, . . . is not this to know both wisdom and virtue?"—Trans.

a husband; but both shall see to it that God's spirit is in their union." That is the motto, and in accordance with it the Talmud and the later codes have multiplied rules and regulations for the guidance of married couples. In the 11th century (to mention but a few) R. Eleazar ben Nathan compiled a special code on the subject, the *Eben Ha-ezer*, and in the 13th century R. Nachman wrote a famous work on the sanctification of marriage.[57] The laws of the *Eben Ha-ezer* were incorporated in the *Shulchan Aruch* and together with the glosses upon them receive recognition to-day. The main ideas throughout are those we have already considered: hallow thy body's strength in accordance with God's will; be careful of thy manhood; be God's servant at all times.[58]

Such was the Jewish view of marriage, which has continued for more than two thousand years. It is well illustrated by that touching story in the Book of Tobit, which may form a fitting conclusion to our considerations under this head.

> And after that they were both shut in together, Tobias rose out of the bed, and said, Sister, arise, and let us pray that God would have pity on us.
>
> Then began Tobias to say, Blessed art Thou, O God of our fathers, and blessed is Thy holy and glorious name for ever; let the heavens bless Thee, and all Thy creatures.
>
> Thou madest Adam, and gavest him Eve his wife for an helper and stay: of them came mankind: Thou hast said, It is not good that man should be alone; let us make unto him an aid like unto himself.
>
> And now, O Lord, I take not this my sister for lust, but uprightly therefore mercifully ordain that we may become aged together.
>
> And she said with him, Amen.
>
> So they slept both that night.—Tobit vii. 4-9.

It may be asked, Why have I treated this aspect of Jewish life at such great length? My answer is simple. I really believe that the rationalization of life, and especially of the sexual life, which the Jewish religion effects cannot be too highly estimated for its influence on economic activities. If religion is at all to be accounted a factor in Jewish economic life, then certainly the rationalization of conduct is its best expression.

To begin with, a number of good qualities or virtues which are indispensable to any economic order owe their existence to rationalization—*e.g.*, industry, neatness, thrift. But the whole of life, if lived in accordance with the ordinances of the "Wise," ministers to the needs of wealth-getting. Sobriety, moderation and piety are surely qualities which stand the business man in good stead. In short, the whole ideal of conduct preached in Holy Writ and in Rabbinic literature has something of the morality of the small shopkeeper about it—to be content with one wife, to pay your debts punctually, to go to church or synagogue on Sunday or Saturday (as the case may be) and to look down with immeasurable scorn on the sinful world around.

But Jewish moral teaching did not spend itself in the mere production of this type of the small respectable shopkeeper. It may even be questioned whether the type is altogether its work. At any rate, it is not of much consequence for economic development. Middle-class respectability as a matter of fact owes its origin to the narrow outlook of the petty trading class. Hence it can have but little to do with capitalism, except in so far as the qualities which that class possessed were the foundation on which capitalism could be built up. But capitalism did not grow out of the qualities, and therefore we must search in other directions for the causes which made the Jews pioneers of capitalism.

The first that suggests itself is the cultivation of family life among Jews, calling forth as it did energies so necessary to economic growth. The cultivation and refinement of family life was undoubtedly the work of the Jewish Rabbis, assisted, it must be added, by the vicissitudes of the Jewish people. In Judaism woman was first held in that high esteem which is the prime postulate for the existence of a sound family life and all that it means for man's conduct. The Rabbis by their laws and regulations affecting marriages, the marital relationship and the education of children and the rest, did all that was humanly possible in the way of outward limitation and influence to establish family life in all its purity. That marriage is considered more sacred among pious Jews than among people of other denominations is demonstrated by the statistics of illegitimate births. These are considerably fewer among Jews than among Christians.[59]

ILLEGITIMATE BIRTHS PER THOUSAND

Year	Country	General Population	Jews
1904	Prussia	2.51	0.66
1905	Würtemberg	2.83	0.16
1907	Hesse	2.18	0.13
1908	Bavaria	4.25	0.56
1901	Russia	1.29	0.14

If the figures for Russia be looked into a little more carefully it will be seen that illegitimate births among Jews vary very much from those among non-Jews. At the same time it must not be forgotten that there is a slight lowering of the standard in sexual morality among Jews. Thus, the following table shows the percentage of illegitimate births in Russia.

ILLEGITIMATE BIRTHS PER HUNDRED IN RUSSIA

Year	Greek Orthodox	Catholics	Protestants	Jews
1868	2.96	3.45	3.49	0.19
1878	3.13	3.29	3.85	0.25
1898	2.66	3.53	3.86	0.37
1901	2.49	3.57	3.76	0.46

Such then was one result of the family life current among Jews and introduced by them. The man contributed to it the best that was in him, and in return he drew from it invigorating strength, courage, and an inducement to maintain and to expand his position in life. Family life of this kind generated centres for masculine energy large enough to set in motion such a mighty economic system as capitalism. For this system calls for great energy, and we can scarcely imagine it being produced except through the agency of psychological influences which appeal not only to the social instincts but also to the family ideal.

It may perhaps be necessary to look below the psychological influences to the physical ones. How curiously moulded must the constitution of the Jew have become through the rationalization of his married life! We see this phenomenon— that a people with strong sexual inclinations (Tacitus speaks of it as *proiectissima ad libidinem gens*) is forced by its religion to hold them in complete restraint. Extra-marital connexions are absolutely forbidden; every one must content himself with one wife, but even with her intercourse is restricted.

The result of all this is obvious. Enormous funds of energy were prevented from finding an outlet in one direction and they turned to others. Knowing as we do the condition of the Jews throughout the Common Era, we shall not be wrong in assuming that economic activities were their chief channel. But we may go further. It is possible to prove that, quite generally, restrained sexual desires and the chase of profits go hand in hand. For the present we have had but little scientific investigation of this fact, so important for all modern sociological problems.[60] That a lordly way of life is usually accompanied by lavishness of money and of love, whereas such qualities as niggardliness, avarice and a setting of much store by money are the ubiquitous partners of a stunted sexual life —these are everyday experiences, and though it would be presumptuous to attempt to solve this most interesting problem with the aid of observations which must perforce be limited, yet for the purpose of my argument they ought not to be omitted, at least as an hypothesis.

We see then that a good deal of capitalistic capacity which the Jews possessed was due in large measure to the sexual restraint put upon them by their religious teachers. The effect of the rationalization of the whole of life on the physical and intellectual powers of the Jew must still be gone into by scientists;[61] at present we have only beginnings of such studies. I refer to the influence of the very wise regulations of sexual intercourse, of eating and drinking and so on. (Incidentally it is worthy of note that Jewish law has long restricted the marriage of the unfit.)

One other point in conclusion. The rationalization of life accustomed the Jew to a mode of living contrary to (or side by side with) Nature and therefore also to an economic system like the capitalistic, which is likewise contrary to (or side by side with) Nature. What in reality is the idea of making profit, what is economic rationalism, but the application to economic activities of the rules by which the Jewish religion shaped Jewish life? Before capitalism could develop the natural man had to be changed out of all recognition, and a rationalistically minded mechanism introduced in his stead. There had to be a transvaluation of all economic values. And what was the result? The *homo capitalisticus,* who is closely related to the *homo Judæus,* both belonging to the same species, *homines rationalistici artificiales.*

And so the rationalization of Jewish life by the Jewish religion, if it did not actually produce the Jewish capacity for capitalism, certainly increased and heightened it.

Israel and the Nations

One of the causes to which the Jew owed his economic progress was, as the reader will remember, the fact that Israel was for generations a stranger and an alien. If we seek to account for this aloofness we shall find its roots in the ordinances of the Jewish religion, shall find that this religion always maintained and broadened the line of separation. As Leroy-Beaulieu, who has studied this aspect of Jewish history with great success, has so well said, "La loi leur donnait l'esprit de clan." The very fact that they had their Law forced the Jews to live apart from the Gentiles. For if they desired to observe the Law they needs must keep to themselves. The Jews created the Ghetto, which from the non-Jewish point of view was a concession and a privilege and not the result of enmity.

But the Jews wished to live separated from the rest because they felt themselves superior to the common people round them. They were the Chosen Race, a People of Priests. The Rabbis did all that was required to fan the flame of pride— from Ezra, who forbade intermarriage as a profanation of Jewish purity, down to this very day, when the pious Jew says every morning, "Blessed art Thou, O Lord, King of the Universe, who has not made me a Gentile (stranger)."

And so they lived separate and apart all through the centuries of the Diaspora, despite the Diaspora and (thanks to the bands which the Law laid upon them) because of the Diaspora—separate and apart, and therefore a group by themselves, or, if you will, a group by themselves and therefore separate and apart.

A group by themselves—they were that already at the time of the Babylonian Exile, which in reality established the internationalism of the Jew. Many of them, especially the wealthier ones, remained behind in Babylon of their own free will, but they retained their Judaism and professed it zealously. They kept up a lively intercourse with their brethren who had returned home, took a sympathetic interest in their fortunes, rendered them assistance and sent them new settlers from time to time.[62]

The bonds of union were in no wise relaxed in the Hellenistic Diaspora. "They kept closely together in the cities and throughout the world. No matter where they pitched their tents, their connexion with Zion was upheld. In the heart of the wilderness they had a native land where they were at home . . . By means of the Diaspora they entered into the world. In the Hellenistic cities they adopted the Greek tongue and Greek manners even if only as the outer garb of their Jewishness" (Wellhausen).

So it continued throughout the centuries of their exile. If anything the bond became strengthened. *"Scis quanta concordia"*—"You know how they hang together!" cries Cicero.[63] So it was; so it still is. "All the Jewries in the Empire and beyond," we read of the rebellion of the year 130 A.D., "were stirred and more or less openly supported the insurgents on the banks of the Jordan."[64] Is it any different to-day when a Jew is expelled from some Russian town or other?

A group by themselves and therefore separate and apart— this is true from earliest antiquity. All nations were struck by their hatred of others, of which they were for the first time accused by Hekateus of Abdera (300 B.C.). Many other ancient writers repeat the indictment,[65] almost always in the same words. Perhaps the best known passage is in Tacitus: *"Apud eos fides obstinata, misericordia in promptu. Sed ad-*

versus omnes alios hostile odium. Separati epulis discreti cubilibus, proiectissima ad libidinem gens, alienarum concubitu abstinent" (*Historia*, V, i. 5). [Amongst themselves they are doggedly faithful and quick to pity, but all strangers they hate as enemies. They neither eat nor intermarry with strangers; they are a people of strong passions, yet they withhold themselves from other men's wives.]

Jewish apologetics never attempted to combat these views:[66] there must therefore have been some foundation for them.

It is true that the Jews kept together so closely and shut themselves off very often on account of the unfriendly treatment they received at the hands of their hosts. But it was not so originally. The Jews wanted to live secluded from their neighbours because of their religion. That this was so appears from their attitude in those lands where they were well treated. Witness one or two instances in the ancient world, of which I have just given illustrations [Tacitus, etc.]. Witness the same tendency in the Middle Ages. Take Arabia in the first century. The Jews there at the period named lived according to the religion which the *Tanaim* and *Amoraim* had formulated—keeping the dietary laws and festivals, the great White Fast and the Sabbath. "Although they could not complain of anything in this hospitable country they yet longed for the return to the Holy Land and awaited the advent of the Messiah every day. . . . They were in direct communication with the Jews of Palestine."[67] Or take Moorish Spain. While the Christians who lived among the Mohammedans forgot their mother tongue (Gothic Latin), no longer understood their sacred books, and were rather ashamed of their Christianity, the Spanish Jews were more and more devoted to their national language, their Holy Writ and their ancient religion.[68] This attitude was clearly reflected in the Jewish poetry and philosophy of the period, the greatest perhaps that mediæval Jewry can boast. In the midst of an Arabic-Spanish world in which they lived and enjoyed the respect of their fellow-citizens, they were strictly "national," that is religious; they drew poetic inspiration from the Messianic hopes and were filled with an unconquerable longing for Zion.[69] One need only mention the great Jehuda Halevy, whose Odes to Zion are the highest expression of the genius of neo-Hebrew poetry.

Like a cloud sailing in the blue of the sky above, Judaism winds its way through history, refreshed by the memories of its hoary and holy past as by a soft breeze. To this very day the pious Jew blesses his children with the words, "The Lord make thee as Ephraim and Manasseh."

What was the effect on economic life of this seclusion and separation of the Jewish social organism? Directly the Jews stepped outside the Ghetto gates their intercourse was with strangers. We have already dealt with the point elsewhere; my reason for calling attention to it again is to show that this attitude was a direct consequence of the teaching of Judaism, that in treating the people among whom they lived as "others," the Jews were but obeying a divine behest. Here, too, their conduct was hallowed, and it received a sanction from the peculiar system of laws relating to "strangers."

The most important and most frequently discussed legal ordinance in this system was that affecting the taking of interest. In the old Jewish theocracy,[70] as in every society in early civilization, loans without interest were the regular means of rendering assistance by a man to his neighbour. But it may be observed that even in the earliest collection of laws interest was allowed to be taken from "strangers."

The Jewish code was no exception. The best example of this may be found in Deuteronomy xxiii. 20. Other passages in the Torah that have reference to interest are Exodus xxii. 25 and Leviticus xxv. 37. They all form the theme of a lively discussion which has been carried on from the days of the *Tanaim* down to the present. The chief instance and at the same time the crux of the matter is in the Talmud, in *Baha Mezia, 70b,* and my own feeling is that for the most part it is an attempt to discount the very clear statement of the Torah by all manner of sophistries. For what does the verse in Deuteronomy say? "Unto a foreigner thou mayest lend upon usury; but unto thy brother thou shalt not lend upon usury." The only doubt is in the wording of the original, which may mean with equal grammatical exactitude, "thou *mayest* lend upon usury" or "thou *shalt* lend upon usury." (It need hardly be added that "usury" with the translators was nothing more or less than our "interest.")

In either case, the pious Jew was allowed to take interest from non-Jews—that is the significant thing as far as we are concerned. Right through the Middle Ages he was not oppressed by the burden of the anti-usury prohibition which weighed upon the Christian. The Jewish law on the subject was never to my knowledge questioned by the Rabbis.[71] On the other hand, there were periods when the "mayest" in the Deuteronomic passage was read as "shalt," periods when the Jew was urged to become a money-lender.

The authors who have dealt with this subject in modern times appear to have overlooked the fact that the Deuteronomic command has been received as one of the laws that regulate the life of the Jew, and that Tradition sanctions money-lending to a stranger on payment of interest. Of the 613 commandments, this is the 198th and may be found likewise in the *Shulchan Aruch*. Modern Rabbis[72] to whom the perfectly clear ordinance in Deuteronomy is somewhat inconvenient (one cannot quite understand why), attempt to explain it away by asserting that "strangers" in the passage is intended not for all non-Jews but only for heathens or idol-worshippers. If this be so, let it not be forgotten that there never was any very distinct conception as to who was, and who was not, an idol-worshipper. Besides, the pious Jew who has committed the 198th command to memory is not likely to draw the fine distinction urged by the learned Rabbis. Sufficient for him that the man to whom he lent money was no Jew, no "brother," no neighbour, but a Gentile.

Now think of the position in which the pious Jew and the pious Christian respectively found themselves in the period in which money-lending first became a need in Europe, and which eventually gave birth to capitalism. The good Christian who had been addicted to usury was full of remorse as he lay a-dying, ready at the eleventh hour to cast from him the ill-gotten gains which scorched his soul. And the good Jew? In the evening of his days he gazed upon his well-filled caskets and coffers, overflowing with sequins of which he had relieved the miserable Christians or Mohammedans. It was a sight which warmed his heart, for every penny was almost like a sacrifice which he had brought to his Heavenly Father.

Apart from this particular question, the stranger was accorded special consideration in the Jewish legal code. Duties towards him were never as binding as towards your "neighbour," your fellow-Jew. Only ignorance or a desire to distort facts will assert the contrary. True, the conception of law and morality as it affected the "stranger" varied from age to age. But there was no change in the fundamental idea that you owed less consideration to the stranger than to one of your own people. That has remained the same from the day when the Torah first became current to our own. That is the impression that is conveyed by an unprejudiced study of the law concerning strangers in the Holy Writ, the Talmud, the Codes and the Responsa literature. There certainly are passages in the Torah which breathe equality between the home-born and the stranger (Exod. xii. 49, xxiii. 9; Lev. xix. 33, 34, xxv. 44-6; Deut. x. 18, 19). But in a question of *halacha* (legal enactment) such as this is, the oral tradition cannot be neglected. Secondly, the passages instanced above all refer to the *Ger*, the non-Jew who had settled in Palestine, seeing that the Jews knew the heart of a *Ger*, "for ye were *Gerim* in the land of Egypt." [In the sentence about interest the word used is *Nachari*, some one from another nation.] As time went on it was but natural that there should be an increase of the cases in Jewish law in which the non-Jew was at a disadvantage as compared with the Jew. So much so that in the latest code they occupy a good deal of space.[73]

What was the importance in economic life of the laws concerning strangers? It was twofold. First, intercourse with strangers was bereft of all considerations, and commercial morality (if I may put it so) became elastic. I admit that there was no absolute necessity for this to come about, but all the conditions were given for it to do so, and it must have been an everyday occurrence in certain circles. "If a non-Jew makes an error in a statement of account, the Jew may use it to his own advantage; it is not incumbent upon him to point it out." So we may read in the *Tur*, and though Joseph Caro did not include this in his law-book, it crept in later as a gloss from the pen of Isserlein. Is it not obvious that the good Jew must needs draw the conclusion that he was not bound to be so particular in his intercourse with non-Jews? With Jews he will scrupulously see to it that he has just weights and a just measure;[74] but as for his dealings with non-Jews, his conscience will be at ease even though he may obtain an unfair advantage. It is not to be denied that in some cases honesty towards non-Jews was inculcated.[75] But to think that this should have been necessary! Besides, this is the actual wording of the law: "It is permissible to take advantage of a non-Jew, for it is written, Thou shalt not take advantage of thy brother." (The context refers not to overreaching, but only to the asking of higher prices from a non-Jew.)

This conception must have been firmly rooted in those districts (*e.g.*, in Eastern Europe) where the study of the Talmud and the casuistry it engendered were universal. The effect it had on the commerce of the Jew has been described by Graetz, surely no prejudiced witness. "To twist a phrase out of its meaning, to use all the tricks of the clever advocate, to play upon words, and to condemn what they did not know . . . such were the characteristics of the Polish Jew. . . Honesty and right-thinking he lost as completely as simplicity and truthfulness. He made himself master of all the gymnastics of the Schools and applied them to obtain advantage over any one less cunning than himself. He took a delight in cheating and overreaching, which gave him a sort of joy of victory. But his own people he could not treat in this way: they were as knowing as he. It was the non-Jew who, to his loss, felt the consequences of the Talmudically trained mind of the Polish Jew."[76]

In the second place, the differential treatment of non-Jews in Jewish commercial law resulted in the complete transformation of the idea of commerce and industry generally in the direction of more freedom. If we have called the Jews the Fathers of Free Trade, and therefore the pioneers of capitalism, let us note here that they were prepared for this rôle by the free-trading spirit of the commercial and industrial law, which received an enormous impetus towards a policy of *laissez-faire* by its attitude towards strangers. Clearly, intercourse with strangers could not but loosen the bonds of personal duties and replace them by economic freedom. Let us glance at this in greater detail.

The theory of price in the Talmud and the Codes, in so far as it affected trade between Jew and Jew, is exactly parallel to the scholastic doctrine of *justum pretium* which was prevalent in Europe throughout the Middle Ages. But as between Jew and non-Jew, there was no just price. Price was formed as it is to-day, by "the higgling of the market."[77]

Be that as it may, the important thing to observe is that already in the Talmud, and still more distinctly in the *Shulchan Aruch,* conceptions of the freedom of industry and enterprise, so entirely alien to the Christian law of Mediæval Europe, are met with. It is a subject deserving of close study and should be taken up by a specialist. For my part, I can do no more here than refer to a few instances. But few though they be, they seem to me to be conclusive evidence on the point in question. My first reference is to a passage in the Talmud which fully recognizes free competition among sellers.

Mishna.—R. Judah was of opinion that a shopkeeper should not distribute nuts among children, because by so doing he gets them into the habit of coming to him. But the Rabbis allow it. Moreover, it is not lawful to spoil prices. But the Rabbis say, "Blessed be his memory."

Gemara.—The question at once arises, what was the reason for the attitude of the Rabbis in the first case? The answer is that the shopkeeper may say to his competitor, "I give the children nuts, you can give them plums." And what is the reason of the Rabbis in the second case? The Mishna forbids price alteration, and yet they say, "Blessed be his memory." The answer is, they bless his memory because he reduces prices (*Baba Mezia,* 60a and b).

In the Codes the reasons have been omitted, and the dry statement of law only is found. "A shopkeeper is allowed to make presents of nuts and other things to the children who come to purchase in his shop, in order to win their custom. Moreover, he may sell at a price below the current one, and the competing tradesmen can do nothing" (*Choshen Mishpat*, 225, § 18).

Similarly, in the laws regulating the conduct of traders who bring their goods to the market town, the following may be read: "Should the strangers sell more cheaply than the native dealers, or should their goods be of a better quality, the natives may not prevent them, for the Jewish public derives benefit therefrom" (*Choshen Mishpat*, 156, § 7).

Once more. "If a Jew is prepared to lend money to a non-Jew at a lower rate of interest than some one else, the latter can do nothing against it" (*Choshen Mishpat*, 156, § 5).

Finally, Jewish law favours industrial *laissez-faire*. So we find in the *Shulchan Aruch:* "If any one commenced a handicraft in his street and none of his neighbours protested, and then one of the other residents in the street wishes to carry on the same calling, the first may not complain that the new-comer is taking the bread out of his mouth, and try to prevent him" (*Choshen Mishpat*, 156, § 5).

Clearly, then, free trade and industrial freedom were in accordance with Jewish law, and therefore in accordance with God's will. What a mighty motive power in economic life!

Judaism and Puritanism

I have already mentioned that Max Weber's study of the importance of Puritanism for the capitalistic system was the impetus that sent me to consider the importance of the Jew, especially as I felt that the dominating ideas of Puritanism which were so powerful in capitalism were more perfectly developed in Judaism, and were also of course of much earlier date.

A complete comparison of the two "isms" is not within my province here. But I believe that if it were made, it would be seen that there is an almost unique identity of view between Judaism and Puritanism, at least, on those points which we have investigated. In both will be found the preponderance of religious interests, the idea of divine rewards and punishments, asceticism *within* the world, the close relationship between religion and business, the arithmetical conception of sin, and, above all, the rationalization of life.

Let me refer to an instance or two. Take the attitude of Judaism and Puritanism to the problem of sex. In one of the best hotels of Philadelphia I found a notice in my room to this effect: "Visitors who may have to transact business with ladies are respectfully requested to leave the door of their room open while the lady is with them." What is this but the old dictum of the Talmud (*Kiddushin*, 82*a*), "Hast thou business with women? See to it that thou art not with them alone"?

Again, is not the English Sunday the Jewish Sabbath?

I would also recall the words of Heine,[78] who had a clear insight into most things. "Are not," he asks in his *Confessions*, "Are not the Protestant Scots Hebrews, with their Biblical names, their Jerusalem, pharisaistic cant? And is not their religion a Judaism which allows you to eat pork?"

Puritanism *is* Judaism.

Whether the first was influenced by the second, and if so, how, are most difficult questions to answer. It is well known, of course, that in the Reformation period there was close intercourse between Jews and certain Christian sects, that the study of Hebrew and the Hebrew Scriptures became fashionable, and that the Jews in England in the 17th century were held in very high esteem by the Puritans. Leading men in England like Oliver Cromwell built up their religious views on the Old Testament, and Cromwell himself dreamed of a reconciliation between the Old and the New Testaments, and of a confederation between the Chosen People of God and the Puritan English. A Puritan preacher of the day, Nathaniel Holmes by name, wished for nothing better than, in accordance with the letter of the prophetic message, to become a servant of God's people and to serve them on bended knee. Public life became Hebraic in tone no less than the sermons in churches. And if only speeches in Parliament had been in Hebrew, you might have believed yourself in Palestine. The "Levellers," who called themselves "Jews" (in opposition to their opponents whom they termed "Amalekites"), advocated the adoption of the Torah as the norm of English legislation.

Cromwell's officers suggested to him to appoint seventy members of his Privy Council according to the number of the members of the Synhedrin. To the Parliament of 1653 General Thomas Harrison, the Anabaptist, was returned, and he and his party clamoured for the introduction of the Mosaic legislation into England. In 1649 it was moved in the House of Commons that the Lord's Day should be observed on Saturday instead of on Sunday. On the banners of the victorious Puritans was inscribed "The Lion of Judah."[79] It is significant that not only the Bible, but the Rabbinical literature as well, was extensively read in large circles of the clergy and laity.

Altogether, then, there appears to be sufficient evidence for the deduction of Puritan doctrines from Jewish sources. The specialists must decide. Here I have been able to do no more than give a hint or two. And in conclusion I would draw attention to a little humorous publication, which appeared in the year 1608 and the contents of which would seem to demonstrate the close connexion between Judaism and Calvinism (which is only Puritanism). It is called, *Der Calvinische Judenspiegel* (the Calvinistic Jewish Mirror), and on page 33 a comparison is drawn between the two religions in the following droll fashion. [The old German is delightful.] "If I am to say on my honour why I am become a Calvinist, I shall have to confess that the one and only reason which persuaded me was that among all the religions I could find none which agreed so much with Judaism, and its view of life and faith. (Here follow a number of parallel statements, partly serious and partly satirical). 8. The Jews hate the name of Mary and tolerate her only when she is made of gold and silver, or when her image is impressed on coins. So do we. We too like Mary farthings and crowns, to which we pay all due respect, for they are useful in business. 9. The Jews everywhere are at pains to cheat the people. So are we. For that very reason we left our country to wander in other lands where we are not known in our true colours, so that by our deceit and cunning . . . we might lead astray the ignorant yokels, cheat them and bring them to us. . . ."

Chapter 12

Jewish Characteristics

The Problem

THE DECISION TO deal in a work of a scientific character with the problem suggested by the title of the present chapter has not been arrived at without a great effort. For it has of late become the fashion to seize upon anything even but faintly savouring of the psychology of nations as the plaything for the lighter moods of dilettanti, whilst descriptions of the Jewish genius have been hailed as the newest form of political sport by coarser spirits, whose rude instincts cannot but give offence to all those who, in our gross age, have managed to preserve a modicum of good taste and impartiality. Unjustifiable juggling with categories in race psychology has already led to the conclusion that it is impossible to arrive at any scientific results in this field of study. Read the books of F. Hertz, Jean Finot and others[1] and you will lay them down with the feeling that it is useless to attempt to find common psychological characteristics among any conglomeration of humans; that French *esprit* is a myth—in fact that there are no Frenchmen, just as there are no Jews. But cross the street, and lo and behold, you are face to face with a specific type; read a book or stand before a picture and almost unconsciously you say, How very German, how thoroughly French!

Is this only the imagining of our fancy?[2]

Nay more. If we think for a moment of human history we must needs construct for ourselves the hypothesis of a sort of "collective soul." When, for example, we talk of the Jewish religion we are bound to connect it with the Jewish people whose genius gave it birth. Or, when we say the Jews had an influence on modern economic development, it follows surely that there must have been something essentially Jewish that brought it about. Otherwise we might as well assert that it would have made no difference to the economic history of

Western Europe if Eskimos had taken the place of Jews, or perhaps even gorillas would have done equally well!

This *reductio ad absurdum* shows plainly enough that there must be some specifically Jewish characteristic. But let us consider the matter from a slightly different point of view. Let us glance at the objective circumstances in the Jewish aptitude for modern capitalism. There was first, as we have seen, the dispersion of the Jews over a wide area. Now without recourse to subjective forces the Diaspora can be as little explained as the effects of the Diaspora. And one thing is evident. The dispersion of a people in itself does not necessarily have either economic or cultural results; nay, very often dispersion may lead to fusion and ultimate disappearance.

It has been claimed—and with truth—that it was the dispersion of the Jews which fitted them to become intermediaries. Granted, but did it also tend to make of them negotiators and private advisers of princes, callings which have from time immemorial been the stepping-stones of the interpreter to higher posts? Were the capacities essential to these new offices not inherent in the Jews themselves?

We have admitted that the dispersion of the Jews was responsible for no little of their success in international commerce and credit. But is not the postulate to this success the fact that the Jews everywhere kept together? What would have happened if, like so many other scattered races, they had not maintained their bonds of union?

Lastly, let us not forget that the Jews came among just those peoples who happened to be mature enough to receive capitalism. But even so, if Jewish influence was strong (and it is so still) in Holland, in England, in Germany, in Austria-Hungary—stronger far than their influence on the Spaniards, Italians, Greeks or Arabs—it was in a large measure due to the contrasts between them and their hosts. For it would seem that the more slow-witted, the more thick-skulled, the more ignorant of business a people is, the more effective is Jewish influence on their economic life. And can this be satisfactorily accounted for except through special Jewish peculiarities?

No matter what was the origin of their innate dissimilarity

from their hosts, the salient point is that this strangeness should have obtained lasting influence in economic life. Once more it is impossible to fathom this without the assumption of inherent Jewish characteristics. That a people or a tribe is hated and persecuted does not furnish sufficient reason for spurring them on to redoubled efforts in their activities. On the contrary, in most cases this contempt and ill-treatment but serve to destroy morals and initiative. Only where man is possessed of exceptional qualities do these become, under the stress of circumstances, the source of regenerated energy.

Again, look at their semi-citizenship. Does not the identical argument hold good here also? It is so obvious as to become almost a truism. Nowhere did the Jews enjoy the same advantages as their fellow-citizens, and yet everywhere they achieved economically much more than the rest of the population. There can be but one explanation for this—the specifically Jewish characteristics.

On the other hand, the legal position of the Jews varied in different countries and at different times. In some States they were allowed to engage in certain occupations; in others these same occupations were forbidden them; in others again, such as England, they were on a perfectly equal footing with the rest of the people in this respect. And yet they devoted themselves almost everywhere to particular callings. In England and America they began their commercial mission by becoming bullion-merchants or storekeepers. And can this be accounted for in any other way than by once more pointing to their peculiar characteristics?

As for the wealth of the Jews, that alone will hardly suffice to explain their great achievements in the sphere of economic activities. A man who possesses vast sums must have a number of intellectual qualities in addition, if his money is to be usefully employed in the capitalistic sense. That surely requires no proof.

Jewish characteristics must therefore exist. It remains only to discover what they are.

Our first thought of the Jews as a unit will naturally be associated with their religion. But before we proceed another step I should like to premise that on the one hand I shall limit the group lumped together under the Jewish religion, and on the other hand, I shall enlarge it. I shall limit it by only considering the Jews since their expulsion from Spain and Portugal, that is, from the end of the Middle Ages. I shall enlarge it by including within the circle of my observations the descendants of Jews, even if they themselves have left the faith.

Moreover, I should like to touch upon the arguments urged against the existence of Jewish peculiarities.

(1) It has been remarked that the Jews of Western Europe and America have to a large extent assimilated with the peoples among whom they dwell. This need not be denied, even if specifically Jewish characteristics were as clear as daylight. Is is not possible for social groups to intermingle? A man may be a German, have all the characteristics of a German, and yet be an individual in the group "international proletariat!" Or take another instance. Are not the German Swiss at one and the same time Swiss and German?

(2) The Jews in the Diaspora, it is maintained, are not a "nation" or a "people" in the commonly accepted meaning of the term,[3] since they are not a political, cultural or linguistic community. The reply to this objection is that there are many other qualifications besides those mentioned (*e.g.,* a common origin) which must be considered. But speaking generally, it is as well not to press a definition too closely.

(3) The differences between the Jews themselves have been made much of. It has been said that there is no homogeneity among Jews, that one section is bitterly opposed to the other. The Western Jews are different from the Eastern Jews, the Sephardim from the Ashkenazim, the Orthodox from the Liberals, the everyday Jew from the Sabbath Jew (to use a phrase of Marx). This also there is no need to deny. But it does not by any means preclude the possibility of common Jewish characteristics. Is it so difficult to conceive of wheels within wheels? Cannot a large group contain lesser groups side by side? Think of the many groups to which an Englishman may belong. He may be a Catholic or a Protestant, a farmer or a professor, a northerner or a southerner and Heaven only knows what else besides. But he remains an

Englishman all the same. So with the Jew. He may belong to one circle within the whole, may possess certain characteristics that mark all individuals in that circle, but he retains the specifically Jewish characteristics nevertheless.

Finally, I must make it plain that I have no intention of outlining all Jewish characteristics. I propose to deal with those only that have reference to economic life. I shall not content myself with the old-fashioned expressions, such as the Jewish "commercialism," the "bartering spirit" and the like. I say nothing of the practice of some to include the desire for profit as a characteristic of a social group. The desire for profit is human—all too human. In fact, I must reject all previous analyses of the Jewish soul (in so far as they touch economic life), and for the following reasons. First, what the Jew was well-fitted for was never clearly enough designated. "For trade" is much too vague a term to be of the slighest use. I have therefore tried to show, in a special chapter, the circle of economic activities for which Jews are specifically fitted. Secondly, mere description is not explanation. If I want to prove that a man has all the capabilities necessary to make him an admirable speculator on the Stock Exchange, it will not be enough if I say that he will make a fine jobber. It is like saying indigence is due to poverty. Yet that is how Jewish economic talents have been treated. Our method will be different. We shall try to discover certain properties of the soul which are congenial to the exercise of economic functions in a capitalistic organism.

And now, having cleared the way, I shall proceed to demonstrate what the real Jewish peculiarities are.

An Attempt at a Solution

It is surprising to find that despite the enormity of the problem there is yet a great degree of unanimity in the different views about the Jews. In literature no less than in actual life, unprejudiced observers agree on one or other point of importance. Read Jellinek or Fromer, Chamberlain or Marx, Heine or Goethe, Leroy-Beaulieu or Picciotto—read the pious or the non-conforming Jew, the anti-Semitic or the philo-Semitic non-Jew—and you get the impression that all of them are conscious of the same peculiarities. This is comforting to one who is about to describe the Jewish genius once more. At any rate, he will say nothing that other people might not have said, even though his standpoint be slightly different. In my own case I shall attempt to show the connexion between the characteristics and the natural gifts of the Jews and the capitalistic economic system. I shall first try to sketch a detailed picture of Jewish qualities and then proceed to bring them into relation with capitalism.

Unlike most other writers on the subject I will begin by noting a Jewish quality which, though mentioned often enough, never received the recognition which its importance merited. I refer to the extreme intellectuality of the Jew. Intellectual interests and intellectual skill are more strongly developed in him than physical (manual) powers. Of the Jew it may certainly be said, "l'intelligence prime le corps." Everyday experience proves it again and again, and many a fact might be cited in its support. No other people has valued the learned man, the scholar, so highly as the Jews. "The wise man takes precedence of the king, and a bastard who is a scholar of a high-priest who is an ignoramus." So the Talmud has it. Any one who is acquainted with Jewish students knows well enough that this over-rating of mere knowledge is not yet a thing of the past. And if you could not become "wise," at least it was your duty to be educated. At all times instruction was compulsory in Israel. In truth, to learn was a religious duty; and in Eastern Europe the synagogue is still called the Shool (Schule, School). Study and worship went hand in hand; nay, study was worship and ignorance was a deadly sin. A man who could not read was a boor in this world and damned in the next. In the popular sayings of the Ghetto, nothing had so much scorn poured upon it as foolishness. "Better injustice than folly," and "Ein Narr ist ein Gezar" (A fool is a misfortune) are both well known.[4]

The most valuable individual is the intellectual individual; humanity at its best is intellectuality at its highest. Listen to what a sensible Jew has to say when he pictures the ideal man, the superman if you like, of the future. He takes it all as a matter of course; those who are differently constituted must surely tremble at the prospect. "In the place of the blind instincts . . . civilized man will possess intellect conscious of purpose. It should be every one's unswerving ideal to crush the instincts and replace them by will-power, and to substitute reflection for mere impulse. The individual only becomes a man in the fullest sense of the word when his natural predisposition is under the control of his reasoning powers. And when the process of emancipation from the instincts is complete we have the perfect genius with his absolute inner freedom from the domination of natural laws. Civilization should have but one aim—to liberate man from all that is mystic, from the vague impulsiveness of all instinctive action, and to cultivate the purely rational side of his being."[5] Only think. Genius, the very essence of instinctive expression, conceived as the highest form of the rational and the intellectual!

One consequence of this high evaluation of the intellect was the esteem in which callings were held according as they demanded more "headwork" or more "handwork." The former were almost in all ages placed higher than the latter. It is true that there may have been, and still may be, Jewish communities in which hard bodily labour is done every day, but this hardly applies to the Jews of Western Europe. Even in Talmud times Jews preferred those callings which necessitated a lesser expenditure of physical energy. As Rabbi said, "The world needs both the seller of spices and the tanner, but happy he who is a seller of spices." Or again, "R. Meir used to say, A man should have his son taught a clean and easy handicraft" (*Kiddushin*, 82b).

The Jews were quite alive to their predominant quality and always recognized that there was a great gulf between their intellectuality and the brute force of their neighbours. One or two sayings popular among Polish Jews express the contrast with no little humour. "God help a man against Gentile hands and Jewish heads." "Heaven protect us against Jewish *moach* (brains) and Gentile *koach* (physical force)." *Moach* v. *Koach*—that is the Jewish problem in a nutshell. It ought to be the motto of this book.

The predominance of intellectual interests could not but lead in a people so gifted as the Jews to intellectual skill.

"Say what you like about a Jew, you cannot say he is a fool." "A gallant Greek, a stupid Jew, an honest Gipsy— all are unthinkable" is a popular saying among Roumanians. And a Spanish proverb has it, "A hare that is slow and a Jew who is a fool: both are equally probable."[6] Who that has had dealings with Jews but will not confirm that on an average they possess a greater degree of understanding, that they are more intelligent than other people? I might even call it astuteness or sagacity, as was remarked by one of the keenest observers of Jews[7] a century or more ago, who characterized them as "intellectual and endowed with great genius for things of the present age," though, he added, "to a less degree than in the past."

"The Jewish mind is an instrument of precision; it has the exactness of a pair of scales": most people will agree with this judgment of Leroy-Beaulieu. And when H. S. Chamberlain speaks of the under-development of Jewish "under-standing" he must surely be using the term in a special sense. He cannot possibly mean by it quick thought, precise analysis, exact dissection, speedy combination, the power of seeing the point at once, of suggesting analogies, distinguishing between synonymous things, of drawing final conclusions. The Jew is able to do all this, and Jellinek, who rightly lays stress[8] on this side of the Jewish character, points out that Hebrew is particularly rich in expressions for activities demanding qualities of the mind. It has no fewer than eleven words for seeking or researching, thirty-four for distinguishing or separating, and fifteen for combining.

There is no doubt that these mental gifts make the Jews prominent as chess-players, as mathematicians[9] and in all calculating work. These activities postulate a strong capacity for abstract thought and also a special kind of imagination, which Wundt has so happily christened the combinatory. Their skill as physicians (ability at diagnosis)[10] may also be traced to their calculating, dissecting and combining minds, which "like lightning, illuminate dark places in a flash."

It is not unknown that often enough Jewish mental ability degenerates into hair-splitting. (When the mill has no corn to grind it grinds itself.) But this does not matter so much as another fact. The intellectuality of the Jew is so strong that it tends to develop at the expense of other mental qualities, and the mind is apt to become one-sided. Let us take a few instances. The Jew lacks the quality of instinctive understanding; he responds less to feeling than to intellect. We can scarcely think of a Jewish mystic like Jacob Böhme, and the contrast becomes still more striking when we remember the sort of mysticism found in the Kabbala. In the same way all romance is alien to this particular view of life; the Jew cannot well sympathize with losing oneself in the world, in mankind or in nature. It is the difference between frenzied enthusiasm and sober, matter-of-fact thought.

Akin to this characteristic is that of a certain lack of impressionability, a certain lack of receptive and creative genius. When I was in Breslau a Jewish student from the far East of Siberia came to me one day "to study Karl Marx." It took him nearly three weeks to reach Breslau, and on the very day after his arrival he called on me and borrowed one of Marx's works. A few days later he came again, discussed with me what he had read, brought back the book and borrowed another. This continued for a few months. Then he returned to his native village. The young man had received absolutely no impressions from his new surroundings; he had made no acquaintances, never taken a walk, hardly knew in fact where it was that he was staying. The life of Breslau passed him by completely. No doubt it was the same before he came to Breslau, and will be the same throughout the future. He will walk through the world without seeing it. But he had made himself acquainted with Marx. Is this a typical case? I think so. You may meet with it every day. Are we not continually struck by the Jew's love for the inconcrete, his tendency away from the sensuous, his constant abiding in a world of abstractions? And is it only accidental that there are far fewer Jewish painters than literary men or professors? Even in the case of Jewish artists is there not something intellectual about their work? Never was word more truly spoken than when Friedrich Naumann compared Max Liebermann [the famous Jewish painter] with Spinoza, saying, "He paints with his brain."

The Jew certainly sees remarkably clearly, but he does not see much. He does not think of his environment as something alive, and that is why he has lost the true conception of life, of its oneness, of its being an organism, a natural growth. In short, he has lost the true conception of the personal side of life. General experience must surely support this view; but if other proofs are demanded they will be found in the peculiarities of Jewish law, which, as we have already seen, abolished personal relationships and replaced them by impersonal, abstract connexions or activities or aims.

As a matter of fact, one may find among Jews an extraordinary knowledge of men. They are able with their keen intellects to probe, as it were, into every pore, and to see the inside of a man as only Röntgen rays would show him. They muster all his qualities and abilities, they note his excellences and his weaknesses; they detect at once for what he is best fitted. But seldom do they see the whole man, and thus they often make the mistake of ascribing actions to him which are an abomination to his inmost soul. Moreover, they seldom appraise a man according to his personality, but rather according to some perceptible characteristic and achievement.

Hence their lack of sympathy for every status where the nexus is a personal one. The Jews' whole being is opposed to all that is usually understood by chivalry, to all sentimentality, knight-errantry, feudalism, patriarchalism. Nor does he comprehend a social order based on relationships such as these. "Estates of the realm" and craft organizations are a loathing to him. Politically he is an individualist. A constitutional State in which all human intercourse is regulated by clearly defined legal principles suits him well.* He is the born representative of a "liberal" view of life in which there are no living men and women of flesh and blood with distinct personalities, but only citizens with rights and duties. And these do not differ in different nations, but form part of mankind, which is but the sum-total of an immense number of amorphous units. Just as so many Jews do not see themselves —do they not deny their obvious characteristics and assert

* Is not this the general modern tendency? Cf. Sir H. Maine's dictum: The progress of Society is from status to contract.—Trans.

that there is no difference between them and Englishmen or Germans or Frenchmen?—so they do not see other people as living beings but only as subjects, citizens, or some other such abstract conception. It comes to this, that they behold the world not with their "soul" but with their intellect. The result is that they are easily led to believe that whatever can be neatly set down on paper and ordered aright by the aid of the intellect must of necessity be capable of proper settlement in actual life. How many Jews still hold that the Jewish Question is only a political one, and are convinced that a liberal régime is all that is required to remove the differences between the Jew and his neighbour. It is nothing short of astounding to read the opinion of so soundly learned a man as the author of one of the newest books on the Jewish Question that the whole of the anti-Semitic movement during the last thirty years was the result of the works of Marr and Dühring. "The thousand victims of the pogroms and the million sturdy workers who emigrated from their homes are but a striking illustration of the power of—Eugen Dühring" (!).[11] Is not this opposing ink and blood, understanding and instinct, an abstraction and a reality?

The conception of the universe in the mind of such an intellectual people must perforce have been that of a structure well-ordered in accordance with reason. By the aid of reason, therefore, they sought to understand the world; they were rationalists, both in theory and in practice.

Now as soon as a strong consciousness of the ego attaches itself to the predominating intellectuality in the thinking being, he will tend to group the world round that ego. In other words, he will look at the world from the point of view of end, or goal, or purpose. His outlook will be teleological, or that of practical rationalism. No peculiarity is so fully developed in the Jew as this, and there is complete unanimity of opinion on the subject. Most other observers start out with the teleology of the Jew; I for my part regard it as the result of his extreme intellectuality, in which I believe all the other Jewish peculiarities are rooted. In saying this, however, I do not in the least wish to minimize the very great importance of this Jewish characteristic.

Take any expression of the Jewish genius and you will be
certain to find in it this teleological tendency, which has
sometimes been called extreme subjectivity. Whether or no
the Indo-Germanic races are objective and the Semitic subjective,[12] certain it is that the Jews are the most subjective of
peoples. The Jew never loses himself in the outer world, never
sinks in the depth of the cosmos, never soars in the endless
realms of thought, but, as Jellinek well puts it, dives below
the surface to seek for pearls. He brings everything into relation with his ego. He is for ever asking why, what for, what
will it bring? *Cui bono?* His greatest interest is always in
the result of a thing, not in the thing itself. It is un-Jewish to
regard any activity, be it what you will, as an end in itself;
un-Jewish to live your life without having any purpose, to
leave all to chance; un-Jewish to get harmless pleasure out of
Nature. The Jew has taken all that is in Nature and made
of it "the loose pages of a text-book of ethics which shall
advance the higher moral life." The Jewish religion, as we
have already seen, is teleological in its aim; in each of its
regulations it has the ethical norm in view. The entire universe, in the Jew's eyes, is something that was made in accordance with a plan. This is one of the differences between
Judaism and heathenism, as Heine saw long ago. "They (the
heathens) all have an endless, eternal 'past,' which is in the
world and develops with it by the laws of necessity; but the
God of the Jews was outside the world, which He created
as an act of free-will."

No term is more familiar to the ear of the Jew than *Tachlis*,
which means purpose, aim, end or goal. If you are to do
anything it must have a *tachlis;* life itself, whether as a whole
or in its single activities, must have some *tachlis,* and so must
the universe. Those who assert that the meaning of Life,
of the World, is not *tachlis* but tragedy, the Jew will reckon
as foolish visionaries.

How deeply the teleological view of things is embedded
in the nature of the Jew may be seen in the case of those
of them who, like the Chassidim, pay no attention to the
needs of practical life because "there is no purpose in them."
There is no purpose in making a living, and so they let their

wives and children starve, and devote themselves to the study of their sacred books. But we may see it also in all those Jews who, with a soul-weariness within them and a faint smile on their countenances, understanding and forgiving everything, stand and gaze at life from their own heights, far above this world. I have in my mind such choice spirits among the literary men of our day as George Hirschfeld, Arthur Schnitzler and George Hermann. The great charm of their work lies in this world-aloofness with which they look down on our hustle and bustle, in the quiet melancholy pervading all their poetry, in their sentiment. Their very lack of will-power is only strength of will in a kind of negative form. Through all their ballads sounds the same soft plaint of grief: how purposeless and therefore how sad is the world! Nature herself is tinged with this sorrow; autumn always lurks in ambush though wood and meadow be bright with gay spring blossoms; the wind plays among the fallen leaves and the sun's golden glory, be it never so beautiful, must go down at last. Subjectivity and the conception that all things must have an aim (and the two are the same) rob the poetry of Jewish writers of *naïveté*, freshness and directness, because Jewish poets are unable simply to enjoy the phenomena of this world, whether it be human fate or Nature's vagaries; they must needs cogitate upon it and turn it about and about. Nowhere is the air scented with the primrose and the violet, nowhere gleams the spray of the rivulet in the wood. But to make up for lack of these they possess the wonderful aroma of old wine and the magic charm of a pair of beautiful eyes gazing sadly into the distance.

When this attitude of mind that seeks for a purpose in all things is united with a strong will, with a large fund of energy (as is generally the case with the Jew), it ceases to be merely a point of view; it becomes a policy. The man sets himself a goal and makes for it, allowing nothing whatever to turn him aside from his course; he is determined, if you like, stiff-necked. Heine in characterizing his people called it stubbornness, and Goethe said that the essence of the Jewish character was energy and the pursuit of direct ends.

My next point is mobility, but I am not quite sure whether

this can be ascribed to all Jews or only to the Ashkenazi (German) Jews. Writers who have sung the praises of the Sephardim (Spanish Jews) always lay stress on a certain dignified air which they have, a certain superciliousness of bearing.[13] Their German brethren, on the other hand, have always been described as lively, active and somewhat excitable.[14] Even to-day you may meet with many Spanish Jews, especially in the Orient, who strike you as being dignified, thoughtful and self-restrained, who do not in the least appear to have that mobility, moral or physical, which is so often noticeable in European Jews. But mobility of mind—quick perception and mental versatility—all Jews possess.

These four elements, intellectuality, teleology, energy and mobility, are the corner-stones of Jewish character, so complicated in its nature. I believe that all the qualities of the Jew may be easily traced to one or more of these elements. Take two which are of special import in economic life—extreme activity and adaptability.

The Jew is active, or if you will, industrious. In the words of Goethe, "No Jew, not even the most insignificant, but is busy towards the achievement of some worldly, temporary or momentary aim." This activity often enough degenerates into restlessness. He must for ever be up and doing, for ever managing something and carrying it to fruition. He is always on the move, and does not care much if he makes himself a nuisance to those who would rest if they could. All musical and social "affairs" in our large towns are run by Jews. The Jew is the born trumpeter of progress and of its manifold blessings. And why? Because of his practical-mindedness and his mobility combined with his intellectuality. The last more especially, because it never strikes deep root. All intellectuality is in the long run shallowness; never does it allow of probing to the very roots of a matter, never of reaching down to the depths of the soul, or of the universe. Hence intellectuality makes it easy to go from one extreme to the other. That is why you find among Jews fanatical orthodoxy and unenlightened doubt side by side; they both spring from one source.

But to this shallow intellectuality the Jew owes perhaps the most valuable of his characteristics—his adaptability—which is unique in history. The Jews were always a stiffnecked people, and their adaptability no less than their capacity to maintain their national traits are both due to the one cause. Their adaptability enabled them to submit for the time being, if circumstances so demanded, to the laws of necessity, only to hark back to their wonted ways when better days came. From of old the Jewish character was at one and the same time resistant and submissive, and though these traits may appear contradictory they only seem so. As Leroy-Beaulieu well said, "The Jew is at once the most stubborn and the most pliant of men, the most self-willed and the most malleable."

The leaders and the "wise" men of the Jewish people were in all ages fully alive to the importance, nay the necessity, of this flexibility and elasticity, if Israel was to continue, and they were therefore never tired of insisting upon it. Jewish literature abounds in instances. "Be as pliant as the reed which the wind blows in this direction and in that, for the Torah can be observed only by him that is of a contrite spirit. Why is the Torah likened unto water? To tell you that just as water never flows up to the heights but rather runs down to the depths, so too the Torah does not abide with the haughty but only with the lowly."[15] Or again, "When the fox is in authority bow down before him."[16] Once more, "Bend before the wave and it passes over you; oppose it, and it will sweep you away."[17] Finally, a supplication from the Prayer Book runs as follows: "May my soul be as the dust to every one."

It was in this spirit that the Rabbis counselled their flocks to pretend to accept the dominant faiths in those countries where their existence depended on the renunciation of their own. The advice was followed to a large extent, and in the words of Fromer, "The Jewish race, by simulating death from time to time, was able to live on and on."

There are very few, if any, make-believe Christians or Moslems to-day. Nevertheless, the remarkable power of the Jew to adapt himself to his environment has more scope than ever. The Jew of Western Europe and America to-day no longer wishes to maintain his religion and his national character intact; on the contrary, he wishes, in so far as the nationalist spirit has not yet awakened in him, to lose his characteristics and to assimilate with the people in whose midst his lot happens to be cast. And lo, this too he can successfully achieve.

Perhaps the clearest illustration of the way in which Jewish traits manifest themselves is the fact that the Jew in England becomes like an Englishman, in France like a Frenchman, and so forth. And if he does not really become like an Englishman or a Frenchman, he appears to be like one. That a Felix Mendelssohn should write German music, that a Jacques Offenbach French and a Sousa Yankee-doodle; that Lord Beaconsfield should set up as an Englishman, Gambetta as a Frenchman, Lassalle as a German; in short, that Jewish talent should so often have nothing Jewish about it, but be in accord with its environment, has curiously enough again and again been urged as evidence that there are no specifically Jewish characteristics, whereas in truth it proves the very opposite in a striking fashion. It proves that the Jews have the gift of adaptability in an eminently high degree. The Jew might go from one planet to another, but his strangeness amid the new surroundings would not continue for long. He quickly feels his way and adapts himself with ease. He is German where he wants to be German, and Italian if that suits him better. He does everything and dabbles in everything, and with success. He can be a pure Magyar in Hungary, he can belong to the Irredenta in Italy, and be an anti-Semite in France (Drumont!). He is an adept in seizing upon anything which is still germinating, and bringing it with all speed to its full bloom.[18] All this his adaptability enables him to do.

I have already said that this peculiar capacity for adaptation is rooted in the four elements of the Jewish character. But perhaps the rationalism of the Jew is responsible for it to a greater degree than the other three. Because of his rationalism he is able to look at everything from without. If the Jew is anything, it is not because he must but because he determines to be so. Any convictions he may have do not spring from his inmost soul; they are formulated by his intellect. His standpoint is not on solid earth but an imaginary castle in the air. He is not organically original but mechanically rational. He lacks depth of feeling and strength of instinct. That is why he is what he is, but he can also be different. That Lord Beaconsfield was a Conservative was due to some accident or other, or some political conjuncture; but Stein and Bismarck and Carlyle were Conservatives because they could not help it; it was in their blood. Had Marx or Lassalle been born in another age, or in another environment, they might quite easily have become Conservatives instead of Radicals. As a matter of fact, Lassalle was already coquetting with the idea of becoming a reactionary, and no doubt he would have played the part of a Prussian Junker as brilliantly as that of socialist agitator.

The driving power in Jewish adaptability is of course the idea of a purpose, or a goal, as the end of all things. Once the Jew has made up his mind what line he will follow, the rest is comparatively easy, and his mobility only makes his success more sure.

How mobile the Jew can be is positively astounding. He is able to give himself the personal appearance he most desires. As in days of old through simulating death he was able to defend himself, so now by colour adaptation or other forms of mimicry. The best illustrations may be drawn from the United States, where the Jew of the second or third generation is with difficulty distinguished from the non-Jew. You can tell the German after no matter how many generations; so with the Irish, the Swede, the Slav. But the Jew, in so far as his racial physical features allow of it, has been successful in imitating the Yankee type, especially in regard to outward marks such as clothing, bearing and the peculiar method of hairdressing.

Easier still, on account of his mental and moral mobility, is it for the Jew to make the intellectual atmosphere of his environment his own. His mental mobility enables him quickly to seize upon the "tone" of any circle, quickly to notice what it is that matters, quickly to feel his way into things. And his moral mobility? That helps him to remove troublesome hindrances, either ethical or æsthetical, from his path. And he can do this with all the more facility because he has only to a small degree what may be termed personal dignity.

It means little to him to be untrue to himself, if it is a question of attaining the wished-for goal.

Is this picture faithful of life? The obvious adaptability of the Jew to the changing conditions of the struggle for existence is surely proof enough. But there is further proof in some of the special gifts which Jews possess. I refer to their undoubted talent for journalism, for the Bar, for the stage, and all of it is traceable to their adaptability.

Adolf Jellinek, in the book we have referred to more than once, has drawn a clever little sketch showing the connexion between the two. "The journalist," he says, "must be quick, mobile, lively, enthusiastic, able to analyze quickly and as quickly to put two and two together; must be able to enter *in medias res*, to have the gist of any question of the day or the central fact of a debate in his mind's eye; must be able to deal with his subject in clear and well-marked outlines, to describe it epigrammatically, antithetically, sententiously, in short arresting sentences, to breathe life into it by means of a certain amount of pathos, to give it colour by means of esprit, to make it spicy by means of seasoning." Are not all these Jewish traits?

The actor's calling, no less than the barrister's, depends for success on his ability to place himself quickly in a strange world of ideas, to take a right view of men and conditions without much difficulty, to form a correct estimate of them and to use them for his own end. The Jew's gift of subjectivity stands him here in good stead, for by its aid he can easily put himself in the position of another, take thought for him and defend him. To be sure, jurisprudence is the bulk of the contents of Jewish literature!

Jewish Characteristics as Applied to Capitalism

Now comes the question, how and in what way did the Jewish characteristics enable Jews to become financiers and speculators, indeed, to engage as successfully in economic activities within the framework of the capitalistic system as to be mathematicians, statisticians, physicians, journalists, actors and advocates? To what extent, that is, does a special talent for capitalistic enterprise spring from the elements in the Jewish character?

Speaking generally, we may say in this connexion what we have already remarked about capitalism and the Jewish religion, that the fundamental ideas of capitalism and those of the Jewish character show a singular similarity. Hence we have the triple parallelism between Jewish character, the Jewish religion and capitalism. What was it we found as the all-controlling trait of the Jewish people? Was it not extreme intellectuality? And is not intellectuality the quality which differentiates the capitalistic system from all others? Organizing ability springs from intellectuality, and in the capitalistic system we find the separation between head and hands, between the work of directing and that of manufacturing. "For the greatest work to be completely done, you need of hands a thousand, of mind but only one." That sums up the capitalistic state of things.

The purest form of capitalism is that wherein abstract ideas are most clearly expressed. That they are part and parcel of the Jewish character we have already seen; there is no occasion to labour the close kinship in this respect between capitalism and the Jew. Again, the quality of abstraction in capitalism manifests itself in the substitution of all qualitative differences by merely quantitative ones (value in exchange). Before capitalism came, exchange was a many-sided, multi-coloured and technical process; now it is just one specialized act—that of the dealer: before there were many relationships between buyer and seller; there is only one now—the commercial. The tendency of capitalism has been to do away with different manners, customs, pretty local and national contrasts, and to set up in their stead the dead level of the cosmopolitan town. In short, there has been a tendency towards uniformity, and in this capitalism and Liberalism have much in common. Liberalism we have already shown to be a near relative of Judaism, and so we have the kindred trio of Capitalism, Liberalism, and Judaism.

How is the inner resemblance between the first and the last best manifested? Is it not through the agency of money, by means of which capitalism succeeds so well in its policy of bringing about a drab uniformity? Money is the common denominator, in terms of which all values are expressed; at the same time it is the be-all and end-all of economic activity in a capitalistic system. Hence one of the conspicuous things in such a system is success. Is it otherwise with the Jew? Does he not also make the increase of capital his chief aim? And not only because the abstractness of capital is congenial to the soul of the Jew, but also because the great regard in which (in the capitalistic system) money is held strikes another sympathetic note in the Jewish character—its teleology. Gold becomes the great means, and its value arises from the fact that you can utilize it for many ends. It needs but little skill to show that a nature intent on working towards some goal should feel itself drawn to something which has value only because it is a means to an end. Moreover, the teleology of the Jew brings it about that he prizes success. (Another point of similarity, therefore, with capitalism.) Because he rates success so highly he sacrifices to-day for to-morrow, and his mobility only helps him to do it all the better. Here again we may observe a likeness to capitalism. Capitalism is constantly on the look-out for something new, for some way of expanding, for abstaining to-day for the sake of to-morrow. Think of our whole system of credit. Does not this characteristic show itself there clearly enough? Now remember also that the Jews were very much at home in the organization of credit—in which values or services which may, or can, become effective some time in the future are made available to-day. Human thought can plainly picture future experiences and future needs, and credit offers the opportunity through present economic activities of producing future values. That credit is extensively found in modern life scarcely requires pointing out. The reason too is obvious: it offers golden chances. True, we must give up the joys that spring from "completely throwing ourselves into the present."[19] But what of that? The Jewish character and capitalism have one more point in common—practical rationalism, by which I mean the shaping of all activities in accordance with reason.

To make the whole parallelism even more plain, let me illustrate it by concrete instances. The Jew is well fitted for the part of undertaker because of his strength of will and his habit of making for some goal or other. His intellectual mobility is accountable for his readiness to discover new methods of production and new possibilities of marketing. He is an adept at forming new organizations, and in these his peculiar capacity for finding out what a man is best fitted for stands him in good stead. And since in the world of capitalism there is nothing organic or natural but only what is mechanical or artificial, the Jew's lack of understanding of the former is of no consequence. Even undertaking on a large scale is itself artificial and mechanical; you may extend a concern or contract it; you may change it according to circumstances. That is why Jews are so successful as organizers of large capitalistic undertakings. Again, the Jew can easily grasp impersonal relationships. We have already noted that he has the feeling of personal dependence only in a slight measure. Hence, he does not care for your hoary "patriarchalism," and pays little attention to the dash of sentimentality which is still sometimes found in labour contracts. In all relations between sellers and buyers, and between employers and employed, he reduces everything to the legal and purely business basis. In the struggle of the workers to obtain collective agreements between themselves and the masters, which shall regulate the conditions of their labour, the Jew is almost invariably on the side of the first.

But if the Jew is well fitted to be an undertaker, still more is he cut out for the part of the trader. His qualities in this respect are almost innumerable.

The trader lives in figures, and in figures the Jew has always been in his element. His love of the abstract has made calculation easy for him; it is his strong point. Now a calculating talent combined with a capacity for working always with some aim in view has already won half the battle for the trader. He is enabled to weigh aright the chances, the possibilities and the advantages of any given situation, to eliminate everything that is useless, and to appraise the whole in terms of figures. Give this sober calculator a strong dose of imagination and you have the perfect speculator before you. To take stock of any given state of things with lightning speed, to see a thousand eventualities, to seize upon the most valuable and to act in accordance with that—such, as we have already pointed out, is the aim of the dealer. For all this the Jew has the necessary gifts of mind. I should like expressly to emphasize the close kinship between the activities of the clever speculator and those of the clever physician who can successfully diagnose a disease. The Jew, because of his qualities, is eminently fitted for both.

A good dealer must be a good negotiator. What cleverer negotiators are there than the Jews, whose ability in this direction has long been recognized and utilized? To adapt yourself to the needs of a market, to meet any specified form of demand, is the one prime essential for the dealer. That the Jew with his adaptability can do this as well as any other is obvious. The second is the power of suggestion, and in this also the Jew is well qualified by his ability to think himself into the situation of another.

Wherever we look the conclusion forces itself upon us that the combination of no other set of qualities is so well fitted, as are those of the Jew, for realizing the best capitalistic results. There is no need for me to take the parallelism further; the intelligent reader can easily do so for himself. I would only direct his attention to one point more before leaving the subject—the parallel between the feverish restlessness of Stock Exchange business, always intent on upsetting the tendency towards an equilibrium, and the restless nature of the Jew.

In another place I have sought to characterize the ideal undertaker in three words—he must be wide-awake, clever and resourceful. Wide-awake: that is to say, quick of comprehension, sure in judgment, must think twice before speaking once, and be able to seize upon the right moment.

Clever: that is to say, he must possess a knowledge of the world, must be certain of himself in his judgment and in his treatment of men, certain in his judgment on a given conjuncture; and above all, acquainted with the weaknesses and mistakes of those around him.

Resourceful: that is to say, full of ideas.

The capitalistic undertaker must have three additional qualities: he must be active, sober and thorough. By sober, I mean free from passion, from sentiment, from unpractical idealism. By thorough, I mean reliable, conscientious, orderly, neat and frugal.

I believe this rough sketch will, in broad outline, stand for the capitalistic undertaker no less than for the Jew.

Chapter 13

The Race Problem

Prefatory Note

STRICTLY SPEAKING the task I had set myself has now been completed. I have tried to show the importance of the Jews in modern economic life in all its aspects, and the connexion between Capitalism and "Jewishness." In other words, I have endeavoured to point out why it was that the Jews have been able to play, and still continue to play, so significant a part in economic life; endeavoured to show that their great achievements were due partly to objective circumstances, and partly to their inherent characteristics.

But here new questions crop up in plenty, and I must not pass them by unanswered, if I desire my most valued readers may not lay aside my book with a feeling of dissatisfaction. It is obvious that any one who has accompanied me to the point where I maintain that specifically Jewish characteristics exist, and that they will account for the great influence of the Jews in the body economic, must be bound to ask, What is the true nature of these characteristics? How have they come about? What will their ultimate effect be?

The answers to these questions may vary considerably. The Jewish characteristics we have noted may be nothing else but, as it were, a function without a corresponding organism; may be only surface phenomena, skin-deep, without any root at all in the human beings that give expression to them; may be but as a feather on a coat—easily blown away; something which vanishes with the disappearance of the person.

Or they may become hardened into a habit and be deep-seated, but yet not sufficiently powerful to be hereditary. Contrariwise, they may be so marked as to pass from one generation to another. In this case, the question presents itself, when did they arise? Were these characteristics always in the Jew, were they in his blood, or have they only been acquired in the course of his history—either in what is termed ancient times, or later? Again, all hereditary qualities may last for ever, or be only a temporary nature—may be, that is, permanent or only transient. Seeing that we are dealing with a social group, it will be necessary here, too, to answer the question, Is the group a racial entity? In a word, are the Jews a subdivision of mankind, differing by blood-kinship from other people? Finally, in a problem of this sort we must deal with the possibility that the peculiar characteristics of the group may be due to admixtures with other groups, or to selection within the group itself.

The problem is many-sided: of that there can be little doubt. And the worst of it is that modern science can give no certain replies to the questions propounded. Attempts have of course been made, but they are not without prejudice, and any one even only superficially acquainted with the subject will be faced by more problems and puzzles than by solutions.

The most pressing need of the moment, so it seems to me—one which alone will be able to withdraw the Jewish Problem from the semi-darkness in which it is enshrouded —is to obtain a clear conception of the questions at issue, and to bring some order into the abundant material at hand. It is almost as though at the point where the general Jewish Question intersects the race problem, a thousand devils had been let loose to confuse the mind of men. As one authority[1] recently urged with regard to the doctrines of heredity: what is most needed is an exact precision concerning elementals. The same is the case to an enormous extent with the question of whether the Jews are a race or not, and perhaps an outsider may contribute something to this end, just because he stands apart from the specialists. This thought emboldens me to attempt to give a résumé of all that is current to-day regarding Jews as a race—of all that is certain, and of the thousand and one theories, to say nothing of the numerous false hypotheses.

The Anthropology of the Jews

Touching the origin of the Jews and their anthropology and ethnology, opinions at the present day are pretty well agreed as to the essential facts. It is generally assumed[2] that Israel, like Judah, arose from the admixture of different Oriental peoples. When, in the 15th century B.C., the Hebrews, then a Bedouin tribe, wished to settle in Palestine they found there an old population long since established—Canaanites, who were probably hegemonic, Hittites, Perizites, Hivites and Jebusites (Judg. iii. 5). Recent research has come to the conclusion, opposed to the older view, that the Israelitish clans largely intermarried with these peoples.

Later, when a portion of the population went into the Babylonian Exile, the admixture of races continued in Palestine. And as for the exiles (whose history in this connexion is of vital importance), we learn much from the latest cuneiform inscriptions concerning their attitude toward intermarriage. The inscriptions show, "without doubt," that there was a gradual fusion between the Jews and the Babylonians. The immigrants called their children by Babylonian names, and the Babylonians theirs by Persian, Hebrew and Aramaic names.[3]

Nothing like so clear are the views as to the relationship to each other of the peoples and clans of which the Jews were composed; still less as to how they can be distinguished from other similar groups; and least of all how they are to be called. A very heated controversy has recently raged about the term "Semites," with the result that in anthropological circles the word is no longer used. The Semite controversy, like that on the Aryans, only shows how vicious it is to allow linguistic concepts to interfere in the anthropological divisions of mankind. It is generally accepted that the Semites are all those peoples whose speech is Semitic, but that anthropologically they belong to different and differing groups.[4]

My own view is that the controversy as to the exact demarcation of the civilized Oriental peoples is a little futile. Nor does our ignorance on this point much matter. One thing however is certain—that all of them, the Egyptians, the Babylonians, the Assyrians, the Phœnicians and the Jews, by virtue of their origin and earliest history, belong to one class, which may perhaps be termed "Desert" or "Desert-edge" Peoples. The assumption that a fair, blue-eyed tribe from the North intermingled with these is now almost unanimously regarded as a fable. The theory of the ubiquity of the Germans[5] will have to be but coldly entertained as long as no more convincing proofs are forthcoming than the reddish hair of Saul, or the dolichocephalic skull of the mummy of Rameses II.

What, then, was the anthropological history of the group of peoples in which the Jews originated? A common answer as regards the Jews was that they continued to mix with their non-Jewish neighbours in the Diaspora as they had done before. Renan, Loeb, Neubauer and others believe that the modern Jews are in large measure the descendants of heathen proselytes in the Hellenistic Age, or of marriages between Jews and non-Jews in the early centuries of the Common Era. The existence of fair Jews (to the extent of 13 per cent.), especially in Eastern Europe, lent probability to this opinion. But to-day, so far as I can make out, the entirely opposite view generally prevails—that from the days of Ezra to these the Jews have kept strictly apart. For more than two thousand years they have been untouched by other peoples; they have remained ethnically pure. That drops of alien blood came into the Jewish body corporate through the long centuries of their dispersion no one will deny. But so small have these outside elements been that they have not influenced to any appreciable degree the ethnical purity of the Jewish people.

It seems pretty clear now that in the past the number of proselytes admitted into Judaism was considerably over-estimated. There is no doubt that in the Hellenistic and early Christian periods Judaism won adherents among the heathen peoples. (The subsequent centuries were of no consequence at all, with the exception of one case only.) Both the Roman and the Jewish Law made provision for such converts. But we may assume with certainty that all of them were the so-called "Proselytes of the Gate"—that is, they worshipped God in accordance with Jewish teaching, but they were not circumcised, nor were they allowed to marry Jewesses. Nearly all of them eventually drifted into Christianity. As a matter of fact, in the time of Pius circumcision was again allowed to the Jews, but the rite was expressly forbidden to be performed on proselytes. In this way conversion to Judaism was made a punishable offence. This in all probability was not the intention of the framers of the prohibition, but its effect was soon recognized, and it was extended.[6] For Severus "forbade conversion to Judaism on pain of grave penalties."

But even if we allow foreign admixtures among the Jews in the early Christian Age, it could never have amounted to very much when we think of the millions of Jews who presumably existed at the time, and anyhow the stranger elements came from peoples closely akin to the Jews.

As for the centuries that followed the entry of the Jews into European history, we may take it that proselytizing ceased almost entirely. Throughout the Middle Ages therefore the Jews received but little of non-Jewish blood. The remarkable conversion of the Chozars in the 8th century cannot be regarded as an exception to this statement, for their realm was never very extensive. In the 10th century it was limited to a very small area in the western part of the Crimea, and in the 11th the tiny Jewish State disappeared altogether. Only a small remnant of the Chozars live in Kieff as Karaites. Hence, even if the whole of the Chozars professed Judaism, the ethnical purity of the Jews could have been affected but little. As a matter of fact, however, it is very doubtful whether any others than the ruling family, or the upper classes, became Jews.[7]

Mixed marriages thus remain as the only possible source whence Jewish blood might be made impure. Certainly marriages between Jews and non-Jews must have occurred in some periods of Jewish history. Mixed marriages were probably numerous—a not extravagant assumption—in those epochs in which the band of Jewish solidarity was somewhat loosened—say, the last pre-Christian century, or the 12th and 13th in Spain. Even so, such relaxations never lasted for any considerable time; Jewish orthodoxy soon regained the upper hand, to the exclusion of non-Jews. What the Pharisees achieved in the first-named period resulted in the second from the Maimonides schism, and this had such reactionary consequences that marriages with Christian and Mohammedan women were annulled.[8]

But there are indications that such marriages were to be found. They were expressly forbidden at the early Spanish Councils. For instance, the 16th Canon of the Council of Elovia (304) provides that "the daughters of Catholics shall not be given in marriage to heretics, except they return to the Church. The same applies to Jews and schismatics." The 64th Canon of the Third Council of Toledo (589) forbids Jews to have Christian women either as wives or mistresses; and if any children spring from such unions they must be baptized. Once more, the 63rd Canon of the Fourth Council of Toledo (633) makes it incumbent upon Jews who have Christian wives to accept Christianity if they wish to continue to live with them.[9] It seems hardly likely, however, that marriages against which these canons were issued were very numerous. And anyhow, as the children of such marriages were lost to Judaism, Jewish racial purity could not have suffered much by them.

Similarly, it is improbable that there was any admixture of Jews with the Northern peoples. There was an opinion current that the Jews in Germany up to the time of the Crusades lived among their Christian neighbours, and had free intercourse with them in every direction. But this view is hardly credible, and Brann, one of the best authorities on German Jewish history, has declared the assumption of even the least degree of assimilation at this period to be "an airy fancy, which must vanish into nothingness when the inner life of the Jews of those days is understood."[10]

There remain the fair Jews. They have been regarded as

a proof of Jewish admixture with the fair races of the North. But no scholar of repute looks upon these as the outcome of legitimate unions between Jews and their Slav neighbours. On the other hand, one hypothesis[11] has found credence— that the fair Jews are the children of illegitimate unions between Jews and Russians, either in the ordinary way or forcibly on the occasion of pogroms. But the weakness of this assumption is obvious. Even if it did explain the existence of fair Jews in Russia, it would be of no use at all for accounting for fair Jews in Germany, in Southern lands, in North Africa and in Palestine.

There is really no necessity to look for an explanation of the fair Jews in the admixture of races. All dark peoples produce a number of variants, and this is a case in point.[12]

We come back then to the fact that for some twenty centuries the Jews have kept themselves ethnically pure. One proof of this is found in the similarity of the anthropological characteristics of the Jews all over the globe, and, moreover, in that the similarity has been remarkably constant through the centuries. "Differences in treatment or environment have not been able to blur a common type, and the Jews more than any other race stand as a proof that the influence of heredity is much more powerful than that of environment" (E. Auerbach).

The anthropological homogeneity of the Jewish stock at the present time has been established by numerous anatomical experiments and measurements.[13] The only doubtful question is whether the ancient contrast between Ashkenazim [German Jews] and Sephardim [Spanish Jews] extends to their anthropology. There are two conflicting opinions on the subject,[14] but I believe the basis of either is not sufficiently conclusive to justify an independent judgment. It must be added, though, that personal observation would seem to warrant the belief that there was some anthropological difference between the two. Look at your spare, elegant Spanish Jew, with his small hands and feet and his thin, hooked nose, and then at his German brother, stout and bow-legged, with his broad, fleshy Hittite nose. Do they not appear as two distinct types to the ordinary observer? There is as yet no scientific ground to explain the difference.

Another controversial argument is whether the Jews of to-day are a separate entity, distinct from their neighbours physiologically and pathologically. There can be no doubt that from this point of view Jews do exhibit certain peculiarities in many respects—early puberty, little liability to cancer, especially cancer of the womb, strong disposition for diabetes, insanity, and so forth. There are people, however, who cannot look upon these things as physiological and pathological Jewish traits, but explain them as resultants of the social position of the Jews, of their religious practices, and so on.[15] Here also the ground has not been sufficiently prepared to warrant a definite statement.

It is different with the physiognomy of the Jew. Physiognomy, as is well known, is the outcome of two causes—of certain facial forms and of their particular expression. You cannot weigh or measure either, and therefore this is a matter that must be left entirely to common observation. Now, just as the colour-blind distinguish no colours, so those who cannot see differences in men's faces know nothing of physiognomy. When, therefore, some writers[16] say that in the case of three-quarters of cultivated and wealthy Jews they cannot with certainty tell that they are Jews merely from their faces, then there is nothing to urge in reply. But a keen observer will most decidedly be able to tell. Jewish physiognomy is still a reality, and few will deny it. Undoubtedly there are individuals among Jews who do not look one whit Jewish. But there are also very many individuals among Gentiles who look very Jewish. I should not like to go so far as some do,[17] and say that the Hapsburgs because of their heavy lips, or the Louis of France because of their hooked noses, were Jewish-looking. But among Oriental peoples (including possibly the Japanese) we do come across Jewish types. This in no wise detracts from the anthropological unity of the Jews. If it proves anything, it only points to a common origin of the Jews and the Oriental peoples. (It might be mentioned, by the way, that the lost Ten Tribes have been located in

Japan—a somewhat fantastic conjecture, but having something in its favour in the striking similarity of the Japanese and Jewish types.) To consider the Jewish physiognomy as an expression of decadence, or to account for it, as Ripley does, as a result of Ghetto life, is not very conclusive in face of the undeniable Jewish types depicted on the monuments of ancient Egypt and Babylonia. Look at the picture of Jewish captives in the epoch of Shishak (973 B.C.), or of the Jewish ambassadors at the court of Salmanasar[18] (884 B.C.), and you will be convinced that from those days to our own, a period of nearly three thousand years, few changes have marked the Jewish type of countenance. This is but another proof of the proposition that the Jewish stock is an anthropological entity, and that its characteristics have been constant through the ages in a most extraordinary fashion.

The Jewish "Race"

In view of all this, may we speak of a Jewish race? The answer would depend on the connotation of the word "race." But to define it is not easy, for there are probably as many definitions as there are writers on it.[19] It is, of course, open to any one to say, Such and such things I look upon as the mark of race, and if I apply my standard the Jews are or are not a race, as the case may be. But a procedure of this kind is more of the nature of a game. What is needed is a scientific definition. But how? Many methods have been tried —anthropological differences, skull measurements, biological experiments and their application—but all with no absolute result. It would, however, be a fallacy to conclude that because hitherto no satisfactory classification of the human species has been achieved, therefore no anthropological differences really exist. An Eskimo *is* different from a Negro, and the South Italian from the Norwegian. We do not require anthropology to tell us that.

So with the Jews. It may be difficult to class them, but anthropological peculiarities of their own they surely have. When therefore one distinguished scholar[20] writes: "I recognize only a Jewish religious community; of a Jewish race

I know nothing," we must regard it as a hasty expression uttered in the heat of the moment. The objection to it is that we can easily place a "Jewish national community" with a common history beside the "Jewish religious community."

So with anthropological characteristics which mark off the Jew from the non-Jew. I am firmly of opinion that the Jews, no matter where they may be found, are an anthropological group differing from, let us say, the Swede or the negro. "A religious community" will not suffice.

After all, is it not a controversy about words? Some will have it that there is no Jewish race. Well and good. But they admit Jewish anthropological peculiarities. It is a thousand pities that there is no satisfactory term by which to describe them. "A people" will not serve, for the definitions of "people" are no less numerous than those of "race." But what does the name matter? The thing certainly is there, and I should have no hesitation in speaking of the Jewish race, or, if you will, of the Jewish "race."

Let me conclude this section with one or two wise words written by Arthur Ruppin,[21] that excellent authority on the Jew, words that appear to me to be among the best that have been uttered on the subject: "The term 'race' should not be stretched too far. If we include in it such groups as developed their special anthropological characteristics in prehistoric times, and have since kept themselves without admixture with other groups, then in reality there are no 'races' among white-skinned peoples, seeing that all of them have intermingled over and over again. As for the Jews, whether they had common racial features in prehistoric times and have preserved them through the centuries, is a detail of no great significance. What does matter is this—that it is certain that those who professed the Jewish religion formed a well-defined group distinct from their surroundings, even as late as the end of the 18th century, after many generations of strict avoidance of marriage with non-Jews. The community which has descended from this group may be called, for lack of a better name, a race, more particularly, 'the Jewish race.' "

How the Jewish Genius Remained Constant

The question of greatest interest in these anthropological considerations is to discover whether any connexion exists between the somatic characteristics of the Jew and his intellectual qualities. We want to make sure whether the latter are in his blood, so to say, *i.e.*, whether they are racial or no. To discover this it will be necessary to see whether the characteristics we have observed in modern Jews were to be found among Jews in ancient times also; whether they reach back to their earliest history, or whether they appeared at a later date, and if so, when.

The result will be that we shall observe that Jewish intellectual qualities have remained constant, that certain characteristics, certain peculiar features of the Jewish soul may be traced as far back as the formation of the Jewish ethnical group. We cannot prove all this directly, because we have no reliable accounts of the Jewish popular character dating from early times. What we do possess are brief and scanty expressions of opinions, valuable, however, as far as they go. It is of great interest, for example, to note that the Pentateuch (in four places—Exod. xxxii. 9, xxxiv. 9; Deut. ix. 13 and 27) asserts of the Jews what Tacitus said of them later —that they are a stiffnecked people. No less interesting is Cicero's statement that they hang together most fraternally, or Marcus Aurelius's that they are a restless people, to whom he cries, "O ye Marcomanni, O ye Quadi, O ye Sarmatæ, at length have I found a race more restless than you!"; or finally Juan de la Huarte's that their intellect is keen and well fitted for worldly things.

The first point to note is:—

(1) The attitude of the Jews to the peoples among whom they dwelt all through the Diaspora. In the last century or so we have seen this to be one of aloofness. Before capitalism came and set them free, Jews were looked upon as "strangers," as "semi-citizens." They were hated and persecuted in all lands, but everywhere they knew how to preserve and maintain themselves.

274 / The Origin of the Jewish Genius

How was it in antiquity? How later? The same spectacle confronts us, ever since the Jews came into contact with other peoples. Everywhere there was opposition, persecution and ill-treatment. To begin with the Egyptians: "They abhorred the children of Israel" (Exod. i. 12). Paul of Tarsus went so far as to say that the Jews "were contrary to all men" (1 Thess. ii. 15). In the Hellenistic period, in Imperial Rome —the same story of hate and plunder and death. Philo and Josephus both record dreadful Jewish pogroms in Alexandria in the first century of our era. "Hatred of the Jew and ill-treatment of him are as old as the Diaspora itself" (Mommsen).

Under the Cæsars their lot was no different: "I am just sick of these filthy, noisy Jews," said Marcus Aurelius. Then, in the time of Theodoric, massacres and wholesale plundering were the order of the day, as later in the 7th century under the Longobards. And the East was like the West; the 6th century in Babylon was as dark as the 7th in Northern Italy. Even in the Pyrenean Peninsula, where they enjoyed much that was good, the end was bitter: Christian and Moslem both laid hands upon them.

These instances might be multiplied. They are all expressions of hatred of the Jew in Christian and non-Christian environments alike. Can the phenomenon be explained without the assumption of the existence of Jewish characteristics, which remained constant no matter where the Jew was placed? The answer must surely be in the affirmative. The hatred of the Jew could not have been the result of a passing mood on the part of all these peoples.

Then again, everywhere and at all times the Jews were semi-citizens. Sometimes indeed they were not in this category because the law placed them there. On the contrary. There were many cases in antiquity where Jews were assigned privileged positions, by virtue of which they were excused certain duties of the citizen (e.g., military service), or had exceptional advantages in regard to legal enactments. Nevertheless they took no full share in the life of the State in which they were domiciled. The Greek inhabitants of Cæsarea, a city on Jewish soil and built under Jewish rule, denied citizen rights to the Jews, and Burnus, Nero's minister, upheld their decision.[22] There was little change in this respect during the Middle Ages.

How are we to account for this generally prevailing treatment? Differing States adopted a similar policy towards the Jew: does it not seem clear that it was due to some special characteristic of his? If you like, say it was the strict adherence to the letter of the Jewish religion. But something it must have been.

And yet, despite all oppression, the Jew was not crushed. He knew how to maintain himself from the oldest times onward. Perhaps it was because of the curious mixture of stubbornness and elasticity which we have noted in Jews of modern days. They might be crushed never so relentlessly, but like a Jack-in-the-box they were soon up again. How they withstood the onslaught of the Roman Emperors, who used all the weapons at their command to stamp them out! Despite their efforts, there was again in the 3rd century a Patriarch at Jerusalem recognized by the government, with a jurisdiction of his own. In antiquity, in the Middle Ages, in this our own time, the peoples have summed up their judgment of the Jew in the one word—stubborn: *"ostinato come un ebreo."*

The peculiar mixture of determination and elasticity is most wonderfully exhibited by the Jews in their bearing towards governments, where their religion was concerned. To it they owed most of their enemies; because of it they suffered hardships untold. Yet they would not give up their beloved faith. And when pressure was severe, many Jews pretended to have forsworn their religion only to be able to carry out its precepts in secret. We know of this conduct in connexion with the Marannos, but it is as old as the Diaspora itself. When you read of the thousands of crypto-Jewish heathens, crypto-Jewish Mohammedans, crypto-Jewish Christians, you are astounded at this unique event in human history. The more so as it was the most religious Jews, teachers and leaders, who had recourse to the sham conversions in order to save their lives. Recall the case of R. Eleazar ben Parta, who was active under Hadrian as a pretended heathen;[23] that of Ismael ibn Negrela, who, as R. Samuel, held discourses on the Talmud and answered questions of religious practice, and as Vizier of the Mohammedan King Habus, began his master's ordinances with the formula *Chamdu-l-Illahi* and ended them with urging those to whom they were addressed to live according to the laws of Islam;[24] that of the great Maimonides, who sought to give excellent reasons for his pretended conversion to Mohammedanism;[25] that of Sabbatti Zevi, the false Messiah, who though he acknowledged Mahomet yet did not lose the respect of his followers; that of the Neapolitan Jew Basilus, who made a pretence of having his sons baptized in order to be able to carry on the trade in slaves under their name,[26] since this branch of commerce was forbidden the Jews; that of the thousands and thousands of Marannos who, after the expulsion of the Jews from the Pyrenean Peninsula, appeared to all the world as Christians and returned to the faith of their fathers at the very first opportunity that presented itself. What remarkable people must these have been who combined such determination with such elasticity!

We have thus noted that many Jewish characteristics developed to their fullest in the Diaspora. But

(2) Is the Diaspora itself explicable as a result of only outward circumstances? Does it not itself rather bear witness to special characteristics? Or to put the question somewhat differently, would it have been possible to scatter any other people over the face of the earth as the Jews were scattered?

The experience of exile the Jews tasted in quite early days. Most people have heard of Tiglath-Pileser, who dragged a part of the Jewish population to Media and Assyria; of the later Babylonian Exile; of Ptolemy Lagi, who forced very many Jews to settle in Egypt and planted a Jewish colony in Cyrene; of Antiochus the Great, who brought two thousand Jewish families from Babylon and peopled with them the centre of Asia Minor, Phrygia and Lydia. Mommsen calls the settlement of Jews outside Palestine "an invention of Alexander or of his generals."

In all these cases the temptation is strong to ascribe the dispersion of the Jews to outward circumstances, seeing that in most of the cases the Jews were carried away from their homes against their will. There appears to be nothing therefore in these dispersions that would point to inherent Jewish characteristics. Such a conclusion would be hasty. Is there not this possibility—that if the Jews had not possessed certain qualities they might never have been transplanted? The enforced settlements must have had some purpose. Either they were beneficial to the land from which the Jews were taken, or (what was more probable) to the land or the town where they were settled. Either they were feared in their own country as firebrands of sedition, or they were accounted such valuable citizens for their wealth or their industry that they were made the nucleus of new settlements, or they were held to be so trusty that they were utilized by rulers to strengthen their hold on turbulent centres (as was done by Ptolemy Lagi in Cyrene).

But many Jews may have forsaken Palestine for what might be termed economic reasons: there was not sufficient room for the maintenance of an increasing population. Considering the size and the productiveness of Palestine, emigration on these grounds must have been of frequent occurrence. But this points to a national characteristic—viz., an increasing population due, as is known, to physiological and psychological causes alike. Furthermore, that economic pressure led to emigration was traceable to another national peculiarity. In this respect the Jews have been compared to the Swiss. They, too, leave their homes because the country is unable efficiently to maintain them all. But they only emigrate because they have the energy and the determination to do better for themselves. The Hindoo does not emigrate. If the population increases, he is content with his smaller portion of rice.

But to regard all Jewish dispersion as enforced is probably one-sided. We cannot possibly explain so general a phenomenon, which moreover remains the same through the ages, without assuming a voluntary migration. What precisely this was due to—whether to a migrative instinct, or to inability to remain on one piece of soil for long—does not much matter. But some special characteristic will have to be associated with this people to account for their travelling so easily from land to land, no less than for their settlement in large cities, a proclivity shown by the Jews already in very early times. Herzfeld, who has compiled probably the most complete list of Jewish settlements in the Hellenistic Age, draws attention to the striking fact that of the settlements 52 are in towns, and of these 39 were wealthy commercial centres.[27]

It would appear from all this that Jewish characteristics were by no means developed in the Diaspora, or as the Jewish historians assume, in the Middle Ages, but that the Diaspora itself was the result of these characteristics. The characteristics were there first, at least in embryo.

(3) So, too, with their religion. When it is asserted that the Jew of to-day is a product of his religion, that he has been made what he is, almost artificially, by means of a well thought-out policy of some man or group of men, and not organically, I am ready to admit the statement. My own presentation of this very subject in a previous chapter attempted to show what enormous influence the Jewish religion had, more especially on the economic activity of the Jew. But I want to oppose the view promulgated by H. S. Chamberlain with all my power. I want to make it clear that the religion of the Jew would have been impossible but for the special characteristics of the Jew. The fact that some man, or group of men, was able to give expression to such wonderful thoughts necessarily postulates that the individual or the group was specially gifted. Again, that the whole people should accept their teachings not merely by way of lip-service, but with deep and sincere inwardness—can we explain this except by the supposition of special national characteristics? To-day we can no longer free ourselves from the opinion that every people has, in the long run, the religion best suited for it, and that if it adopts another religion it keeps on changing it to suit it to its needs.

I believe, therefore, that we may deduce the special characteristics of the Jewish people from the special characteristics of the Jewish religion. From this standpoint many traits of the Jewish character adduced from Jewish legends may be placed very far back, certainly as early as the Babylonian Exile. That I shall proceed in this as the authors of anti-Semitic catechisms do, and infer from the somewhat questionable story of Isaac, Jacob and Esau, and their cheating of each other, a tendency on the part of the Jews for swindling, need not be feared. No one, I hope, will think so badly of me. Cheating is an element found in all mythologies. We need only cast our eyes on Olympus or Valhalla to see the gods cheating and swindling each other in the most shameless fashion. No. What I mean is that the fundamental characteristics of the Jewish religious system which we have already examined—Intellectuality, Rationalism, Teleology—are also the characteristics of the Jewish people, and they must have been in existence (I would repeat, at least in embryo) even before the religion was developed.

(4) My next point is the remarkable similarity in the economic activities of the Jews throughout almost all the centuries of history. In asserting that this is a proof that Jewish characteristics were constant, I am setting myself in opposition to the prevailing views. I differ not only from those who believe that the economic activities of the Jews have changed in the course of time, but also from those who agree with me that it was a constant factor in their development. From the latter I differ because we do no agree as to what those activities were.

What is the generally accepted view of Jewish economic history? I believe it may be traced to Heine, and is something to this effect. Originally the Jews were an agricultural people. Even in the Diaspora, it is said, the Jews tilled the soil, avoiding all other pursuits. But in the 6th and 7th centuries of our era they were forced to sell their holdings and had, willy-nilly, to look out for other means of livelihood. What did they do? They devoted themselves to trade, and for something like five centuries continued in this calling. Again Fate pressed heavily upon them, for the Crusades engendered much anti-Jewish feeling in commercial circles, and the growing trading

class in each country organized themselves into gilds, and
excluded the Jews from the markets, which they retained as
the exclusive preserves of members of their corporations.
Once more the Jews had to cast about for new occupations.
All channels were closed to them; the only possibility left was
to become money-lenders. So they became money-lenders,
and before long enjoyed privileges as such because the usury
laws meted out special treatment to them.

Such is the almost semi-official view prevalent in Jewish
circles, certainly among assimilationists, but also among a
goodly number of Jewish nationalists.

There is another view to which some historians, Jewish
and Gentile (among the former Herzfeld), have given currency. It is that the Jews have always been a commercial
people, from the age of King Solomon onwards, throughout
the Diaspora, down to our own times.

I regard both views as wrong, certainly as one-sided, and
I hope to give my reasons in a sketch of the economic history
of the Jews which I shall furnish.

From the period of the Kings to the end of the national
independence—we may even say up to the codification of
the Talmud—the Jewish people were a self-contained, self-
sufficing economic unit. Its surplus commodities it sent to
foreign lands, and its constituent units produced all they
needed, or at best, supplemented their own work by simple
bartering with their neighbours. We should describe the
whole by saying that we had here single economic units satisfying their own wants, with which was connected a certain
amount of hired labour; there was something of the nature
of the manorial system, and there were some handicrafts.
Where these are found little trade is possible. But how about
the numerous merchants in Palestine, of whom we read in
the time of the Kings? How account for them? To speak of
merchants in the ordinary interpretation of the term is to
misunderstand the nature of the economic organization of the
country in Solomon's day. It was nothing but an extensive
manorial system, something like that of Charlemagne, and
obviously required the distribution of commodities. But this

was not commerce. "The chief officers (they corresponded to the *villici*) that were over Solomon's work were 550. . . . And King Solomon made a navy of ships in Ezion-geber. . . . And Hiram sent in the navy his servants, shipmen that had knowledge of the sea, with the servants of Solomon. And they came to Ophir and they fetched from thence gold, four hundred and twenty talents, and brought it to King Solomon" (1 Kings ix. 23, 26-28).

This and similar passages have been taken to denote a flourishing international commercial intercourse, even a monopoly of trade. But there is no need of this explanation at all. It is perfectly simple when we think of the royal household as a manor on a large scale, from which the servants, in company with those from another large manor, were sent forth to distant lands in order to bring back commodities that were needed at the King's court. The economic independence of the royal household further appears in the story of the building of the Temple. Solomon asks Hiram to send him "a man cunning to work in gold, and in silver and in brass, and in iron and in purple, and in crimson and in blue, and that can skill to grave all manner of gravings, to be with the cunning men that are with me. . . . Send me also cedar-trees, fir-trees and algum-trees, out of Lebanon: for I know that thy servants can skill to cut timber in Lebanon; and behold my servants will be with thy servants. . . . And behold I will give to thy servants, the hewers that cut timber, twenty thousand measures of beaten wheat, and twenty thousand measures of barley, and twenty thousand baths of wine, and twenty thousand baths of oil" (2 Chron. ii. 7ff.). The same applies to a later passage in the same book (2 Chron. viii. 4), "And Solomon built Tadmor in the wilderness and all the store cities which he built in Hamath." Store cities tell of the manor and its wealth in kind rather than of commerce.

The other passages on which the theory is based that an extensive trade was carried on in later times hardly warrant this deduction.[28] True, we learn that the Babylonian exiles were wealthy (Ezra i. 46; Zech. vi. 10, 11), but no indication is given of their callings. There is not one iota of evidence in the Bible for the contention of Graetz that they had obtained their riches in commerce. Perhaps the cuneiform inscriptions brought from Nippur may support such an assumption. But to refer the prophecy of Ezekiel about the destruction of Tyre (Ezek. xxvi. 2) to jealousy of the Phœnicians, and then on that basis to establish the suggestion that even in the pre-Exilic period Palestine was largely a trading country, appears to me to be somewhat bold.

That we cannot be too careful in reasoning of this kind is made abundantly manifest by the interpretation put upon the famous passage in Proverbs (vii. 19, 20), where the wiles of the adulteress are described. "For the goodman is not at home, he is gone a long journey; he hath taken a bag of money with him: he will come back at the full moon." Was the husband a merchant? Perhaps, but he may have been a farmer who had left home to pay his rent to the bailiff in a distant town, and at the same time to buy a couple of oxen there.

There is no clear proof, therefore, for the existence of commerce as a specialized calling. On the other hand, there are passages which support my view that the manorial system was prevalent even at a later period. Take, for example, Nehemiah ii. 8, where the letter is mentioned in which Asaph, the keeper of the King's forest, is asked to give timber to make beams for the gate of the castle. The injunction in Leviticus (xix. 35, 36) about just weights and measures does not in itself militate against this theory.

But this does not mean that there were no traders. There must have been, even in the period of the Kings, but they were only retail dealers. Do we not read of them in the Book of Kings (1 Kings xx. 34), where the defeated Benhadad, King of Syria, offers Ahab to build streets for bazaars in Damascus as his father had done in Samaria? Or in Nehemiah (iii. 32), where we are told that the goldsmiths and the merchants built their shops in a particular quarter? How this last statement can be construed to mean that there must have been highly respected merchant gilds (Bertholet)

I cannot understand. You can almost see the small shopkeepers at the Sheep Gate.

That there was an international exchange of commodities, even in the earliest times, cannot of course be denied. There must have been extensive trade and great merchants, who exchanged the surplus produce of Palestine for the articles of luxury which they brought with them.[29] "Judah, and the land of Israel, they were thy (Tyre's) traffickers: they traded for thy merchandise wheat of Minnith and pannag [a kind of confection] and honey and oil and balm" [Ezek. xxvii. 17]. But the extraordinary thing is that these great merchants were never Jews, but always foreigners. The caravans that crossed the country were led by Midianites, Sabæans, Dedanites, men of Keder, but not by Jews.[30] Even retail trade, when the Proverbs were written, was in the hands of Canaanites. Ousted from trade in their own land, the Jews were hardly likely to have had any influence in the international trade of those times. The great international merchants were Phœnicians, Syrians or Greeks.[31] "Absolute proofs that Jewish emigration was chiefly for commercial ends are wanting entirely."[32] In view of all this I see no reason for regarding the passage in Josephus, which describes the position of the Jews in his days, as prejudiced and one-sided. It was in all probability true to fact. What does he say? "As for ourselves, therefore, we neither inhabit a maritime country, nor do we delight in merchandise" (*Contra Apion*, i. 12).

The centuries that followed brought little change in these conditions. In the Talmud those sayings predominate that would point to the prevalence among Jews, at least in the East, of small independent economic units, each sufficient for its own needs. It would be a mistake to speak of commercial activity. Granted we hear[33] that man accounted blessed who is able to become a spice-seller, and need not do laborious work. But surely the retail trader is meant, and not the great merchant. In fact trade, and more particularly over-sea trade, found little favour with the Rabbis. Some even go so far as to damn all manner of markets, pinning their faith to that economic organization where there is no need for the exchange of commodities. "R. Achai ben Joshia used to say, Unto whom may he be likened who buys fruit in the market? Unto a little child whose mother has died, which, when taken to the houses of other mothers who feed their own babes, yet remains unsatisfied. Whoso buys bread in the market is like to a man who digs the grave in which he will be buried."[34] Rab (175–247) constantly impressed upon his second son that "better was a small measure from the field than a large one from the vat" (i.e., warehouse).[35] Or again, "The Rabbis taught: four kinds of grain bring no blessing—the payment of a scribe, the fee of an interpreter, the earnings that flow from orphans' property and the profits derived from over-sea trade." Why the latter? "Because miracles do not happen every day."[36]

So much for the East. What of the West? Here, too, the Jews were not great merchants. Throughout the Imperial period and the succeeding early Middle Ages the Jew, like the Syrian, if he were a "trader" was only a poor chapman, a mere grasshopper who got entangled between the feet of the royal merchants of Rome, just like the small Polish dealer of the 17th and 18th centuries, who made himself a nuisance to the merchants of that day. All that we can discover regarding Jewish trade in the early mediæval period fits beautifully into the picture. The Jews, in short, were never merchants so long as commerce, and especially intermunicipal and international commerce, remained partly a robbing expedition and partly an adventure—that is to say, until modern times.

If this is so—if the Jews never were a trading people from of old—are those correct who hold that they were agriculturists? Certainly, in so far as their economic organization was the manorial one. But that is not all. The occupation to which Jews devoted themselves in later times and which, in the view of Jewish historians, was forced upon them against their will, was well-known and practised even in the earliest periods. I refer to money-lending, and I attach the greatest importance to the establishment of this fact. The economic history of the

Jews throughout the centuries makes it appear that money-lending always played a very great, nay, an extraordinarily great, part in the economic life of the people. We meet with it in all phases of Jewish history, in the age of national independence as in the Diaspora. Indeed, a community of peasant proprietors is fine game for money-lenders. Always the creditors are Jews, anyhow after the Exodus. In Egypt it appears the Jews were the debtors, and when they left, as the official report narrates, they carried away what had been lent to them. "And I will give this people favour in the sight of the Egyptians, and it shall come to pass when ye go, ye shall not go empty" (Exod. iii. 21). "And the Lord gave the people favour in the sight of the Egyptians, so that they let them have what they asked . . ." (Exod. xii. 36). Thereafter the position changed. Israel became the creditor and other peoples became its debtors. Thus the promise made by God was fulfilled, the promise that may rightly be called the motto of Jewish economic history, the promise which indeed expresses the fortunes of the Jewish people in one sentence: "The Lord thy God will bless thee as He promised thee: and thou shalt lend unto many nations, but thou shalt not borrow" (Deut. xv. 6).[37]

The oldest passage which points to a highly developed system of borrowing in ancient Israel is that in Nehemiah (vi. 15):—

> Then there arose a great cry of the people and of their wives against their brethren the Jews. For there were that said, We, our sons and our daughters, are many: let us get corn, that we may eat and live. Some also there were that said, We are mortgaging our fields, and our vineyards and our houses: let us get corn because of the dearth. There were also that said, We have borrowed money for the king's tribute upon our fields and our vineyards. Yet now our flesh is as the flesh of our brethren, our children as their children: and lo, we bring into bondage our sons and our daughters to be servants, and some of our daughters are

brought into bondage already: neither is it in our power
to help it, for other men have our fields and our vineyards.
And I was very angry when I heard their cry and these
words. Then I consulted with myself and contended with
the nobles and the rulers, and said unto them, Ye exact
usury, every one of his brother. . . . Restore, I pray you,
to them even this day their fields, their vineyards, their
olive-yards and their houses, also the hundredth part of the
money, and of the corn, the wine and the oil, that ye exact
of them.

The picture here drawn is clear enough. The people were
divided into two sections, an upper wealthy class, which
became rich by money-lending, and the great mass of agricultural labourers whom they exploited. This state of affairs
must have continued, in despite of Nehemiah and other re-
formers, throughout the whole history of the Jews in Palestine
and Babylon. We need only refer to the Talmud for proof.
In some of the Tractates, after the study of the Torah nothing
occupies so much space as money-lending. The world of
ideas which the Rabbis had was crammed full with money
business. A decision of Rabina (488–556), one of the last
of the Amoraim (*Baba Mezia,* 70*b*), sounds almost like the
creation of a money-lending monopoly for the Rabbis.
Throughout the three Tractates called *Baba,* there are numerous examples from the business of money-lending and from
the rise and fall of interest, and numerous discussions about
money and problems of money-lending. The unprejudiced
reader of the Talmud cannot but come to this conclusion: in
the Talmudic world there must have been a good deal of
money-lending.

With the Diaspora the business only extended. How far
money-lending was regulated among the Jews in the Egyptian
Diaspora, four or five centuries before the Common Era, may
be seen from the Oxford Papyrus (MS. Aram. cl. P)[38]:—

 . . . Son of Jatma . . . you gave me money . . . 1000 segel
of silver. And I am ready to pay by way of interest 2 hallur

of silver / per month for each segel until the day whereon I repay the money to you. The interest / for your money is thus to amount to 2000 hallur every month. And if in any month I pay you no / interest, then the amount of interest shall be added to the principal and shall bear interest itself. I undertake to pay you month by month / out of my salary which I receive from the Treasury, and you will give me a receipt (?) for the whole / sum and for the interest that I will pay you. And if I have not repaid the whole of your / money by the month of Roth in the year . . . then your money shall be doubled (?) / and also the interest I have yet to pay, and month by month I must be made to pay the same / until the day I repay you the whole / Witness, etc.

In the Hellenistic and Imperial periods rich Jews were found supplying crowned heads with money, and the poorer Jews lent to the lower classes. The Romans were not unacquainted with Jewish business.[39] It was the same in the pre-Islamic period among the Arabs, to whom the Jews lent money at interest, and who regarded this business as being natural to the Jew, as being in his blood.[40]

When the Jews first appeared on the scene in Western Europe it was as money-lenders. We have already noted that they acted as financiers to the Merovingians, which means, of course, mainly as creditors.[41] They went further in Spain; there, where they had complete freedom of movement, the common people were soon in their debt. Long before there was a Jewish (i.e., money-lending) question in other States, the legislative authorities in Castile were dealing with the problem of debts owing to Jews, and dealing with it in such a way as to show that it was of no small practical importance.[42] That money-lending became the principal calling of the Jews after the Crusades will be admitted on all hands.

We come, then, to this conclusion, that from the earliest times money-lending was a prime factor in the economic history of the Jews.

The time has really arrived when the myth that the Jews

were forced to have recourse to money-lending in mediæval
Europe, chiefly after the Crusades, because they were debarred
from any other means of livelihood, should be finally disposed of. The history of Jewish money-lending in the two
thousand years before the Crusades ought surely to set this
fable at rest once and for all. The official version that Jews
could not devote themselves to anything but money-lending,
even if they would, is incorrect. The door was by no means
always shut in their faces; the fact is they preferred to engage in money-lending. This has been proved by Professor
Bücher for Frankfort-on-the-Main, and the same may be
done for other towns as well. The Jews had a natural tendency
towards this particular business, and both in the Middle Ages
and after rulers were at pains to induce Jews to enter into
other callings, but in vain. Edward I made the attempt in
England;[43] it was also tried in the 18th century in the Province
of Posen,[44] where the authorities sought to direct the Jews to
change their means of livelihood by offering them bounties if
they would. Despite this, and despite the possibility of being
able to become handicraftsmen and peasants like all others,
there were, in 1797, in the southern towns of Prussia, 4164
Jewish craftsmen side by side with 11,000 to 12,000 Jewish
traders. The significance of these figures is borne in upon
us when we note that though the Jewish population formed
5 or 6 per cent. of the whole, the Christian traders totalled
17,000 or 18,000.

It may be urged, however, that the practice of usury, even
when it is carried on quite voluntarily, need not be accounted
for by special racial attributes. Human inclinations of a general kind will amply explain it. Wherever in the midst of a
people a group of moneyed men dwell side by side with
others who need cash, be it for consumption, be it for production, it soon comes about, especially where the legal
conditions governing money-lending are of a primitive kind,
that the one class becomes the debtors and the other the
creditors.

True. Wherever rich and poor lived together, the latter borrowed from the former, even when there was as yet no money in existence—in which case the debts were in kind. In the earliest stages of civilization, when the two classes felt themselves members of the same brotherhood, the lending was without interest. Later, especially when some intercourse with strangers sprang up, the borrower paid the lender a certain quantity of corn or oil or (where a money economy had already established itself) gold over and above the principal, and the custom of giving interest gradually became universal.

In this there is no difference between the ancient, the mediæval or the modern world. All three were acquainted with money-lending and "usury," which was never confined to the members of any one race or religion. Think of the agrarian reforms in Greece and Rome, which prove conclusively that the economic conditions in these countries at certain times were exactly like those in Palestine in the days of Nehemiah.* In the ancient world the temples were the centres of the money-lending business, for in them were stored vast quantities of treasure. If at the Jerusalem Temple money-lending was carried on—what is by no means established: the Talmudic tractate (*Shekalim*) which deals with Temple taxes clearly forbids the utilization of what remained over from certain sacrifices for purposes of business—I say *if* such were the case, then there was nothing extraordinary in this: all temples in antiquity lent money. The temples of Babylonia, we are informed,[45] were like so many great business houses. The temples at Delphi, at Delos, at Ephesus, at Samos were no different.[46] And in the Middle Ages the churches, the monasteries, the houses of the various Knights and other religious orders took the place of the ancient temples in this respect. Despite the prohibitions of the Church against usury, they were the centres of a brisk trade in money. Is it any different to-day? The German peasant on the marshes of

* Cf. A. E. Zimmern, *The Greek Commonwealth,* p. 111 ff. —Trans.

the North Sea coast who has managed to make a little money knows of nothing better to do with it than to lend it at interest to a needy neighbour.

To increase one's fortune by means of interest on loans is so easy and pleasant, that everybody who is able makes the attempt. Every period wherein the demand for money is great gives opportunity enough (the periods, that is, of the so-called credit crises—regularly followed, by the way, in recent European history by Jewish persecutions).

Everybody, then, does it—gladly does it. The desire to take interest on money is pretty generally prevalent. But is the ability to do so? This leads me to my next proof in support of the view that Jewish characteristics have remained constant—

(5) The capacity of the Jew for money-dealing.

It is well-known that in the Middle Ages many authorities, whether individual rulers or corporations, almost begged the Jews to come to their city in order to carry on money-lending. All sorts of privileges were held out to them. The Bishop of Speyer is a case in point. He thought it would give his city a certain *cachet* to count a number of rich Jews among its in-habitants. Some of the cities of Italy in the 15th and 16th centuries actually made agreements with the wealthiest Jewish money-lenders that they should come and establish loan-banks and pawnshops.[47]

Why should these requests have been made, and these privileges offered? Why should just Jews and no others have been invited to found money-lending concerns? No doubt to some extent it was because good Christian men were not willing to soil their souls by the nefarious trade, and Jews were called in to stand between them and damnation. But was this all? Does it not appear rather that the Jews had a special capacity for the business? They were the cleverest, the most gifted money-lenders, and that is why they were in demand. How else should we be able to account for their success, which for centuries brought them so much riches? Anybody can be a lender, but not everybody can be a successful lender. For that special capacities and attributes are necessary.

Turn to the pages of the Talmud and you will find that money-lending was no mere dilettante business with the Jews. They made an art of it; they probably invented (certainly they utilized) the highly organized machinery of lending.

The time has come, it seems to me, for a trained economist to deal thoroughly with the economic side of the Talmud and of Rabbinic literature generally. I hope this book may act as some spur to this end. All I can do here is to point the way, so that some successor of mine may find it the more easily. I shall briefly note some of the passages which appear to me to bear witness to an extensive acquaintance with economic problems, and more particularly those bearing on credit. When we recall the period in which the Talmud came into being (200 B.C. to 500 A.D.) and compare what it contains in the field of economics with all the economic ideas and conceptions that the ancient and the mediæval worlds have handed down to us, it seems nothing short of marvellous. Some of the Rabbis speak as though they had mastered Ricardo and Marx, or, to say the least, had been brokers on the Stock Exchange for several years, or counsel in many an important money-lending case. Let me cite an instance or two.

(a) A profound acquaintance with the nature of the precious metals. "R. Chisda said, There are seven kinds of gold: ordinary gold, best gold, gold of Ophir (1 Kings x. 11), fine gold (1 Kings v. 18), drawn gold, heavy gold and Parvayin gold" (Joma, 45a).

(b) The idea that money is a common denominator in terms of which commodities are exchanged is fully developed. The best proof of this is the legal decision that the act of purchasing becomes complete not as soon as the price has been paid, but when the commodity is delivered. The whole of the 4th section of Baba Mezia is illustrative of this point.

(c) There is a clear conception of the difference between credit for production and for consumption. In the case of the first, interest is permitted; not so, from a Jew, in the case of the second. "If A rents a field from B at a rental of 10 measures of wheat and then requests B to lend him 200 zuz for the improvement of the field, promising a total payment of 12 measures of wheat—that is permissible. But may you offer to give more in renting a shop or hiring a ship? Rab Nachman (235–320), on the authority of Rabba bar Abuha, was of opinion that sometimes it was permissible to give more for a shop in order to be able to hang pictures up in it, and for a ship too, in order to place a mast on it. The pictures in the shop will attract many people and so increase profits, and the mast on the ship will enhance the ship's value" (*Baba Mezia,* 69*b*).

(*d*) Law and rules of practice point to an extraordinarily developed system of credit agreements. After reading the 4th and 5th sections of *Baba Mezia* you feel as though you had just laid down the report of an Enquiry into Money-lending in Hesse twenty or thirty years ago, where a thousand and one gins and traps were introduced into money-lending compacts. The *Prosbol,* too (by means of which it was possible to ensure the existence of a debt even over the year of release), is a sign of a highly organized system of lending (Section 10 of *Sheviith*).

(*e*) The treatment of deposits is handled in a way which shows practical knowledge of the subject. "If any one deposits moneys with a banker, the latter may not make any use of them if they are in one bundle. If, however, they are loose, he may, and if they are lost he is held responsible. But if the moneys are deposited with a private individual, whether they are in one bundle or loose, he may make no use of them whatever; and if they should be lost he is not bound to replace them. R. Meir (100–160) held that a shopkeeper was regarded as a private individual in this respect; but R. Judah (136–200) was of the contrary opinion, and said that the shopkeeper was like the banker. . . . " (*Baba Mezia,* 43*a*).

(*f*) Finally I would mention the Jewish gift for figures. The Talmudists all had it, but it was to be found in earlier ages also. The exact statistical lists in the Bible and the later literature must have struck every one. One French writer remarks on the topic: "The race possessed a singular capacity for calculation—a genius, so to say, for numbers."[48]

Apart from all these considerations, the very success of the Jews in their money-lending activities effectively demonstrates a special capacity for the business. And the success was manifested in

(6) Jewish wealth.

That ever since the race began some Jews amassed huge fortunes can be easily shown, nor can it be doubted that the average wealth of all Jews was fairly high. In all ages and in all lands Jewish riches were proverbial.

We may begin with King Solomon, whose wealth was renowned even among wealthy Oriental potentates—although he did not acquire it by successful trading (though you never can tell!). Later we read that some of the Jewish exiles in Babylon were in a short time able to send gold and silver to Jerusalem (Zech. vi. 10, 11). That Jews played a great part in the economic life of the Euphrates country during the Exile appears from the commercial contracts dug up at Nippur.[49] Those who returned with Ezra brought great opulence with them (Ezra i. 6–11), and in the subsequent period the wealth of the priests was notorious.[50] Noticeable are the large number of rich men, some of them very rich, among the Talmudic Rabbis. It would not be difficult to compile quite a respectable list of such of them as were renowned for their wealth. Certainly, in any view, the rich Rabbis were in the majority.[51]

In the Hellenistic Diaspora likewise the impression cannot be avoided that the standard of wealth among Jews was pretty high. Wherever Jews and Greeks lived side by side, as in Cæsarea,[52] the former were the more opulent. There must have been a specially great number of wealthy Jews among those of Alexandria. Of very rich Alabarchs we are actually told, and we have already mentioned the position of the Alexandrian Jews as financiers of crowned heads.

It was not one whit otherwise in the early Middle Ages.

We have it on record that many Jews in those days were blessed with the good things of the world in abundance. In Spain they offered money to Reccared if he would annul anti-Jewish legislation,[53] and in the early period of Mohammedan rule we learn that the Arabs envied them their wealth.[54] Cordova, in the 9th century, had "several thousand(?) Jewish families who were well off."[55] And more to the same effect.[56]

There is no need to labour the statement that in the later Middle Ages the Jews were wealthy. It is a generally accepted fact.[57] And for what is called the modern period I have myself adduced proofs enough in this book.

We shall be justified in the conclusion, therefore, that from King Solomon to Barney Barnato Jewish opulence runs through history like a golden thread, without ever once snapping. Is this merely accidental? If not, what was it due to—subjective or objective causes?

Objective factors, *i.e.*, outward forces, have certainly been hinted at to explain Jewish wealth. In the first place, the Jews were early taught to look for their chief happiness in the possession of money; in the second, the insecurity of their position forced them to accumulate their wealth in easily movable forms—in gold or ornaments, which they could take about with them, which they could hide or carry off without much difficulty. These causes undoubtedly go a good way to account for the growth of Jewish wealth, but they by no means suffice to explain it completely. We must not forget that the outward forces referred to above, in order to produce the result they did, could not but have influenced a people possessing certain special gifts. But let that pass. Again, the facts instanced could only have been of any effect in the Diaspora. Let that also pass. The great weakness of this explanation is that it tells us merely why the Jews had any desire to become wealthy, and, incidentally, that their wealth took a particular form. The desire in this case is of little moment; it does not make clear why it was realized. Hence we must look for other causes. Besides, the desire to become rich has been universal ever since Alberich robbed the Maidens of the Rhine-gold.

Another explanation has therefore been suggested for Jewish wealth. The Jews, it has been rightly pointed out, for centuries occupied a position of inequality with their Christian neighbours, and therefore had less occasion to spend as much as the latter. The conception of social status, with varying standards of comfort for each, was unknown among them, and therefore also the thousand and one artificial wants that were associated with the idea. "It is certain," remarks a writer who has dealt with this aspect of the problem in a most delicate fashion,[58] "that a Jew, compared with a Christian of the same income, was bound to become the richer of the two, seeing that the Christian had very many opportunities of spending money which were denied to the Jew, for the simple reason that the former belonged to the ruling class, and the latter was only tolerated. As for the rich Jew, his circumstances were different from those of the Christian, for he had no need to consider what was demanded in his social class. Thus, any luxuries he cared to enjoy were not necessarily in accordance with his status."

Doubtless this is one explanation of the wealth of the Jews, and will account also for the specifically Jewish economic standpoint, which we have noted above. To it were due such ideas as that of free competition, that your expenses should be limited by your income—a conception utterly foreign to a feudal society—and that saving, associated with Jews from earliest times, was good. Let me recall an old German proverb:—

> Selten sind sieben Dinge:
> Eine Nonne, die nicht singe,
> Ein Mädchen ohne Liebe,
> Ein Jahrmarkt ohne Diebe,
> Ein Geissbock ohne Bart,
> Ein Jude der nicht spart,
> Ein Kornhaus ohne Mäuse,
> Und ein Kosak ohne Läuse.

[Rare are seven things:
A nun who never sings,
A maid without a lover,
A fair without a robber,
A goat of beard bereft,
A Jew that knows no thrift,
A granary without mice,
And a Cossack without lice.]

To the saving habit of the Jews may be traced the tendency to accumulate capital. One sometimes hears it said that Jewish money remains in a business longer than Christian money, and increases more quickly to boot. In olden times the Jew could not enter the charmed circle of the feudal landed gentry, and so his money was not spent in keeping up the appearances demanded by his status. If he saved, his money had perforce to be invested in commercial enterprise, unless, of course, he lent it out directly at interest, as the Jews of Hamburg of the 17th century were in the habit of doing. Glückel von Hameln and her friends, whenever they had any surplus, always lent it out on security. The money fructified and increased.

All these considerations are valuable as far as they go. But they do not go far enough satisfactorily to explain the phenomenon of Jewish wealth. It is all very well pointing to objective forces in any problem. We must not forget, however, that those forces might not effect the particular result they did if the men and women whom they influenced were not constituted in a particular way. A people does not become thrifty because of the stress of outward circumstances alone. The merest tyro knows that. Besides, nowadays, when the Ghetto walls have long since fallen, and the Jew enjoys perfect equality when he may become a landed proprietor and regulate his life in accordance with the most rigid requirements—nowadays, too, I say, Jews are thriftier than Christians. Look at a few statistics. In Baden, in the years 1895 to 1903, capital increased in the case of Protestants from 100 to 128.3 per cent., in the case of Jews from 100 to 138.2 per cent. This is striking enough, but it becomes even more so when we remember that during the same period the incomes of Protestants grew from 100 to 146.6 per cent., those of Jews from 100 to 144.5 per cent.

When all is said the possible causes hitherto mentioned would only explain why already existing wealth was increased. Not one can satisfactorily answer the question, How was it in the first place obtained? There is only one answer. Wealth is got by those who have a talent for it. From the wealth of the Jews, therefore, may be deduced special Jewish characteristics or attributes.

Is the Jewish Genius Natural or Artificial?

What is the result of all our considerations in the previous section? That in all probability the anthropological character of the Jews, no less than their intellectual attributes, has remained constant for thousands of years.

What does this prove? Are we to conclude that the Jewish genius is rooted in race? Those who have a dogmatic faith in race unhesitatingly say yes. We however, who are trying to proceed scientifically, must say no. Nothing as yet has been proved.

A brief reference to the methods of some of the believers in the race-theory[59] will show how unreliable their conclusions are. They start out with the assumption that the Jews are a race. Since every race must have specific characteristics, Jews have theirs. In other words, their specific characteristics are rooted in their race. But for this there is no actual proof. If the truth must be told, we know nothing whatever of the connexion between somatic or anthropological features and intellectual capacities.

What the race-theorists have produced is a new sort of religion to replace the old Jewish or Christian religion. What else is the theory of an Aryan, or German, "mission" in the world but a modern form of the "chosen people" belief? All well and good, but let no one be deceived into imagining that this is science. It is faith, and faith and science had best be kept apart.

As we have said, there is no certain connexion between somatic attributes and intellectual capacities. The constancy of each may be purely accidental; it may arise anew in every generation or may be carried on by the aid of tradition. And among a people who were attached to tradition as the Jews were, this assumption seems likely enough. The Jews were shut off from others, they possessed a strong love of family, their religious practices were scrupulously observed, the Talmud was energetically studied in every generation—all these supplied, as it were, the machinery for carrying on certain peculiarities from one generation to another merely by education alone.

This is one view. Yet Jewish characteristics *may* spring from the blood. Again, there are those who would trace them to environment. The Jewish religion, Ghetto life, the dealing in money for so many centuries have all three been instanced to account for the specifically Jewish type of character. There may be something in this. Only possibly, as I have tried to show, these influences instead of being causes may be results.

I propose in the next chapter to analyse the Jewish genius, laying special stress on the following points in the order given: (1) The original aptitudes of those races from which the Jews sprang as exhibited in their mode of life. (2) How the various elements mingled. (3) Which of these aptitudes survived under the influences of Jewish history. Finally, if these considerations should prove insufficient, we shall venture the hypothesis: (4) that certain characteristics grew up in the course of history. We shall see, however, that there will be no need to have recourse to this hypothesis, since the Jewish genius can be adequately explained along the first three lines. If this be so, then one result will have been established: that the Jewish characteristics are rooted in the blood of the race, and are not in any wise due to educative processes.

Chapter 14

The Vicissitudes of the Jewish People

IF ANY ONE wished in a sentence to account for the importance of the Jews in the world's civilization, and more particularly in economic life, he could do so by saying that it was due to the transplanting of an Oriental people among Northern races, and the culture union of the two. A similar assertion has been made regarding the civilizations of the classical world, of the Greek more especially, and also of that of the Italian Renaissance. It has been suggested that they resulted from the mixture of Northern peoples, who had wandered into a Southern environment, with the autochthonous inhabitants—a brilliant hypothesis, not without an element of truth in it.

But the statement concerning the Jews is no hypothesis: it is an established fact, capable of abundant proof. The capitalistic civilization of our age is the fruit of the union between the Jews, a Southern people pushing into the North, and the Northern tribes, indigenous there. The Jews contributed an extraordinary capacity for commerce, and the Northern peoples, above all the Germans, an equally remarkable ability for technical inventions.

It is clear, therefore, what we must have in view in our considerations of the Jewish genius and its enormous influence. Not whether the Jews were Semites, or Hittites, or of some other stock, not whether they are "pure," or "mixed," is the important thing, but that they are an Oriental folk transplanted into an environment both climatically and ethnically strange, wherein their best powers come to fruition.

They are an Oriental people—that is to say, one of those peoples whose habitat was in that part of the globe lying between the Atlas Mountains in the West, and the Persian Gulf in the East; one of those races baked by the sun in the dry, burning climate of the great deserts of North Africa,

Arabia and Asia Minor, or of their border-lands; the races which brought their special characteristics to maturity amid their peculiar environment which had never altered since the Ice Age, a period of some twelve or sixteen thousand years.

The whole of this region, from which the Jews also hailed, is an extensive sandy desert, with here and there an oasis where man and beast can dwell. In the larger of these watered valleys arose, as is well known, the earliest civilizations of the world—in Egypt, in Mesopotamia and in Palestine. All three are comparatively small fertile patches; all are true oases in the desert, and theirs was an essentially oasis civilization. The cultivable area of Egypt was about as large as the Prussian Province of Saxony is to-day [about 5,500,000 acres, according to the *Statesman's Year Book*]; Mesopotamia at its widest extent was only about half the size of the Plain of Lombardy [about 4500 square miles, according to the same authority]; Palestine, the land of the whole people of Israel, was smaller still, being no larger than perhaps Baden [about 5000 square miles]; while Judæa, the Southern Kingdom, and therefore the home of the Jews, was as extensive as the Duchies of Anhalt and Saxe-Coburg and Gotha together [about 1600 square miles]. But these oases, and Palestine more especially, were themselves broken by deserts, Judæa being particularly badly treated by Nature. Its southern end extended past Hebron and Beersheba, right into the modern sandy waste.

All agriculture in these countries was the tillage of oases. What does this mean? It means that the soil collected by almost artificial means, and that the great aim of the farmer was to gather the water necessary for the growth of vegetation. This was the case in Palestine, where the cultivation of the soil depended on the water-supply. Drought is the scourge that the farmer fears most. Every year he trembles lest the arid waste should stretch its arms and embrace his strip of land, tended with so much care and tribulation. Every moment he is in dread lest the desert send him its scorching winds, or its locust-swarms. And above all, he fears the desert wastes because of the marauding bands who may fall upon him, robbing, killing, pillaging as they cross the country, sometimes even taking possession of his holding if the fancy seize them. These children of the desert, whom we now call Bedouins, and of whom the oasis-dwellers were once themselves a part, were nomadic shepherds. Their raids hastened the rise of strong cities with stout walls, behind which the inhabitants of the plain could take refuge. Sometimes the desert crept right into them, and so at all times they were filled with the spirit of the sandy wastes.

Such a tribe of restless wandering Bedouins were the Hebrews, when about the year 1200 B.C. they fell upon Canaan, plundering and killing as they went, and finally deciding to settle there, and rest from all their wanderings. Which meant, that if possible they would do nothing, but that the natives would work for them—the aim of every conquering people. Such was Jehovah's promise: "I will lead you unto the land which I promised you, a land of great and goodly cities which thou buildedst not, and houses full of all good things which thou filledst not, and cisterns hewn out which thou hewedst not, and vineyards and olive-trees which thou plantedst not, and thou shalt eat and be full" (Deut. vi. 10, 11).

Once there, what did the Hebrews do in this promised land? What sort of economic organization did they establish? We cannot, of course, speak as to the details,[1] but one or two things we may imagine. Probably, as we have seen, the powerful and mighty among them after having conquered large tracts of land instituted a sort of feudal society. Part of the produce of the land they took for themselves, either by way of rent in kind, by farming it out to tax-collectors, or by means of the credit nexus. In any case, a large number of Hebrews lived in the towns, receiving rent or interest from the subject population who worked on the soil, either as "colonists," or "free peasants," or whatever term was used in the Orient for this class. Some of the conquering tribes may have become impoverished and themselves sunk to the level of unfree farmers, but they were hardly the influential ones. This position was held by those who inhabited the West

Jordan lands, principally Judah, sections of Simeon and Levi and others. In those districts cattle farming only was possible: "Judah's teeth are white with milk." Other tribes, such as Reuben and Gad, remained east of the Jordan as semi-nomads, rearing cattle, and half the tribe of Manasseh crossed the Jordan to return thither. But all the tribes alike must have been impregnated with the nomadic spirit. Were this not the case, it would be exceedingly difficult to understand the rise and growth of the Jewish religious system.

It should not be forgotten that the Holy Scriptures of the Jews in which their religion is embodied, especially the Pentateuch, is the literature of a nomadic people. Their God, who triumphs over the false gods, is a desert and pastoral divinity. The traditions of the nomad state were maintained by Ezra and Nehemiah in the conscious re-establishment of the Jehovah cult, in doing which they paid no heed to the intervening period of agriculture. The Priestly Code "takes care not to mention the settled life in Canaan. . . it strictly limits itself to the wanderings in the wilderness, and in all seriousness wants to be regarded as a desert Code."[2] Open the historical books or the majority of the Prophets, that desert choir, include the Psalms also, and you everywhere find metaphors and similes taken from shepherd life. Only occasionally do you meet with the peasant "sitting contentedly at the door of his house in the shade of the fig-tree." Jehovah is the good Shepherd (Psa. 23) who will gather the remnants of Israel "as a flock in the midst of their pasture" (Micah ii. 12). And what does the Sabbatical year mean but that you cease being a peasant for the time being, and become an Israelite of the old sort? Israel never quite gave up its division into families and clans; it was always composed of tribes, like most shepherd peoples. There seems to be little doubt that even as late as the 5th century B.C. there must have been a strong dash of the nomads, certainly in the ruling classes, but probably also in the great mass of the people. Else how would it have been possible to saddle them for any length of time with a nomadic religion?

It may be asked, Were not the nomad tendencies of those

days perchance a harking back to an earlier state? Did not perhaps the old wandering instincts, which in the previous centuries had been lulled to sleep, awake again under the influences of the Exile? It is quite likely, and what is more, the vicissitudes of the Jewish people since the Babylonian Exile could not but arouse any slumbering desert and nomad feelings within them. On this point I would lay especial stress. Hence, even if we were inclined to assume that the Children of Israel lived a settled life for five hundred years after the conquest of Canaan, it is perfectly clear that all the powers on earth seemed to have conspired together not to allow this state to become permanent. Scarcely had the plant taken root (so far as it could in so hot a country) than it was pulled up. The Jew's inherent "Nomadism" or "Saharaism" (if I may coin the words) was always kept alive through selection or adaptation. Throughout the centuries, therefore, Israel has remained a desert and nomadic people.

There is nothing new in this conclusion. But one does not establish it without some scruple of conscience. Why? Because anti-Semitic pamphleteers rudely pounce upon it and make capital out of it for their abuse. That, of course, can be no reason for doubting its truth, or neglecting to take cognizance of it as an explanation of Jewish characteristics. What should be done to oppose the prejudiced scribblers is to analyse the problem most carefully, and present an illuminating view of its importance. Up to the present little has been achieved in this direction; what has been done has been childish and spitefully distorted. No wonder that the idea that the Jew has always been a nomad has been received with scorn and jest by some people. It would have been much more to the point if these same people had been able to prove that it was wrong. This has never yet been seriously attempted. The chain of reasoning which runs: Agriculture was practised in Palestine in olden times; the Jews lived in Palestine then; therefore the Jews were agriculturists, is on the face of it a little weak. And another point. The term nomad is not meant to imply obloquy or disgrace. At most, objection may be taken to the robbing. But why should there be any dishonour attached to a brave Bedouin tribe which, under such a doughty leader as, say, King David, lived on plunder? Why should they appear less worthy, or call forth less sympathy, than an agricultural tribe of Negroes somewhere in the wilds of Africa? It is obvious, of course, that when I use the term "nomad" as applied to later Jewish history, I want it to bear not its secondary meaning, which it has acquired in the lapse of time, but its original connotation in all its pristine strength.

Having cleared the air a little, let us now attempt to prove that our conclusion is true. Throughout the centuries Israel has remained a desert and nomadic people, either by the process of selection or of adaptation.

We have already mentioned the possible effect of the Exile in calling forth slumbering nomadic instincts. In reality, if the truth be told, we can form no clear conception of what the Exile meant, neither of the journey into it, nor of the return home. It only seems possible on the assumption that the Jews then were still nomads or semi-nomads. One can scarcely conceive the conquest of an agricultural people; whereas the forcible transplanting of nomad tribes is not unknown to-day.[3] Moreover, the assumption seems to be supported by the story of the Captivity. "And he carried away all Jerusalem and all the princes and all the mighty men of valour, even ten thousand captives, and all the craftsmen and the smiths; none remained save the poorest sort of the people of the land." And after the second expedition of the Babylonians, "the captain of the guard left of the poorest of the land to be vine-dressers and husbandmen" (2 Kings xxiv. 14 and xxv. 12). Jeremiah's version of the story agrees with this (Jer. xxxix. 10).

Whoever the exiles may have been, it is pretty certain that the actual agriculturists were not among them. These remained behind even after the second batch of exiles had been carried away captive. The passage in Jeremiah would seem to lend probability to my view that the soil was tilled by unfree villeins who, when their lords were led to Babylon, became independent husbandmen. It is not assuming too much to regard these men as the descendants of the original inhabitants whom the Hebrews had conquered. From the age of the Captivity, therefore, the population of Judæa had a thinner stream of Jewish blood in their veins than the Babylonian exiles, who were more or less the Jewish aristocracy, the cream of the people, as it were. This was indeed the view that obtained currency in later times. Even in Judæa itself it was admitted that the Babylonian Jews were of the very best stock, and an old Jewish saying helped to confirm the belief. "The Jews in the Roman Diaspora compared as to their descent with those in Judæa are like the mixed dough to the pure flour, but Judæa itself is only dough compared with Babylon."[4] And R. Ezekiel (220–299) excuses that good man, Ezra, for having returned to Palestine by saying that he took the families of doubtful origin away with him, and so left those that remained free from the danger of mixing with them(!).[5]

We come then to this conclusion. The Exile was a kind of selective process whereby the best elements of Jewry, never favourable to an economy of settled life, were forced to revive the inherent nomad instincts within them, and to gain their livelihood as townsmen, *i.e.*, traders. This does not mean that none of them became husbandmen. Far from it. The Babylonian Talmud certainly makes it appear that some devoted themselves to agriculture, but the conditions must have been those prevalent in Palestine, where an aristocracy of wealth lived in the towns on the work of (non-Jewish?) peasants. Such at any rate is the impression of the typical state of affairs. But there were exceptions too. Do we not read of many an ancient Rabbi who himself walked behind the plough? What is of consequence, however, is that the prevailing conditions in the Exile were by no means exceptional. On the contrary, they were normal. Even before the Exile many Jews had settled in Egypt and other lands in a kind of voluntary Diaspora. Those who left Palestine were no doubt the men in whom the old nomadic instincts were not yet quite dead, and their self-imposed exile only called them forth the more. We never find these wandering Jews, be their origin Judæa or Palestine, establishing agricultural colonies or independent settlements of any sort, as most other emigrants did. But what do we find? That Jewish settlers scattered themselves in all corners of the inhabited globe among foreign nations, preferably in the large towns, where they sought their livelihood.[6] We never hear of their return to their native hearth after having saved up sufficient money to keep them in affluence, as the Swiss, Hungarian or Italian emigrants do to-day. The only bonds that bound them with home were religious. If they ever do go back, it is only at the annual Passover pilgrimage, like real nomads that they are.

Little by little Palestine ceased to be the centre of Jewish life, and Jews became more and more scattered. Even as late as the destruction of the Second Temple (70 A.D.), the Jews in the Diaspora outnumbered those in Judæa. Perhaps there was some reason for this. That the country, even when it was most densely populated, could maintain more than a million, or a million and a half souls is scarcely likely. (To-day the inhabitants number at most 650,000.) As for Judæa, it had no more than 225,000 inhabitants, and Jerusalem no more than 25,000.[7] There certainly was a larger number outside Palestine already at the commencement of the Common Era. In the Egypt of the Ptolemies it is said that out of a total population of seven or eight millions, one million were Jews.[8] Nor was Egypt unique in this respect. It would have been difficult indeed to name one spot which, in the words of Strabo quoted by Josephus, was not inhabited and dominated (!) by Jews. Philo gives a list of countries that had a Jewish population in his day, and adds that they were settled in numerous cities of Europe, Asia, Lybia, on the mainland and on islands, on the coast and inland. We hear the same thing from a Sibylline Oracle, composed towards the end of the 2nd century,[9] while Jerome informs us that they were to be found "from sea to sea, from the British to the Atlantic Oceans, from the West to the South, from the North to the East, the world through."[10] How densely packed they were in the Rome of the early Empire may be gathered from the account of the visit of King Herod to the capital of the Cæsars, wherein we are told that no less than 8000 Jews resident in Rome accompanied him to Augustus. Again, in the year 19 A.D., 4000 freedmen of military age who "professed the Egyptian and Jewish superstition" were sentenced to be deported to Sardinia.[11]

But enough. No matter how many Jews were in the Diaspora in the pre-Christian age, so much is certain, that when the Second Temple fell, Israel was already scattered over the face of the earth.[12] Nor did the ant-heap become quiescent in the Middle Ages; for Jewish wanderings continued apace. That, too, is certain.

What direction did the wanderings take? About the end of the 5th century Babylon was emptied, at first slowly and then with speed, the Jews migrating to all points of the globe—to Arabia, India and Europe. Again in the 13th century streams of emigrants from England, France and Germany journeyed partly to the Pyrenean Peninsula, where there was already a large number of Jews from Palestine and Babylon, and partly to the kingdoms of Eastern Europe, which were likewise not without their Jewish inhabitants, who had settled there as far back as the 8th century, having arrived from the Byzantine Empire *via* the Black Sea. Then, towards the end of the Middle Ages, Spain and Portugal on the one hand and Russia and Poland on the other were the two great basins outside the Orient wherein the Jews had settled. From each of these the wandering commenced afresh; we have already seen what course it took. The Spanish Jews first, then, after the Cossack pogroms in the 17th century, the Russian Jews began to disperse over the earth. This process of emigration from Russia and Poland was a steady one, until towards the end of the 19th century there was a volcanic eruption and hundreds of thousands sought a refuge in the New World.[13]

So this people was driven from place to place—tribe of the wandering foot whose fate has been so touchingly expressed in the legend of the Wandering Jew.[14] The constant insecurity of their position made it impossible for them to think of settling down on the soil. As a matter of fact, however, they seldom had any inclination that way. All that we know of Jewish life in the Diaspora points to the conclusion that only an insignificant number of Jews devoted themselves to agriculture even in those lands where no difficulties were placed in their path. Perhaps Poland in the 16th century is the best instance. There they appear to have taken up farming. But even in Poland they showed a preference for city life. For every 500 Christian merchants in the Polish towns of the period there were to be found 3200 Jewish merchants.[15]

Yes, they became town-dwellers—whether voluntarily or by stress of circumstances is of no consequence—and town-dwellers they have remained. More than half the Jews of the world to-day are to be found in cities with over 50,000 inhabitants. In Germany this applies to about 43.6 per cent. of the Jews (1900), in Italy, Switzerland, Holland and Denmark to about four-fifths, and to all the Jews of England and the United States.

Now the modern city is nothing else but a great desert, as far removed from the warm earth as the desert is, and like it forcing its inhabitants to become nomads. The old nomadic instincts have thus through the centuries been called forth in the Jew by the process of adapting himself to his environment, while the principle of selection has only tended to strengthen those instincts. It is clear that in the constant changes to which the Jews were subjected, not those among them that had an inclination to the comfortable, settled life of the farmer were the ones likely to survive, but rather those in whom the nomadic instincts were strong.

This hot-blooded, restless people that had wandered not forty, but four thousand years in the wilderness came at last to its Canaan, to its promised land, where it should be able to repose from all its travels—it came to the Northern countries, meeting nations there who, while the Jews were hurrying from one oasis to another, had dwelt on their soil and smelt of the earth, who differed from the Jews as a horse of the Ardennes differs from a fiery Arab charger.

It will soon be of little moment whether the nations of Northern, Central and Eastern Europe are called Aryans or by some other name. The latest researches, it is true, would make it appear that most of them were indeed Aryans.[16] But the name tells us nothing. What is of importance is that they were all peoples from the cold North, and never able to acclimatize themselves in the warm lands of the South.[17] To consider them as Aryans is misleading. For then we shall have to include the dark Indian too, and obviously the fair, blue-eyed Europeans have little in common with him, except perhaps their language. In other respects they have peculiarities all their own. What these are may easily be seen by looking at those peoples as they are to-day, and if we had to characterize them in one word which should be in contrast to desert it would be forest. Forest and desert are indeed the two great opposites which sum up differences in countries and their inhabitants. Forests are of the North—those Northern forests with the murmur of their brooks, where the mist clings fast to the tree-trunks and the toads have their habitation "in the dank moss and the wet stones," where in winter the faint sunlight glistens on the rime and in summer the song of birds is everywhere. To be sure, there were forests on Lebanon's height, as there are forests to-day in the South of Italy. But who that has set foot in a Southern forest will not at once perceive that it has small affinity with the forests of the North, will not at once realize that "even in Italy the forest tells the heart and the eye something very different from the Alpine forest, or that on the Baltic shore? The South Italian forest is full of harmonies, permeated with clear light and ineffable blue, pliant and yet vigorous in its aiming skyward and in its bending before the moaning wind; it seems a sacred grove" (Hehn). But our Northern forests—they have a charm and a mystery about them at once intimate and fearful. Desert and forest, sand and marsh—those are the great opposites, depending in the long run on differences in the moisture of the air, and so creating dissimilar environments for the activities of man. In the one case the Fata Morgana is Nature's symbol, in the other the cloud of mist.

In olden times the characteristics of the Northern climes were even more strongly marked than to-day. The Romans' picture of Germany shows us a rude land, covered with bogs and dense forests, a land of leaden skies, with a misty and moist atmosphere, whose winters are long and wildly stormy. For thousands of years peoples and races (our ancestors) dwelt in the damp woods, the bogs, the mists, the ice and the snow and the rain. They hewed down the woods, made the land habitable and pitched their tents where axe and plough had gained for them a strip of the wilds. From the very first they seemed to be rooted in the soil; from the very first it would seem that tillage was never quite absent. But even if we try to imagine these Northern folk as "nomads," theirs is a very different kind of life from that of a Bedouin tribe. We feel that they are more tied to the hearth than even an agricultural people in an oasis-land. The Northerners are settlers even when they only breed cattle; the Bedouins are always nomads, even though they till the soil.

This is so because man is brought into closer touch with Nature in the North than in the hot countries. Man is part and parcel of Nature even if he only beats the woods as a huntsman, or as a shepherd breaks a path through the thickets for his flocks. I am inclined to say, even at the risk of being ridiculed as a modern mystic, that in the North there are between Nature and even the most prosaic of men tender bonds of love and friendship, unknown to the Southerner. In the South, as has been rightly observed, man regards Nature only as an instrument in the work of civilization. Even when he is a tiller of the soil, he is a stranger to Nature. In the South there is no country life, no living in and with Nature, no attachment to bush and tree, heath and meadow, wild creature and free bird.

Is it not clear that these varying and varied environments must produce different results, must influence men in different ways? Would it be too much to assume that the Jewish characteristics as we have seen them have been affected by, nay, have even received their peculiar impress from the thousands of years of wandering in the wilderness? The answer of course is yes, and if in the following pages I try to prove it, I must nevertheless admit that the present state of our knowledge of biology is inadequate to show *how* environ-

ment has bearing on the anatomical and physiological character of man, and therefore also on his psychical disposition.
The direction which our inquiries under this head should
take has been laid down by Juan Huarte de San Juan, that
wise old 16th-century Spanish physician whom I have already
mentioned, in his splendid book, *Examen de ingenios,* in
which he makes a serious attempt (the first of its kind) to
give a biological and psychological explanation of Jewish
characteristics by referring to the vicissitudes of the Jewish
people. The ideas of this profound thinker, who treated of
some of the problems of human selection in a manner which
for that period was certainly remarkable, appear to me to
be worth saving from an undeserved oblivion, and I shall
here give them in outline.[18]

Huarte mentions four causes which contributed to make
the Jews what they are: (1) A hot climate. (2) An unfruitful
soil. (3) The peculiar food of the people during their forty
years' wandering in the wilderness: they subsisted on Manna;
the water they drank was exceedingly pure, and the air they
breathed very rare. In such circumstances there was a tendency (as Aristotle had already pointed out) for children
to be born who were keen of intellect (*hombre de muy agudo
ingenio*). (4) "When the Children of Israel entered into possession of the Promised Land they were faced with so many
difficulties, scarcity, hostile raids, conquests and tribulations
of all sorts, that the misery of it had the effect of adding to
their intellectual genius a fiery, dry and parched temperament.
. . . Continual melancholy and a never-ending wretchedness
together resulted in collecting the blood in the brain, the liver
and the heart, and a process of blood consuming and burning
ensued. . . . This produced much burnt black gall (*melancolia
por adustion*). Of this almost all the Jews still have a great
deal and it results . . . in craft, cunning and spite (*solercia,
astucia, versacia, malicia*)." The author then proceeds to
answer the objection, that in the three thousand years since
their feeding on Manna the Jews very probably lost the characteristics they then acquired, by saying that once certain
tendencies enter into the system they become second nature

and are passed on for many generations. He is ready to admit, however, that possibly the Jews are not quite as sagacious as they used to be.

Into the depths to which the Madrid physician descends I cannot take the reader. We should not find anything but unproved theories there. We shall therefore remain above ground and content ourselves with noting the connexion between Jewish psychological qualities and the vicissitudes of the Jewish people.

The intellectuality of the Jew, we saw, was his most striking attribute, the one which embraced many others. It can be very easily accounted for when we recall that from the very earliest period of their history, when they tended their flocks beside the still waters, the Jews never had to perform hard manual labour. The curse that fell on Adam and Eve when they were expelled from the Garden of Eden, that man should eat bread in the sweat of his face, did not at any time bear heavily on the Jew—that is, if we take the words in their literal meaning and exclude mental worry and anxiety. Shepherd life calls for care, combination and organization, and all subsequent vocations which the Jews adopted (whether voluntarily or forcibly is of no consequence) demanded but little bodily work, though much mental effort. The family history of most of us leads through two or three generations to the plough or the anvil or the spinning-wheel. Not so with the Jews. For centuries and more they were for the most part never peasants or craftsmen, never makers of anything, but only thinkers—brain-workers. It was therefore only to be expected that certain gifts and capacities should be developed in them in the course of time. Given the Jewish mode of life, an exceptional intellectuality cannot but be deduced from it.

But more than this: the special Jewish intellectuality is of a kind associated with sandy or stony deserts. The Jews are rational, are fond of abstraction. Once more we are reminded of the contrast between desert and forest, between North and South. The sharp outlines of the landscape in hot, dry countries, their brilliant sunshine and their deep shadows, their clear, starlit nights and their stunted vegetation—cannot all these be summed up in the one word abstraction? The opposite to this is surely what is concrete, as all things of the North are, where the water flows abundantly, where the landscape is as varied as it is rich, where Nature is prolific in wood and field, and the earth sends up its fragrance. Is it accidental that astronomy and the art of reckoning first arose in the hot lands where the nights are ever brilliant, and was developed among peoples whose pastoral pursuits taught them to count? Can we think of the Sumerians who invented the cuneiform script[19] as a Northern people? Or, on the other hand, can we imagine the peasant of the misty North as he follows his plough, or the huntsman chasing deer in the forest, as either of them able to conceive the abstract idea of numbers?

So with rational thinking and searching after causes. That also leads us into the world of the South with its artificially produced, never natural vegetation, with the eternal insecurity of Bedouin life as the dominating factor of existence. And contrariwise, tradition is associated with the comfortable, secure and peaceful existence of the Northern farmer and with his misty and mysterious surroundings. That the appreciation of life and growth should be able to develop, or at least to develop more freely, among the luxuriant Nature of the North than among the dead vegetation of the South is not at all unlikely. And as the desert, so the town, in depriving man of his piece of fruitful mother earth destroys in him the feeling of communion with all living things, breaks the bond of fellowship between him and animals and plants, and so deadens all true understanding of organic Nature. On the other hand, the city sharpens his intellectual capacities, enabling him to search, to spy-out, to organize, to arrange. To be constantly on the alert is the nature of the nomad; to have to be constantly on the alert was what their fate forced on the Jews—to be constantly alive to new possibilities, new goals, new combinations of events; in a word, to order life with some end in view.

The Jew is adaptable and mobile. Adaptability and mobility are the principal qualities the nomad must possess if he is to

survive the struggle for existence. Your settled peasant could
not make any use of these virtues. "The law of desert life
prescribes the greatest mobility both of person and of property. Camel and steed must be able to carry the nomad and
all his substance speedily from one halting-place to the next,
for his stock of provisions is not great and is soon exhausted,
and besides he must be able to flee from the onslaughts of his
foe with the rapidity of a lightning flash. . . This mobility
even in ordinary circumstances necessitates a certain measure
of organizing talent on the part of the tribal leaders."[20] (The
soil tiller has no need of this.) "The plough and the ox seem
lazy things enough when compared with the lance, the arrow
and the horse of the nomad."[21] So too the country when
compared with the town. Turn to the history of the Jews,
and observe how from the moment they crossed the Jordan
until this very day towns have engendered in them a high
degree of mobility.

Always then we have the contrast between the nomad and
the dweller by the hearth, the contrast to which may be
ascribed, on the one hand determination to reach some goal,
on the other, joy in work for what it is worth. In the case
of the Jews their thousand years' wanderings only developed
this nomad virtue in them. The promised land throughout
their journeyings was always before them; it was always something to be reached, something to be achieved, something to
which they looked forward, like a traveller who has no delight
in his wandering. The more hopeless the present became, the
richer were the blessings which the future held out; everything that was was accounted as a bubble, all reality as without content, all action as senseless; only the result of action—
success, the end in view—had a value. In this chain of
tendencies the stress laid on results was to a large extent
responsible for the utilization of money for lending purposes,
and, indeed, for the whole of the capitalistic nexus. The importance attached by the Jew to results of action may have
been cause and effect at once of their capitalistic undertakings.

Now, for the attainment of some given end, no less than
for mobility, a large measure of physical and intellectual

energy is essential. The first ancestors of the Jews must have been possessed of a great deal, and the sojourn of the Jews amid Northern peoples only served to increase it still more. It is plainly manifest that the contact with the North perfected the inherent powers of the Jew. One need but compare his achievements here with those in Southern lands to see the truth of this statement. The process of selection, by weeding out the unfit, only made bodily and mental energy still more the possession of a people whose Southern origin already inclined them to it.

As the spirits of the two types of peoples differed, so also their respective expressions. Water, wood and fragrant earth have their fairy tales, their myths, their songs; so have desert and oasis. Delightful as it would be to follow this side-issue, we can here only call attention to it and perforce pass on to the consideration of the different economic system associated with each type of people.

The economic differences may be traced, at bottom, to the contrast between the nomadic and the agricultural life, between Saharaism and "Sylvanism." From the wood which is cleared, from the marsh which is drained, from the soil which the ploughshare turns up arose that economic organization of society which was dominant in Europe before Capitalism came—the feudal, manorial system, resting on the ideas that production should be only for consumption, that every man should have his niche to work in, and that every society should have differences in status. The peasant's holding, strictly marked off as it was from his neighbour's, gave prominence to the idea of each man's limited sphere of activities, of "the estate to which it had pleased God to call him"; there he was to remain and work in the traditional way.

From the endless wastes of sand, from the pastoral pursuits, springs the opposite way of life—Capitalism. Economic activities here are not circumscribed for each man, but are those of the breeder (shepherd) with his boundless outlook, where to-morrow may undo the work of to-day, but where also in a few years' time stock may increase tenfold. Sheep and kine multiply quickly, but as quickly they may be decimated by hunger or disease. Hence, only in the shepherd's calling, never in the farmer's, could the idea of gain have taken root, and the conception of unlimited production have become a reality. Only in the shepherd's calling could the view have become dominant that in economic activities the abstract quantity of commodities matters, not whether they are fit or sufficient for use. Only in the shepherd's calling was counting a prime necessity. Moreover, the rationalism which, as we have seen, is inseparable from nomadic life, here entered into play, and it is not too much to say that "Nomadism" is the progenitor of Capitalism. The relation between Capitalism and Judaism thus becomes more clear.

Now desert and wandering, though they influenced the Jewish character in no small degree, were not the only forces which moulded the Jewish spirit. There were others, not as effective as the first, but supplementary to them.

The first was money, of which the Jews were the guardians. This left its mark on their nature, but at the same time it was in consonance with it. For in money, the two factors that go to make up the Jewish spirit are united—desert and wandering, Saharaism and Nomadism. Money is as little concrete as the land from which the Jews sprang; money is only a mass, a lump, like the flock; it is mobile; it is seldom rooted in fruitful soil like the flower or the tree. Their constant concern with money distracted the attention of the Jews from a qualitative, natural view of life to a quantitative, abstract conception. The Jews fathomed all the secrets that lay hid in money, and found out its magic powers. They became lords of money, and, through it, lords of the world—as I tried to describe in the first chapter of this book.

Did they go in search of money, or was it first forced upon them and did they then gradually accustom themselves to the stranger? Both explanations, it would seem, have much in their favour.

In the beginning it looks as though a great deal of money flowed into their possession almost naturally—or more correctly stated, the precious metals, which they afterwards turned into coin. I believe it has never yet been pointed out that large quantities of gold and silver must have accumulated in Palestine in the period of the Kings. We are told of David that he brought back from his raiding expeditions much of both metals, not to mention the tribute he received in gold and silver. "And Joram brought with him vessels of silver and vessels of gold and vessels of brass; these also did King David dedicate unto the Lord with the silver and gold that he dedicated of all the nations which he subdued" (2 Sam. viii. 10–11).

The stories we read of the use of gold and silver, both in the making of the Tabernacle and in the building of the Temple, border on the fabulous, and apparently it was no exaggeration to say that "the King made silver and gold to be in Jerusalem as stones" (2 Chron. i. 15)—certainly not when we remember the exact statistical information on the subject. The voyages of King Solomon's ships to Ophir must have opened up a veritable California in those days. No wonder that the prophet Isaiah lamented that "their land is full of silver and gold, neither is there any end of their treasures" (Isa. ii. 7).

What happened to all these quantities of the precious metals? The Rabbis of the Talmud considered this question and came to the conclusion that it remained with Israel. "This is what R. Alexandrai taught. Three things returned whence they came: Israel, Egypt's money (cf. Exod. xii. 35 and 1 Kings xiv. 25) and the tablets of the Ark."[22] But of course a more convincing proof will hardly be adducible. Be that as it may, the important thing is that an enormous supply of the precious metals had accumulated in Israel at an early stage in its history. To this was added the moneys obtained through the centuries in all parts of the world. Nor must we overlook the streams of treasure that were directed to Palestine, partly as Temple taxes and partly as the offerings of pious pilgrims. Cicero (*pro Flacco*, c. 28) deplored the large sums that were annually taken to Jerusalem from Italy and all the provinces. Both channels must have given no small yield, as would appear from several interesting incidents. Mithridates, for instance, seized 800 talents of the Temple taxes and deposited them in the island of Cos. Cicero relates that Flaccus captured while on its way to Jerusalem the money which the Jews of four cities of Asia Minor (Apamea, Laodicea, Pergamum and Adramyttium) had sent, and that the spoil from the first-named city alone amounted to a hundred pounds of gold. And then the pilgrims! Their number must have been exceedingly large, though it was not quite 2,700,000, as Josephus reports, and though there were not quite 380 synagogues in Jerusalem for the convenience of the visitors. Certain it is, however, that the pilgrim bands were like reservoirs from which money flowed in all directions, and many a man must have become wealthy and therefore able to lend money at interest. Perhaps the priests may be instanced; we are told that they generally obtained large dowries and were not disinclined for a little money-lending business.[23]

The next question of importance is whether the Jews themselves discovered the secret power of money, whether it was they who instituted the mechanism of lending, or whether they learnt it from the Babylonians. It seems pretty well established now that money circulated freely in Babylon prior to the arrival of the Jews, though we have no details of any value as to the extent to which money-lending was developed. Possibly the seeds of Jewish monetary activities may have been germinating with their cousins, the Babylonians. It does not matter much which of these kindred peoples first grew golden fruit. The main thing is that later events forced money-lending upon the Jews, and so made them specialists in it. For their constant wanderings necessitated their having their wealth in a form easily portable, and what more adaptable for this than money and jewellery? Money was their sole companion when they were thrust naked into the street, and their sole protector when the hand of the oppressor was heavy upon them. So they learned to love it, seeing that by its aid alone they could subdue the mighty ones of the earth. Money became the means whereby they—and through them all mankind—might wield power without themselves being strong. With the fine threads of money-lending a people who were socially of little moment were able to bind the feudal giant, much as the Lilliputians did to Gulliver.

So much then for money as one factor in Jewish development. I come now to another, which some regard as of even greater import. I refer to the Ghetto.

The Ghetto undoubtedly influenced the social status of the Jews in a very peculiar way: it made of them despised pariahs. Even to-day the greater portion of Ghetto Jews belong socially to the lower classes, and are so considered by their brethren in faith. At one time in their history the contrast between the Ghetto Jew and his liberated brother found tangible expression in the attitude of the Sephardim (Spanish Jews) towards the Ashkenazim (German Jews). The former looked down on the latter with contempt, regarding them as importunate beggars who were a nuisance. This is the vein of bitter sarcasm in which a German Jew wrote to a Portuguese co-religionist about the middle of the 18th century (when the relation between the two sections was most strained) [24]: "I am aware, Sir, that the Portuguese Jews have nothing in common with those of Germany except a religious rite, and that their upbringing and their manners utterly differentiate between them as far as social life is concerned. I am also aware that the affinity between the two is a tradition of very ancient date, and that Vercingentorix, the Gaul, and Arminius, the German, were nearer relatives to Herod's father-in-law than you are to the Son of Ephraim." Pinto, the Sephardi Jew, expresses himself in a similar tone in his well-known reply to the attacks which Voltaire made on the Jews as a whole.[25] Pinto is anxious that the Spanish Jews should not be put in the same boat as the German Jews; they are two distinct nations. "A Jew of London," he says, "as little resembles a Jew of Constantinople as the latter does a Chinese Mandarin. A Portuguese Jew of Bordeaux and a German Jew of Metz have nothing in common." "Mons. de Voltaire cannot ignore the delicate scruples of the Portuguese and Spanish Jews in not mixing with the Jews of other nations, either by marriage or otherwise." Pinto proceeds to say that if a Sephardi Jew in Holland or England were to make a German Jewess his wife, his relatives would disown him and he would not even be given burial in their cemetery.

This opposition very often found practical expression, more especially on the part of the Sephardim, who in their own eyes were the aristocracy of Jewry and who were afraid lest their social position should be endangered by the arrival of Jews from more easterly countries. Thus, in 1761 the Portuguese Jews (or Marannos) of Bordeaux were able to get an order passed to the effect that within fourteen days all alien Jews were to leave the city. Pinto and Pereira were the prime movers in the matter, and they used every endeavour to rid themselves of the "vagabonds"—their own co-religionists from Germany and France.[26] In Hamburg the Sephardim occupied a position of official superiority over the German Jews; the latter having to give undertakings to the former that no shady commercial practices would be carried on.

The reason for the dislike between the Sephardim and the Ashkenazim, more especially of the former towards the latter, may be found in the different social positions occupied by each. But no doubt the feeling was strengthened by the distinctly marked aristocratic consciousness of the Sephardim, who held that they were of purer origin than the Ashkenazim, that their blood was bluer, that their family pride had always been a spur to them as long as they lived in the Pyrenean Peninsula to do noble deeds, and had thus been a protection against all things base.[27]

We have here possibly touched on a chord which will help us to apprize at its true worth the influence of the Ghetto for Jewish life. Perhaps the conception of *noblesse oblige* held by the Spanish and Portuguese Jews—their aim to make the highest virtues theirs—may explain why they had no Ghettos, and will not need to be regarded as an effect of Ghetto life. In other words, perhaps a section of the Jews lived the Ghetto life because they were by nature inclined that way. It is difficult to say why some continued in the Ghetto while others soon freed themselves. We have not sufficient information for the decision. Nor can we assert without hesitation (though much would seem to point to it) that the Sephardim represented the result of a process of social selection among Jews. But it is not assuming too much to say that differences in their vicissitudes are traceable to differences in their natures. These differences must not, however, be made too much of. Their Jewishness was little influenced by them. Jews they were all, whether Sephardim or Ashkenazim. But in the case of the latter, Ghetto life produced certain habits, certain mannerisms which always clung to the Ghetto Jew, and often affected his economic activities. In part they were the habits of low social grades generally, but in Jews, with their peculiar temperament, they assumed curious features—a tendency, for instance, to petty cheating, obtrusiveness, lack of personal dignity, tactlessness and so on. These things must have played some part in the Jewish conquest of the feudal economic strongholds; in what way precisely we have already had occasion to see.

But these mere externals must not be exaggerated. In social intercourse with Jews they may appear of some importance to this or that person; but we doubt whether any great weight should be attached to them in considering Jewish economic achievements. Without question the Jews could not have won their dominant position in the world by the aid of these mannerisms alone.

Another aspect of Ghetto life is of more consequence. I refer to its influence in making the inherent Jewish characteristics more marked and more one-sided. If, as we have already observed, these characteristics sprang from a want of settledness on the part of the Jew, it is obvious that the Ghetto only intensified it. But it was already there, already innate in the Jew.

The Ghetto had the same effect in another direction by giving prominence to, and emphasizing the twin forces which were responsible for the constancy in Jewish peculiarities—religion and pure breeding.

The religion of a people is, of course, the expression of its soul: that has been the view that we have taken in this book. But all the same, an exclusive formalistic religion like

Judaism must in its turn strongly influence its adherents, more especially in the direction of unifying their life and giving it a common stamp. How this expressed itself we have also considered; I would here only remind the reader of its rationalizing tendencies.

And as with religion so with the physiological side of life, which is so closely akin to it. That also intensified the inbreeding of the Jews, which they had practised for hundreds of years.

I have just remarked that with the Jews inbreeding is closely akin to religion. One may go even further and say that it is a direct consequence of the central idea of the religion, the idea of election. This has been demonstrated recently in a series of studies, one of the best of which perhaps is by Alfred Nossig, who writes as follows:[28] "A striking biological result of the idea of election is the existence of the Jews, and their power of reproduction, not yet abated. The Mosaic conception of 'an everlasting people' would seem to be realizing itself." Dietary and marriage laws are safeguards for the continuance of the race. "These ethical treasurers of highest worth were of course shielded against destruction through intermixture with less carefully reared races. The result of the prohibition of mixed marriages was that the factor which is supreme in race culture—heredity—was maintained in its pristine strength, and the advantages that have been mentioned not merely remained constant but increased from generation to generation." "Inbreeding has thus resulted in making Jewish inherited characteristics more and more marked and intense, so that it becomes exceedingly difficult to oust them by intermixture. For it has been proved that the intensity of heredity, like all other organic functions, has become strengthened by constant practice."[29]

Religion and inbreeding were the two iron hoops that bound the Jewish people and kept them as one body through the centuries. Suppose that the hoops were to become loose, what then? To answer this very difficult question was not the task I set myself. For as long as we find the Jews exercising their particular influence on economic life—and they still do so—we may take it that the hoops are yet strong. I did not in this book intend to go beyond considering that influence, and showing the genesis of the Jewish genius which made it possible—that influence which has been so fateful in economic life and for modern culture as a whole.

Notes and References

Notes and References

Abbreviations

Monatsschrift = *Monatsschrift für Geschichte und Wissenschaft des Judentums.*

J.Q.R. = *Jewish Quarterly Review.*

Z.D.S.J. = *Zeitschrift für Demographie und Statistik der Juden.*

R.E.J. = *Revue des Études Juives.*

Chapter 1

1. Jakob Fromer, *Das Wesen des Judentums* (1905), p. 144. No authority cited.

2. *Zeitschrift für Demographie und Statistik der Juden* [*Z.D.S.J.*], iii., 140, 145.

3. J. Thon, "Taufbewegung der Juden in Oesterreich," in *Z.D.S.J.*, iv., 6.

4. Théophile Malvezin, *Histoire des Juifs à Bordeaux* (1875), p. 105.

5. *E.g.,* Lucien Wolf, "Jessurun Family" in *Jewish Quarterly Review* [*J.Q.R.*], i. (1889), 439.

6. *E.g.,* B. C. Weiss, *Histoire des réfugiés protest.,* i. (1853), pp. 164, 377, 379, 383; ii., 5.

7. Sigmund Mayer, *Die ökonomische Entwicklung der Wiener Juden,* p. 7.

Chapter 2

1. To give the numbers of Jews who were scattered in different lands is impossible. Attempts to do this have indeed been made, but the results were nothing more than conjectures. Perhaps the

best of these is I. Loeb, *Le nombre des Juifs de Castile et d'Espagne au moyen Age,* in *Revue des Études Juives,* xiv. (1887), p. 161. Loeb bases a good many of his calculations on the number of Jews resident in the different localities to-day. Nevertheless I shall give the results of his researches. He believes there were about 235,000 Jews in Spain and Portugal in 1492. The number had remained pretty constant for some two hundred years. Of the total, 160,000 lived in Castile (Andalusia, Granada, etc.) and 30,000 in Navarre. What happened to all these Jews? Loeb maintains that 50,000 were baptized, 20,000 perished as a result of the expulsion, and 165,000 emigrated as follows: 90,000 to Turkey, 2000 to Egypt and Tripoli, 10,000 to Algiers, 20,000 to Morocco, 3000 to France, 9000 to Italy, 25,000 to Holland, Hamburg, England and Scandinavia, 5000 to America, and 1000 to various other countries.

Supplementary to these figures let me quote the report of the well-informed Venetian Ambassador, who says, "Si giudica in Castilia ed in altre province di Spagna il terzo esser Marrani un terzo dico di coloro che sono cittadini e mercanti perchè il populo minuto è vero cristiano, e cosi la maggior parte delli grandi." Vicenzo Querini (1506) in Alberi, *Rel. degli Amb.,* Series I, vol. i., p. 29.

2. For the fate of the Marannos in Portugal see M. Kayserling, *Geschichte der Juden in Portugal* (1876), pp. 84, 167. Further particulars may be found in J. H. Gottheil's *The Jews and the Spanish Inquisition,* in *J.Q.R.,* xv. (1903), p. 182; in Elkan Adler's *Auto da Fè and Jew,* ib., xiii., xiv., xv. (recently issued in book form).

3. Cf. B. Sieveking, *Genueser Firanzwesen,* ii. (1899), p. 167, with Schudt, *Jüdische Merkwürdigkeiten,* i. (1714), p. 128.

4. Frankfort (Main) was the goal of the Jews expelled from the other South-German towns in the 15th and 16th centuries. But Holland must also have contributed its quota, as would appear from the close commercial relations between Frankfort and Amsterdam in the 17th and 18th centuries. According to F. Bothe, *Beiträge zur Wirtschafts- und Socialgeschichte der Reichsstadt Frankfurt* (1906), p. 70, the number of Jews in Frankfort increased twenty-fold. In 1612 there were about 2800; in 1709 the official census gives 3019, out of a total population of 18,000. We are tolerably well informed as to the origin of the Jews in

Frankfort, thanks to the assiduous industry of A. Dietz in his *Stammbuch der Frankfurter Juden: Geschichtliche Mitteilungen über die Frankfurter jüdischen Familien von* 1549-1849 (1907). For the period prior to 1500 see Karl Bücher, *Bevölkerung von Frankfurt am Main* (1886), pp. 526-601.

In Hamburg the Jews first settled (ostensibly as Catholics) in 1577 or 1583. They came from Flanders, Italy, Holland, Spain and Portugal, and it was not until the 17th century that immigrants from the East (Germany especially) began to arrive. According to Count Galeazzo Gualdo Priorato there were some 40 or 50 German-Jewish houses in Hamburg in 1663 side by side with the 120 of Portuguese Jews. See *Zeitschrift für Hamburgische Geschichte,* iii., p. 140. For a general account of the Jews of Hamburg, see A. Feilchenfeld, *Die älteste Geschichte der deutschen Juden in Hamburg,* in the *Monatsschrift für Geschichte und Wissenschaft des Judentums,* vol. 43 (1899); also M. Grunwald, *Portugiesengräber auf deutscher Erde* (1902) and *Hamburgs deutsche Juden* (1904).

From the end of the 17th century onward the Jews increased rapidly in Hamburg. About the middle of the 18th century we hear of a "terrible crowd of Jews," estimated (much too highly, of course) at between twenty and thirty thousand. Cf. C. L. von Griesheim, *Die Stadt Hamburg* (1760), p. 47.

5. Risbeck, *Briefe eines reisenden Franzosen über Deutschland an seinen Bruder in Paris* (1780). Quoted in H. Scheubbe, *Aus den Tagen unserer Grossväter* (1873), pp. 382 ff.

6. We have a wealth of information about the Jews in Bordeaux in the fine work of Malvezin (cf. Chapter 2), which is really invaluable. Of the Jews in Marseilles we are told much in Jonas Weyl's "Les juifs protégés français aux échelles du Levant et en Barbarie," in *Rev. de Études Juives,* vol. xii. (1886). For the Jews of Rouen see Gosselin, "Documents inédites pour servir à l'histoire de la marine normande et du commerce rouennais pendant les xvi et xvii siècles" (1876). Pigeonneau, who quotes this book in his *Histoire du commerce,* ii, p. 123, speaks of course of "the naturalized Spaniards and Portuguese."

We ought to mention also Maignial, *La Question juive en France en* 1789 (1903), a book based on an extensive acquaintance with sources, written with skill and judgment. Not only does it present a good account of the Jewish Question in France in 1789, but it also shows how that problem developed.

In Paris there were not many Jews before the 19th century, though some of them were very influential. A good deal of information will be found concerning the Jews of Paris in the 18th century in the books of Léon Kahn, *Les juifs à Paris depuis le vi siècle* (1889); *Les juifs sous Louis XV* (1892), and *Les juifs à Paris au xviii siècle* (1894). Good as these books are, they do not deal with every aspect of the question.

Much valuable material dealing with the history of the Jews in France will be found scattered in the *Revue des Études Juives* [*R.E.J.*] (from 1880 onwards).

7. The history of the Jews in Holland has been treated by H. J. Koenen, *Geschiedenes der Joden in Nederland* (1843), which has not been surpassed. Also worth mentioning are the following: M. Henriques Pimentel, *Geschiedkundige Aanteekeningen betreffende de Portugesche Israeliten in den Haag* (1876); S. Back, *Die Entstehungsgeschichte der portugiesischen Gemeinde in Amsterdam* (1883); E. Italie, *Geschiedenes der Israelitischen Gemeente te Rotterdam* (1907).

8. Ranke, *Französische Geschichte,* vol. iii., p. 350.

9. Schudt, *Jüdische Merkwürdigkeiten,* i. (1714), p. 271; cf. also p. 277.

10. In addition to the literature mentioned in note 6, see also Carmoly in the *Revue Orientale* (1841) i., 42, 168, 174, and Graetz, *Geschichte der Juden,* vol. 9, pp. 292, 354, 490.

11. See L. Guiccardino, *Totius Belgii Descriptio* (1652), p. 129, and cf. Ehrenberg, *Zeiltalter der Fugger,* ii. (1896), p. 3.

12. Cf. Macaulay's [History] iv., p. 320, and Ehrenberg, *op. cit.,* ii., p. 303.

13. The history of the Jews in England has been abundantly and efficiently dealt with. A mine of information (though it must be used with care) will be found in *Anglia Judaica, or the History and Antiquities of the Jews in England,* by D'Blossiers Tovey (1738). Among later works the pioneer was that of James Picciotto, *Sketches of Anglo-Jewish History* (1875), which is deficient in that it does not always mention authorities. H. S. Q. Henriques

in his *Return of the Jews to England* (1905) has written on this subject from the legal point of view.

A complete account of the history of the Jews in England will be found in Albert M. Hyamson's admirable *A History of the Jews in England* (1908). The author has skilfully utilized the material at his disposal in special articles and papers, and has presented a rounded off study of the whole subject. The *J.Q.R.* (first appeared in 1889) contains much miscellaneous material. Also the publications of the Anglo-Jewish Historical Exhibition (1888).

For the Cromwellian period the following may be mentioned: Lucien Wolf, *The Middle Age of Anglo-Jewish History*, 1290-1656, in the Publications of the Anglo-Jewish Historical Exhibition, No. 1. Significant for the position of the Jews in England at the end of the 15th century is the fact that a Jew commenced legal proceedings quite openly and was confident of winning his case. A century later there were Jewish industrial undertakers in England, cf. *Calendar of State Papers*, 1581-90, p. 49 (quoted in L. Wolf's paper). There must have been quite a number of Jews in England at the beginning of the 17th century. A publication of 1625, *The Wandering Jew telling fortunes to Englishmen* (also quoted in Mr. Wolf's paper), says: "A store of Jews we have in England; a few in Court; many i' the city; more in the country."

14. *Anglia Judaica*, p. 302, "as I have been well inform'd," writes Tovey.

15. A good instance is that of J. F. Richter, who works out the thesis for Nuremberg. For the old Jewish community in Nuremberg, see *Allgemeine Judenzeitung*, 1842, No. 24. Cf. also the Eighth Report of the Historische Verein für Mittelfranken, and M. Brann, "Eine Sammlung Fürther Grabschriften," in *Gedenkbuch zur Erinnerung an David Kaufmann* (1900).

16. A most interesting document in support is given by D. Kaufmann in his "Die Vertreibung der Marranen aus Venedig im Jahre 1550," in the *J.Q.R.*, vol. 13 (1901), p. 520.

17. Hyamson's *History of the Jews in England*, p. 174.

18. M. Bloch, *Les juifs et la prospèritè publique à travers l'histoire* (1899), p. 11. The Ordinance contains the following remarkable words, "Vous devez bien prendre garde que la jalousie du commerce portera toujours les marchands à être d'avis de les chasser."

19. Malvezin, *Les juifs à Bordeaux,* p. 132.

20. Malvezin, p. 175.

21. S. Ullmann, *Studien zur Geschichte des Juden in Belgien bis zum* 18. *Jahrhundert* (1909), p. 34

22. Émile Ouverleaux, "Notes et documents sur les juifs de Belgique," in *R.E.J.,* vol. 7, p. 262.

23. Thurloe, *Collection of State Papers,* iv, p. 333. Cf. also the letter of Whalley, p. 308.

24. J. Müller in his anti-Jewish book, *Judaismus* (1644). Cf. also Reils, "Beiträge zur älteren Geschichte der Juden in Hamburg," in the *Zeitschrift des Vereins für Hamburgische Geschichte,* vol. 2, p. 412.

25. Ehrenberg, *Grosse Vermögen,* p. 146.

26. M. Grunwald, *Hamburgs deutsche Juden bis zur Auflösung der Dreigemeinden,* 1811 (1904), p. 21.

27. Arnold Kiesselbach, *Die wirtschafts- und rechtsgeschichtliche Entwicklung der Seeversicherung in Hamburg* (1901), p. 24.

Chapter 3

1. Hyamson, p. 178.

2. *Anglia Judaica,* p. 292.

3. Thanks to the work of R. Markgraf, *Zur Geschichte der Juden auf den Messen in Leipzig vom* 1664-1839 (a doctoral dissertation, 1894), from which the figures in the text have been taken. For the short period 1675-99 Max Freudenthal, "Leipziger Messgäste" in *Monatsschrift,* vol. 45 (1901), p. 460, is even better than Markgraf, for he draws from the actual Fair Books, where Markgraf depends on the documents in the Leipzig archives, which are of later date. Freudenthal shows that between 1671 and 1699, 18,182 Jews visited the fairs, apart from those who had special permits. Markgraf, however, for the same period has traced only

14,705. Freudenthal's study appeared in book form in 1902 under the title of *Die jüdischen Besucher der Leipziger Messe.*

4. Markgraf, p. 93; Freudenthal, p. 465. Cf. R. Funke, *Die Leipziger Messen* (1897), p. 41.

5. See, for example, No. 21 of the *Judenreglements* of the year 1710 in C. L. von Griesheim, *Die Stadt Hamburg, Anmerkungen und Zugaben* (1759), p. 95.

6. E. Baasch, "Hamburgs Seeschiffahrt und Warenhandel" in the *Zeitschrift des Ver. für Hamburg. Geschichte,* vol. 9 (1894), pp. 316, 324. Cf. A. Feilchenfeld, "Anfang und Blütezeit der Portugiesengemeinden," in *Hambg. Ztschrift.,* vol. 10 (1899), p. 199.

7. *Encyclopédie methodique.* "Manufactures," i., 403-4.

8. Cf. H. J. Koenen, *Geschiedenes der Joden in Nederland* (1843), p. 176 ff. Also H. Sommershausen, "Die Geschichte der Niederlassung der Juden in Holland und den holländischen Kolonien," in *Monatsschrift,* vol. ii.

9. For jewellery and pearls, see for Hamburg Griesheim, *op. cit.,* p. 119; for North Germany I am indebted to Dr. Bernfeld, of Berlin, for information; for Holland, see *Jewish Encyclopædia,* article "Netherlands"; E. E. Danekamp, *Die Amsterdamer Diamantindustrie,* quoted by N. W. Goldstein in his article in the *Z.D.S.J.* (vol. iii., p. 178) on *Die Juden in der Amsterdamer Diamantindustrie;* for Italy, see D. Kaufmann, "Die Vertreibung der Marranen aus Venedig," in the *J.Q.R.*
As for silks, the Jews were for centuries engaged in this industry, which they transplanted from Greece into Sicily and later to France and Spain. Cf. Graetz v.², p. 244. In the 16th century they dominated the silk trade in Italy (cf. David Kaufmann, *loc. cit.*), and in the 18th century in France. In 1760 the wardens of the Lyons Silkweavers' Guild termed the Jewish nation "la maîtresse du commerce de toutes les provinces." See J. Godard, *L'Ouvrier en Soie* (1899), p. 224. In 1755 there were 14 and in 1759, 22 Jewish silk merchants in Paris. See Kahn, *Juifs des Paris sous Louis XV,* p. 63. It was the same tale in Berlin.

10. How the Jews developed the wholesale textile trade in Vienna may be seen from the personal experiences of S. Mayer in his *Die ökonomische Entstehung der Wiener Juden,* p. 8 ff.

An ordinance of the City Council of Nuremberg, bearing date December 28, 1780, calls silk, velvet and wool "Judenware." Cf. H. Barbeck, *Geschichte der Juden in Nürnberg und Fürth* (1878), p. 71.

11. For the sugar trade with the Levant, see Lippmann, *Geschichte des Zuckers* (1890), p. 206; D. Kaufmann, *loc. cit.*; for sugar trade with America, see M. Grunwald, *Portugiesengräber auf deutscher Erde* (1902), p. 6 ff.; A. Feilchenfeld, "Anfang und Blütezeit der Portugiesengemeinde in Hamburg," in the *Zeitschrift des Vereins für Hamburg. Geschichte*, vol. 10 (1899), p. 211. Cf. also Risbeck, *op. cit.*

12. "Controlling the Cotton Trade." See art. "America, U.S. of," in *Jewish Encyclopædia* (i. 495).

13. More especially for Hamburg, see Feilchenfeld, *loc. cit.*

14. Moses Lindo, the principal pioneer in the indigo trade, arrived in South Carolina in 1756 and invested £120,000 in indigo. Between 1756 and 1776 the production of indigo increased fivefold. Cf. B. A. Elgas, *The Jews of South Carolina* (1903), see also art. "South Carolina," in *Jewish Encyclopædia*.

15. Risbeck, *op. cit.*, vol. ii., under Frankfort.

16. Quoted by Bloch, *op. cit.*, p. 36.

17. See Richard Markgraf, *op. cit.*, p. 93.

18. Cf. Hyamson, pp. 174, 178. Also the report sent by the rulers of Antwerp to the Bishop of Arras, quoted by Ullmann, *op. cit.*, p. 35, "they have brought much wealth with them, especially silver, jewels and many ducats."

Chapter 4

1. When Don Isaac Abarbanel was writing his commentary on the Book of Jeremiah (1504) he saw a document brought from India by Portuguese spice merchants wherein it was reported that they had met many Jews in that country. Quoted by M. Kayserling, *Christopher Columbus* (1894), p. 105. Cf. also Bloch, *op. cit.*, p. 15.

2. As Manasseh ben Israel mentions in his "Humble Address" to Cromwell. For this document, see *Jewish Chronicle,* November and December, 1859. Cf. also de Barrios, *Hist. universal Judayca,* p. 4.

3. G. C. Klerk de Reus, *Geschichtlicher Überblick der . . . niederländisch-ostindischen Compagnie* (1894), xix. For Coen, see p. xiv.

4. J. P. J. Du Bois, *Vie des Gouverneurs généraux . . . ornée de leurs portraits en vignettes au naturel* (1763).

5. *E.g.,* Francis Salvador. Cf. art. "Salvador," in *Jewish Encycl.,* also Hyamson, p. 264.

6. In 1569 wealthy Amsterdam Jews furnished the Barentz Expedition. Cf. M. Grunwald, *Hamburgs deutsche Juden* (1904), p. 215.

7. See art. "South Africa," in the *Jewish Encycl.*

8. Dr. J. H. Hertz, *The Jew in South Africa* (1905).

9. Art. "Commerce" in *Jewish Encycl.*

10. The literature concerning Jews and America is pretty extensive. I can only mention the most important works here. To begin with, there is the *Jewish Encyclopædia* (an American publication), which has some excellent articles relating to American conditions. Then I must mention the *Transactions* of the Jewish Historical Society of America (begun in 1895), a veritable mine of information on American Jewish (also economic) history, more especially in the colonies in North and South America in the 17th and 18th centuries. There are some valuable speeches in *The 250th Anniversary of the Settlement of the Jews in the U.S.A.* (1905).

Further, see Markeus, *The Hebrews in America;* C. P. Daly, *History of the Settlement of the Jews in North America* (1893); M. C. Peters, *The Jews in America* (1906). The first two books appear to be out of print.

11. In connexion with the 400th anniversary of the discovery of America, a number of works have made their appearance showing to what extent Jews participated in the actual discovery. The best of these is M. Kayserling, *Christopher Columbus und der*

Anteil der Juden, etc. (1894). Some others are: F. Rivas Puiq-cerver, *Los Judios y el nuevo mundo* (1891); L. Modona, *Gli Ebrei e la scoperta dell' America* (1893). Cf. also art. "Discovery of America," in *Jewish Encycl.*, and address by Oscar Strauss in the 250*th Anniversary*, etc., p. 69.

12. M. Kayserling, *loc. cit.*, p. 112; Juan Sanchez, of Saragossa, the first trader. Cf. also Kayserling's "The Colonization of America by the Jews," in the *Transactions* of the Jewish Historical Society of America, vol. 2, p. 73.

13. G. F. Knapp, "Ursprung der Sklaverei in den Colonien," in the *Archiv für Soziale Politik*, ii., p. 129.

14. Oscar Strauss, *loc. cit.*, p. 71.

15. Ritter, "Über die geographische Verbreitung des Zucker-rohrs," in the *Berichten der Berliner Akademie* (1839), quoted by Lippmann, *Geschichte des Zuckers* (1890), p. 249.

16. According to Max J. Kohler, "Phases of Jewish Life in New York before 1800," in the *Transactions* of the Jewish Hist. Soc. of America, vol. ii., p. 94.

17. Art. "America," in *Jewish Encycl.* Cf. G. A. Kohut, "Les juifs dans les colonies hollandaises," in the *R.E.J.* (1895), vol. 31, p. 293.

18. H. Handelmann, *Geschichte von Brasilien* (1860), p. 412.

19. P. M. Netscher, *Les Hollandais au Brésil* (1853), p. 1. For the wealthy Jewish family of Souza, cf. M. Kayserling, *Geschichte der Juden in Portugal* (1867), p. 307; M. Grunwald, *Portugiesengräber* (1902), p. 123.

20. M. J. Kohler, *op. cit.*

21. Art. "America," in *Jewish Encycl.*

23. *Ibid.*

22. *Transactions* of Jewish Hist. Society of America, ii. 95. Cf. also Netscher, p. 103.

24. There was no actual expulsion; in fact the treaty of peace of 1654 granted Jews an amnesty. But the fateful words were added, "Jews and other non-Catholics shall receive the same treatment as in Portugal." That was sufficient. For the treaty, see

Aitzema, *Historia,* etc. (1626), quoted by Netscher [see note 19], p. 163.

25. H. Handelmann, *loc. cit.,* pp. 412-13.

26. For Jews in Barbados, see John Camden Hatten, *The Original Lists, etc.* (1874), p. 449; Ligon, *History of Barbados* (1657), quoted by Lippmann *op. cit.,* p. 301; Reed, *The History of Sugar and Sugar-yielding Plants* (1866), p. 7; M'Culloch, *Dictionary of Commerce,* ii., p. 1087. Cf. also C. P. Lucas, *A Historical Geography of the British Colonies, e.g.* ii. (1905), 121, 274, 277.

27. For Jews in Jamaica, see M. Kayserling, "The Jews in Jamaica," etc., in the *J.Q.R.,* vol. 12 (1900), 708 ff.; Hyamson, *loc. cit.,* chapter xxvi. Numerous extracts from contemporary records will be found in Kohler's "Jewish Activity in American Colonial Commerce," in *Transactions* of Jewish Hist. Society of America, vol. 10, p. 59. Cf. also the same writer's paper in the *Transactions,* vol. 2, p. 98.

28. The letter of the Governor to Secretary of State Lord Arlington, quoted by Kayserling in *J.Q.R.,* vol. 12, p. 710.

29. Monumental inscriptions of the British West Indies, collected by Captain J. H. Lawrence Archer, quoted by Kohler, "Phases of Jewish Life," *op. cit.,* p. 98.

30. For Jews in Surinam the most important authority is the *Essai sur la colonie de Surinam avec l'histoire de la Nation Juive Portugaise y établie,* etc., 2 vols., Paramaribo (1788). Koenen, in his *Geschiedenes der Joden in Nederland* (1843), p. 313, speaks of this work as "de hoofdbron . . . voor de geschiedenes der Joden in die gewesten." I have not been able to see a copy. Newer treatises on the subject have brought to light a good deal of fresh material. We may mention R. Gottheil, "Contributions to the History of the Jews in Surinam," in *Transacions* of Jewish Hist. Society of America, vol. 9, p. 129; J. S. Roos, "Additional Notes on the History of the Jews of Surinam," *Transactions,* vol. 13, p. 127; P. A. Hilfman, "Some Further Notes on the History of the Jews in Surinam," *Transactions,* vol. 16, p. 7. For the connexion between Surinam and Guiana see Samuel Oppenheimer, "An Early Jewish Colony in Western Guiana, 1658-1666, and its relation to

the Jews in Surinam," in *Transactions*, vol. 16, pp. 95-186. Cf. also Hyamson, ch. xxvi, and Lucas.

31. For Jews in Martinique, Guadeloupe, and Santo Domingo, see Lippmann, *op. cit.*, p. 301; A. Cahen, "Les Juifs de la Martinique au xvii sc.," in *R.E.J.*, vol 2; Cahen, "Les Juifs dans les Colonies françaises au xviii sc.," in *R.E.J.*, vols. 4 and 5; Handelmann, *Geschichte der Insel Hayti* (1856).

32. Lucien Wolf in the *Jewish Chronicle*, Nov. 30, 1894, quoted by Kohler in *Transactions*, vol. 10, p. 60.

33. *The 250th Anniversary of the Settlement of the Jews in the U.S.* (1905), p. 18.

34. *The 250th Anniversary*, etc.

35. John Moody, *The Truth about the Trusts* (1905), pp. 45, 96, etc.

36. Art. "California," in *Jewish Encycl.* (which is a particularly good one).

37. There are others who maintain that even before the Brazilian refugees arrived a number of wealthy Jewish traders from Amsterdam settled in the colony of the Hudson. Cf. Albion Morris Dyer, "Points in the First Chapter of New York Jewish History," in *Transactions* of Jewish Hist. Soc. of America, vol. 3, p. 41.

38. The letter is quoted in full by Kohler, "Beginnings of New York Jewish History," in *Transactions*, vol. 1, p. 47.

39. See *Transactions*, vol. 1, p. 41; vol. 2, p. 78; vol. 10, p. 63; Kohler, "Jews in Newport," *Transactions*, vol. 6, p. 69. Kohler often quotes Judge Daly, *Settlement of the Jews in North America* (1893).

40. Address by Governor Pardell, of California, in *The 250th Anniversary*, etc., p. 173.

41. See art. "Alabama," in *Jewish Encycl.*

42. See art. "Albany," in *Jewish Encycl.*

43. B. Felsenthal, "On the History of the Jews in Chicago," in *Transactions*, vol. 2, p. 21; H. Eliassof, "The Jews of Chicago," in *Transactions*, vol. 2, p. 117.

44. Lewis N. Dembitz, "Jewish Beginnings in Kentucky," in *Transactions*, vol. 1, p. 99.

45. J. H. Hollander, "Some Unpublished Material relating to Dr. Jacob Lumbrozo of Maryland," in *Transactions*, vol. 1.

46. D. E. Heinemann, "Jewish Beginnings in Michigan before 1850," in *Transactions*, vol. 13, p. 47.

47. D. Philipson, "The Jewish Pioneers of the Ohio Valley," in *Transactions*, vol. 8, p. 43.

48. Henry Necarsulmer, "The Early Jewish Settlement at Lancaster, Pa.," in *Transactions*, vol. 3, p. 27.

49. Henry Cohen, "The Jews in Texas," in *Transactions*, vol. 4, p. 9; Henry Cohen, "Henry Castro, Pioneer and Colonist," in *Transactions*, vol. 5, p. 39. Cf. also H. Friedenwald, "Some Newspaper Advertisements in the 18th Century," in *Transactions*, vol. 6.

50. "Einiges aus dem Leben der amerikanisch-jüdischen Familie Seligman aus Bayersdorf in Bayern," in Brüll's *Monatsblättern* (1906), p. 141.

51. Leon Hühner, "The Jews of Georgia in Colonial Times," in *Transactions*, vol. 10, p. 65; Hühner, "The Jews of South Carolina from the Earliest Settlement to the End of the American Revolution," in *Transactions*, vol. 12, p. 39; Chas. C. Jones, "The Settlement of the Jews in Georgia," in *Transactions*, vol. 1, p. 12.

52. B. A. Elgas, *The Jews of South Carolina* (1903).

53. L. Hühner, "Asser Levy, a noted Jewish Burgher of New Amsterdam," in *Transactions*, vol. 8, p. 13. Cf. also Hühner, "Whence came the First Jewish Settlers of New York?" in *Transactions*, vol. 9, p. 75; M. J. Kohler, "Civil Status of the Jews in Colonial New York," in *Transactions*, vol. 6, p. 81.

54. For Jews who in the 18th century carried on business in their own tongue in New York cf. J. A. Doyle, *The Colonies under the House of Hanover* (1907), p. 31.

55. Chas. C. Jones, "The Settlement of the Jews in Georgia," in *Transactions*, vol. 1, pp. 6, 9.

56. M. Jaffé, "Die Stadt Posen," in *Schriften des Vereins für S. P.*, vol. 119, ii. 151.

57. Simon Wolf, "The American Jew as Soldier and Patriot," in *Transactions*, vol. 3, p. 39.

58. According to Dr. Fischell's *Chronological Notes of the History of the Jews in America*.

Chapter 5

1. Perhaps our conclusion would have to be a different one if we were to recall the fact that the elements of the modern State were already developed in the later decades of the Middle Ages, chiefly in Italy and Spain, and that Jewish statesmen occupied influential positions in both these countries. It is to be regretted that the history of modern States has never (so far as I am aware) been written from this point of view; I believe much that is profitable would result. Of course there is little in common between the writers on the history of the Jews in Spain and Portugal, say Lindo, de los Rios, Kayserling, Mendes dos Remedios, and those who treat of the rise of the State in the Pyrenean Peninsula, say Ranke or Baumgarten.

2. Lucien Wolf, "The First English Jewry," in *Transactions* of the Jewish Historical Society of England, vol. 2. Cf. Hyamson, pp. 171-3.

3. Hyamson, p. 269; Picciotto, *Sketches of Anglo-Jewish History* (1875), p. 58.

4. "Und bedient sich Frankreich jederzeit ihrer Hülffe, bey Krieges-Zeiten seine Reuterey beritten zu machen." T. L. Lau, *Einrichtung der Intraden und Einkünfte der Souveräne*, etc. (1719), p. 258.

5. Quoted by Liebe, *Das Judentum* (1903), p. 75.

6. Art. "Banking," in *Jewish Encycl.*

7. *Mémoire of the Jews of Metz of the 24 March*, 1733, given in part by Bloch, *op. cit.*, p. 35.

8. Quoted by Bloch, *op. cit.*, p. 23.

9. Extracts from the *Lettres patentes*, in Bloch, *op. cit.*, p. 24.

10. For the Gradis, see T. Malvezin, *op. cit.*, p. 241; Graetz, Die Familie Gradis," in *Monatsschrift*, vol. 24 (1875), 25 (1875).

11. M. Capefigue, *Banquiers, fournisseurs*, etc. (1856), pp. 68, 214, etc.

12. Quoted in *Revue de la Révolution française* (1892), 16, 1.

13. *Historische Nachlese zu den Nachrichten der Stadt Leipzig*, edited by M. Heinrich Engelbert Schwartze (1744), p. 122, quoted by Alphonse Levy, *Geschichte der Juden in Sachsen* (1900), p. 58.

14. Bondy, *Zur Geschichte der Juden in Böhmen*, vol. i., p. 388.

15. I quote this from Liebe, *Das Judentum* (1903), pp. 43, 70, who mentions the facts without giving his authorities.

16. König, *Annalen der Juden in den preussischen Staaten, besonders in der Mark Brandenburg* (1790), pp. 93-4.

17. The document of 28 June, 1777, given by A. Levy, *op. cit.*, p.74; also S. Haenle, *Geschichte der Juden im ehmaligen Fürstentum Ansbach* (1867), p. 70.

18. *Geschichte Philanders von Sittewaldt das ist Straffs-Schriften Hanss Wilhelm Moscherosch von Wilstätt* (1677), p. 779.

19. F. von Mensi, *Die Finanzen Österreichs von* 1701-1740 (1890), p. 132. Samuel Oppenheimer, "Kaiserlicher Kriegsoberfaktor und Jud" (as he was officially styled and as he called himself), saw to the needs of the armies in all the campaigns of Prince Eugene (p. 133).

20. Cf. for instance the petition of the Vienna Court Chancery of May 12, 1762, given by Wolf, *Geschichte der Juden in Wien* (1894), p. 70; *Komitätsarchiv Neutra Iratok*, xii-3326 (according to information supplied by Mr. Jos. Reizman); *Verproviantierung der Festungen Raab, Ofen und Komorn durch Breslauer Juden* (1716), see Wolf, *loc. cit.*, p. 61.

21. H. Friedenwald, "Jews mentioned in the Journal of the Continental Congress," in *Transactions* of the Jewish Hist. Soc. of America, vol. i., pp. 65-89.

22. I have already mentioned the more important works on the history (not excepting the economic history) of the Jews in England, France, Holland and America (see notes 6, 7, 13 of Chapter 1; note 10, Chapter 2); here I would refer to those dealing with the same subject for Germany and for Spain. There is no complete study of the history of the Jews in Germany, and we are forced therefore to go to local monographs and essays in learned periodicals. In any case the economic history of the German Jews has been treated in a somewhat stepmotherly way, and we find little that is useful in such works as L. Geyer's *Die Geschichte der Juden in Berlin*, 2 vols. (1870-71). Recently Mr. Ludwig Davidsohn, a pupil of mine, went carefully through the Berliner Staatsarchiv for the purpose of establishing the economic position of the Jews. The results of his labours have not yet been printed, but I have been able to use some of them. A good deal may be found in Grunwald's *Portugiesengräber auf deutscher Erde* and his *Hamburgs deutsche Juden bis zur Auflösing der Dreigemeinde* (1904). For a particular here and there one may turn (but care is needed) to König, *op. cit.*, as also to *Die Juden in Österreich*, 2 vols. (1842).

As for learned journals, they are not of much use for economic history. The chief of them is the *Monatsschrift für Geschichte und Wissenschaft des Judentums* (begun 1851). Others are the *Allgemeine Zeitung des Judentums* (begun 1837) and Brüll's *Populärwissenschaftliche Monatsblätter* (begun 1888), both with more or less propagandist ends in view. The *Zeitschrift für Demographie und Statistik des Judentums* (begun 1905) deals with questions of economic history only occasionally.

Sometimes one comes across papers in the general historic reviews or in local journals which shed a flood of light on Jewish economic history. But a complete list of these it would be impossible to give here.

The history of the Jews in Spain has been sufficiently dealt with. But unfortunately its economic aspect has been almost entirely neglected. I know of no more needful thing than an economic history of the Jews in the Pyrenean Peninsula, and I wish that some economic historian would undertake to write it. It would most certainly illuminate the general economic history of Europe in a most surprising fashion. For the present, however, we must perforce consult general histories of the Jews in Spain, and of these perhaps the best is M. Kayserling's *Geschichte der Juden in Spanien und Portugal*, 2 vols. (1861-7). The principal work in Spanish is D. José Amador de Los Rios, *Historia social, politica y religiosa de los Judios de España y Portugal*, 3 vols. (1875-8), but for our purpose it is of little use. A book of a different kind is E. H. Lindo's *The History of the Jews of Spain and Portugal* (1848). It contains extracts from the legal enactments affecting Jews and the decisions of the Cortes, and thus has a special value of its own.

For Portugal the most important work is now by J. Mendes dos Remedios, *Os Judeus em Portugal*, vol. i. (1895) up to the expulsion.

It ought to be mentioned also that the volumes of Graetz, *Geschichte der Juden*, which treat of the Spanish period (7 and 8) are of great use, because of the abundance of material which they contain. So far as my experience goes they have not been surpassed by any later work.

With regard to monographic studies on the position of the Jews in the economic life of the Pyrenean Peninsula, I do not know of any. But this may be due to my ignorance. Anyhow, the Jewish libraries of Breslau and Berlin contain nothing under this head. The work of Bento Carqueja, *O capitalismo moderno e as suas origens em Portugal* (1908), only just touches the problem so far as the Jews are concerned.

23. H. J. Koenen, *op. cit.*, p. 206.

24. Cf. art. "Banking" in *Jewish Encycl.*

25. For the position of the Jews in English finance during the 17th and 18th centuries we have many records. Cf. Picciotto, p. 58; Hyamson, pp. 171, 217, 240, 264, etc.; Lucien Wolf, *The Re-settlement of the Jews in England* (1888); the same author's "Crypto-Jews under the Commonwealth," in *Transactions* of the Jewish Historical Society of England, vol. i. (1895); likewise his "The Jewry of the Restoration (1660-1664)," reprinted from *The Jewish Chronicle* (1902).

26. L. Wolf, *The Jewry of the Restoration*, p. 11.

27. G. Martin, *La grande industrie sous Louis XIV* (1899), p. 351.

28. Victor de Swarte, *Un banquier du Trésor royal au xviii siècle, Samuel Barnard—sa vie—sa correspondance*, 1651-1739 (1893).

29. Kahn, *Les juifs de Paris au* xviii *sc.* (1894), p. 60.

30. Graetz, *Geschichte der Juden,* vol. 10, p. 40.

31. Wolf, *Ferdinand II,* Appendix 4, quoted by Graetz, vol. 10, p. 41.

32. The actual wording from *Die Juden in Österreich,* vol. 2 (1842), p. 41.

33. *Die Juden in Österreich,* vol. 2, p. 64; F. von Mensi, *op. cit.,* p. 132. In the 18th century the most important creditors of the State were (in succession) Oppenheimer, Wertheimer, Sinzheimer; the last-named had owing to him in 1739 no less than five million gulden. F. von Mensi, p. 685. Cf. also David Kaufmann, *Urkundliches aus dem Leben Samson Wertheimers* (1892). For the earlier period, see G. Wolf, *Ferdinand II und die Juden* (1859).

34. F. von Mensi, p. 148.

35. G. Liebe, *op. cit.,* p. 84.

36. Art. "Abensur Daniel," in *Jewish Encycl.*

37. A. Levy, "Notes sur l'histoire des Juifs en Saxe," in *R.E.J.,* vol. 26 (1898), p. 259. For Berend (Behrend) Lehmann, *alias* Jisachar Berman, see B. H. Auerbach, *Geschichte der israelitischen Gemeinde Halberstadt* (1866), p. 43; for his son Lehmann Berend, see p. 85.

38. Auerbach, *loc. cit.,* p. 82 (for Hanover); see also S. Haenle, *op. cit.,* pp. 64, 70, 89; for more cases of Hofjuden, see L. Müller, "Aus fünf Jahrhunderten," in the *Zeitschrift des historischen Vereins für Schwaben und Neuburg,* vol. 26 (1899), p. 142.

39. F. von Mensi, p. 409.

40. *Memoiren der Glückel von Hameln* [published in the original Yiddish by D. Kaufmann (1896)], German translation (privately printed) in 1910, p. 240.

41. M. Zimmermann, *Josef Süss Oppenheimer, ein Finanzmann des* 18ten *Jahrhunderts* (1874).

42. Address by Louis Marshall in *The 250th Anniversary of the Settlement of the Jews in the U.S.,* p. 102.

43. H. Friedenwald, *op. cit.,* p. 63.

44. W. Graham Sumner, *The Financiers and the Finances of the American Revolution,* 2 vols. (1891).

Chapter 6

1. For a legal consideration of the question, see Brunner, *Endemanns Handbuch,* vol. 2, p. 147, and Goldschmidt, *Universalgeschichte des Handelsrechts* (1891), p. 386. Cf. also Knies, *Der Credit* (1876), p. 190.

2. I give the "credit relationship" its most extended meaning in the sense that you create duties between persons by the one giving an economic value to the other and the second promising a *quid pro quo* in the future.

3. Cf. F. A. Biener, *Wechselrechtliche Abhandlungen* (1859), p. 145.

4. The view of Kuntze and others. See Goldschmidt, *op. cit.,* p. 408.

5. Goldschmidt, *loc. cit.,* p. 410, who puts the question in the form of a query, leaving the answer vague. See on the other hand A. Wahl, *Traité théor. et pratique des titres au porteur* (1891), vol. 1, p. 15.

6. Cf. Kuntze, "Zur Geschichte der Staatspapiere auf den Inhaber," in the *Zeitschrift für das ges. Handelsrecht,* vol. 5, p. 198; the same writer's *Inhaber Papiere* (1857), pp. 58, 63; Goldschmidt, *op. cit.,* pp. 448-9; Sieveking in *Schmollers Jahrbuch* (1902); and above all, G. Schaps, *Zur Geschichte des Wechselindossaments* (1892), p. 86. Cf. also Biener, *op. cit.,* pp. 121, 137.

7. Goldschmidt, p. 452; Schaps, p. 92.

8. The text is given in D. Kaufmann's article in the *J.Q.R.,* vol. 13 (1901), p. 320, "Die Vertreibung der Marranen aus Venedig im Jahre 1550."

9. Graetz, vol. 8, p. 354; vol. 9, p. 328.

346 / Notes and References

10. So far as I am aware, this question has never yet been asked: What part did the Jews play in the Genoese fairs? It will be most difficult to give a satisfactory answer, because the Jews in Genoa were forced, especially after the Edict of Expulsion in 1550, to keep secret their identity. Probably also they changed their names and made a pretence of accepting Christianity. Nevertheless, it would be worth while to make the attempt. Anyhow, we have here one instance where in the post-mediæval period a great financial and credit system was developed without the clear proof of Jewish influence. It may be, of course, that the proof has slipped my observation; in that case I should be glad to have my attention drawn to it.

The best account of the Genoese fairs will be found in Ehrenberg's *Zeitalter der Fugger,* vol. 2, p. 222, and Endemann, *Studien in der römisch-kanonischen Wirtschafts- und Rechtslehre,* vol. 1 (1874), p. 156. Endemann bases his conclusions chiefly on Scaccia and R. de Turris, while Ehrenberg also relied on documents in the Fugger archives.

11. Possibly earlier, in the case of the Company of the Pairiers, to whom was transferred in the 12th century the mill in Toulouse, du Basacle, by means of securities (*uchaux* or *saches*). Cf. Edmund Guillard, *Les opérations de Bourse* (1875), p. 15.

12. Cf. K. Lehmann, *Die geschichtliche Entwickelung des Aktienrechts* (1895).

13. J. P. Ricard, *Le Négoce d' Amsterdam* (1723), pp. 397-400.

14. This is the conclusion arrived at by André E. Sayous, "Le fractionnement du capital social de la Compagnie néerland des Indes orientales," in *Nouv. Rev. Historique du droit franç. et étrangers,* vol. 25 (1901), pp. 621, 625.

15. Cf. Endemann, *op. cit.,* vol. 1, p. 457.

16. See instances—1422 in Palermo and 1606 in Bologna—in Goldschmidt, p. 322.

17. The most important collection of documents concerning the history of banking in Venice is still Elia Lattes' *La libertà delle banche e Venezia dal secolo xiii al xvii secondo i documenti inediti del R. Archivio dei Frari ec.* (1869). The subject has been dealt with by Ferrara, "Gli antichi banchi di Venezia" in *Nuova*

Antologia, vol. xvi.; E. Nasse, "Das venetianische Bankwesen in 14, 15, und 16 Jahrhundert," in the *Jahrbuch für Nationalökonomie,* vol. 34, pp. 329, 338. To show the share of the Jews in Venetian banking would be a welcome piece of work. But it would be most difficult of accomplishment because, so far as I can judge, the Jews in Venice already in the 15th century were the most part New Christians, often holding high offices and having Christian names.

18. Macleod, *Dictionary of Political Economy,* art. "Bank of Venice" (? authorities), quoted by A. Andréades, *History of the Bank of England* (1909), p. 28.

19. "Gallicioli Memorie Venete," ii., No. 874, in Graetz, vol. 6, p. 284.

20. S. Luzzato, *Dis. circa il stato degli Hebrei in Venezia* (1638), ch. 1, and pp. 9a, 29a. The figures need not be taken too seriously; they are only an estimate.

21. See, for instance, D. Manuel Calmeiro, *Historia de la economia politica en España,* vol. 1, p. 411; vol. 2, p. 497.

22. See A. Andréades, *History of the Bank of England* (1909), p. 28. That will certainly have to be the conclusion if importance is attached to the scheme (1658) of Samuel Lambe (printed in *Somer's Tracts,* vol. vi). Andréades actually dates the first idea of the Bank from Lambe's scheme. There was a scheme previous to that—Balthasar Gerbier's in 1651, and between that year and 1658 Cromwell had allowed the Jews to settle in this country. For my own part I cannot admit "the superiority" of Lambe's scheme. But other writers also lay stress on the very great share of the Jews in the establishment of the Bank of England.

23. For instances of public debt bonds, see Walter Däbritz, *Die Staatsschulden Sachsens in der Zeit von 1763 bis 1837,* Doctoral Dissertation (1906), pp. 14, 55; E. von Philippovich, *Die Bank von England* (1885), p. 26; also, Ehrenberg, *Fugger* [note 10, Chapter 6], vol. 2, pp. 141, 299.

24. Ad. Beer, *Das Staatsschuldenwesen und die Ordnung de Staatshaushalts unter Maria Theresia* (1894), p. 13.

25. Cf. F. von Mensi, *op. cit.,* p. 34.

26. Witness a pamphlet little known generally (even Däbritz, *op. cit.*, has overlooked it), to which I should like to call attention. It has a very long title: "Ephraim justifié. Mémoire historique et raisonné sur l'Etat passé, présent et futur des finances de Saxe. Avec le parallèle de l'Oeconomie prussienne et de l'Oeconomie saxonne. Ouvrage utile aux Créanciers et Correspondans, aux Amis et aux Ennemis de la Prusse et de la Saxe. Adressé par le Juif Ephraim de Berlin à son Cousin Manassés d'Amsterdam. Erlangen. A l'enseigne de 'Tout est dit.' " 1785.

27. Cf. (Luzac) *Richesse de la Hollande,* vol. 2 (1778), p. 200. Also vol. 1, p. 366. Luzac, besides his own personal experiences, must have also used Fermin, *Tableau de Surinam* (1778).

28. Chief among them Kuntze, *Die Lehre von den Inhaberpapieren* (1857), p. 48, which is still unsurpassed. We may mention besides, Albert Wahl, *Traité théorique et pratique des titres au porteur français et étrangers,* 2 vols. (1891).

The best history of mediæval credit instruments is that of H. Brunner, *Das französische Inhaberpapier* (1879). Cf. also his "Zur Geschichte des Inhaberpapiers in Deutschland," in the *Zeitschrift für das gesammte Handelsrecht,* vols. 21 and 23. For Holland, see F. Hecht, *Geschichte der Inhaberpapier in den Niederlanden* (1869), p. 4.

By the way, it is interesting to note that credit instruments have been said to be of Hellenic origin. Cf. Goldschmidt, "Inhaber- Order- und exekutorische Urkunden im Klassischen Altertum," in *Zeitschrift für Rechtsgeschichte Roms,* vol. 10 (1889), p. 352.

But Goldschmidt's view is not generally accepted. Cf. Benedict Frese, *Aus dem gräko-ägyptischen Rechtsleben* (1909), p. 26. Another criticism of Goldschmidt's theory may be found in H. Brunner, "Forschungen zur Geschichte des deutschen und französischen Rechts," in his *Gesammelte Aufsätze* (1894), p. 604.

Brunner also deals with the same problem in his *Französische Inhaberpapier,* pp. 28, 57.

Made casually by Kuntze, but rejected by Goldschmidt in the *Zeitschrift für Rechtsgeschichte,* vol. 10, p. 355.

Also rejected by Salvioli, *I titoli al portatore nella storia del diritto italiano* (1883).

29. Cf. L. Auerbach, *Das judische Obligationenrecht,* vol. 1 (1871), p. 270. Other passages from rabbinic literature are given

in Hirsch B. Fassel, *Das mosaisch-rabbinische Zivilrecht,* vol. 2, Part 3 (1854), § 1390; Frankel, *Der gerichtliche Beweis nach mosaischem Recht* (1846), p. 386; Saalschütz, *Mosaisches Recht,* 2 vols. (1848), p. 862.

30. For the Mamre, cf. L. L'Estocq, *Exercitatio de indole et jure instrumenti Judæis usitati cui nomen "Mamre" est* (1775), § vii; J. M. G. Besekes, *Thes. jur. Camb.,* Part II (1783), pp. 1169, 1176; P. Bloch, *Der Mamran, der judisch-polnische Wechselbrief.*

31. Ehrenberg, *op. cit.,* vol. 2, p. 141.

32. Brunner, *op. cit.,* p. 69.

33. Schaps, *op. cit.,* p. 121.

34. *Ibid.*

35. Cf. F. Hecht, *op. cit.,* p. 44.

36. Hecht, p. 96.

37. Däbritz, *op. cit.,* p. 53.

38. Kuntze, *op. cit.,* p. 85.

39. Straccha, *Tract. de assicur.* (1568).

40. A. Wahl, *op. cit.,* vol. 1, pp. 15, 84.

41. Hecht, *op. cit.,* p. 37.

42. Cf. J. H. Bender, *Der Verkehr mit Staatspapieren* (2 ed., 1830), p. 167.

43. "Ex diversis animi motibus in unum consentiunt, id est in unam sententiam decurrunt" (Ulp., L. I. § 3, *D. de pact.,* 2, 14).

44. Cf. Goldschmidt, *op. cit.,* p. 393.

45. I am indebted for what follows above all to L. Auerbach, *op. cit.,* vol. 1, pp. 163, 251, 513. This work (unfortunately uncompleted) is written in a most suggestive fashion and deserves to be widely known. For it is one of the best accounts of Talmudic law in existence. Of much less importance, yet useful nevertheless, are the works of Saalschütz, *op. cit.;* H. B. Fassel, *op. cit.;* J. J. M. Rabbinowicz, *Législation du Talmud,* vol. 3 (1878); Frankel, *op. cit.* On the basis of Goldschmidt's translation of the Talmud, J. Kohler attempted a "Darstellung des talmudischen

Rechts" in *Zeitschrift für vergleichende Rechtswissenschaft*, vol. 20 (1908), pp. 161-264. Cf. the criticism of V. Aptowitzer in the *Monatsschrift* (1908), pp. 37-56.

46. Otto Stobbe, *Die Juden in Deutschland während des mittelalters* (1866), pp. 119, 242; Sachsenspiegel, III, 7, § 4.

47. Goldschmidt, *op. cit.*, p. 111.

48. (Isaac de Pinto) *Traité de la circulation du crédit* (1771), pp. 64, 67-68. Cf. also E. Guillard, *op. cit.*, p. 534. See also Däbritz, *op. cit.*, p. 18, for illustrations.

49. Ehrenberg, *Fugger*, vol. 2, p. 244. We owe most of what we know about the history of the Stock Exchanges to Ehrenberg.

50. Cf. Kaufmann, *op. cit.*

51. Van Hemert, *Lectuur voor het ontbijt en de Theetafel*, VII^de. Stuk, p. 118, quoted by Koenen, *op. cit.*, p. 212.

52. H. Stephanus, *Francofordiense Emporium sive Francofordienses Nundinæ* (1574), p. 24.

53. Quoted by Ehrenberg, *Fugger*, vol. 2, p. 248.

54. *Memoirs*, p. 297.

55. Given by M. Grunwald, *op. cit.*, p. 21.

56. S. Haenle, *op. cit.*, p. 173. *Die Juden in Österreich*, vol. 2 (1842), p. 41.

57. In a report of the Sous-Intendant, M. de Courson, dated 11 June, 1718, quoted by Malvezin, *op. cit.*

58. E. Meyer, "Die Literatur für und wider die Juden in Schweden in Jahre 1815," in *Monatsschrift*, vol. 57 (1907), p. 522.

59. H. Sieveking, "Die Kapitalistische Entwickelung in den italienischen Städten des Mittelalters," in the *Vierteljahrsschrift für Soziale- und Wirtschaftsgeschichte*, vol. 7, p. 85.

60. Saravia della Calle, "Institutione de' Mercanti," in *Compendio utilissimo di quelle cose le quali a Nobili e Christiani mercanti appartengono* (1561), p. 42. Also, art. "Börsenwesen" in *Handwörterbuch der Staatswissenshaften*.

61. H. Sieveking, *Genueser Finanzwesen*, vol. i. (1898), pp. 82, 175.

62. The most reliable sources for the history of Stock Exchange dealing in Amsterdam in the first decades of the 17th century are the Plakate of the States General, which prohibit this sort of business. Reference should also be made to the controversial pamphlets of the period on this topic, more especially those written by the opponent of stock and share dealing, Nicolas Muys van Holy. See Laspeyres, *Geschichte der volkswirtschaftlichen Anschauungen* (1863). Not to be omitted is also de la Vega's book, about which more in due course. For the subsequent period there is much valuable material in books on Commerce, notably J. P. Ricard, *Le négoce a'Amsterdam* (1723), from whom later writers quote. The works of Joseph de Pinto dating from the second half of the 18th century [see note 48], are also very useful. Of recent books the following may be mentioned: G. C. Klerk de Reus, *op. cit.*, S. van Brakel, *De Holland, Hand. Comp. der xvii. eeuv* (1908).

63. In the periodical *De Koopman*, vol. 2, pp. 429, 439, quoted by Ehrenberg, *Fugger*, vol. 2, p. 333.

64. Pinto, *De la Circulation, op. cit.*, p. 84.

65. Kohler, *op. cit.*

66. Israel, *op. cit.*

67. Ehrenberg, *Fugger*, vol. 2, p. 336, gives a fairly lengthy extract from this remarkable book.

68. *Extrait d'un mémoire présenté en* 1692, from the Archives of the French Foreign Office, published in the *Revue historique*, vol. 44 (1895). I am indebted to my friend André E. Sayous, of Paris, for having called my attention to this article.

69. "The Anatomy of Exchange Alley, or a System of Stock-jobbing" (1719). Printed in J. Francis's *Stock Exchange* (1849), Appendix.

70. Art. "Brokers" in *Jewish Encycl.*

71. J. Piccotto, *op. cit.*, p. 58.

72. *Universal Dictionary of Trade and Commerce*, vol. 2 (1755), p. 554.

73. Tovey, *Anglia Judaica*, p. 297.

74. As would appear from a complaint of the Christian merchants, of the year 1685, mentioned by Ehrenberg, *Fugger*, vol. 2, p. 248.

75. M. Grunwald, *op. cit.*, p. 6.

76. Postlethwayt, *Dictionary*, vol. 1, p. 95.

77. Joseph Jacobs, "Typical Character of Anglo-Jewish History," in *J.Q.R.*, vol. 10 (1898), p. 230.

78. Ranke, *Französische Geschichte*, vol. 4³, p. 399.

79. Mélon, *Essai pol. sur le commerce* (1734), éd. Davie, p. 685.

80. See Ehrenberg, *Fugger*, vol. 2, p. 142.

81. (Du Hautchamp) *Histoire du système des Finances sous la minorité de Louis XV*, vol. 1 (1739), p. 184.

82. Oscar de Vallée, *Les Manieurs d'argent* (1858), p. 41.

83. P. A. Cochut, *Law, son système et son époque* (1853), p. 33.

84. E. Drumont, *La France Juive* (1904), vol. 1, p. 259.

85. All the figures are from *Von den Gilde-Dienern Friedrich Wilhelm Arendt und Abraham Charles Rousset herausgegebenen Verzeichnissen . . . der gegenwärtigen Aelter-Manner*, etc. (1801).

86. In the *Hamburger Münz- und Medaillenvergnügen* (1753), p. 143, No. 4, there is a coin struck in commemoration of the trade in stocks and shares.

87. Raumburger, in the preface to his *Justitia selecta Gent. Eur. in Cambiis*, etc.

88. Kiesselbech, *op. cit.*, p. 24.

89. The case is mentioned and discussed by von Gönner, *Von Staatsschulden, deren Tilgungsanstalten und vom Handel mit Staatspapieren* (1826), § 30.

90. *Dictionary*, vol. 2, p. 533. Cf. also the very informing article, "Monied Interest," p. 284.

91. See articles "Monied Interest" and "Paper Credit" in Postlethwayt, vol. 2, pp. 284 and 404.

92. D. Hume, *Essays*, vol. (1793), p. 110.

93. Adam Smith, *Wealth of Nations*, ch. 3.

94. Von Gönner, *op. cit.*, § 31.

95. Pinto, *op. cit.*, pp. 310-11.

96. Ehrenberg, *Fugger*, vol. 2, p. 299.

97. I must content myself with mentioning the following three works which appear to me to be the best: *Das Haus Rothschild. Seine Geschichte und seine Geschäfte*, 2 Parts (1857); John Reeves, *The Rothschilds: the Financial Rulers of Nations* (1887); R. Ehrenberg, *Grosse Vermögen*, etc., vol. 1, "Die Fugger-Rothschild-Krupp" (2nd ed., 1905).

98. J. H. Bender, *Der Verkehr mit Staatspapieren* (2nd ed., 1830), p. 145.

99. *E.g.*, von Gönner, *op. cit.*, p. 60; Bender, p. 142.

100. *Das Haus Rothschild*, vol. 2, p. 216.

101. A. Crump, *The Theory of Stock Exchange* (1873). Reprinted 1903, p. 100.

102. Von Mensi, *op. cit.*, p. 54.

103. Ad. Beer, *op. cit.*, p. 43.

104. J. H. Bender, *op. cit.*, p. 5.

105. J. Francis, *Stock Exchange*, p. 161.

106. *Das Haus Rothschild*, vol. 2 (1857), p. 85.

107. The best books on this period in Germany are, despite their prejudice and one-sidedness, Otto Glagau's *Der Börsen- und Gründungsschwindel in Berlin* (1876) and *Der Börsen- und Gründungsschwindel in Deutschland* (1877). These books are particularly useful for the short historical sketches of the different companies, giving the names of the founders and the first directors. Cf. also the annual issues of Saling's *Börsenpapieren*, and Rudolf Meyer, *Die Aktiengesellschaften*, 1872-3 (which, however, deal

only with banks). The figures given in the text were supplied by Mr. Arthur Loewenstein, at my request.

108. M. Wirth, *Geschichte der Handelskrisen* (3rd ed., 1883), p. 184.

109. Riesser, *Entwicklungsgeschichte der deutschen Grossbanken* (1905), p. 48.

110. For a glorification of this policy see J. E. Kuntze, *op. cit.*, p. 23.

111. A. Beer, *op. cit.*, p. 35.

112. C. Hegemann, *De Entwickelung des französischen Gross-bankbetriebes* (1908), p. 9.

113. Books of reference are given fully in J. Plenge, *Gründung und Geschichte des Crèdit mobilier* (1903).

114. Model-Loeb, *Die Grossen Berliner Effectenbanken* (1895), p. 43—an excellent book, from which the information in the text is taken in so far as it is not my own personal knowledge.

115. Cf. R. Ehrenberg, *Fondsspekulation* (1883), and Adolf Weber, *Depositenbanken und Spekulationsbanken* (1902).

116. See for instance A. Gomoll, *Die Kapitalistische Mause-falle* (1908). Despite its curious title the book deals seriously with Stock Exchange speculations and is one of the best pieces of work recently published.

117. Mostly from local histories, too numerous to mention here.

Chapter 7

1. König, *op. cit.*, p. 97.

2. "Zur Geschichte der Juden in Danzig," in *Monatsschrift*, vol. 6 (1857), p. 243.

3. M. Güdemann, "Zur Geschichte der Juden in Magdeburg," in *Monatsschrift*, vol. 14 (1865), p. 370.

4. Quoted by Liebe, *op. cit.*, pp. 91-2.

5. Regesten, in Hugo Barbeck's *Geschichte der Juden in Nürn-berg und Fürth* (1878), p. 68.

6. See, for instance, the conduct of the Berlin Retailers' Gild as related in Geiger's *Geschichte der Juden in Berlin,* vol. 2 (1871), pp. 24, 31.

7. Josiah Child, *Discourse on Trade,* 4th ed., p. 152. Child reports the prevailing opinion without saying one word by way of criticism. But he does make it clear that the accusation levelled against the Jews is no crime at all.

8. See extracts from the polemical pamphlets of the period in Hyamson, p. 274.

9. Given in Léon Brunschvicg, "Les Juifs en Bretagne au 18 sc.," in *R.E.J.,* vol. 33 (1876), pp. 88, 111.

10. "Les Juifs et les Communautés d'Arts et Métiers," in *R.E.J.,* vol. 36, p. 75.

11. M. Maignial, *La question juive en France en* 1789 (1903), contains a great deal of material from which the prevailing feel-ing among French merchants against the Jews in the 17th and 18th centuries becomes apparent.

12. "L'admission de cette espèce d'hommes ne peut être que très dangereuse. On peut les comparer à des guêpes qui ne s'intro-duisent dans les ruches que pour tuer les abeilles, leur ouvrir le ventre et en tirer le miel qui est dans leurs entrailles: tels sont les juifs."—Requête des marchands et négociants de Paris contre l'admission des Juifs (1777), p. 14, quoted by Maignial, *op. cit.,* p. 92.

13. The opinion of Wegelin is given by Ernst Meyer, *op. cit.,* pp. 513, 522.

14. Czacki, *Rosprava o Zydach,* p. 82; cf. Graetz, vol. 9, p. 443. Almost word for word the same cry is heard from Rumania, cf. Verax, *La Roumanie et les Juifs* (1903).

15. Maignial, p. 92.

16. Philander von Sittewaldt, *op. cit.*

17. Georg Paul Hönn, *Betrugs-Lexicon, worinnen die meisten*

*Betrügereyen in allen Ständen nebst denen darwider guten Theils
aienenden Mitteln endeckt,* Dritte Edition (1724).

18. *Allgemeine Schatzkammer der Kaufmannschaft oder voll-
ständiges Lexikon aller Handlungen und Gewerbe,* vol. 2 (1741)
p. 1158.

19. *Charakteristik von Berlin. Stimme eines Kosmopoliten in
der Wüste* (1784), p. 203.

20. J. Savary (Œuvre posthume, continué . . . par Phil-Louis
Savary), *Dictionnaire universel de Commerce,* vol. 2 (1726), p.
447.

21. *Allgemeine Schatzkammer,* vol. 1 (1741), p. 17.

22. *Allgemeine Schatzkammer,* vol. 3 (1742), p. 1325.

23. This is only the expression of the mediæval view. It is
excellently well discussed in R. Eberstadt, *Französische Gewer-
berecht* (1899), p. 378.

24. D. Defoe, *The Complete English Tradesman,* 1st ed., 1726.
I have used the 2nd edition in 1 vol. (1727), and the 5th edition in 2 vols. (1745), published after the author's death. The
passage cited in the text is from the 1st ed., p. 82.

25. *Allgemeine Schatzkammer,* vol. 3, p. 148.

26. *Ibid.,* vol. 4, p. 677.

27. *Ibid.,* vol. 3, p. 1325.

28. *Ibid.,* vol. 3, p. 1326.

29. *Ibid.,* vol. 1, p. 1392—"Sächsischen Krämer-Ordnungen"
of 1672, 1682, and 1692, § 18.

30. See the highly instructive Letter (No. 19 in the 2nd ed.,
corresponding to No. 22 in the 5th) "Of fine shops and fine
shews."

31. Jules de Bock, *Le Journal à travers les âges* (1907), p. 30,
quoted in F. Kellen, *Studien über das Zeitungswesen* (1907), p.
253.

32. Much useful information, especially as regards England,

will be found in Henry Sampson's *History of Advertising from the Earliest Times* (1875), pp. 76, 83.

33. M. Postlethwayt, *A Universal Dictionary of Trade and Commerce*, 2 vols. (1741), 2nd ed. (1757), vol. 1, p. 22. Postlethwayt calls his work a translation of Savary's *Lexicon*, but in reality there are so many additions in it that it may be regarded as original. It should be mentioned by the way that the work is an invaluable source of information concerning economic conditions in England in the 18th century.

34. Savary, *Dict. du Commerce* (1726), Suppl. 1732.

35. P. Datz, *Histoire de la Publicité* (1894), p. 161, contains a facsimile of the whole of the first issue of *Les Petites Affiches*.

36. *Allgemeine Schatzkammer*, vol. 4, p. 677.

37. D. Defoe, *op. cit.*, vol. 5², p. 163.

38. Cf. G. Martin, *La grande industrie sous Louis XV* (1900), p. 247.

39. Josiah Child, *A New Discourse of Trade*, 4th ed., p. 159.

40. Such teaching is met with as early as the later 16th century. Saravia della Calle, whom I regard as of supreme importance in the history of the theory of just price, goes so far as to deduce it from the relationship of supply and demand. His work, together with that of Venuti and Fabiano, is printed in the *Compendio utilissimo*.

41. (Mercier) *Tableau de Paris*, vol. 11 (1788), p. 40.

42. "A Paris on court, on se presse parce qu'on y est oisif; ici l'on marche posément, parce que l'on y est occupé." Quoted by J. Godard, *L'Ouvrier en Soie*, vol. 1 (1899), pp. 38-9.

43. Memoirs of the Rev. James Fraser, written by himself. *Selected Biographies*, vol. 2, p. 280; Durham's *Law Unsealed*, p. 324, quoted by Buckle, *History of Civilization*, vol. 2, p. 377.

44. Durham's *Exposition of the Song of Solomon*, quoted by Buckle, *loc. cit.*

45. *Allgemeine Schatzkammer*, vol. 4 (1742), p. 666.

46. See, for instance, Mercier, *Tableau de Paris*, vol. 2, p. 71.

47. Samuel Lambe, in his scheme for a national bank [see note 22, Chapter 6] speaks of the low commercial morality of English merchants as compared with the reliability of (say) the Dutch.

48. Owen Felltham in his *Observations* (1652), quoted by Douglas Campbell, *The Puritan in Holland, England, and America*, vol. 2 (1892), p. 327.

49. This accusation was levelled against the Jews from the early mediæval period down almost to this very day. Cf. G. Caro, *Sozial- und Wirtschaftsgeschichte der Juden*, vol. 1 (1908), p. 222; Bloch, *op. cit.*, p. 12; article "Juden," in *Allgemeine Schatzkammer;* von Justi, *Staatswirtschaft*, vol. 1 (1758), p. 150. For Germany more especially, see Liebe, *Das Judenthum in der deutschen Vergangenheit* (1903).

50. According to a Minute Book of the Portuguese community in Hamburg—A. Feilchenfeld, "Die älteste Geschichte der deutschen Juden in Hamburg," in *Monatsschrift*, vol. 43 (1899), p. 279.

51. Geyler von Kaiserberg's sermon on the 93rd "Narrengeschwärm," in S. Brandt's *Narrenschiff* (to be found in the collection called *Das Kloster*, vol. 1, p. 722, published by J. Scheible). Cf. Oskar Franke, *Der Jude in den deutschen Dichtungen des 15, 16, und 17 Jahrhunderts* (1905), especially section 4.

52. Quoted by A. M. Dyer, *op. cit.*, p. 44.

53. Will. Ussellinx, quoted by Jameson, in *Transactions* of the Jewish Historical Society of America, vol. 1, p. 42. For Usselinx, see E. Laspeyres, *Volkswirtschaftliche Ansichten der Niederlande* (1863), p. 59.

54. Savary, *op. cit.*, vol. 2, p. 449.

55. See *Transactions* of the Jewish Historical Society of America, vol. 3, p. 44.

56. Josiah Child, *Discourse on Trade*, 4th ed., p. 152.

57. Cf. R. Ehrenberg, *Grosse Vermögen*, 2nd ed., p. 147.

58. *Annalen der Juden,* pp. 106-17.

59. Liebe, *Das Judentum,* p. 34.

60. Risbeck, *op. cit.* Cf. also Scheube, *op. cit.,* p. 393.

61. *Uber das Verhältniss der Juden zu den Christen in den deutschen Handelsstädten* (1818), pp. 171, 252, 270, 272.

62. See *R.E.J.,* vol. 33, p. 111.

63. H. Bodemeyer, *Die Juden. Ein Beitrag zur Hannoverschen Rechtsgeschichte* (1855), p. 68.

64. See Albert Wolf, "Etwas über jüdische Kunst und ältere jüdische Künstler," in *Mitteilungen zur jüdischen Volkskunde,* edited by M. Grunwald, vol. 1 (1905), p. 34.

65. See Ehrenberg, *Grosse Vermögen,* p. 147.

66. The documents are printed in Kracauer's "Beiträge zur Geschichte der Frankfurter Juden im 30 jährigen Kriege," in *Zeitschrift für die Geschichte der Juden in Deutschland,* vol. 3 (1899), p. 147. Cf. Schudt, *op. cit.,* vol. 2, 164.

67. *Ibid.*

68. *Ibid.*

69. *Annalen der Juden, op. cit.,* pp. 97, 106-17.

70. *Ibid.*

71. *Versuch über die jüdischen Bewohner der österreichischen Monarchie* (1804), p. 83. Contains much valuable material.

72. L. Holst, *Judentum in allen dessen Teilen aus einem staatswissenschaftlichen Standpunkte betrachtet* (1821), pp. 293-4.

73. "Les fripiers de Paris qui sont à la plus part Juifs," Noel du Fail, *Contes d'Eutrapel,* xxiv, quoted by G. Fagniez, *L'économie sociale de la France sous Henry IV* (1897), p. 217.

74. Mercier, *Tableau de Paris,* vol. 2, p. 253. In Breslau this method of attracting custom is not unknown, and is called "Ärmelausreissgeschäfte."

75. Romani, *Eines edlen Wallachen landwirtschaftliche Reise*

durch verschiedene Landschaften Europas. Zweyter Theil (1776), p. 150. Cf. Schudt, vol. 2, p. 164.

76. *Über das Verhältniss,* etc., p. 184.

77. Jules de Bock, *op. cit.,* p. 30.

78. Max J. Kohler, *op. cit.*

79. Bloch, *op. cit.,* p. 30.

80. Hyamson, *Jews in England,* p. 274.

81. S. Kahn, "Les Juifs de Montpellier au 18 siècle," in *R.E.J.,* vol. 33 (1896), p. 290.

82. Leon Brunschvicg, *op. cit.,* p. 111.

83. "Requête des marchands," etc., p. 234.

84. L. Kahn, *Les Juifs de Paris au XVIII sc.,* p. 71.

85. Justin Godard, *L'Ouvrier en Soie* (1899), p. 224.

86. For Wegelin's view, see Meyer, *op. cit.,* p. 522.

87. Cf. Czacki, *op. cit.;* Graetz, *op. cit.;* and Verax, *op. cit.*

88. *Annalen,* p. 97.

89. F. Bothe, *Beiträge zur Wirtschafts- und Sozial-Geschichte der Reichstadt Frankfurt* (1906), p. 74.

90. *Bericht der Kriegs- und Domänenkammer über den wirtschaftlichen Niedergang des Herzogtums Magdeburg* (1710), quoted by Liebe, *Das Judentum,* p. 91.

91. Romani, *op. cit.,* p. 147.

92. In *Geschichte der Juden in der Reichstadt Augsburg* (1803), p. 42.

93. Von Mensi, *op. cit.,* p. 367.

94. *Allgemeine Schatzkammer,* vol. 2, p. 1158.

95. Will. Usselinx, quoted by Jameson, in *Transactions* of the Jewish Historical Society of America, vol. 1, p. 42. For Ussellinx, see E. Laspeyres, *Volkswirtschaftliche Ansichten der Niederlande* (1863), 1. 59.

96. Mercier, *op. cit.*

97. *R.E.J.*, vol. 33, p. 111, in Kahn, *op. cit.*

98. Lambe, *op. cit.*

99. *Le cri du citoyen contre les juifs de Metz* (18 *sc.*), quoted by Maignial, *op. cit.*

100. See Bothe, *op. cit.*, p. 74.

101. Felltham, *op. cit.* "Cette nation ne fait fabriquer que des étoffes inférieures et de mauvaise qualité."

102. Quoted by Liebe, *Das Judentum*, p. 91.

103. N. Roubin, "La vie commerciale des juifs contadines en Languedoc," in *R.E.J.*, vols. 34, 35, and 36.

104. *Uber das Verhältniss*, etc., p. 254.

105. Liebe, *op. cit.*

106. *Juden, sind sie der Handlung schädlich?* (1803), p. 25.

107. Graetz, vol. 9, p. 445.

108. Romani, *op. cit.*, p. 148.

109. I am indebted to Mr. Josef Reizman for kindly calling my attention to this passage.

110. Child, *Discourse on Trade*, p. 152.

111. Hyamson, p. 274.

112. *R.E.J.*, vol. 33, p. 290.

113. L. Holst, *op. cit.*, p. 290.

114. See note 61, Chapter 7, p. 239.

115. Holst, *op. cit.*, p. 288.

116. *R.E.J.*, vol. 36.

117. *R.E.J.*, vol. 33, p. 289.

118. *Annalen*, p. 90.

119. From a Memorandum, dated January 9, 1786, of the

Hungarian Court Chancery; again I am indebted to Mr. Josef Reizman.

120. Königlichen Staatsarchiv (Mr. Ludwig Davidsohn informed me of it).

121. "In the U.S.A. the most striking characteristic of Jewish commerce is found in the large number of department stores held by Jewish firms." Art. "Commerce," in *Jewish Encycl.* (vol. 4, p. 192).

122. See the lists of firms in J. Hirsch, *Das Warenhaus in Westdeutschland* (1910).

123. *Juden, sind sie der Handlung schädlich?*, p. 33.

124. Henry Sampson, *A History of Advertising* (1875), p. 68.

Chapter 9

1. For a fuller account of the subject of this chapter, see an article of mine, "Der Kapitalistische Unternehmer," in *Archiv für soziale Wissenschaft und Soziale Politik*, vol. 29.

Chapter 10

1. M. Kayserling, *op. cit.*, p. 708.

2. An account of the Jewish world-famed firms of his time is given by Manasseh ben Israel in his Humble Address to Cromwell. The story of the single families may be found in the *Jewish Encyclopedia*, which is especially good for biographies.

3. "Lettres écrites de la Suisse, d'Italie," etc., in *Encycl. mèth. Manuf.*, vol. 1, p. 407. Cf. the opinion of Jovet, quoted by Schudt, *Jüdische Merkwürdigkeiten*, vol. 1, p. 228.

4. The *Spectator*, No. 495.

5. *Revue Historique*, vol. 44 (1890).

6. Graetz, vol. 5, p. 323.

7. These instances of Jewish diplomatists are generally known. The number could easily be added to. Any one specially interested in this question should refer to Graetz, where abundant material will be found (*e.g.*, vol. 6, pp. 85, 224; vol. 8. ch. 9, etc.).

8. M. Kayserling, *Christopher Columbus* (1894), p. 106.

9. H. J. Koenen, *op. cit.*, p. 206.

10. Edmund Bonaffé, *Dictionnaire des amateurs français au XVII siècle* (1881), p. 191.

11. Friedländer, *Sittengeschichte Roms,* vol. 3, p. 577.

12. (v. Kortum) *Über Judentum und Juden* (1795), p. 165.

13. *Ibid.*, p. 90.

14. *R.E.J.*, vol. 23 (1891), p. 90.

15. M. de Maulde, *Les juifs dans les Etats français du Saint-Siège* (1886). The legal position of the Jews generally is treated fully in the current Jewish histories, most of which are in reality nothing more than the history of the legal position of the Jews. Indeed, a goodly number of their authors imagine they are writing economic history when all the time it is just legal history they are dealing with. For records, consult the article "Juden" in Krünitz (vol. 31) and Schudt, *Jüdische Merkwurdigkeiten* (specially for Frankfort). For France, see Halphen, *Recueil des lois, etc., concernant les Israëlites* (1851); for Prussia, L. von Rönne and Heinrich Simon, *Die früheren und gegenwärtigen Verhältnisse der Juden in den sämtlichen Landesteilen des preussischen Staates* (1843). All the laws quoted in the text I have taken from this collection. A. Michaelis, *Die Rechtsverhältnisse der Juden in Preussen seit dem Beginn des 19 Jahrhunderts: Gesetze, Erlasse, Verordnungen, Entscheidungen* (1910).

16. Cf. B. Bento Carqueja, *op. cit.*, pp. 73, 82, 91.

17. Wagenaar, *Beschrijving van Amsterdam,* quoted by Koenen, *op. cit.*, p. 142. Further, for the wealth of the Dutch Jews (greatly exaggerated) see Schudt, vol. 1 (1714), p. 277; vol. 4 (1717), p. 208. Cf. M. Mission, *Reise nach Italien* (1713), p. 43. Of newer books, M. Henriquez Pimentel, *op. cit.*, p. 34.

18. *Memoiren*, p. 134.

19. Savary, *Dict.*, vol. 2 (1726), p. 448.

20. Lucien Wolf, *The Jewry of the Restoration*, 1660-1664, p. 11.

21. See H. Reils, "Beiträge zur ältesten Geschichte der Juden in Hamburg," in *Zeitschrift des Vereins für hamburgische Geschichte*, vol. 2 (1847), pp. 357, 380, 405; and M. Grunwald, *op. cit.*, pp. 16, 26, 35.

22. In M. Grunwald's *Hamburgs deutsche Juden*, pp. 20, 191.

23. F. Bothe, *Die Entwickelung der direkten Besteuerung der Reichsstadt Frankfurt* (1906), p. 166, Tables 10 and 15.

24. Kracauer, *op. cit.*, p. 341.

25. Alexander Dietz, *Stammbuch der Frankfurter Juden* (1907), p. 408.

26. L. Geiger, *Geschichte der Juden in Berlin* (1871), vol. 1, p. 43.

Chapter 11

1. M. Lazarus, *Ethik des Judentums* (1904), pp. 67, 85, etc. [There is an English edition of this book issued by the Jewish Publication Society of America.]

2. Hermann Cohen, "Das Problem der jüdischen Sittenlehre. Eine Kritik (adverse) von Lazarus' Ethik des Judentums," in *Monatsschrift*, vol. 43, p. 385.

3. *Orach Chajim*, § 8.

4. Quoted by F. Weber, *Altsynagogale Theologie* (1880), p. 273.

5. J. Wellhausen, *Israelitische und jüdische Geschichte*, p. 340.

6. Graetz, vol. 4, p. 411. Graetz also has an excellent appreciation of the Talmud (one-sided of course, and optimistic), and its influence in Judaism.

7. J. Fromer, *Vom Ghetto zur modernen Kultur* (1906), p. 247.

8. M. Kayserling, *Columbus* (1894), ch. vi.

9. *Das Haus Rothschild,* vol. 1 (1857), p. 186.

10. This is not the place to enter into an account of the results of Biblical criticism. All I can do here is to mention a few books that may serve as an introduction to the subject: Zittel, *Die Entstehung der Bibel* (5th ed., 1891); for the history of the Pentateuch, Adalbert Merx, *Die Bücher Moses und Josua* (1907), and Ed. Meyer, *Die Entstehung des Judentums* (1896).

11. W. Frankenberg, "Die Sprüche, übersetzt und erläutert," in *Handkommentar zum Alten Testament,* herausgegeben von D. W. Nowack. On p. 16 there is a list of books for the Wisdom Literature. See also Henri Traband, *La loi mosaïque, ses origines et son développement* (1903), p. 77.

12. Cf. M. Friedländer, *Geschichte der jüdischen Apologetik* (1903).

13. Books about the Talmud form a small library in themselves. I can only mention one or two to serve as an introduction to the subject. The best is H. L. Strack's *Einleitung in den Talmud* (4th ed., 1908), which also contains a pretty full bibliography. For Talmudic Ethics, see Salo Stein's *Materialien zur Ethik des Talmud* (1904). Talmudic scholars, however, do not apprize this book very highly. A more recent book is by J. Fromer, who has occupied himself with Talmudic and later Jewish literature. See his *Die Organization des Judentums* (1908), which is intended to serve as an Introduction to a big Encyclopedic Dictionary of the Talmud, which Fromer has planned. Another book which deals with the sources is E. Schürer, *Geschichte des jüdischen Volkes im Zeitalter Jesu Christi,* in 3 vols. The first (2nd ed., 1890) in § 3 contains an extensive bibliography. In addition, the standard Jewish histories, especially Graetz, deal with this aspect of Jewish literature.

To comprehend the spirit of the Talmud it is necessary to read the text itself. There is a German translation (almost complete) by Lazarus Goldschmidt. The Talmud has this characteristic: that although the sections follow each other in some fixed order, yet not one of them is strictly limited as regards its subject matter. They all deal with practically the whole field of Talmudic subjects. Hence by studying one or more of the (63) Tractates, it is comparatively easy to obtain a fair notion of the contents of the whole, and certainly, to find one's way about in the great sea. Specially to be recommended is the Tractate *Baba Mezia* and its two sister tractates [*Baba Kama* and *Baba Bathra*]. There is a good edition of *Baba Mezia,* with an introduction and a translation by Dr. Sammter (1876).

A special branch of Talmudic literature is composed of the so-called "Minor Tractates," usually found in an appendix to the Talmud, though often published separately. These are *Derech Erez Rabba* (3rd century), *Aboth, Aboth de R. Nathan, Derech Erez Zutta* (9th century, according to Zunz). Zunz calls them Ethical *Hagadoth* because of their obvious intention of teaching practical wisdom. They have had no small influence on the development of the Jewish people and are therefore of great interest to us here. Next to the Bible, these tractates enjoyed a widespread popularity. They formed the principal reading of the layman, unacquainted with the Talmud. They were (are) found in Prayer Books and devotional literature. Some of them have been issued in German translations. *R. Nathan's System der Ethik und Moral,* translated by Kaim Pollock (1905). *Derech Erez Zutta,* translated by A. Tawrogi (1885). *Derech Erez Rabba,* translated by M. Goldberg (1888). We must also mention the *Tosephta,* which contains the teaching not included in the *Mishna.* This also dates from the period of the *Tanaim* and is arranged like the *Mishna.*

Finally, a word as to the Rabbinical commentaries or *Midrashim,* which are partly *halachic* [*i.e.,* legal] and partly *hagadic* [*i.e.,* moral and edifying]. The oldest of them, mostly *halachic,* are *Mechilta* (on Exodus), *Siphra* (on Leviticus), and *Siphre* (on Numbers and Deuteronomy).

The *Targumim* are the Aramaic translations of the O.T.

14. There is no good translation of the *Shulchan Aruch.* The only available one is by Löwe (1837), which is incomplete and one-sided. On the other hand, the *Orach Chajim* and the *Jore Deah* have been published in a German dress by Rabbi P. Lederer (1906 and 1900), but not in a complete form.

As for works on the *Shulchan Aruch,* they are mostly of the nature of apologetic pamphlets. Anti-Semites have turned to the *S. A.* for material to attack Jews and Judaism; and Jewish scholars have naturally replied. We may mention, for instance, A. Lewin, *Der Judenspiegel des Dr. Justus* (1884), and D. Hoffmann, *Der*

Schulchan Aruch und die Rabbiner über das Verhältniss der Juden zu Andersgläubigen (1885). Thus there is no subjective treatment of the *Shulchan Aruch*, though it deserves as thorough a consideration as the Talmud. The only strictly scientific book with which I am acquainted and which should be mentioned in this connexion is S. Bäck's *Die religionsgeschichtliche Literatur der Juden in dem Zeitraume vom 15-18 Jahrhundert* (1893), reprinted from Winter and Wünsche, *Die jüdische Literatur seit Abschluss des Kanons*, vol. 2. But Bäck's book is not big and his treatment therefore can only be of the nature of a sketch.

15. Paul Volz, *Jüdische Eschatologie von Daniel bis Akiba* (1903).

16. Fürst, *Untersuchungen über den Kanon des Alten Testaments nach den Uberlieferungen in Talmud und Midrasch* (1868).

17. L. Stern, *Die Vorschriften der Thora, welche Israel in der Zerstreuung zu beobachten hat. Ein Lehrbuch der Religion für Schule und Familie* (4th ed., 1904), p. 28. This book, which may be looked upon as a type, gives the view current in strictly orthodox circles.

18. Cf. Rabbi S. Mandl, *Das Wesen des Judentums* (1904), p.14. Mandl relies on J. Gutmann, *Uber Dogmenbildung und Judentum* (1894). Cf. also S. Schechter, "The Dogmas of Judaism," in *J.Q.R.*, vol. 1 (1889), pp. 48, 115. As is well known, Moses Mendelssohn was the first to express (in his *Jerusalem*) the idea that Judaism has no dogmas, with some degree of insistence.

19. The best that I am acquainted with is Ferdinand Weber's *System der altsynagogalen palästinensischen Theologie aus Targum, Midrash und Talmud* (1880).

20. Stern, *op. cit.*, p. 5.

21. Döllinger, *Heidentum und Judentum* (1857), p. 634.

22. Rutilius Namatianus, "De reditu suo," in Reinach's *Textes d'auteurs grecs et romains relatifs au judaisme*, vol. 1 (1895), p. 358.

23. Stern, *op. cit.*, p. 49; S. R. Hirsch, *Versuche über Jissroëls Pflichten in der Zerstreuung* (4th ed., 1909), §711.

24. Cf. Weber, *op. cit.*, p. 49. Weber has worked out this idea

of contract in Judaism better than any other writer. The treatment in the text owes much to him, as will be apparent. I have also utilized his references. In this particular instance, cf. *Sifre*, 12*b*, *Wajjikra Rabba*, c. 31.

25. *Aboth*, II, near the beginning.

26. Cf. Weber, *op. cit.*, pp. 270, 272.

27. *Ibid.*, p. 292.

28. R. Joseph Albo, *Ikkarim*, a book on the principles of Judaism, dating from the 15th century. W. and L. Schlesinger have issued a German translation [of the Hebrew] (1844). This particular problem is dealt with in ch. 46.

29. S. R. Hirsch, *op. cit.*, ch. 13, especially §§ 100 and 105.

30. J. F. Schröder, *Talmudisch-rabbinisches Judentum* (1851), p. 47.

31. Graetz, vol. 2, p. 203 and note 14; J. Bergmann, *Jüdische Apologetik im neutestamentlichen Zeitalter* (1908), p. 120. For the spirit of ancient Judaism, see Wellhausen, *op. cit.*, ch. 15.

32. H. Deutsch, *Die Sprüche Salomons nach der Auffassung in Talmud und Midrasch* (1885).

33. J. F. Bruch, *Weisheitslehre der Hebräer* (1851), p. 135.

34. Rabbi S. Schiffer, *Das Buch Kohelet. Nach der Auffassung der Weisen des Talmud und Midrasch* (1884).

35. Cf. Graetz, vol. 4, p. 233; Wellhausen, *op. cit.*, pp. 250, 339; and also the well-known works of Müller, Schürer, and Marti.

36. Mandl, *op. cit.*, p. 14.

37. S. R. Hirsch, *op. cit.*, § 448.

38. A number of similar extracts from Talmudic literature will be found in S. Schaffer, *Das Recht und seine Stellung zur Moral nach talmudischer Sitten- und Rechtslehre* (1889), p. 28.

39. M. Lazarus, *op. cit.*, p. 22. Lazarus has worked out the idea that to be holy means to overcome your passions, exceedingly well, though he approaches very closely to Kant's system of Ethics.

40. *Kiddushin*, 30*b*, *Baba Bathra*, 16*a*.

41. Cf. Schaffer, *op. cit.*, p. 54.

42. Cf. Fassel, *Tugend- und Rechtslehre des Talmud* (1848), p. 38.

43. Albo's *Ikkarim* [note 28], ch. 24, deals fully with this.

44. Cf. S. Bäck, *op. cit.*, Preface; also M. Lazarus, *op. cit.*, p. 20.

45. Stern, *op. cit.*, p. 126.

46. *Aboth de R. Nathan*, xxi. 5 [also *Aboth*, III, 14].

47. G. F. Oehler, *Theologie des A.T.* (3rd ed., 1891), p. 878.

48. Lazarus, *op. cit.*, p. 40.

49. *Aboth de R. Nathan*, xvi. 6.

50. Cf. Eccles. 1, 8; Prov. x. 8; x. 10; x. 31; xiv. 23; xvii. 27, 28; xviii. 7, 21; xxi. 23; Ecclus. iv. 34 (29); v. 15 (13); ix. 25 (18); xix. 20, 22.

51. Stern, *op. cit.*, No. 127*a*.

52. Cf. also Prov. xii. 27; xiii. 11; xviii. 19; xxi. 20. For further passages in praise of labour, cf. L. K. Amitai, *La sociologie selon la lègislation juive* (1905), p. 90.

53. Hirsch, *op. cit.*, § 448.

54. *Ibid.*, § 463; and Stern, *op. cit.*, p. 239.

55. Hirsch, *op. cit.*, § 443, almost identically expressed by Stern, *op. cit.*, Nos. 125, 126.

56. J. Fromer, *op. cit.*, p. 25.

57. *Iggeret ha-Kodesh*, first published in 1556; translated into Latin by Gaffareli; cf. Graetz, vol. 7, p. 46.

58. Hirsch, *op. cit.*, § 263. Cf. also § 264, § 267.

59. The figures are taken from Hugo Nathansohn, "Die unehelichen Geburten bei den Juden," in *Z.D.S.J.*, vol. 6, (1910), p. 102.

60. We may mention as one of the foremost authorities S. Freud. See his *Sammlung kleiner Schriften zur Neurosenlehre* (2nd series, 1909).

61. See Dr. Hoppe, "Die Kriminalität der Juden und der Alkohol," in *Z.D.S.J.*, vol. 3 (1907), p. 38; H. L. Eisenstädt, "Die Renaissance der jüdischen Sozialhygiene," in *Archiv für Rassen- und Gesellschaftsbiologie,* vol. 5 (1908), p. 714; L. Cheinisse, "Die Rassenpathologie und der Alkoholismus bei den Juden," in *Z.D.S.J.*, vol. 6 (1910), p. 1. It can be proved with great certainty that the Jew's freedom from the evil effects of alcohol (as also from syphilis) is due to his religion.

62. Wellhausen, *op. cit.,* p. 119.

63. Cicero, *Pro Flacco,* ch. 28.

64. Mommsen, *Römische Geschichte,* vol. 5, p. 545.

65. The passages may be found in Felix Stähelin, *Der Antisemitismus des Altertums* (1905). Cf. Reinach, *op. cit.*

66. J. Bergmann, *op. cit.,* p. 157.

67. Graetz, vol. 5, p. 73.

68. Graetz, vol. 5, p. 321.

69. Graetz, vol. 6, pp. 140, 161.

70. A comprehensive account of laws on interest in the old Jewish legal system will be found in J. Heicl, Das *alttestamentliche Zinsverbot (Biblische Studien,* herausgegeben von O. Bardenhewer, vol. 12, No. 4, 1907).

71. Cf. a collection of "Responsa" by Hoffmann, in *Schmollers Forschungen,* vol. 152.

72. Cf. Fassel, *op. cit.,* p. 193; E. Grünebaum, *Die Sittenlehre der Juden andern Bekenntnissen gegenüber* (2nd ed., 1878), p. 414; the same writer's "Der Fremde nach rabbinischen Begriffen," in *Geigers jüdische Zeitschrift,* vols. 9 and 10; D. Hoffmann, *op. cit.,* p. 129; Lazarus, *op. cit.,* § 144. Lazarus is curiously incomplete. What he says in his third chapter about the duty of Israel towards non-Jews does his heart all credit, but it is hardly in accord with historic truth.

73. Cf. *Choshen Mishpat,* §§ 188, 194, 227, 231, 259, 266, 272, 283, 348, 389, etc.

74. "When he appears before the divine Judge, the first question that man is asked is, Have you been straightforward and honest in business?" *Sabbath,* 31*a.* This Talmudic quotation is the motto of a little book (privately printed) dealing with passages concerning honesty, *Das Biblisch-rabbinische Handelsgesetz,* by Rabbi Stark.

75. *Choshen Mishpat,* § 231. The passage given in the text is from § 227.

76. Graetz, vol. 10, pp. 62, 81.

77. *Choshen Mishpat,* § 227; *Baba Mezia,* 49*b.*

78. In addition, see John G. Dow, "Hebrew and Puritan," in *J.Q.R.,* vol. 3 (1891), p. 52.

79. Graetz, vol. 9, pp. 86, 213; vol. 10, p. 87; Hyamson, p. 164; *J.Q.R.,* vol. 3, p. 61.

Chapter 12

1. Cf. also R. S. Woodworth, "Racial Differences in Mental Traits," in *Bulletin mensuel des Institut Solvay* (1910), No. 21.

2. Anatole Leroy-Beaulieu, *Israël chez les nations* (1893), p. 289; also cf. H. St. Chamberlain, *Die Grundlagen des 19 Jahrhunderts* (3rd ed., 1901), p. 457. [An English edition of this book is now to be had.]

3. I cannot here enter into a disquisition of the various meanings attached to the terms People, Nation, Nationality. The reader will find all that he needs in that excellent study of F. J. Neumann, *Volk und Nation* (1888). See, too, Otto Bauer, *Die Nationalitätenfrage und die Sozialdemokratie* (1907); F. Rosenblüth, *Zur Begriffsbestimmung von Volk und Nation* (1910).

4. A. Jellinek, *Der jüdische Stamm in Sprichwörtern* (2nd series, 1882), pp. 18, 91.

5. J. Zollschan, *Das Rassenproblem unter besonderer Berück-sichtigung der theoretischen Grundlagen der jüdischen Rassenfrage* (1910), p. 298.

6. Jellinek, *op. cit.*, (3rd series, 1885), p. 39.

7. Juan Huarte de San Juan, *Examen de ingenios para las Sciencias. Pomplona* (1575), (Biblioteca de autores Españoles, lxv, p. 469).

8. Jellinek, *op. cit.* This book by the well-known Rabbi of Vienna is one of the very best that has been written on the Jewish spirit. Good, too, is the booklet of D. Chwolson, *Die semitischen Völker* (1872), which criticizes Renan's *Histoire générale et système comparé de langues Sèmitique* (1855). A third writer who in my opinion has looked deep into the Jewish soul is Karl Marx, in his *Judenfrage* (1844). What has been said about the Jewish spirit since these men (all Jews!) wrote is either a repetition of what they said or a distortion of the truth.

9. For Jews as mathematicians, see M. Steinschneider in *Monatsschrift*, vols. 49-51 (1905-7).

10. For Jews as physicians, see M. Kayserling, "Zur Geschichte der jüdischen Aerzte," in *Monatsschrift*, vols. 8 (1859) and 17 (1868).

11. Zollschan, *op. cit.*, p. 159.

12. C. Lassen, *Indische Altertumskunde*, vol. 1 (1847), p. 414.

13. "Une certaine gravité orgueilleuse et un fierté noble fait le caractère distinctif de cette nation," Pinto, "Reflexions," etc., in the *Lettres de quelques juifs*, vol. 1, p. 19.

14. J. M. Jost, *Geschichte des Judentums und seiner Sekten*, vol. 3 (1859), p. 207.

15. *Derech Erez Zutta*, ch. viii.

16. *Megilla*, 16.

17. *Midrash Rabba* to Genesis, 1, 44.

18. "Développer une chose qui existe en germe, perfectionner ce qui est, exprimer tout ce qui tient dans une idée qu'il n'aurait pas trouvée seul."—M. Murel, *L'esprit juif* (1901), p. 40.

19. K. Knies, *Credit*, vol. 1, p. 240; vol. 2, p. 169.

Chapter 13

1. F. Martius, "Die Bedeutung der Vererbung für Krankheitsenstehung und Rassenerhaltung," in *Archiv für Rass. und Ges. Biologie,* vol. 7 (1910), p. 477.

2. Some of the most important of recent works on the ethnology and anthropology of the Jews are the following: von Luschan, "Die anthropologische Stellung der Juden," in *Korrespondenzblatt für Anthropologie,* vol. 23 (1892); Judt, *Die Juden als Rasse* (1903). On the historic side, much light has been thrown on the problem by Ed. Meyer, *Die Israeliten und ihre Nachbarstämme* (1906). Side by side with this excellent book may be placed one somewhat older, A. Bertholet, *Die Stellung der Israeliten und der Juden zu den Fremden* (1896). That the whole literature on Babylonia must be mentioned here goes without saying, *i.e.,* the works of Winkler, Jeremias, and others. Recently there appeared a book by W. Erbt, *Die Hebräer. Kanaan im Zeitalter der hebraischen Wanderung und hebraischen Staatengründung* (1906).

3. H. V. Hilprecht, *The Babylonian Expedition of the University of Pennsylvania.* Series A, Cuneiform Texts, vol. 9 (1898), p. 28; the same author's *Explorations in Bible Lands during the 19th Century* (1903), p. 409.

4. Cf. von Luschan, "Zur phys. Anthropologie der Juden," in *Z.D.S.J.,* vol. 1 (1905), p. 1.

5. The chief exponent of this theory is Ludwig Wilser, who has set forth his view in numerous articles, and at great length in his book, *Die Germanen* (1903). His chief opponent is Zollschan, *op. cit.,* p. 24.

6. Mommsen, *Römische Geschichte,* vol. 5, p. 549.

7. Graetz, vol. 5, pp. 188, 330, 370.

8. Graetz, vol. 7, p. 63.

9. All these instances in Lindo [see note 22, Chapter 5], p. 10.

10. In his criticism of Hoeniger, who holds the view expressed in the text as applicable to Cologne. Others who have supported Brann are Lau, Kuessen, and A. Kober, *Studie zur mittelalterlichen Geschichte der Juden in Köln am Rhine* (1903), p. 13.

11. Maurice Fishberg, "Zur Frage der Herkunft des blonden Elements im Judentum" in *Z.D.S.J.*, vol. 3 (1907), pp. 7, 25. A contrary view in the same journal, vol. 3, p. 92, is Elias Auerbach's "Bemerkungen zu Fishbergs Theorie," etc.

12. Cf. F. Sofer, "Über die Plastizität der menschlichen Rassen," in *Archiv für Rass. und Ges. Biologie*, vol. 5 (1908), p. 666; E. Auerbach, "Die jüdische Rassenfrage," in the same journal, vol. 4, p. 359; also vol. 4, p. 370, where von Luschan expounds an almost identical view. Cf. also Zollschan, *op. cit.*, pp. 125, 134, etc.

13. See the results in Judt, *op. cit.* Cf. also A. D. Elkind, *Die Juden. Eine vergleichend-anthropologische Untersuchung* (1903). I know the book only from the review by Weinberg in *Archiv für Rass. und Ges. Biologie*, vol. 1 (1904), p. 915. Cf. also Elkind's "Anthropologische Untersuchungen über die russ.-polnischen Juden," in *Z.D.S.J.*, vol. 2 (1906), pp. 49, 65, and his other essay in vol. 4 (1908), p. 28; Leo Sofer, "Zur Anthropologische Stellung der Juden," in *Pol. anthrop. Revue*, vol. 7 (cf. review of this in *Z.D.S.J.*, vol. 4, p. 160). Cf. E. Auerbach, *op. cit.*, p. 332; Aron Sandler, *Anthropologie und Zionismus* (1904), though his results are not first-hand; Zollschan, *op. cit.*, pp. 125, 134, etc.

14. The theory of "racial differences" between Ashkenazim and Sephardim is supported by S. Weissenberg, "Das jüdische Rassenproblem," in *Z.D.S.J.*, vol. 1 (1905); M. Fishberg, "Beiträge zur phys. Anthropologie der nordafrikanischen Juden," ditto. Opponents of the view are most of the authors mentioned in note 13.

15. For an all-round consideration of this question see Leo Sofer, "Zur Biologie und Pathologie der jüdischen Rasse," in *Z.D.S.J.*, vol. 2 (1906), p. 85. For further views, see the issues *Biologie*, vol. 4 (1907), pp. 47, 149: Siegfried Rosenfeld, "Die Sterblichkeit der Juden in Wien und die Ursachen der jüdischen Mindersterblichkeit."

16. F. Hertz, *Moderne Rassen-Theorie* (1904), p. 56.

17. C. H. Stratz, *Was sind Juden? Eine ethnographisch-anthropologische Studie* (1903), p. 26.

18. Illustrations in Judt, *op. cit.*, and elsewhere. Cf. also L. Messerschmidt, *Die Hettiter* (1903).

19. Cf. Hans Friedenthal, *Über einen experimentalen Nachweis von Blutsverwandtschaft* (1900). Also appeared in the author's *Arbeiten aus dem Gebiete der experimentellen Physiologie* (1908); also Carl Bruck, "Die biologische Differenzierung von Affenarten und menschlichen Rassen durch spezifische Blutreaktion," reprinted from the *Berliner Klinischen Wochenschrift,* vol. 4 (1907), p. 371.

20. Von Luschan, "Offener Brief an Herrn Dr. Elias Auerbach," in *Archiv für Rassen und Ges. Biologie,* vol. 4 (1907), p. 371.

21. A. Ruppin, "Die Mischehe," in *Z.D.S.J.,* vol. 4, p. 18.

22. Mommsen, *Römische Geschichte,* vol. 5, p. 529.

23. M. Braunschweiger, *Die Lehrer der Mischna* (1890), p. 27.

24. Graetz, vol. 6, p. 22.

25. Graetz, vol. 6, 320.

26. Gregor. Ep. ix. 36, in Schipper, p. 16.

27. Herzfeld, *Handelsgeschichte der Juden des Altertums,* p. 204.

28. Herzfeld has perhaps dealt most fully with these questions. But besides many errors of textual interpretation he is also wrong as regards the dates of documents. He still maintains the chronology current before the age of criticism, and therefore places most of his sources in the pre-exilic period.

29. For the Talmudic period, see Herzfeld, *op. cit.,* p. 118, where over a hundred imports into Palestine are given.

30. A. Bertholet, *op. cit.,* p. 2.

31. Cf. Büchsenschütz, *Besitz und Erwerb im griechischen Altertum* (1869), p. 443.

32. L. Friedländer, *Sittengeschichte Roms,* vol. 3, p. 571.

33. *Kiddushin,* 82*b*.

34. *Aboth de R. Nathan,* xxx. 6.

35. *Pesachim,* 113*a*.

36. *Pesachim, 50b.* Cf. also the articles "Welthandel" and "Handel" in J. Hamburger's *Real-Encyklopädie des Judentums* (1883, 1886) for more material under this heading.

37. A. Bertholet, "Deuteronomium" (1899), in Marti's *Kurz. Handkommentar zum A.T.* On the passage in the text, Bertholet remarks that it refers to a period in which Israel is scattered all over the globe as a people of traders, and is a force in the world because of its wealth. Bertholet informs me that he regards the passage xv. 4-6 as a later addition to the text, and because the words appear to point to an extensive distribution of Israel he would incline to assign them to the Greek period after Alexander.

But for myself I cannot believe that the Jews were then a scattered *commercial* people. In order to make quite sure that I had not overlooked important passages I wrote to Professor Bertholet to ask him on what grounds he based his opinion. In his reply he referred me to Prov. vii. 19; xii. 11; xiii. 11; xx. 21; xxiii. 4; xxiv. 27; xxviii. 19, 20, 22; Ecclus. xxvi. 29–xxvii. 2. These passages deal with the dangers of wealth, and I have already discussed them in another connexion. None of them, however, appear to me to point to trade on a large scale. Certainly Prov. vii. 19 *may* have reference to a travelling trader, but not necessarily. And when we are told of Tobit (to whom also Professor Bertholet referred) that he was King Enemessar's "agorastes" and as such had a comfortable income, does not that rather point to a feudal state of society? Again, Ananias, a merchant at the court of Adiabene (of whom Josephus tells), may have been a Hofjude. Of course, I do not deny that Jews participated in international trade. But I contend that this was not characteristic of them. What was characteristic was the business of lending, and of this it may be said, as Bertholet does, that Israel was then (in the period after Alexander) a power in the earth.

38. I am indebted to Professor Bertholet for calling my attention to this document.

39. E. Renan, *Les Apôtres* (1866), p. 289.

40. J. Wellhausen, *Medina vor dem Islam* (1889), p. 4.

41. Cf. Aronius, *Regesten zur Geschichte der Juden im fränkischen und deutschen Reiche bis zum Jahre* 1273 (1902), Nos. 45, 62.

42. Cf. Lindo, *op. cit.*, p. 73.

43. Statutes of Jewry, in Cunningham, *Growth of English Industry and Commerce,* vol. 1 (1905), p. 204.

44. Wassermann, "Die Entwickelung der jüdischen Bevölkerung in d. Provin. Posen," in *Z.D.S.J.*, vol. 6 (1910), p. 37.

45. F. Delitzsch, *Handel und Wandel in Altbabylon* (1910), p. 33. Cf. Heicl, *Alttestamentliches Zinsverbot* (1907), p. 32, and especially p. 54.

46. Weber, article "Agrargeschichte im Altertum," in *Handwörterbuch der Staatswissenschaften.* Cf. also Marquardt, *Römische Staatsverwaltung,* vol. 2, p. 55.

47. In the years 1436 and 1437 a number of Jewish pawnbrokers were invited to Florence by the city council, in order to assist the poor who were in need of cash. Cf. M. Ciardemi, *Banchieri ebrei in Firenze nel secolo XV e XVI* (1907).
When the city of Ravenna was about to join itself to the Republic of Venice, one of the conditions of its adhesion was that wealthy Jews should be sent there to open a loan bank, so that the poverty of the population might be lessened. Cf. Graetz, vol. 8, p. 235.
"We have seen that the business of finance in the period up to 1420 was gradually increasing in the hands of the Jews of Rome; from 1420 to 1550 circumstances were even more favourable, and hence we find a still greater growth. Indeed, it became customary for the Italian communes to make regular agreements with Jews concerning money-lending." Cf. Theiner, Cod. dipl. 3, 335, in Paul Rieger's *Geschichte der Juden in Rom* (1895), p. 14.

48. A. Moreau de Jonnès, *Statistique des peuples de l'antiquité,* vol. 1 (1851), p. 98. For censuses in the Bible, cf. Max Waldstein in *Statistische Monatsschrift,* Vienna (1881).

49. A. Jeremias, *Das alte Testament im Lichte des alten Orients* (2nd ed., 1906), p. 534.

50. F. Buhl, *Die sozialen Verhältnisse der Israeliten* (1899), pp. 88, 128.

51. Biographies of the Talmudic Rabbis are frequent enough. Cf. Strack, *op. cit.;* Graetz, in vol. 4; A. Sammter in the Appen-

dix to his translation of *Baba Mezia* (1876) and M. Braunschweiger, *Die Lehrer der Mishna* (1890).

52. Mommsen, *Römische Geschichte*, vol. 5, p. 529.

53. The 58th Canon of the 4th Council of Toledo (633), quoted
by Lindo, *op. cit.*, p. 14.

54. J. Wellhausen, *op. cit.*, vol. 4, p. 14.

55. Cf. Graetz, vol. 5, p. 345.

56. Cf. Graetz, vol. 5, pp. 11, 39, 50; also the passages in
Schipper, *op. cit.*, pp. 20, 35; Aronius, *op. cit.*, Nos. 45, 62, 173,
206, 227, etc. How Caro, *op. cit.*, p. 83, arrives at the contrary
conclusion it is not easy to perceive.

57. For the period up to the 12th century, see the references
in Schipper, *op. cit.*, also my *Moderne Kapitalismus,* vol. 1.

58. K. F. W. Freiherr von Diebitsch, *Kosmopolitische, unpartei-
ische Gedanken über Juden und Christen* (1804), p. 29.

59. I cannot give a complete bibliography of all the works on
biology, anthropology, ethnology, etc. Only a few will be mentioned for the guidance of the reader.

The works of Moritz Wagner appear to me to be of great value:
Die Darwinsche Theorie und das Migrationsgesetz (1868); *Über
den Einfluss der geographischen Isolierung und Kolonienbildung
auf die morphologische Veränderung der Organismen* (1871); *Die
Enstehung der Arten durch räumliche Sonderung* (1889).

Ludwig Gumplovicz, *Der Rassenkampf* (1883); *Die soziolo-
gische Staatsidee* (2nd ed., 1901); Ward, *Reine Soziologie*, vol. 1;
L. Woltmann, *Politische Anthropologie* (1903).

For the question of heredity, see H. E. Ziegler, *Die Vererbungslehre in der Biologie* (1905); W. Schallmeyer, *Vererbung
und Auslese* (2nd ed., 1910); R. Sommer, *Familienforschung und
Vererbungslehre* (1907); F. Martius, *Das pathologische Verer-
bungsproblem* (1909); J. Schultz, *Die Maschinentheorie des
Lebens* (1909); W. Bölsche, *Das Liebesleben in der Natur* (1909).

Chapter 14

1. For the social and economic conditions in ancient Palestine there are not many books to hand. Perhaps the best is F. Buhl's work [note 50, Chapter 13]. A more recent book is Max Lohr's *Israels Kulturentwickelung* (1911).

2. Wellhausen, *Proleg.*, p. 10; cf. Budde, *The Nomadic Ideal in the O.T.* (1895).

3. F. Ratzel, *Völkerkunde*, vol. 3, p. 47.

4. *Kiddushin*, 71*a*. Cf. Graetz, vol. 4, p. 273.

5. Graetz, vol. 4, p. 321.

6. For a list of Biblical passages in support, see Herzfeld, *Handelsgeschichte der Juden des Altertums*, note 9.

7. For this estimation, see Buhl, *op. cit.*, p. 52.

8. Philo, *in Flaccum*, 6 (II, 523, Mangey), in Stähelin, *op. cit.*, p. 33.

9. L. Friedländer, *Sittengeschichte Roms*, vol. 3, p. 570.

10. Cassel, in the article "Juden" in Ersch and Gruber, p. 24.

11. Tacitus, *Annal.*, II, 85; Suetonius and Josephus mention only Jews.

12. The best accounts of the Diaspora will be found in Graetz, vol. 3, p. 90; Frankel, "Die Diaspora zur Zeit des zweiten Tempels," in *Monatsschrift*, vol. 2, p. 309; Herzfeld, *op. cit.*, p. 200, and note 34.

13. An excellent example of Jewish migration within one particular country is furnished by the history of the Jews in the province of Posen. In 1849 there were 21 localities (out of a total of 131) with a population of 30 to 40 per cent. of Jews while in 4 there were 41 to 50 per cent. Jews, in 3 over 50 per cent. But in the last half century the Jewish population of the Posen province has shrunk considerably. Cf. E. von Bergmann, *Zur Geschichte der deutschen, polnischen und jüdischen Bevölk-*

erung in der Provinz Posen (1883); *Zwanzig Jahre deutscher Kulturarbeit* (1906); B. Breslauer, *Die Abwanderung der Juden aus der Provinz Posen* (1909). For the expulsion of the Jews from Vienna at the close of the 17th century cf. David Kaufmann, *Die letzte Vertreibung der Juden aus Wien und Niederösterreich; ihre Vorgeschichte* (1625-1670) *und ihre Opfer* (1889).

14. L. Neubaur, *Die Sage vom ewigen Juden* (2nd ed., 1893).

15. According to Gratian, *Vita Joh. Commendoni,* II, c. 15; Victor von Karben, *De Vita et Moribus Judæorum* (1504); Graetz, vol. 9, p. 62.

16. J. Ranke, *Der Mensch,* vol. 2, p. 533.

17. Ratzel, *Völkerkunde,* vol. 3, p. 743.

18. Juan Huarte de San Juan, *op. cit.,* p. 409.

19. F. Delitzsch, *op. cit.,* p. 12.

20. A. Wahrmund, *Das Gesetz des Nomadentums* (1887), p. 16.

21. Ratzel, *op. cit.,* vol. 3, p. 56.

22. *Pesachim,* 87*b.* Cf. also 119*b.*

23. W. Erbt, *Die Hebräer* (1906), p. 166.

24. *Ephraim justifié* (1758). L'éditeur à Mr. André de Pinto, Juif Portugais, Citoyen et négociant d'Amsterdam.

25. Pinto, "Réflex. critiques sur le premier chap. du vii tome des œuvres de M. Voltaire (1762)," in the *Lettres de quelques juifs,* (5th ed., 1781), p. 10.

26. Graetz, vol. 11, p. 54.

27. "L'idée, où ils sont généralement, d'être issus de la Tribe de Juda, dont ils tiennent que les principales familles furent envoyées en Espagne du temps de la captivité de Babylone, ne peut que les porter à ces distinctions et contribuer à cette élévation de sentimens qu'on remarque en eux."—Pinto, *op. cit.,* p. 17.

28. A. Nossig, "Die Auserwähltheit der Juden im Lichte der Biologie," in *Z.D.S.J.*, vol. 1. Cf. in same volume essay of Curt Michaelis; also his "Prinzipien der natürlichen und sozialen Entwicklungsgeschichte der Menschheit" (*Natur und Staat*, vol. 5) (1904), p. 63.

29. A. Sandler, *op. cit.*, p. 24.

Bibliographical Note

Bibliographical Note*

(Prepared in association with Benjamin N. Nelson)

IN THE REFERENCES alluded to in the Introduction only very scanty attention was given to the vast literature on the social and economic history of the Jews in languages other than German and originating after the beginning of the first World War. This emphasis was intentional, because I wanted to show that German scholars contemporary with Sombart held views on the subjects treated in *The Jews and Modern Capitalism* which not only contradicted his conclusions but made many of them nugatory. But since Sombart's work constitutes in a way a beginning in a new direction of research in the social history of the Jews, some attention must be paid to the literature, particularly in languages other than German, which deals with the topics touched upon in this book.

It would be a foolhardy attempt to compile a comprehensive list of works on the social and economic history of the Jews. In order to limit the scope of this bibliographical note, I have decided to exclude works which appeared before 1911, and which either were or should have been used by Sombart. Another factor which permits me to limit the length of this note is the ready availability of several excellent and exhaustive bibliographies which are listed below in section 1, entitled "Bibliographical Aids."

Since these bibliographies contain exhaustive guides to the literature I have found it permissible to limit the other parts of this note to the listing chiefly of works which originated in the last fifteen years. I have attempted also to stress contributions in the English language. In the second section (§2) I enumerate a series of studies on the general problem of the history of capitalism and

* I am greatly indebted to my friend, Professor Benjamin N. Nelson, of the University of Minnesota for many valuable suggestions made in connection with the Introduction, and, above all, his cooperation on this note. Advice on the Introduction was also given by Daniel Bell and Preston S. Cutler. Needless to say that I alone am responsible for the final form in which the Introduction and this note appear.

the "capitalist spirit" and in the last section (§3) a number of works on Jewish history and culture and its relation with modern capitalism and its manifestations.

It might perhaps be of interest to note some of Sombart's later references to Jewish history and problems. The chief references to Jews in his writings on social history are:

Der Bourgeois, Munich, 1913. *Passim,* but esp. pp. 131-132, 299-302, 337-348, 383-384. (This work was published in an English translation by M. Epstein under the title, *The Quintessence of Capitalism,* London, 1915. The corresponding page references to the English translation are pp. 100-101, 232-235, 263-266, 294-295. A new edition of this translation is scheduled for the Fall of 1951 by *The Free Press,* Glencoe, Ill.)

Krieg und Kapitalismus, Munich, 1913. Esp. pp. 64-65 and 147-149.

Luxus und Kapitalismus, Munich, 1913. Esp. pp. 149, 156.

Der moderne Kapitalismus, 5th and later edn., Munich, 1922 and later years. *Passim,* but esp. vol. I, pp. 303-306, 622-628, 635-637, 839-840, 889-892, 896-919; vol. II, pp. 560 f., 721-722; vol. III, (1927 and later), pp. 21-22, 381-383, 394-395.

Der proletarische Sozialismus, Jena, 1924. Esp. vol. I, pp. 74-75, 82-84; vol. II, pp. 152-156, 298-300, 517-518.

It is interesting to note on the basis of these works that Sombart assigns to the Jews a decisive role not only in the development of capitalism, but also of socialism. Similarly he finds that Jews are leading figures both in the capitalist as well as in the socialist camp. In spite of Sombart's assurance of his objectivity in matters of social history, it is interesting to note that he discovers the Jewish influence in the development of capitalism at a time when he is, on the whole, critical of capitalist economy, whereas, after World War I, when he has become a violent opponent of Marxian socialism, he finds that "proletarian socialism" is strongly influenced by Jewish thought. These facts lead us to suppose that Sombart's attitude towards the Jews was not entirely objective and without bias. Although it would probably be exaggerated to call the Sombart of the early period an anti-semite, there are strong anti-Jewish tendencies in his *Die Zukunft der Juden,* Leipzig, 1912.

By 1933 Sombart had become a full-fledged supporter of the Nazi philosophy. (See his *Deutscher Sozialismus,* Berlin-Charlottenburg, 1934, esp. pp. 185 ff.; translated by Karl F. Geiser under the title *A New Social Philosophy,* Princeton, 1937, esp. pp. 171 ff., and 176 ff.)

§ 1. Bibliographical Aids

BARON, SALO W. *Bibliography of Jewish Social Studies.* New York, 1941. Jewish Social Studies Publications, No. 1.

——. *The Jewish Community: Its History and Structure to the American Revolution.* 3 vols., Philadelphia, 1942. See Vol. III for the Notes and References.

——. *A Social and Religious History of the Jews.* 3 vols., New York, 1937. See Vol. III for the Notes and References.

FISCHOFF, EPHRAIM. "The Protestant Ethic and the Spirit of Capitalism: The History of a Controversy." *Social Research,* XI (1944), 53-77.

GABRIELI, GIUSEPPE. *Italia judaica. Saggio d'una bibliografia storica e archeologica degli Ebrei d'Italia.* Rome, 1924.

GERTH, HANS and HEDWIG. "Bibliography on Max Weber." *Social Research,* XVI (1949), 70-89.

JOURNALS (only the most important journals are listed):
..*Annales d'histoire économique et sociale.* Paris, I (1929) ff.
 The Economic History Review. London, I (1927) ff.
 Jewish Social Studies. New York, I (1939) ff.
 Journal of Economic History. New York, I (1941) ff.
 Monatsschrift für Geschichte und Wissenschaft des Judentums. Frankfurt am Main, I (1851) ff.
 Revue des études juives. Paris, I (1880) ff.
 Vierteljahrschrift für Sozial-und Wirtschaftsgeschichte. I-XIII (1903-13), Leipzig; XIV (1918) ff., Stuttgart.

LUZZATTO, GINO. "The Study of Medieval Economic History in Italy: Recent Literature and Tendencies." *Journal of Economic and Business History,* IV (1932), 708-27.

NELSON, BENJAMIN N. *The Idea of Usury: From Tribal Brother-hood to Universal Otherhood.* Princeton, 1949. History of Ideas Series, No. 3. For the Selected References, see esp. pp. 165-220.

NUSSBAUM, F. L. "The Economic History of Renaissance Europe," *The Journal of Modern History,* XIII (1941), 527-545.

POSTAN, M. M. "Studies in Bibliography: I. Mediaeval Capitalism." *Economic History Review,* IV (1933), 212-27.

SAPORI, ARMANDO. "Il commercio internazionale nel Medioevo," in *VIIIe Congrès International des Sciences Historiques, Zürich, 1938.* Paris, n.d., [1938]. Vol. II., pp. 374-377.

ROTH, CECIL. See *The Cambridge Medieval History,* VII (Cambridge, 1932), 937-47.

TAWNEY, R. H. "Studies in Bibliography: II. Modern Capitalism." *Economic History Review,* IV (1934), 336-56.

§ 2. History of Capitalism and the "Capitalist Spirit"

BEARD, MIRIAM. *A History of the Businessman.* New York, 1938.

————. See also §3 below under I. Graeber and S. H. Britt.
   In the first work there is a notable and instructive section (pp. 114-123) on the medieval Jewish merchant and money-lender. Throughout the book occur interesting remarks on Jewish participation in business and trade.

BRODERICK, JAMES, S.J. *The Economic Morals of the Jesuits: An Answer to Dr. H. M. Robertson.* London, 1934.
   Denies the charge that the Jesuits of the 16th and 17th centuries displayed exceptional sympathy for the ethics of capitalism.

DOREN, ALFRED VON. *Storia economica dell'Italia nel medioevo.* Trans. from the German by Gino Luzzato. Padua, 1937.
   The standard economic history of medieval Italy. Indispensable as a general guide to medieval trade and monetary problems in the Mediterranean basin.

DE ROOVER, RAYMOND. *Money, Banking, and Credit in Mediaeval Bruges: Italian Merchant Bankers, Lombards, and Money-Changers.* Cambridge, Mass., 1948. The Mediaeval Academy of America, Publications no. 51.

Emphasizes the paramount role played by Italians in the commercial and financial life of medieval and early modern Bruges and Flanders generally. Other studies by the author, listed in his bibliography, directly contradict Sombart's views on the evolution of accounting methods and commercial instruments, notably the bill of exchange.

FANFANI, AMINTORE. *Cattolecismo e protestantismo nella formazione storica del capitalismo.* Milan, 1934.

A recapitulation of the debate between Weber and Sombart and their critics on the problems of the relation between religious ethic and the growth of capitalism.

FIFOOT, C. H. S. *History and Sources of English Law: Tort and Contracts.* London, 1949.

Splendid essays and materials.

GORIS, JAN. *Les colonies marchandes méridionales à Anvers de 1488 à 1567.* Louvain, 1925.

Analyzes the activities of the outstanding merchants and firms of Portugal, Spain, Italy, and other lands at the great "fairs" of Antwerp.

HOLDSWORTH, SIR WILLIAM W. *A History of English Law.* 12 vols., London, 1922-1938.

Vol. VIII contains a masterly account of the development of commercial and maritime law, Continental as well as English.

KULISCHER, JOSEPH. *Allgemeine Wirtschaftsgeschichte des Mittelalters und der Neuzeit.* 2 vols., Munich and Berlin, 1928-29. (Handbuch der mittelalterlichen und neueren Geschichte, hgb. von G. von Below und F. Meinecke.)

A noted guide to the literature and problems.

LEJEUNE, JEAN. "Réligion, morale et capitalisme dans la societé liègeoise du xviii siècle." *Revue belge de philologie et d'histoire,* XXII (1943), 109-54.

The author of the fundamental treatise on the formation of capitalism in Liege here summarizes the evidence on the ties between religion, morality, and the growth of enterprise in 17th century Belgium.

LEMOINE, R. J. "Les étrangers et la formation du capitalisme en Belgique." *Revue d'histoire économique et sociale*, XX (1932), 252-336.

A review of the literature on the role of strangers in the evolution of Belgian capitalism. Sombart's views are criticized as gross exaggerations (p. 282).

NELSON, BENJAMIN N. "The Usurer and the Merchant-Prince; Italian Businessmen and the Ecclesiastical Law of Restitution." *The Tasks of Economic History* (Annual Supplement to the *Journal of Economic History*), VII (1947), 104-22.

Exhibits the steps by which the merchant-prince (e.g., Antonio) became exempt from the stigma attached by the Church and public opinion generally to the usurer-pawn-broker, whether Jew or Christian (e.g., Shylock).

PIRENNE, HENRI. *Economic and Social History of Medieval Europe.* Trans. by E. H. Clegg. New York, 1937.

————. "Les périodes de l'histoire sociale du capitalisme." Académie Royale de Belgique. *Bulletins de la classe des lettres et des sciences morales et politiques. 1914.* Pp. 258-99. Trans. without notes under the title "The Stages in the Social History of Capitalism," *American Historical Review*, XIX (1914), 494-515.

Sombart's theories received little support from the renowned Belgian historian. The latter's notion of the "social stages" in the history of capitalism is a most significant rendering of the dynamics of European economic development.

RICHARDS, R. D. *The Early History of Banking in England.* London, 1925.

Sombart's claims are flatly contradicted in the conclusion to this scholarly work. The author writes: "The contemporary documentary evidence thus shows that it is inaccurate to say that the Jews had a 'very great share in the establishment of the Bank of England,' that English finance in the seventeenth century was 'very extensively controlled by Jews," that Jews were 'the principal participants in the first English loan,' and 'that a very large part of the capital of the Bank of

England came from the Dutch.'" (P. 219, and see in index *s.v.* "Jews.")

ROBERTSON, HECTOR M. *Aspects of the Rise of Economic Individualism: A Criticism of Max Weber and His School.* Cambridge, 1933.

Although chiefly directed against Max Weber's thesis of the relation between protestantism and capitalism, this study traces the early development of capitalism back to the catholic ethic and philosophy of the waning middle ages.

SANBORN, FREDERIC R. *Origins of the Early English Maritime and Commercial Law.* New York and London, 1930. With a Foreword by Sir William W. Holdsworth.

Indicates the profound influence of continental law (Roman, canon, maritime, municipal) on the English developments. (Cf. essay by Rabinowitz in §3 below.)

SÉE, HENRI. *Histoire économique de la France.* Paris, 1948.

————. *Modern Capitalism: Its Origin and Evolution.* Trans. by Homer B. Vanderblue and Georges F. Doriot. New York, 1928.

————. *Science et philosophie de l'histoire.* Paris, 1928.

Sée's chief criticisms of Sombart (and Max Weber) will be found in his essay on the reputed contributions of the Jews and Puritans to the development of capitalism in the last-mentioned volume.

TAWNEY, R. H. *Religion and the Rise of Capitalism.* New York and London, 1926. Reprinted by Penguin Books, Inc. New York, 1947. Contains the 1937 Preface.

————. Introduction to Thomas Wilson, *A Discourse upon Usury.* London, 1925.

Two contemporary "classics."

USHER, ABBOT PAYSON. *The Early History of Deposit Banking in Mediterranean Europe.* Vol. I. Cambridge, Mass., 1943. In progress.

Emphasizes the role of Italians and Spaniards in the innovation of advanced commercial and financial techniques which contributed to the creation of deposit banking.

VAN DILLEN, J. G., ed. *History of the Principal Public Banks. Accompanied by Extensive Bibliographies of the History of Banking and Credit in Eleven European Countries.* The Hague, 1934.

The insignificance of Jewish influence in the formation of the great *public* banks of Europe will readily be noted in this compilation of excellent monographs by celebrated authorities.

WAETJEN, HERMANN. *Das holländische Kolonialreich in Brasilien.* Gotha, 1921.

A careful and well-documented study on Dutch colonization in Brazil, notably during the seventeenth and eighteenth centuries, containing considerable material on the role played by Jews in Dutch overseas enterprise.

WEBER, MAX. *The Protestant Ethic and the Spirit of Capitalism.* Trans. by Talcott Parsons. London, 1930. With a Foreword by R. H. Tawney.

————. *General Economic History.* Trans. by Frank H. Knight. New York and London, 1927. New edition, Glencoe, Illinois: The Free Press, 1950.

As indicated in the Introduction, it was the first-mentioned of Weber's studies, the celebrated *Protestant Ethic,* which stimulated Sombart to issue his *The Jews and Modern Capitalism.* Weber's *General Economic History* contains a number of that master's most significant criticisms of Sombart's theses.

§ 3. Jewish History and Culture in its Relation to Modern Capitalism

ALTMANN, BERTHOLD. "Jews and the Rise of Capitalism: Economic Theory and Practice in a Westphalian Community." *Jewish Social Studies,* V (1943), 163-86.

A study of the economic history of the Jews of Paderborn, Westphalia, in the seventeenth and eighteenth centuries. On the basis of the data collected in the area of this essay the general validity of Sombart's thesis is subjected to serious doubt.

ANCHEL, ROBERT. *Les juifs de France.* Paris, 1946.

A concise and eminently readable history of Jews in France with special emphasis on the period from the eighteenth century on.

ARENDT, HANNAH. "Privileged Jews." *Jewish Social Studies,* VIII (1946), 3-30.

A careful and well-documented analysis of the political status and the economic functions of "Court Jews" and other privileged Jews and their dependence on the non-Jewish institutions of the society in which they moved. The essay throws light on the dichotomy in the character structure between privileged and non-privileged Jews.

BARON, SALO W. "The Economic Views of Maimonides." In *Essays on Maimonides,* edited by Salo W. Baron. New York, 1941, 127-264.

An elaborate study of Maimonides' teachings on economic matters.

———. See above in § 1.

BLOOM, HERBERT I. *The Economic Activities of the Jews of Amsterdam in the Seventeenth and Eighteenth Centuries.* Williamsport, Pennsylvania, 1937.

A well-documented account of the Jewish contribution to Dutch economic life before 1795.

COLORNI, V. *Legge ebraica e leggi locali.* Milan, 1945.

Valuable material on the legal status of the Jews in Italian history.

———. "Prestito ebraico e communità ebraiche nell'Italia centrale e settentrionale con particolare riguardo alla communità di Mantova." *Rivista di storia del diritto italiano,* VIII (1935), 406-58.

The most complete summary available of the spread and activity of Jewish pawnshops in Italy from the fourteenth to the sixteenth centuries.

CRESPI, E. *La morale commerciale nell'ebraismo.* Trieste, 1934.

A criticism of Sombart's theories which are declared to be partially unfounded and partially supported by inconclusive evidence.

DUBNOW, SIMON N. *Weltgeschichte des jüdischen Volkes.* Trans. from the Russian by A. Steinberg. 10 vols., Berlin, 1925-1929.

EPSTEIN, M. "Review of *Die Juden und das Wirtschaftsleben*" in *Economic Journal*, XXI (1911), 445-47.

FINKELSTEIN, LOUIS, ed. *The Jews: Their History, Culture, and Religion.* 2 vols., New York, 1949.
    Notable essays and bibliographies by various authors, each a well-known specialist in his field.

GRAEBER, ISACQUE and STEUART HENDERSON BRITT. *Jews in a Gentile World: The Problem of Anti-Semitism.* New York, 1942.
    Particular attention is called to the following papers: SAMUEL KOENIG, "The Socioeconomic Structure of an American Jewish Community;" MIRIAM BEARD, "Anti-Semitism—Product of Economic Myth;" JACOB LESTSCHINSKY, "The Position of the Jews in the Economic Life of America."

JACOBS, JOSEPH. *Jewish Contributions to Civilization: An Estimate.* Philadelphia, 1919.
    Chapters vi-viia afford an extensive review of the evidence. They are entitled: "Jews and Commerce," "Jews and Capitalism," and "Excursus on Sombart."

KISCH, GUIDO. *The Jews in Medieval Germany.* Chicago, 1949.
    An examination of the status of the Jew in medieval German law and society. Pp. 567-605 contain an exhaustive bibliography on medieval Germanic Law and economic conditions and its relevance to Jewish law and economic life.

———. "The Jewish Law of Concealment," *Historica Judaica*, I (1938), 3-30.
    A critical evaluation of Sombart's thesis that the so-called "Hehlerrecht" of medieval Germany is based on Talmudic sources.

KOHLER, M. J. "Review of *Die Juden und das Wirtschaftsleben*" in *American Economic Review*, II (1912), 81-84.

LESTSCHINSKY, JACOB. "Capitalism, Role of Jews in." *The Universal Jewish Encyclopedia*, New York, 1941. Vol. III, pp. 28-33.

LÉVY, RAPHAEL-GEORGES. "Le role des juifs dans la vie écono-mique." *Revue des études juives,* LXII (1911), 161-189.

A critical review of the German edition of Sombart's *Die Juden und das Wirtschaftsleben.*

NELSON, BENJAMIN N. "Blancardo (the Jew?) and the Restitu-tion of Usury in Medieval Italy." *Studi in onore di Gino Luzzatto,* I (Milan, 1949), 96-116.

Queries the reliability of some of the evidence advanced to prove the dominance of Easterners, notably Jews in Genoese trade in the mid-twelfth century.

—— and JOSHUA STARR. "The Legend of the Divine Surety and the Jewish Moneylender." *Annuaire de philologie et d'histoire orientales et slaves,* VII (1939-1944), 289-338.

Surveys the evolution in East and West of a noted folktale, not previously perceived to have many of the essential ele-ments of the Merchant of Venice. The penultimate section of the study is entitled "The Earliest Prototype of Shylock?"

NEUMANN, ABRAHAM A. *The Jews of Spain: Their Social, Political and Cultural Life during the Middle Ages.* 2 vols., Philadel-phia, 1942.

PARKES, JAMES. *The Jew in the Medieval Community: A Study of His Political and Economic Situation.* London, 1938.

Part iii, entitled "The Royal Usurer," will be found es-pecially relevant.

RABINOWITZ, JACOB J. "The Influence of Jewish Law on the De-velopment of the Common Law." In *The Jews,* edited by Louis Finkelstein, I, 497-527.

A sensational paper which in some respects makes greater claims for the influence of Jewish law on Western thought than does Sombart. Rabinowitz traces the common law vari-ants of the following legal institutions to Jewish sources: the right of judgment creditors to seize the land of forfeiting debtors, the recognizance, the general release, warranty of real property, the Anglo-American dower, the mortgage, the conditional or penal bond, trial by jury, and the notion of supremacy of law in the thirty-ninth clause of Magna Carta. For contrasting statements of influences shaping the common law of contracts, see above under FIFOOT, HOLDSWORTH,

SANBORN in § 2 and also note the general trend of analysis in the work of KISCH.

REICH, NATHAN. "Capitalism and the Jews: A Critical Examination of Sombart's Thesis," *Menorah Journal,* XVIII (1930), 5-19.
A lively and informed discussion for the general reader.

ROTH, CECIL. *The History of the Jews in England.* Oxford, 1941.

———. *The History of the Jews in Italy.* Philadelphia, 1946.

———. *A History of the Marranos.* Philadelphia, 1934.
Eminently readable histories by a seasoned scholar.

SAYOUS, ANDRÉ E. "Les Juifs." *Revue économique internationale,* XXIV. 1 (1932), 491-535.

———. Preface to S. Jankélévitch's translation of Sombart's *L'apogée du capitalisme.* Paris, 1932. Vol. I, i-lxxvi, esp. at ix-x.
There is hardly a phase of the development of European capitalism about which Sayous failed to publish a monograph or book. His paper on "The Jews" provides abundant citations to special investigations by himself and others on all aspects of Sombart's account of the development of the European economy from the twelfth to the twentieth centuries.

STRAUSS, RAPHAEL. "The Jews in the Economic Evolution of Central Europe." *Jewish Social Studies,* III (1941), 15-40.

TAEUBLER, EUGEN. "Zur Handelsbedeutung der Juden in Deutschland vor Beginn des Städtewesens" in *Beiträge zur Geschichte der deutschen Juden: Festschrift zum 70. Geburtstage Martin Philippsons.* Leipzig, 1916, pp. 370-81.
An analysis of the participation of Jews in the trading relations of early medieval Germany. This essay is strongly influenced by Sombart.

TORO, ALFONSO, editor. *Los Judíos en la Nueva España: Selección de Documentos del Siglo XVI.* Mexico, 1932.
A collection of documents relating to Jewish settlement in Mexico and Central America in the sixteenth century.

VAN DILLEN, J. G. "De economische positie en betekenis der Joden in de Republiek en in in de Nederlandse Koloniale wereld," in H. Brugmans and A. Frank, eds., *Geschiedenis der Joden in Nederland*, Amsterdam, 1940, vol. I, pp. 561 ff.

An account similar in scope to that of H. I. Bloom (see above), written less with a view to state detailed historical events but rather to provide an over-all picture of Jewish economic life in Holland before 1795.

Index

Index.

Index

Abensur, Daniel, 75
Aboab, Jacob, 182
Abdul-Rahman III, Caliph, 173
Acoste, Lord d', 182
Adaptability of the Jew, 251-55, 313-14
Advertising,
  beginnings of, 130-32, 144-45
  prototype of, 168
Agrippa, King, 173
Aguilar, Baron d', 101
Alaska Commercial Company, 59
Albrecht, Cardinal, 70
Alexander, Alabarch, 173
Alexandrai, Rabbi, 317
Alexandria, marine insurance in, 90
Alhadib family, 170
Aliens, Jews as, 174-76
Allgemeine Elektrizitäts-Gesellschaft, 119
Almanach perpetuum, 51
Alphonso VI, of Spain, 173
Altschul, Richard, 59
America,
  colonial settlement in, 52-66
  discovery of, 50-52
Americanism, 62
American Revolutionary War,
  financiers of, 75
  purveyors of, 70
Amschel, Mayer, 110
Amsterdam,
  bill-broking in, 97-98
  refuge of Jewish exiles, 37, 41
Amsterdam Stock Exchange, 98-100, 109, 171
Anglia Judaica, 38
Anglo-Californian Bank, 59
Anne, Queen, of England, 72, 101
Anthropological homogeneity, Jewish, 269
Anthropology of the Jews, 265-71

Antiochus the Great, 276
Antwerp,
  Custom of 1582, 89
  refuge of Jewish exiles, 38, 40-41
Apostasy, tendency to, 31
Aptitude for modern capitalism, Jewish, 157-260
  capitalistic undertaker, defined, 162-68
  characteristics, Jewish, 238-60
  objective circumstances in, 169-86
  problem, the, 159-61
  religion, significance of, 187-237
Aquinas, Thomas, 128
Aristotle, 311
Arminius, 319
Arnold, 121
Arnstein family, 74
Aryans, 308-09
Asher, Rabbenu, 87, 91
Asher, Rabbi Jacob ben, 192, 195, 198
Ashkenazim (German) Jews, 72, 183, 241, 251, 319, 320, 321
Asphalt Trust, 58
Astrolabe, discovery of, 51
Auerbach, L., 93
Augsburg, expulsion of Jews from, 36
Augsburger Allgemeine Zeitung, 114
Aurelius, Marcus, 273, 274
Australia, colonial settlement in, 50
Austria,
  bill-broking in, 97
  financiers of, Jews as, 73-75
  government loans, floating of, 112
  purveyors in, 70

Baba Mezia, 291, 292
Babylonian Exile, 265, 279, 303, 304-05
Baierdorf family, 75
Ballin, 121
Bank of Amsterdam, 85
Bank of England, 85, 101
Bank of Hamburg, 85
Bank of St. George, Genoa, 82
Bank of the United States, 64
Bankers' Almanack, 115
Banknotes, 78, 83-85
Bankruptcies, fraudulent, 135
Banks and banking, origin of, 84-85
speculative, 115-17
Barbados, colonial development, 55
Bernard's Bill, Sir John, 106
Barnato, Barney, 294
Basilus, 276
Bavarian State Lottery, 106
Beaconsfield, Lord, 253, 254
Bedouin tribes, 301
Behrend family, 75
Belisarius, 174
Bendix, Nathan, 184
Benjamin of Tudela, 168
Berend, Meyer, 184
Berens, Meyer, 184
Berens, Salomon, 184
Berentz, Leffmann, 75
Berlin, wealth of Jews in, 184
Berliner, 119, 121
Berliner Discontogesellschaft, 117
Berliner Handelsgesellschaft, 117
Berlin Stock Exchange, 104-05
Bernard, Samuel, 73, 104
Bertholet, 282
Besançon fairs, bill of exchange in, 81
Bible, the, 87, 192-93, 196, 198, 209, 282
Bills of exchange, 78, 79, 80-82
Bischopfield, 89
Bismarck, Otto von, 254
Blackwell, Alderman, 182
Bleichröder, S., 117
Boards of Directors, membership of, 121-22
Böhme, Jacob, 246

Bonds, public debt, origin of, 85-93
Bookkeeping, divine, 202-05
Bordeaux, bill-broking in, 97
refuge of Jewish exiles, 37, 40
Borsig, 121
Brann, M., 268
Brazil, colonial settlement in, 53-55, 62
expulsion of Jews from, 53
Bücher, Professor, 288
Bueno de Mesquita family, 71
Burnus, 275

Caesarea, 275, 293
Calculator, speculating, 166-67, 259
Calvinische Judenspiegel, Der, 237
Calvinism, Judaism and, 237
Candace, Queen, of Ethiopia, 173
Cape Colony, colonial settlement in, 50
Capitalism, definition of, 162
Jewish aptitude for modern, 157-260
Jewish characteristics applied to, 255-60
Judaism, Puritanism and, 187, 202, 206, 235-37, 316
Capitalist point of view, growth of, 124-56
Carcere family, 170
Carlyle, Thomas, 254
Caro, Rabbi Joseph, 87, 195, 198-99, 232
Carvajal, Antonio Fernandez, 68, 72
Casten, Marx, 184
Castro, Henry, 64
Catering business, 155
Catherine of Braganza, Queen, of England, 72, 182
Cerfbeer family, 73
Chamberlain, H. S., 242, 245, 278
Characteristics, Jewish, 238-60
adaptability, 251-55, 313-14

applied to capitalism, 255-60
energy, 251, 314-15
impressionability, lack of, 246-47
intellectuality, 243-48, 279, 312-13
mobility, 250-51, 254-55, 313-14
personal relationships, lack of understanding of, 247-48
problem, the, 238-42
rationalism, practical, 248-49, 253-54, 279, 316
solution, attempt at, 242-55
subjectivity, 249-50, 255
teleology, 248-50, 279
Charlemagne, 173, 280
Charles II, of England, 55, 72, 182
Charles V, 67
Charles Alexander, of Würtemberg, 75
Charlotte, Elizabeth, 103
Cheating and falsifying, 127, 134-36, 279
Child, Sir Josiah, 126, 132, 140, 152-53
Choshen Mishpat, 87
Chozars, the, 267
Cicero, 228, 273, 317, 318
Civil War, American,
   Jewish soldiers in, 66
   purveyors in, Jews as, 70
Claudius, Emperor, 173
Cleveland, Grover, 58
Code of Jacob ben Asher (the *Turim*), 192, 234
Code of Joseph Caro (the *Shulchan Aruch*), 192, 195, 198-99, 223, 231, 234, 235
Code of Maimonides, 192, 234
Cohen, Rabbi Shabbatai, 91
Colbert, Jean Baptiste, 39, 67
Collection for the Improvement of Husbandry and Trade, The, 130
Cologne, expulsion of Jews from, 36
Colonial expansion, Jews in, 49-66
Columbus, Christopher, 36, 51-52, 185
Comic Lexicon of Cheating,

127, 134-35, 149
Commerce in economic life, predominance of, 77-123
Commercialization of industry, 117-23
Company promotion, 113-17
Competitive dealing, 129-30
Complete English Tradesman, 131
Comstock Lodes, 59
Conegliano family, 170
Confusion de confusiones, etc., 99
Conqueror, the, 165
Cordova, Jacob de, 64
Cordova, Spain, 294
Costa family, 170
Council of Elovia (304), 269
Council of Trade (Paris), 56
Councils of Toledo, 268
Court Jews, status of, 69, 73, 75, 76, 120, 173
Credit,
   public, see Public credit system
   standardization of, 78
Crédit mobilier, 117
Cromwell, Oliver, 38, 39, 67, 71, 98, 236-37
Crump, A., 113
Crypto-Jews, 31-33, 38, 54, 71, 275
Customers, attracting new, 154

Da Costa, Moses or Anthony, 101
Da Costa family, 72
Da Gama, Vasco, 36
Dalembert family, 73
Dangeau, Marquis de, 73
Daniel, Zacharias, 184
Darmstädter Bank, 117
Da Sylva, Francisco, 182
Da Sylva Brothers, 72
David, King, 304, 317
Davidson, Benjamin, 59
Dazevedo, Isaac, 183
De Foe, Daniel, 130, 131
De la Vega, Don Joseph, 99, 108
Del Banco, Simon, 184
Delmonte, Baron, 182
Delmonte family, 71

De Pass, Aaron and Daniel, 50
Deutsch, Felix, 119, 121
Deutsche Bank (1870), 117
Discoverer, the, 164-65
Dispersion of the Jews, 169-74, 267-78, 306-08
Dormido, Solomon, 100
Dühring, Eugen, 248
Dupont family, 73
Dutch East India Company, 49, 83, 97-98
Dutch West India Company, 61, 98
Dyer, Albert, 59

East Indies, colonial settlement of, 49
Eben Ha-ezer, 221, 223
Economic life,
   commerce in, predominance of, 77-123
   shifting centre of, 34-43
Edward I, of England, 38, 288
Egypt, 300, 306
Eichthal family, 114
Eisenmenger, 197
Electrical industry, commercialization of, 118-19
Elias, Philip, 183
Elias, Solomon, 70
Elijah the Prophet, 203
Elizabeth I, of England, 38
Elkan, Moses, 74
Energy of the Jew, 251, 314-15
England,
   company promotion in, 115
   economic growth of, 35
   financiers of, Jews as, 71-73
   government loans, floating of, 112-13
   international trade in, 44
   purveyors in, 68-69
   refuge of Jewish exiles, 38, 39
   stock exchange in, 100-03
   underselling practiced in, 146
   wealth of Jews in, 182-83
English East India Company, 82
Erfurt, expulsion of Jews from, 36
Eskeles family, 74
Espinosa family, 82

Essenes, the, 213
Ethics, Jewish, 188, 199, 214-27
Examen de ingenios, 311
Exchange,
   local code regulating, 93-95
   stock, *see* Stock exchanges
Ezekiel, Rabbi, 305
Ezekiel the Prophet, 282
Ezra the Prophet, 193, 201, 293, 302, 305

Family life, Jewish, 224-26
Farmers' and Merchants' Bank, Los Angeles, 59
Ferdinand, of Spain, 51
Ferdinand, Emperor, of Austria, 74
Financiers, the Jews as, 70-76
Finot, Jean, 238
Fonterosa, Suzanna, 52
Fould, Benjamin, 117
Fould family, 73, 114
Fraenkel family, 75
France,
   advertising in, 131, 132
   capitalistic competition in, 126, 127
   company promotion in, 115, 117
   economic growth of, 35
   financiers of, Jews as, 73
   government loans, floating of, 113
   international trade in, 45-46
   purveyors in, 69
   refuge of Jewish exiles, 37, 39-40
   stock exchange in, 103-04
   underselling practiced in, 146
Francia, George and Domingo, 183
Francis, John, 100, 102
Frank, Aaron, 101
Frankford-on-the-Main,
   bill-broking in, 96
   insurance business in, 108
   refuge of Jewish exiles, 37
   stock-jobbing in, 102, 104, 105
   wealth of Jews in, 184
Frankfort Stock Exchange, 104, 105

Frederick II (the Great), of Prussia, 67, 75
Frederick Augustus, Elector of Saxony, 70, 75
Frederick William, of Prussia, 67, 75
French East India Company, 73
Friedlaender, Moritz, 59, 121
Fromer, Jacob, 31, 242, 252

Gambetta, Léon, 253
Garcia de la Riega, Don Celso, 52
Gemara, the, 194, 195, 196, 234
Genetic method of study, 28-29
Genius, Jewish, origin of, 262-323
  constancy of, 273-97
  natural or artificial?, 297-98
  race problem, the, 263-98
  vicissitudes of the Jewish people, 298-323
General Privileges of 1750, Prussian, 177-78
General store, the, 154-55
General Treasury for Merchants, 127
Genoa, expulsion of Jews from, 37
Genoa fairs, bill of exchange in, 81-82
Geographical Society of Madrid, 52
Germanus, John Baptist, 89
Germany,
  advertising in, 131
  bill-broking in, 96-97
  capitalistic competition in, 125
  company promotion in, 115, 116
  credit instruments in, 89-90
  economic growth of, 35
  expulsion of Jews from, 36
  financiers of, Jews as, 73-75
  international trade in, 44-45
  public debt bonds in, 85
  purveyors to, 70
  stock exchanges in, 104-06
  underselling practiced in, 147
  wealth of Jews in, 181-82, 183-85

Gerstle, Lewis, 59
Ghentsche Post-Tijdingen, 130
Ghetto life, 319, 320-21
Gideon, Sampson, 72, 101
Gilds, merchant and craft, 126, 140, 141, 179
Giudetti, 89
Glazier family, 59
Godchaux family, 73
Goethe, Johann Wolfgang von, 242, 250
Goldschmidt, Moses, 183
Goldsmid, Abraham and Benjamin, 113
Gompertz, Leimann, 70
Gonzales, Gaspar, 40
"Good" wares, stress on, 132
Government loans, floating of, 111-13
Gradis, Abraham, 69
Gradis family, 69, 170
Graetz, Heinrich, 73, 138, 195, 233, 282
Greenbaum, Sigmund, 59
Guadeloupe, colonial development in, 56
Guggenheim family, 58

Hagen (of Cologne), 121
Haggada, the, 196
Hagiographa, the, 196
Halevy, Jehuda, 229
Halske, 119
Hamburg,
  bill-broking in, 97
  economic growth of, 35
  international trade in, 45
  refuge of Jewish exiles, 37, 41-42
  stock-jobbing in, 102, 104, 105
  wealth of Jews in, 183-84
Hamburg Stock Exchange, 104, 105
Hamm, Moses, 183
Hanassi, Rabbi Judah (the Prince), 194, 203
Handbook of German Joint-Stock Companies, 122
Haroun al Rashid, Caliph, 173
Harrison, General Thomas, 237
Hart, Moses, 101
Hausemann, David, 117

Hebrews, the ancient, 301-02
Heine, Heinrich, 110, 236, 242, 249, 250, 279
Heine, Solomon, 117
Hekateus of Abdera, 228
Hellanistic philosophy, 194
Hellman and Newmark, Los Angeles, 59
Helphen family, 73
Henry IV, 95
Heredity, doctrines of, 264
Hermann, George, 250
Herod, King, 306-07
Herschel, Mayer, 70
Hertz, F., 238
Hertz, Isaac, 184
Herzfeld, 278, 280
Heyman, Berend, 183
Heymann, Mangelus, 184
Hillel, school of, 193
Hiram, King, of Tyre, 281
Hirsch, Baron, 115
Hirschfeld, George, 250
Hittites, 299
Holland,
    bill of exchange in, 80
    credit instruments in, 89
    economic growth of, 34
    financiers of, Jews as, 71
    international trade in, 46
    public debt bonds, 86-87
    refuge of Jewish exiles, 37, 41
    stock exchange in, 98-100
Holmes, Nathaniel, 236
Homen, Manuel Lopez, 182
Hönn, George Paul, 127
Houghton, John, 130
Huarte de San Juan, Juan, 273, 311-12
Huguenots, 32
Hume, David, 107
Hyrkanus, Rabbi Dosa ben, 219

Illegitimate births, statistics of, 225
Inbreeding of the Jews, 322
India, colonial settlement in, 50
Industry, commercialization of, 117-23
Inferior goods, trade in, 149-50
Inquisition, the, 36, 41, 54
Insurance business, 90, 108

Intellectuality of the Jews, 243-48, 279, 312-13
Intermarriage, attitude toward, 205
International trade, quickening of, 44-48
Inventor, the, 164
Isaac, Alexander, 184
Isaac, Rabbi, 206
Isaiah the Prophet, 317
Ishmael, 203
Islam, 194, 201, 276
Israel, 265, 303, 304
    the nations and, 227-35
Israel, Manasseh ben, 38, 41, 98
Isserlein, Rabbi Moses, 199
Italy,
    economic decline of, 34
    expulsion of Jews from, 37
Itzig family, 75

Jamaica, colonial development in, 55-56
James II, of England, 173
Jellinek, Adolf, 242, 245, 249, 255
Jewish law, credit instruments and, 87, 92-93, 94
Jews, the,
    adaptability of, 251-55, 313-14
    aliens, 174-76
    anthropology of, 265-71
    aptitude for modern capitalism, 157-260
    centre of economic life and, 34-43
    characteristics of, 238-60
    cheating and falsifying of, 127, 134-36, 279
    colonial settlement by, 49-66
    contributions to modern economic life by, 25-156
    court, see Court Jews
    crypto-, 31-33, 38, 54, 71, 275
    definition of, 30-31
    dispersion of, 169-74, 276-78, 306-08
    economic importance of, 42-43
    energy of, 251, 314-15

ethics of, 188, 199, 214-27
fair, 266, 268-69
financiers, 70-76
genius of, origins, 261-323
German, *see* Ashkenazim Jews
impressionability, lack of, 246-47
inbreeding of, 322
intellectuality of, 243-48, 279, 312-13
international trade and, 44-48
inventiveness of, 29
living standard of, 152-53
mobility of, 250-51, 254-55, 313-14
physiognomy of, 270-71
Portuguese, *see* Marannos
public life, exclusion from, 179-81
purveyors, 68-70, 174
race problem, 263-98
religion of, *see* Religion, Jewish
rationalism of, 248-49, 253-54, 279, 316
semi-citizens, 176-81, 240, 273-76
Spanish, *see* Sephardim Jews
subjectivity of, 249-50, 255
success of, causes for, 169
teleology, 248-50, 279
vicissitudes of, 299-323
wealth of, 181-86, 293-97
Joachim II, of Prussia, 75
Joan, Queen, of Portugal, 52
John II, of Portugal, 51
John Philip, Bishop, of Würzburg, 74
Josephus, Flavius, 173, 188, 274, 306, 318
Joshia, Rabbi Achai ben, 284
Judaea, 300, 306
Judah, 302
Judaism, *see* Religion, Jewish
Julius, Samuel, 70
"Just price," theory of, 133
Justus, Dr., 197

Kabbala, the, 195, 246
Kalonymus, 173
Kempinsky, 155

Kinkherle, Joseph, 74
Koppore, Morris, 64
Krupp, Alfred, 121
Kuhn, Loeb & Company, 58

Lagi, Ptolemy, 276, 277
Laissez-faire, industrial, 235
Lassalle, Ferdinand, 253, 254
Law, John, 104
Lazard Frères, 59
Lazarus, Abraham, 184
Legal code regulating exchange, evolution of, 93-95
Legal practice, Jewish influences in, 88-93
Leghorn, refuge of Jewish exiles, 37
Lehmann, Berend, 75
Leipzig fairs, trading by Jews at, 44-45, 48
Leopold I, Emperor, of Austria, 70, 74, 97
Leroy-Beaulieu, Anatole, 227, 242, 245, 252
Levantine trade, 34, 45-46, 170
Levi, Asser, 63
Levy, Benjamin, 72
Levy, Hayman, 145
Liberalism, capitalism and, 256
Liebermann, Max, 246
Liebmann, Gomperz and Joost, 75
Life, rationalization of, in Judism, 214-27
Lilienthal, Philip N., 59
Lindo, Moses, 65
Lipman family, 84
Lippold, 75
London, advertising in, 130
London, Paris and American Bank, 59
London *Spectator,* 171
London Stock Exchange, 100-03, 109, 113
Longobards, 274
Long Parliament, the, 71
Lopez, Ildefonso, 174
Lopez, Manasseh, 72, 101
Lopez, Miguel, 182
Lopez, Rodrigo, 38
Lopez family, 170

Lost Ten Tribes of Israel, 270-71
Louis XI, of France, 67
Louis XIV, of France, 69, 73, 104
Louis XV, of France, 73
Ludewig, Stattskanzler, 74, 97
Luxury articles, trade in, 46-47

Machado, Moses, 71
Magnus Barford Saga, 168
Mahamad, the, 136
Maimon, Solomon, 138
Maimonides, 192, 195, 199, 276
Maine, Sir H., 247 n.
Mallet Frères, 117
Mamre (Mamram, Mamran), 88, 89, 90
Managing directors, membership of, 122
Mangelus, Philip, 184
Marannos, the, 31, 36, 37, 38, 39, 51, 71, 82, 84, 89, 190, 275, 320
Marburger, Moses and Jacob, 74
Maria Theresa, Empress, of Austria, 74
Marks, Simon, 50
Marine insurance, 90
Marlborough, General Lord, 101
Marriage, Jewish view on, 223
Marseilles, refuge of Jewish exiles, 37, 39
Martinique, colonial development in, 56
Marx, Carsten, 184
Marx, Karl, 241, 242, 254
Mary, Queen, of Hungary, 40-41
Maurice of Saxony, Field Marshal, 69
May, Michel, 75
Mazarin, Cardinal, 67
Medina, Sir Solomon, 68-69, 72, 101
Megalopolis, Rev. John, 139, 140
Mels, Francis, 71
Memoirs of Glückel von Hameln, 137-38, 182, 213-14

Mendelssohn, Felix, 253
Mendelssohn & Company, 117
Mendes da Costa, Ferdinando, 101, 183
Mendes family, 170
Mesopotamia, 300
Meyer, Isaac, 70
Meyer, J., 75
Meyer, Jonas, 69
Millaud, Polydore, 145
Mishna, the, 194, 196, 215, 234
Mithridates, 317
Mixed marriages, 267-68
Mobility of the Jew, 250-51, 254-55, 313-14
Model family, 70, 75
Modern Capitalism, 30
Modern state, foundation of, 67-76
    financiers, Jews as, 70-76
    purveyors, Jews as, 68-70
Modyford, Thomas, 55
Mohammed the Prophet, 192, 201
Money and Trade Considered, 104
Money-lending activities, 185-86, 231-32, 284-93, 318
Montefiore, 50
Mordecai, Abraham, 63
Morris, Robert, 75
Mosenthal, Adolph, 50
Mosenthal, James, 50
Mosenthal, Julius, 50
Moses, 196, 214, 221
Moses the Mathematician, 51
Moyses, Lemte, 75
Muys van Holy, Nicolas, 98
Myer, H. H., 121
Myers, Joel, 50

Nachman, Rabbi, 223
Naples, expulsion of Jews from, 37
Nathan, Abraham, 184
Nathan, Rabbi Eleazar ben, 223
Nathan, Samson, 183
Nathan family, 75
National Bank of Texas, 64
Naturalization Bill of 1753 (England), 126, 146
Naumann, Friedrich, 246
Negrela, Ismael ibn, 276

Nehemiah the Prophet, 286, 302
Netherlands, refuge of Jewish exiles, 38, 40-41
Neubauer, 266
Nevada Bank, 59
New Amsterdam, refuge of Jewish exiles, 61, 65
Newburg, Philip, 64
New commodities, trade in, 47
New York *Mercury,* 145
Nieuhoff, 54
Norden, Benjamin, 50
North American Commercial Company, 59
Nossig, Alfred, 322
Nunez, Maria, 182
Nuremburg, expulsion of Jews from, 36

Offenbach, Jacques, 253
Old Testament, the, 192-93, 196, 198, 209
Oppenheim (of Cologne), 117
Oppenheimer, Elias, 183
Oppenheimer family, 70, 74
Organizer, the, 165-66
Orthodox Jews, 241
Otto II, Emperor, 173
Oulman, Abraham, 146
Oxford Papyrus, 286

Pakuda, bachja ibn, 213
Palestine, 300, 304, 306
Papenheim, Alex, 183
Pardel, Governor, of California, 63
Parente, Ventura, 74
Paris Stock Exchange, 103-04
Parta, Rabbi Eleazar ben, 276
Paul of Tarsus, 274
Pechmann, Baron, 147
Pereira, Moses Lopez, 101, 321
Pereire, Isaac and Emil, 117
Pereire family, 73, 170
Petites Affiches, Les, 131
Petit Journal, 145
Pfefferkorn, 197
Pharisees, 189, 268
Philip II, 35, 36
Philo, 306
Physiognomy of the Jews, 270-71

Picciotto, J., 101, 242
Pinto, Joseph de, 98, 107-08, 182, 319-20
Pinto family, 71
Plautus, 201
Poland,
  capitalistic competition in, 126
  underselling practiced in, 147
Portugal,
  economic decline in, 34
  expulsion of Jews from, 36
Possession, doctrine of, 208
Postlethwayt, M., 102, 106, 130
Prester, John, 173
Priest, Albert, 59
Production, cost of, 151-52, 153-54
Promissory notes, 93-94
Prophetic Books, the, 193, 196
Prussian Edicts of 1737 and 1750, 125, 147, 179
Public credit system, transformation in, 76
  industry, commercialization of, 117-23
  securities, origin of, 77-93
    banknotes, 78, 83-85
    bill of exchange, 78, 79, 80-82
    bonds, public debt, 85-93
    buying and selling, 93-111
    creation of, 111-17
    stocks and shares, 82-83
Public life, exclusion of Jews from, 179-81
Punishments, idea of, in Judaism, 207-14
Puritanism, capitalism and, 187, 202, 236-37
Purveyors, the Jews as, 68-70, 174
Pyrard, F., 54

Rabbinic law, credit instruments and, 87, 88
Race, the Jewish, 271-72
Race problem, the, 263-98
  anthropology of the Jews, 265-71
  Jewish genius,
    constancy of, 273-97

natural or artificial?, 297-98

Jewish "race," the, 271-72

Ranke, 103

Rat, Frau, 137

Rathenau, 121

Rationalism,
economic, 162, 175
of the Jew, 248-49, 253-54, 279, 316

Ratisbon, expulsion of Jews from, 36

Ready money, supply of, 48

Reccared, 294

Reformed Judaism, 199

Religion, Jewish, significance in economic life, 187-237, 278-79, 302, 321-22
asceticism in, 212-13
capitalism and, 187, 202, 206, 235-37, 316
dogmas of Judaism, 197
dualism, 216-17
ideas of, fundamental, 199-206
importance of, 187-92
Israel and the nations, 227-35
life, rationalization of, 214-27
mysteries, lack of, 200-02
proselytes admitted into, 266-67
rewards and punishments, idea of, 207-14
sources of, 192-99

Renan, 266

Rewards, idea of, in Judaism, 207-14

Richelieu, Cardinal, 67, 174

Rodrigues, Gomez, 183

Röhling, 197

Rome, 306-07

Roosevelt, Theodore, 58

Rosenfeld, John, 59

Rothschild, Baron Amschel, 191, 209-10

Rothschild, Nathan, 110, 168

Rothschild, S. M., 117

Rothschild, William Charles, 191

Rothschild, House of, 73, 109-11, 114, 117

Rothschild family, 170, 181

Rouen, refuge of Jewish exiles, 37

Rubens, Simon, 79

Ruppin, Arthur, 272

St. Thomas, West Indies, 52, 53

Salomon, Berend, 184

Salomon, Elias, 183

Salomon, Haym, 75

Salvador, Francis and Joseph, 72

Samuel, Rabbi, 276

San Domingo, colonial development in, 56

Saniheg, Gabriel, 51

Santangel, Louis de, 51

Sardinia, 307

Sassoon family, 170

Saul, King, 266

Savannah, Georgia, colonial development in, 65

Savary, 127, 131, 140, 182

Schickler Brokers, 117

Schiesser, Samuel, 183

Schlesinger, Wolf, 74

Schmieles, Jacob B. B., 74

Schnitzler, Arthur, 250

Schubert, Benedict, 64

Scribes, 189, 193

Securities,
banknotes, 78, 83-85
bill of exchange, 80-82
bonds, public debt, 85-93
buying and selling, 93-111
legal code regulating exchange, evolution of, 93-95
stock exchange, the, 77, 86, 95-111
creation of, 111-17
industry, commercialization of, 117-23
origin of, 77-93
stocks and shares, 82-83

Seligman, David, 64

Seligman, Joseph, 64

Seligman Brothers (William, Henry, Jesse and James), 59, 64-65

Semi-citizens, Jews as, 176-81, 240, 273-76

Semite controversy, 265

Semites, 265, 299

Sephardim (Spanish) Jews, 72, 182, 183, 241, 251, 319, 320, 321
Severus, Emperor, 267
Shammai, school of, 193
Shaprut, Chasdai ibn, 173
Short measure, practice of, 151
Shulchan Aruch, see Code of Joseph Caro
Sibylline Oracle, 306
Siemens, Werner von, 119, 121
Sigismund, King, of Poland, 126
Sinzheim, Lewel, 74
Sloss, Louis, 59
Smelters' Trust, 58
Smith, Adam, 107, 108, 112
Solomon, Joel, 183
Solomon, King, 281, 293, 317
Sombart, 191 n., 213 n., 221 n.
South Africa, colonial settlement in, 50
South America, colonial settlement in, 52-55
South Sea Bubble, 72, 73
Souza, Antonio de, 71
Souza, Thomé de, 53
Spain, banking business in, 84-85
economic decline of, 34
expulsion of Jews from, 36
international trade in, 46
Spanish Succession, wars of the, 69, 73
Speculation, 167
Speculative banking, 115-17
Speyer, Bishop of, 290
Spinoza, Baruch, 246
States-General, 174
Statesman's Year Book, 300
Statistical method of study, 27-28
Steinhart, Ignatz, 59
Stevenson, Robert Louis, 222 n.
Stock exchanges, 77, 86, 95-111, 112, 118, 124, 171
Stocks and shares, origin, 82-83
Stolen property, dealing in, 136-37
Strabo, 306
Strassburg, expulsion of Jews from, 36
Strousberg, Dr., 115

Studendolus, Marcus, 89
Stuyvesant, Peter, 61, 98
Suasso family, 71, 72
Subjectivity of the Jews, 249-50, 255
Substitution, principle of, 150-51
Suess-Oppenheimer, 75
Sugar industry, development of, 53-57
Surinam, colonial development in, 56
mortgage-banking with, 86
Sutro, Adolph, 59
Sweden, capitalistic competition in, 126
underselling practiced in, 147
Sylva, Duarte de, 182
Synhedrium, 189, 237

Tacitus, 228-29, 273
Talmud, the, 87, 94-95, 190-91, 192, 194, 196, 197-98, 206, 208, 209, 212, 221, 230, 232, 233, 234, 283, 286, 291, 298, 305
Talmudic colleges, 194
Tanchuma Chukkath, 189
Telegraph Trust, 58
Teleological outlook of the Jews, 248-50, 279
Textiles, trade in, 47
Thirty Years War, 73
Tiglath-Pileser, 276
Tobacco Trust, 58
Torah, the (Pentateuch), 188, 193, 196, 198, 201, 202, 209, 230, 232, 252
Torlonia (of Rome), 117
Torres, Louis de, 51
Trader, the, 163, 164, 166-68
Traité du crédit et de la circulation, 107-08
Transvaal, colonial settlement in, 50
Tur, the, 198
Turnover, increase in, 153
Twain, Mark, 57

Ukba, Mar, 203
Ullmann, H. E., 106

Ulm, expulsion of Jews from, 36
Underselling, practice of, 131-32, 146-49
Undertaker, capitalist, 162-68, 259-60
Union Trust Company, 59
United States, growth of, Jewish factor in, 57-66
Usury, practice of, 288-90

Van den Meeren, Nicholas, 40
Variety in trade, 47-48
Vecuho, Jose, 51
Vega, Samuel de, 182
Venice,
  banknotes in, 84
  bill of exchange in, 80-81
  economic decline of, 34
  expulsion of Jews from, 37, 39
Vercingentorix, 319
Vicissitudes of the Jewish people, 299-323
Voltaire, 319
Von Halle, Abraham, 184
Von Hameln, Glückel, 96, 137-38, 140, 182, 183, 214, 296
Von Rosheim, Joselman, 70
Von Sittewald, Philander, 127

Vossische Zeitung, 145

Walpole, Horace, 72
Warschauer Co., Robert, 117
Waste-product business, 154
Wealth of Nations, 107
Wealth of the Jews, 181-86, 293-97
Weber, Max, 235
Weil, A., 109
Werner, Dr., 31
Wertheimer, W. Z., 108
Wertheimer family, 70, 74
West Indies, colonial settlement in, 55-57, 62
Westinghouse Electric Company, 165-66
William III, of England, 68, 71, 72, 85, 100, 101
Wisdom Literature, the, 193, 211, 221
Worms, Jacob, 69
Wormser family, 59

Yad Hachazaka, 198

Zacuto, Abraham, 51
Zagnoni Brothers, 89
Zevi, Sabbatti, 276
Zimmern, A. E., 289 n.